Handbook of Mental Performance

This extensive overview of mental performance optimization techniques offers both a state-of-the-art reference resource and comprehensive tool for those engaged in the management and implementation of mental performance programs.

The book is written by a combination of academic and operational experts from a wide range of high-performance domains, including the military, space programs, academia, executive coaching, and elite athlete coaching, who complement scientific analyses and overviews of current knowledge with their own experience. Divided into three parts, the book begins by providing a broad conceptual framework through which to embed the latter technical content. Part two looks specifically at the interventions, knowledge, skills, and techniques needed to improve mental performance for both individuals and teams. The final section pulls together the theory of the previous parts, taking a more practical approach by covering implementation, methodological plans on how to appraise new techniques, lessons learned based on the practical experience of the authors, and considerations regarding the necessary learning environment for mental performance improvement.

Pairing an overview of all available neurological, cognitive, and psychological interventions aimed at improving mental performance with a review of their implementation, this is a go-to guide for practitioners involved in managing mental performance and program managers looking at the implementation of a mental performance policy across a wide range of domains. It will also be of interest for courses on performance psychology and human performance in both an academic and professional environment.

Nathalie Pattyn, MSc, MD, MPsy, PhD is Human Performance Professor, Royal Military Academy, Belgium, and Invited Researcher at the Université de Montréal, Canada.

Robin Hauffa, MD is a senior psychiatric resident at the Military Hospital in Berlin, Germany and the former Medical Advisor at the German Special Operations Component Command. He also serves as the Human Performance Advisor to the NATO SOF Medicine Development Initiative, Security and Defense Medicine at University College Cork, Ireland.

Handbook of Mental Performance

Lessons from High Performance Domains

Edited by

Nathalie Pattyn and Robin Hauffa

Routledge
Taylor & Francis Group
LONDON AND NEW YORK

Cover Image: Getty Images © Bannosuke

First published 2024
by Routledge
4 Park Square, Milton Park, Abingdon, Oxon, OX14 4RN

and by Routledge
605 Third Avenue, New York, NY 10158

Routledge is an imprint of the Taylor & Francis Group, an informa business

British Library Cataloguing-in-Publication Data
A catalogue record for this book is available from the British Library

ISBN: 978-1-032-45849-6 (hbk)
ISBN: 978-1-032-45844-1 (pbk)
ISBN: 978-1-003-37896-9 (ebk)

DOI: 10.4324/9781003378969

Typeset in Times New Roman
by Newgen Publishing UK

Graphics created by Anthony Levasseur and Marc Vermeersch.

Multiple Funding Bodies: Royal Higher Institute for Defence; U.S. Army Research Institute of Environmental Medicine; Canadian Forces Morale and Welfare Services.

This book is dedicated to the fond memory of Rune Giske, who showed a rare combination of academic rigour and operational relevance.

Contents

Contributors

Deanna Beech, KBR-POTFF, USA.

Erin L. Beatty, Canadian Forces Morale and Welfare Service, Ottawa, ON, Canada.

Maarten Bocksteins, EY, Brussels, Belgium.

Susan Charlesworth, Charlesworth Human Performance, UK.

Jesper Corneliussen, Danish Special Operation Command, Denmark.

Aisha Cortoos, Brainwise, Overijse, Belgium; Better Minds at Work, Antwerp, Belgium.

Jessica Couse, U.S. Army Research Institute of Environmental Medicine, Natick, MA, USA.

Silvia DeGirolamo, KBR – POTFF, USA.

Nicole Ekon, U.S. Army Research Institute of Environmental Medicine, Natick, MA, USA.

Don Harris, Faculty of Engineering, Environment and Computing, Coventry University, Coventry, UK.

Robin Hauffa, German Joint Command Special Operations, Potsdam, Germany.

Kristin J. Heaton, U.S. Army Research Institute of Environmental Medicine, Natick, MA, USA.

Audrey Hildebrandt, U.S. Army Research Institute of Environmental Medicine, Natick, MA, USA.

Koen Hogenelst, Nederlandse Organisatie voor Toegepaste Natuurwetenschappelijk Onderzoek (TNO), Netherlands.

Martin I. Jones, Tactical Athlete Performance Centre, Buckinghamshire New University, UK.

Anders Kjærgaard, Danish Special Operation Command, Denmark.

Helen Kilding, Human Sciences Programme, Defence Technology Agency, New Zealand Defence Force.

Heikki Mansikka, Department of Mathematics and Systems Analysis, Aalto University, Helsinki, Finland; Department of Military Technology, Finnish National Defense University, Helsinki, Finland.

Dietrich Manzey, Alumnus Technical University Berlin, Germany.

Antonio Martin, CIUSSS NÎM Research Center, Montreal, Canada.

Paige Mattie, Mental Performance Consultant, Ottawa, ON, Canada.

Adrianna Mendrek, Bishop's University, Sherbrooke, QC, Canada.

William Neumeier, U.S. Army Research Institute of Environmental Medicine, Natick, MA, USA.

Nathalie Pattyn, Royal Military Academy, Brussels, Belgium; Université de Montréal, Canada.

Caitlin Ridgewell, U.S. Army Research Institute of Environmental Medicine, Natick, MA, USA.

Claus Rønnow Pedersen, Danish Special Operation Command, Denmark.

Marion Trousselard, Institut de Recherche Biomédicale des Armées (IRBA), France.

Joern Ungerer, German Army Special Operations Forces, Germany.

Jeroen Van Cutsem, Royal Military Academy, Brussels, Belgium; Vrije Universiteit Brussel.

Nicholas van den Berg, Royal Military Academy, BEL & CIUSSS NÎM, Montréal.

Martine Van Puyvelde, Royal Military Academy, Brussels, Belgium.

Kai Virtanen, Department of Mathematics and Systems Analysis, Aalto University, Helsinki, Finland; Department of Military Technology, Finnish National Defense University, Helsinki, Finland.

Jenny Wilhelmsson, Swedish Armed Forces.

Paul Wylleman, Sport Psychology and Mental Support (SPMB) & Brussels Olympic Research and Education Centre (BOREC), Vrije Universiteit Brussel, Brussel, Belgium; Expert Psychology & Olympic Welfare Officer, Team Belgium.

Part 1

Foundation

1 Introduction

For the purpose of this handbook, mental performance includes the physiological, cognitive and behavioural aspects of performance that need to be closely integrated and trained with professional training (which might be physical, intellectual, technical…) to holistically address the way high performers function cognitively. We chose "mental performance", as this is a term all high-performance fields we address in this handbook will understand in terms of relevance. As described in our chapter on ethical caveats, the distinction between optimization vs. enhancement needs to be clarified. Currently, performance optimization is described as maximizing available resources to allow the individual to reach their full potential, whereas enhancement includes invasive techniques to attempt to go beyond that inherent individual potential. This is also discussed in the chapter on pharmacological interventions, and actually describes whether the drugs are adequate performance enhancers. This is clearly an attempt at an enhancement technique; whereas other techniques and interventions are considered optimization (e.g., breathing); and some are still the matter of debate (e.g., neurostimulation or biofeedback).

This distinction thus raises ethical issues, which are not new. David Morell's novel "First Blood" (1972), which most people know as the mainstream movie "Rambo", discusses this ethical dilemma of the armed forces: that soldiers may not easily reintegrate as functional members of civilian society, and that armed forces as employers have a duty of care towards their potential as "mean, lean, killing machines", both towards the individual and towards the civil society they need to function in. So how far are we willing to go to enhance human performance? Should we jeopardize performers' health and well-being in the process? If so, to what extent? If performers are willing to put themselves at risk, how much constraint should we, as a society, impose unto that individual freedom? These questions have to be kept in mind when designing and/or managing a program.

Our current industrialized Western society has replaced collective ideals with individual goals. Achieving the best version of oneself has become paramount in this worldview. As emphasized by Paul Verhaeghe (2014) in his book "What About Me? The Struggle for Identity in a Market-Based Society", we live under the pressure to become the best version of ourselves, in a free-market economy that has forced a pay-for-performance approach to essentially non-marketable subjects like health, interpersonal relationships, happiness, and even death.

The economic boom in the service economy targeting health and well-being has translated to the niche of people needing to achieve exceptional performance. According to a Grand View Research Report from 2020 regarding the US economy: "The global personal development market size was valued at USD 38.28 billion in 2019 and is expected to grow at a compound annual growth rate (CAGR) of 5.1% from 2020 to 2027. Increasing consciousness about self-recognition and the pursuit of happiness is expected to drive the demand for personal development programs

DOI: 10.4324/9781003378969-2

during the forecast period. Individuals are gradually looking for ways to attain physical as well as emotional fitness." Bluntly put: there is a lot of money to be made in convincing people they need whatever one sells to improve their performance. And high-performance environments are a nexus of this economy, as they are optimal testbeds, potential clients (albeit in a niche market), but above all, heavy-weight marketing arguments to sell a similar or downgraded version of whatever product or service to the general public. If all the consultants, hardware and service advertising "being used/having worked by/for the SAS" (the emblematic UK tier 1 special forces unit, the Special Air Service) were really what they advertise, there would be more SAS operators in the UK than conventional forces.

This economic drive has thus created products and services of varying quality, the likes of which could be "brain training", "neurocognitive performance enhancement", "neurolinguistic programming", "brain gym", "cortical stimulation", "performance optimization"... One could easily get lost in the terminology in the field, especially considering the current boom in commercial services offering to improve all aspects of mental functioning. This is exactly why our group of experts decided it was not only timely but also urgent to provide a state-of-the-science answer regarding available tools, techniques, and interventions aiming at improving mental performance. This author team originated as part of a NATO Research Task Group regarding mental performance optimization in 2018, and expanded to other contexts considering the societal relevance and interest from other fields.

This handbook is to be used as a reference work. It is structured in three distinct parts.

The first part contains the "foundation" chapters: this introduction; the scientific foundation, i.e., all the notions related to physiology and psychology that are necessary to fully grasp the content of the subsequent parts; a description of the most common mental performance degradation conditions (stress and mental fatigue); and a description of ideal performance states.

The second part is the state-of-the-art technical content regarding interventions, knowledge, skills, and techniques to improve mental performance. This part is reductionist in nature, and is also the most technical, cutting up the inherent necessary holistic approach to performance in order to focus on the available evidence regarding each topic. The authors have strived to summarize the relevant literature findings, to allow the reader a critical appraisal of the information, and a reference framework in which to place future knowledge.

The third and last part of the report brings these pieces back together in a more practical approach, with chapters covering implementation in various high-performance contexts; lessons learned based on the practical experience of the author team; and reflections regarding ethics or the necessary learning environment for mental performance training. Topics that are not addressed (in the spirit of keeping the volume of information manageable) are those where a sufficient level of knowledge and expertise is available in other sources, and which are not specific to mental performance, like sleep, nutrition, or physical activity (to name the three pillars of health defined by the World Health Organization).

This handbook is thus aimed at subject matter experts, to offer them a compilation of the available knowledge, as well as the product of decades of combined experience from the members of the author team. For communities already implementing mental performance management or training, this compilation will allow for a check on current practice, to identify possible improvement or development strategies. For those aiming to kickstart a program from scratch, this work was intended to provide a robust foundation and thus a solid head start.

2 Scientific Foundation

Nathalie Pattyn, Jeroen Van Cutsem, Antonio Martin, Robin Hauffa, and Joern Ungerer

Aims and overview

The current chapter aims to provide a summary of the necessary theoretical background concepts used in this handbook. We define mental performance and frame the vocabulary and notions that are used throughout the following chapters. This chapter provides an overarching framework for a psychophysiological concept of performance, detailing the scientific descriptions of the different systems in physiology and psychology we draw on for the study of mental performance enhancement.

First, we set the scene, and explain how and why we choose the scientific approach, and what this entails exactly.

We then define mental performance and delve a little deeper into cognitive psychology concepts which precisely describe the machinery of information processing, or how our brains analyze input, make decisions, and act on those. This terminology is often used in reports describing performance enhancement, hence its basic understanding is necessary to be able to critically appraise those.

The next subsection will provide the necessary background physiological concepts, focusing on the human nervous system, with an emphasis on brain physiology and the autonomic nervous system.

Our last section will present a psychophysiological approach to stress and mental fatigue. Stress is the paramount example of a psychophysiological concept; its study laid the foundation for autonomic nervous system physiology; and it is ever present in elite performance.

Why do we choose our foundation to be scientific?

For all scientific authors, there is a "before and after" phenomenon regarding the COVID pandemic. We have seen science being commented, criticized, abused, misunderstood, and praised like never before. Which underscores the need for a bit more emphasis on what we call scientific methodology. Yes, it is tedious, does not make for light reading, and the level of detail and accuracy required seems at loggerheads with the current Zeitgeist, calling for pop-culture-like easily understandable statements. However, mental performance training is precisely one of the fields where this scientific rigor is most distorted. In our concluding chapter, we even decided to devote a whole section on "shiny object evaluation", which is actually the topic of a proper scientific discipline, epistemology, to provide the reader with a basic hoax-debunking arsenal. Beyond health and wellbeing, which are already billion-dollar markets, lies the still developing field of performance optimization, which is only in its infancy.

DOI: 10.4324/9781003378969-3

Mental performance: what's in a name?

The accurate evaluation of mental performance and its applications are widely investigated topics. A first problem is raised when trying to define mental performance. In layman's terms, it would be a single concept, reflecting one's efficiency of information processing in the execution of any given task. To neuropsychologists, cognitive performance is a window to the brain, a way to the diagnosis of brain lesions, and a way to investigate the localization and processes underlying several functions. For cognitive psychologists, there is no such thing as this overarching mental performance, but an interaction of different dimensions of cognition (which is these scientists' denomination of mental performance), such as perception, attention, or memory. We will detail this a bit further in a following section. To the applied specialist (e.g., aviation psychologist, sport psychologist, performance psychologist, human factors engineer), mental performance would be the efficiency with which certain tasks are performed in specific (i.e., professional) environments.

Who may be concerned?

As briefly defined previously, three distinct fields can be differentiated, with different views on mental performance and different interests. First, there is the clinician's field. The historical background of neurology and neuropsychology is based on testing (Chaytor & Schmitter-Edgecombe, 2003). Before brain-imaging techniques allowed for precise anatomical diagnostics, the description of lesions was derived from impaired cognitive functions. Therefore, normative research to associate well-defined functions with performance on well-defined tests was developed.

The second field related to mental performance is experimental, or cognitive, psychology. Pioneers' work reflects what remains to be the major difficulty when studying mental processes: we have gained access to the visualization of brain structures and of their activity, but not to the content of information within the information exchanges. Wundt, who set up the first experimental psychology laboratory in 1879 used introspection by trained observers; James (1890) studied memory through its output, remembered items; and Watson (1924) declared that scientific psychology had to focus on objective and measurable variables, like reaction times or accuracy. Despite the tremendous progresses in cognitive science, researchers still have to deal with the fact that there is no direct measure of cognitive processes: the input can be manipulated, the output can be measured, ever-evolving technology allows for a glimpse in the physiological and anatomical basis of the process, but there is still no gold standard providing an undisputable direct quantification.

The third field where mental performance is a relevant topic, is the operational environment: every setting involving humans to accomplish specific tasks. The interest for this human part of the system gave rise to a new discipline: human factors, originating from engineering, psychology and medicine. In this area, the measurement of mental performance has implications for personnel selection, management and productivity enhancement, safety and well-being. Therefore, it is applicable to every possible professional activity. The main sector to have driven substantial advances in the discipline is aviation. The reason is obvious: while there is research to be done to enhance the efficiency of every employee in every kind of activity, an individual's errors in any industrial setting would probably only decrease productivity and/or profit, but human errors in aviation always make for headline news. A relative newcomer to this field is the sports world, where coaching has evolved over the past two decades from a more personality-based clinical approach to a more cognitive-based performance approach.

When looking at these three different fields, it is clear that their aims in the approach of mental performance are different. However, it would be oversimplifying to completely separate them, since the tools used for measurement of cognitive functioning show several similarities, and since these tools are the cornerstone of any approach to improve mental performance.

This issue of measurement tools raises the following questions. Is it possible to accurately monitor the quality of an individual's performance as experienced in everyday life? Are there specific markers allowing to predict potential failures? Which kind of tests could be used to generate these predictive markers?

Methodological issues in the quantification of cognitive performance

This question of instruments to use takes us back to the methodological problem of cognitive psychology: there are no existing instruments to directly measure mental processes. The tasks used to do so are always indirect measures, whether using subjective self-reports, peer evaluation, or psychometrics. Three issues will be discussed in this section: the ecological validity of cognitive tests, the individual versus population-based approach, and the inclusion of an emotional dimension to testing.

Ecological validity

A first issue in using experimental setups as part of these indirect measurements is ecological validity: can the results of a test readily be generalized to real-world performance? This has been a widely discussed topic in both neuropsychology and cognitive psychology for decades. In neuropsychology, Chaytor and Schmitter-Edgecombe (2003) discussed the growing demand for neuropsychological evaluations in non-clinical settings, e.g., by schools, employers, insurance companies, and others. Heinrichs (1990) pointed out that test inferences had to be judged by both their validity and their utility. He stated that medically referenced neuropsychological assessment had substantial validity, but that its utility, in terms of diagnostic decision-making, was becoming less important. In contrast, ecological and rehabilitative assessments had the potential for great utility, considering the growing demand, but the database to establish validity is limited. In cognitive psychology, there is a known trade-off in achieving the desirable combination of experimental rigor and ecological validity.

This issue is especially relevant when dealing with operational applications: do the results of carefully designed tests in laboratory conditions reflect the functioning of the human central executive when performing specific tasks in the real world? Indeed, the latter could involve multitasking, task switching, parallel processing of information from different categories, emotional appraisal, social influences, and motivational factors. The tests included in most of the well-known batteries are derived from theoretical tools that were intended as paradigms to isolate and describe specific cognitive processes in well-controlled conditions. There is no direct evidence indicating that the interaction of all these separate modalities in real-world human processing can be summarized by test results on each separate dimension. Despite the numerous commercial applications claiming the opposite, no definitive answer exists. Experimental evidence suggests that a reliance on cognitive testing only may lead to overly optimistic estimates about operational performance (Caldwell, 1995). However, making the choice of a totally naturalistic approach may improve the predictive value of the chosen measures, but deprives the experimenter of theoretical insights to qualify this performance. In pilots' selection, for example, the question has been repeatedly raised about whether the test results of selection really reflect future operational abilities, or whether it is only related to succeeding in qualification training. An example of the laboratory-like approach in aviation psychology is to proceed (1) to the cognitive task analysis of successful pilots on-the-job, which allows to decompose the overall performance and identify the modalities in information processing that are crucial to their specific performance, then (2) to the design of appropriate tests measuring these modalities with the necessary validation studies, then (3) to apply these tests for selection, and last (4) to perform longitudinal studies on applicants to check whether selection through these procedures was successful, by quantitative (success rates) and qualitative (causes of failure, related or not to the previously established model) analysis. This is a scientific method – and one of the reasons why science has lost momentum in applied environments is the necessary time for data collection, analysis, and validation. A more naturalistic approach would be to focus on the predictive value of the selection procedure, with less emphasis on construct validity, as is the case when flight simulators are used in aviation, or "screening flights", instead of standardized laboratory-derived cognitive testing.

Both approaches, as well as combinations, have been applied, with the strengths and weaknesses inherent to each. Thus, the question can be summarized as follows: do these tests reflect or predict a candidate's ability to become a qualified pilot, implying a causal link, or do they serve as a kind of general cut-off allowing a selection on objective criteria, known to correlate with future performance, with less emphasis on their significance?

This issue is of major importance in the evaluation of techniques and devices advertised as tools to improve mental performance, for it is a reflection of how our rational performance culture craves objective measures with cut-offs. However, there is a necessary caution regarding any type of tool or measure, and it is related to the complexity of the assessment of mental performance, which is exactly why we decided to provide this background in the current handbook.

Individual versus population-based approach

Another methodological issue is whether the assessment of mental performance should be individually tailored, or population based. All cognitive tests are first validated through investigation on a broad population, thus allowing for robust inferential statistical analysis. Ideally, an external criterion exists, to which the test results can be compared, to assess their validity. This is what happens when a new test or treatment is devised in medicine, to allow for the evidence-based approach. However, regarding mental performance, it brings us back to the cornerstone issue: there is no gold standard to assess any type of performance. There are proxies of varying quality, relevance, validity – depending on the topic, population, situation – but there are no gold standards.

The typical approach in cognitive psychology involves applying analysis of variance to assess whether the effect of an experimental manipulation in the studied sample can be generalized to a population level, with individual differences being relegated to the error term. This classical approach, called "nomothetic" explains why research on human performance in elite performers, with its niche population, or other extreme environments (i.e., with small sample size) is by definition a never-ending story, since there are not enough subjects to draw solid conclusions (e.g., Casler & Cook, 1999). The choice of the differential sensitivity of a task is related to this issue. If the aim of a study is the assessment of individual capability (e.g., for selection), the chosen tool should be a task showing minimal variance due to stressors (or more generally, to environmental conditions and situations) and maximal variance over individuals, as long as this variance is related to the dimension one aims to measure. On the other hand, if the aim is the assessment of specific stressors, the task to use should show minimal variance across individuals and maximal variance due to the stressor(s) (AGARDograph Report No. 308, NATO Human Factors Working Group, 1989). The question then becomes more complex when both aspects are mixed, when there is a need for the operational evaluation of the influence of stressors on specific individuals, selected according to well-defined abilities (i.e., therefore not being part of a normal population distribution on the tested parameters). The counterpart of the nomothetic approach, also referred to as the extensive approach, is the idiographic approach, also referred to as the intensive approach: the assessment of a single individual, which is done routinely through case-studies. Indeed, in neuropsychology, there are seldom groups of patients with exactly the same deficit. Therefore, some cases are considered as unique and studied as such, with comparisons to a group of closely matched controls.

Neuropsychology has thus made peace (by designing different statistical analysis methods) with the uniqueness of its study participants. However, applied environments like spaceflight, for example, still try to apply population-based approaches to small or very small sample sizes in order to apply what our scientific culture still considers to be the highest level of scientific quality studies. However, in the field of physiology, the added value of considering individual differences as more than noise is slowly gaining momentum. For example, the 2020 symposium of the Physiological Society was focused on that precise topic, and themed "Variability: How to Deal with It, Interpret It, and Learn from It".

Emotional and motivational factors

A last issue is the acknowledgment of the involvement of emotional and motivational factors in human everyday cognitive functioning. The conceptual framework of "decoupling" emotion and cognition prevailed in cognitive research for a long time. For example, in research about memory, every effort was made to isolate, i.e., decouple, memory from variations in other cognitive systems and from the influence of emotional and motivational factors. It is of course possible to study memory apart from every other cognitive influence, and it has delivered an impressive body of knowledge, but it is clear that it is functionally integrated with other systems and that everyday cognitive functioning is never free of emotional and motivational influence. However, for a long time, the attitude of "pure" cognitive scientists towards emotions may have been summarized as follows: "emotion is a factor which may be important for cognitive functioning but whose inclusion at this point would unnecessarily complicate the cognitive-scientific enterprise" (Gardner, 1985). This approach might have worked for isolating specific processes to be tested in laboratory conditions but could be falling short in reflecting real-life cognitive functioning.

Since the end of the 20th century, a more integrative view of neurosciences has prevailed, finding its way into pop culture through the 1995 book "Descartes' error: Emotion, reason and the Human Brain" from Antonio Damasio. However, several decades later, performance culture in Western society still views mental performance management mainly as buying additional RAM to our central executive. Any holistic approach including experiential and subjective dimensions will be dismissed as fluffy. And devices promising brain stimulation and the increase of certain well-targeted cognitive processes are in high demand, despite the less-than-flimsy evidence of their efficacy. In one of the following sections, we delve deeper into the issue of stress as a psychophysiological construct, as it is the emotional reaction most likely to affect an elite performer in an acute way.

Methodological solutions

Since mental performance can only be assessed through indirect measurements, and considering the different trade-offs we already explored, it seems impossible for one of those measurements to meet all the requirements expressed above. Therefore, a way to maximize both the understanding of human cognition and the operational validity of cognitive measurements is to use the method of converging operations (Eysenck & Keane, 2000, p. 523). This involves using a variety of approaches to consider a given problem from different perspectives, like triangulation in signal processing. When the findings from these different approaches are similar, this increases the allowed confidence in the validity of these results and in the usefulness of these approaches. When the findings are dissimilar, this indicates the need for further research to clarify the results. For the evaluation of mental performance, there are four possible approaches.

Subjective evaluation

The first one is subjective evaluation, which can be done by the subject (self-report), or by peers, or by experts (which typically takes place when instructors evaluate a candidate, or when coaches evaluate an athlete). Self-report reminds of the introspective method used by Wundt in the 19th century. The validity of this method has been widely investigated in neuropsychology and symptom management, for it is still the only available information to evaluate the impact of some pathologies. A well-known example is the investigation of memory function through reports of personal memories: the only possible access to this information is reported by the patient. There are two basic requirements to be fulfilled before considering the use of self-reports for cognitive processes: the studied process must be available to consciousness (which is not the case for most of the human information processing) and there must be an optimal collaboration of the subjects. However, because it depends on perception, it will be biased by the subject's perceptive filters, which can be situational, emotional, or both. Therefore, the replicability may be low. Optimal collaboration raises issues of social desirability and deception, narrowing the number of contexts in which self-reports might be useful. Several studies compared the correlation of self-reports and test results in the evaluation of functional status and cognitive performance. One of the examples that gained instant social-media-fame in recent years was the Dunning–Kruger effect (Kruger & Dunning, 1999). The title of their original publication speaks for itself: "Unskilled and unaware of it: how difficulties in recognizing one's own incompetence lead to inflated self-assessments". The main finding of their study is that the accuracy of self-report regarding one's performance actually evolves with the level of expertise. Novices will grossly overestimate their abilities in a variety of domains, according to what the authors describe as a lack of metacognitive ability, which would allow them to distinguish their errors. Expertise is thus a crucial moderator to take into account when relying on self-report.

According to Hoeymans, Feskens, Van den Bos, and Kromhout (1996), self-reports and test results provide complementary information: they measure related, but different dimensions of the same problem. Despite the expressed need for caution in interpreting the results, self-reports can thus provide useful insights. Furthermore, the method requires little investment, is not time consuming and is logistically easy to implement.

Cognitive testing

Cognitive testing, as included in standardized test batteries has already been discussed. The major advantage of these tests is the objective output (the most common are reaction times and error rates) allowing robust statistical comparisons, either between individuals or for a same individual over time and settings. Such tests are also quite easy to implement. However, since most of them are reducing their scope to a limited modality of cognitive processing, they may lack ecological validity, as discussed before. Practice effect is also a concern: to avoid the confounding influence of this effect, several protocols include extensive practice sessions. However, increasing the stability of the performance through multiple practice sessions may decrease the sensitivity to factors that might be investigated. Such a trade-off implies an a priori choice by the investigator, which has not been well-documented yet for operational settings.

Physiological measures

A third approach is psychophysiology. Physiological indicators are objective measurements which provide information regarding the state of the organism. This approach has seen substantial growth in the past decades, driven by the refining of available technology and methods, as is the case in functional brain-imaging techniques, or in wearable sensors. We have entered the era of the "quantified self", where the majority of our target populations of elite performers now wears some kind of monitoring device (usually through a wristwatch) to allow, at its most simple, a quantification of physical activity. However, the interpretation of proxy recordings (regarding metabolism, sleep, and stress status, to name just a few which are advertised) may sometimes not be clear, as the implemented algorithms may have been adapted to the commercial market by cutting the corners of scientific rigor. This means the claims which are sold are not backed up by science.

However, physiology is a very useful proxy in performance assessment because of the approach related to behavioural energetics (which we will detail in a following section). The overall rationale is to measure not only the output of information processing, such as a reaction time or decision-making, but also the cost of the process, in terms of physiological activation, both in terms of quality and quantity. As with every method, there is a caveat, and regarding physiological measurements these may reflect a specific arousal. Indeed, although the illusion of visualizing the mental process may be created, for the experimenter gains access to real-time processing data, these remain indirect measurements. With careful experimental design, variations in the recorded data can be attributed with lesser or higher probability to the experimental manipulation, but this attribution remains probabilistic.

Task simulations

The last method for evaluating performance is simulating real-world tasks. Task simulations have the highest face validity, since they are close to executing real-life complex tasks (e.g., a flight simulator). In a military culture, this could be termed as the "train-as-you-fight" approach. However, this complexity can make it difficult to implement and hard to standardize, since their validity relies on the tailoring to specific tasks. Furthermore, for complex tasks, a potential decrement would be difficult to interpret, since the degraded modality could be hard to identify. Since neuropsychological assessment is more and more concerned with ecological validity, as discussed before, a growing number of studies use task simulations to be able to issue statement about everyday performance, rather than about specific neuropsychological impairments. For example, researchers investigating prospective memory used a simulation of a shopping task (Farrimond, Knight & Titov, 2006), and real-life cognitive skills have been evaluated through the virtual reconstitution of a street scene (Titov & Knight, 2005). Despite all the whistles and bells about augmented and virtual reality, these offer only a range of tools within this category, not a new paradigm. However, the correct use of these methods depends mainly on the research question. If the effect of external variables, e.g., intake of caffeine under different pharmacological forms and doses, on a given performance, e.g., driving, is the focus of research, the use of a driving simulator is a coherent choice. If the research question is about the locus of performance effects of caffeine, the use of task simulation will not allow investigators to isolate the different components of this ability.

Conclusion

As stated before, using the method of converging operations enhances the informational value of cognitive investigations. It seems therefore critical to rely on several indicators, which have to be chosen by balancing their respective strengths and weaknesses in the function of the research question and the experimental setting. In the light of this brief overview on the definition and the assessment of mental performance, we hope we have conveyed the necessary caution when assessing so-called "scientific results" regarding mental performance-enhancing techniques. The following section will delve into a more detailed account of cognitive psychology, to try and "demystify" some of the jargon used in the description of mental performance.

Cognitive psychology

Cognitive psychology concerns the understanding of how people think, learn, remember, and solve problems, exploring the intricate workings of the mind to uncover the underlying processes that drive human behaviour. Understanding key cognitive psychology concepts is crucial for individuals working in a wide range of high mental performance domains. For example, aviation psychologists might focus on the cognitive processes involved in pilot decision-making, situation awareness, and multitasking under high-pressure situations (for a practical illustration of this, we refer to Chapter 11, where a case study in aviation psychology is presented), whereas human factors engineers aim to optimize the interaction between humans and technology, considering cognitive processes to design systems and interfaces that enhance performance and reduce errors. In such contexts, cognitive psychology contributes by understanding and enhancing mental processes to facilitate optimal performance, whether it is in the cockpit, on the field, in the workplace, or in complex environments. The application of cognitive psychology principles can lead to interventions and strategies that improve attentional control, memory, and decision-making skills, ultimately enhancing overall mental performance.

Cognitive processing

As discussed before, the most common outcome variables of cognitive tests are reaction time and error rates. Reaction time is the time that elapses between the presentation of a stimuli and a behavioural response, and is thus interpreted as the outcome of processing speed. Two types of reaction time are simple reaction time and choice reaction time. Simple reaction time is when a person reacts as quickly as possible to a single stimulus such as a tone, light, or symbol. In contrast a choice reaction time requires the person to make the correct choice regarding the response to a specific stimuli presented at the time (Deary, Liewald, & Nissan, 2011). Reaction time is influenced by a number of factors.

Age is one such factor: individuals' processing speed tends to decrease across the life span. The decrease is slow from young adulthood to middle age when the slowing becomes more pronounced after one reaches one's 50s and seems to plateau once people reach their 70s (Welford, 1977; Jevas and Yan, 2001; Luchies et al., 2002; Der and Deary, 2006). Reaction time represents an important component of the decline of higher level cognitive function observed in older populations (Madden, 2001; Salthouse, 1996). Interventions with the elderly to improve their step performance and decrease their falls have been shown to impact both simple and choice reactions times (Okubo, Schoene, & Lord, 2017), which indicates a link with physical fitness as well.

Indeed, reaction time is one of the cognitive outcomes that is influenced by physical fitness. Smith et al. (2010) reports a meta-analysis that among older individuals aerobic training as well as combined aerobic and strength training conferred multiple neurocognitive benefits including improved processing speed. A review from Bherer, Erickson, and Liu-Ambrose (2013) also concludes that aerobic exercise for older adults has broad spectrum benefits including neurocognitive outcomes such as reaction time. A meta-analysis from Chang, Labban, Gapin, and Etnier (2012) examined the effect of a single acute session of exercise. Results indicated that a consistent small positive effect of exercise on cognitive performance including choice reaction time was observed for three periods: during exercise, immediately following exercise, and after a brief delay.

Fatigue is another significant factor of influence with reaction time (see also section "Mental fatigue"). The first scientific investigation of how fatigue affects reaction times and error rates was by Mackworth (1948), in response to a very practical request from the UK Royal Air Force during WWII. The question was how long radar operators could accurately detect potential enemies, and thus how long they could be kept on duty. This initial practical enquiry started a whole field of study, namely sustained attention. Van den Berg and Neely (2006) compared individuals' performance on a monotonous simple reaction time task that required low rates or response over a two-hour time period. Individuals completed this task well rested and partially sleep deprived and results showed that found that reaction times were slower when individual were sleep deprived. Cote et al. (2009) randomly assigned individuals to three, five, or eight hours of sleep per night for two nights. They reported a dose-dependent deterioration in reaction time, meaning those with the least sleep performed worse while those on the eight-hour sleep schedule showed stable performance. Electroencephalography (EEG) data showed that three- and five-hour sleep groups experienced greater physiological sleepiness relative to baseline with those in the three-hour group having widespread EEG slowing later during the day. High-frequency EEG observed in the restricted sleep groups reflects compensatory efforts. Naps have been investigated as a countermeasure for fatigue during work periods. Takahashi et al. (2004) studied workers on a day shift who were allowed to take a 15-minute afternoon nap on the job. Workers' attitude toward the intervention was positive and they reported higher levels of alertness but no changes in reaction time were observed. Smith, Kilby, Jorgensen, and Douglas (2007) found that a 30-minute nap during a night shift for health workers had a positive impact on reaction times (faster responding) and subjective measures of alertness and that these persisted through the remainder of the shift but that it was not sufficient to return performance back to the baseline of the beginning of their shift.

Another factor influencing processing speed is the overall arousal of the individual. This has become an area of research in itself, which we will describe in a further section regarding stress and behavioural energetics.

The information-processing model

Cognitive psychology emerged as a reaction to behaviourism, which focused on observable behaviours while largely ignoring internal mental processes of the mind. The advent of computers provided a powerful metaphor for understanding the human mind. Psychologists began conceptualizing the mind as an information-processing system similar to a computer, with input, processing, output, and storage. The information-processing framework continues to help strongly how applied scientists create better tools, training, and strategies that align with how different aspects of our minds naturally function, ultimately improving outcomes in various practical settings. For example, the development of one of the firsts serial models of memory by Richard Atkinson and Richard Shiffrin (1968) led scientists with an organized model introducing specific tasks and strategies, targeted at specific aspects of memory and clarified their capacity limits.

The mind as a computer metaphor often assumed static and rule-based systems, akin to the programming of a computer. However, advances in neuroscience, particularly in the understanding of embodied cognition and neural plasticity, challenged this assumption (Jones et al., 2006). Neural plasticity refers to the brain's ability to reorganize itself by forming new connections throughout life, whereas embodied cognition relates to the active adaptation and reconfiguration of our cognitive systems by interacting with the environment. This is where new advances in artificial intelligence and neural networks are opening new areas of understanding how our minds constantly change after making interpretations of incoming information (Pfeifer & Lida, 2004).

The information processing models of cognition are crucial for improving mental performance because they provide a systematic framework for developing interventions, strategies, and technologies that align with cognitive processes. In the following sections, we describe some of the most influential cognitive models of attention, executive functions, and memory. Understanding each cognitive system helps when designing effective interventions (whether targeting selective, sustained, or divided attention, for example) to optimize task performance (e.g., designs minimizing factors of cognitive load and the likelihood of errors).

What is attention?

Attention is the linchpin of elite performance, transcending its evolutionary role in survival to become the cornerstone of excellence in various domains. It serves as the silent architect of focused awareness, the key differentiator between ordinary and extraordinary achievements. In the realm of elite soldiers, attention is the razor's edge that hones situational awareness, enabling rapid, precise responses in the midst of chaos. For athletes, it is the finely tuned focus that elevates performance to the pinnacle of precision and grace. Grounded in the principles of cognitive psychology and neuroscience, attention emerges not just as a survival tool but as the catalyst that propels individuals to triumph in the face of complexity, making it an indispensable asset for those aspiring to elite feats (Goldstein, 2019; Gazzaniga, Ivry & Mangun, 2018). Attention can be considered a minimal requirement for cognitive processing and mental performance. Attention acts as a gateway, determining which information is processed and which is ignored. It is an essential filter that allocates cognitive resources to relevant stimuli while filtering out distractions. Without attention, cognitive processes would lack direction and focus, hindering the ability to perceive, process, and respond to information effectively. Whether in problem-solving, decision-making, learning, or any cognitive task, attention provides the foundational framework for optimal mental performance. In this sense, attention is a fundamental prerequisite for the entire spectrum of cognitive processing.

Attention is multidimensional in nature, ranging from purely physiological levels of reactiveness (also called arousal) to sustained processing of crucial tasks while avoiding distractors. Each component involves different cognitive processes and neural mechanisms, adding layers of complexity to its study. Attention has traditionally been classified as having three main components: alerting, orienting, and executive control (Petersen & Posner, 2012). Alerting involves achieving a state of readiness to perceive stimuli, acting as the "fuel" that powers the intensity of attention. This is essential for high mental performance, as in high-stress situations a heightened state of alertness primes individuals to rapidly detect threats, process critical information, and make split-second decisions. Thus, ensuring mission success while minimizing risks requires maintaining optimal alertness or cognitive readiness, for instance by ensuring appropriate sleep (Killgore, 2010). Orienting, in turn, is the ability to shift and direct one's focus towards specific stimuli or locations in the environment, allowing us to prioritize and process relevant information, and thus guiding responses to potential threats or strategic details. While orienting can automatically guide responses to salient and unexpected stimuli (for example, enhancing combat skills), relying solely on external cues can divert focus from the task at hand and lead to a loss of concentration on important goals. Finally, executive attention refers to the management and voluntary control of one's focus in situations that require resolving conflicts, shifting focus, and maintaining concentration on relevant tasks (Table 2.1). Executive attention is intimately related to the cognitive system responsible for supervising and coordinating various mental processes online (Baddeley, 2012), and rather than understood as the opposite of orienting, it should be understood as a simultaneous process actively deciding whether to follow external or internal cues, relevance, or instructions (Katsuki & Constantinidis, 2013). Executive attention helps elite performers to prioritize critical details, anticipate potential threats and suppress irrelevant distractions, formulate strategic plans, and shift focus as needed, all of which contribute to enhancing decision-making, response times, and overall cognitive efficiency (Gray, Gaska, & Winterbottom, 2016). Other authors provide an in-depth explanation on the conceptualization of attention in contemporary psychology and neuroscience (Esterman & Rothlein, 2019; Lindsay, 2020).

In today's technologically driven world, attention has become the currency of the digital realm. We are encircled by a myriad of devices, including smartphones, tablets, laptops, and smartwatches, each competing for our cognitive focus. The ubiquity of these gadgets has ushered in an era where our attention is persistently under siege by a barrage of distractions. The fear of

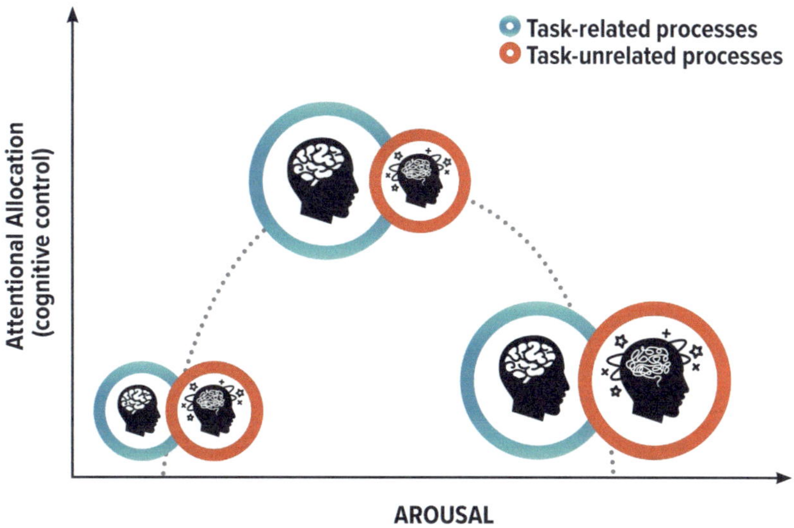

Figure 2.1 At any given task, our performance depends on a sufficient, yet not too elevated, level of arousal. However, an engaged individual cannot rely on a sufficient level of motivation to engage in a task, but also needs to deploy an optimal level of attentional allocation to a specific task in order to sustain task-related information processing, while inhibiting the distraction from task-unrelated processes.

missing out, perpetuated by the constant stream of information and updates, exerts a powerful pull on our minds, increasing our mental load. Notifications, with their intrusive beeps and alerts, punctuate our daily lives, drawing us away from our tasks. These digital interruptions, among others, collectively conspire to fragment our attention, leaving us in a perpetual battle to safeguard our cognitive resources in this ever-connected world.

Attention, as has been introduced, is not an isolated mechanism independent from other psychological functions, indeed we deploy attention towards expected stimuli following plans and motivations based on memorized rules. Knudsen (2007) describes four component processes which are fundamental to attention:

- working memory,
- competitive selection,
- top-down sensitivity control, and
- filtering for stimuli that are likely to be behaviourally important (salience filters).

In focusing on relevant information, a competitive selection process operates (Desimone & Duncan, 1995). Consider an elite athlete in a team sport in action, where attention is divided among factors like opponents' moves, game dynamics, and teammates' positions. Competitive selection prevents overwhelm, prioritizing crucial details through top-down sensitivity control aligned with

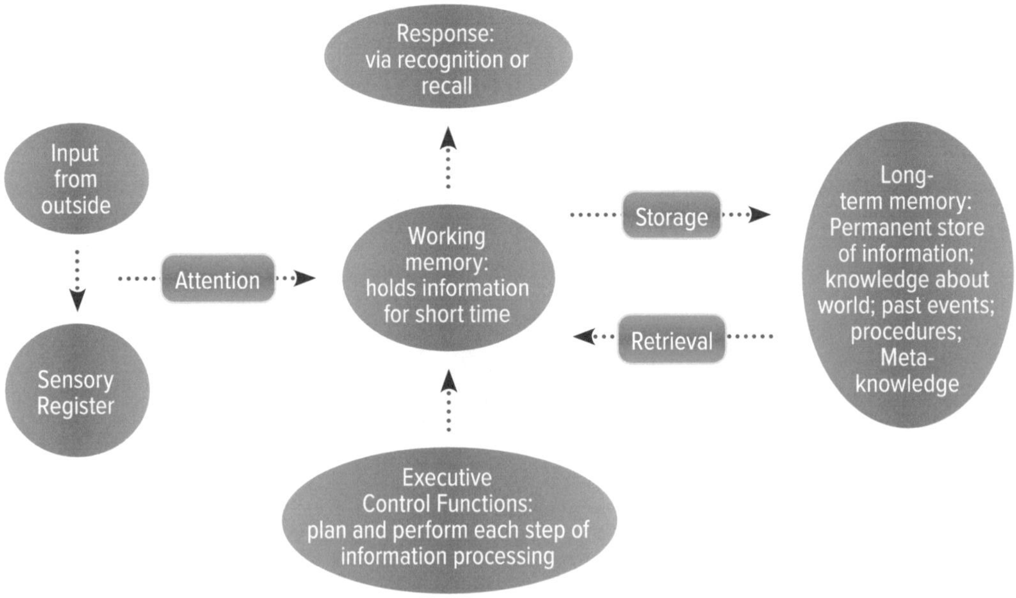

Figure 2.2 A generic information processing model of learning and memory based on the model originally proposed by Atkinson and Shiffrin (1968).

performance goals. This process works with bottom-up salience filters, highlighting important but infrequent cues. These filters can override ongoing tasks, exemplified when an athlete swiftly adapts to sudden changes in the game (Egeth & Yantis, 1997). Egeth and Yantis stress the dynamic interplay of attention between stimuli and goals.

Working memory, in turn, is like your mental notepad, holding onto information briefly for tasks like solving problems or following directions, making it crucial for everyday thinking and decision-making.

Let us proceed to a detailed analysis of each component in this model, encompassing both executive functions and memory.

Executive functions

Executive functions (also typically referred to as cognitive control) refer to a set of higher-order cognitive processes that facilitate goal-directed behaviour, encompassing skills such as working memory, cognitive flexibility, and inhibitory control. These functions are crucial for planning, decision-making, and problem-solving, contributing to adaptive and flexible behaviour (Diamond, 2013). Executive functions are intricately linked not just to attention, but also to elite mental performance (Miyake et al., 2000). In high-stakes environments, such as those encountered by elite athletes, soldiers, musicians, or professionals, the ability to maintain focus, quickly adapt to changing conditions, and inhibit irrelevant information is paramount. Strong executive functions contribute to heightened decision-making precision, efficient problem-solving, and adaptability, all essential for achieving peak performance. Executive functions are implicated in the control and regulation of "lower-level" cognitive processes and goal-directed, future-oriented behaviour. They are activated when confronted by unfamiliar circumstances and are required to optimize our response (Alvarez & Emory, 2006; Gilbert & Burgess, 2008). It is also typically invoked as an important control process when we need to intervene in a lower-level process such as when

Table 2.1 Executive functions

Core executive functions	*High executive functions*
WORKING MEMORY: The ability to temporarily hold and manipulate information for cognitive tasks (see next section on memory).	**PROBLEM-SOLVING:** The skill to effectively solve complex problems by considering various strategies and alternatives.
INHIBITORY CONTROL: The ability to suppress or override automatic or prepotent responses.	**GOAL-SETTING:** The capability to establish and pursue well-defined objectives.
COGNITIVE FLEXIBILITY: The capacity to adapt and switch between different cognitive tasks or mental sets.	**METACOGNITION:** Awareness and understanding of one's own cognitive processes, including monitoring regulating one's thinking.

a routine response process produces an error. As such this serves a crucial adaptation function within the attentional control system (Barkley, 1996; Manly & Robertson, 1997; Stuss et al., 1998; Stuss et al., 2001). Research has identified inhibition (preventing a prepotent response) as well as the ability to switch between tasks as core components of the cognitive control (Baldo et al., 2001; Burgess et al., 1998; Rabbitt, 1997; Troyer et al., 1998; Welsh, Satterlee-Cartmell & Stine, 1999), upon which other high-level executive functions are built (as summarized in Table 2.1). Some of the key high executive functions are problem-solving, goal-setting, and metacognition. Problem-solving is akin to assembling a mental puzzle where individuals strategically manipulate mental representations (Newell & Simon, 1972). The process involves breaking down a complex problem into manageable components, accessing relevant knowledge from long-term memory, and generating potential solutions through trial and error or heuristic strategies. Goal-setting is another key cognitive process where individuals establish specific and challenging objectives, and these objectives are characterized by being Specific, Measurable, Achievable, Relevant, and Time-bound (SMART; Locke & Latham, 2002). Chapter 4 elaborates on goal-setting as a mental skill to enhance performance. Strongly intertwined with both problem-solving and goal-setting, metacognition is a key mechanism involved in self-regulation associated to the ability to evaluate one's mental functions and performance (Rahnev, 2021). The relevance of executive functions in applied performance research is highlighted in Chapter 15, with the description of mental performance in the corporate world.

What is memory?

If attention is the crucial mechanism allowing for outstanding information processing in the present moment, memory can be understood as the ability to retain and recall relevant information from the past. In other words, without memory there is no learning and thus we would be at the mercy of perpetual ignorance, unable to benefit from past experiences or apply acquired knowledge to navigate and adapt to our surroundings. Without memory, elite performance would not exist. Similar to attention, memory is multidimensional in nature, this section covers a broad categorization depending on both the duration for which information is retained and its content.

SENSORY MEMORY

This is the briefest form of memory and pertains to the initial processing of sensory information from the environment (Irwin & Thomas, 2008). It retains information for a very short period, typically of the order of milliseconds to seconds. It can be thought of as a continuation of the present event but removed in time and always modality-specific (Crowder & Surprenant, 2000). However insignificant it can appear, sensory memory is very relevant to elite behavioural performance since it allows for a quick processing of incoming information, with its associated enhanced reaction times, precision in movements and enhanced situational awareness.

SHORT-TERM MEMORY (AND WORKING MEMORY)

Since the inception of scientific memory research, initiated by experiments conducted by Hermann Ebbinghaus in the 1880s, revealing the primacy and recency effects, which highlight the tendency to better remember the first and last items in a list, numerous studies have sought to identify factors influencing memory retention. Initially, the primary goal of retaining items in short-term memory was seen as facilitating their transfer to long-term memory and expanding the concurrent storage capacity of short-term memory for swift retrieval in tasks (Atkinson & Shiffrin, 1968). However, it became evident that this process is not passive; rather, items in short-term memory can be actively manipulated to extract pertinent features (Kail & Hall, 2001; Aben, Stapert & Blokland, 2012). This active processing, now recognized as working memory, plays a pivotal role in efficient long-term storage and enhances decision-making, a critical component of executive functions in contemporary understanding (Baddeley and Hitch, 1974; Baddeley, 2020). Although initial experiments revealed a limitation of short-term retention for about 30 seconds, the most influential result came from studies showing that the active use of information in short-term memory allows for infinite online availability of information of about seven plus or minus two sets of inputs (Miller, 1956).

Critically, working memory is a capacity limited system, meaning that information needs to be constantly maintained or it won't be retained. Because of its limited capacity, information competes to access the system. Here is when attention becomes crucial, helping control and guide working memory, together with other executive functions, to the task-related information processing. This aspect of working memory is called "the central executive". However, working memory is said to have two other main components, being the phonological loop, in charge of rehearsing auditory and verbal information, and the visuo-spatial sketchpad, in charge of stimulating visuo-spatial information (Genovesio, Brasted & Wise 2006, LaBar et al. 1999).

Working memory itself is sensitive to fatigue, similarly to processing speed, such that when people are tired, we see reduced capacity and efficiency of processing (Cote et al., 2009). There has been much interest in working memory training in recent years. The topic is one of considerable controversy. What is difficult to determine from the current evidence is: what exactly is the mechanism of change that underlies working memory training interventions? Are participants increasing their baseline capacity of the system? Or due to the repetitious nature of the hundreds and thousands of memory trials within training studies are participants deriving or deploying memory strategies to improve performance while their basic cognitive capacity remains unchanged? For more discussion of memory training and other interventions see Chapter 8.

LONG-TERM MEMORY

Long-term memory is the system responsible for the storage of information over a longer period, ranging from minutes to a lifetime. It has a much larger capacity compared to short-term memory and requires extra layers of mental preprocessing (Norris, 2017). However, although different, similar genetic and neural mechanisms might be in play (Bailey, Bartsch & Kandel, 1996; Hawkins, Kandel & Bailey, 2006). Long-term memory can be further divided into explicit (declarative) and implicit (non-declarative) memory.

Explicit or declarative memory involves the conscious recollection of information and is divided into two subtypes: episodic and semantic memories. Episodic being the recollection of specific events or experiences in a temporo-spatial context, and semantic memory being the abstract knowledge and facts not tied to specific experiences. Interestingly, flashbulb memories are a particular subset of episodic memories, which are highly emotionally charged. For example, for the 9/11 terrorist attacks in the USA, some people report being able to remember vivid details from the day of the event and the moment they learned thc ncws. No matter how vivid the recollection, these memories are just as vulnerable to inaccuracies as other memories.

In turn, implicit or procedural memory, involves how prior experiences and behaviours, even without conscious awareness, are maintained or improved over time. This includes skills, habits, and unconscious priming effects (i.e., a psychological phenomenon where exposure to a stimulus, a prime, influences a person's response to a subsequent related stimulus). This type of memory is painfully free from explicit explanations and particularly dependent on active practice, the more a task is practiced, the more it becomes automated and freed from executive control.

Conclusion

The purpose of this introduction to cognitive psychology was to highlight some of the mental processes that are constantly at work when people are living their everyday lives. Most individuals can remain unaware of the intricacies of the mind. However, for human performance professionals, it is valuable to consider how the performance we aim to enhance is constructed. Threat discrimination, situational awareness, split second decision-making, planning, etc. collectively rest on these basic and more advanced functions. This understanding comes to the forefront when we desire to deliver specialized training through devices or other skill training programs. It would be wise to consider what is the mechanism of change and whether there is evidence that this capacity is malleable. It is our recommendation to consider these propensities when designing systems and procedures.

How mental is mental performance: a psychophysiological concept of performance

Performance

We have now briefly described the academic fundamental research aiming to uncover the cogs and wheels behind our information processing. At the applied end of the spectrum, what we may call the user end, humans have always striven to increase their mental capacities. During the last decades, cognitive enhancement has received a considerable amount of attention both in the general population and in the academic community. It can be defined as the attempt to increase, in healthy individuals, cognitive functions (Taya, Sun, Babiloni, Thakor, & Bezerianos, 2015; Thakor & Sherman, 2013). As we have described earlier, cognitive functions help the organism to process and organize information to guide behaviour (e.g., reasoning or coordination of motor output). Despite the fact that there are no existing instruments to directly measure mental processes, performance is always an adaptative response to demands of the environment (Homan, 2002; Salehi et al., 2010). Thus, understanding cognitive performance would benefit from the addition of subjective and psychophysiological aspects to the traditionally measured behavioural outcomes (i.e., reaction times and error rates) (Pattyn et al., 2009).

Psychophysiology

Most definitions of psychophysiology emphasize the mapping of the relationships between mechanisms underlying psychological and physiological events (e.g., Hugdahl, 1995).

Psychophysiology is based on the assumption that human perception, thought, emotion, and action are embodied phenomena (Cacioppo, Tassinary & Berntson, 2000) and that an integrated view of the whole organism will provide information which, with the appropriate experimental design, can shed light on human processes. The level of analysis is not on isolated components, but on an integrative view of the interaction between organisms and their environments. No subordination or hierarchical relationship is implied between mind and body.

Several physiological measurements have been used to infer information about mental processes. Two types of recordings can be distinguished: those aiming to record specific brain activity and those targeting systemic activation, fitting with the behavioural energetics approach we will describe later on. Overall, these systemic measures include galvanic skin response (humidity, and therefore conductance, of the skin), pupillary diameter, heart frequency, blood pressure, respiratory frequency, and others. These systemic measures have been used to either reflect the reaction of an organism on exposure to psychological variables (e.g., in mood induction procedures or stress research) or to provide information about resource allocation, the activation level of the overall system.

As stated by Ohman, Hamm, and Hughdahl (2000), nervous systems play a key role in making organisms integrated systems. For researchers, it seems very appealing to use indicators that reflect the state of these nervous systems. Furthermore, these indicators are less dependent on the subjects' collaboration, can give information on mental processes in real time, and are "hard data": objective, reliable, and easily quantifiable. However, physiology is not just a window into the brain and mind: "heart rate, for example, has more important business to mind than informing psychologists about the level of arousal in research participants" (Ohman et al., 2000). This is why many psychologists are often disappointed by psychophysiological results: an important matter of debate is that physiological and psychological measurements often fail to show reliable correlations. Considering a correlation between two measures as reflecting a shared source of variance, reaction time and heart rate could, theoretically, show a correlation based on an experimental variation of cognitive workload. However, while this experimental variation could account for most of the variance observed in reaction time, it will never account for most of the variance observed in heart rate, since the latter is the complex output of countless feedback loops in different systems, mainly tasked with the maintenance of homeostasis for bodily functions (Cacioppo & Tassinary, 1990).

The nervous system

The common denominator of physiological recordings applied in psychophysiological research is to reflect either central, or somatic, or autonomic nervous system activation. In mental performance applications throughout this handbook, we will mainly discuss either central (i.e., brain) or autonomic nervous system (ANS) activation. We will now provide an introductory description of the measures for both.

As depicted in Figure 2.3, the nervous system includes both the central nervous system (CNS) and the peripheral nervous system (PNS). The CNS comprises the brain (i.e., the body's "control centre") and spinal cord, while the PNS contains the nerves or neuronal axons through which the central nervous system interacts with the rest of the body. The CNS receives information about changes in the internal and external environment through afferent sensory nerves. The CNS is responsible for integrating, processing, and coordinating the sensory information and the motor commands. The nervous system is made up of nerve cells called neurons which are responsible for all the connections in this information-transmitting system, and thus also between brain and body. There are three main types of neurons. First, the sensory neurons carry information from the internal and external environment upward toward the CNS. Second, the motor neurons send information

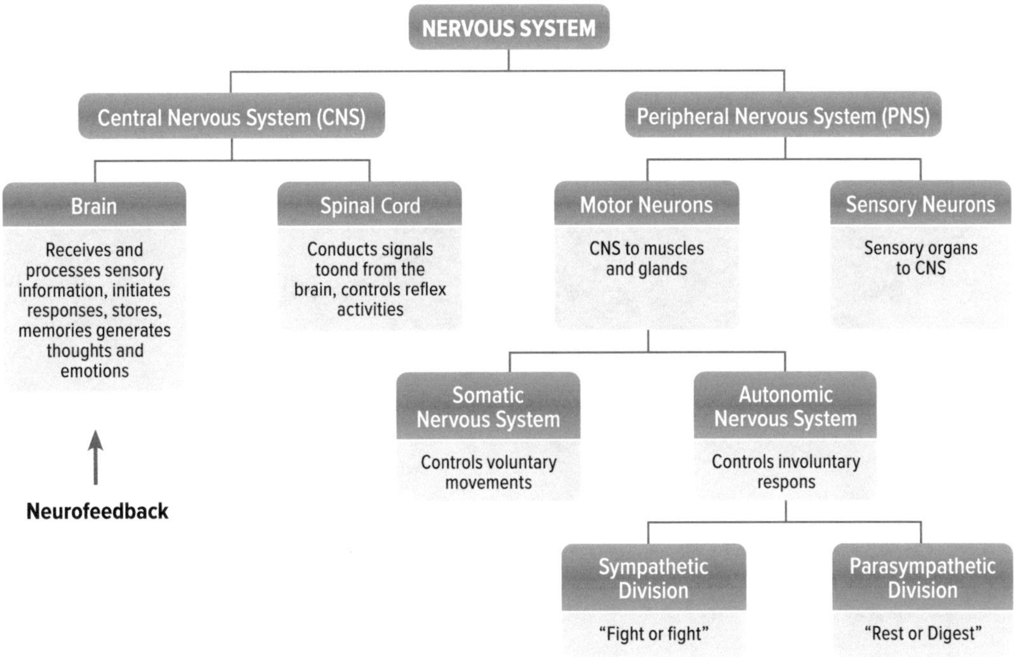

Figure 2.3 Representation of the human nervous system. Adapted from https://kaiserscience.wordpress.com/biology-the-livingenvironment/physiology/brain-and- nervous-system/

downward and away from the CNS to control the activity of muscles. Third, in between sensory and motor neurons, they are the association neurons also called the interneurons. Interneurons mediate simple reflexes as well as being responsible for the highest functions of the brain, the cognitive processes we have described in a previous section.

Brain anatomy

The brain is anatomically divided into three parts: (1) the cerebrum, (2) the cerebellum, and (3) the brainstem (see Figure 2.4 for an overview).

As a result of evolution, the brainstem and the cerebellum, which are included in the primitive or reptilian brain, are responsible for survival. The brainstem relays signals from the spinal cord and directs basic internal functions and reflexes; whereas the cerebellum adjusts body movements, speech coordination, and balance. The cerebrum, the most prominent part of the brain, which includes the cerebral cortex, is responsible for higher mental functions. It is divided by the longitudinal fissure into two hemispheres, i.e., the left and the right hemispheres (see Figure 2.5). The corpus callosum, located underneath the cerebrum at the midline of the brain, allows for communication between both hemispheres. This large connective pathway is connected to the cerebrum by a white fibrous tract. The cerebrum's surface is made of ridges (gyri) and grooves (sulci). These increase the amount of cortex in the cranial cavity and thus the surface area for information processing capability. Some sulci divide each hemisphere into four lobes, named after the cranial bones overlying them: the frontal lobe, the temporal lobe, the occipital lobe, and the parietal lobe (see Figure 2.5).

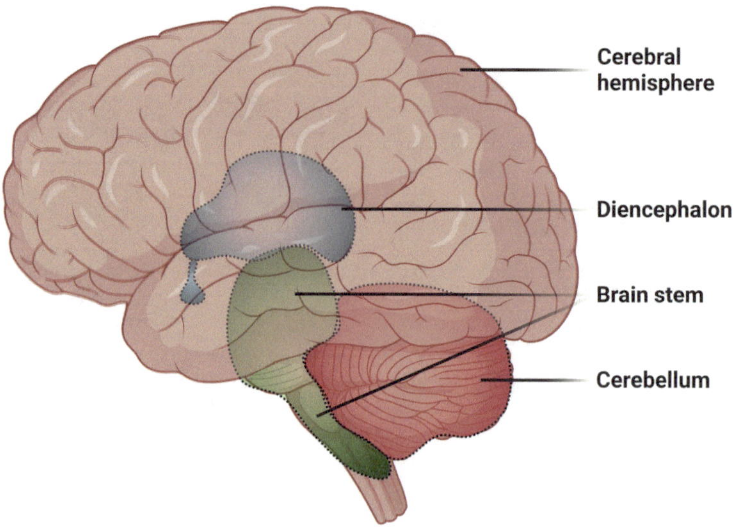

Figure 2.4 The different subdivisions of the brain.

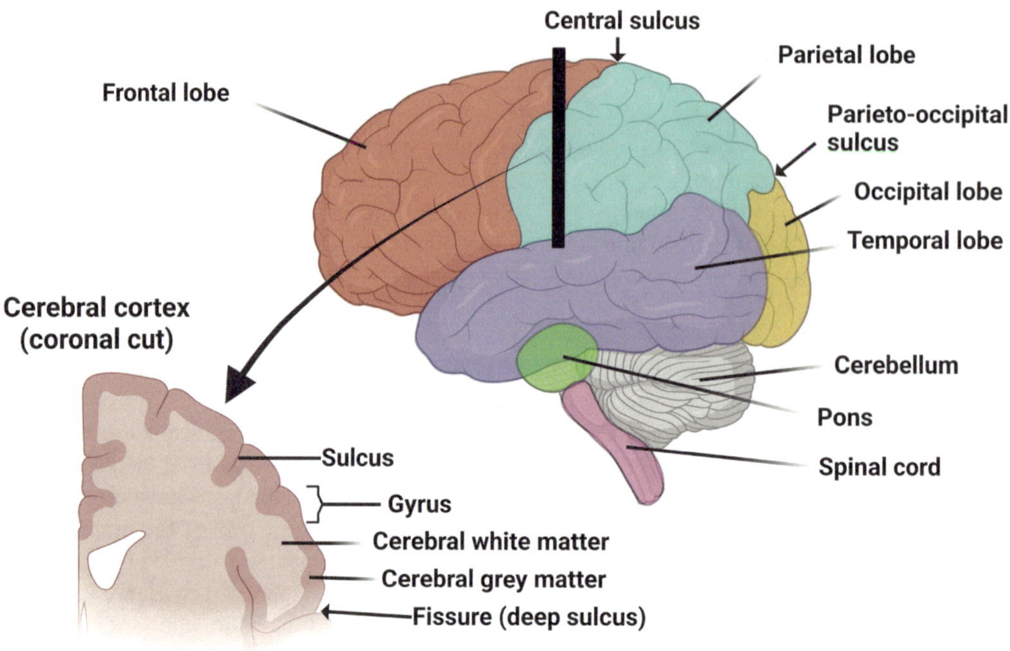

Figure 2.5 Representation of the four lobes for the left cerebral hemisphere. The cerebrum's surface is made of ridges (gyri) and grooves (sulci).

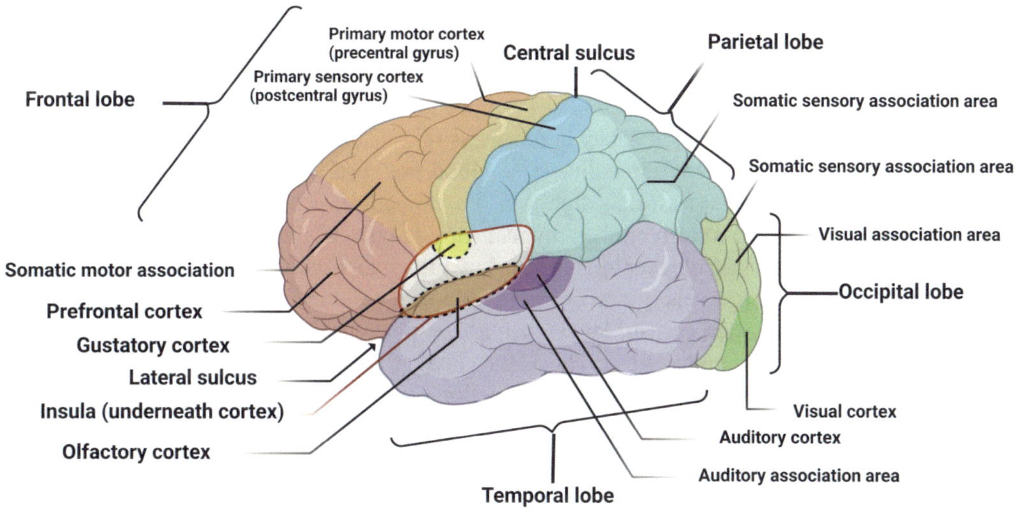

Figure 2.6 The specialized areas of the cerebrum.

The lobes are functional segments and they are specialized in various areas: (1) somatic sensory areas receiving impulses from the body's sensory receptors, (2) primary motor area sending impulses to skeletal muscles, and (3) areas involved in the interpretation such as Broca's area involved in our ability to speak (see Figure 2.6).

Many of the described functions are carried out by both sides of the brain, but some are largely lateralized to one cerebral hemisphere or the other. Areas concerned with some of these higher functions, such as speech (which is lateralized in the left hemisphere in most people), have been identified. While there is some specialization to each hemisphere, the idea of lateralization of functions has been oversimplified in pop culture. Some functions produce activity on both sides of the brain, and the processing of these may be different in different people (e.g., novices vs. experts).

The brain as part of the network: the example of the stress response

Beneath the lobes of the cerebral cortex is a complex network of connections and structures. One of these structures is the limbic system; it is key to understanding emotions, memory, and the fight-or-flight response, which we will describe in more detail in the section about stress. Some of the parts of the limbic system (diencephalon) include: (1) the amygdala, associated with deep emotions and fear; (2) the hippocampus, which is crucial for memory storage and emotions; (3) the anterior thalamic nuclei, which is necessary for sensory data processing, and (4) the thalamus, which relays impulses from all sensory systems to the cerebral cortex, which in turn sends messages back to the thalamus. Below the thalamus, the hypothalamus (the master gland of our endocrine system) controls the survival functions and the autonomic nervous system. Indeed, to respond to a stressful challenge, the brainstem starts the noradrenaline release in a variety of structures as well as the adrenaline release from the adrenal glands (situated just above the kidney). Their release underpins the fight-or-flight response (sympathetic activation).

The fight-or-flight response is also a neuroendocrine response resulting from the activation of a circuit linking the brain and the body (i.e., the hypothalamic–pituitary–adrenal or HPA axis). This links the hypothalamus, the pituitary gland, the adrenal cortex, and the hippocampus together by a bloodstream highway carrying specialized hormones. The hypothalamus is the key brain area regulating many of our hormones. Indeed, the hypothalamus integrates the inputs received from areas of the brain processing emotional information with the inputs coming from regions of the brainstem controlling sympathetic nervous responses to produce a hormonal response activating the pituitary gland. The pituitary gland releases a hormone called adrenocorticotropin (ACTH) into the bloodstream, which in turn stimulates the production of cortisol by the adrenal glands. Cortisol is a steroid hormone which is key in the stress response, as it raises metabolic fuels (e.g., blood sugar or fatty acids), helps adrenaline raise blood pressure, and turns off all the processes that are not essential for survival (e.g., digestion, inflammation, or wound healing). Then, cortisol feeds back to the brain to turn on the amygdala and to turn off the hippocampus. The hippocampus has two types of cortisol receptors: (1) the low mineralocorticoid (MR) receptor, activated by the normally circulating levels of cortisol in the bloodstream; and (2) the high glucocorticoid (GR) receptor, activated when cortisol levels increase, if in excess, the activity of the receptor is sustained to shut down the hippocampus. This is the classical curve relating optimal stress to brain function, which we will discuss in the upcoming section on stress.

Electrophysiological recordings of the brain: EEG

The physiological activity of the brain can be measured, quantified, and investigated through different imaging techniques. These techniques are based either on hemodynamic (i.e., blood flow) changes, which is the case for functional magnetic resonance imaging (fMRI); metabolic activity, for example, positron emission tomography (PET scan) or near infrared spectroscopy (NIRS); or electromagnetic recording, which is the oldest brain "imaging" technique, electroencephalography (EEG). Since the techniques reviewed and described in subsequent chapters do not use any other functional brain imagery method, we will focus on EEG.

In EEG, brain-related electrical potentials are recorded from the scalp. EEG signals always represent the potential difference between two electrodes, an active electrode and the so-called reference electrode. Electrodes are located on the head according to an internationally accepted standard, the 10–20 system, which thus standardizes the recording of electrical activity in specific areas (see Figure 2.7).

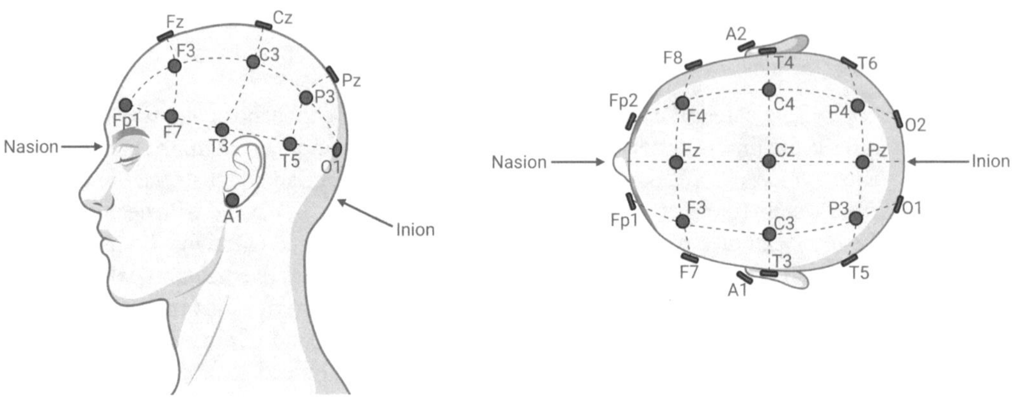

Figure 2.7 10–20 system is an internationally recognized method to describe the location of the scalp electrodes. The system is based on the relationship between the location of a sensor and the underlying area of cerebral cortex. The number 10–20 refers to the f fact that the distance between adjacent electrodes are either 10% or 20% of the total front-back or right-left distance of the skull. The lobe is identified by a letter (F = frontal; C = central; P = parietal; T = temporal; O = occipital) and the hemisphere by a number (even numbers on the right hemisphere and odd numbers on the left hemisphere).

One single electrode can detect changes in the field potential of thousands to millions of neurons (see Figure 2.7) on the surface of the cortex across a localized area. To communicate together, neurons use an electrochemical event which is called the action potential. The action potential is a discharge caused by fast opening and closing of sodium (Na^+) and potassium (K^+) ion channels in the neuron membrane. Nerve fibres behave like electrical conductors, and so an action potential generated at one point creates another gradient of voltage between the active and resting membranes adjacent to it. In this way, the action potential is actively propelled in a wave of depolarization that spreads from one end of the nerve fibre to the other.

Once an individual neuron has completed an action potential, it begins to repolarize to rejuvenate itself. The time period needed to do this is called a refractory period, in which no further communication can take place. Tracking these discharges over time reveals the electrical brain activity. Either visual or spectral analysis (fast Fourier-transform) of the recorded brain activity indicates that neurons oscillate within a range of distinct frequency ranges. Raw EEG contains various EEG frequency components, ranging from the lowest to the highest as delta, theta, alpha, beta, and gamma. The patterns of EEG frequencies vary, depending on the measured brain location and the activities performed. Each of these specific frequency ranges is obtained by a rhythmic pacemaker property of neurons, either by intrinsically generating oscillations in electrical voltage, or by interacting with other neurons in an excitatory/inhibitory pattern, or in a combination of the above (Steriade, Jones, & Llinas, 1990).

EEG oscillations appear to be dependent on interactions between the cortex and the thalamus, which both produce intrinsically rhythmical activities. Whereas the thalamus has been critically implicated in the pacing of such rhythmical activities, the cortex provides the coherent output in response to thalamic input and generates the clear majority of oscillations that can be recorded at the scalp. Nonetheless, the drivers behind many of these oscillations have yet to be confirmed. Chapter 7 (Neurostimulation Tools) and Chapter 9 (Biofeedback) will apply these notions of neurophysiology.

The autonomic nervous system

The ANS is called autonomic, or self-governing, because it acts independently, not requiring voluntary action or consciousness from the subjects. As we will further discuss in Chapter 6, in the section related to breathing techniques, this classical neuro-anatomical distinction is challenged by breath control, which is the only vital function with a leverage for voluntary control. The ANS is subdivided into two anatomically and functionally distinct systems: the sympathetic branch and the parasympathetic branch. Figure 2.8 gives a schematic representation of the activity of both branches of the ANS on a range of effector organs. This figure does not provide an anatomically precise view of the system but shows a good summary of the antagonist effects on various organs. These effects have been applied in psychophysiological research to infer the activity of the ANS. For example, the use of pupillary diameter as a proxy for arousal, which, as shown on Figure 2.8, increases with sympathetic stimulation.

This usual textbook description (e.g., Carlson, 2017) of this part of the peripheral nervous system, is a concept of two antagonizing branches innervating the same effector organs, which status is always a result of the shifting balance between both. Both branches are the sympathetic and the parasympathetic nervous system, where the action of the sympathetic is usually described as activating, whereas the parasympathetic is considered the inhibiting, or relaxing mode. The interaction of both has been described as responsible for the homeostasis, the fact the human body was designed to warrant a constant "milieu intérieur", one of the founding concepts of human physiology, dating back to Claude Bernard (1857, in Carlson, 2017).

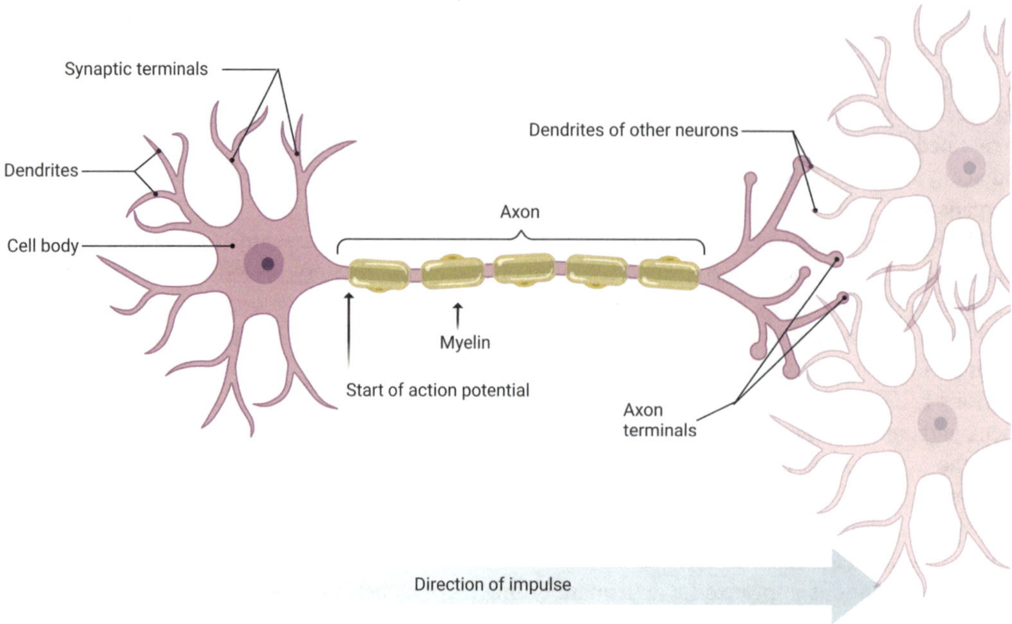

Figure 2.8 A nerve cell, or a neuron, consists of many different parts. A neuron is composed by a soma (cell body + nucleus), several dendrites and a unique axon. The dendrites receive the information/the signals/the message while the cell body is the metabolic unit. When a message arrives and needs to be transmitted to another neuron, this message is called an action potential. The axon is the emitting unit of this message. The message is transmitted to the other cell inn a chemical form through the synaptic terminals. This chemical will excite or inhibit the receiving cell. Nerve conduction is thus an electrochemical process.

The ANS description and the history of stress physiology go hand in hand, which is why we are introducing some concepts here that will be further detailed in the following section on stress. Indeed, Cannon's first description of the "fight-or-flight" response (1914) and Selye's (1936) work on the General Adaptation Syndrome both put the stress response in the spotlight, with the "emergency function" (i.e., sympathetic activation) of the ANS as the centre of gravity, and more specifically the sympathetic part, ensuring energy mobilization. In physiology research, this view described stress as a neural circuit (hypothalamus–adrenal medulla) on top of the hormonal one (pituitary–adrenal cortex) (Öhman, Hamm & Hughdahl, 2000). Psychology applied the concept to behavioural energetics, describing the psychophysiological integration of the stress response. This was an important stepping stone to the motivational concept of generalized drive. After Moruzzi and Mangoun's (1949, in Caccioppo et al., 2000) description of the reticular activating system, the ANS was seen as the "peripheral core" of the arousal and activation dimension (Malmo, 1965). Thus, the use of ANS innervated organs status (e.g., heart rate or skin conductance) measures in psychophysiology was seen as an indicator for an underlying one-dimensional concept of arousal and activation, thus providing information about the motivational status of the organism.

The most recent functional descriptions of the ANS see the emergence of the neurovisceral integration perspectives (Thayer & Lane, 2000; Thayer & Brosschoot, 2005; Friedman, 2007). These models encompass the integrative regulation of cognitive, emotional, and physiological response. They also emphasize the need for a flexible regulation, to allow for optimal adaptation of an organism to changing environmental demands, and thus for optimal functioning. The concept of homeostasis, with its ideal of internal stability, where labile physiology is an indicator for pathology, is replaced by allostasis, stressing the fact that different circumstances demand different allostatic set points (and thus that there is no single optimum value for each physiological parameter), and that the integration and regulation of this variability thus needs to happen at a systemic, and not a local level. Rather than a stable "milieu intérieur", these models emphasize healthy functioning as a dynamic steady state, where the constant physiological variability allows for a stable outcome, through a constant adaptation of the organism. To quote the editorial of a 2006 issue of Clinical Autonomic Research: "Autonomic neurology is emerging as a key nexus of cognitive neuroscience, behavioural neurology, and neuropsychiatry" (Goldstein & Silverman, 2006). The last decade has seen a growing acknowledgement that the ANS is not as autonomic as previously thought, such as the PNS is not as peripheral (Buijs, 2013).

This brain–body connection is not new, it was already suggested 150 years ago, by Claude Bernard (Bernard, 1858, 1898; in Thayer & Lane, 2000). He claimed that the prefrontal cerebral cortex has a regulatory function on the activity of subcortical circuits related to the motivated response. Decades later, Thayer and Lane (2000) called this network of neural structures related to physiological, cognitive, and emotional regulation, the Central Autonomic Network (CAN) (Thayer & Lane, 2000). This network allows the brain to control visceromotor, neuroendocrine, and behavioural responses, all of which are necessary for adaptive behaviour.

Figure 2.9 shows an overview of the different peripheral effectors used in psychophysiological research to infer the autonomic activation status. One of these has a special status: breathing. Breathing is an exception to the other ANS innervated functions, because it is the only vital physiological activity that can be bypassed by free will in awake and conscious individuals. Furthermore, breathing has a reciprocal influence on the ANS, which is the basis for all relaxation and breathing techniques. As such, breathing is a window to influence the overall activation or arousal of an organism, which is why it is of paramount importance in all psychophysiological self-regulation techniques. This will be detailed in the chapters on breathing techniques and relaxation (Chapter 6), and biofeedback (Chapter 9).

Stress

We have already described how stress has been of paramount importance in the description of the autonomic nervous system. We have also summarized how the whole nervous system governs the stress reaction as a neuro-hormonal circuitry. This section aims at giving readers an overview of the most commonly used theories and the terminology. Stress will always be discussed when targeting performance monitoring, management, or enhancement in elite performers, because it is such a basic component of the high-performance environment.

Stress: the basics from physiology research

Fight-or-flight response

The fight-or-flight response was first described by Cannon (1914). It describes the effects of acute stressors on the body, mediated by the sympathetic adrenomedullary system (SAM) in the first phase and the hypothalamic pituitary adrenal axis (HPA) in the second phase (Godoy, Rossignoli, Delfino-Pereira, Garcia-Cairasco, & de Lima Umeoka, 2018). The fight-or-flight response is characterized by the effects of catecholamines on the body. Reactions include, but are not limited to, bronchodilatation, tachycardia, arterial dilatation (skeletal muscles and coronary arteries), mydriasis, glycogenolysis, and lipolysis (basically the red side of the Figure 2.9). Even though the typical examples for this response show an "all-in" response, the single reaction depends mainly on the amount of catecholamines released. This is based on the perceived threat level.

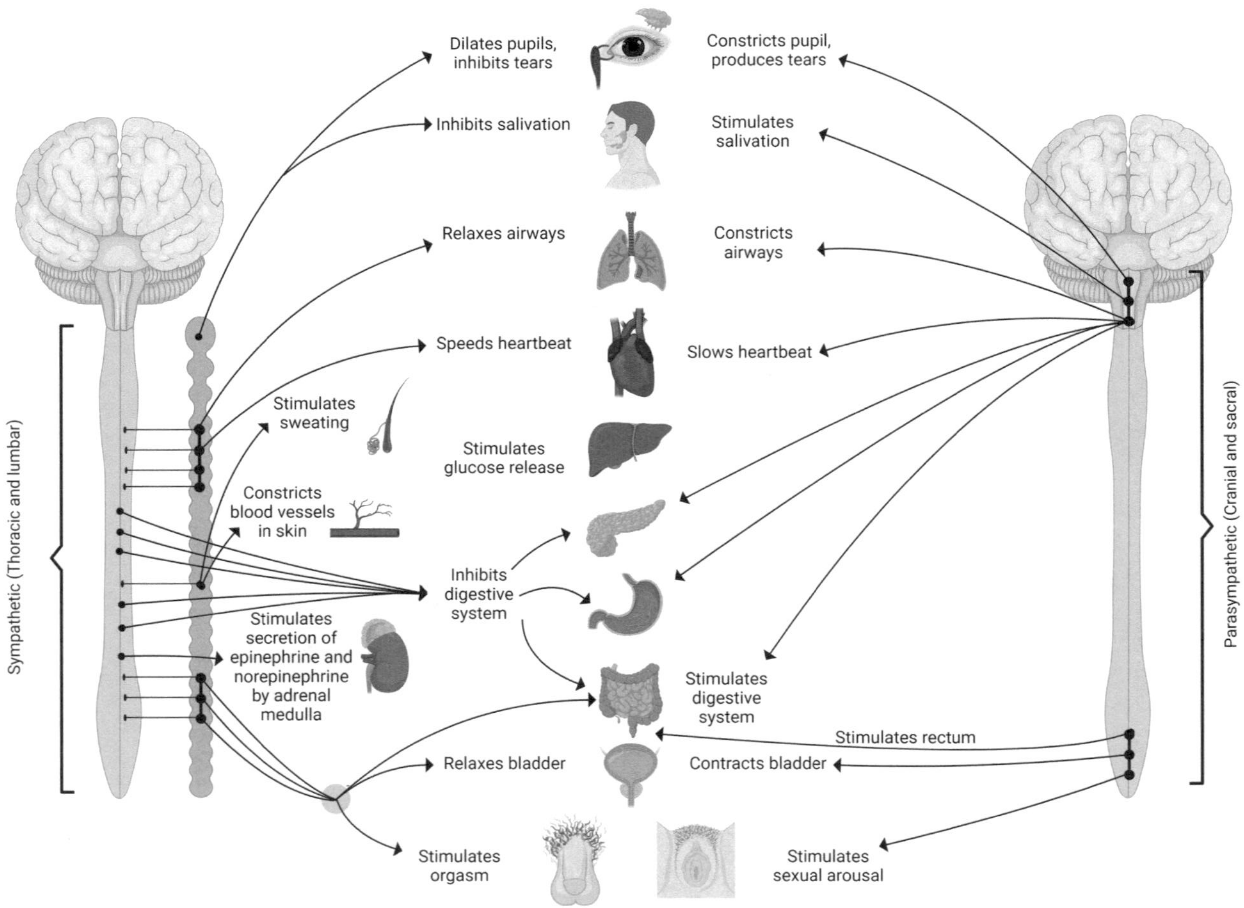

Figure 2.9 The anatomical and functional distinction between both branches of the autonomic nervous system. This figure also illustrates, albeit in a simplified way, the functional interpretation of systemic measures in psychophysiology: galvanic skin conductance, for example, is used as a reflection of sympathetic activity because of the sympathetic stimulation of sweating.

The fight-or-flight response has been well researched and is described down to the molecular level. It is, however, not sufficient to describe all aspects of stress, as experienced by human beings. Indeed, this response is remarkably preserved throughout evolution, and can thus be investigated through animal models. However, the complexity of human information processing, including perception (which, as we described earlier, is the process of conferring meaning to signals form our environment), adds a rich layer to the basic physiology.

General adaptation syndrome

The General Adaptation Syndrome (GAS) is based on the work of Hans Selye (1936), with subsequent revisions in the following decades. The GAS is defined as "integrated syndrome of closely interrelated adaptive reactions to non-specific stress[ors] itself" (Hans Selye, 1950). The key element of this theory is the uniform (i.e., non-specific) response pattern of the organism, independent from the type of the stressor. The model postulates three stages: (1) the alarm phase, characterized by acute manifestations; (2) resistance phase, when the acute manifestations disappear; and (3) exhaustion phase, when the first stage reaction may be present again or when it may result in the collapse of the organism (Hans Selye, 1936). Even though the alarm phase is often seen as equivalent to the fight-or-flight response, the comparison is not fully accurate. Whereas the popular understanding of the fight-or-flight response is often limited to acute perceived threat and its activation of the SAM system (which is also not fully accurate), the GAS is more focused on exposure to noxious stimuli and its activation of the HPA axis. The GAS should be understood as a much more comprehensive stress model. This understanding is important for comprehension of the resistance and exhaustion phase of the GAS. The resistance phase is characterized as the activation of nervous and hormonal defence mechanisms, allowing the organism to adapt and subsequently prevent damage and maintain homeostasis, or at least try to reach a new equilibrium, albeit a deleterious one considering the metabolic cost. According to Selye (1956) the interaction of the GAS with the damaging effects of the stressors, (negative) effects of the defence and internal and external conditioning (factors specific to the situation of the individual, like genetics, environmental factors, treatment) can lead to very different diseases of adaptation. The GAS will thus hardly ever occur in its pure form. The adaptability of the organism is not indefinite, as many of the changes caused by the activation of defence mechanisms will express harmful consequences to the organisms if held up for too long. Remember how we described cortisol as being the metabolic key to the stress reaction, by inhibiting all processes irrelevant for immediate survival (such as digestion, reproduction, immunity, etc.). If the noxious stimulus cannot be eliminated, the organism will go into the exhaustion phase and eventually die.

This model is extremely useful in explaining typical symptoms related to prolonged exposure to external and internal stimuli, like reduced performance, sleep problems, disturbance of the circadian rhythm, fatigue, psychosomatic complaints, recurrent infections etc., which are typical "side-effects" of the adaptation phase. However, since the GAS, just as the fight-or-flight response, stems from fundamental physiological research, it fails to address the mechanisms of "cognitive transformation" of objective stimuli to perceived threatful or distressing stimuli (Krohne, 2001). Furthermore, it does not properly address the influence of coping strategies as reaction to noxious stimuli.

Stress: what's in a name?

According to the Merriam Webster dictionary, stress is defined as a "constraining force or influence, such as […] a physical, chemical, or emotional factor that causes bodily or mental tension and may be a factor in disease causation […]" and also as "a state resulting from a stress[…]". As shown by this definition, the general use of the term is diffuse and describes the origin as well as the effect of the "constraining force or influence". A closer look at the scientific use of the term reveals a similar divergent use. Whereas some models focus on the stimulus, others focus more on the reaction. Modern stress theory usually focuses on a transactional approach, highlighting the interaction of the stimulus and the individual exposed to the stimulus. However, none of these models fully cover the complexity of stress. This is even more true for simplistic adaptations by popular science. On the other hand, in particular the simplified adaptations are often used as a theoretical basis for interventions to improve physical and mental performance, resilience, mental health, and well-being.

For the sake of stringent argumentation and uniformity of nomenclature, this chapter will refer to stimuli or the cause of the reaction as the stressor, and the reaction or effect itself as stress (an approach which we also use in Chapter 14, when describing the specific environment of spaceflight). Be aware that this differentiation is neither commonly accepted nor fully accurate. The term stressor does not only refer to psychological or emotional stimuli, but also to physical (e.g., physical trauma, heat, cold), biological (bacteria, viruses), and chemical stimuli.

Acute and chronic stressors

When looking at stress models, it is useful to differentiate between acute and chronic stressors. Acute stressors are most commonly referred to as singular, extraordinary stimuli with a sudden, recognizable start, with a short duration, and a foreseeable end. The stimulus is perceived as immediate physical or psychological threat, and will commonly lead to a non-specific, uniform stress response. Chronic stressors are often episodic, recurring stimuli with a long duration and without foreseeable end. The single stimulus itself is often not perceived as an immediate threat. However, cumulative exposure to such stimuli can result in a number of specific and non-specific stress responses.

Eustress and distress

Whereas stress in the general meaning is seen as something negative, the physiological models above are merely describing the physiological response. A typical argument in classes about stress is: "I need a certain amount of stress to perform to my best". A further development of the GAS by Hans Selye (1956), focusing more on the psychological (and also sociological) aspects of stress, resulted in introducing the concept of an optimal level of stress. In contrast to the early versions of the GAS, in this model stress is defined as "the nonspecific response of the body to any demand made upon it", moving away from the term of the noxious stimulus. Selye argues that every individual needs a certain amount of stress in order to be "happy". The specific amount however differs widely between individuals. As long as a person stays within a certain range of his or her optimal level of stress, they will experience the demands made upon them as eustress. Over- or understimulation on the other hand will result in distress that has an adverse effect on performance and well-being, based on the GAS model. In both cases, the response is mediated by the same systems (SAM and HPA). While there is some similarity between this model and the Yerkes–Dodson law (Yerkes and Dodson, 1908; see below), the eustress–distress model is more focused on mid- and long-term level of stimulation than on the specific situation.

Further adaptation by popular science has altered the model beyond recognition by incorporating simplified versions of other models (e.g., the appraisal process of the transactional stress model, or the Yerkes–Dodson law – we will discuss both in later paragraphs). The popular eustress–distress model thus focuses on the different perception of the stimulus and the different interpretation of the response as well as the subsequent effect on performance. Despite the model as it is used today having a lot of face validity, it lacks proper theoretical foundation and fails to address the mechanisms of interpretation of the stimulus and the response as positive or negative. The main value of the original model was to explicitly address positive responses to certain levels of stimulation, which resulted in plenty of research on the mechanisms of appraisal and coping. We therefore suggest not using this model at all, but referring to the transactional stress model (Lazarus, 1991) or the conservation of resources theory (Hobfoll, 1989) for models of psychological stress, the theory of challenge and threat states in athletes (Jones, Meijen, McCarthy, & Sheffield, 2009) for a sport-focused model, and the Yerkes–Dodson law (Yerkes & Dodson, 1908) or the catastrophe model (Fazey & Hardy, 1988) for the connection of arousal and performance.

Stress models: the forest and the trees

Transactional stress model

This transactional stress model is based on the work of Lazarus (1991, for the most recent version of the model). In general stress is defined as a relational concept between individuals and their environment. "Psychological stress refers to a relationship with the environment that the person appraises as significant for his or her well-being; and in which to demand, tax or exceed available coping resources" (Lazarus & Folkman, 1986). Psychological stress is thus not defined by a specific kind of external or internal stimulus nor a specific or nonspecific response pattern. The key factor to understanding this model are (1) the process of primary and secondary appraisal and (2) coping.

In the primary appraisal process, a stimulus is classified as relevant versus irrelevant. Evaluation is based on three main questions: relevance, congruence, and ego involvement: (1) is the event or the stimulus relevant to the affected individual's current goals; and how significant is the perceived impact (goal relevance)? (2) If an event is classified as relevant, evaluation takes place, how will this event affect achievement of that goal (goal congruence)? The possible outcomes are goal congruent, if it is beneficial, or goal incongruent if it has a negative impact on achieving that goal and is thus harmful or threatening. (3) The third factor is called ego involvement or goal content, where appraisal of the type of goal affected is concerned. Which of my goals are affected and how strong is the impact? Primary appraisal is not only relevant for determining if a specific situation, e.g., incoming fire, is relevant for the outcome of the specific task, e.g., completing the mission; it also concerns the possible effect on overarching personal goals like survival, performing well, or avoiding failure. The results of the primary appraisal are highly relevant for the emotional response to the stimulus and subsequently also for the secondary appraisal process.

"Secondary appraisal concerns the options and prospects for coping" (Lazarus, 1991). The three decisions of secondary appraisal are "blame or credit", "coping potential", and "future expectations". Blame or credit focuses on the questions of "who is responsible?" and "how much control does the originator have over the event?" Blame as well as credit can be directed outwards or inwards. While this might not be relevant in a short-term tactical situation (e.g., the firefight again) it is highly relevant for other work-related stressors, like interpersonal interactions, time pressure, high workload, or dealing with organizational constraints and restraints. The question on coping potential mainly deals with whether and in what way the available coping mechanisms are suitable to meet the demands upon the affected individual. The last question addresses how the individual expects the situation to turn out with regards to his or her goals, including the possibilities of effective or ineffective coping. The result of primary and secondary appraisal depends highly on specific factors within the individual, leading to "typical" appraisal patterns in an individual. The resulting mediating appraisals for the same situation can thus differ highly from one individual to another, based on their individual appraisal pattern. The appraisal process leads to three distinguished types of mediating appraisals: threat, harm, and challenge (this, of course only applies when the primary appraisal process yields goal incongruence). Be aware that events that are generally seen as positive can have anticipated effects that are goal incongruent. If the goal of a

Special Forces operator for a mission is to prove himself in combat, and during the mission he does not have the chance to engage the enemy, this can be a threat to achieving his goal. Depending on the hierarchy of his goals (prove oneself in combat versus achieving mission success), the mediating appraisal of the overall situation could still be "threat" with the subsequent negative emotions and thus require coping.

It is noteworthy, that most of the appraisal processes happen unconsciously and are not modifiable by choice. According to Lazarus and Folkman (1984) the different kinds of mediating appraisals are "embedded in specific types of emotional reactions, thus illustrating the close conjunction of the fields of stress and emotions" (Krohne, 2001). Based on the appraisal process, the individual will express certain emotions categorized as positive emotions, negative emotions, and borderline cases (such as hope, contentment, relief, or compassion; Lazarus, 1991). It is important to understand, that the expression of negative emotions is not necessarily detrimental to well-being or performance, but essential to initiate a coping process that will allow an individual to reach or adapt goals.

Coping is defined as "the cognitive and behavioural efforts made to master, tolerate or reduce external and internal demands and conflicts among them" (Folkman & Lazarus, 1980). A majority of the literature on coping focuses heavily on coping in reaction to harm, threat, or challenge appraisals. In reality, coping consists mostly of different single acts forming a coping episode (Krohne, 2001). The single coping act can be classified either as problem-focused or emotion-focused. Problem-focused coping acts are aimed directly at the actual person–environment relationship, either by acting on the environment or acting on oneself. It often involves planful actions. This could include eliminating a physical threat, addressing a conflict at work in order to solve it, or the adaptation of internal goals. Emotion-focused coping relates to internal elements with the goal to try reducing negative emotional states or reevaluating the impact of the situation on achieving a certain goal. Examples are employment of breathing techniques or mindfulness in order to reduce negative emotional states, but also reframing a situation as a challenge and not as a threat. Other emotion-focused coping techniques can focus on altering attention deployment, e.g., focusing exercises or avoidance of certain stimuli. As mentioned earlier, a coping episode usually consists of multiple single coping acts. A typical example is the use of a breathing technique to reduce the impact of the emotions anger and fear in a competition situation, followed by actively refocusing on the task ahead, and then developing a plan how to best activate recovery.

The main advantage of this model is the fact that it focuses on psychological stress and puts big emphasis on the specific situation of the affected individual. Many of the interventions used in mental skills training (be it in the field of performance enhancement, resiliency training, or clinical interventions) are based on modification of the coping process with the goal to subsequently alter the (re-)appraisal process, allowing clients to achieve a challenge or beneficial appraisal of the situation instead of staying in a threat or harm state.

Theory of challenge and threat states in athletes (TCTSA)

The theory of challenge and threat states in athletes was proposed by Jones et al. (2009) and is based on the biopsychosocial model of challenge and threat (Blascovich & Mendes, 2000; Blascovich & Tomaka, 1996), the model of adaptive approaches to competition (Skinner & Brewer, 2004), and "other related contemporary approaches to understanding athletes' perceptions and experiences of an upcoming competition". TCTSA aims to explain why athletes perceive an upcoming competition as challenge or threat, how they respond emotionally and physiologically and how the perception as challenge or threat influences performance. Based on past research, the general assumption is that the challenge state is associated with more favourable physiological changes, more helpful emotional states, and increased performance, whereas the threat state will be associated with less favourable physiological changes, more unhelpful emotional states, and decreased performance.

Performance psychological interventions will often aim to bring athletes into the challenge state during a competition. By revealing the mechanisms behind the appraisal process in the subsequent responses, the TCTSA allows development of interventions based on the specific situation of athletes. As there are a lot of similarities between athletes' approaches to competition and elite soldiers or pilots' approaches to a mission, or elite musician's approach to performance, it seems feasible to adapt the theory to elite performers in general. This section will therefore focus on the appraisal within the TCTSA.

The perception of a competition, performance, or mission as threat or challenge is based on demand appraisal and resource appraisals. Both are influenced by the dispositional style of the individual. Demand appraisals include perception of danger, uncertainty, and required personal effort to succeed. For a Special Forces operator this could include appraisal of known enemy strength and equipment (danger of mission failure, injury or death), unknown factors and missing or inaccurate intel (uncertainty), and recognition of the required physical and mental effort to complete his or her specific task (effort). Demand appraisal thus determines the relevance of the situation. Resource appraisals are connected to the individual's resources to cope with the demands of the specific situation. They include skills, knowledge, abilities, dispositional factors, and available external support. A Special Forces operator could, for example, see a mission as challenge when he has sufficient shooting skills, has performed well in training or past missions (experience), and is facing an enemy who is insufficiently trained and equipped (knowledge). The classification as threat or challenge is hereby based on three interrelated constructs: self-efficacy, perceptions of control, and goal orientation, which determine how effective the available resources are perceived to be in meeting the demands.

Perceived self-efficacy is the expectation of a person that he or she can successfully complete a task based on their own competencies. The concept of self-efficacy is mainly based on the work of Bandura (1986). High self-efficacy beliefs in the competencies required to complete a certain task, e.g., the upcoming mission, are associated with a challenge state whereas low self-efficacy beliefs are associated with a threat state. Self-efficacy perception is based on accomplishments, vicarious experiences, verbal persuasion, and physiological status (sometimes also referred to as arousal). Based on the work of Bandura (1997), Maddux (1995), Schunk (1995), and Treasure and Monson (1996), Jones et al. (2009) state that imaginary experiences and emotional states "may contribute as additional sources of self-efficacy information".

Control is an essential part of self-efficacy, as high perceived self-efficacy can only occur when the individual feels they have enough control over the situation, so they can effectively use their skills. Based on Skinner (1996), the three aspects of control are objective control, perceived (or subjective) control, and experiences of control. Objective control refers to the actual control present in the situation or the individual. In a tactical context, a pre-planned high-risk arrest is associated with higher objective control than being surprisingly attacked during a patrol. Subjective control in contrast is based on the individual's belief of how much control is actually available. For the example of the surprise attack on a patrol, the perceived level of control can be very high (e.g., due to pre-planned and sufficiently trained procedures for such a case), despite the lack of objective control. Many researchers argue that subjective control is a more powerful predictor of functioning (and thus performance) than objective control (e.g., Skinner, 1996; Averill, 1973; or Burger, 1989). Experiences of control are based on the feelings of the individual in the situation and depend on "external conditions, subjective interpretations and individual actions" (Jones et al., 2009). In the military context, high experiences of control are usually present when a mission runs according to the plan (including the contingency plans) or an operator or unit have the ability to actively influence the situation as opposed to purely reacting to enemy actions.

The last construct relevant for resource appraisal is goal orientation. The TCTSA is distinguishing four types of achievement goals that are highly relevant for determination of threat state or challenge state. In general, achievement goals can be classified as mastery goals that focus on "developing competence through mastering tasks" and performance goals which focus on "demonstrating competence relative to others" (Jones et al., 2009). Each of these split into approach and avoidance goals, leading to a 2 × 2 framework of achievement goals. The valances "approach" and "avoidance" reflect the motivational pattern behind the goal. In approach goals, the motivation is to achieve a certain favourable outcome, whereas in avoidance goals, the motivation is to prevent a certain unfavourable outcome. Examples for mastery approach goals (MAp) could be "I want to minimize the number of personal errors during the performance of this aria" or "I want to improve my personal best time on the 200m". In contrast, mastery avoidance goals (MAv) are "I don't want to make more than X personal errors during the performance of this aria" or "I don't want to score more than X in the 200m". Performance approach goals (PAp) are, for example, phrased like "I want to perform better during the test run than my buddy" or "I want to be the best shooter in my team". Typical performance avoidance goals (PAv) are "I don't want to score below-average in the shooting task" or "I don't want to be the weakest performer in my team." Jones et al. propose that focus on approach goals is associated with reaching a challenge state, especially when the focus is on mastery approach goals. Mastery avoidance goals on the other hand are linked to a threat state.

In summary, the TCTSA proposes that challenge states are associated with high self-efficacy, a perception of control, and focus on approach goals, whereas a threat state is associated with low self-efficacy, low perceived control, and focus on avoidance goals. These notions will be further applied in Chapter 3 (Ideal performance states).

Yerkes–Dodson law and beyond

YERKES–DODSON LAW

The Yerkes–Dodson law is a psychological construct based on the original work of Yerkes and Dodson (1908) which has undergone multiple reinterpretation and adaption throughout the last decades. The common understanding is an inverted U-shaped relationship between arousal and performance, which is based on a publication of Hebb (1955). Performance increases with arousal up to a certain point (optimal level of arousal), but decreases with even higher levels of arousal for complex tasks. For simple tasks there is no or very limited decrease of performance.

The scientific accuracy of the reinterpretation that led to the common understanding that we have today is questionable (see Teigen, 1994, for a detailed discussion). Nonetheless it is present in many textbooks and psychological encyclopedias and is ubiquitously used in performance psychology and the general assumption has been positively tested repeatedly (e.g., Humphreys and Revelle, 1984; Anderson, 1994; Pattyn et al., 2008).

The Yerkes–Dodson Law is a very useful model to explain the importance of arousal management within the operational environment. When using the model it should be emphasized that the optimal level of arousal highly varies in-between individuals, depending on the specific situation, the specific task, and internal factors (e.g., baseline "stress level", personality traits, or appraisal patterns).

CATASTROPHE MODEL OF ANXIETY AND PERFORMANCE

The catastrophe model of anxiety and performance was introduced by Fazey and Hardy (1988). The model explains the relationship between the independent variables cognitive anxiety and physiological arousal with the dependent variable performance by introducing the three-dimensional model based on the "cusp catastrophe model". The development of this model was necessary because research findings and anecdotal evidence contradicted the two-dimensional performance–arousal connection described by the Yerkes–Dodson law in elite sports. Contrary to the expectations based on the Yerkes–Dodson law, athletes performance would not decrease slowly after reaching

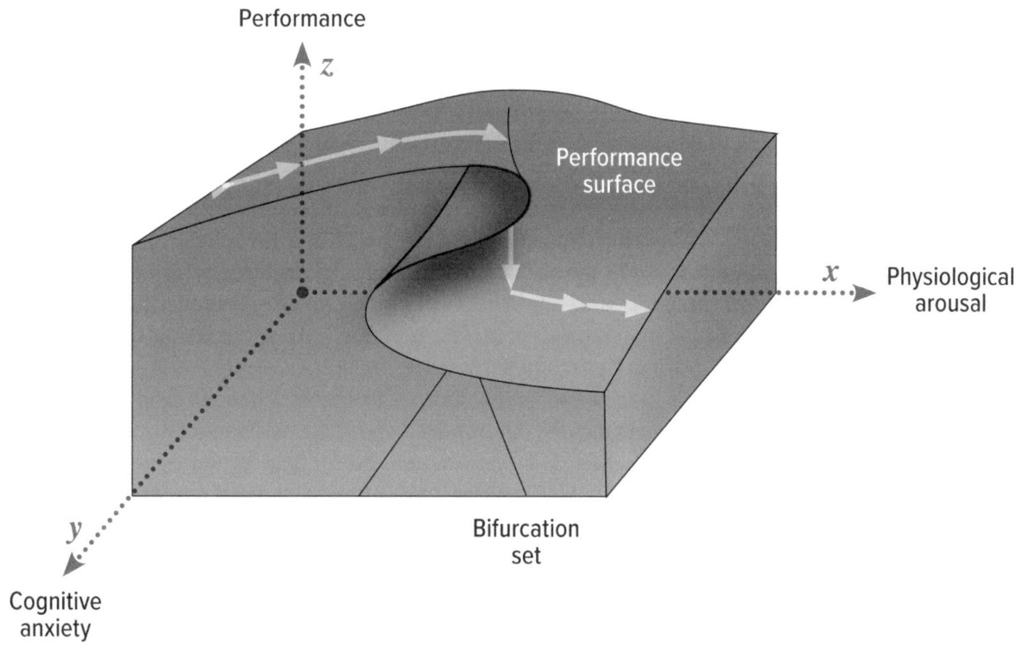

Figure 2.10 Fazey & Hardy's (1988) catastrophe model of the relationship between anxiety and performance.

the cusp but rather drastically drop and not increase again with decrease in arousal. Within the model, the unidimensional variable "arousal" was split into "cognitive anxiety" and "physiological arousal". The resulting three-dimensional model is displayed in Figure 2.10. When cognitive anxiety is low, for example, in training situations or during rehearsal, the relationship between physiological arousal and performance is an inverted U, as proposed by the Yerkes–Dodson law (rear of Figure 2.10). In situations with high physiological arousal, e.g., during a competition, a critical mission or high physical workload, there is a strong negative correlation between cognitive anxiety and performance, as displayed on the right side of Figure 2.10. So in situations with high cognitive anxiety, such as key phases of the mission or performance, the effect of physiological arousal on performance depends on the exact height of cognitive anxiety and physiological arousal (front of Figure 2.10). Small increases in either physiological arousal or cognitive anxiety can easily push the performer over the cusp and result in detrimental effects on performance.

Ideal performance states

Based on the stress and performance models discussed above it is obvious that performance not only depends on objective skill levels, but is highly dependent on the physiological and psychological state in the specific situation. For maximum utilization of specific skills during a performance event, it is essential that operators are in, or close to, an ideal/optimal performance state when executing a mission. Understanding the key factors that enable a performer to reach such a state must be the foundation of all interventions that aim to influence mental performance. The determinants that are associated with ideal performance states are (1) perception of the situation as challenge rather than as threat and (2) reaching an optimal level of arousal at the right time. Elite performers will intuitively use coping strategies and mental skills to alter the situational appraisal and the arousal level by influencing multiple, underlying factors associated with them. For instance, using imagery techniques to increase self-efficacy, focus on approach goals, and practice mindfulness to reduce the impact of non-helpful emotions in order to reach a challenge state, while using a breathing technique to reduce arousal. This can happen consciously or unconsciously. The goal of mental performance optimization is to increase performers' capabilities and capacities to utilize coping strategies and mental skills, and reach an ideal performance state, even under extreme circumstances. This entails that performers learn to identify when they are inside or outside this state and subsequently have a robust set of techniques available to bring themselves into the state of ideal performance. The development of a robust set of coping strategies and mental skills should include the refinement of existing resources and acquisition of new resources by education, practice, and application in performance situations. The technical chapters of the current handbook specifically describe the interventions targeting those coping strategies.

Challenge appraisal, arousal management, and resources to manipulate appraisal and arousal are highly dependent on intrapersonal factors. Therefore, individual performance counselling in addition to group educational approaches will yield better results than group education alone. However, since for many elite performers, performance will often be in team context, a systemic approach is needed, which is why Chapter 11 of the present handbook is devoted to team performance. In the following section, we will briefly introduce these systemic approaches for a professional application.

Stress and performance in professional context

Model of professional gratification crises

The model of professional gratification crises according to Siegrist (1996) proposes that the extent to which someone is rewarded for his labour, is crucial for their health and well-being. Gratification can come from money, recognition, status, level of control, job security, or career opportunities. According to Siegrist, when periods of high personal work input and effort are not followed by the expected reward, emotional, psychological, and physical stress occur.

Person–environmental model (person–environment fit theory)

Building on the Personal Environment Fit model by Lewin (1946), Edwards (1996) postulates that stress arises through a bad fit between the person and their environment. Two constellations, which can result in the experience of stress, are described. The first one is characterized by a mismatch between the requirements of the environment and the capabilities of the individual to manage these requirements. The second one refers to an imbalance between the needs of the person and the existing resources of the environment.

Linking stress and performance to potential interventions: behavioural energetics

To understand how people can learn coping strategies in order to counteract the potential negative effect of stress on performance, we will summarize some notions from the previously described models.

As we have described, the notion of stress is polysemic and involves a multitude of physiological and psychological mechanisms. Its definitions can be multiple and ambiguous, to the point of calling it an "umbrella concept" (Fink, 2010; Lancry, 2007). Stress has alternatively been considered as: (1) an external constraint (i.e., stressor) disturbing the balance of an organism, (2) a response to a stimulus, or (3) the interaction between the organism and the environment. The work of Cannon (i.e., the theory of homeostasis) (Cannon, 1929) and especially of Selye allowed for the wider diffusion of the term in the medical world and beyond.

Stress appears to be an inevitable part of life, an adaptive response to demands of the environment, which allows the body to prepare for performance (Homan, 2002; Salehi et al., 2010). Understanding how an individual intellectualizes stress determines his or her adaptative response or coping strategies which lead us to the more dynamic explanation of stress proposed by Lazarus and Folkman (1984), i.e., the transactional theory of stress (Lazarus & Folkman, 1984). This model refers to stress "as a product of a transaction between a person (including multiple systems: cognitive, physiological, affective, psychological, neurological) and his or her complex environment". Indeed, the term transactional implies that the individual and the environment have a dynamic reciprocal and bidirectional relationship (Delongis, Folkman, Lazarus, & Gruen, 1986; Folkman, Lazarus, Dunkel-Schetter, DeLongis, & Gruen, 1986). As we have described, this model has been built around a concept mediating the link between such a transaction and its short- and long-term consequences: the cognitive assessment or cognitive appraisal. This appraisal admits an underlying adaptative function of finding a balance between the realities of the environment and the interests of the person and operationalizing by means of two distinct subjective processes, the so-called "primary" appraisal and the so-called "secondary" appraisal (Lazarus & Folkman, 1984). Primary appraisal reflects the nature and degree of risk that an event may entail. The qualification of an event as "stressful" also results from the "secondary" appraisal. During this process, an individual evaluates the resources or coping strategies at his or her disposal for addressing the perceived threats. The process of reappraisal is ongoing and requires a constant reevaluation of both the nature of the stressor and the resources available for responding to it. However, as mentioned by Lazarus and Folkman (1991), not all stressors "are amenable to mastery" (Lazarus & Folkman, 1991, p. 205). Stressors that are unmanageable and lead to strains require interventions to reverse or slow down those effects.

Stress management refers to "tertiary" interventions employed to treat and repair harmful repercussions of stressors that were not coped with sufficiently (Glazer & Liu, 2017). There are many ways that people strive to cope with stressors and feelings of stress in their lives. Stress management techniques are more general and range from cognitive (mindfulness, cognitive therapy, meditation) to physical (yoga, leisure activities, deep breathing) to environmental (music, pets, nature). As described in the section on the nervous system, some theoretical brain–body integration models (e.g., Friedman, 2007) highlight the importance of a well-developed information processing system for humans to cope with stress, which requires a "functional reserve", the equivalent of a charged battery. The reserve model explains the inter-individual differences in stress effects by referring to differences in the cognitive processes or neural networks underlying task performance. People with higher reserve can "optimize or maximize performance through differential recruitment of brain networks, which perhaps reflect the use of alternate cognitive strategies" (Stern, 2002, p. 451). Moreover, according to Baevsky and colleagues (2005), the functional reserve of an organism correlates to the person's normal range of variability and flexibility of the autonomic nervous system (Baevsky et al., 2005), which has been verified in real-life stress situations regarding performance (Pattyn et al., 2010; Pattyn et al., 2013). As previously introduced, this type of autonomic flexibility has also been described in the neurovisceral integration model (Friedman, 2007; Hansen, Johnsen, & Thayer, 2009; Thayer & Lane, 2000, 2009) which identified a flexible neural network associated with self-regulation and adaptability that might help the organism to respond effectively to demands from the environment.

Mental fatigue

As described in section "Ideal performance states" performance not only depends on objective skill levels, but is highly dependent on the physiological and psychological state in the specific situation. Throughout their career, elite performers learn to identify when they are inside or outside this state and subsequently have a robust set of techniques available to bring themselves into the state of ideal performance (which is the topic of the next chapter). However, a factor that often challenges the ability to stay in an ideal mental performance state in real-life situations is mental fatigue.

Mental fatigue: what is it?

Mental fatigue (also known as cognitive fatigue) is a psychophysiological state induced by prolonged mental exertion. It is experienced as feelings of tiredness and lack of energy, as a reduction in cognitive performance, or as an increase in the effort required to maintain performance (Ackerman, 2011).

In a laboratory setting, the standard method to induce mental fatigue is a prolonged cognitive computer task (Boksem & Tops, 2008). Although the characteristics of the ideal mentally fatiguing computer task are to date still actively debated (O'Keeffe et al., 2020), two of the most important characteristics appear to be task duration and task complexity (Borragán et al., 2017). Subsequently, prolonged cognitive tasks engaging executive functions such as working memory, response inhibition, and planning became the golden standard to induce mental fatigue in a lab-based setting. Prolonged performance on such tasks will eventually trigger mental fatigue (Lim et al., 2010) and often impair both the performance on the mentally fatiguing task itself (i.e., time-on-task effect) as well as on subsequent tasks that engage similar executive functions (i.e., the carryover effect) (Boksem et al., 2005; Habay, Van Cutsem, et al., 2021; Van Cutsem et al., 2017). Moreover, as previously mentioned, the usage of such laboratory-based tasks enables researchers to control for multiple confounding variables (e.g., muscle fatigue) and gain specific theoretical insights. However, the downside is that, as described in section "Ecological validity", it is difficult and/or too simplistic to translate laboratory-based study results to the complex real-life situations performers need to perform in. For example, within sport sciences this critique has also been put forward and, for this reason, scientists have started to incorporate more ecologically valid tasks in their study designs. For example, Coutinho et al. (2017), used a whole-body coordination task to induce mental fatigue. The whole-body coordination task consisted of seven different ladder drill exercises requiring motor coordination, sustained attention, cognitive processing, and perceptual skills, making this task much more ecologically valid in terms of soccer performance compared to a computer-based cognitive task (Coutinho et al., 2017). In addition, besides a more fundamental stream of mental fatigue research, a more applied stream of mental fatigue research has emerged (Russell, Jenkins, Halson, Juliff, Connick, et al., 2022; Russell, Jenkins, Halson, Juliff, & Kelly, 2022; Russell, Jenkins, Halson, & Kelly, 2022; Thompson et al., 2020). Mental fatigue has been monitored by embedded sport scientists in English academy soccer players (Thompson et al., 2020) and in international elite netballers (Russell, Jenkins, Halson, Juliff, Connick, et al., 2022; Russell, Jenkins, Halson, Juliff, & Kelly, 2022; Russell, Jenkins, Halson, & Kelly, 2022). Based on this research it was concluded that practitioners should be aware that athletes report instances of elevated mental fatigue across camps and competition, that mental fatigue is not limited to competition, and thus is recommended to be monitored during periods of training and preparation for competition (Russell, Jenkins, Halson, Juliff, & Kelly, 2022). In addition, perceived mental fatigue can clearly be differentiated from physical fatigue, tiredness, stress, mood, and motivation (Russell, Jenkins, Halson, Juliff, Connick, et al., 2022). Sport-related activities such as the journey to an away match and playing a match were observed to trigger mental fatigue (Thompson et al., 2020).

In terms of the carryover effect, executive functions such as working memory, response inhibition, and planning are crucial to optimally perform in both physical and mental tasks. As such, in theory, it does not matter whether the mentally fatiguing task and/or the subsequent tasks also include a high physical component and are highly physically fatiguing, as long as similar executive functions are addressed in both the mentally fatiguing and the subsequent task, mental fatigue-associated carryover effects are prone to occur and performance on the subsequent task will be perceived as harder and/or performance will drop. The references mentioned in the above paragraph already partly demonstrated this reasoning, in that sense, that papers like the one of Coutinho et al. (2017) and Thompson et al. (2020) demonstrate that cognitively demanding physical tasks, despite being physical tasks, also result in mental fatigue. In the case of Coutinho et al. (2017), the mental fatigue that was induced by a 20-min cognitively demanding whole-body coordination task (i.e., ladder drill exercises), eventually also resulted in carryover effects, as it was reported that during the subsequent small-sided soccer game the players' tactical behaviour was affected by mental fatigue in such a way that players spent less time in the lateral synchronization when mentally fatigued (i.e., an altered positioning strategy; Coutinho et al., 2017). Another example that backs up the reasoning on the role of similar executive function in observing carryover effects in a sequential task paradigm, is the research that has been performed on the impact of mental fatigue on sport-specific performance (Habay, Van Cutsem, et al., 2021). Habay, Van Cutsem, et al. (2021) conducted a systematic review on this topic and gathered 21 studies that, in general, demonstrated the negative impact of mental fatigue (mostly induced with a computer-based task) on a myriad of sport-specific psychomotor performance, including decision-making, reaction time, and accuracy. This field of research points out that also the combination of a computer-based mentally fatiguing task and a sport-based subsequent task does not prevent carryover effects from occurring. Nonetheless, the fact that the addition of physical load in a sequential task paradigm does not seem to counteract the occurrence of mental fatigue-associated performance decrements, does not mean that physical activity cannot positively impact mental fatigue (Jacquet et al., 2021; Oberste et al., 2021). A study from Oberste et al. (2021) included 99 healthy adults, mentally fatigued them with a 60-min cognitively demanding test battery and subsequently evaluated which activity provided the best recovery, 30 min of moderate aerobic exercise on a cycle ergometer, 30 min of a simple lower body stretching routine (= active control treatment), or watching a popular sitcom (= passive control treatment). Their results suggest that, both compared to the active and passive control treatment, a single bout of acute moderate aerobic exercise supports regeneration of cognitive flexibility performance and of subjective well-being (Oberste et al., 2021). Also in the study of Proost et al. (2023) a relieving effect of physical activity on mental fatigue was identified. Following a 60-min mentally fatiguing Stroop task, the self-reported feeling of mental fatigue was higher compared to after watching a 60-min documentary. However, immediately following a subsequent leg extension task, in which participants had to perform 100 extensions at a low intensity, the self-reported mental fatigue did not differ anymore between both conditions. Moreover, the quick drop in self-reported mental fatigue was associated with an increase in alpha power (i.e., brain activity) in the brain during the physical task, suggesting that participants may have entered a state of focused internal attention to counter the effects of (mental) fatigue (Proost et al., 2023). These results, again, demonstrate the mental fatigue-relieving effects of physical activity both on a subjective, objective, and neurophysiological level.

Based on the above, it can be assumed that different work-related activities of any performer will trigger mental fatigue (e.g., deployment preparations, staff meeting, or during training camps) and that this mental fatigue will impair performance in general (i.e., both mental and physical) (Habay, Van Cutsem, et al., 2021; Kurzban et al., 2013; Pattyn et al., 2018; Van Cutsem et al., 2017). A vast amount of studies have already demonstrated the presence of a negative effect of mental fatigue on many aspects of daily life (Chaudhuri & Behan, 2004; McCormick et al., 2012; Van Cutsem et al., 2017). In the workplace, mental fatigue has been found to predict an increased risk of error (McCormick et al., 2012), and, in addition, it is also one of the most common symptoms experienced by individuals with neurological disorders (Chaudhuri & Behan, 2004). Mental fatigue has been reported to deteriorate both cognitive (Kurzban et al., 2013; Pattyn et al., 2018) and physical performance (Habay, Van Cutsem, et al., 2021; Van Cutsem et al., 2017), and subsequently negatively impact work-related activities (Mackworth, 1948; McCormick et al., 2012), sport performance (Habay, Van Cutsem, et al., 2021; Van Cutsem et al., 2017), and general well-being (Smith, 2018).

How is mental fatigue assessed/monitored?

Markers of mental fatigue are usually categorized in three main areas: subjective, behavioural and (neuro)physiological. Subjectively, increased feelings of tiredness, lack of energy (Boksem & Tops, 2008), and decreased motivation (Boksem et al., 2006) and alertness have been reported (van der Linden et al., 2006). Behaviourally, mental fatigue is recognized as a decline in performance (accuracy and/or reaction time) on a cognitive task (Marcora et al., 2009; Mockel et al., 2015; Wascher et al., 2014). Finally, alterations in brain activity (Cook et al., 2007; Habay, Proost, et al., 2021; Van Cutsem et al., 2022; Wascher et al., 2014) have been shown to be a physiologic manifestation of mental fatigue. For example, Cook et al. (2007) used functional magnetic resonance imaging (fMRI) to determine the association between feelings of mental fatigue and brain responses and found that mental fatigue was significantly related to brain activity during the mentally fatiguing cognitive task but not during the finger tapping or the simple auditory monitoring tasks. Changes in all three of these areas (subjective, behavioural, and physiological) do not have to be present for mental fatigue to be present. For instance, cognitive performance does not necessarily decline when one is mentally fatigued, since compensatory effort (e.g., indicated by alterations in brain activity or as a result of increased motivation) may alleviate this (Hopstaken et al., 2015; Mockel et al., 2015). Hopstaken et al. (2015) identified that the detrimental effects of fatigue on the subjective, behavioural, and physiological measures could be reversed by increasing the task rewards. Increasing the rewards led to task reengagement in spite of previous signs of fatigue (Hopstaken et al., 2015). Importantly, the compensatory effort needed to reverse the mental fatigue effects and reengage was accompanied by increased pupil diameter and brain activity changes (i.e., an increase in the amplitude of an event-related brain potential, named the P3).

To date, the in-the-field measurement of mental fatigue is mostly performed via subjective reports (Russell, Jenkins, Halson, Juliff, Connick, et al., 2022; Russell, Jenkins, Halson, Juliff, & Kelly, 2022; Russell, Jenkins, Halson, & Kelly, 2022; Thompson et al., 2020). However, based on the above paragraph it is obvious that to monitor mental fatigue multiple measurements should be combined. Monitoring mental fatigue based on a single marker (see Friedl, 2018, for an example on elevated heart rate) will provide unreliable feedback in terms of fatigue and performance. For example, recent research from Russell, Jenkins, Halson, and Kelly (2022) demonstrated that salivary biomarkers of stress are not associated with the self-reported feeling of mental fatigue across a 16-week pre-season in elite female athletes. This stresses again that, like for the quantification of mental performance itself, it is critical to rely on several indicators and jointly interpret them. This reasoning is further substantiated by research of Van Cutsem et al. (2022), reporting that the mental fatigue-associated impact on performance is complex, even in a controlled laboratory environment, and that factors like subjective self-evaluation, peripheral autonomic activation, and metabolic and brain activity interact to determine performance. In the study of Van Cutsem et al. (2022), participants had to perform once a 90-min mentally fatiguing Stroop task and once watch a 90-min documentary; where both 90-min tasks were preceded and followed up by a 10-min flanker task that was completed in the MRI scanner; specific mental fatigue-markers were associated with a time-on-task effect and others with the carryover effect. A drop in flanker performance was observed from pre to post and this drop was linked with a physiological deactivation (i.e., an increase in parasympathetic activity). In addition, an increase in the level of subjective mental fatigue with prolonged performance on the 90-min Stroop task was found, and this was associated with a decrease in response inhibition-associated brain activity in both grey and white matter.

To operationalize the in-the-field measurement of mental fatigue in the future, multiple mental fatigue-markers should be combined in a wearable (Friedl, 2018). This wearable would then be connected to an algorithm that combines the information of all mental fatigue-markers and provides an actionable output to the performer (e.g., the application of a mental fatigue countermeasure). Moreover, the inputs that the algorithm receives should, preferably, also be task unrelated. So that the wearable and algorithm can be used in different settings and during different performer-related activities. The monitoring of mental fatigue undoubtedly holds premise. However, once mental fatigue has occurred and performance drops and this is flagged by the wearable/algorithm, the negative impact of mental fatigue is already in play. The ultimate goal is of course to prevent the negative impact of mental fatigue. To do that, we should monitor for markers that indicate the risk of getting mentally fatigued is rising, and to determine those markers it is crucial to elucidate the underlying mechanisms of mental fatigue.

What are the underlying mechanisms?

To date, the mechanistic discussion on mental fatigue can be illustrated by the underload/overload spectrum that is provided by Pattyn et al. (2008, 2018). Within this spectrum, that was originally developed in the sustained attention literature (Pattyn et al., 2008), a mental fatigue-associated drop in performance can be related to underload or overload. Underload is linked to insufficient workload and/or arousal, which might cause engagement to drop and/or motivation to decrease. Subsequently, underload could lead to boredom, task withdrawal, and a drop in performance (Kurzban et al., 2013). In contrast to underload, overload is related to a high mental workload and/or arousal. Prolonged high mental workload could, like underload, also result in task withdrawal (e.g., the task is perceived as too difficult, and performance is dropped) and/or in a depletion of resources and the impossibility to maintain performance. The term 'resource' has been interpreted differently depending on the field of research. For example, in vigilance research it is often seen as attention, while in exercise science it has been defined as a metabolic fuel (e.g., glucose) (Pattyn et al., 2018). Besides a depletion of resources, the overload account has also been related to an accumulation of energy-related metabolites (e.g., an accumulation of adenosine (Marcora et al., 2009; Martin et al., 2018; Van Cutsem & Marcora, 2021) and glutamate (Wiehler et al., 2022)). Related to this last interpretation (i.e., mental fatigue is linked to an accumulation of substances in the brain) a recent study of Wiehler et al. (2022) provided some compelling evidence. They went beyond the subjective report of effort and fatigue and attempted to pinpoint the neurophysiological mechanism of cognitive control (Wiehler et al., 2022). These authors operationalized and objectified mental fatigue as a state in which more impulsive decisions are taken. Subsequently, they monitored mental fatigue throughout an approximate high-demand and low-demand workday with an economic choice-task (i.e., a task in which impulsivity is an outcome parameter) and measured whether a difference in specific brain metabolites could be measured at the end of the high-demand workday vs. the low-demand workday. Their results demonstrate that only during the high-demand workday did participants became more impulsive throughout the day (i.e., more mentally fatigued), and that this was associated with a higher glutamate concentration and glutamate/glutamine diffusion in a cognitive control brain region (i.e., lateral prefrontal cortex). Moreover, during the decision-making process in the economic choice-task, a reduction in pupil dilation was associated with the increased impulsivity (Wiehler et al., 2022).

Building further on the evidence that is reported in the study of Wiehler et al. (2022), it appears that a focus on cognitive control could serve to monitor a valid precursor of mental fatigue. Applied to the underload/overload account, cognitive control indeed precedes the occurrence of mental fatigue in both the underload and overload setting. In the underload account, cognitive control is necessary to withstand boredom and task withdrawal, while in the overload account, cognitive control is exerted to perform on a challenging task. Prolonged cognitive control in both the underload and overload setting lead to the subjective experience of effort, which eventually leads to mental fatigue (Kurzban et al., 2013). Therefore, to develop a wearable and algorithm that provides actionable output before mental fatigue occurs, cognitive control and the perception of effort seem to be the constructs that we need to be able to monitor.

The discussion on the possible mechanisms underlying mental fatigue and its effects is of great value, as this will not only optimize the functioning of mental fatigue monitoring methods, but it will also give rise to the development of new methods to counteract mental fatigue, both in daily life as well as in a work-related environment.

How to counteract it?

Besides real-time performance monitoring systems, the search to unravel the mechanisms underlying the mental fatigue-associated drop in performance will also result in the possibility to optimize and individualize the already available mental fatigue countermeasures (Proost et al., 2022). In a recent systematic review of Proost et al. (2022) an overview was provided of the mental fatigue countermeasures that currently have been explored. Behavioural (e.g., napping, listening to music, physical exercise), physiological (e.g., caffeine, odours,), and psychological (e.g., mindfulness) countermeasures have been evaluated and most of them were found to positively counteract a mentally fatigued state in a behavioural and/or subjective way (Proost et al., 2022).

In section "Mental fatigue: what is it?" we already mentioned the research demonstrating the positive effect of physical activity on mental fatigue. Jacquet et al. (2021) tested two non-bioactive strategies to counteract mental fatigue: physical activity and listening to music. They used a 32-min cognitively demanding task to induce mental fatigue and evaluated the impact on performance via an arm-pointing task that the participants had to perform before and after the 32-min task. Participants performed this sequence of tasks three times, and each time the post arm-pointing task was separated from the 32-min task by 20 min. Once this 20-min gap was filled up with 15 min of physical activity, once with 15 min of listening to music, and once with 15 min of discussion. The arm-pointing task performance was deteriorated only in the condition where they had to discuss for 15 min, suggesting that practicing physical activity and listening to music could be efficient strategies to counteract the negative effects of mental fatigue on motor performances. Besides physical activity, the most promising countermeasures that were put forward by Proost et al. (2022) were the use of caffeine before and/or during the occurrence of mental fatigue and the use of a noticeable and pleasant odour during a mentally fatiguing task/activity. In addition, the use of strategies (e.g., rewards) to increase motivation seems to be a promising psychological method to counteract mental fatigue. Based on the studies of Azevedo et al. (2016) and Franco-Alvarenga et al. (2019) it appears that caffeine is able to reduce mental fatigue-related decrements in sport-related endurance performance and that a 5-mg/kg dosage is sufficient to do so. Moreover, also in terms of cognitive performance, caffeine has been demonstrated to successfully counteract mental fatigue and its impact on performance (Ataka et al., 2008). In the study of Ataka et al. (2008), a supplementation protocol of 200 mg/day for 7 days was found to successfully improve task performance during fatigue-inducing mental tasks. In terms of odours, Kato et al. (2012) designed an interesting study that showed the positive effects of intermittent presentation of odours on cognitive-motor performance and brain activity during mental fatigue. They used citral, green (cis-3-hexanal), and menthol odours to stimulate the olfactory bulb during a 60-min computer-based task, and found that the typical time-on-task increase in reaction time was smaller when the odours where presented compared to when not. Moreover, also on a neurophysiological level the odours counteracted mental fatigue, as in terms of brain activity P3 amplitudes were higher in the odour conditions.

The above illustrates that a wide variety of mental fatigue countermeasures have been evaluated and found to be, partly, successful (Proost et al., 2022). In terms of the practical application of these mental fatigue countermeasures this of course generates new questions. Such as: which mental fatigue countermeasure should I take? When should I take it? Is it worth combining multiple countermeasures? To begin with, the answers on these questions will greatly depend on each specific situation an elite performer finds him/herself in. For example, during a long game or ride with no possibility to take a break, an easy-to-consume nutritional countermeasure could be the preferred option to counteract mental fatigue (e.g., the intake of caffeine). On the other hand, when performing a task in which breaks are allowed (e.g., a day of work), behavioural interventions such as listening to music for 20 min could specifically be of added value to deal with mental fatigue. Nevertheless, to provide in-detail practical guidelines for the real-life application of mental fatigue countermeasures, more research has to be performed on the underlying mechanisms and the optimal dosage and timing of application/intake (Proost et al., 2022). Besides countermeasures, studies are also being conducted on the possibility to the train the brain to be more resistant to mental fatigue and its effects. The so-called Brain Endurance Training seeks to increase the load on the brain during endurance performance, to induce adaptations in specific cortical areas of the brain (e.g., anterior cingulate gyrus) and as such increase resistance to mental fatigue and its negative effects on endurance performance (Marcora et al., 2015). In the specific case of endurance performance, the extra load is added by performing a cognitive computer task while cycling on a stationary bike. For elite performers, a mental fatigue-toolbox including training and countermeasure strategies would of course be ideal.

Future research on this topic should specifically focus on inter- and intraindividual variability in the response to mental fatigue countermeasures and/or resistance training, as this research could result in the determination of the state and trait factors that impact the efficacy of a specific mental fatigue countermeasure and/or resistance training (Habay et al., 2023). By combining insight into the mechanisms and into the state and trait factors of efficacy of the countermeasures and resistance training, the application of mental fatigue countermeasures and training strategies could be optimized and individualized (e.g., genetic profiling).

References

Aben, B., Stapert, S., & Blokland, A. (2012). About the distinction between working memory and short-term memory. *Frontiers in psychology*, *3*, 301. https://doi.org/10.3389/fpsyg.2012.00301

Ackerman, P. (2011). *Cognitive fatigue: Multidisciplinary perspectives on current research and future applications* (P. Ackerman, Ed.). American Psychological Association.

Aerospace Medical Panel Working Group 12 North Atlantic Treaty Organization Advisory Group for Aerospace Research and Development (1989). *Human performance assessment methods* (Rep. No. AGARDograph-AG-308).

Alvarez, J. A., & Emory, E. (2006). Executive function and the frontal lobes: a meta-analytic review. *Neuropsychology Review*, 16(1), 17–42.

Anderson, K. J. (1994). Impulsivity, caffeine, and task difficulty: A within-subjects test of the Yerkes-Dodson law. *Personality and Individual Differences*, 16(6), 813–829. doi:https://doi.org/10.1016/0191- 8869(94)90226-7

Ataka, S., Tanaka, M., Nozaki, S., Mizuma, H., Mizuno, K., Tahara, T., . . . Watanabe, Y. (2008). Effects of oral administration of caffeine and D-ribose on mental fatigue. *Nutrition*, 24(3), 233–238. https://doi.org/10.1016/j.nut.2007.12.002

Atkinson, R. C., & Shiffrin, R. M. (1968). Human memory: A proposed system and its control processes. In *Psychology of learning and motivation* (Vol. 2, pp. 89–195). Academic press.

Averill, J. R. (1973). Personal control over aversive stimuli and its relationship to stress. *Psychological Bulletin*, 80(4), 286–303. doi:10.1037/h0034845.

Azevedo, R., Silva-Cavalcante, M. D., Gualano, B., Lima-Silva, A. E., & Bertuzzi, R. (2016). Effects of caffeine ingestion on endurance performance in mentally fatigued individuals. *European Journal of Applied Physiology*, 116(11-12), 2293–2303. https://doi.org/10.1007/s00421-016-3483-y

Baddeley, A. (2012). Working memory: Theories, models, and controversies. *Annual review of psychology*, *63*, 1–29. https://doi.org/10.1146/annurev-psych-120710-100422

Baddeley, A. (2020). Working memory. In *Memory* (71–111). Routledge. www.taylorfrancis.com/chapters/edit/10.4324/9780429449642-4/working-memory-alan-baddeleyv

Baddeley, A. D., & Hitch, G. J. (1974). Working memory. In G. H. Bower (Ed.), The psychology of learning and motivation, 8(47– 89). New York: Academic Press.

Baevsky, R. M., Baranov, V. M, Chernikova, A. G., Funtova, I. I., Pashenko, A. V., Tank, J. (2005). Results of cardiorespiratory system autonomic regulation investigations during long term International Space Station missions: Experiment "PULSE". *Joint 9th European symposium on life sciences research in space & 26th Annual Internation Gravitational Physiology Meeting, 26th Jun-1st Jul 2005*. Cologne, Germany.

Bailey, C. H., Bartsch, D., & Kandel, E. R. (1996). Toward a molecular definition of long-term memory storage. *Proceedings of the National Academy of Sciences*, *93*(24), 13445–13452. https://doi.org/10.1073/pnas.93.24.13445

Baldo, J. V., Shimamura, A. P., Delis, D. C., Kramer, J., and Kaplan, E. (2001). Verbal and design fluency in patients with frontal lobe lesions. *Journal of the International Neuropsychological Society,* 7, 586–596.

Bandura, A. (1986). *Social foundations of thought and action: A social cognitive theory*. Englewood Cliffs, NJ, US: Prentice-Hall, Inc.

Bandura, A. (1997). *Self-efficacy: The exercise of control*. New York, NY, US: W H Freeman/Times Books/Henry Holt & Co.

Barkley, R. A. (1996). Linkages between attention and executive functions. In G. R. Lyon, & N. A. Krasnegor, (Eds.), *Attention, memory, and executive function* (pp. 307–325). Baltimore, MD, US: Paul H. Brookes Publishing Co.

Bherer, L., Erickson, K. I., & Liu-Ambrose, T. (2013). A review of the effects of physical activity and exercise on cognitive and brain functions in older adults. *Journal of aging research*, 2013. 2013:657508. doi: 10.1155/2013/657508. Epub 2013 Sep 11. PMID: 24102028; PMCID: PMC3786463.

Blascovich, J., & Mendes, W. (2000). Challenge and threat appraisals: The role of affective cues. In J. P. Forgas (Ed.), *Feeling and thinking: The role of affect in social cognition* (pp. 59–82). Paris: Cambridge University Press.

Blascovich, J., & Tomaka, J. (1996). The biopsychosocial model of arousal regulation. In M. P. Zanna (Ed.), *Advances in experimental social psychology* (Vol. 28, pp. 1–51), Academic Press.

Boksem, M. A., Meijman, T. F., & Lorist, M. M. (2005). Effects of mental fatigue on attention: an ERP study. *Brain Res Cognitive Brain Research*, 25(1), 107–116. https://doi.org/S0926-6410(05)00118-7 [pii]

Boksem, M. A., Meijman, T. F., & Lorist, M. M. (2006). Mental fatigue, motivation and action monitoring. *Biological Psychology*, 72(2), 123–132. https://doi.org/10.1016/j.biopsycho.2005.08.007

Boksem, M. A., & Tops, M. (2008). Mental fatigue: Costs and benefits. *Brain Research Reviews*, 59(1), 125–139. https://doi.org/10.1016/j.brainresrev.2008.07.001

Borragán, G., Slama, H., Bartolomei, M., & Peigneux, P. (2017). Cognitive fatigue: A Time-based Resource-sharing account. *Cortex,* 89, 71–84. https://doi.org/10.1016/j.cortex.2017.01.023

Burger, J. M. (1989). Negative reactions to increases in perceived personal control. *Journal of Personality and Social Psychology*, 56(2), 246–256. doi:10.1037/0022-3514.56.2.246

Burgess, P. W., Alderman, N., Ernslie, H., Evans, J., & Wilson, B. A. (1998). The ecological validity of tests of executive function. *Journal of the International Neuropsychological Society,* 4, 547–558.

Buijs, R. M. (2013). The autonomic nervous system: A balancing act. *Handbook of Clinical Neurology,* 117, 1–11. https://doi.org/10.1016/B978-0-444-53491-0.00001-8.

Cacioppo, J. T., & Tassinary, L. G. (1990). Inferring psychological significance from physiological signals. *American Psychologist,* 45, 16–28.

Cacioppo, J. T., Tassinary, L. G., & Berntson, G. G. (2000). *Handbook of psychophysiology*. (2nd ed.) Cambridge: Cambridge University Press.

Caldwell, J. (1995). Assessing the impact of stressors on performance – Observations on levels of analyses. *Biological Psychology,* 40, 197–208.

Cannon, W. B. (1914). The interrelations of emotions as suggested by recent physiological researches. *The American Journal of Psychology*, 25(2), 256–282. doi:10.2307/1413414

Cannon, W. B. (1929). Organization for physiological homeostasis. *Physiological Reviews*, 9(3), 399–431.

Carlson N. R. (2017). *Physiology of behaviour*. (12th ed.) Harlow: Pearson.

Casler J. G., & Cook J.R. (1999). Cognitive performance in space and analogous environments. *International Journal of Cognitive Ergonomics,* 3, 351–372.

Chang, Y. K., Labban, J. D., Gapin, J. I., & Etnier, J. L. (2012). The effects of acute exercise on cognitive performance: a meta-analysis. *Brain Research,* 1453, 87–101.

Chaudhuri, A., & Behan, P. O. (2004). Fatigue in neurological disorders. *Lancet*, 363(9413), 978–988. https://doi.org/10.1016/S0140-6736(04)15794-2

Chaytor, N. S., & Schmitter-Edgecombe, M. (2003). The ecological validity of neuropsychological tests: A review of the literature on everyday cognitive skills. *Neuropsychology Review,* 13, 181–197.

Cook, D. B., O'Connor, P. J., Lange, G., & Steffener, J. (2007). Functional neuroimaging correlates of mental fatigue induced by cognition among chronic fatigue syndrome patients and controls. *Neuroimage*, 36(1), 108–122. https://doi.org/10.1016/j.neuroimage.2007.02.033

Cote, K. A., Milner, C. E., Smith, B. A., Aubin, A. J., Greason, T. A., Cuthbert, B. P., & Duffus, S. E. (2009). CNS arousal and neurobehavioral performance in a short-term sleep restriction paradigm. *Journal of Sleep Research,* 18(3), 291–303.

Coutinho, D., Gonçalves, B., Travassos, B., Wong, D. P., Coutts, A. J., & Sampaio, J. E. (2017). Mental fatigue and spatial references impair soccer players' physical and tactical performances. *Frontiers in Psychology,* 8, 1645. https://doi.org/10.3389/fpsyg.2017.01645

Crowder, R. G., & Surprenant, A. M. (2000). Sensory stores. In A. E. Kazdin (Ed.), *Encyclopedia of psychology* (Vol. 7, pp. 227–229). Oxford University Press.

Deary, I. J. D., Liewald, & J. Nissan. (2011). A free, easy-to-use, computer-based simple and four-choice reaction time programme: The Deary-Liewald reaction time task. *Behavior Research Methods* 43(1), 258–268.

Delongis, A., Folkman, S., Lazarus, R. S., & Gruen, R. J. (1986). Appraisal, coping, health status, and psychological symptoms. *Journal of Personality and Social Psychology*, 50(3), 571–579. https://doi.org/10.1037/0022-3514.50.3.571

Der, G., & I. J. Deary. (2006). Age and sex differences in reaction time in adulthood: Results from the United Kingdom health and lifestyle survey. *Psychology and Aging*, 21(1), 62–73.

Desimone, R., & Duncan, J. (1995). Neural mechanisms of selective visual attention. *Annual Review of Neuroscience*, 18, 193–222.

Diamond, A. (2013). Executive functions. Annual Review of Psychology, 64, 135–168. https://doi.org/10.1146/annurev-psych-113011-143750

Edwards, J. R. (1996). An examination of competing versions of the person-environment fit approach to stress. *The Academy of Management Journal*, 39(2), 292–339. doi:10.2307/256782

Egeth, H. E., & Yantis, S. (1997). Visual attention: Control, representation, and time course. *Annual Review of Psychology*, 48(1), 269–297.

Esterman, M., & Rothlein, D. (2019). Models of sustained attention. *Current opinion in psychology, 29*, 174–180. https://doi.org/10.1016/j.copsyc.2019.03.005

Eysenck, M. W., & Keane, M. T. (2000). *Cognitive psychology*. (4th ed.) Hove: Psychology Press.

Farrimond, S., Knight, R. G., & Titov, N. (2006). The effects of aging on remembering intentions: Performance on a simulated shopping task. *Applied Cognitive Psychology*, 20, 533–555.

Fazey, J., & Hardy, L. (1988). *The Inverted-U Hypothesis: A catastrophe for sport psychology: British association of sports sciences and the national coaching foundation.*

Fink, G. (2016). Stress: Definition and history. In Fink, G. (Ed.). Stress: Concepts, Cognition, Emotion, and Behavior. Academic Press, 2016. https://doi.org/10.1016/C2013-0-12842-5

Folkman, S., & Lazarus, R. S. (1980). An analysis of coping in a middle-aged community sample. *Journal of Health and Social Behavior,* 21(3), 219–239. doi:10.2307/2136617

Folkman, S., Lazarus, R. S., Dunkel-Schetter, C., DeLongis, A., & Gruen, R. J. (1986). Dynamics of a stressful encounter: Cognitive appraisal, coping, and encounter outcomes. *Journal of Personality and Social Psychology*, 50(5), 992.

Franco-Alvarenga, P. E., Brietzke, C., Canestri, R., Goethel, M. F., Hettinga, F., Santos, T. M., & Pires, F. O. (2019). Caffeine improved cycling trial performance in mentally fatigued cyclists, regardless of alterations in prefrontal cortex activation. *Physiology & Behavior,* 204, 41–48. https://doi.org/10.1016/j.physbeh.2019.02.009

Friedl, K. E. (2018). Military applications of soldier physiological monitoring. *Journal of Science and Medicine in Sport*, 21(11), 1147–1153. https://doi.org/10.1016/j.jsams.2018.06.004

Friedman, B. (2007). An autonomic flexibility–neurovisceral integration model of anxiety and cardiac vagal tone. *Biological Psychology*, 74(2), 185–199. https://doi.org/10.1016/J.BIOPSYCHO.2005.08.009.

Gardner, H. (1985). *The mind's new science*. New York: Basic Books.

Gazzaniga, M. S., Ivry, R. B., & Mangun, G. R. (2018). "Cognitive Neuroscience: The Biology of the Mind." W. W. Norton & Company.

Genovesio, A., Brasted, P. J., & Wise, S. P. (2006). Representation of future and previous spatial goals by separate neural populations in prefrontal cortex. *Journal of Neuroscience*, 26, 7305–16.

Gilbert, S. J., & Burgess, P. W. (2008). Executive function. *Current Biology*, 18(3), R110-R114.

Glazer, S., & Liu, C. (2017). Work, stress, coping, and stress management. *Oxf. Res. Encycl. Psychol.*

Godoy, L. D., Rossignoli, M. T., Delfino-Pereira, P., Garcia-Cairasco, N., & de Lima Umeoka, E. H. (2018). A comprehensive overview on stress neurobiology: basic concepts and clinical implications. *Frontiers in Behavioral Neuroscience*, 12(127). doi:10.3389/fnbeh.2018.00127

Goldstein, E. B. (2019). "Cognitive psychology: Connecting mind, research, and everyday experience." Cengage Learning.

Goldstein, M. A. & Silverman, M. E. (2006). Autonomics and cognition. *Clinical Autonomic Research* (2006) 16, 86–89. DOI 10.1007/s10286-006-0339-2

Gray, R., Gaska, J., & Winterbottom, M. (2016). Relationship between sustained, orientated, divided, and selective attention and simulated aviation performance: Training & pressure effects. *Journal of applied research in memory and cognition, 5*(1), 34–42. https://doi.org/10.1016/j.jarmac.2015.11.005

Habay, J., Proost, M., De Wachter, J., Díaz-García, J., De Pauw, K., Meeusen, R., . . . Roelands, B. (2021). Mental fatigue-associated decrease in table tennis performance: Is there an electrophysiological signature? *International Journal of Environmental Research and Public Health*, 18(24). https://doi.org/10.3390/ijerph182412906

Habay, J., Uylenbroeck, R., Van Droogenbroeck, R., De Wachter, J., Proost, M., Tassignon, B., . . . Roelands, B. (2023). Interindividual variability in mental fatigue-related impairments in endurance performance: A systematic review and multiple meta-regression. *Sports Medicine Open,* 9(1), 14. https://doi.org/10.1186/s40798-023-00559-7

Habay, J., Van Cutsem, J., Verschueren, J., De Bock, S., Proost, M., De Wachter, J., . . . Roelands, B. (2021). Mental fatigue and sport-specific psychomotor performance: A systematic review. *Sports Medicine*. https://doi.org/10.1007/s40279-021-01429-6

Hawkins, R. D., Kandel, E. R., & Bailey, C. H. (2006). Molecular mechanisms of memory storage in Aplysia. *The Biological Bulletin, 210*(3), 174–191. https://doi.org/10.2307/4134556

Hebb, D. O. (1955). Drives and the C. N. S. (conceptual nervous system). *Psychological Review*, 62(4), 243–254. doi:10.1037/h0041823

Heinrichs, R. W. (1990). Current and emergent applications of neuropsychological assessment – problems of validity and utility. *Professional Psychology-Research and Practice,* 21, 171–176.

Hobfoll, S. (1989). Conservation of Resources: A new attempt at conceptualizing stress. *The American Psychologist,* 44, 513–524. doi:10.1037/0003-066X.44.3.513

Hoeymans, N., Feskens, E. J. M., van den Bos, G. A. M., & Kromhout, D. (1996). Measuring functional status: Cross-sectional and longitudinal associations between performance and self-report (Zutphen Elderly Study 1990-1993). *Journal of Clinical Epidemiology,* 49, 1103–1110.

Homan, W. J. (2002). *Stress Coping Strategies for Commercial Flight Crewmembers*, Journal of Aviation/Aerospace Education & Research, 12(1). DOI: https://doi.org/10.15394/jaaer.2002.1592

Hopstaken, J. F., van der Linden, D., Bakker, A. B., & Kompier, M. A. (2015). A multifaceted investigation of the link between mental fatigue and task disengagement. *Psychophysiology,* 52(3), 305–315. https://doi.org/10.1111/psyp.12339

Hughdahl, K. (1995). *Psychophysiology: The mind-body perspective.* (1st ed.) Cambridge, MA: Harvard University Press.

Humphreys, M. S., & Revelle, W. (1984). Personality, motivation, and performance: A theory of the relationship between individual differences and information processing. *Psychological Review*, 91(2), 153–184. doi:10.1037/0033-295X.91.2.153

Irwin, D. E., & Thomas, L. E. (2008). Visual sensory memory. *Visual memory*, *1*(9), 9-43.

Jacquet, T., Poulin-Charronnat, B., Bard, P., Perra, J., & Lepers, R. (2021). Physical activity and music to counteract mental fatigue. *Neuroscience,* 478, 75–88. https://doi.org/10.1016/j.neuroscience.2021.09.019

James, W. (1890). *The principles of psychology* (Vol. 1). New York: Henry Holt & Co.

Jevas, S., & Yan, J. H. (2001). The effect of aging on cognitive function: A preliminary quantitative review. *Research Quarterly for Exercise and Sport* 72, A-49.

Jones, M., Meijen, C., McCarthy, P. J., & Sheffield, D. (2009). A theory of challenge and threat states in athletes. *International Review of Sport and Exercise Psychology*, 2(2), 161–180. doi:10.1080/17509840902829331

Jones, S., Nyberg, L., Sandblom, J., Neely, A. S., Ingvar, M., Petersson, K. M., & Bäckman, L. (2006). Cognitive and neural plasticity in aging: General and task-specific limitations. *Neuroscience & Biobehavioral Reviews*, 30(6), 864–871.

Kail, R., & Hall, L. K. (2001). Distinguishing short-term memory from working memory. *Memory & cognition*, *29*(1), 1-9. https://doi.org/10.3758/BF03195735

Kato, Y., Endo, H., Kobayakawa, T., Kato, K., & Kitazaki, S. (2012). Effects of intermittent odours on cognitive-motor performance and brain functioning during mental fatigue. *Ergonomics*, 55(1), 1–11. https://doi.org/10.1080/00140139.2011.633175

Katsuki, F., & Constantinidis, C. (2013). *Bottom-Up and Top-Down Attention. The Neuroscientist, 20(5), 509–521.* https://doi.org/10.1177/1073858413514136

Killgore WD. Effects of sleep deprivation on cognition. Prog Brain Res. 2010;185:105-29. doi: 10.1016/B978-0-444-53702-7.00007-5. PMID: 21075236.

Knudsen, E. I. (2007). Fundamental components of attention. *Annual Review if Neuroscience,* 30, 57–78.

Krohne, H. W. (2001). *Stress and Coping Theories*. The International Encyclopedia of the Social and Behavioral Sciences, 22, 15163–15170. https://doi.org/10.1016/B0-08-043076-7/03817-1

Kruger, J., & Dunning, D. (1999). Unskilled and unaware of it: How difficulties in recognizing one's own incompetence lead to inflated self-assessments. *Journal of Personality and Social Psychology*, 77(6), 1121– 1134. https://doi.org/10.1037/0022-3514.77.6.1121

Kurzban, R., Duckworth, A., Kable, J. W., & Myers, J. (2013). An opportunity cost model of subjective effort and task performance. *Behavioral and Brain Sciences*, 36(6), 661–679. https://doi.org/10.1017/S0140525X12003196

LaBar, K. S., Gitelman, D. R., Parrish, T. B., & Mesulam, M. (1999). Neuroanatomic overlap of working memory and spatial attention networks: A functional MRI comparison within subjects. *Neuroimage*, (10), 695–704.

Lancry, A. (2007). Incertitude et stress. *Le Travail Humain*, 70(3), 289–305.

Lazarus, R. S. (1991). Progress on a cognitive–motivational–relational theory of emotion. *American Psychologist*, 46(8), 819–834. doi:10.1037/0003-066X.46.8.819

Lazarus, R. S., & Folkman, S. (1984). *Stress, appraisal, and coping*. New York: Springer Pub. Co.

Lazarus, R. S., & Folkman, S. (1986). Cognitive theories of stress and the issue of circularity. In Appley, M.H., Trumbull, R. (eds) *Dynamics of stress: Physiological, psychological, and social perspectives*. (pp. 63–80). The Plenum Series on Stress and Coping. Boston, MA: Springer. https://doi.org/10.1007/978-1-4684-5122-1_4

Lazarus, R. S., & Folkman, S. (1991). *The concept of coping. Stress and coping: An anthology*, 3rd ed. New York, NY, US: Columbia University Press.

Lim, J., Wu, W. C., Wang, J., Detre, J. A., Dinges, D. F., & Rao, H. (2010). Imaging brain fatigue from sustained mental workload: An ASL perfusion study of the time-on-task effect. *Neuroimage*, 49(4), 3426–3435. https://doi.org/10.1016/j.neuroimage.2009.11.020

Lindsay, G. W. (2020). Attention in psychology, neuroscience, and machine learning. *Frontiers in computational neuroscience*, *14*, 29. https://doi.org/10.3389/fncom.2020.00029

Locke, E. A., & Latham, G. P. (2002). Building a practically useful theory of goal setting and task motivation: A 35-year odyssey. *American psychologist*, *57*(9), 705. https://psycnet.apa.org/doi/10.1037/0003-066X.57.9.705

Luchies, C. W., J. Schiffman, L. G. Richards, M. R. Thompson, D. Bazuin, & A. J. DeYoung. (2002). Effects of age, step direction, and reaction condition on the ability to step quickly. *The Journals of Gerontology, Series A*, 57(4), M246.

Mackworth, N. H. (1948). The breakdown of vigilance during prolonged visual search. *Quarterly Journal of Experimental Psychology,* 1, 6–21.

Madden, D. J. (2001). Speed and timing of behavioural processes. In J. E. Birren & K. W. Schaie (Eds.), *Handbook of the psychology of aging*, 5th ed. (pp. 288–312). San Diego: Academic Press.

Maddux, J. E. (1995). Self-efficacy theory: An introduction. In J. E. Maddux (Ed.), *Self-efficacy, adaptation, and adjustment: Theory, research, and application.* (pp. 3–33). New York, NY, US: Plenum Press.

Malmo, R. B. (1965). Physiological gradients and behaviour. *Psychological Bulletin,* 64, 225–234.

Manly, T., & Robertson, I. H. (1997). Sustained attention and the frontal lobes. In P. Rabbitt (Ed.), *Methodology of frontal and executive function* (pp. 135–153). Hove, UK: Psychology Press.

Marcora, S. M., Staiano, W., & Manning, V. (2009). Mental fatigue impairs physical performance in humans. *Journal of Applied Physiology (1985)*, 106(3), 857–864. https://doi.org/10.1152/japplphysiol.91324.2008

Marcora, S. M., Staiano, W., & Merlini, M. (2015). *A randomized controlled trial of Brain Endurance Training (BET) to reduce fatigue during endurance exercise ACSM annual meeting.* San Diego.

Martin, K., Meeusen, R., Thompson, K. G., Keegan, R., & Rattray, B. (2018). Mental fatigue impairs endurance performance: A physiological explanation. *Sports Medicine.* https://doi.org/10.1007/s40279-018-0946-9

McCormick, F., Kadzielski, J., Landrigan, C. P., Evans, B., Herndon, J. H., & Rubash, H. E. (2012). Surgeon fatigue: A prospective analysis of the incidence, risk, and intervals of predicted fatigue-related impairment in residents. *Archieves of Surgery*, 147(5), 430–435. https://doi.org/10.1001/archsurg.2012.84

Miller, G. A. (1956). The magical number seven, plus or minus two: Some limits on our capacity for processing information. *Psychological Review, 63*(2), 81–97. https://doi.org/10.1037/h0043158

Miyake, A., Friedman, N. P., Emerson, M. J., Witzki, A. H., Howerter, A., & Wager, T. D. (2000). The unity and diversity of executive functions and their contributions to complex "frontal lobe" tasks: A latent variable analysis. *Cognitive Psychology*, 41, 49–100.

Mockel, T., Beste, C., & Wascher, E. (2015). The effects of time on task in response selection–An ERP study of mental fatigue. *Scientific Reports*, 5, 10113. https://doi.org/10.1038/srep10113

Newell, A., & Simon, H. A. (1972). *Human problem solving.* Prentice-Hall.

Norris, D. (2017). Short-term memory and long-term memory are still different. *Psychological Bulletin, 143*(9), 992–1009. https://doi.org/10.1037/bul0000108

O'Keeffe, K., Hodder, S., & Lloyd, A. (2020). A comparison of methods used for inducing mental fatigue in performance research: Individualised, dual-task and short duration cognitive tests are most effective. *Ergonomics*, 63(1), 1–12. https://doi.org/10.1080/00140139.2019.1687940

Oberste, M., de Waal, P., Joisten, N., Walzik, D., Egbringhoff, M., Javelle, F., . . . Zimmer, P. (2021). Acute aerobic exercise to recover from mental exhaustion – a randomized controlled trial. *Physiology & Behavior,* 241, 113588. https://doi.org/10.1016/j.physbeh.2021.113588

Ohman, A., Hamm, A., & Hugdahl, K. (2000). Cognition and the autonomic nervous system. In J. T.Cacioppo, L. G. Tassinary, & G. G. Berntson (Eds.), *Handbook of psychophysiology* (pp. 533–575). Cambridge,MA: Cambridge University Press.

Okubo, Y., Schoene, D., & Lord, S. R. (2017). Step training improves reaction time, gait and balance and reduces falls in older people: A systematic review and meta-analysis. *British Journal of Sports Medicine*, 51(7), 586–593.

Pattyn, N., Mairesse, O., Cortoos, A., Morais, J., Soetens, E., Roelands B, van den Nest A, Kolinsky, R. (2013). Cardiac reactivity and preserved performance under stress: two sides of the same coin? *International Journal of Psychophysiology*, 2014 Jul;93(1), 30–7. doi: 10.1016/j.ijpsycho.2013.03.008. Epub 2013 Mar 23. PMID: 23528304

Pattyn, N., Migeotte, P.-F., Morais, J., Soetens, E., Cluydts, R., & Kolinsky, R. (2009). Crew performance monitoring: Putting some feeling into it. *Acta Astronautica*, 65(3–4), 325–329. https://doi.org/10.1016/j.actaastro.2009.01.063

Pattyn, N., Migeotte, P. F., Neyt, X., den Nest, A. van, & Cluydts, R. (2010). Comparing real-life and laboratory-induced stress reactivity on cardio-respiratory parameters: Differentiation of a tonic and a phasic component. *Physiology and Behavior,* 101(2), 218–223. https://doi.org/10.1016/j.physbeh.2010.04.037

Pattyn, N., Neyt, X., Henderickx, D., & Soetens, E. (2008). Psychophysiological investigation of vigilance decrement: boredom or cognitive fatigue? *Physiology & Behavior*, 93(1–2), 369–378. https://doi.org/10.1016/j.physbeh.2007.09.016.

Pattyn, N., Van Cutsem, J., Dessy, E., & Mairesse, O. (2018). Bridging exercise science, cognitive psychology, and medical practice: Is "Cognitive Fatigue" a remake of "The Emperor's New Clothes"? *Frontiers in Psychology*, 9, 1246. https://doi.org/10.3389/fpsyg.2018.01246

Petersen S.E., Posner M.I. The attention system of the human brain: 20 years after. Annu Rev Neurosci. 2012;35:73–89. doi: 10.1146/annurev-neuro-062111-150525. Epub 2012 Apr 12. PMID: 22524787; PMCID: PMC3413263.

Pfeifer, R., & Iida, F. (2004). Embodied artificial intelligence: Trends and challenges. *Lecture Notes in Computer Science*, 3139(1–26). Berlin, Heidelberg: Springer. https://doi.org/10.1007/978-3-540-27833-7_1

Proost, M., Habay, J., De Wachter, J., De Pauw, K., Marusic, U., Meeusen, R., . . . Van Cutsem, J. (2023). The impact of mental fatigue on a strength endurance task: Is there a role for the movement-related cortical potential? *Medicine & Science in Sports Exercise*. https://doi.org/10.1249/MSS.0000000000003322

Proost, M., Habay, J., De Wachter, J., De Pauw, K., Rattray, B., Meeusen, R., . . . Van Cutsem, J. (2022). How to tackle mental fatigue: A systematic review of potential countermeasures and their underlying mechanisms. *Sports Medicine*. https://doi.org/10.1007/s40279-022-01678-z

Rabbitt, P. (1997). Introduction: Methodologies and models in the study of executive function. In: Rabbitt, P. (Ed.), *Methodology of frontal and executive function* (pp. 1–38). Hove, UK: Psychology Press.

Rahnev, D. (2021). Visual metacognition: Measures, models, and neural correlates. *American Psychologist, 76*(9), 1445–1453. https://doi.org/10.1037/amp0000937

Russell, S., Jenkins, D. G., Halson, S. L., & Kelly, V. G. (2022). Mental fatigue increases across a 16-week pre-season in elite female athletes. *Journal of Science and Medicine in Sport*, 25(4), 356-361. https://doi.org/10.1016/j.jsams.2021.12.002

Russell, S., Jenkins, D. G., Halson, S. L., Juliff, L. E., & Kelly, V. G. (2022). How do elite female team sport athletes experience mental fatigue? Comparison between international competition, training and preparation camps. *European Journal of Sport Science*, 22(6), 877–887. https://doi.org/10.1080/17461391.2021.1897165

Russell, S., Jenkins, D. G., Halson, S. L., Juliff, L. E., Connick, M. J., & Kelly, V. G. (2022). Mental fatigue over 2 elite netball seasons: A case for mental fatigue to be included in athlete self-report measures. *International Journal of Sports Physiology and Performance*, 17(2), 160–169. https://doi.org/10.1123/ijspp.2021-0028

Salehi, B., Cordero, M. I., & Sandi, C. (2010). Learning under stress: The inverted-U-shape function revisited. *Learning & Memory (Cold Spring Harbor, N.Y.)*, 17(10), 522–530. https://doi.org/10.1101/lm.1914110

Salthouse, T. A. (1996). The processing-speed theory of adult age differences in cognition. *Psychological Review,* 103, 403-428.

Schunk, D. H. (1995). Self-efficacy and education and instruction. In J. E. Maddux (Ed.), *Self-efficacy, adaptation, and adjustment: Theory, research, and application* (pp. 281-303). New York, NY, US: Plenum Press.

Selye, H. (1936). A Syndrome produced by diverse nocuous agents. *Nature*, 138(3479), 32–32. doi:10.1038/138032a0

Selye, H. (1950). Stress and the general adaptation syndrome. *British Medical Journal*, 1(4667), 1383.

Selye, H. (1956). *The stress of life*. McGraw-Hill.

Siegrist, J. (1996). Adverse health effects of high-effort/low-reward conditions. *Journal of Occupational Health Psychology*, 1(1), 27–41. doi:10.1037/1076-8998.1.1.27

Skinner, E. A. (1996). A guide to constructs of control. *Journal of Personality and Social Psychology*, 71(3), 549–570. doi:10.1037/0022-3514.71.3.549

Skinner, N., & Brewer, N. (2004). Adaptive approaches to competition: Challenge appraisals and positive emotion. *Journal of Sport & Exercise Psychology*, 26(2), 283–305.

Smith, A. P. (2018). Cognitive fatigue and the well-being and academic attainment of university students. *Journal of Education, Society and Behavioral Science*, 24(1–12). https://doi.org/10.9734/JESBS/2018/39529

Smith, P. J., Blumenthal, J. A., Hoffman, B. M., Cooper, H., Strauman, T. A., Welsh-Bohmer, K., ... & Sherwood, A. (2010). Aerobic exercise and neurocognitive performance: A meta-analytic review of randomized controlled trials. *Psychosomatic Medicine,* 72(3), 239.

Smith, S. S., Kilby, S., Jorgensen, G., & Douglas, J. A. (2007). Napping and nightshift work: Effects of a short nap on psychomotor vigilance and subjective sleepiness in health workers. *Sleep and Biological Rhythms*, 5(2), 117-125.

Steriade, M., Jones, E. G., & Llinás, R. R. (1990). *Thalamic oscillations and signaling*. John Wiley & Sons.

Stern, Y. (2002). What is cognitive reserve? Theory and research application of the reserve concept. *Journal of the International Neuropsychological Society*, 8(3), 448–460.

Stuss, D. T., Alexander, M. P., Hamer, L., Palumbo, C., Dempster, R., Binns, M., Levine, B., & Izukawa, D. (1998). The effects of focal anterior and posterior brain lesions on verbal fluency. *Journal of the International Neuropsychological Society,* 4, 265–278.

Stuss, D. T., Floden, D., Alexander, M. P., Levine, B., & Katz, D. (2001). Stroop performance in focal lesion patients: Dissociation of processes and frontal lobe lesion location. *Neuropsychologia,* 39, 771–786.

Takahashi, M., Nakata, A., Haratani, T., Ogawa, Y., & Arito, H. (2004). Post-lunch nap as a worksite intervention to promote alertness on the job. *Ergonomics*, 47(9), 1003–1013.

Taya, F., Sun, Y., Babiloni, F., Thakor, N., & Bezerianos, A. (2015). Brain enhancement through cognitive training: A new insight from brain connectome, 9(April), 1–19. https://doi.org/10.3389/fnsys.2015.00044

Teigen, K. H. (1994). Yerkes-Dodson: A law for all seasons. *Theory & Psychology,* 4(4), 525–547. doi:10.1177/0959354394044004.

Thakor, N. V, & Sherman, D. L. (2013). *Neural Engineering*. (B. He, Ed.). Boston, MA: Springer US. https://doi.org/10.1007/978-1-4614-5227-0

Thayer J. F., & Brosschot, J. F. (2005). Psychosomatics and psychopathology: Looking up and down from the brain. *Psychoneuroendocrinology*, 30, 1050–1058.

Thayer, J. F., Hansen, A. L., Saus-Rose, E., Johnsen, B. H. (2009). Heart rate variability, prefrontal neural function, and cognitive performance: the neurovisceral integration perspective on self-regulation, adaptation, and health. Ann Behav Med. 37(2):141-53. doi: 10.1007/s12160-009-9101-z. Epub 2009 May 8. PMID: 19424767.

Thayer, J. F., & Lane, R. D. (2000). A model of neurovisceral integration in emotion regulation and dysregulation. *Journal of Affective Disorders*, 61, 201–216.

Thompson, C. J., Noon, M., Towlson, C., Perry, J., Coutts, A. J., Harper, L. D., . . . Meyer, T. (2020). Understanding the presence of mental fatigue in English academy soccer players. *Journal of Sports Science,* 38(13), 1524–1530. https://doi.org/10.1080/02640414.2020.1746597

Titov, N., & Knight, R. G. (2005). A computer-based procedure for assessing functional cognitive skills in patients with neurological injuries: The virtual street. *Brain Injury,* 19, 315–322.

Treasure, D. C., & Monson, J. (1996). Relationship between self-efficacy, wrestling performance, and affect prior to competition. *Sport Psychologist*, 10(1), 73–83. Retrieved from https://ucc.idm.oclc.org/login?URL=http://search.ebscohost.com/login.aspx?direct=true&db=s3h&AN=9604 071256&site=ehost-live

Troyer, A. K., Moscovitch, M., Winocur, G., Alexander, M. P., & Stuss, D. (1998). Clustering and switching on verbal fluency: The effects of focal frontal- and temporal-lobe lesions. *Neuropsychologia,* 36, 499–504.

Van Cutsem, J., & Marcora, S. (2021). The effects of mental fatigue on sport performance; An update. In C. Englert & I. Taylor (Eds.), *Handbook of self-regulation and motivation in sport and exercise*. Routledge/Taylor & Francis Group. https://doi.org/10.4324/9781003176695

Van Cutsem, J., Marcora, S., De Pauw, K., Bailey, S., Meeusen, R., & Roelands, B. (2017). The effects of mental fatigue on physical performance: A systematic review. *Sports Medicine*. https://doi.org/10.1007/s40279-016-0672-0

Van Cutsem, J., Van Schuerbeek, P., Pattyn, N., Raeymaekers, H., De Mey, J., Meeusen, R., & Roelands, B. (2022). A drop in cognitive performance, whodunit? Subjective mental fatigue, brain deactivation or increased parasympathetic activity? *It's complicated! Cortex,* 155, 30-45. https://doi.org/10.1016/j.cortex.2022.06.006

Van Den Berg, J., & Neely, G. (2006). Performance on a simple reaction time task while sleep deprived. *Perceptual and Motor Skills,* 102(2), 589-599.

van der Linden, D., Massar, S. A., Schellekens, A. F., Ellenbroek, B. A., & Verkes, R. J. (2006). Disrupted sensorimotor gating due to mental fatigue: Preliminary evidence. *International Journal of Psychophysiology,* 62(1), 168-174. https://doi.org/10.1016/j.ijpsycho.2006.04.001

Wascher, E., Rasch, B., Sanger, J., Hoffmann, S., Schneider, D., Rinkenauer, G., . . . Gutberlet, I. (2014). Frontal theta activity reflects distinct aspects of mental fatigue. *Biological Psychology,* 96, 57–65. https://doi.org/10.1016/j.biopsycho.2013.11.010

Welford, A. T. (1977). Motor performance. In J. E. Birren & K. W. Schaie (Eds.), *Handbook of the psychology of aging* (pp. 450–496). New York: Van Nostrand Reinhold.

Wiehler, A., Branzoli, F., Adanyeguh, I., Mochel, F., & Pessiglione, M. (2022). A neuro-metabolic account of why daylong cognitive work alters the control of economic decisions. *Current Biology*, 32(16), 3564–3575.e3565. https://doi.org/10.1016/j.cub.2022.07.010

Yerkes, R. M., & Dodson, J. D. (1908). The relation of strength of stimulus to rapidity of habit-formation. *Journal of Comparative Neurology and Psychology*, 18(5), 459–482. doi:10.1002/cne.920180503

3 Ideal Performance States

Integrating Physiology, Cognition, and Emotion

Martin I. Jones and Paige Mattie

What is a performance state?

A performance state is broadly conceived as the consequence of a state of mind, or a way of thinking and feeling, that supports the striving toward and achievement of desired goals. Fundamentally, mental skills (i.e., goal setting, self-talk, relaxation) improve performance through changes in the way performers think, feel, and behave. Put differently, the ideal performance state mediates the relationship between the practice of mental skills and task performance. That said, mental skills are not the only way to change an individual's performance state. For example, sleep deprivation, poor nutrition, and environmental variables (i.e., hypoxia, cold, and heat) can undermine the way a performer thinks and feels, and therefore need consideration when building an ideal performance state.

There are many different constituents of the ideal performance state, and it is highly likely that significant individual differences exist when characterizing the experience of ideal performance. To that end, Gardner and Moore (2012) stated that there is no single nomothetic ideal performance state and that in fact, people can perform while experiencing an assortment of cognitive, emotional, and physiological states (Hanin, 1980). Even though it is true that there are a range of "mindsets" that facilitate performance, it is also true that a range of mindsets will also degenerate performance. For example, ways of thinking that are characterized by catastrophe, maladaptive perfectionism, procrastination, and narcissism (to name but a few) are likely to impede progression toward valued goals.

While it is not within the scope of the current chapter to analyze the full range of the possible constituents of the ideal performance state (cf. Dalgaard-Nielsen & Holm, 2019) we do suggest some core components of the ideal performance state that we have observed in high performers, which generalize to all performance contexts and are trainable. These qualities and capabilities are self-efficacy, self-regulation, and attentional control.

In athletic performance, the idea of an ideal performance state in a sporting context can be traced to the concept of an individual zone of functioning (IZOF) first proposed by Hanin (1997). Hanin (1997, 2000) described the relationship between arousal, emotional states, and sport performance and highlighted the individual differences in how people react to stress (i.e., anxiety). Specifically, some people (sometimes) performed better under low anxiety and others under high anxiety. Essentially, each person has a zone of functioning that depends on the interaction of environmental demands and the personal resources that allow them to perform optimally. Deviations from this zone can hinder performance (Hanin, 2000).

Hanin (2000) extended the concept of the IZOF beyond just anxiety to encompass a variety of emotional states, distinguishing between emotions that facilitate or debilitate performance. For

DOI: 10.4324/9781003378969-4

example, performers may find certain emotions, like excitement or anger, either conducive or detrimental to their performance. However, the IZOF model does not consider the antecedents of these emotions.

Despite being introduced in sports in the 1990s, the idea of a performance state (although not necessarily labelled in that way) is not new. In fact, ideal states of functioning predate psychology and are a feature of most classical theories of philosophy. Cognitive theories of emotion (e.g., Beck, 1963; Beck & Haigh, 2014; Ellis, 1962) focus on the concept that emotions are determined by cognitive processes. These theories of emotion lean heavily on Greco-Roman philosophical traditions, specifically Stoicism. The Stoic Philosopher Epictetus stated that "It's not things that upset you; it's your judgments about those things." This precept is like Beck's (1963) suggestion that emotions are the result of our perceptions, interpretations, and thoughts about events rather than the events themselves. Beck's theory particularly emphasizes how certain patterns of distorted thinking (cognitive distortions) can lead to emotional distress, particularly in disorders such as depression and anxiety. Ellis' (1962) approach also links emotional disturbances with irrational and illogical beliefs. Like Epictetus, Ellis suggested that it is not events themselves that cause emotional distress but rather the beliefs and interpretations we attach to these events. Ellis formulated the ABC model to explain this process: "A" stands for the activating event, "B" for the belief about the event, and "C" for the consequent emotion. Ellis argued that by identifying and challenging these irrational beliefs and replacing them with more rational and logical ones, individuals could alter their emotional responses and alleviate psychological distress. In this way, the ideal performance state is one that recognizes what is under one's control and what is not. Specifically, an ideal performance state involves indifference to uncontrollable events (such as opponents, crowds, and external judgement) and focus on controllable factors such as beliefs, attitudes, and judgements. While the outcome of a competition would be considered uncontrollable and therefore requires indifference, it is accepted that there are preferred indifferents, for example, winning. It is normal to prefer winning over losing, health over illness, and wealth over poverty; however, the ideal performance state involves focused attention on controllable factors, and the concepts of winning, health, and wealth should not occupy attention as they can be sources of frustration, anger, and sadness if obstacles prevent their acquisition, or if they are removed or lost.

In the context of high performance, more specifically in the military, Dalgaard-Nielsen and Holm (2019) refer to the Special Operations Forces (SOF) mindset as an extraordinary commitment to mission success by means of some combination of qualities and capabilities that cut across from units and countries. Some aspects of the ideal performance state will be relatively stable (i.e., personality traits), whereas others will require specific training over time (i.e., mental skills training). We will focus on the latter and encourage readers to consider the chapters on mental skill training (Chapter 4) or the restorative techniques (Chapter 5) as a potential route to help achieve an ideal performance state.

Before delving into constructs that could comprise an ideal performance, state a word of caution. The ideal performance state is not a panacea for performance. Notwithstanding the role of environment and equipment, performers who lack physical fitness, health (although a caveat is needed here regarding mental health, as is discussed in Chapter 12), technical and tactical skill and awareness, adequate nutrition, sufficient sleep and recovery, and supportive and cohesive relationships will not perform optimally even if they have an optimal mindset built upon excellent mental skills. The ideal performance state forms one part of a broad developmental system that contributes to performance alongside other pillars of human performance (i.e., sleep, nutrition, physical activity, training, equipment, and strategy). However, we contend that if performers are self-assured and they believe (and have the capability to) exert control over the environment and their internal world (i.e., thoughts and emotions), they improve their chances of achieving their desired goals.

Self-efficacy

Self-efficacy is a person's beliefs about their capabilities to execute a course of action to achieve a designated goal or standard of performance. Self-efficacy also represents an individual's perceived capability to act in a way that influences events in his or her life. Self-efficacy beliefs determine how people feel, think, motivate themselves, and behave and effectively describes how the person regulates his or her behaviour when interacting with the environment (Bandura, 1997). Self-efficacy theorists support the reciprocal nature of the relationship between efficacy beliefs and behaviour by stating that the behaviour will not be indulged in unless the efficacy perceptions are sufficient. Self-efficacy is dynamic rather than representing a stable and inherent character of the person.

Self-efficacy is not a mental skill, but rather a consequence (and antecedent) of using mental skills (McCrory, Cobley, & Marchant, 2013). Self-efficacy is often either (or both) a mediator and a moderator of the relationship between mental skill use and performance. For example, as shown in the goal setting chapter (Chapter 4), self-efficacy is a predictor of goal setting (people with high self-efficacy beliefs set challenging goals) and setting goals can increase self-efficacy as positive feedback on goal attainment is received (Locke & Latham, 2019).

Self-efficacy beliefs determine how people think, feel, motivate themselves, and behave (Bandura, 1993). For example, whether someone practices mental skills or techniques can be determined by their efficacy beliefs about whether they can use the skill (e.g., assumptions about ability to control imagery). However, Bandura (1977) clearly stated that efficacy beliefs alone will not produce desired performance. Efficacy beliefs need to coexist alongside skill, ability, and incentives (and arguably group dynamics such as leadership and cohesion, when performance is a team outcome). When appropriate conditions are in place, self-efficacy beliefs are a major determinant of goals, effort, and persistence during stressful situations (Bandura, 1977).

Self-efficacy beliefs can also be divided into process and outcomes components. Specifically, efficacy expectations are beliefs related to the ability to carry out a particular behaviour or cognition. For example, a belief that one can successfully adhere to a mental skills program comprising ten minutes of practice five times each week. Conversely, outcome expectations are beliefs of whether behaviour will produce a particular result. For example, a belief that such a mental skills program will produce the increased performance in each task (e.g., marksmanship) that was desired at the beginning.

Self-efficacy beliefs are situation-specific (Bandura, 1977), and while trait self-efficacy is a measure of one's typical or general self-efficacy beliefs, it is crucial to recognize that people can have high self-efficacy beliefs in one context and low self-efficacy beliefs in another context. Equally, efficacy beliefs at different times in the same context can change. Therefore, self-efficacy beliefs should be assessed in relation to specific behaviours or thoughts. Self-efficacy beliefs are typically unrelated to habitual actions (e.g., brushing one's teeth). When desired outcomes require effect, planning, and the traversing of obstacles, self-efficacy emerges as a strong predictor of behaviour, particularly when the desired outcomes are complex, challenging, or unpleasant (e.g., vigorous exercise).

Self-efficacy will vary along the dimensions of magnitude, strength, and generality (Bandura, 1986). The magnitude of self-efficacy refers to the ordering of tasks by difficulty, such as feeling that one can achieve simple short-term goals but is incapable of achieving complex long-term goals. The strength of self-efficacy refers to the assessment of one's capabilities for performing a particular task. For example, a person can subjectively rate their likelihood of maintaining ten minutes of mindful meditation every day. The generality of self-efficacy refers to the extent to which efficacy expectations from one situation generalize to other situations. For example, efficacy beliefs gained through completing an introduction to mental skills to completion of a train the trainer course for mental skills development. Self-efficacy judgements can generalize but will be strongest for activities like the activity experienced. Self-efficacy in dissimilar activities can be enhanced through counselling, for example, a practitioner stimulating reflection on how the activities might be similar.

Sources of self-efficacy beliefs include mastery experiences, vicarious experiences, social persuasion, and physiological experiences. The most influential source of self-efficacy beliefs is mastery experiences. If people have experienced success in the past, they build a robust self-efficacy (i.e., I have done it before, I can do it again). Previous failures can have the opposite effect, though. According to Bandura (1977) the negative impact of occasional failures is likely to be reduced if strong efficacy is built through repeated success. Bandura (1977, p 195) stated "Indeed, occasional failures that are later overcome by determined effort can strengthen self-motivated persistence, if one finds through experience that even the most difficult obstacles can be mastered by sustained effort." The relationship between mastery experiences and self-efficacy is moderated by the difficulty of the earlier challenges. If people derive their efficacy beliefs from mastery experiences of accomplishing easy tasks, they can be discouraged by failure when faced with challenging tasks. The most robust mastery experiences, by which self-efficacy is formed, come from overcoming hindrances and demonstrating perseverance.

The second source of self-efficacy comes through vicarious experiences provided by similar (to oneself) role models. Seeing people who are like oneself succeeding in a task influences the observer's belief that she can also thrive in the same task (i.e., if she can do it, so can I). The opposite is also true, however. If the observer sees someone similar fail at a task her self-efficacy could be eroded. Equally, Bandura (1977) suggested that seeing others perform potentially threatening activities without adverse consequences can engender expectations in observers that they too will improve if they persist in their efforts (even if they initially experience task failure).

The perceived similarity of the role model and the observer is paramount. If the observer perceives the role model to be significantly different from them, the observer's self-efficacy is unlikely to be changed if the role is successful. If the role model is perceived to be substantially more talented or competent and fails, the observer's self-efficacy would likely be eroded despite perceived dissimilarity (i.e., "if she can't do it, there's no way I can").

The third source of self-efficacy is social persuasion. When exposed to positive verbal persuasion from significant others (i.e., respected peers, team leaders, coaches), an individual's self-efficacy can be increased. If verbal persuasion includes feedback concerning the individual's capabilities to master a given activity or achieve a particular outcome, the individual is likely to mobilize effort and sustain the effort. In contrast, in the absence of feedback, or if verbal persuasion undermines beliefs about personal capabilities, the individual may dwell on self-doubt and harbour thoughts of their own deficiencies in the face of obstacles. It is harder to instil self-efficacy by social persuasion alone than to undermine it. Unrealistic enhancements in self-efficacy are quickly disconfirmed by disappointing results of one's efforts. However, individuals who have been persuaded that they lack capabilities avoid challenging activities and give up quickly in the face of difficulties.

Persuasion can come from self-talk (i.e., motivational self-talk, see also Chapter 4) and is particularly valuable when social persuasion is impossible (i.e., when on one's own; Bandura, 1977). However, if self-talk and social persuasion experienced in sequence or in parallel are incongruent, self-talk might not be enough to buffer the egregious effects of negative social persuasion.

The final (and weakest) way of modifying self-efficacy is to reduce stress reactions and to alter negative emotional inclinations and misinterpretations of bodily sensations during periods of emotional arousal. The vital aspect of this source of self-efficacy is the perception of the emotion or physical sensation, not the strength of the experience. Individuals who can experience emotions, stress reactions, and other bodily sensations (e.g., increased breathing) as energizing factors or facilitators of performance are likely to have higher self-efficacy than those who experience the same stimuli as an enervator of performance. Diminishing emotional arousal can reduce avoidance behaviour and consequently, methods to alleviate stress reactions during periods of emotional arousal (e.g., breathing, relaxation, reappraisal, biofeedback) could help reinterpret their bodily sensations as signals of upcoming performance rather than fear or stress (Bandura, 1977).

The consequences of high self-efficacy include perceiving difficult tasks as challenges to be approached as opposed to threats to be avoided. In the presence of failure, people with high self-efficacy beliefs sustain their efforts. They can rebound from defeat while recovering or maintaining their high self-efficacy. Bandura (1997) suggested that self-efficacy positively influences motivation and performance indirectly. That is, self-efficacy influences the probability that a person will choose to engage or remain engaged in a goal pursuit. Self-efficacy directly influences goal striving because efficacy beliefs directly determine the strength of effort applied to the goal (particularly if feedback on the goal is absent).

Self-regulation

Many performance tasks (e.g., training, exercises, deployments, expeditions, competitions) require performers to engage in processes that guide them towards goals, disengage from one task to achieve another or avoid maladaptive or harmful states. Examples of these processes could include the effort a performer is willing to offer, pain and fatigue tolerance, enforcing wakefulness when sleepy, and decisions about pacing or rationing. These processes, where performers regulate or alter their internal states to achieve desired outcomes, encapsulate the idea of self-regulation.

Like self-efficacy, self-regulation represents a critical mediator and moderator of the relationship between mental skill use and performance. Zimmerman (2000, p14) defined self-regulation as "self-generated thoughts, feelings, and actions that are planned and cyclically adapted to the attainment of personal goals." Self-regulation may also be viewed as the ongoing, dynamic, and adaptive control of one's internal state (i.e., thoughts, emotions) and behaviours, as opposed to regulating or being regulated by others. Therefore, self-regulation is an intrinsic process that is aimed at adjusting one's mental and physiological state to adapt to a context. McCormick et al. (2019) stated that self-regulation enables an individual to monitor and improve their goal-directed activities in different situations and contexts, using self-oriented feedback loops. A self-oriented feedback loop involves the evaluation of one's behaviour concerning their standards and the environment (Zimmerman, 2000).

Researchers and practitioners have used several different labels (i.e., psychological constructs) interchangeably to represent the idea of adaptive control of one's internal state and behaviour. For example, Nigg (2017) noted that terms including (but not limited to) executive control, executive functioning, emotional regulation, reactive control, impulse control, and self-control had been used synonymously with self-regulation.

In most cases, despite the differences in the label used, the researchers were broadly interested in examining the adaptive processes and systems that people use to control and adjust themselves. While it is not within the scope of this chapter to provide a detailed discussion and debate of the conceptual and empirical distinctiveness of self-regulation and the aforementioned psychological constructs, it is worth noting that some researchers, practitioners, and performers might not explicitly use self-regulation to describe the idea of regulating oneself. However, they ostensibly mean adaptive control of one's internal state and behaviour. Thus, practitioners should strive to be adaptive and use the lexicon of the performer or group while applying the theory of self-regulation.

Several models, frameworks, and theories of self-regulation exist. However, most of these models, frameworks, and theories share core components; for example, most theorists recognize that self-regulation is not static but instead develops through critical periods from early life into adulthood and beyond. The development of the self-regulation "skill" may manifest over time through the accumulation and aggregation of low-level capacities (i.e., the ability for positive self-talk in response to stress) in line with the development (or breakdown) of physical and neural systems (i.e., through injury or disuse) and the gradual internalization of control through repeated exposure and practice. From a practitioner's perspective, it is therefore essential to acknowledge that self-regulation is amenable to change (positively and negatively) and may take time to develop.

Most models of self-regulation also share a dual process logic that necessitates a clarification of what is being regulated rather than what is regulating (Nigg, 2017). Dual processes in self-regulation can take many forms. For example, automatic/deliberate, bottom-up/top-down, exogenous/endogenous, or type I/type II. In most cases, the dual dichotomous states represent one top-down control aspect of self-regulation and one bottom-up, often an automatic/reactive process. Given that top-down conscious systems can activate, suppress, magnify, or bias the bottom-up process, top-down self-regulation is commonly used to regulate bottom-up processes.

Bottom-up (automatic, type I, reactive) processes are stimulus-driven, rapid, and do not require conscious control. They are (typically) elicited by external stimuli (via human senses) and are not unitary. For example, bottom-up processes could be habits, reflexes, innate responses, conditioned learning, and avoidant behaviours. In most models of self-regulation, bottom-up processes are the targets of top-down control. For example, a mountaineer must regulate the desire to stop or slow down during a physically demanding climb if he wishes to attain his goal of breaking a record (e.g., the quickest ascent of the North face of the Eiger). Bottom-up processes can also be regulatory. For example, the bottom-up process can prime, activate, or modify a top-down process. Pain and fatigue are bottom-up signals, which can be overridden by top-down control, but which have a signal function towards the organism, in terms of available resources to face a demand.

One particular type of self-regulation that is relevant to high performance is emotion regulation. Emotional regulation refers to the process by which an individual influences his or her experience of emotions when they have them, which feelings they have, and how they express those emotions (Gross, 1998). Kich, Mars, Toni, and Roelofs (2018) stated that emotion regulation, which is also known as emotion control, denotes all the conscious and non-conscious regulatory strategies by which the physiological, behavioural or subjective component of an emotional response is altered or controlled.

Emotional regulation characterizes an individual's ability to switch between different emotion control strategies, especially in unfamiliar and rapidly changing situations when the best course of action is ambiguous. Because of this volatility and uncertainty, performers in physically and cognitively extreme environments will likely require a range of emotional regulation strategies to operate optimally. Lane, Bucknall, Davis, and Beedie (2012) stated that military personnel experience intense emotions in a range of different situations and that emotion regulation strategies differ between situations. As such, Lane and colleagues recommended that instructors encourage personnel to become cognizant of their beliefs in emotions that help performance, and the strategies that they use to regulate these emotions. The result of this approach will be greater awareness of similarities and differences between emotion regulation strategies used in different situations and how these could transfer across situations or contexts (e.g., from sport to military operations).

Emotional regulation is distinct from similar processes, such as coping. Coping is typically viewed as the removal of negative experiences to bring oneself back into a state of equilibrium. Conversely, emotional regulation can also include processes aimed at maintaining or magnifying positive emotion, regulating how these emotions are displayed, and (when appropriate) downregulating negative emotions. While emotion regulation efforts can be utilized to cope, emotional regulation strategies exclusively target the regulation of emotional experience (Beatty & Janelle, 2020).

Gross's (1998) process model of emotional regulation specifies five categories of regulatory processes by which responses to emotional experiences might be regulated. The five categories are situation selection, situation modification, attention deployment, cognitive change, and response modulation. Performers can employ the five emotion regulation processes and may be effective at varying points during an emotional experience. Emotion regulation strategies can be both conscious and unconscious within a variety of areas, tasks, and situations.

Within the process model of emotional regulation, antecedent-focused strategies are enacted before the complete activation of a particular emotion. The antecedent-focused strategies have implications for the type of response (i.e., behaviour) in which the individual may participate and the future manifestation of emotional reactions. For example, an astronaut might receive a negative assessment of his performance on a re-entry drill from a teammate and feel angry. The astronaut might resist the urge to complain to other teammates about the negative feedback and reframe the situation to consider whether his performance might warrant better preparation next time. The other type of strategy in the process model of emotional regulation, a response-focused strategy, refers to actions taken after the trajectory of emotion has unfolded. Therefore, the same astronaut who was angry because of perceived negative feedback from a teammate may remain angered by the input. Still, his body language does not reflect his anger while he talks to his teammates to gain further clarification on his performance.

Antecedent-focused emotion regulation strategies include situation selection, which involves either approaching or avoiding situations in anticipation of a given emotional outcome. For example, a performer might avoid a member of the human performance team that had previously frustrated them. The next antecedent-focused strategy is situation modification, which encompasses altering the physical aspects of situations to avoid an anticipated emotional outcome. For example, an athlete might complete her physical training in a gym away from the team if a strength and conditioning coach has angered her. Another antecedent focused emotional regulation strategy is attentional deployment. This strategy involves focusing on specific aspects of a given situation to control an expected emotional response. For example, a performer could focus on how the feedback from a teammate might provide insight into the performance of a room clearance drill. Finally, cognitive change entails an internalized version of situational modification. For example, the performer could interpret his anger as an opportunity to focus more on the value of the content of a human performance program.

An example of a response-focused strategy, response modulation, involves either upregulating or downregulating a strong response. In contrast with antecedent-focused strategies, the performer could apply this response-focused strategy after the emotion response tendencies have been generated. In this way, the performer strives to influence the process of response tendencies in becoming a behavioural response. For example, a military operator might attempt to suppress anxiety when about to disembark from a helicopter, or a ballet dancer might attempt to suppress "stage fright" before going onto stage.

The capability to successfully regulate emotions is central to human performance outcomes within high-performance environments, including the success of future missions and survival in military units (Janelle & Hatfield, 2008). For example, effective emotion regulation could influence behaviour towards other teammates, satisfaction, tactical decision-making, and motivation to complete a given task. Performers could train self-regulatory skills through exposure to training that imposes self-regulatory demands, where psychological adaptation is beneficial. For instance, employing extreme environments during adventurous training can impose physiological and psychological stress on participants, which require regulation of emotion (i.e., negative emotion derived from exposure to cold and wet conditions). Similarly, training that includes sequential task protocols could also increase the demand for self-regulatory resources. Finally, alternative stressors that could increase the significance for appraisals could consist of increasing the importance of the stressor; for example, creating head-to-head competition (do Carmo et al., 2020), or manipulating instructor feedback and behaviour towards others (Beedie, Lane, & Wilson, 2012).

Conclusion

In conclusion, the concept of an ideal performance state is multifaceted and significantly influenced by both internal and external factors. Mental skills like goal setting, self-talk, relaxation, or attentional control play a pivotal role in shaping an individual's performance state, demonstrating the crucial link between mental strategies and task execution. However, these mental skills are just a part of a broader spectrum that includes physical health, nutrition, sleep, and environmental factors.

Importantly, self-efficacy emerges as a central component in this framework, influenced by a variety of sources and significantly impacting an individual's approach to challenges and setbacks. Bandura's emphasis on the reciprocal nature of efficacy beliefs and behaviour underlines the dynamic and context-specific nature of self-efficacy. Similarly, self-regulation, characterized as an intrinsic process of managing one's internal state, is key in navigating towards desired outcomes, particularly in high-pressure or demanding situations.

This comprehensive understanding of performance states underscores the necessity of a holistic approach to performance enhancement. It's not just about developing mental skills but also about recognizing and addressing the multitude of factors that contribute to one's performance state.

References

Bandura, A. (1977). Self-efficacy: Toward a unifying theory of behavioral change. *Psychological Review*, 84, 191–215.

Bandura, A. (1986). Social foundations of thought and action. *Englewood Cliffs,* NJ, 1986(23-28).

Bandura, A. (1993). Perceived self-efficacy in cognitive development and functioning. *Educational Psychologist*, 28, 117–148. doi: 10.1207/s15326985ep2802_3

Bandura, A. (1997). Self-*efficacy: The exercise of control*. New York: Freeman

Beatty, G. F. & Janelle, C. M. (2020) Emotion regulation and motor performance: an integrated review and proposal of the Temporal Influence Model of Emotion Regulation (TIMER). *International Review of Sport and Exercise Psychology*, 13, 266–296. doi:10.1080/1750984X.2019.1695140

Beck, A. T. (1963). Thinking and depression. I. Idiosyncratic content and cognitive distortions. *Archives of General Psychiatry*, 9, 36–46.

Beck, A. T., & Haigh, E. A. (2014). Advances in cognitive theory and therapy: The generic cognitive model. *Annual Review of Clinical Psychology*, 10, 1–24.

Beedie, C. J., Lane, A. M., & Wilson, M. G. (2012). A possible role for emotion and emotion regulation in physiological responses to false performance feedback in 10 mile laboratory cycling. *Applied Psychophysiology and Biofeedback*, 37, 269–277. doi: 10.1007/s10484-012-9200-7

do Carmo, E. C., Barroso, R., Renfree, A., da Silva, N. R., Gil, S., & Tricoli, V. (2020). Affective feelings and perceived exertion during a 10-km time trial and head-to-head running race. *International Journal of Sports Physiology and Performance*, 1–4. Advance online publication. doi:10.1123/ijspp.2019-0586

Dalgaard-Nielsen, A., & Holm, K. F. (2019). Supersoldiers or rulebreakers? Unpacking the mind-set of special operations forces. *Armed Forces & Society*, 45(4), 591–611.

Ellis, A. (1962). *Reason and emotion in psychotherapy*. New York: Stuart.

Gardner, F. L., & Moore, Z. E. (2012). Mindfulness and acceptance models in sport psychology: A decade of basic and applied scientific advancements. *Canadian Psychology/Psychologie Canadienne*, 53, 309. doi:10.1037/a0030220

Gross, J. J. (1998). The emerging field of emotion regulation: An integrative review. *Review of General Psychology*, 2, 271–299. doi: 10.89-2680/98/$3.00

Hanin, Y. L. (1980). A study of anxiety in sport. In W. F. Straub (Ed.), *Sport psychology: An analysis of athlete behavior* (pp. 236–249). Ithaca, NY: Movement Publications.

Hanin, Y. L. (1997). Emotions and Athletic Performance: Individual Zones of Optimal Functioning Model. *European Yearbook of Sport Psychology*, 1(29-72).

Hanin, Y. L. (Ed.). (2000). *Emotions in sport*. Champaign, Illinois: Human Kinetics.

Janelle, C. M., & Hatfield, B. D. (2008). Visual attention and brain processes that underlie expert performance: Implications for sport and military psychology. *Military Psychology*, 20, 39–69. doi: 10.1080/08995600701804798

Koch, S. B., Mars, R. B., Toni, I., & Roelofs, K. (2018). Emotional control, reappraised. *Neuroscience & Biobehavioral Reviews*, 95, 528–534. doi: 10.1016/j.neubiorev.2018.11.003

Locke, E. A., & Latham, G. P. (2019). The development of goal setting theory: A half century retrospective. *Motivation Science*, 5, 93. doi: 10.1037/mot0000127

McCormick, A., Meijen, C., Anstiss, P. A., & Jones, H. S. (2019). Self-regulation in endurance sports: theory, research, and practice. *International Review of Sport and Exercise Psychology*, 12(1), 235–264. doi:10.1080/1750984X.2018.1469161

McCrory, P., Cobley, S., & Marchant, P. (2013). The effect of psychological skills training (PST) on self-regulation behavior, self-efficacy, and psychological skill use in military pilot-trainees. *Military Psychology*, 25, 136–147. doi: 10.1037/h0094955

Nigg, J. T. (2017). Annual Research Review: On the relations among self-regulation, self-control, executive functioning, effortful control, cognitive control, impulsivity, risk-taking, and inhibition for developmental psychopathology. *Journal of Child Psychology and Psychiatry*, 58(4), 361–383.

Zimmerman, B. J. (2000). Attaining self-regulation: A social cognitive perspective. In M. Boekaerts, P.R. Pintrich, & M. Zeidner (Eds.), *Handbook of Self-Regulation* (pp. 13–39). San Diego, CA: Academic Press.

Part 2

Scientific Evidence Base

4 Self-talk, Goal Setting, and Visualization

Martin I. Jones and Paige Mattie

Introduction

This chapter introduces common performance-enhancing strategies performers use in high-pressure contexts (e.g., military, sport, business, performing arts) and describes how individuals operating in these contexts and human performance practitioners can use these strategies in their mental performance programs.

In many high-performance environments, there can be a temptation to lean on technological advancements to provide the critical edge. This is particularly true in volatile, uncertain, complex, and ambiguous (VUCA) environments or those that are isolated, confined, and extreme (ICE) where new technologies can make operators more effective (i.e., doing the right things) and more efficient (i.e., doing things right). There is no doubt that technology can produce effects at a reduced cost, with fewer resources, or can support people when they otherwise cannot complete an assigned task (e.g., during the night). However, the first of truth of special operations states that humans are more important than hardware. No matter which technology is applied, there will always be a human in the loop, either pressing a button, programming, and operating a system, or pulling the trigger. It is, therefore, critically important that the performance of these humans is optimized to ensure that the technology works are intended. This is true of all types of technology, from the advanced (e.g., space stations) to the relatively simple (e.g., a bayonet). The quality and sophistication of tools and techniques are not the primary determinants of success – it is the human.

The core of high performance lies in the cognitive, emotional, and behavioural virtues of the individual. Mental skills training focuses on developing strategies before, during, and after events to manage the unique psychological (and physical and social) stressors that emerge in VUCA and ICE environments. The performance-enhancing strategies described in this chapter enable individuals to increase their chances of success by contributing to a broad developmental system of high performance (e.g., genetic, physical, technological, social). The phrase that "Humans are more important than hardware" serves as a guiding principle for mental skills training. It underlines the necessity of investing in the psychological development of performers, ensuring that they are mentally equipped to navigate the complexities and pressures of high-stakes environments. This chapter will delve into how performers and human performance practitioners can implement this principle, designing mental training programs that utilize evidence-based performance-enhancing strategies.

DOI: 10.4324/9781003378969-6

Self-talk

How we think and talk to ourselves (self-talk, inner speech, inner talk, sub-vocal speech, mental verbalization, internal monologue, internal dialogue, and self-statements; Morin, 2005) is associated with how we feel and act. Most commonly, self-talk (the term we will use in the current chapter) is experienced by the person speaking in their voice but with no sound being produced. However, some people hear different accents or dialects (e.g., those of a significant other), and there are large individual differences in the frequency with which individuals experience self-talk.

Self-talk, as a performance-enhancing strategy, is based on the hypothesized link between thoughts and behaviour. Therefore, scholars and practitioners have recommended that people attempt to regulate how they think, as the quality of our thoughts can influence the performance of tasks. Self-talk is particularly relevant for performers who experience "dead time' when maladaptive thoughts can creep in. During this time, intrusive, maladaptive, and task-irrelevant cognitions can creep into one's awareness. For instance, a military operator might start thinking about risk, previous missions, or the consequences of future action while in transit to a mission. In this example, self-talk can cue task-relevant and adaptive thoughts, thereby blocking out potentially hazardous intrusive cognitions.

Several authors have shown that self-talk is used in high-performance and high-pressure settings. For example, Adler et al. (2013) conducted a survey and interview study of 121 service personnel from nine NATO nations and reported that self-talk was used to maintain optimism. Similarly, Arthur et al. (2017) described the positive relationship between using self-talk training and performance in the UK Parachute Regiment's "P-company" airborne selection course. In a sporting context, Hase et al. (2019) conducted a three-group, randomized control trial (instructional self-talk, motivational self-talk, or control) on dart-throwing performance while measuring cognitive and cardiovascular reactivity as a proxy for a challenge or threat state (i.e., Blascovich 2008. The results revealed that motivational but not instructional self-talk improved performance (i.e., hits closest to the bullseye) compared with the control condition; however, self-talk did not influence challenge and threat states. Saint-Martin et al. (2020) examined the self-reported cognitions and emotions of Olympic and Paralympic swimmers to understand how these athletes prepared for elite-level performance. The results of a series of semi-structured interviews revealed that these elite athletes used a range of techniques to manage their cognitive and emotional responses to high-pressure competition. For example, the athletes used motivational and instructional self-talk, often in combination with other psychological techniques (e.g., imagery), to change cognitions or emotions before and during the performance.

What is self-talk?

Theodorakis, Weinberg, Natsis, Douma, and Kazakas (2000) defined self-talk as "what people say to themselves either out loud or as a small voice inside their head" (p. 254). This definition addresses two central aspects of self-talk. Firstly, self-talk can be said either covertly or overtly; secondly, self-talk comprises statements addressed to oneself and not others.

Hatzigeorgiadis, Zourbanos, Galanis, and Theororakis (2011) stated that people often verbalize thoughts to themselves by expressing feelings ("Awesome!"; "Terrible!"), ask themselves questions ("Why did you miss that shot?"), and give themselves instructions ("Recheck your map in 1000 paces"). As a psychological strategy, self-talk uses our capacity for internal dialogue and shapes the words and phrases used to influence our behaviour.

Using one's self-talk to influence emotions and behaviour is not a new concept. Plato's Socrates is thought to have stated that thinking is merely inner speech that makes us aware of our existence. Similarly, the Stoics recognized the value of self-talk in helping people live virtuous and tranquil lives. Like modern psychotherapists, the Stoics advocated addressing the content of self-talk to help alter emotional responses and function more effectively. The Stoics (and subsequently psychologists) recognized that self-talk is controllable, and through carefully planned and executed self-talk, people can exert control over their response to uncontrollable events. Therefore, the value of self-talk to performers as a controllable response in an uncontrollable, unpredictable, and volatile environment is evident.

Essentially, self-talk is the recognition of the influence that the way people think about themselves influences how they behave. Self-talk interventions utilize that recognition and leverage our capacity to choose our way of thinking (and internal dialogue) regardless of outside events. Although people spontaneously talk to themselves, self-talk as a performance-enhancing cognitive strategy involves carefully planning and repeating particular words and phrases to achieve specific outcomes. For example, people may use self-talk for performance enhancement, confidence enhancement, to learn new techniques, or with non-performance-related issues (e.g., coping with family stress).

Is all self-talk the same?

Valence

Self-talk is a multidimensional and diverse psychological skill. The valence dimension is arguably the most understood (albeit one of the less valuable) dimension of self-talk. The valence dimension of self-talk concerns the dialogue's nature as either a positive or a negative statement. Statements are assigned the label "positive self-talk" when they are (for example) framed as praise and "negative self-talk" when they are framed as criticism. While this simple dichotomy is somewhat appealing, it is less helpful in applying self-talk because of the paradoxical consequences of self-talk valence. For some people, positive self-talk is indeed performance-enhancing. However, for others, positive praise like self-talk could inhibit performance by introducing complacency. Equally, negative criticism like self-talk could promote improved performance by stimulating motivation. Other individual differences (e.g., self-esteem and personality traits) influence the interpretation of the self-talk valance. Therefore, coaches and human performance practitioners should be careful when training "positive" self-talk or discouraging "negative" self-talk without considering the individual's phenomenology of self-talk.

Overtness

Self-talk can be covert, where the dialogue is articulated sub-vocally (like a voice inside the mind), or overt, where the self-talk is told so others can hear. There appears to be no difference between overt and covert self-talk in performance effects; however, some people might feel embarrassed vocalizing their thoughts. Sometimes, deliberate overt self-talk is inappropriate because of the requirement for silence (i.e., reconnaissance tasks). That said, overt self-talk could trigger social support and communal coping that could influence performance, particularly in team-based assignments. This type of self-talk is commonly observed in sports performances. For example, spectators at tennis matches often hear players shouting "COME ON" following the completion of a point.

Dual process

In psychology, dual-process theories describe how thoughts (in this case, self-talk) arise differently. Both Hatzigeorgiadis and Biddle (2008) and Hardy, Oliver, and Tod (2009) discriminated between two different types (i.e., dual processes) of self-talk. The first type is the self-talk that is an organic, automatic, spontaneous, and potentially intrusive experience. The other type is a deliberate mental strategy that employs specific cues or goals. Van Raalte, Vincent, and Brewer (2016) have made a similar differentiation. They used the labels system one and system two self-talk to represent the more spontaneous and automatic self-talk vs. the more intentional self-talk. According to Van Raalte et al. (2016), system one self-talk brings recent experiences into awareness. This awareness represents the emotionally charged reaction to a stimulus (i.e., pain, situational factors). System two self-talk results from consideration and planning and may lead to logical instructional, motivational, and task-focused self-talk. System one self-talk could represent the individuals' core self-evaluations (i.e., "I am terrible," expressing low perceived confidence). System one could also represent the depletion of cognitive resources. Therefore, practitioners should be wary of reading into the content of system one self-talk without considering how the self-talk manifests.

Intentional self-talk may be used to reframe spontaneous self-talk. Reframing will most likely occur if the consequences of automatic system one self-talk are maladaptive (i.e., anger, frustration, and self-loathing). For example, a performer might react to negative bodily sensations (e.g., "my back hurts, you are weak, I am never going to finish"). The performer could then attempt to regulate the maladaptive thoughts by telling himself to "stop and calm down". Next, he might apply an intentional and instructional cue. This cue could focus on a specific aspect of the task (e.g., "focus on putting one foot in front of the other; I will finish this march").

Intentional self-talk can be cognitively demanding. Thought-stopping and reframing will incur a cognitive cost and could ultimately impede performance over time if the thought stoppage depletes mental resources and manifests in mental fatigue. Equally, intentional self-talk requires working memory; therefore, using concise cues is more optimal than a long pre-planned monologue. Using brief cues frees up working memory and other attentional resources available to complete different tasks (Van Raalte et al., 2016). Performers could find that the regulation of their self-talk is viable in relatively benign or low-stress training scenarios. However, self-talk regulation might break down in volatile, uncertain, contested, and ambiguous (VUCA) training, selection, and performance environments where cognitive demands are high. Therefore, self-talk cues should be concise to spare mental resources and then practiced in VUCA training environments where possible.

Self-generated or assigned?

An additional consideration to add to the various dual-process theories of self-talk is whether the self-talk is self-generated (typically automatic system one self-talk) or whether the self-talk is assigned. Assigned self-talk could represent intentional system two self-talk but typically relates more to self-talk statements that a coach, mentor, or human performance practitioner generates on behalf of (or in collaboration with) the performer (usually in preparation for an anticipated situation). This type of self-talk is valuable for performers with limited experience in each situation because it allows someone with more expertise to help generate task-relevant cues. In terms of effectiveness, self-generated and assigned self-talk are likely to be effective but moderated by situational and individual variables (e.g., task novelty and trait anxiety).

Does self-talk work?

A large body of literature suggests that self-talk improves performance (Tod, Hardy, & Oliver, 2011). Researchers and practitioners, for instance, Hardy, Jones, and Gould (1996), have promoted self-talk as a critical component of performance psychology programs. However, as with most mental skills, it is essential to consider the types of outcomes. Self-talk likely exerts different-sized effects on various aspects of performance or types of tasks.

McCormick, Meijen, and Marcora (2015) conducted a systematic review to identify practical psychological interventions that improved endurance performance. They found consistent support for using various psychological skills, including self-talk. Detailed analysis of the results revealed that motivational self-talk reduced the perception of effort and increased time to exhaustion in a cycling task (Blanchfield et al., 2014). Self-talk also improved non-athletes' performances in a 10-km cycling time trial, compared with neutral self-talk (Barwood et al., 2015). Finally, self-talk increased the amount of work completed by non-athletes during 20 minutes of cycling (Hamilton et al., 2007).

Hatzigeorgiadis et al. (2011) examined 32 studies that showed self-talk interventions on sports performance. Their meta-analysis revealed a positive moderate-sized relationship between goal setting and task performance. They found the most robust relationships when the task performance involved fine motor skills (compared with gross motor skills) and when tasks were novel (versus well-learned). Hatzigeorgiadis and colleagues considered the different types of self-talk rather than considering self-talk as a homogeneous experience. Self-talk that was designed to provide instruction (i.e., "keep your eye on the target") was more effective when outcomes involved fine motor tasks compared with self-talk that was designed to be motivational (i.e., "you can win"). Finally, Hatzigeorgiadis et al. revealed that trained (i.e., system two) self-talk was more effective at influencing task performance than untrained (i.e., spontaneous, system one) self-talk. Performers and human performance practitioners must carefully consider the types of training and the associated desired outcomes. While self-talk is generally performance (and learning) enhancing, the task's nature can influence the effect size.

A challenge with all self-talk research is the accurate measurement of inner speech. The content of human thought cannot be observed or recorded by any objective measurement tool. Consequently, we rely on self-reporting self-talk, which is confounded by metacognitive skills (i.e., one's capacity to think about thinking). Given the sensitivities and pressures around many training procedures in high-pressure and high-performance exercises and operations (i.e., spaceflight, military), it is practically impossible to study self-talk "in the wild" by using think-aloud protocols, interviews, and thought listing that researchers use in other performance domains (e.g., sport). Therefore, most self-talk research in close proximity to performance typically involves non-elite athletes as the consequences of performance are reduced compared with professional athletes, military personnel, astronauts, and front-line medical professionals.

Why does self-talk influence performance?

Tod et al. (2011) suggested that the relationship between self-talk and performance is mediated by cognitive (i.e., attention), motivational, behavioural, and affective mechanisms. However, they recognized that there was limited research in 2011 to demonstrate the salience of each mechanism. The same is accurate at the time of writing this chapter.

Many researchers believe that self-talk is indirectly related to performance by helping people focus attention, increase motivation, increase confidence (self-efficacy), and manage arousal (Hardy, 2006). Specifically, adaptive self-talk (typically intentional and positive) can positively influence the performance of tasks. Maladaptive (usually spontaneous, intrusive, and often negative) can negatively affect the performance of tasks. However, positive and intentional self-talk can be debilitative (i.e., paralysis by analysis). Moreover, negative spontaneous self-talk can be facilitative (i.e., motivational).

People may use self-talk for different functions. The two main functions researchers have described in the performance psychology and consulting psychology literature are motivational and instructional self-talk. Motivational self-talk serves the purpose of influencing psychological or physiological arousal. For example, a performer could use a set of cues to "psych up" and build confidence to complete a specific task. Instructional self-talk refers to the focusing of attention on a particular prompt. For example, a performer could use deliberate cues to focus on a technique, strategy, or the kinaesthetic attributes of the skill's execution (Theodorakis, Hatzigeorgiadis, &

Zourbanos, 2012). The dichotomy of motivational and instructional self-talk could apply to the content and the function of the discourse (i.e., the consequences). For example, instructional cues could also have a motivational effect.

Using self-talk is likely to change performance because of cognitive mechanisms. Specifically, individuals use self-talk to initiate or increase attentional control toward task-relevant stimuli or decrease interfering thoughts. Self-talk likely influences motivation toward a task, mainly if the self-talk content's function is motivational and can influence effort and task-relevant and performance-enhancing behaviour. In addition to motivation influencing behaviour, Tod and colleagues noted that other behavioural mechanisms explain the self-talk and performance relationship. For example, individuals use instructional self-talk to talk through a specific movement (mainly if the movement patterns are not well learned). Finally, self-talk could exert an emotional change that subsequently changes performance. For example, individuals could use self-talk to reappraise an irrational thought to help them experience anxiety as excitement or to reduce debilitative stress.

Antecedents of self-talk

The content and function of self-talk are influenced by different antecedents that practitioners can target during attempts to intervene to change performance. Figure 4.1 shows the potential precursors to inform whether self-talk is used, the self-talk content, the timing, and the final performance. It is worth noting that many of the possible antecedents are not well-researched. Therefore, the antecedents are theoretically grounded but hypothesized. There is a lack of evidence to substantiate causal relationships between specific antecedents and self-talk experiences.

Whether an individual adopts self-talk as a mental skill to strive for optimal performance or excellence will depend on various factors. Hardy, Oliver, and Tod (2009) suggested that personality factors might be related to the use of self-talk. For example, negative self-concept or trait pessimism might be reflected in the valance of (particularly system one) self-talk. Similarly, motivational dispositions (e.g., the general desire to demonstrate superiority over others vs. mastering a task and referencing competence based on improvement) have also been linked to self-talk use. Harwood, Cumming, and Fletcher (2004) revealed that junior athletes with a higher task mastery and moderate superiority goal profile used significantly more positive self-talk in practice and competition than athletes with lower task mastery and higher superiority goal orientation dispositions.

Individual perception of the utility of self-talk influences performance. Also, the understanding that one can regulate system one self-talk and apply system two self-talk is likely to change the content and timing of self-talk experiences. Practitioners could use peer instruction activities to help sell the benefits of strategic self-talk. For example, describing role models' stories of when they used self-talk and how it influenced their performance. The belief that individuals can execute self-talk skills can be addressed through practice in training. Positive feedback from peers and instructors, role modelling, and increasing an operator's awareness of positive physical sensations when using self-talk (i.e., decreased somatic anxiety and increased physical arousal) can help change a person's self-talk beliefs.

According to Hardy et al. (2009), people will use self-talk based on their information processing preference. Specifically, some people favour information in text and verbal instructions or visual demonstrations and imagery. Although there is little evidence to substantiate this claim, Hardy and colleagues supposed that athletes with a verbal cognitive processing preference would likely use self-talk more frequently than athletes with a non-verbal processing preference.

The final antecedent that could influence self-talk experiences is the individual's perceptions of situations. Tasks perceived as too easy or too tricky could produce different types and functions of self-talk. For example, a simple task may require motivational self-talk to psych up. In contrast, a problematic task might require more instructional self-talk, mainly if the task requires skills that are not well-developed. Hardy et al. (2009) also suggested that peers, teammates, and significant others (e.g., instructors and leaders) can influence self-talk experiences. Specifically, the valence of statements from significant others could be matched in the self-talk of operators. Similarly, overt self-talk could be used to initiate social support from others.

Moderators of self-talk and task performance

Moderators are variables that influence the direction (e.g., positive or negative effect) and vary the relationship's strength. For example, skills might improve performance for novices but do not affect an expert. In this case, the level of expertise is a moderating variable.

Competence

The competence of the individual using self-talk is likely to moderate the relationship between self-talk and task performance. Several studies have suggested that elite athletes use different self-talk types (i.e., diverse content and function) compared with non-elite athletes. This is likely due to experience, with elite athletes having more experience using self-talk in a wider range of activities (i.e., training, competition, and injury) that have enabled a personalized mental framework of where and when self-talk can be used and which forms of self-talk are most appropriate given the situation, cognitive responses, and emotions. Similarly, successful vs. unsuccessful athletes have reported using different types of self-talk. Individuals competent at a given skill might use self-talk for motivational or tactical reasons (i.e., psych up, environment cues). In contrast, individuals not skilled in a given ability could employ self-talk to help execute the capabilities (i.e., instructions through movement phases). This divergence in self-talk may be attributed to the varying psychological demands and experiences faced by performers at different levels of competition. Compared with novices and less successful performers, elite performers, often exposed to higher stakes and more intense, VUCA and ICE environments, might develop more sophisticated or targeted self-talk strategies to cope with these pressures. Their self-talk might encompass a broader range of content, focusing not just on motivation or encouragement but also on strategic aspects of performance, technical execution, and emotional regulation. It is difficult to demonstrate causation; however, the difference in self-talk between elite and novice performers emphasizes the role of mental strategies in achieving and maintaining high performance.

Task complexity

The nature of the task being performed is also likely to moderate the relationship between self-talk and performance. In this case, the issue could be conceived as a matching task and self-talk function. Specifically, suppose the individual uses instructional self-talk to focus attention on a technical aspect of a task. In that case, the performance of the given task will only be improved if the task is technical. Conversely, if the task is not technical and does not require instructional self-talk, the self-talk-to-performance relationship's strength will be attenuated. If the task requires a change in effort, motivational self-talk content will produce a more significant effect than instructional self-talk.

Emotion

Van Raalte et al. (2016) proposed emotional matching of self-talk. Emotional matching assumes that self-talk congruent with the emotions or arousal level of the individual will be more effective than incongruent self-talk. For example, when arousal levels are high, and there is an associated emotional response (e.g., anxiety), the self-talk will improve performance if it matches the emotion (i.e., I am pumped – I feel excited, rather than calm).

Language

The type of language used also appears to be a significant moderator of effect. Kross et al. (2014) considered whether first-person or third-person self-talk was critical. A series of studies by Kross and colleagues suggested using one's name and other non-first-person pronouns to refer to the self-represented, a form of self-distancing that could influence performance in specific situations. Specifically, Kross et al. reported that using third-person self-talk promoted self-distancing, enhanced participants' ability to regulate their thoughts, feelings, and behaviour under stress, and helped them appraise anxiety-provoking events in more challenging, less threatening terms.

When using self-talk as a motivational strategy during painful or unpleasant bodily sensations, Kross and colleagues' findings suggest that using one's first name, for example, "Come on, Smith, you can do this", might be more effective than using a personal pronoun "come on, I can do this". The reason behind this quirk of language appears to be a psychological distancing between the self and the experience. For example, the pain is happening to Smith, not me. The consequence of the psychological distance is a greater capacity to exert self-control (i.e., keeping pace while in pain). Equally, using a name or a non-first-person pronoun could promote self-distancing, allowing individuals to think objectively about irrational thoughts and be more accepting of their experiences.

Practical application

Greene (2019) described a situation where psychologists could use self-talk in coaching for special operations forces. Greene described an assessment and selection practice where prospective

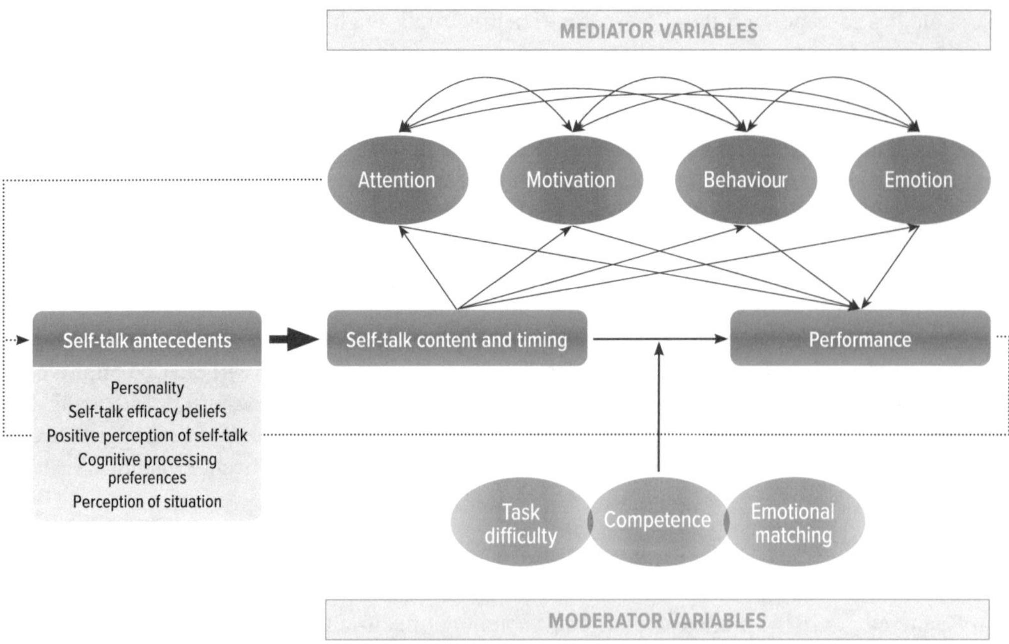

Figure 4.1 Applied mediational model of self-talk and performance.

operators were instructed to jump into 12 feet (3.6m) of water, plunge to the bottom of the pool, and then push off back to the surface to breathe. The prospective operators must repeat the cycle of dunking and re-emerge for several minutes with their hands bound behind their backs. Greene noted that for many candidates, the anticipation of this exercise is intimidating and anxiety-provoking. While waiting to start the activity, there is ample opportunity for self-talk to exacerbate fear and self-doubt. To prepare for this situation, a psychologist can educate the candidates on the dimensions and moderators of self-talk and their potential consequences. This education could help the candidates to recognize when and how their self-talk might negatively influence their performance on the task. The candidates could also practice intentional self-talk by analyzing "what if" scenarios. For example, if the candidate anticipates worry about drowning (i.e., "I cannot do this – I am going to die"). The self-talk cue could focus on drawing attention to a task-relevant behaviour (i.e., "keep kicking") and employ third-person self-talk as a method of self-distancing (it is OK, Smith, you are worried about drowning, that's normal given the task, but the rational thing is to focus on your technique and control your arousal). Finally, the self-talk can be a benign cue to distract the candidate from this worrisome thought (i.e., counting backward from 100).

Goal setting

In the high-pressure and high-performance contexts, it is essential to set goals (e.g., pass a selection or qualification course, win an event, complete an objective) and have the resources for goal pursuit, staying on track, stopping futile goal striving, and not overextending oneself while attempted to achieve desired outcomes. Therefore, this section aims to introduce goal setting as a performance-enhancing strategy, describe why goal setting improves performance, and discuss how to improve the goal setting and goal implementation process.

Adopting goal-setting and implementation techniques can directly influence ideal performance states and indirectly improve performance. For example, researchers (McEwan et al., 2016) have shown that setting goals increases self-efficacy and can focus the performer's attention on relevant tasks. Moreover, Locke and Latham (2002) revealed that setting goals (specifically challenging goals) led to the highest levels of effort and task performance, both of which are necessary for all elite performers. Therefore, we believe that goal setting and implementation present elite performers and coaching practitioners with a simple technique that could be integrated into any mental performance program under one's control.

What is goal setting?

Goal setting is a cognitive technique many people use, based on the premise that conscious goals affect action. In its most basic form, goal setting is a process of creating a discrepancy in achievement. When setting goals, the individual describes a difference between where she is currently and where she wants to be. She then sets about reducing that discrepancy with action. The action required to achieve the goal is broadly labelled goal striving and goal implementation. For clarity, when talking about goal setting, we refer to both setting goals and the processes needed to achieve those goals.

According to Locke and Latham (2002), a goal is "the object or aim of an action, for example, to attain a specific standard of proficiency, usually within a specified time" (p. 705). Goals are defined as end states that people have not yet attained (and are focused on achieving in the future) and are committed to approaching or avoiding (Moskowitz, 2012). Goals are thus an objective or aim an individual is trying to accomplish. The pursuit of goals is not always elevated to a conscious level. Goal setting, however, is a cognitive endeavour. Goal setting is the process of articulating and pursuing one's goals.

To demonstrate the importance of goal setting, consider the similarity of land navigation and goal setting. Like navigation, goal setting requires forethought about where one is going and how one will get there. A military operator might be tasked with navigating from one destination to another in a pre-determined time. It is doubtful that the operator will set off having received his coordinates, hoping for the best. They will take out a map, plot the coordinates, take a compass bearing, consider the land's contour, avoid apparent pitfalls, discuss the route with teammates, and carefully consider their pace count. Like land navigation, goal setting will only be successful if the individual sets off with a plan.

Most people have experience setting a performance goal (e.g., passing a selection course, improving personal best timings, running 5 km in under 20 minutes) or creating a new year's resolution. Though many people have experience setting goals, only some have experience achieving them. The reasons why people do not achieve goals are complex and often multifaceted. It is abundantly clear that simply stating that you desire a change is not enough. Perhaps the goal was framed in a negative tone or was too vague. Maybe things got in the way, or it became apparent that goal-striving was futile, but they kept going anyway. Therefore, to achieve desired goals, performers and human performance professionals need to consider the antecedents of goals, the mechanisms of the effect, and the boundary conditions that influence the strength and direction of effects. Essentially, by understanding the "how" of goal setting and goal pursuit, individuals will know how to set goals, strive for goals, and understand what has gone wrong (and make changes) when goal attainment goes awry. By learning about goal setting, we hope that performers and human performance professionals can play the goal-setting detective to investigate goal-setting and implementation processes in the past and consider new techniques and strategies to inform future achievement.

Does goal setting work?

The short answer to the question in this subheading is yes – goal setting does work! A large body of evidence suggests that goal setting improves the performance of a range of tasks through changes in motivation, effort, attention, and self-efficacy (more of that in the next section). Not only that, setting goals increases subjective well-being and satisfaction (Latham & Locke, 2007).

Goal-setting theorists broadly state that goal-setting positively influences the performance of a range of tasks in diverse situations (assuming that the goal is attainable). Arguably, the most prominent theory on goal-setting and performance was developed by industrial and organizational psychologists Locke and Latham (1984, 1990) for task performance in the workplace. Researchers have studied goal setting in several contexts despite the initial focus on the workplace. Locke and Latham's (1990) theory of goal setting has been developed over the past 30 years by groups of researchers across achievement (i.e., education) and performance (i.e., sport) domains. Goal setting has beneficial effects in sport, psychotherapy, creativity, leadership, negotiation, health care, entrepreneurship, and the military (Locke & Latham, 2019) because of shared concerns across high-performance contexts with achievement, cognitive processes, and social processes.

Goal setting is a consistently applied tool within sport and performance (Orlick & Partington, 1988; Weinberg & Butt, 2014). Several researchers have conducted meta-analyses to examine the size and direction of the relationship between goal setting and performance. Within each context (e.g., sport, physical activity, and health care), the performance metric is different. Still, the idea that goal setting improves performance is consistently reported (Locke & Latham, 1990). For example, McEwan et al. (2016) conducted a systematic review and meta-analysis of multicomponent goal-setting interventions to change physical activity behaviour. McEwan and colleagues searched for studies that included controlled experimental trials where participants in the intervention conditions set physical activity goals and their physical activity behaviour was compared to participants in a control group who did not set goals. They found 45 articles that fit the bill and reported that goal setting positively affected physical activity behaviour. An important finding from McEwan and colleagues was a high degree of heterogeneity in how coaches and physical activity professionals delivered goal-setting interventions. There appear to be multiple components of goal-setting interventions that, when delivered, can strengthen the effect of the goal-setting intervention.

Why does goal setting work?

Locke and Lathan (2006) stated that four mechanisms explain why goal setting positively influences performance. Firstly, challenging goals (aka goal difficulty) lead to greater effort and persistence than moderately complex, easy, or vague goals (i.e., "do my best"). Secondly, goals direct effort, attention, and action toward goal-relevant actions at the expense of irrelevant actions. Thirdly, having goals may motivate individuals to use existing abilities. By having plans in place, individuals might initiate a "pull" of stored task-relevant knowledge into awareness and start searching for new knowledge. Finally, because performance is a function of motivation and ability, goal effects depend on the requisite task knowledge and skills.

A core tenet of Locke and Latham's theory is that a specific goal is better than a vague goal (i.e., do my best) or no goal. If the goal is also challenging to the individual (i.e., difficult to pursue and achieve), the level of performance is higher than when the goal is easy. However, it is essential to recognize that if the goal is too challenging and exceeds the individual's abilities, performance variation will be more likely attributable to other individual differences (not goal setting).

The relationship between goal setting and performance is not simple or linear. A time lag between the assignment of the goal and performance can manifest while people search for appropriate strategies to achieve their goals. Locke and Latham (2002) suggested that four mechanisms mediate the relationship between goals and performance. First, setting goals directs attention toward goal-related activities and away from irrelevant activities. This effect occurs cognitively and behaviourally (Locke & Latham, 2002). For example, an individual with a specific learning goal (e.g., learning how to use a new technology) will likely pay attention to goal-relevant instruction. Moreover, they will probably pay less attention to what they perceive as irrelevant teaching. Next, they will likely practice using the technology to achieve proficiency.

Second, goals can motivate an individual. More challenging (than easy) goals lead to a higher strength of effort. Third, goals influence persistence in tasks relevant to goal pursuit. When individuals control their time on a task, challenging, compared with manageable goals, can prolong effort (i.e., physical, cognitive, and personal effort). However, there is often a trade-off between time and intensity of effort (Locke & Latham, 2002). When individuals set very difficult goals, the consequence can be a faster and more intense work rate for a short period. Conversely, challenging goals can result in slow work and reduced intensely for an extended period.

Finally, goals can influence action by adopting task-relevant strategies and knowledge (Healey, Tincknell-Smith, Ntoumanis, 2019). People use the knowledge and skills they possess that are relevant to goal attainment. For example, suppose the goal involves navigation. In that case, individuals will use their knowledge of map reading without needing additional conscious planning to exert effort and persist until the goal is attained (Locke & Latham, 2002). If goal pursuit is not automatic, people apply skills from a repertoire previously used in related contexts. If the quest toward a goal involves engaging in new skills or strategies, the individual will engage in deliberate planning to enable them to attain their goals. People with high self-efficacy to develop a new plan will be more likely to create effective task strategies than those low in self-efficacy.

Goal attributes

Performers and human performance practitioners can break down goal attributes into goal content, intensity, and temporality. Goal content refers to the nature of the activity or the desired outcome. Typically, these contents are labelled as either outcome or process goals; however, other labels are sometimes used (e.g., learning and performance goals). An outcome goal is usually the desired endpoint (e.g., passing a course), whereas process goals reflect the steps required to reach the destination. Individuals could set goals in isolation (i.e., setting only outcome goals) or as a combination (i.e., process and outcome goals). For most people, effective and efficient goal setting inevitably involves combining the two types of goals, but usually at different times. For example, an individual might set an outcome goal once per year but then set different process goals (based on perceived progress and feedback) as they set off on their journey toward goal attainment.

Goal intensity refers to the strength with which the goal is pursued and reflects the perceived resource requirements demanded by the goal. Goal intensity also demonstrates the importance of the goal to the individual. It will typically manifest in the effort and determination the individual shows when striving toward their goal. Goal importance is closely related to self-efficacy. Unimportant goals can suffer from a lack of traction or can be easily derailed in the presence of obstacles. The importance of the goal is a critical consideration when setting goals on behalf of someone else (versus using self-set goals). The coach or human performance practitioner must consider goal intensity when setting a goal for someone else.

Goal temporality reflects the timing of the goal. Individuals can set goals for the distant future (i.e., long-term goals), for a time soon (i.e., intermediate goals), or for the immediate future (i.e., short-term goals). As with goal content, most goal-setting systems include combinations of the different temporal types. For example, the outcome goal of becoming an astronaut might necessarily be a long-term goal (because of the time it takes to pass selection and qualify). An intermediate goal might form part of the process by tracking back from the endpoint of selection and qualification, such as submitting paperwork and attending a briefing course before selection. A short-term goal might focus the performer's attention on what they must do that day or week to facilitate their chances of achieving a long-term outcome. For example, a short-term process goal could be to complete specific physical workouts that day, and a short-term outcome goal could be to record a particular number of activities by the end of the month. Short-term goals are compelling in increasing self-efficacy because individuals gain positive feedback concerning their capacity to master a task. Long-term goals are captivating because of their capacity to change behaviour and cement positive habits.

Another goal-setting approach evident in blogs, websites, self-help books, and health and fitness publications is SMART (i.e., Specific, Measurable, Achievable, Realistic, and Timed; Doran, 1981). Many individuals use the variations of the SMART acronym to help set goals that address each letter of the acronym. The SMART acronym is catchy and easily remembered; however, it does not provide the setter of the goal with relevant information that helps them strive toward their goal or adapt to changing circumstances. Consequently, we observe that many people with knowledge of SMART (in place of a more detailed understanding of goal-setting theory) do not consistently achieve their desired outcomes. According to Healey, Tincknell-Smith, and Ntoumanis (2019), understanding goal taxonomies and recommendations (e.g., SMART) is overly simplistic. Consequently, they do not reflect goal setting and goal striving in the real world. Similarly, Maitland and Gervis (2010) suggested that if coaches and human performance practitioners rely on simplistic goal-setting processes without considering athletes' wider social and motivational choices, such as why they pursue explicit goals, the goal-setting practice might be ineffective.

Moderators of goal-setting and performance

Burton, Naylor, and Holliday (2001) stated that goal setting is a paradox because it is a straightforward technique that is complicated in practice. The technique is complicated in practice because of moderators that, when applied or omitted, change the size and direction of the effect. A moderator variable influences the strength of a relationship between two other variables (i.e., goal setting and performance). In the context of goal setting, researchers have suggested that goal commitment, goal importance, self-efficacy, feedback, framing, suitable task strategies, and task complexity moderate the relationship between goal setting and performance.

Goal commitment

The goal–performance relationship is most robust when people are committed to their goals. Goal-setting theorists have suggested that goals that an individual is not committed to attaining or pursuing have little influence on performance. A lack of goal commitment manifests in the absence of effort, strategy, and attention toward task-relevant activities. It may be a function of perceived (in)competence or (a lack of) belief in an individual's ability to execute a goal-pursuit strategy and attain goals. Goal commitment is more important for goal-setters when the goal is challenging. When goals are straightforward, fewer personal resources are required to achieve the goal (i.e., little effort) than challenging goals. Therefore, commitment to a difficult goal is necessary because challenging goals need people to do "something" that they would not already be doing (i.e., increased effort, strategy, and attention). Practitioners can facilitate goal commitment by helping to make goal attainment relevant to people, including the importance of the outcomes they expect because of working to attain a goal. Next, practitioners can help build a belief that the individual can achieve the goal (self-efficacy). When goals stretch personal resources, goal pursuit can be less satisfying than easy goals (because they are tough). However, when people achieve challenging goals, they report higher satisfaction, probably because of the gravitas of performing a socially desirable goal that is difficult enough to put most people off (i.e., gaining promotion).

Self-efficacy

Self-efficacy is one's belief that one can execute a course of action to accomplish a task or achieve a given outcome. In goal setting, a strong belief that one can execute a course of action to achieve desired goals manifests in setting more challenging goals and having high commitment.

Self-efficacy beliefs are partially based on previous experiences (i.e., "I have achieved before and can achieve again"). However, they also reflect appraisals of one's current capabilities and the specific conditions that will enhance or inhibit performance. Individuals with high self-efficacy set challenging goals and can maintain effort and drive when confronted with high task demands and obstacles. People with low self-efficacy are beset with self-doubt when faced with challenging circumstances (Locke & Latham, 1990). High self-efficacy is performance-enhancing because goals are challenging, and those with high efficacy beliefs stay the course and can cope with adverse situations along the way.

Human performance practitioners and leaders can raise the self-efficacy of performers by ensuring adequate training to increase perceptions of mastery (i.e., "I have done it in training; I can do it again"). Next, leaders can identify relevant role models to instil the belief that if someone similar can achieve their goal, so can they. Persuasive communication (e.g., giving operators information and confidence about strategies that facilitate goal attainment) can also help build strong efficacy beliefs. Finally, transformational leaders raise the efficacy of operators through inspiring messages.

Feedback

People require feedback during the goal-setting process to help set achievable goals and assess their progress. Feedback allows people to decide whether they need to exert more or the same effort to attain their goals. Feedback can also stimulate the individual (or leader) to change a goal-pursuit strategy or outcome. Feedback can come from knowledge of results, communication with significant others (i.e., training staff, peers), self-reflection, perception of bodily sensations (i.e., anxiety), and biofeedback. Practitioners and leaders should tailor the nature of feedback based on the goal and individual differences of the goal-setter. For example, a long-term outcome-focused goal set in close collaboration with a respected leader would require additional feedback to a self-set short-term process goal. Similarly, the type of feedback delivered to someone with high perceived competence would differ from someone with low perceived competence.

Task complexity

Locke and Latham (2002) stated that as the complexity of the task rises, and greater level skills and strategies have yet to become automatized, goal effects depend on the operator's ability to discover appropriate task strategies. Because people vary significantly in their ability to find appropriate task strategies, the effect size for goal setting is smaller on complex than on simple tasks. Moreover, because complex tasks require a greater variety of strategies to secure desired outcomes, there are more points of failure and more effort needed to execute the range of strategies in pursuit of a goal.

Suitable task strategies

Implementation intentions involve considering how the goal-setter will enact their goals and how they will overcome hindrances to their goal attainment. Specifically, when, where, and how a person intends to pursue a goal. To form an implementation intention, the performer needs to identify a future goal-relevant situational cue and a related planned response to that cue. For example, "If situation X arises, I will initiate behaviour Y."

Therefore, goal implementation intentions include the time and place where goal-related behaviour will commence and cease, which cues will initiate action, and existing habits to which the goal-related actions can be attached. For example, an implementation intention to help someone achieve a goal of passing a physical activity test could look like this: "I will complete ten pull-ups at 0700 on my door frame pull-up bar every morning. I will boil a kettle to make a cup of coffee. While the kettle boils, I will complete my pull-ups. I will not drink my coffee until I have completed my pull-up goal for the day." Similarly, a musician may create an implementation intention related warming up by practicing scales. For example, "I will complete five minutes of a pentatonic scale on my guitar while sitting alone before the rest of the band arrives. I, therefore, need to arrive at the studio 15 minutes before the scheduled start time (and therefore need to consider obstacles that could prevent this). Getting to the studio and sitting on a recognizable stool will signal the moment to start the practice; I will start a timer on my phone and will complete all the positions of an A minor scale before moving to B minor, C minor, and so on until the timer goes off. After the timer sounds, putting my guitar back into the case will signal the end of the exercise. If the engineer is in the studio, I will inform her of my plan and ask her to give me some privacy while I am practicing." Implementation intentions improve goal setting because they delegate control over the commencement of the intended goal-directed behaviour to a specified opportunity by creating a solid link between a cue and a response.

Implementation intentions also help people avoid following futile goal-attainment strategies. People often fail to disengage from faulty goals because of a strong self-justification motive (i.e., people adhere to the irrational belief that deliberate decisions must be good). The effect of sticking with a futile goal, even if feedback on goal progress reinforces futility, can be reduced through implementation intentions. In this example, the cue could be consistent negative feedback (or absence of positive feedback), and the response could be switching to available alternative means or goals.

Other suitable task strategies include how the operator will recognize and avoid obstacles and leverage environmental factors (e.g., feedback and social support) to achieve their goals. The goal-setting process can help operators consider things that have gone wrong in the past and use the experience of others to conduct "what if" planning. Performers can execute negative imagery and "what if" plans alone, in teams, and with the support of leaders and human performance practitioners. This form of negative imagery, where performers think about what could go wrong, can help bring obstacles and mitigation plans into consciousness. This process results in greater self-efficacy that the performer can overcome obstacles and achieve their goals despite the path sometimes being blocked.

Framing

Framing encapsulates the thinking and language used when setting a goal. We previously discussed how difficult goals could increase performance; however, this might not happen if the performer views the goal as threatening. Whether a person judges a high goal as a challenge versus a threat makes a difference in that person's performance. As such, how the performer frames the goal is a significant moderator. Individuals can set goals positively using positive language. For example, "I will maintain my concentration, effort, and strategy to stay on top of the heptathlon table." Equally, the performer could frame the same goal negatively. For example, "I will not let my concentration lapse, which will decrease the chances of winning." When framing goals, it is helpful to reflect on how much goal statements focus on failure versus success and the usefulness of effort (the latter being better).

Self-set goals?

Who should set goals? Should the performer set the goal for themselves, or should a leader or practitioner set it for them? When someone else sets a goal for you, it is known as an assigned goal, whereas when the individual develops the goal or is part of the discussion, it is known as a participatory goal. Locke and Latham (2015) revealed that participatory and assigned goals effectively improve performance. However, some researchers have found that those who set participative goals set higher goals than those assigned goals. These higher-set goals were likely to reflect greater goal difficulty and commitment to participatory goals than assigned goals. Locke and Latham (2015) suggested that assigned goals affect self-set goals and mediate the former. Assigned goals influence self-set goals through self-efficacy beliefs. Specifically, if a coach or leader sets a high goal, it can communicate the assertion that the operator can achieve. The resultant self-set goal will also be high because of the confidence gained from their coach or leader's expression. Self-set goals are the most immediate cause of goal-directed action (Locke & Latham, 2015) and should be set in combination with (or in the absence of) assigned goals.

Practical application

Greene (2019) described a situation where psychologists could use goal setting in coaching for Special Operations Forces (SOF). In the previous section on self-talk, we used the example of plunging to the bottom of the pool during assessment and selection. Greene suggested that candidates could use goal setting to increase task performance in this scenario. For example, to prepare for evaluation and selection, a psychologist can educate the performers on goal content and help them consider moderating variables that might influence the strength and direction of a relationship between goal setting and performance. The candidates might be encouraged to consider how and when they can receive feedback on their goal pursuit and whether they are participatory or assigned goals. This education could help candidates recognize when or where behaviour (or cognition) needs to change to pursue goals (i.e., implementation intentions). The candidates could set goals for different parts of a selection course, and their previously learned self-talk skills could form part of their implementation intentions. In a systematic review of the psychology of mountaineering, Jackman et al. (2020) reported that elite climbers typically used goal setting to regulate cognition, emotion, and behaviour on the mountain. Specifically, mountaineers would use short-term process goals, for example, considering the route toward a particular feature of the climb and setting goals that enable the climber to ascend to the feature safely. Jackman et al. also noted that mountaineers also adopted goal flexibility, particularly recognizing when the process goals were becoming unattainable (i.e., dangerous) or when competing goals (e.g., rescue missions) would be more important and therefore take precedence.

Imagery and visualization

Imagery, or visualization, refers to the deliberate mental practice of specific skills, tasks, or strategies typically employed to optimize performance. Sport and exercise psychology researchers have put forward various definitions of imagery, including the following early definition by White and Hardy (1998): "An experience that mimics real experience. We can be aware of 'seeing' an image, feeling movements as an image, or experiencing an image of smell, tastes, or sounds without experiencing the real thing. Sometimes, people find that it helps to close their eyes. It differs from dreams in that we are awake and conscious when we form an image" (p. 389).

Mental imagery, like other cognitive skills, could complement, versus replace, physical and technical training. Researchers have demonstrated that employing imagery just before skill execution can improve motor skill performance in sport-related (Murphy & Woolfolk, 1987) and strength-related performance (Lee, 1990; Perkins, Wilson & Kerr, 2001). Researchers have also shown that optimal performance outcomes are achieved by concurrently applying both physical practice and imagery, where using imagery itself does not produce greater performance benefits than physical practice (Feltz & Landers, 1983).

Imagery researchers have identified several imagery modalities that match modes of sensory perception in humans. In particular, imagery can be auditory (i.e., sound), gustatory (i.e., taste), kinaesthetic (i.e., feel), olfactory (i.e., smell), tactile (i.e., touch), and visual (i.e., sight). Mental imagery has been applied for decades in pilot training, and is consistently cited as a factor of success in pilot performance (e.g., Hohmann & Orlick, 2014). Researchers concerned with performance in sport settings have primarily been concerned with visual and kinaesthetic imagery; however, the other sensory modalities could be equally crucial for performers when creating an imaginary experience (i.e., imaging the sound of rotor blades and the heat from the engines before disembarking from a helicopter). Kinaesthetic imagery is defined as how it feels to perform a movement or action (Callow & Waters, 2005). Internal visual imagery refers to mental practice in which the performer views the performance environment from their vantage point (i.e., through their own eyes). External visual imagery refers to mental practice from the perspective of an observer's position, akin to watching oneself on television.

Performers can employ multiple modalities within one imagery training session, and it is commonly found that athletes will employ multiple imagery modalities or perspectives, switching back/forth between them as required. For example, a performer using imagery to mentally practice a pistol shot could feel the weapon in hand and the physical mechanics of drawing the pistol from a holster to the shooting position (kinaesthetic imagery) while also fixating on a target through the firearm sights (internal imagery) and observing the recoil and successful shot on target from the perspective of a peer standing behind him (external imagery).

The type of imagery that could be employed depends on the kind of skill or task being imaged. The internal visual perspective produces a more accurate motor performance for slalom-line-based activities (Callow, Roberts, Hardy, Jiang & Edwards, 2013). In contrast, the external visual perspective is more effective for form-based tasks or movement patterns (Hardy & Callow, 1999). Researchers suggest combining kinaesthetic and visual imagery may lead to more robust cognitive representations and motor performance than internal visual imagery alone (Callow, Jiang, Roberts & Edwards, 2017).

Imagery researchers distinguish between imagery *function* and *content,* where function refers to one's purpose for engaging in imagery training or practice (i.e., to improve consistency in skill execution). In contrast, content pertains to the skill, strategy, or technique being imaged (i.e., achieving a particular performance outcome in a specific environment).

Paivio (1985) proposed an influential theoretical framework for imagery use for performance enhancement. Paivio suggested that imagery can be applied for cognitive and motivational functions, each of which is applied at a specific or general level. Additional research into this Functional Model of imagery (Hall et al., 1998) further differentiated the Motivational-General function into (i.e., Mastery and Arousal functions, described below). The functional model of imagery suggests that imagery can be employed for the following five distinct purposes. Cognitive Specific (CS) imagery refers to practice of specific skills or techniques (i.e., execution of proper technical skills or physical movement patterns, including correction to technique). Cognitive General (CG) imagery pertains to the mental practice of tactics, plans, or strategies. Motivational-specific (MS) imagery includes images of specific goal-oriented events or achievements (i.e., achievement of a personal best time in a physical training task). It is often employed to enhance motivation or task commitment. Motivational general mastery (MG-M) is used to maintain confidence and mental toughness and involves images of a performer feeling confident and in control of the performance environment. Motivational General-Arousal (MG-A) imagery practice regulates cognitive or physiological arousal (e.g., holding heart rate before a room entry) and includes emotion regulation.

It is suggested that the *function* of imagery employed should match the desired outcome of the imagery practice. For example, an athlete aiming to achieve better self-regulatory control in high-stress environments would use motivation-general arousal imagery, imaging oneself regulating activation in context. In contrast, a performer mentally rehearsing tactics/battle procedures in the context of a military operation might benefit from employing cognitive-general imagery.

The PETTLEP Model of imagery use has been put forth by Holmes and Collins (2001) and has been shown to improve physical performance (i.e., skill acquisition and execution) and psychological process (Lindsay et al., 2023; Morone et al., 2022; Simonsmeier et al., 2021; Toth, 2020). This model purports that for imagery practice to be effective, it must be as similar as possible to the performance context to which the imagery practice applies. The need for similarly is based on functional equivalence, which reveals a neural overlap between imagery and the production of actual movements. Specifically, when people use imagery, the same brain areas activate as when they execute the skill for real. Put another way, brain activation imagery is equivalent to actual movement. Scott, Wright, Smith, and Holmes (2022) noted that it is not essential to include all the PETTLEP components for effective imagery interventions, nor should PETTLEP serve as a checklist to tick through when designing or evaluating interventions. Rather, PETTLEP should serve as a guiding framework for performers and practitioners when discussing and executing imagery.

To make the imagery experience as accurate as possible (or similar to the real thing), operators can incorporate specific imagery elements that simulate the performance environment and experience. Physical Context refers to the physical nature of the task or skill being imaged. It includes movement patterns, physiological responses, stance or physical position, and any relevant equipment to perform the task (e.g., combats, weapon, and gear). Environment pertains to details of the performance environment, including operational or training area, weather, team members, and any other sights and sounds characteristic of the performance environment (e.g., dust, gunfire, over-pressure). Task pertains to the nature of the task being imaged (e.g., attentional requirements or demands, degree of fatigue).

In contrast, Timing suggests that the functionally equivalent pace for imaging any skill is at the "real-time" rate (i.e., the time required to perform that skill in a real-life environment). Learning pertains to one's level of experience or mastery with a particular task, and the content of the mental imagery should evolve to reflect skill development and technique as learning occurs and the performer becomes more proficient in the task. Emotion pertains to the incorporation of relevant emotions into mental practice. For example, a feeling of relief or accomplishment upon mission completion or the experience of nervous excitement when stacking up at the door. The final element, Perspective, suggests that either an internal (first-person) or external (third-person) vantage point may be assumed in imagery training and practice, both of which have been shown effective in imagery interventions (Hardy & Callow, 1999). The perspective preferred is often related to the type of task being practiced, with the external perspective being particularly beneficial for imaging tasks focused on body positioning or form (Cumming & Williams, 2013).

In addition to incorporating the seven categories of information outlined in the PETTLEP model, several recommendations for the effective use of imagery for performance enhancement are put forth in the sport psychology literature. First, imagery practice should be polysensory and include information from each of the sense organs where applicable (i.e., vision, auditory, olfactory information, gustatory, tactile). Second, the individual must be able to exert control over mental images. This controllability aspect is one aspect of imagery that improves with practice. Third, mental practice should assume a positive focus, whereby the individual practices performing a skill or movement pattern successfully versus unsuccessfully (Nordin & Cumming, 2005). In one examination of shooting performance in low-threat and high-threat conditions, Colin, Nieuwenhuys, Visser, and Oudejans (2014) found that imaging successful shot execution was critical to successful shooting performance under both threat and low-threat conditions, compared to a control group. Fourth, temporal characteristics of imagery training should mirror real-world requirements, whereby the speed at which a performer mentally images a particular skill coincides with the temporal requirements in a physical context. Others have suggested (O & Hall, 2009) that practicing imagery in a "slow-motion" format may be effective for particularly complex skills or difficult components of skills.

Scott, Wright, Smith, and Holmes (2022) provided a summary of 20 years of PETTLEP imagery research, stating that PETTLEP has emerged as one of the most dominant models for structuring the content of imagery interventions. In support of this assertion, Smith et al. (2021) revealed that sports psychology scholars and practitioners have reported using PETTLEP in at least 43 different sports across 13 countries, with novices, Olympians, and World Champions. However, based on advances in neuroscience and imaging techniques since the inception of PETTLEP, Scott et al. (2022) recommended that PETTLEP be adapted in line with these recent advancements. The main adaptation to PETTLEP proposed by Scott and colleagues was the integration of (video-based) action observation. Action observation in the context of imagery training refers to a cognitive process where an individual observes someone else performing an action, often a skilled movement or a complex task, and mentally simulates doing the same action themselves (Scott et al., 2022). This mental process is based on the concept that observing an action activates similar neural pathways in the brain as actually performing the action. The video also helps the performer recall salient stimulus and response propositions (a core element of PETTLEP) in the absence of verbal cues. Therefore, in practice, performers could replace the traditional imagery script with a video (or dynamic photographs). For example, Lu et al., 2020 explored the efficacy of action observation within a PETTLEP framework, specifically focusing on enhancing the accuracy of three-point shots in basketball. Lu and colleagues sampled college basketball players and randomized them into groups where they observed videos of themselves executing three-point shots in either a first-person or third-person perspective (or control condition that only received physical training). The players then engaged in imagery, visualizing the action in the same perspective as the one shown in their respective videos. Lu and colleagues' results demonstrated significant performance improvements in the players who viewed both first- and third-person videos compared with the control group. Lu et al. did not find a significant performance difference between the two video perspective groups, indicating that both provided essential visual cues for the task.

Imagery effectiveness

The evidence for the effectiveness of mental imagery in enhancing performance is strong (e.g., Lindsay et al., 2023; Morone et al., 2022; Simonsmeier et al., 2021; Toth, 2020). Evidence suggests that, during imagery, neural activations are evident in similar areas of the brain as those used for executing action (e.g., Guillot et al., 2009). However, research on imagery effectiveness is further challenged by including imagery within multimodal mental skill interventions alongside other cognitive skills (e.g., self-talk, relaxation training, goal setting). Thus, it is difficult to identify the contribution of imagery per se to the overall improvement in performance (Weinberg, 2008). Despite these research issues, Simonsmeier et al. (2021) suggested that the influence of "third" variables can be ruled out based on the results of their meta-analysis of the effect of imagery on sports performance. Simonsmeier and colleagues revealed that the cumulative impact of imagery-based interventions was observed to be moderately strong, exhibiting an effect size of $d = 0.431$, with a 95% confidence interval ranging from 0.298 to 0.563. Imagery interventions improved motor skills, motivational factors, and emotional responses. When examining all outcomes collectively, it was evident that combining imagery with physical practice yielded better results than physical practice alone, highlighting the distinct benefits of imagery in conjunction with physical training.

Imagery ability is an important consideration from both research and practice standpoints. Most people can learn to form an image in the "mind's eye". However, it has recently emerged (Zeman, Dewar, & Della Sala, 2015) that a small percentage of the population cannot form a voluntary mental image. Thus, the term "aphantasia" was coined to describe this subset of the population. Even though aphantasia is rare, it is important to acknowledge individual variability in imagery ability and the possibility that some performers will not be able to execute this psychological strategy (and therefore may become frustrated if advised to do so).

Measurement

Measurement of imagery use is typically done via validated self-report measures, each assessing a distinct dimension of imagery use, such as imagery ability, vividness, or frequency of imagery use.

Among the available measures to assess imagery ability are the Sport Imagery Ability Questionnaire (SIAQ; Williams & Cumming, 2011), which measures the ability to image sport-specific cognitive and motivational imagery content; the Movement Imagery Questionnaire-Revised (MIQ-R; Hall & Martin, 1997) which assesses kinaesthetic and visual imagery; the Vividness of Motor Imagery Questionnaire (VMIQ-2; Roberts et al. 2008), measuring the vividness of kinaesthetic and visual imagery; and the Vividness of Visual Imagery Questionnaire (VVIQ; Roberts, Callow, Hardy, Markland & Bringer, 2008). The Sport Imagery Questionnaire (SIQ; Hall et al. 1998) measures the frequency with which certain types of images are employed.

Practical application

Imagery has been applied in sports for various purposes, including improving and maintaining confidence, sustaining concentration, regulating emotional responses, developing and fine-tuning sport-specific skills, and rehearsing tactics strategy (Weinberg & Gould, 2003). A performer can utilize imagery to enhance performance by incorporating the principles of the PETTLEP model. For instance, a basketball player could engage in a detailed mental rehearsal prior to a game. Through imagery, the athlete vividly envisions the game setting, incorporating the sounds of the crowd, the feel of the ball, and the scent of the gymnasium to create a multi-sensory experience. Employing kinaesthetic imagery, the player "feels" the dribbling motion, the jump, muscle tension, and the release of a three-point shot. They use internal imagery to visualize the flight of the ball from their own eyes, following its trajectory to the basket. Then, they switch to an external perspective, observing their form and the ball's entry into the net as if watching a video replay, reinforcing technique. The athlete could apply Motivational Specific (MS) imagery to envision a successful play or scoring the winning basket, which boosts motivation and confidence. Concurrently, they utilize Motivational General Mastery (MG-M) imagery to picture themselves as composed and confident, enhancing self-efficacy and mental toughness. When feeling anxious, they might use Motivational General-Arousal (MG-A) imagery to regulate their heart rate and emotions, maintaining an optimal arousal level for peak performance.

References

Adler, A. B., Delahaij, R., Bailey, S. M., Van den Berge, C., Parmak, M., van Tussenbroek, B., ... & Castro, C. A. (2013). NATO survey of mental health training in army recruits. *Military Medicine*, 178, 760–766.

Arthur, R. A., Fitzwater, J., Roberts, R., Hardy, J., & Arthur, C. A. (2017). Psychological skills and "the Paras": The indirect effects of psychological skills on endurance. *Journal of Applied Sport Psychology,* 29, 449–465.

Barwood, M. J., Corbett, J., Wagstaff, C., McVeigh, D., & Thelwell, R. C. (2015). Motivational self-talk improves 10 km time trial cycling compared to neutral self-talk. *International Journal of Sports Physiology and Performance,* 10, 166–171.

Blanchfield, A. W., Hardy, J., De Morree, H. M., Staiano, W., & Marcora, S. M. (2014). Talking yourself out of exhaustion: The effects of self-talk on endurance performance. *Medicine and Science in Sports and Exercise,* 46, 998–1007.

Callow, N., Jiang, D., Roberts, R., & Edwards, M. G. (2017). Kinesthetic imagery provides additive benefits to internal visual imagery on slalom task performance. *Journal of Sport and Exercise Psychology,* 39, 81–86. doi: 10.1123/jsep.2016-0168

Callow, N., Roberts, R., Hardy, L., Jiang, D., & Edwards, M. G. (2013). Performance improvements from imagery: Evidence that internal visual imagery is superior to external visual imagery for slalom performance. *Frontiers in Human Neuroscience*, 7, 697. doi: 10.3389/fnhum.2013.00697

Callow, N., & Waters, A. (2005). The effect of kinesthetic imagery on the sport confidence of flat-race horse jockeys. *Psychology of Sport and Exercise,* 6, 443–459. doi: 10.1016/j.psychsport.2004.08.001

Colin, L., Nieuwenhuys, A., Visser, A., & Oudejans, R. R. (2014). Positive effects of imagery on police officers' shooting performance under threat. *Applied Cognitive Psychology,* 28, 115–121. doi: 10.1002/acp.2972

Cumming, J., & Williams, S. E. (2013). Introducing the revised applied model of deliberate imagery use for sport, dance, exercise, and rehabilitation. *Movement & Sport Sciences-Science & Motricité,* 82, 69–81. doi: 10.1051/sm/2013098

Doran, G. T. (1981). There's a SMART way to write management's goals and objectives. *Management Review,* 70, 35–36.

Feltz, D. L., & Landers, D. M. (1983). The effects of mental practice on motor skill learning and performance: A meta-analysis. *Journal of Sport Psychology,* 5, 25–57.

Greene III, C. H. (2019). Coaching military special-operations forces. *Consulting Psychology Journal: Practice and Research,* 71, 107–119.

Guillot, A., Collet, C., Nguyen, V. A., Malouin, F., Richards, C., & Doyon, J. (2009). Brain activity during visual versus kinesthetic imagery: an fMRI study. *Human brain mapping*, 30(7), 2157-2172.

Hall, C. R., Mack, D. E., Paivio, A., & Hausenblas, H. A. (1998). Imagery use by athletes: Development of the Sport Imagery Questionnaire. *International Journal of Sport Psychology,* 29, 73–89.

Hall, C. R., & Martin, K. A. (1997). Movement Imagery Questionnaire--Revised. *Journal of Imagery Research in Sport and Physical Activity*.

Hamilton, R. A., Scott, D., & MacDougall, M. P. (2007). Assessing the effectiveness of self-talk interventions on endurance performance. *Journal of Applied Sport Psychology,* 19, 226–239.

Hardy, J. (2006). Speaking clearly: A critical review of the self-talk literature. *Psychology of Sport and Exercise,* 7, 81–97.

Hardy, J., Oliver, E., & Tod, D. (2009). A framework for the study and application of self-talk within sport. In S. Mellalieu and S. Hanton (Eds.), *Advances in applied sport psychology: A review* (pp 37–74). Oxford, UK: Routledge.

Hardy, L., & Callow, N. (1999). Efficacy of external and internal visual imagery perspectives for the enhancement of performance on tasks in which form is important. *Journal of Sport and Exercise Psychology,* 21, 95–112.

Hardy, L., Jones, J. G., & Gould, D. (1996). *Understanding psychological preparation for sport: Theory and practice of elite performers*. London, UK: John Wiley & Sons Inc.

Harwood, C., Cumming, J., & Fletcher, D. (2004). Motivational profiles and psychological skills use within elite youth sport. *Journal of Applied Sport Psychology,* 16, 318–332.

Hase, A., Hood, J., Moore, L. J., & Freeman, P. (2019). The influence of self-talk on challenge and threat states and performance. *Psychology of Sport and Exercise*, 45, 101550.

Hatzigeorgiadis, A., & Biddle, S. J. (2008). Negative self-talk during sport performance: Relationships with pre-competition anxiety and goal-performance discrepancies. *Journal of Sport Behavior,* 31, 237–253.

Hatzigeorgiadis, A., Zourbanos, N., Galanis, E., & Theodorakis., Y. (2011). Self-talk and sports performance: A meta-analysis. *Perspectives on Psychological Science,* 6, 348–356.

Hohmann, M., & Orlick, T. (2014). Examining the psychological skills used by elite Canadian military pilots. *Mission of the Journal of Excellence,* 16, 4–19.

Holmes, P. S., & Collins, D. J. (2001). The PETTLEP approach to motor imagery: A functional equivalence model for sport psychologists. *Journal of Applied Sport Psychology*, 13, 60–83. doi: 10.1080/10413200109339004

Jackman, P. C., Hawkins, R. M., Burke, S. M., Swann, C., & Crust, L. (2020). The psychology of mountaineering: A systematic review. *International Review of Sport and Exercise Psychology,* 1–39.

Kross, E., Bruehlman-Senecal, E., Park, J., Burson, A., Dougherty, A., Shablack, H., ... & Ayduk, O. (2014). Self-talk as a regulatory mechanism: How you do it matters. *Journal of Personality and Social Psychology,* 106, 304–324.

Latham, G. P., & Locke, E. A. (2007). New developments in and directions for goal setting research. *European Psychologist,* 12, 290–300.

Lee, C. (1990). Psyching up for a muscular endurance task: Effects of image content on performance and mood state. *Journal of Sport and Exercise Psychology*, 12(1), 66-73.

Lindsay, R. S., Larkin, P., Kittel, A., & Spittle, M. (2023). Mental imagery training programs for developing sport-specific motor skills: A systematic review and meta-analysis. *Physical Education and Sport Pedagogy*, 28(4), 444–465.

Locke, E. A., & Latham, G. P. (1984). *Goal setting: A motivational technique that works!* Englewood Cliffs, NJ: Prentice Hall.

Locke, E. A., & Latham, G. P. (1990). *A theory of goal setting and task performance*. Englewood Cliffs, NJ: Prentice Hall.

Locke, E. A., & Latham, G. P. (2002). Building a practically useful theory of goal setting and task motivation: A 35-year odyssey. *American Psychologist,* 57, 705.

Locke, E. A., & Latham, G. P. (2006). New directions in goal setting theory. *Current Directions in Psychological Science,* 15, 265–268.

Locke, E. A., & Latham, G. P. (2015). Breaking the rules: a historical overview of goal-setting theory. In *Advances in motivation science* 2(99-126). Elsevier.

Locke, E. A., & Latham, G. P. (2019). The development of goal setting theory: A half century retrospective. *Motivation Science*, 5, 93–105. doi: 10.1037/mot0000127

Lu, F. J., Gill, D. L., Lee, Y. C., Chiu, Y. H., Liu, S., & Liu, H. Y. (2020). Effects of visualized PETTLEP imagery on the basketball 3-point shot: A comparison of internal and external perspectives. *Psychology of Sport and Exercise,* 51, 101765.

Maitland, A., & Gervis, M. (2010). Goal setting in youth football: Are coaches missing an opportunity? *Physical Education and Sport Pedagogy,* 15, 323–343.

McCormick, A., Meijen, C., & Marcora, S. (2015). Psychological determinants of whole-body endurance performance. *Sports Medicine,* 45, 997–1015.

McEwan, D., Harden, S. M., Zumbo, B. D., Sylvester, B. D., Kaulius, M., Ruissen, G. R. …et al. (2016).The effectiveness of multi-component goal setting interventions for changing physical activity behaviour: A systematic review and meta-analysis. *Health Psychology Review*, 10, 67–88, doi: 10.1080/17437199.2015.1104258

Morin, A. (2005). Possible links between self-awareness and inner speech: Theoretical background, underlying mechanisms, and empirical evidence. *Journal of Consciousness Studies,* 12, 115–134.

Morone, G., Ghanbari Ghooshchy, S., Pulcini, C., Spangu, E., Zoccolotti, P., Martelli, M., ... & Iosa, M. (2022). Motor imagery and sport performance: A systematic review on the PETTLEP model. *Applied Sciences*, 12(19), 9753.

Moskowitz, G. B. (2012). The representation and regulation of goals. In H. Aarts & A. J. Elliot (Eds.), *Frontiers of social psychology. Goal-directed behaviour* (pp. 1–47). Psychology Press.

Murphy, S. M., & Woolfolk, R. L. (1987). The effects of cognitive interventions on competitive anxiety and performance on a fine motor skill accuracy task. *International Journal of Sport Psychology.*

Nordin, S. M., & Cumming, J. (2005). More than meets the eye: Investigating imagery type, direction, and outcome. *The Sport Psychologist,* 19, 1–17. doi: 10.1123/tsp.19.1.1

O, J., & Hall, C. (2009). A quantitative analysis of athletes' voluntary use of slow motion, real time, and fast motion images. *Journal of Applied Sport Psychology,* 21, 15–30. doi:10.1080/10413200802541892

Orlick, T., & Partington, J. (1988). Mental links to excellence. *The Sport Psychologist,* 2, 105–130.

Paivio A. (1985). Cognitive and motivational functions of imagery in human performance. *Canadian Journal of Applied Sport Sciences. Journal Canadien Des Sciences Appliquees Au Sport*, 10, 22S–28S.

Perkins, D., Wilson, G. V., & Kerr, J. H. (2001). The effects of elevated arousal and mood on maximal strength performance in athletes. *Journal of Applied Sport Psychology*, 13(3), 239–259.

Roberts, R., Callow, N., Hardy, L., Markland, D., & Bringer, J. (2008). Movement imagery ability: development and assessment of a revised version of the vividness of movement imagery questionnaire. *Journal of Sport and Exercise Psychology*, 30(2), 200-221.

Saint-Martin, S. V., Turner, M. J., & Ruiz, M. C. (2020). Mental preparation of olympic and paralympic swimmers: Performance-related cognitions and emotions, and the techniques used to manage them. *Journal of Physical Education and Sport*, 20(6), 3569–3578. https://doi.org/10.7752/jpes.2020.06481

Scott, M. W., Wright, D. J., Smith, D., & Holmes, P. S. (2022). Twenty years of PETTLEP imagery: An update and new direction for simulation-based training. *Asian Journal of Sport and Exercise Psychology*, 2(2), 70-79.

Simonsmeier, B. A., Andronie, M., Buecker, S., & Frank, C. (2021). The effects of imagery interventions in sports: A meta-analysis. *International Review of Sport and Exercise Psychology*, 14(1), 186–207.

Smith, D., Wright, D. J., Holmes, P. S., & Colyer, E. (2021). The use of PETTLEP imagery by sport psychology practitioners. *Report as Part of a REF Impact Case Study Titled: The PETTLEP Model for Motor Imagery. International Application in Sport Psychology Training and Practice*, 1–15.

Theodorakis, Y., Hatzigeorgiadis, A., & Zourbanos, N. (2012). Cognitions: Self-talk and performance. In S. M. Murphy (Ed.), *The Oxford handbook of sport and performance psychology* (pp. 191–212). Oxford University Press.

Theodorakis, Y., Weinberg, R., Natsis, P., Douma, I., & Kazakas, P. (2000). The effects of motivational and instructional self-talk on improving motor performance. *The Sport Psychologist*, 14, 253–271.

Tod, D., Hardy, J., & Oliver, E. (2011). Effects of self-talk: A systematic review. *Journal of Sport and Exercise Psychology,* 33, 666–687.

Toth, A. J., McNeill, E., Hayes, K., Moran, A. P., & Campbell, M. (2020). Does mental practice still enhance performance? A 24 Year follow-up and meta-analytic replication and extension. *Psychology of Sport and Exercise,* 48, 101672.

Van Raalte, J. L., Vincent, A., & Brewer, B. W. (2016). Self-talk: Review and sport-specific model. *Psychology of Sport and Exercise,* 22, 139–148.

Weinberg, R. (2008). Does imagery work? Effects on performance and mental skills. *Journal of imagery research in sport and physical activity*, 3(1).

Weinberg, R. S., & Butt, J. (Eds.). (2014). Goal-setting and sport performance: Research Findings and Practical Applications. In A.G. Papaioannou and D. Hackfort (Eds) *Routledge Companion to Sport and Exercise Psychology* (pp. 343–355).

Weinberg, R. S., & Gould, D. (2023). *Foundations of sport and exercise psychology*. Human kinetics.

White, A., & Hardy, L. (1998). An in-depth analysis of the uses of imagery by high-level slalom canoeists and artistic gymnasts. *The Sport Psychologist*, 12, 387–403.

Williams, S. E., & Cumming, J. (2011). Measuring athlete imagery ability: The sport imagery ability questionnaire. *Journal of Sport and Exercise Psychology*, 33(3), 416-440.

Zeman, A., Dewar, M., & Della Sala, S. (2015). Lives without imagery–Congenital aphantasia. *Cortex*, 73, 378-380.

5 Restorative Techniques

Mindfulness, Relaxation, Breathing, and Yoga

Nathalie Pattyn, Deanna Beech, Jenny Wilhelmsson, Helen Kilding, and Adrianna Mendrek

Introduction

Restorative techniques all share a common denominator in terms of physiological effect. If we refer to the description of the autonomic nervous system in Chapter 2, these four techniques will enhance the activity of the parasympathetic branch. As already discussed in Chapter 2, the historical focus in autonomic physiology lies on the sympathetic branch, the stress reaction, and the formidable energy mobilization potential this offers. However, if we use an economics metaphor, to be able to spend (energy), one must first capitalize. The way we "put money in the bank", when it comes to autonomic energy, is by rest, recovery, and restoration.

In terms of acute effects, these techniques, when practiced regularly and thus mastered to a certain proficiency level, can also be activated fast, in times when a sharp focus requires a "rebalance" of anabolic and catabolic forces. There is no free lunch: to reap the benefits of restorative techniques, regular practice is key. Hence the need to present several techniques, to allow for practitioners to identify which one best suits the needs of their performers.

Mindfulness

Introduction

This section provides a brief review of the developments in this field, discusses the evidence for claims that mindfulness can be performance enhancing, explores the application of mindfulness for high performers, and describes how to implement mindfulness programs. While there are many definitions of mindfulness in the literature, Kabat-Zinn (2003) proposed the operational definition most referenced when he stated that mindfulness is "the awareness that emerges through paying attention on purpose, in the present moment, and nonjudgmentally to the unfolding of experience moment by moment" (2003, p. 145). In more psychological terms this would be the process of "selecting a stimulus event to have stimulus control over a selected response" (Moran, 2016).

Mindfulness interventions have been employed for decades in psychotherapy. In third wave therapies such as Acceptance and Commitment Therapy (ACT) and Mindfulness Based Cognitive Therapy (MBCT) the focus is on taking a dimensional or contextual approach to addressing an individual's mental performance (Bach & Moran, 2008; Barraca, 2012; Hayes et al., 2004; Kahl, Winter & Schweiger, 2012). Interventions from these therapies aim to change the individual's relationship to their thoughts, feelings, sensations, and behaviours. This is achieved through the practice of committing to pay maximal attention to select stimuli while remaining unhindered (i.e.,

DOI: 10.4324/9781003378969-7

detached) by irrelevant stimuli and accepting the information that this presents, instead of trying to change it or becoming emotionally engaged with it. From this perspective, mindfulness practice can be described as the practice of committed action (Moran, 2016). It's a form of mental control (Barraca, 2012). Describing the practice of mindfulness from this nomenclature separates it from its historically spiritual roots in the meditative tradition of Eastern cultures.

A brief historical review: mindfulness in Western culture

Modern-day interest in the benefits of mindfulness was sparked by Jon Kabat-Zinn while he was a PhD candidate in Molecular Biology at MIT. He was introduced to the practice of mindfulness by a visiting lecturer, Philip Kapleau. When he and his colleges were looking for a method to help chronic pain patients who were no longer responding well to medical intervention, they proposed the MBSR (Mindfulness Based Stress Reduction) in 1979 at the Stress Reduction Clinic (now called the Center for Mindfulness) at the University of Massachusetts (UMass). The program aimed to help patients recognize and accept their experiences, even pain, by being mindfully aware of it and accepting it (i.e., changing their relationship with the pain experience). The program showed significant improvement in pain management and set in motion more than 40 years of research into the benefits and applications of mindfulness.

Over that time, and as the evidence of effectiveness of this approach grew, pseudo-scientific studies gave way to more scientifically rigorous research utilizing randomized controlled trials and physiological measures. Meta-analyses of these studies show support for the benefits of mindfulness for chronic pain and sleep (Zou et al., 2018), headaches (Gu et al., 2018), depression (Sorbero et al., 2015; Lenz, Hall, & Bailey Smith, 2016), and even obesity (Rogers et al., 2017). Interestingly, while it is often assumed that there is solid support for mindfulness as an adjunct treatment for anxiety disorders, the meta-analyses do not all agree. Two meta-analyses found support for mindfulness as a treatment for anxiety (Vøllestad et al., 2012; Franca & Milbourn, 2015) and one did not (Strauss, 2014). Overall, most studies find mindfulness to be beneficial as an adjunct treatment, rather than a sole treatment modality (Sorbero et al., 2015).

Mindfulness to enhance performance in applied environments

Kabat-Zinn was also the first to apply the technique of mindfulness to athletic performance (Bühlmayer et al., 2017). In 1985 he found that mindfulness training enhanced the performance of rowers on the Denmark Olympic team. However, this did not spark the same research storm as his pain management findings. It was not until the body of evidence around the clinical benefits of mindfulness began to amass that interest in the application of mindfulness to sports began to grow (Bühlmayer et al., 2017).

As with the clinical application of mindfulness, early studies often lacked scientific rigor (Chiesa, Calati & Serretti, 2011), but over time well-structured programs and researched applications were developed. The two most prominent programs include the Mindfulness-Acceptance and Commitment approach (MAC; Gardner & Moore, 2004; 2007), and the Mindfulness Sport Enhancement Program (MSPE; Kaufman, Glass, & Arnkoff, 2009). Both programs involve group-based mindfulness exercises conducted several times a week for seven and four weeks, respectively. Brief mindfulness interventions with as few as four sessions have also been shown to be beneficial (Tang et al., 2007). Still other studies have found performance benefits using non-sport focused programs, such as the earlier mentioned MBSR program, as well as general mindfulness training (Sappington & Longshore, 2015). For a reasonably comprehensive review of mindfulness interventions in sport psychology see the book "Mindfulness and Performance" edited by Baltzell and Summers (2016).

The body of evidence for the benefits of mindfulness on well-being and performance have not been lost on the military. With the increasingly complex and cognitively challenging environments of today's missions, units are seeking every advantage possible. Programs in mindfulness training have been implemented throughout the US Military (Jha et al., 2015; Jha et al., 2019a), particularly across US Special Forces units (Zanesco et al., 2019), and in Great Britain (Carter & Mortlock, 2019), the Netherlands (Tilborg et al., 2019), Norway (Meland et al., 2015a,b), Denmark (Bijlsma et al., 2018), and many other countries. Feasibility studies have shown that mindfulness training programs can be successfully implemented in elite units like Special Forces, and they result in enhanced mental performance of the operators (Meland et al., 2015a; Stanley & Jha, 2009; Stanley et al., 2011). By practicing sustained attention and the reorientation of attention back to the task at hand, operators improve their ability to monitor situations in extreme environments to ensure awareness of salient cues. With this practiced meta-awareness of information, they are then able to view the content of their attention dispassionately and flexibly, which allows for improved accuracy in decision-making and execution as the information is observed without bias or prejudgment (Meland, 2016; Bernstein et al., 2019).

Mindfulness has also been shown to improve the management of operational stress (Johnson et al., 2014; Meland, 2015a), and has protective benefits for those going into high stress environments (Jha et al., 2010; Jha et al., 2016; Röthlin, Horvath, Birrer & Holtforth, 2016). While elite performers have proven their ability to effectively cope in high-stress situations, the additional economy of mental resources that is achieved by avoiding unnecessary stress-activation allows for continued optimal mental processing (judgement, strategizing, and problem-solving) in the information dense, fast-paced, fluid, operational climates of today's high-performance professional environments (Meland, 2016; Jha et al., 2019a). For a solid review of the benefits of mindfulness as a cognitive training technique see the scientific report of NATO Research Task Group HFM-302, "Deploying Mindfulness to Gain Cognitive Advantage: Considerations for Military Effectiveness and Well-Being" (Jha, Rogers, Shoomaker, & Cardon, 2019a). Figure 5.1 summarizes the mechanisms, facets, and components through which mindfulness provides a cognitive advantage.

How does it work?

It is broadly acknowledged that there are two styles of mindfulness meditation practice: focused attention (FA) and open monitoring (OM) (Lutz et al., 2008; Malinowski, 2013; Tang et al., 2015). In FA meditation, the practitioner sustains the attentional focus on a chosen object (most commonly one's breath) and returns it to this anchor each time the mind wanders. Accordingly, it is theorized that FA develops three attentional control processes, along with their underpinning neural networks: (a) the monitoring faculty that remains vigilant to mind-wandering while attention is sustained to the anchor (alerting network); (b) the ability to detect mind-wandering (salience network) and to disengage from it (executive network); and (c) the ability to redirect the focus to the anchor (orienting network) (Lutz et al., 2008; Malinowski 2013). Some proficiency in FA meditation is required to transition to OM practice, in which the aim is to remain solely in the monitoring state maintaining an open, nonreactive attention to all arising and passing mental events. OM would further develop the practitioner's meta-awareness of inner mental processes, including mind-wandering (Lutz et al., 2008).

Casedas et al. (2020) performed a meta-analysis to investigate whether mindfulness meditation training enhanced executive functions, which would be expected according to the cognitive description of FA meditation. Their overview of 13 studies revealed a small-to-medium effect (average effect size of 0.34) of mindfulness meditation training in enhancing executive control; more specifically working memory, inhibitory control, and cognitive flexibility. In their systematic review of 20 included studies, Bondar et al. (2021) aimed to answer the question whether mindfulness had

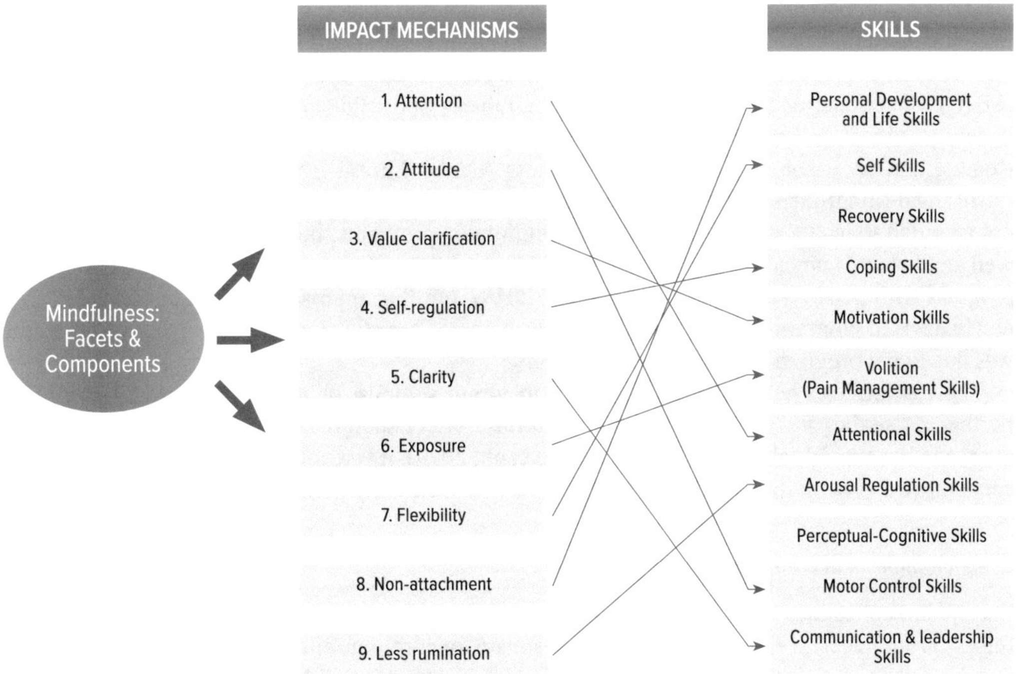

Figure 5.1 Mindfulness: Facets and components translating to cognitive and emotional mechanisms to impact skills.

a tangible effect on physiological measures of neural activity. The main finding that emerged was the potential enhancing effect of mindfulness practice on performance-monitoring abilities, but with no consistent changes regarding neural activity. These inconsistencies might be explained by a mix of investigations of novice and expert practitioners. Indeed, the seminal studies showing an effect of mindfulness meditation were performed on participants like Buddhist monks (e.g., Kral et al., 2018).

Implementing mindfulness training in a performance-enhancement framework

First, it is recommended that education on the benefits of mindfulness be conducted to foster interest in the tool and identify volunteers for the program. Then, gold standard programming would include a pre-intervention assessment of the client's level of mindfulness and other performance variables of interest, a structured mindfulness intervention, and then a post-intervention assessment using the same measures. For an evaluation and comparison of available instruments see the extensive review by Park, Reilly-Spong & Gross (2013), as well as Chapter 17 on program evaluation. The quantitative data produced by these assessments demonstrates the benefits of the program to both the individual clients and, if necessary, the larger organization.

The most evidence-based programs in mindfulness training have been conducted over four to eight weeks with eight hours of direct training time. The training usually involves a combination of didactic education, in-class practice, and homework-based practice. The four-week program appears to be an ideal length as it is a more compressed, and thus easier to incorporate into work schedules, and still reliably provides the cognitive and stress-reduction benefits of the longer programs. Some studies have shown benefits with less than four weeks of training (Tang et al., 2007), but these results are not consistently observed. For example, Zanesco et al. (2019) found that when training is compressed to two weeks the resulting effectiveness is reduced to negligible. Handbooks with the structure of pre-developed programs are available: Mindfulness-Acceptance and Commitment (MAC) by Gardner & Moore (2007), the Mindfulness Sport Enhancement Program (MSPE) by Kaufman, Glass, & Arnkoff (2009), the Mindfulness-Based Attention Training (MMFT) by Jha, Rogers, and Morrison (2014), the Mindfulness Mental Fitness Training (MMFT) by Stanley (2014), and Mindfulness and Acceptance in Sport by Henriksen, Hansen, & Larsen (2020). This is not intended to be a comprehensive list of mindfulness programs, but these programs are already well studied and manualized. It is also possible to modify an already existing mindfulness training program with good results (Röthlin & Birrer, 2019), but this approach is not recommended. If a newly devised program were to fail to show the expected benefits it would be unclear whether this was due to the program or to some other factor.

The training can be effectively provided in group settings, or through individual coaching. Further, as studies have shown that there is a dose effect such that the more one practices, the more one benefits (Rooks et al., 2017; Zanesco et al., 2019), it is recommended that participants be encouraged to incorporate their at-home practice into their daily performance routines.

Common implementation challenges

Jha and her colleagues (2019a) identified several challenges in the process of implementing mindfulness programs with elite forces, and these resonate for corporate clients as well. The first problem that the authors note is the operators' perception that it is "not 'worth' the time". In an environment full of very active people the perception that mindfulness training is sitting and "doing nothing" runs counter to the culture. A successful strategy to switch this perception is to point out that while practicing mindfulness you are physically not active, but you are mentally very active as you work to train your attention. Have them set a challenge or goal for themselves. Suggest that the operator start with a short practice time, such as starting with five to ten minutes a day. Identify a regular time in their day that can easily be dedicated to the task. When they realize that it is difficult to focus their minds for even this short timeframe, the data is present to help them understand that improving their attention and ability to monitor the present moment will benefit these abilities in mission-critical operations.

It is also often evident when the topic of mindfulness is broached that some perceive it to be a "fluffy-headed" or a "hippie" thing to do. And, since the practice does owe its origins to the Buddhist tradition, there are those that believe they will be required to change or adopt a specific belief system or world view (Jha et al., 2019a). In these situations, education is needed to uncouple this cognitive training task from its spiritual roots and ensure a solid understanding of the cognitive and physiological benefits.

Others may feel that "if you need to train your mind, it must mean that your mind is weak" (Jha et al., 2019a). When this sentiment arises, it can be countered with the example of the classic training model. Training is needed to get stronger and faster, and once these goals are met it must be continued in order to maintain the gains. Everyone works hard to stay average on a team of all stars. Mental training is the same. In a group of intellectually gifted operators mental training can give them the cognitive advantage, which then translates into a performance advantage. Further, Jha and her colleagues (2019a) point out that everyone is affected by the high operational tempo across elite units and mindfulness training can "allow for longer periods of mission-related physical and mental training with less compromise to the integrity of body and mind."

Finally, tech savvy personnel may feel that mindfulness is not a "modern technological" solution (Jha et al., 2019a). However, it is precisely because of the increasingly complex, information saturated and rapid changing nature of the modern work environment that our elite performers need to be able to "observe with discernment, orient with precision, decide without bias, and act with awareness" (Jha et al., 2019a); skills that are enhanced through mindfulness training.

Summary

There is considerable evidence to support the conclusion that mindfulness helps regulate emotions, enhances one's sense of well-being, improves pain management, benefits sleep, and buffers against stress. Research and recent application of this multi-modal technique to the military has also shown that it can enhance mission critical skills such as focused attention, situational awareness, improved perceptual accuracy, and cognitive flexibility in decision-making. And yet, mindfulness is an abstract concept to grasp, a difficult skill to learn, and not everybody will be open to trying it. In addition, it takes time and time is a precious commodity in this community. Inevitably, within Special Operations Foreces (SOF) populations, as in the general population, after trying to practice mindfulness there will still be those that report that they just do not get it and those that find it a game changer.

Relaxation

Introduction

The capacity to manage and regulate physical and mental activation levels is essential to maintaining the readiness and effectiveness of high performers, both during their core professional tasks and across other life domains. The relevance of relaxation to this population centres around managing relaxation during action as part of self- regulation, i.e., as a downregulator, for preparation and recovery pre- or post-action. As such, relaxation is the technique of choice to promote recovery, through an enhanced parasympathetic activation (we refer to Chapter 2 for the detailed neurophysiological background). Techniques and skills to facilitate the sensation and perception of readiness and fatigue are of utmost importance for safety in execution and task completion, as well as in promoting health and well-being in demanding occupational areas.

This section is not an exhaustive review on the field of relaxation, as the concept spans several disciplines involving psychology and physiology. The aim is to explore the utility of relaxation training to high performers, and reflect on points of reference regarding relaxation training as part of a mental performance program.

Conceptualization

Relaxation generally refers to a state of mind and body and includes specific techniques, methods, or procedures actively applied as downregulators to attain or maintain either an ideal performance state (i.e., zone control), or to facilitate recovery when "switching off" might be challenging. Several attempts to frame the concept of relaxation have been presented over the years, mostly in clinical practice, including this informative reflection by Schilling and Poppen (1983, p. 99): "Relaxation can be regarded as a complex response class involving responses in the physiological, cognitive and overt behavioural areas. Relaxation training typically focuses on one area and the effects are assumed to generalize to other members of the response class."

The physiological modifications due to relaxation training, which may include decreased blood pressure, heart rate, oxygen consumption, and muscle tension, were described in the 1970s by Herbert Benson as the Relaxation Response (RR; Benson & Klipper, 2000; see also Gonzales, Vranceanu, Mahaffey, Laroche, & Park, 2016; Lazar et al., 2000). In some restful environments or pleasurable activities (e.g., exposure to nature, listening to music), a relaxed mind and body may come naturally. In other more demanding or chaotic situations, relaxation might be more challenging and require the active use of specific techniques (e.g., slow breathing; Zaccaro et al., 2018), which would then allow to enter a state of relaxation (e.g., psychological relaxation states [R-States]; Smith et al., 2000).

Scientific evidence

One of the earliest published reports by Edmund Jacobson used progressive relaxation (PR; Jacobson, 1987) and found that more relaxed individuals were not startled by sudden noise (see McGuigan & Lehrer, 2007). Several techniques, methods, or procedures with distinct features are available nowadays in the multitude of relaxation literature. They include (but are not limited to) progressive muscle relaxation (PMR) and autogenic training (AT), and can include techniques to manage anxiety and stressful cognitions. In sport psychology, Pineschi and Di Pietro (2013) stated that: "Among these techniques (i.e., psychophysiological techniques), the best known are relaxation techniques that can be defined as means through which individuals are able to reduce their muscle and psychological tension voluntarily" (p. 182). Furthermore, in sports, relaxation training has been linked to recovery (Bonnar, Bartel, Kakoschke, & Lang, 2018; Crowther, Sealey, Crowe, Edwards, & Halson, 2017; Kenttä & Hassmén, 1998; Pelka, 2017), which, considering the physiological basis for the training, is unsurprising (as discussed in the introduction to the current chapter). Kellman et al. (2018) presented relaxation as part of psychological recovery strategies to mitigate cognitive exhaustion in athletes. They suggested that "the improvement of performance (in sports) is not achieved through a high quantity of recovery activities but, rather, through a high-quality, well-matched, and individualized approach to recovery" (p. 243). Research in different worksite settings also explored relaxation related to regulating strain and recovery (e.g., PMR during lunch breaks; Krajewski, Wieland, & Sauerland, 2010). Similarly, relaxation improved sleep during naps (e.g., involving PMR, hypnosis, and paradoxical interventions; Debellemaniere et al., 2018). To summarize, relaxation training can be viewed as a way of increasing an individual's resources to meet demands placed on them (see Bates et al., 2010, for more details).

Relaxation in applied settings

There are significant crossovers between the demands of elite military personnel, top corporate executives, and elite sports performers; although there are also key differences (notably the level of physical engagement, the duration of time where high performance is required, the predictability of the environment, and the scale of consequences for poor performance). Despite these differences, one can agree on the common denominator of "high stakes performance environments". It is thus logical that results from one elite domain would have relevance to another elite domain. In a study examining the effects of relaxation training and mindfulness training, Rooks and colleagues (2007) found that relaxation training for elite soccer players led to a decrease in anxiety and an increase in positive mood and perceptions of efficacy during periods of high demand. They also found that relaxation training had positive effects pre and post sporting season. A similar result was found in elite rock climbers, where relaxation and visualization training was found to promote better performance, especially in those with high self-efficacy (Ilham, 2021). It is important to note that often relaxation training for elite populations has the greatest effect when combined with additional techniques. This observation is supported by the conclusions made by Kellman and colleagues in their review, who noted that relaxation techniques should be integrated as an essential component in elite athletes' training regimens (Kellman, Pelka, & Beckmann, 2017).

Positive effects of relaxation (i.e., PMR) have been described extensively in active duty military (McCallie, Blum, & Hood, 2006). Relaxation training has been explored during preparations for duty (i.e., predeployment training; e.g., Hourani et al., 2011; Lewis et al., 2015; Oded, 2011;

Pagnini, Phillips, Bercovitz, & Langer, 2019) and linked to recovery (i.e., as part of a personal performance plan; DeWiggins, Hite, & Alston, 2010). Di Nicola et al. (2007) investigated stress management and deployment. They suggested that implementing relaxation training may be a preventive intervention to stress and anxiety, and the skills acquired would be helpful in demanding situations (i.e., balancing strain). Furthermore, Stetz et al. (2011) investigated the usage of technology-enhanced relaxation (i.e., virtual reality and guided imagery) on relaxation training for military medics and found effects on anxiety levels. Also, using psychological skills (e.g., imagery; discussed in Chapter 4) to induce a relaxed state has been described as beneficial for stress management in high-performance conditions (Hohmann & Orlick, 2014). In a study examining elite military recruits, Fitzwater, Arthur, and Hardy (2018) found that groups trained in relaxation skills were rated as higher performers and as having greater mental toughness than a group that did not receive this training.

Designing relaxation training

The purpose of relaxation training is to condition the mind and body to relax in demanding circumstances, using a specific stimulus. There is limited consensus in the literature on whether using one technique or a combination of techniques during relaxation training is most effective. Dendato and Diener (1986) found that a combination of relaxation techniques (i.e., deep muscle relaxation) and cognitive reframing was effective in reducing test anxiety. Also, Reiss et al. (2017) found effects on test anxiety levels when combining relaxation techniques with cognitive behavioural therapy relative to using relaxation alone. For military use, Joshi (2019) suggested applying different techniques sequentially and stated that even "A short three to ten-minute systematic relaxation is useful after any vigorous physical exercise, daily physical training, or a hatha yoga practice" (p. 3). This sequential approach may allow the mind to rest, apprehend, and integrate the benefits of activities performed (i.e., enhancing recovery and readiness). Taken together, relaxation training is likely to be most effective when combining techniques and it is likely that offering a combination or variety of techniques will lead to better uptake and integration among high performers.

Notably, adverse effects are rarely identified in the research literature (see Rees, 2011, for more detail), but the possibility of no effect or even adverse effects should not be ignored. As Lehrer (1982) reflected, "perhaps some individuals attribute unpleasant properties to the bodily feelings of relaxation. They may feel that it signifies vulnerability, lack of control over anger or sexual desire, extreme passivity, etc." (p. 424). Lehrer also discussed the effectiveness of progressive relaxation. Lehrer focused on muscular skills to relax (i.e., somatic orientation) versus modified techniques (i.e., cognitive or behavioural orientation). He implied that a specific technique might be more potent than another depending on underlying components (i.e., what it is used for), in addition to varying individual preferences in the targeted audience.

Furthermore, Matsumoto and Smith (2001) stated that more profound benefits of relaxation training may be delayed in time or manifest as an after effect. A detailed and informative presentation of relaxation from a stress management perspective can be found in Lehrer, Woolfolk, and Sime (2007) and from a practitioner's more hands-on perspective, in Smith (2005). The design of relaxation training is influenced by several components such as individual characteristics, context, and relaxation goals. Importantly, programs are likely to be most beneficial when they are flexible and take into account individual differences.

PROGRESSIVE MUSCLE RELAXATION (PMR) TRAINING

Progressive muscle relaxation (i.e., PR; Jacobson, 1987; see also Bernstein, Borkovec, & Hazlett-Stevens, 2000) is a non-pharmacological deep muscle relaxation involving a systematic and conscious switch between tensing and releasing specific muscle groups. The aim is to differentiate a tense state from a relaxed state and facilitate relaxation through tension and release. While initial training may incorporate whole body relaxation, the number of muscle groups targeted may decrease with training, resulting in relaxation in "one step". To facilitate relaxation in "one step", PMR may be linked to the use of cue words and brief mental imagery, to condition specific stimuli as "anchors".

BEHAVIOURAL RELAXATION TRAINING (BRT)

Behavioural relaxation training (BRT; Chung, Poppen, & Lundervold, 1995; Lundervold & Poppen, 2004; Schilling & Poppen, 1983; Tatum, Lundervold, & Ament, 2006) is a procedure to teach individuals structured relaxation through presenting a number of relaxed behaviours involving instructions, modelling, prompting, shaping, reinforcement, and corrective feedback. The training consists of observing and evaluating outcomes of overt and measurable relaxed behaviours involving head, eyes, throat, shoulders, hands, body, feet, breath, and mouth. A benefit of this technique is that there is a qualitative measure for it, which may be helpful for users and future research. The Behavioural Relaxation Scale (BRS) assesses overt relaxed behaviours and could be used as a feedback or measurement tool in training.

AUTOGENIC TRAINING (AT)

Autogenic training (AT) is credited to Johannes H. Schultz and was introduced in the 1930s (see Linden, 2007, for more detail). AT is a self-induced deep relaxation or a quasi-hypnotic state achieved through subvocal instructions. It involves consciously directing and focusing the mind on specific inner sensations such as heaviness and warmth or coolness, cardiac regulation, and respiration, in order to regulate arousal. AT aims at reinforcing independence and self-control, with the intent of minimizing the need for external direction, for example, from a trainer or device.

Recommendations for implementation in high-performance environments

When considering implementing relaxation training as either a stand-alone intervention, or as part of a broader program, it is important to consider the suitability of the approach for the specific target audience, the credibility and evidence base of the intervention, and how the techniques will be applied in an operational environment. Specifically, the following points should be considered when implementing relaxation training in high-performance environments:

- Individuals differ in which techniques are more suitable to them, both in terms of subjective preference and physiological suitability; therefore a variety of techniques and skills should be included: one size does not fit all.
- While relaxation is in essence an individual skill, the dynamics of a group may influence (either positively or negatively) how easily or effectively the techniques can be applied. In highly competitive environments, the automatic comparison individuals perform with each other must be taken into account.
- Environmental considerations as to where, when, and with whom to practice relaxation training. Supervised or guided training in a calm setting is generally more manageable, at least at the beginning of training.
- Individually assess and evaluate the efficacy of training using different measurements methods such as journalling or other qualitative measures, or biofeedback to demonstrate the effectiveness (or lack thereof) of the techniques.

- Reflection on if and how relaxation skills can be used in circumstances outside the performance environment.

Conclusion

The environment in which high performers choose to operate is often high intensity and likely to lead to heightened states of activation and stress, both physical and mental. Having techniques to manage this level of activation might be vital in demanding situations (e.g., a managed arousal state can contribute to situational awareness and thus to safety in execution and task completion). Relaxation training may contribute to a sensation of readiness and facilitate recovery, as it per se involves reducing tension for the body and mind. The one caveat to mention is that relaxation is a skill which needs to be acquired and maintained to show its beneficial effects, meaning it will not do any good if not practiced on a regular basis (similarly to the dose-response effect discussed for mindfulness on the previous section). Therefore, techniques and sequence of techniques should be carefully selected to ensure they are effective in the specific environment and group culture, to ensure continued practice.

Relaxation is not a new concept, and many studies highlight the beneficial effects of relaxation training in different settings and populations. Relaxation training has been used broadly, often with the aim of increased calmness or to reduce tension. The connection to performance and task execution is somewhat indirect through stress management and recovery, however, a better management of arousal is also related to a better ability to focus. Relaxation training is likely to have positive outcomes for preparation (i.e., self-efficacy) and for task execution in high-risk professions. The adverse effects of relaxation training seem unlikely but are not negligible, and the consideration should always be given to the specific performance outcome sought when implementing this as a performance intervention. Evaluating and adapting relaxation training to the individual is highly recommended, as there will be an individual variability in which techniques are most efficacious, as well as variation in which environments are most conducive to these techniques. Relaxation training is a powerful tool both as a stand-alone intervention and as part of a broader mental performance program, and on balance is likely to have positive impacts on high performers both in terms of operational effectiveness and quality of life.

Breathing

Introduction

Breathing (or technically speaking the ventilation part of it) is the only process sustaining vital functions that can be controlled both voluntarily and autonomously (e.g., during sleep). This unique feature is also why breath is key in all the discussed restorative techniques, and why yoga (discussed in the following section) uses breathwork as a cornerstone of its holistic approach. Breathing is, literally, our action window to the autonomic nervous system (see Chapter 2 for a more detailed description). As the recent bestseller "Breath" (Nestor, 2020) demonstrates, breathwork has profound implications for basic health and well-being, and for advanced performance management.

Breathing serves the ultimate vital function of the exchange of gases (oxygen and carbon dioxide) and thermoregulatory processes (Kreiman & Sidtis, 2011). At rest, an adult typically breathes around 17,280 to 23,040 times per day, at a rate of 12 to 16 breaths per minute. Stress, excitement, pain, and physical activity typically increase breathing rate. Soldiers engaged in extended load carriage over mixed terrain, or athletes engaged in anaerobic physical activity display respiration rates of up to 50 breaths per minute (Looney et al., 2018). This section will explore how manipulating our breathing can impact cognitive performance, positively and negatively. First, the mechanisms of breathing and breath control will be introduced followed by a review of the various breath training concepts that have been studied. Finally, the evidence for the efficacy of individual breath training techniques for applied high-performance contexts will be discussed.

Basics of breathing

One breath consists of one inhalation (air is pulled in to the lungs) followed by one exhalation (air is pushed out of the lungs). During inhalation, the diaphragm and the external intercostal muscles contract to expand the chest cavity and the rib cage, pulling air in. During exhalation, the diaphragm and external intercostal muscles relax causing the chest cavity to return to its original volume, forcing air out of the lungs.

Under normal conditions, breathing (depth and rate) is controlled automatically, unconsciously, and continually by the respiratory centre in the brainstem, and the control impulses are relayed by the autonomic nervous system (ANS). Breathing rate and depth adjust based on the amount of carbon dioxide, oxygen, and level of acidosis in the arterial blood (Kenney, Willmore & Costill, 2015). During exercise, chemoreceptors detect the increase in carbon dioxide levels, which alerts the brain's respiratory centre to increase the speed and depth of breathing to help eliminate excess carbon dioxide and provide more oxygen. This is known as metabolic control of breathing (Kenney, Willmore & Costill, 2015). Over-breathing (hyperventilation), because of a stress stimulus, shock, or illness, causes considerable losses of carbon dioxide and therefore a rise in the pH of extracellular fluids (through the process of respiratory alkalosis), which triggers symptoms such as gasping, trembling, and choking. During mental stress, the sympathetic branch of the ANS is activated, signalling the body to go into "fight-or-flight" mode (for a detailed description of the stress reaction, we refer to Chapter 2). During this reaction, stress hormones are released and physical symptoms such as tachycardia (faster heartbeat), hyperventilation, and vasoconstriction (constricted blood vessels) are experienced.

Breathing can also be controlled voluntarily, or behaviourally, in response to a given stimulus, or to achieve a desired physiological effect. The difference between voluntary and automatic (metabolic) breathing is that automatic breathing requires no attention to maintain, whereas voluntary breathing involves a given amount of focus (Kenney, Willmore & Costill, 2015). Inhalation leads to an increase in sympathetic activity and an increase in heart rate, while exhalation leads to an increase in parasympathetic activity and a decrease in heart rate (Grossman & Taylor, 2007); as such, altering breathing rate and inhalation/exhalation ratio can be used to modulate physiological arousal and anxiety (Cappo & Holmes 1984; Van Diest et al., 2014). This variation in heart rate during the breathing cycle is perfectly normal and is referred to as respiratory sinus arrhythmia (RSA), which we discuss in more details in Chapter 9 (Biofeedback).

Humans can breathe through their nose, through their mouth, or a combination of the two. At rest, healthy humans typically breathe through the nose which has a number of benefits:

- Filtration of particulates in the air
- Improved oxygen transportation due to increased resistance to air flow (more time for full ventilation of the lungs)
- Humidification of inspired air

Sovik (2000) suggests that optimal breathing (at rest) is diaphragmatic, nasal (both inhalation and exhalation), smooth, deep, even, quiet, and free of pauses.

Breath training

Several researchers (e.g., Van Diest et al., 2006; Pattyn et al., 2010) have suggested that breathing is the most sensitive physiological parameter to stress. When stress is experienced, breathing typically becomes faster and shallower which can compromise short-term performance and long-term health. Controlling this response and training the breath can have the opposite effect.

According to Sovik (2000), breath training has three purposes: (1) to increase the ability to sustain relaxed attention on the flow of breath, (2) to refine and control respiratory movements for optimal breathing, and (3) to integrate awareness and respiratory functioning in order to reduce stress and enhance psychological functioning. Breathing techniques typically have one of three functions: (1) to calm and focus the mind, (2) to strengthen respiratory muscles and respiratory efficiency, and (3) to promote relaxation and recovery.

Breath training and breathing techniques are associated with short- and long-term effects in the general population, some of which may be advantageous to the high performer. However, few techniques have been scientifically investigated in this population. Evidence for various techniques is presented below. See also the sections on mindfulness and yoga, as well as Chapter 9, regarding biofeedback, for a review of the effectiveness of multi-modal techniques which incorporate controlled breathing.

Diaphragmatic (belly) breathing

All breathing uses the diaphragm muscle and the external intercostal muscles to some extent, but if the diaphragm is not fully engaged, the chest cavity and rib cage will not expand and contract optimally. This is referred to as chest breathing. Diaphragmatic breathing (or belly breathing, or abdominal breathing, or full yogic breathing) involves full expansion of the abdomen, followed by full expansion of the rib cage, and is integral to efficient, deep breathing. The technique helps fill the lungs from bottom to top, impacting the amount of air taken into the body and thus how much oxygenated blood is available throughout the body (Ungerleider, 2005). The goal of diaphragmatic breathing is to focus awareness on the breath (which is the technique described in mindfulness as Attention Focus), making it slower and deeper. The model created by Noble and Hochman (2019), building on the decades of work of Lehrer and colleagues (Lehrer et al., 2000; 2003; 2009) suggests that slow, deep breathing (0.1 Hz; six breaths per minute) induces a functional state of alert relaxation and can boost memory consolidation.

As introduced in Chapter 2, respiratory patterns are closely related to affective and autonomic arousal states, with quick, shallow, thoracic breathing associated with anxiety, tension, and unpleasant affect, and slow, deep, abdominal/diaphragmatic breathing associated with relaxation and pleasant affect (Boiten, Frijda, & Wientjes, 1994). Diaphragmatic breathing may help treat insomnia (Jereth et al., 2019) and manage pain (Zautra et al., 2010; Busch et al., 2012), which both have implications for mental performance in high performers.

In direct relation to mental performance, Soni et al. (2015) assessed the effect of controlled deep breathing on psychomotor and higher mental functions. One hundred healthy participants (52 females and 48 males aged between 18 and 25 years) took part in a six-week course of controlled deep breathing (five seconds of maximal inhalation followed by five seconds of maximal exhalation, once a day for ten minutes, six days a week). Scores on a rapid fire arithmetic deviation test (score out of 20), a letter finding task (time to complete) and a seven playing card recall test (score out of 10 for correct recall and sequence), measures of attention, memory, and reasoning, improved significantly after training. Reductions in state anxiety and timed maths test performance following the taking of deep breaths have also been seen in children (Khng, 2017) and older, maths-anxious college students (Brunye et al., 2013).

Recent studies have explored the effectiveness of deep breathing in conjunction with biofeedback. Ma et al. (2017) looked at the effect of diaphragmatic breathing on sustained attention, negative affect, and stress in healthy adults. Participants assigned to a deep breathing intervention group (average respiratory rate of four breaths/min) received intensive training, employing a real-time feedback device, for 20 sessions, implemented over eight weeks, while the control group received nothing. All participants completed pre- and post-tests of sustained attention and affect, and salivary cortisol concentration was measured. The breathing group showed a significant decrease in negative affect and cortisol level (suggesting decreased stress levels), and a significant increase in sustained attention after the intervention.

De Couck et al. (2019) examined the effects of two deep breathing patterns on heart rate variability (HRV), an index of parasympathetic tone and vagal nerve activity, and on stress and decision-making performance. Increasing parasympathetic tone and vagal nerve activity is one way to control the autonomic response to anxiety (Gill, 2004). One group performed five minutes of slow breathing with equally long inhalations and exhalations and with a short holding-phase in between (symmetric group), a second group performed five minutes of slow breathing with a long inhalation and an even longer extended exhalation (skewed group), and a third group watched an emotionally neutral film (control). Both types of breathing pattern significantly increased time and frequency domain HRV parameters, reflecting reduced anxiety, while viewing the film did not. In the second phase of the study, 56 students were randomized to perform two minutes of the skewed breathing (experimental group) or to wait for two minutes (control group) before performing a 30-minute, challenging, decision-making task with multiple choice answers. While individuals in the control group reported elevations in stress levels, those in the experimental group did not and the experimental group provided a significantly higher percentage of correct answers than the control group. These findings have important implications for situations where time available to practice (or implement) a breathing technique is limited.

Tactical breathing

Tactical breathing (also known as combat, paced, square, or box breathing) is basically a "rebranding" of a known breathing pattern in pranayama to gain acceptance in tactical populations (military, security, firefighters, etc.). Its aim is to slow heart rate and reduce anxiety by regulating the sympathetic-parasympathetic balance of the autonomic nervous system (for a review, see Grossman, 1983). The same principles of diaphragmatic breathing are employed, but for fixed time periods.

The technique typically involves inhaling deeply (abdominally) through the nose for four seconds, holding for four seconds, exhaling through the mouth over four seconds and then holding again for four seconds, before repeating four times (Grossman and Christensen 2008). The slow holding of breath allows carbon dioxide to build up in the blood. Increased blood carbon dioxide enhances the cardio-inhibitory response of the vagus nerve during exhalation, which stimulates the parasympathetic response. Regular practice is essential, to ensure that the technique becomes automatic and can be used effectively during stressful times to improve performance.

Tactical breathing has been presented as a tool that can be used in at least three contexts: (1) before a stressor creates a peak in stress (i.e., in moments of apprehension), (2) while stressed and performing duties (i.e., with minimal intrusion on task performance), or (3) while stepping back from a task (i.e., when becoming overwhelmed by stress and stepping back becomes necessary to regain control) (Bouchard et al., 2012). Bouchard et al. (2012) assessed the efficacy of using visual and auditory biofeedback while soldiers were immersed in a 3D videogame (15 minutes per day for three days) to practice tactical breathing. On Day 4, all participants (21 in the experimental group and 20 in a control group who did not receive the training) underwent a simulated ambush with an improvised explosive device, where they had to provide first aid to a wounded soldier. Salivary cortisol was measured when waking up and before and after the live simulation. Heart rate was measured at baseline, during an apprehension phase, and during the live simulation. Practicing stress management training (SMT) was effective in reducing stress, as evidenced by cortisol and HRV responses. Although the breathing training was part of a wider stress management training programme called ImPACT (Immersion and Practice of Arousal Control Training), the operational relevance of this study cannot be ignored.

Pranayama (yogic breathing)

Pranayama is the formal practice of controlling the breath. Prana is a Sanskrit word that means life force and ayama means extending or stretching. As described in more detail in the following section on yoga, pranayama or breath regulation is considered an essential component of yoga through its influence on physiological systems.

There are many variations of pranayama: the complete yoga breath (conscious deep filling of the lungs through abdominal, ribcage, and clavicular breathing, followed by full emptying of the lungs); interval breathing (in which the duration of inhalation and exhalation are altered); Nadi Shodhana (alternate nostril breathing); Kapalabhati (short, sharp inhalations and exhalations); Ujjayi (or ocean breath); Sitali (a cooling breath utilizing the tongue), to name a few. Each varies the pace, rhythm, and depth of the inhalation, retention, and exhalation to achieve a specific result, be that relaxation, invigoration, heating, or cooling.

Saoji et al.'s (2019) review of a range of pranayama exercises highlighted "advantageous effects of yogic breathing on the neurocognitive (e.g., reaction time and spatial task performance), psychophysiological (e.g., heart rate variability and blood pressure), respiratory (e.g., forced vital capacity and peak inspiratory flow rate), biochemical and metabolic functions (e.g., oxygen consumption and oxidative stress) in healthy individuals." Slow pranayama breathing techniques have shown the most practical and physiological benefits. Fast breathing pranayama can cause hyperventilation, which may hyperactivate the sympathetic nervous system, stressing the body more. These techniques require a level of expertise outside the scope of "basic" tools teaching. Slow, deep pranayamic breathing has been shown to decrease oxygen consumption, heart rate, and blood pressure, and to increase parasympathetic activity (Jerath et al., 2019. Pranayama breathing has also been shown to positively affect immune function, hypertension, asthma, autonomic nervous system imbalances, and psychological or stress-related disorders (Jerath et al., 2019. The same authors hypothesized that "slow breathing pranayama breathing techniques activate the parasympathetic nervous system, thus slowing certain physiological processes down that may be functioning too fast or conflicting with the body homeostasis."

Carter and Carter (2016) highlighted that the potential for yogic breathing to optimize human performance and overall well-being is not well known, which was further emphasized by Nestor (2020), but that breathing techniques such as alternate nostril, Sudarshan Kriya, and Bhastrika utilize rhythmic breathing to guide individuals into a deep meditative state of relaxation and promote self-awareness. The same authors suggested that breath-based meditation is easier for beginning practitioners when compared to other forms of meditation (Carter & Carter, 2016), which is related to the "entry level" form of mindfulness focusing on the breath. Recent results from a randomized control trial of four weeks of Bhastrika training (three 30-minute sessions per week) showed not only an effect on anxiety and affect regulation, but also connectivity changes in fMRI supporting these behavioural results (Novaes et al., 2020).

ALTERNATE NOSTRIL BREATHING (NADI SHODHANA)

According to Swift et al. (1988), "nasal breathing (as opposed to mouth breathing), increases circulation, blood oxygen and carbon dioxide levels, slows the breathing rate, and improves overall lung volumes." Stress, physical activity, and injury typically result in an increase in mouth breathing.

Beyond regular nostril breathing, alternate nostril breathing also has its origins in yoga and involves alternatively blocking the right and left nostrils while air is inhaled, or exhaled, through the other. The aim is to improve relative nostril efficiency, which has been shown to improve performance on cognitive tasks associated with the hemisphere contralateral to the dominant nostril (Shannahoff-Khalsa, 1991).

A typical protocol involves an initial exhalation through both nostrils, followed by closing the right nostril with the thumb of the right hand and then inhaling slowly through the left nostril. After complete inhalation, the left nostril is closed with the little and ring fingers of the right hand, followed by a retention period with both nostrils blocked, and then the right nostril is opened to allow exhalation. The participant then inhales through the right nostril, practices retention with both nostrils blocked, followed by exhalation through the left nostril. This cycle is repeated for a given time. Participants are advised to close their eyes and focus their attention on the breath throughout the exercise.

Telles et al. (2007) compared the effects of right, left, and alternate nostril breathing on performance on a letter-cancellation task, which is a left-hemisphere dominant task that measures attentional skill and visuomotor ability. There were fewer errors following 30 minutes of right and alternate nostril yoga breathing, possibly due to enhancement of contralateral hemisphere function.

Pal et al. (2004) compared the effects of three months of slow, alternative nostril breathing versus a fast breathing technique (deep, fast inspiration and expiration for one minute, 8–10 times, with three minutes rest between). Both groups practiced their breathing technique twice per day, for 30 minutes at a time. Extended practice of slow ANB increased parasympathetic activity and decreased sympathetic activity, whereas no significant changes in autonomic functions were observed in the fast breathing group.

Centering

According to Nideffer (1992), centering is "a breathing technique designed to produce physical balance and mental focus." It involves a deep breath (diaphragmatic breathing), an awareness of muscle tension, and a strong exhalation to relax the muscles. Orlick (1990) has suggested that in real situations, the one-breath relaxation technique is the most useful. Centering has a second aspect which is mental focus, whereby attention is refocused on the task at hand, which is similar to mindfulness. Nideffer (1994) states that "it is this process that sets the stage for optimal performance." Although improved performance in the practice environment in sport has been observed following centering, the impact on performance in a real-world, competition, or operational environment has not been studied. In our opinion, this is an example of how a given technique (focused attention using the breath as anchor) is popularized under different names.

Breath awareness

Awareness of breath (or Anapanasati in Buddhism) is a component of most other breathing techniques, so it is hard to determine the effects of breath awareness alone. Telles et al. (2012) randomly assigned 140 Indian Army soldiers to a breath awareness group, a yoga group, or a meditation music group. All groups performed two 45-minute sessions, with a digit-letter substitution task (a measure of cognitive function) and a state anxiety subscale administered immediately before and after. Digit-letter substitution scores increased for all groups but state anxiety only decreased after yoga and listening to meditation music, not breath awareness. Pozuelos et al. (2019) looked at the impact of three weeks of mindful breath awareness training on behavioural and neural indicators of inhibitory control and metacognition. Performance on a Go/No-Go task and concurrent neural activity (via EEG) was assessed before and after training. Compared to a waitlist control group, the training group showed enhanced conflict and response monitoring, suggesting that breath awareness training improves metacognitive processes. The training group also showed improved impulsiveness response. Magnitude of change correlated with accumulated training time, highlighting the importance of ongoing practice. Finally, Levinson et al. (2014)

found that four weeks of breath counting training improved mindfulness (measured via breath counting accuracy pre- and post-training) and decreased mind wandering, compared to working memory training and a no-training control. Again, this can be categorized as a breathing technique or a mindfulness exercise.

Cardiac coherence training or heart rate variability biofeedback

Despite the name, cardiac coherence is actually a breathing technique training, aiming at enhancing heart rate variability. As described in Chapter 9, a slow paced breathing will activate the vagus nerve (the tenth cranial nerve), which also innervates the cardiac pacemaker (the sinus node in the right atrium). As this is mostly used in a biofeedback training setting, this technique will be discussed in the relevant section of Chapter 9 (Biofeedback).

Wim Hof method

The Wim Hof Method is a combination of breathing exercises, cold exposure, mindful meditation, and self-therapy. It is the only method in this enumeration that is representative of a novel phenomenon in therapeutic approaches: the race between pop culture and science.

As perfectly summarized by Lindfors (2021), the "Wim Hof Method" is "an exemplary representation of what scholars have called therapeutic cultures, which, they argue, are increasingly important indices of changing values, political contexts, and contemporary understandings of the self." As an anthropologist, Lindfors described the way participants' non-reactive engagement with the cold teaches swimmers to acknowledge, face, and adapt to their (negative) emotions, and enables them to deal with discomfort or stressful encounters in day-to-day life more generally.

Supporters of this technique cite thousands of enthusiastic practitioners, and a much discussed original article of supporting academic research (Kox et al., 2014), which compared two groups on the reaction after an experimental endotoxemia (an infusion of a low concentration of the bacteria *Escherichia coli*). These authors compared a trained group (following 10 days of training) with an untrained group (hence not possibly ruling out a placebo effect), and the final number of included participants in each group was six. The physiological responses (cardiorespiratory and immune mediators) differed significantly between both groups. The same authors have published follow-up investigations (Zwaag et al., 2022), yet the clinical relevance of the findings remains to be demonstrated.

As with many popular self-help methods stemming from personal experience, the danger of such an approach lies in the lack of nuance and acknowledgement of interindividual vulnerabilities. No doubt thousands of practitioners experience beneficial effects of applying those principles in their daily life. However, the lack of medical screening for those to whom this might represent a medical risk (people with vascular disorders, patients suffering from neurological conditions such as epilepsy or migraine) is a real concern. No researcher in psychophysiology, or no medical professional with a robust knowledge of physiology will doubt that exercises like hyperventilation or cold exposure have profound effects. Yet, in acknowledging these profound effects, the foundational principle of medical ethics, "Primum non nocere" (First, do no harm), comes to mind. Popularizing these techniques in the hands of non-trained practitioners (not affiliated to regulating bodies, with no notions of ethics or deontology) is what does not sit well with the medical community, and why many practitioners are reluctant to implement this method as part of their arsenal.

Relevance for high performers

Although evidence for the effectiveness of breathing techniques to enhance mental performance in real-life situations is limited, evidence from experimental paradigms and scenarios shows promise, particularly with respect to paced diaphragmatic (tactical/combat) breathing and alternate nostril breathing.

Alternate nostril breathing may help reduce anxiety and increase focus in stressful situations (Kamath et al., 2017) but session durations of practical relevance to operational environments have not been studied. Session duration has typically been 15, 30, or 45 minutes, immediately prior to the stress challenge, which is likely impractical for a performer, especially in unpredictable contexts, but reflects that breathing control is a form of conditioning and like all other conditioning, it will suffer extinction if not practiced. The effects on long-term health and well-being, and on self-regulation of arousal, can only be measured after the adoption of breathing techniques as part of one's lifestyle. Tactical/combat breathing on the other hand usually relies more on the acute effect of breathing exercises.

Deep, alternate nostril breathing may also help the retention of newly learned motor skills (Yadav & Mutha, 2016), both immediately and after 24 hours. This finding has implications for any type of skill training where better retention of learned motor skills is desirable (musicians, military, athletes).

Studies looking at the impact of unilateral (single) nostril breathing have similar limitations to alternate nostril techniques (e.g., long session durations, non-military population/tasks), but the impact of left nostril breathing on subsequent spatial task performance (Jella & Shannahoff-khalsa, 1993) and spatial memory (Joshi & Telles, 2008) should be noted, and further exploration of the impact of variations of this technique on domain-specific mental performance is recommended.

Increases in sustained attention and arousal control seen after diaphragmatic breathing in conjunction with biofeedback (Bouchard et al., 2012; Ma et al., 2017) are relevant, but further study is required to which extent training load/duration can be reduced, whilst achieving similar results. Modifications in respiratory patterns come naturally to some individuals after one lesson, but it may take up to six months to replace bad habits and ultimately change the way one breathes (Sovik, 2000). However, Gallego et al. (2001) observed that if a voluntary act is repeated, "learning occurs, and the neurophysiological and cognitive processes underpinning its control may change." The short (two-minute) skewed, diaphragmatic breathing protocol of De Couck et al. (2019) and its impact on subsequent decision-making bodes well in this respect. It should be noted, however, that the effects of diaphragmatic breathing may be moderated by both gender and susceptibility to the effects of anxiety, thus studies in specific operational populations, using operationally valid metrics (specific to one's performance domain), are required.

Conclusion

Breath training is a relatively cheap, accessible, and low-risk tool in the mental performance toolkit. Although further studies are required to establish the performance-specific benefits of breath training protocols to help justify their inclusion in human performance programmes, there is sufficient evidence to suggest that such investigation is warranted. Chapter 9 will build further on the integration of breathing techniques in biofeedback training programs.

This section has highlighted the most effective techniques based on current evidence, and techniques which merit further attention. As real-life performers usually need to fulfil many different tasks (we refer to the experience brief in Chapter 15 for a striking example), and breathing can be used to optimize arousal level, performers should be aware of the relationship between their own arousal level and optimal functioning and use breathing to both increase and decrease arousal level in a bid to enhance performance. Optimal breathing at rest (diaphragmatic, nasal, smooth, deep, even, and quiet) must first be mastered before it can be reliably executed under pressure. Opportunities to incorporate breathing practices into an performer's existing routine of physical training, yoga practice, marksmanship training (for the military) etc., should be explored, to potentially improve efficiency of practice and ultimately increase long-term adherence and efficacy.

Yoga

Scope and purpose of this section

This section presents a concise definition of what we mean when we use the term "yoga", and how this content can be relevant to the performance enhancement in operational populations. As yoga is by definition holistic, despite the focus of the present handbook on mental performance enhancement, we have looked into physiological effects of yoga that could be relevant for mental performance. The available evidence regarding effects in the high-performance population has been reviewed exhaustively, and we will end with practical recommendations for use and implementation, eventually formulating an answer to the question whether yoga is a potentially useful tool to implement for performance enhancement.

What do we call yoga?

Any attempt at a rigorous scientific approach to the study of yoga must first acknowledge the inherent complexities of yoga. The Indian tradition considers yoga as a way of life, encompassing five different types of yoga, which cover all aspects of the human existence and aspirations: Jnâna yoga, or the intellectual discipline, more philosophical in nature; Bhakti yoga, or the devotional love for the divine, more religious in nature; Raja yoga, the search for mental stillness and control, more meditational in nature; Karma yoga, or the selfless service aiming at detaching oneself from the results of one's actions, more altruistic in nature; and finally what most Westerners would call yoga, being Hatha yoga, the yoga of the physical body, using the well-known poses (asana) and breathing techniques (pranayama). In terms of terminology, we will thus focus in this chapter on hatha yoga, knowing that we hereby already adopt a reductionist approach which is contradictory to the discipline of yoga itself. However, regarding implementation in our specific populations, hatha yoga is quite approachable: it uses the physical aspects of breathing and physical exercise, which our population is already familiar with; and it is applicable at an individual level, hence being in control of the person. Yoga is holistic, not only toward the human organisms, but in what contemporary psychology would call a "systemic" way: humans are interconnected in systems, with other human beings, and, in the biggest picture, with the whole universe.

Despite our focus on hatha yoga, it would be foolish to ignore the meditation or mental part of the practice, as this is one of the key elements that defines yoga as a different activity from physical exercise. Considering the fact we devote a separate section to mindfulness, which is in essence the westernized version of meditation, we will not describe its benefits or implementation here. However, in the classical teachings, the practice of hatha yoga is seen as the path to meditation. In summary: controlling the body to control the mind.

How yoga differs from physical exercise

From an almost philosophical point of view, there is a fundamental difference in the scientific approach of the Western society to physical activity and the holistic approach of yoga. The Western rational materialistic tradition is by nature reductionist, focusing only on the physical activity of the body in terms of biomechanics of movement and biochemistry of energy consumption. The holistic spiritual approach of yoga encompasses the physical, mental, emotional, and spiritual well-being of the human organism. As summarized by Broad (2012): "A complicating factor [to the application of the instruments and techniques of the academic sports establishment to the study of yoga's fitness claims] is that yoga, taken as a singular [physical] activity, represents an oversimplification rooted in the discipline's timeless image" (p. 49).

An example of the hardcore dualism of Western science is the delay in the acknowledgements of the contribution of mental states to physical performance, which is currently a booming area of research in exercise physiology (for an overview of the overlap and difference of the concept of fatigue in exercise science and psychology, see Pattyn, Van Cutsem, Dessy, & Mairesse, 2018).

Physiologically, exercise will always trigger a sympathetic stimulation, of varying magnitude depending on its intensity. Yoga on the other hand, as demonstrated by one of the most upheaving studies in the field (Chaya, Kurpad, Nagendra, & Nagarathna, 2006), lowers the metabolic rate, something that most contemporary styles, which adopt more dynamic practices, may have lost.

Physiology: Western and yogic concepts, and how they relate

The main conceptual difference between yoga and physical activity, even when looking only at the physical part, is the conscious use of breathing as an integral part of the practice in yoga. And this use of breathing is linked to the metabolic effects. Indeed, as we discussed in the previous section, breathing is considered the "gateway to the autonomous nervous system" (Pattyn, 2009), and hence the main avenue of intervention in all self-regulation techniques, from autogenous training in relaxation, to attentional focus (on breathing) in meditation and in yoga (for a review, see Zaccaro, Piarulli, Laurino, Garbella, Menicucci, Neri & Gemignani, 2018). In hatha yoga, pranayama is the use of breath to control bodily states.

The key physiological overlap that allows for a better understanding of the effects of yoga is between ancient yogic texts and Western science on the description of the autonomic nervous system. Without going too deep in this description and comparison, we can summarize that what Vedic texts (the ancient traditional Sanskrit texts covering the historical roots of yoga) called the nadis (being energetic channels in the body) are anatomically and functionally coherent with the medulla oblongata (which is a part of the most "basic" machinery of the brain, located between the spine and the rest of the central nervous system, and responsible for the control of autonomic vital functions), the sympathetic and the parasympathetic nervous system (for a detailed overview of these neurophysiological concepts, we refer to Chapter 2). And it is exactly the balance between sympathetic and parasympathetic nervous system that is targeted by yoga, and which underlies most of the beneficial effects identified through Western scientific research (for a summary, see Goyal and Thakur, 2018).

Furthermore, as we described in Chapter 2, this balance between sympathetic and parasympathetic activity plays a key role in contemporary models of stress and performance.

The paramount importance of breathing

Pranayama, as extensively described in the previous section, is the name of the practice of breath regulation, both on its own or during asanas (yogic poses). It covers much more than the simplified derived breathing exercises that are applied in most relaxation techniques, which are basically slow-paced breathing at a rhythm of approximately six cycles per minute (for a more detailed description of this slow-paced breathing effects, we refer to Chapter 9). Pranayama encompasses exercises varying all components of the breathing cycle: inhalation, exhalation, retention after inhalation, retention after exhalation; as well as rhythmic variations ranging from extreme slowing to extreme acceleration of the breathing frequency. As we already emphasized, breathing is currently the only way to consistently influence our physiological autonomic functions on a voluntary basis. Whereas Western scientists investigating the effects of breathing have focused on the slow-paced breathing at 0.1 Hz (which is known to induce the so-called "Mayer wave" in the heart rate variability power spectrum), Indian scientists have investigated a much wider range of pranayama exercises (for a review, see Saoji, Raghavendra & Manjunath, 2019). The slow-paced breathing induces a shift in the autonomic balance towards a more important parasympathetic activation (e.g., Lehrer, 2007), which is basically a way to relax, or to support mindfulness. This is a notion that we discuss in several other sections of this handbook: mindfulness, relaxation, breathing techniques, and biofeedback. On the other hand, the full range of pranayama exercises offers a toolbox to achieve either a physiological activation or deactivation, depending on the needs and aims of the practitioner. Regarding effects on performance, this offers a much more diverse intervention leverage than solely a "slowing-down" response.

Evidence base for physical and mental performance improvement

Physical effects relevant to mental performance

With regard to the physiological models of stress and performance (which we described in Chapter 2), the effect of yoga on autonomic flexibility is expected to impact the ability of individuals to self-regulate, and thus to adapt to varying performance demands. Several authors, among which are Saoji et al. (2019), Goyal and Thakur (2018), and Tyagi, Cohen, Reece, Telles, and Jones (2016), have summarized the effects of yoga practice on autonomic function as basically improving homeostasis. Considering the results of Tyagi et al. (2016), which showed a higher baseline vagal tone, as well as a higher autonomic reactivity to a mental workload in regular yoga practitioners, one can expect the practice of yoga to have a beneficial effect on cognitive performance, considering the numerous links in psychophysiological research between autonomic flexibility and emotion regulation on the one hand (e.g., Thayer, Ahs, Fredrikson, Sollers, & Wager, 2012) or between autonomic flexibility and cognitive performance (e.g., Pattyn et al., 2014 on the other hand. However, the one study linking yoga practice to autonomic flexibility and to cognitive performance is still missing.

Apart from autonomic nervous system physiology, yoga practice has also been demonstrated to influence central nervous system functioning. A seminal investigation by Streeter et al. (2007) showed asana practice increased GABA levels in the brain, as measured by MR spectroscopy. Streeter et al. (2010) confirmed the results, and provided additional information: these GABA increases were specific to asana practice, since a control group performing intensity-matched walking failed to exhibit them. Furthermore, the GABA increases were associated with improved mood and decreased anxiety. Considering the fact that GABA is a neurotransmitter serving an inhibitory function and playing a role in the control of anxiety, and that elevated GABA is associated with greater self-control and self-regulatory functioning, the potential to influence the levels of this neurotransmitter is of great importance. Another element pointing towards a direct link between GABA activity and yoga practice is that these GABA increases showed a dose-response relationship with the frequency of the practice and the experience of the practitioner. In other words: these investigations showed the benefit of asana practices in both physiological and mood domains, and the increase of these benefits with a sustained practice. Apart from neurotransmitter studies, several investigations using functional MRI (fMRI) or electroencephalography (EEG) reported the effects of an integrative yoga practice on the central nervous system. The review from Desai, Tailor, and Bhatt (2015) clearly shows effects on cortical and subcortical structures, along with EEG changes. The most solidly confirmed EEG change was an increase in alpha wave activity. Moreover, depending on the experimental paradigms, findings also revealed a diminished activation of the amygdala, a smaller amygdala volume, an increase in frontal lobe activity, a decreased activation due to negative stimulus content, and a higher white matter connectivity in the insula in yoga practitioners. This review thus confirms the effect of yoga on the central nervous system, be it in terms of local activation or morphology.

The area that has probably been the most widely researched when it comes to yoga, is the effects on overall fitness and health. In 1998, the US National Institute of Health initiated a funding campaign on yoga research. This funding surge is reflected in the build-up of publications from the last decade looking into potential therapeutic or preventive effects of yoga practice. These cover the major health care challenges of our Western society: cardiovascular diseases, metabolic diseases, and mental health. However, we will not address clinical populations in this handbook. Despite the practice of yoga inducing a hypometabolic state, a regular practice of asanas, pranayama, and meditation showed a marked significant effect on overall physical fitness, with a reduction in weight and BMI and an increase in VO2max (Udhan, Wankhede & Phatale, 2018). This investigation was conducted rigorously in a sample of 200 healthy individuals being followed up for six months, making it the most significant study to date with regard to health effect in a non-clinical population.

Specific effects of pranayama

The overview of available evidence on the effects of pranayama (in the previous section) does not allow to establish a causal relationship between the physiological changes yielded by the practice and the cognitive performance effects, yet one is tempted to jump to the conclusion that the modulation of breathing allows for a modulation of arousal, with performance effects that relate to this shift in arousal. For example, the increase in reaction speed after the exercise of Bhastrika (Bhavani et al., 2003 & 2012), which induces a controlled hyperventilation, and thus a shift towards sympathetic activation; or Pradhan (2013), showing an increase in error rate after Kapalabhati practice (another exercise involving controlled hyperventilation). This clearly suggests an increase in arousal and thus a modified speed-accuracy trade-off in performance (see Chapter 2 for a more detailed account on the relationship between autonomic arousal and performance). Apart from Telles et al. (2013), no investigation attempted to link the physiological effects with the cognitive effects, which would allow to confirm or disconfirm the causal or modulating relationship between both.

Cognitive performance effects

Most performance studies investigating the effects of yoga either focus on physical performance, or on a clinical population (elderly people with cognitive impairments, psychiatric populations, or chronic disease patients). Three studies investigated specific cognitive effects in healthy adult populations: Telles et al. (2012) Gothe et al. (2013), and Bowden et al. (2012). However, these differ in whether they measured acute effects (i.e., right after a yoga session) or chronic effects (i.e., after an intervention period of regular yoga practice).

As reviewed by Gothe and MacAuley (2015), this distinction between acute and chronic effect is an important one. Indeed, if we aim to identify long-lasting benefits from an intervention regarding mental performance, the effects of a regular practice seem the most appropriate (as we already mentioned in the previous sections regarding mindfulness and relaxation). On the other hand, if we aim to add to a performer's toolbox for managing critical situations here and now, acute effects are definitely important. Acute studies showed a stronger overall effect of yoga on cognition ($g = 0.56$, standard error = 0.11, 95% confidence interval = 0.33-0.78, $p < .001$). The effect was strongest for memory ($g = 0.78$, $p < .001$), followed by attention and processing speed measures ($g = 0.49$, $p < .001$) and executive functions ($g = 0.39$, $p < .003$).

Bowden et al. (2012) found no significant improvements in working memory under the n-back task after five weeks of intervention. Researchers discuss that these insignificant findings may have been due to a small sample size via a high attrition rate. A within subject study conducted by Gothe et al. (2013) yielded significant improvements in working memory using the n-back task and inhibitory control using the flanker task immediately after Hatha yoga as compared with the aerobic exercise and baseline control sessions in an undergraduate female sample. Telles et al. (2012) performed a randomized controlled trial in a large participants cohort (N = 140) and revealed significant improvements in working memory and selective attention using the Digit Letter Substitution task after an acute bout of Hatha yoga.

Evidence in military populations

All evidence available on military populations comes from investigations carried out in the Indian army. Three cohort studies of more than 100 participants each looked at cognitive performance, physical acclimation to altitude, vigilance, sleep, and anxiety (Himashree, Mohan, & Singh, 2016; Telles, Bhardwaj, Kumar, Kumar, & Balkrishna, 2012; Telles, Kala, Gupta, Verma, Vishwakarma, Agnihotri, Gandharva, & Balkrishna, 2019). Control groups either performed relaxing tasks or physical training. There were no significant effects on cognitive performance: the improvement was present in the control group as well, and the control intervention was listening to meditation music. However, the intervention in this study lasted only for nine days (Telles et al., 2012). Himashree et al. (2016) showed striking results to altitude acclimatization after 60 days of intervention, which consisted of a comprehensive package of asana practice, pranayama practice, and meditation. The participants in the yoga group exhibited significantly improved pulmonary function (FVC & FEV), physical fitness (VO2max), metabolic profile (fasting sugar, blood urea, cholesterol, and triglycerides) and quality of life indices (risk factor for coronary heart disease and anxiety score). Regarding the quality of sleep and daytime functioning, Telles et al. (2019) showed an increased daytime vigilance paired with a decreased anxiety and more daytime napping in the yoga group.

These interesting results must not obfuscate the fact that the adhesion of participants to an intervention is paramount to its effect (Dessy et al., 2020). This means that an Indian cohort in a military population might not be readily comparable with a Western cohort.

Evidence in other applied settings

Most recent investigations regarding yoga in athletes combine some sort of mindfulness or meditation training to the intervention, and do not measure performance variables as such, but rather the level of "flow" state or the perceived stress and anxiety of the participants. Goddard et al. (2021) reviewed the literature on "flow" intervention in athletes, and the current focus of applied research seems to move away from the reductionistic investigation of a single intervention, to a "package" evaluation, probably serving the applied community better in its adaptability to individual preferences, yet impeding progress in the mechanistic understanding of action mechanisms. Sierra-Palmeiro et al. (2023) showed that a five-month intervention of weekly hatha yoga (with sessions covering meditation, asanas and pranayama) in rhythmic gymnasts improved psychological variables such as self-regulation and team cohesion, but also their competition ratings on all relevant aspects (difficulty, technicality, execution, and overall score). Unfortunately, this investigation did not report any kind of control measures, thereby making it impossible to rule out a placebo effect.

In musicians, either professionals or advanced students, the current trend in applied research mirrors the "package" investigations studying a combination of diverse interventions, usually combining mindfulness and yoga (e.g., Bartos et al., 2022). However, as emphasized by Adams (2012), yoga can help to address both performance anxiety and musculoskeletal issues in this population. The fact that most published research reports effects on performance anxiety, is probably more related to the turnover time of scientific activities than to a lack of effect in the musculoskeletal domain, where prevention interventions need to be investigated over several years to actually show significant effects.

Implementation recommendations

Regarding the question whether yoga is a potentially useful tool to implement for performance enhancement in operational environments, the answer would be yes, considering the non-existent hardware investment costs, the "portability" of the technique for a population that travels often and spends a lot of time away from its home base, and the "collateral benefits" in terms of health and well-being. If the World Health Organization promotes the wide diffusion of yoga as a tool for preventive medicine and well-being enhancement, it means the evidence base is robust enough (WHO). Two caveats remain: the first one is the quality of the practice, the second one is the possible resistance to change in the target population.

The quality of the practice highly depends on the proficiency, knowledge, and experience of the teacher. Unlike physical activity, there are no international standards to certification of yoga teachers. There are several international bodies attempting to unify standards of practice. For example, the US-based "Yoga Alliance" created the RYT 200 and RYT 500, respectively, for teachers having followed a 200-hours and 500-hours certifying training in one of the programs recognized by the Alliance. Furthermore, if taught or practiced improperly, yoga can actually cause physical damage, especially in a competitive population that might focus on the athletic aspects of asanas, and hereby injure themselves.

The stereotypes held about yoga practice make it difficult to reconcile with the organizational culture of high-performance environments. Nevertheless, the integrative body/mind approach is similar to the one from eastern-rooted martial arts, and high performers might be the most adaptive audience to something akin to a paradigm change in the rigid, traditional, overly materialistic (in the philosophical sense of the term) male culture, especially regarding a practice that is linked to the attainment of a performance edge.

The physiological aspects of the practice will often be the most accessible stepping stones. Physical exercise and its benefits are highly regarded in athletic and military populations, and a brief introduction to the self-regulatory advantages of breathing can produce sufficient adhesion to get started with pranayama practice, especially if the full spectrum of the offered self-regulation is emphasized: not only the meditative, calming aspects, but also the focusing energizing aspects.

Summary and conclusion

The major advantage of restorative techniques in a performance-enhancing approach is to allow for a better self-regulation, directly linking in to ideal performance states (as described more extensively in Chapter 3). Despite a possible low initial attractiveness in a population that may be more "tech-hungry", the evidence base for these approaches, combined with their low implementation cost, and independence from any kind of infrastructure make them extremely interesting choices. Considering their holistic nature, it is difficult to design the "gold standard" of therapeutic effect studies, namely randomized double-blind clinical trial like investigations.

The crucial element in the success of their implementation is the trained professional who will deliver the training. Credibility and deontology are key factors in the choice of the right person.

References

Adams, A.D. (2012). *Yoga and Saxophone Performance: The Integration of Two Disciplines*. Arizona State University, Department of Music, Doctoral dissertation.

Bach, P. A., & Moran, D. J. (2008). *ACT in practice: Case conceptualization in acceptance and commitment therapy*. ProQuest Ebook Central.

Baltzell, A., & Summers, J. (2017). The Power of Mindfulness Meditation Training in Sport (MMTS) (1st ed. 2017). Springer International Publishing. https://doi.org/10.1007/978-3-319-70410-4

Barraca. (2012). Mental control» from a third-wave behavior therapy perspective. *International Journal of Clinical and Health Psychology,* 12(1), 109–121.

Bartos, L. J., Funes, M. J., Ouellet, M. et al. (2022). A feasibility study of a program integrating mindfulness, yoga, positive psychology, and emotional intelligence in tertiary-level student musicians. *Mindfulness*, 13, 2507–2528. https://doi-org.myezproxy.vub.ac.be/10.1007/s12671-022-01976-7

Bates, M. J., Bowles, S., Hammermeister, J., Stokes, C., Pinder, E., Moore, M., ... Burbelo, G. (2010). Psychological Fitness. *Military Medicine,* 175(8), 21.

Benson, H., & Klipper, M. Z. (2000). *The relaxation response.* New York: HarperCollins Publishers. (Original work published 1975).

Bernstein, A., Hadash, Y., & Fresco, D. (2019). Metacognitive processes model of decentering: Emerging methods and insights. *Opinion in Psychology,* 28, 245–251.

Bernstein, D. A., Borkovec, T. D., & Hazlett-Stevens, H. (2000). *New directions in progressive relaxation training: A guidebook for helping professionals*. Westport: Praeger Publishers.

Bhavanani, A. B., Madanmohan, Udupa K. (2003). Acute effect of Mukh bhastrika (a yogic bellows type breathing) on reaction time. *Indian Journal of Physiology and Pharmacology*, Jul;47(3), 297–300. PMID: 14723315

Bhavanani, A. B., & Ramanathan, M, Kt H. (2012). Immediate effect of mukha bhastrika (a bellows type pranayama) on reaction time in mentally challenged adolescents. *Indian Journal of Physiology and Pharmacology*, Apr-Jun;56(2), 174–80. PMID: 23387247

Bijlsma, T., Muis, S., & Tilborg, A. (2018). Mindfulness in Dutch military – train your brain. In A. Rocha & T. Guarda (Eds.). *Developments and Advances in Defense and Security*, Vol 94, 183–192: Springer International Publishing. Switzerland.

Boiten, F.A., Frijda, N.H., Wientjes, C.J. (1994). Emotions and respiratory patterns: review and critical analysis. *Int J Psychophysiol*. Jul;17(2):103–28. doi: 10.1016/0167-8760(94)90027-2. PMID: 7995774.

Bondár, R. Z., Bertollo, M., di Fronso, S., & Robazza, C. (2021). *Mindfulness to performance enhancement: A systematic review of neural correlates, International Review of Sport and Exercise Psychology.* DOI: 10.1080/1750984X.2021.1949742

Bonnar, D., Bartel, K., Kakoschke, N., & Lang, C. (2018). Sleep interventions designed to improve athletic performance and recovery: A systematic review of current approaches. *Sports Medicine,* 48, 683- 703. https://doi.org/10.1007/s40279-017-0832-x

Bouchard, S., Bernier, F., Boivin, E., Morin, B., & Robillard, G. (2012). Using biofeedback while immersed in a stressful videogame increases the effectiveness of stress management skills in soldiers. *PLoS One*, 7(4), e36169. doi: 10.1371/journal.pone.0036169. Epub 2012 Apr 27

Bowden D., Gaudry C., An S. C., Gruzelier J. (2012). A comparative randomised controlled trial of the effects of brain wave vibration training, iyengar yoga, and mindfulness on mood, well-being, and salivary cortisol. *Evid Based Complementary and Alternative Medicine*, 2012, 234713. doi: 10.1155/2012/234713. Epub 2011 Dec 15. PMID: 22216054; PMCID: PMC3246835

Broad, W. J. (2012). *The science of yoga*. New York: Simon & Schuster.

Brunye T.T., Mahoney C.R., Giles G.E., Rapp D.N., Taylor H.A., Kanarek R.B. (2013). Learning to relax: Evaluating four brief interventions for overcoming the negative emotions accompanying math anxiety. *Learning and Individual Differences*, 27, 1–7.

Bühlmayer, L., Birrer, D., Röthlin., P., Faude, O., & Donath, L. (2017). Effects of mindfulness practice on performance-relevant parameters and performance outcomes in sports: A meta-analytical review. *Sports Medicine,* 47, 2309–2321. doi:10.1007/s40279-017-0752-9

Busch, V., Magerl, W., Kern, U., Haas, J., Hajak, G., & Eichhammer, P. (2012). The effect of deep and slow breathing on pain perception, autonomic activity, and mood processing–an experimental study. *Pain Medications*, *Feb*;13(2), 215–28. doi: 10.1111/j.1526-4637.2011.01243.x. Epub 2011 Sep 21. PMID: 21939499

Cappo B.M. & Holmes D.S. (1984). The utility of prolonged respiratory expiration for reducing physiological and psychological arousal in non-threatening and threatening situations. J. Psychosom. Rcs. 28(4):265–73 DOI: 10.1016/0022-3999(84)90048-5

Carter, A., & Mortlock, J. (2019). *Mindfulness in the military: Improving mental fitness in the UK Armed Forces using next generation team mindfulness training*. Institute for Employment Studies. www.employment-studies.co.uk/system/files/resources/files/IES_MoD_mindfulness_report- 525.pdf

Carter, K. S., & Carter, R. (2016). Breath-based meditation: A mechanism to restore the physiological and cognitive reserves for optimal human performance. *World Journal of Clinical Cases*, 4, 99–102.

Cásedas, L., Pirruccio, V., Vadillo, M. A. et al. (2020). Does mindfulness meditation training enhance executive control? A systematic review and meta-analysis of randomized controlled trials in adults. *Mindfulness*, 11, 411–424. https://doi-org.myezproxy.vub.ac.be/10.1007/s12671-019-01279-4

Chaya, M. S, Kurpad, A. V., Nagendra, H. R., & Nagarathna, R. (2006). The effect of long term combined yoga practice on the basal metabolic rate of healthy adults. *BMC Complement and Alternative Medicine*, Aug 31;6, 28. doi: 10.1186/1472- 6882-6-28. PMID: 16945127; PMCID: PMC1564415

Chiesa, A., Calati, R., & Serretti, A. (2011). Does mindfulness training improve cognitive abilities? A systematic review of neuropsychological findings. *Clinical Psychology Review*, 31(3), 449–464. https://doi.org/10.1016/j.cpr.2010.11.003.

Chu, L. C. (2010). The benefits of meditation vis-à-vis emotional intelligence, perceived stress and negative mental health. *Stress & Health: Journal of the International Society for the Investigation of Stress*, 26(2), 169–180. https://doi-org.ezproxy.vccs.edu:2443/10.1002/smi.1289.

Chung, W., Poppen, R., & Lundervold, D. A. (1995). Behavioral relaxation training for tremor disorders in older adults. *Biofeedback and Self-Regulation*, 20(2). doi:10.1007/BF01720969

Coffey, K., Hartmann, M., & Fredrickson, B. L. (2010). Deconstructing mindfulness and constructing mental health: Understanding mindfulness and its mechanisms of action. *Mindfulness,* 1, 235–253.

Crowther, F., Sealey, R., Crowe, M., Edwards, A., & Halson, S. (2017). Team sports athletes' perceptions and use of recovery strategies: A mixed-methods survey study. *BMC Sports Science, Medicine and Rehabilitation*, 9(6). doi:10.1186/s13102-017-0071-3

De Couck, M., Caers, R., Musch, L., Fliegauf, J., Giangreco, A., & Gidron, Y. (2019). How breathing can help you make better decisions: Two studies on the effects of breathing patterns on heart rate variability and decision-making in business cases. *International Journal of Psychosocial,* 139, 1–9.

Debellemaniere, E., Gomez-Merino, D., Erblang, M., Dorey, R., Genot, M., Perreaut-Pierre, … & Chennaoui, M. (2018). Using relaxation techniques to improve sleep during naps. *Industrial Health,* 56, 220–227. doi:10.2486/indhealth.2017-0092

Delizonna, L., Williams, R., & Langer, E. (2009). The effect of mindfulness on heart rate control. *Journal of Adult Development*, 16(2), 61–5. DOI: 10.1007/s10804-009-9050-6

Dendato, K. M., & Diener, D. (1986). Effectiveness of cognitive/relaxation therapy and study-skills training in reducing self-reported anxiety and improving the academic performance of test-anxious students. *Journal of Counseling Psychology*, 33(2), 131–135. https://doi.org/10.1037/0022- 0167.33.2.131

Desai, R, Tailor, A, & Bhatt, T. (2015). Effects of yoga on brain waves and structural activation: A review. *Complementary Therapies in Clinical Practice*. May;21(2), 112–8. doi: 10.1016/j.ctcp.2015.02.002. Epub 2015 Mar 9. PMID: 25824030

Dessy, E., Mairesse, O., van Puyvelde, M., Cortoos, A., Neyt, X., & Pattyn, N. (2020). Train Your Brain? Can we really selectively train specific EEG frequencies with neurofeedback training. *Frontiers Human Neuroscience*. Mar 10;14, 22. doi: 10.3389/fnhum.2020.00022. PMID: 32210777; PMCID: PMC7077336

DeWiggins, S., Hite, B., & Alston, V. (2010). Personal performance plan: Application of mental skills training to real-world military tasks. *Journal of Applied Sport Psychology*, 22(4), 458–473. https://doi.org/10.1080/10413200.2010.500606

Di Nicola, M., Occhiolini, L., Di Nicola L., Vellante, P., Di Mascio, R., Guizzardi, M., … Ballone, E. (2007). Stress management and factors related to the deployment of Italian peacekeepers in Afghanistan. *Military Medicine,* 172(2), 140. doi:10.7205/milmed.172.2.140

Fitzwater, J. P. J., Arthur, C. A., & Hardy, L. (2018). "The tough get tougher": mental skills training with elite military recruits. *Sport, Exercise, and Performance Psychology*, 7(1), 93–107. https://doi.org/10.1037/spy0000101

Franca, R., & Milbourn, B. (2015). A meta-analysis of Mindfulness Based Interventions (MBIs) show that MBIs are effective in reducing acute symptoms of depression but not anxiety. *Australian Occupational Therapy Journal,* 62(2), 147–148.

Gallego, J., Nsegbe, E., Durand, E. (2001). Learning in respiratory control. *Behav Modif.* Sep;25(4):495-512. doi: 10.1177/0145445501254002. PMID: 11530713.

Gardner, F., & Moore, Z. (2004). A mindfulness-acceptance-commitment-based approach to athletic performance enhancement: Theoretical considerations. *Behavioral Therapy*, 35(4), 707–23.

Gardner, F., & Moore, Z. (2007). *The psychology of enhancing human performance: The mindfulness-acceptance-commitment approach.* Springer Publishing Company: New York: NY.

Gill S., Kolt G.S., Keating J. (2004). Examining the multi-process theory: an investigation of the effects of two relaxation techniques on state anxiety. Journal of Bodywork and Movement Therapies, 8, 288–296. doi:10.1016/j.jbmt.2003.11.002

Gonzales, A., Vranceanu, A-M., Mahaffey, B., Laroche, K., & Park, E. R. (2016). Mental and physical health outcomes following the Relaxation Response Resiliency Program (3RP) in a clinical practice setting. *European Journal of Integrative Medicine*, 8(5), 756–761. https://dx.doi.org/10.1016/j.eujim.2016.05.002

Gothe, N., Pontifex, M. B., Hillman, C., & McAuley, E. (2013). The acute effects of yoga on executive function. *Journal of Physical Activity and Health*, May;10(4), 488–95. doi: 10.1123/jpah.10.4.488. Epub 2012 Jul 9. PMID: 22820158

Gothe, N. P., & McAuley, E. (2015). Yoga and Cognition: A meta-analysis of chronic and acute effects. *Psychosomatic Medicine*, Sep;77(7), 784–97. doi: 10.1097/PSY.0000000000000218. PMID: 26186435

Goyal, R. K., & Thakur, A. K. (2018). A status report on autonomic nervous system: The Indian research scenario during the last five years. *Proc Indian Natn Sci Acad 84 No.* 1 March 2018 pp. 3–14. DOI: 10.16943/ptinsa/2018/49305

Grossman, D., & Christensen, L. W. (2008). *On combat. The psychology and physiology of deadly conflict in war and in peace (3rd ed.)* Warrior Science Publications.

Grossman, P. (1983). Respiration, stress, and cardiovascular function. *Psychophysiology*, May;20(3):284–300. doi: 10.1111/j.1469-8986.1983.tb02156.x. PMID: 6408680.

Grossman, P., & Taylor, E. W. (2007). Toward understanding respiratory sinus arrhythmia: relations to cardiac vagal tone, evolution and biobehavioral functions. *Biol Psychol.* Feb;74(2):263–285. doi: 10.1016/j.biopsycho.2005.11.014. Epub 2006 Nov 1. PMID: 17081672.

Gu, Hou, J.-C., & Fang, X.-M. (2018). Mindfulness meditation for primary headache pain: A meta- analysis. *Chinese Medical Journal,* 131(7), 829–838. https://doi.org/10.4103/0366-6999.228242.

Hagan, J. E., & Schack, T. (2017). The influence of indigenous culture on sport psychology practice: Challenges and prospects. *Psychology and Behavioral Science International Journal.* 2017; 7(4), 555719. DOI: 10.19080/PBSIJ.2017.07.555719

Hayes, S., Follette, V., & Linehan, M. (2004). *Mindfulness and Acceptance: expanding the cognitive- behavioral tradition.* Guilford Press.

Henriksen K., Hansen J., & Larsen C.H. (Eds). *Mindfulness and Acceptance in Sport*. Routledge, Milton Park, UK

Himashree, G., Mohan, L., & Singh, Y. (2016). Yoga practice improves physiological and biochemical status at high altitudes: A Prospective case-control study. *Alternative Therapies in Health and Medicine*, Sep;22(5), 53–9. PMID: 27622961

Hohmann, M., & Orlick, T. (2014). Examining the psychological skills used by elite Canadian military pilots. *Journal of Excellence*, 16.

Holiday, R. (2014). *The obstacle is the way: The timeless art of turning trials into triumph.* New York: Portfolio/Penguin.

Hourani, L. L., Kizakevich, P. N., Hubal, R., Spira, J., Strange, L. B., Holiday, D. B., … McLean, A. N. (2011). Predeployment stress inoculation training for primary prevention of combat-related stress disorders. *Journal of Cyber Therapy & Rehabilitation*, 4(1).

Howell, A., & Buro, K. (2010). Relations among mindfulness, achievement-related self-regulation, and achievement emotions. *Journal of Happiness Studies*, 12(6), 1007–1022. https://doi.org/10.1007/s10902-010-9241-7.

Ilham, D. (2021). The effect of visualization, relaxation, and self-efficacy on the performance of men speed world record athletes category. *International Journal of Human Movement and Sports Sciences*, 9(1), 48–55.

Jacobson, E. (1987). Progressive relaxation. *The American Journal of Psychology*, 100(3-4), 522–537. https://doi.org/10.2307/1422693

Jella, S. A., & Shannahoff-khalsa, D. S. (1993). The effects of unilateral forced nostril breathing on cognitive performance. *International Journal of Neuroscience*, 73(1-2), 61–68.

Jerath, R., Beveridge, C., & Barnes, V. A. (2019). Self-regulation of breathing as an adjunctive treatment of insomnia. *Front Psychiatry*, Jan 29;9:780. doi: 10.3389/fpsyt.2018.00780. eCollection 2018

Jha, A., Morrison, A., Parker, S., & Stanley, E. (2016). Practice is protective: Mindfulness training promotes cognitive resilience in high-stress cohorts. *Mindfulness*, 7(1), 1–13. doi: 10.1007/s12671-015- 0465-9

Jha, A., Rogers, S. L., & Morrison, A. (2014). Mindfulness training in high stress professions: Strengthening attention and resilience. In R. Baer (Ed.), *Mindfulness-based treatment approaches: clinician's guide to evidence base and applications*, pp. 347–366. Academic Press. https://doi.org/10.1016/B978-0-12-416 031-6.00015-3

Jha, A., Rogers, S. L., Schoomaker, E., & Cardon, E. (2019a). Deploying mindfulness to gain cognitive advantage: Considerations for military effectiveness and well-being. *NATO Science and Technology Conference Proceedings*, pp. 1–14.

Jha, A., Zanesco, P., Witkin, J., Rooks, J., & Rogers, S. (2019b). Does mindfulness training help working memory 'work' better? *Current Opinion in Psychology*, 28, 273–278.

Jha, A. P., Morrison, A. B., Dainer-Best, J., Parker, S., Rostrup, N., & Stanley, E. A. (2015). Minds "at attention": Mindfulness training curbs attentional lapses in military cohorts. *PloS one*, 10(2), e0116889.

Jha, A. P., Stanley, E. A., Kiyonaga, A., Wong, L., & Gelfand, L. (2010). Examining the protective effects of mindfulness training on working memory capacity and affective experience. *Emotion*, 10(1), 54–64. https://doi.org/10.1037/a0018438

John, S., Verma, S., & Khanna, G. (2011). The effect of mindfulness meditation on HPA-axis in pre- competition stress in sports performance of elite shooters. *National Journal of Integrated Research Medicine*, 2, 15–21.

Johnson, D. C., Thom, N. J., Stanley, E. A., Haase, L., Simmons, A. N., Shih, P. A., Thompson, W. K., Potterat, E. G., Minor, T. R., & Paulus, M. P. (2014). Modifying resilience mechanisms in at-risk individuals: A controlled study of mindfulness training in marines preparing for deployment. *American Journal of Psychiatry*, 171(8), 844–853. https://doi.org/10.1176/appi.ajp.2014.13040502.

Joshi, A. V. (2019, February). *Warrior pose: Building readiness through resilience — yoga, and meditation*. [Occasional Paper]. JSOU Press.

Joshi, M., & Telles, S. (2008). Immediate effects of right and left nostril breathing on verbal and spatial scores. *Indian Journal of Physiology and Pharmacology*, 52, 197–200.

Kabat-Zinn. (2003). Mindfulness-based interventions in context: Past, present, and future. *Clinical Psychology (New York, N.Y.)*, 10(2), 144–156. https://doi.org/10.1093/clipsy/bpg016

Kabat-Zinn, Jon. (2017). Defining Mindfulness. Mindful.org, 11 Jan 2017. Retrieved on 30 Sep 2019. www.mindful.org/jon-kabat-zinn-defining-mindfulness/

Kahl, K., Winter, L., & Schweiger, U. (2012). The third wave of cognitive behavioural therapies: What is new and what is effective? *Current Opinion in Psychiatry*, 25(6), 522–528. https://doi.org/10.1097/YCO.0b013 e328358e531

Kamath, A., Urval, R. P., & Shenoy, A. K. (2017). Effect of alternate nostril breathing exercise on experimentally induced anxiety in healthy volunteers using the simulated public speaking model: A Randomized Controlled Pilot Study. *Biomed Research International*, 2017, 2450670. doi: 10.1155/2017/2450670. Epub 2017 Oct 11

Kaufmann, K., Glass, C., & Arnkoff, D. (2009). Evaluation of mindful sport performance enhancement (MSPE): A new approach to promote flow in athletes. *Journal of Clinical Sport Psychology*, 25(4), 334- 356.

Kellman, M., Bertollo, M., Bosquet, L., Brink, M., Coutts, A. J., Duffield, R., ... Beckmann, J. (2018). Recovery and performance in sport: Consensus statement. *International Journal of Sports Physiology and Performance*, 13, 240–245. https://doi.org/10.1123/ijspp.2017-0759

Kellman, M., Pelka, M., & Beckmann, J. (2017). Psychological relaxation techniques to enhance recovery in sport. In M. Kellman & J. Beckman. (Eds.), *Sport, recovery and performance*, interdisciplinary insights. London: Routledge.

Kenney W.L., Wilmore J.H. & Costill D.L. (Eds). *Physiology of Sport and Exercise*, 6th Edition. Human Kinetics, Champagne, IL, USA.

Kenttä, G., & Hassmén, P. (1998). Overtraining and recovery. A conceptual model. *Sports Medicine*, 26(1), 1–16. doi:10.2165/00007256-199826010-00001

Khng, K. H. (2017). A better state-of-mind: Deep breathing reduces state anxiety and enhances test performance through regulating test cognitions in children. *Cognition and Emotion*, 31, 1502–1510.

Kilpatrick, L., Suyenobu, B. Y., Smith, S. R., Bueller, J. A., Goodman, T., Creswell, J. D., Tillisch, K., Mayer, E. A., & Naliboff, B. D. (2011). Impact of mindfulness-based stress reduction training on intrinsic brain connectivity. *NeuroImage (Orlando, Fla.)*, 56(1),290–298. https://doi.org/10.1016/j.neuroimage.2011.02.034

Kim, J., &Tennant, K. (1993). Effects of visualization and Danjeon breathing on target shooting with an air pistol. *Perceptual and Motor Skills,* 77, 1083–1087.

Kox, M., van Eijk, L. T., Zwaag, J., van den Wildenberg, J., Sweep, F. C, van der Hoeven, J. G., & Pickkers, P. (2014). Voluntary activation of the sympathetic nervous system and attenuation of the innate immune response in humans. *Proc Natl Acad Sci U S A.*, May 20;111(20), 7379–84. doi: 10.1073/pnas.1322174111. Epub 2014 May 5. PMID: 24799686; PMCID: PMC4034215

Krajewski, J., Wieland, R., & Sauerland, M. (2010). Regulating strain states by using the recovery potential of lunch breaks. *Journal of Occupational Health Psychology*, 15(2), 131–139. doi:10.1037/a0018830

Kral, T. R. A., Schuyler, B. S., Mumford, J. A., Rosenkranz, M. A, Lutz, A., & Davidson, R. J. (2018). Impact of short- and long-term mindfulness meditation training on amygdala reactivity to emotional stimuli. *Neuroimage*, Nov 1;181, 301–313. doi: 10.1016/j.neuroimage.2018.07.013. Epub 2018 Jul 7. PMID: 29990584; PMCID: PMC6671286

Kreiman, J., & Sidtis, D. (2011). *Foundations of Voice Studies: An Interdisciplinary Approach to Voice Production and Perception.* Wiley-Blackwell. https://doi.org/10.1002/9781444395068

Lardone, A., Liparoti, M., Sorrentino, P., Rucco, R., Jacini, F., Polverino, A., Minino, R., Pesoli, M., Baselice, F., Sorriso, A., Ferraioli, G., Sorrentino, G., & Mandolesi, L. (2018). Mindfulness meditation is related to long-lasting changes in hippocampal functional topology during resting state: A magnetoencephalography study. *Neural Plasticity,* article ID 5340717. doi:10.1155/2018/5340717

Lazar, S. W., Bush, G., Gollub, R. L., Fricchione, G. L., Khalsa, G., & Benson H. (2000). Functional brain mapping of the relaxation response and meditation. *NeuroReport: For Rapid Communication of Neuroscience Research*, 11(7), 1581–1585.

Lee, L., Kulubya, E., Goldin, P., Goodarzi, A., & Girgis F. (2012). Review of the neural oscillations underlying meditation. *Frontiers in Neuroscience.* Retrieved on Jan 6, 2019. Doi.org/10.3389/fnins.2018.00178.

Lehrer, P., Vaschillo, E., Trost, Z., & France, C. R. (2009). Effects of rhythmical muscle tension at 0.1Hz on cardiovascular resonance and the baroreflex. *Biological Psychology*, Apr;81(1), 24–30. doi: 10.1016/j.biopsycho.2009.01.003. Epub 2009 Jan 22. PMID: 19428965

Lehrer, P. M. (1982). How to relax and how not to relax: A re-evaluation of the work of Edmund Jacobson — I. Behaviour Research and Therapy. doi:10.1016/0005-7967(82)90063-8

Lehrer, P. M. (2007). Biofeedback training to increase heart rate variability. *Principles and Practice of Stress Management,* 3, 227–248.

Lehrer, P. M., Vaschillo, E., & Vaschillo, B. (2000). Resonant frequency biofeedback training to increase cardiac variability: Rationale and manual for training. *Appl Psychophysiol Biofeedback*, Sep;25(3):177–91. doi: 10.1023/a:1009554825745. PMID: 10999236

Lehrer, P. M., Vaschillo, E., Vaschillo, B., Lu, S. E., Eckberg, D. L., Edelberg, R., Shih, W. J, Lin, Y., Kuusela, T. A, Tahvanainen, K. U, Hamer, R. M. (2003). Heart rate variability biofeedback increases baroreflex gain and peak expiratory flow. *Psychosomatic Medicine,* Sep-Oct;65(5), 796–805. doi: 10.1097/01.psy.0000089200.81962.19. PMID: 14508023

Lehrer, P. M., Woolfolk, R. L., & Sime, W. E. (Eds.). (2007). *Principles and practice of stress management (3rd ed.).* New York: The Guilford Press.

Lenz, Hall, J., & Bailey Smith, L. (2016). Meta-analysis of group mindfulness-based cognitive therapy for decreasing symptoms of acute depression. *The Journal for Specialists in Group Work,* 41(1), 44–70. https://doi.org/10.1080/01933922.2015.1111488

Levinson, D. B., Stioll, E. L., Kindy, S. D., Mery, H. L., & Davidson, R. J. (2014). A mind you can count on: Validating breath counting as a behavioural measure of mindfulness. *Frontiers in Psychology*, 2014 Oct 24;5, 1202. doi: 10.3389/fpsyg.2014.01202. eCollection 2014

Lewis, G. F., Hourani, L., Tueller, S., Kizakevich, P., Bryant, S., Weimer, B., & Strange, L. (2015). Relaxation training assisted by heart rate variability biofeedback: Implication for military predeployment stress inoculation protocol. *Psychophysiology,* 52, 1167–1174. doi:10.1111/psyp.12455

Linden, W. (2007). The Autogenic training method of J. H. Shultz. In P. M. Lehrer, R. L. Woolfolk, & A. Lindfors, *Qualia of Stress and Bodily Enregisterment in Ice Swimming. Signs and Society*, Volume 9, Issue 2, Spring 2021, pp. 155–175.

Lindfors, A. M. (2021). Qualia of Stress and Bodily Enregisterment in Ice Swimming. *Signs and society*, 9(2) 155–175. https://doi.org/10.1086/714857

Looney, D.P., Santee, W.R., Blanchard, L.A., Karis, A.J., Carter, A.J., Potter, A.W. (2018). Cardiorespiratory responses to heavy military load carriage over complex terrain. *Appl Ergon*, 73,194–198. doi: 10.1016/j.apergo.2018.07.010. Epub 2018 Jul 24. PMID: 30098635

Lundervold, D. A., & Poppen, R. (2004). Biobehavioral interventions for older adults coping with essential tremor. *Applied Psychophysiology and Biofeedback*, 29(1), 63–73. doi:10.1023/b:apbi.0000017864.06525.eb

Lutz, A., Slagter, H. A., Dunne, J. D., & Davidson, R. J. (2008). Attention regulation and monitoring in meditation. *Trends in Cognitive Sciences*, 12(4), 163–169.

Ma, X., Yue, Z., Gong, Z. Q., Zhang, H., Duan, N. Y., Shi, Y. T., Wei, G. X., & Li, Y. F. (2017). The effect of diaphragmatic breathing on attention, negative affect and stress in healthy adults. *Frontiers in Psychology*, Jun 6;8, 874. doi: 10.3389/fpsyg.2017.00874. eCollection 2017

Malinowski, P. (2013). Neural mechanisms of attentional control in mindfulness meditation. *Frontiers in Neuroscience,* 7, 8.

Manna, A., Raffone, A., Perrucci, M., Nardo, D., Ferretti, A., Tartaro, A., Londei, A., Gratta, C., Olivetti Belardinelli, M., & Romania. G. (2010). Neural correlates of focused attention and cognitive monitoring in meditation. *Brain Research Bulletin*, 82(1-2), 46–56. doi:10.1016/j.brainresbull.2010.03.001

Matsumoto, M., & Smith, J. C. (2001). Progressive muscle relaxation, breathing exercises, and abc relaxation theory. *Journal of Clinical Psychology*, 57(12), 1551–1557. doi:10.1002/jclp.1117

McCallie, M. S., Blum, C. M., & Hood, C. J. (2006). Progressive muscle relaxation. *Journal of Human Behavior in the Social Environment*, 13(3), 51–66. https://doi.org/10.1300/J137v13n03_04

McGuigan, F. J., & Lehrer, P. M. (2007). Progressive relaxation. origins, principles, and clinical applications. In P. M. Lehrer, R. L. Woolfolk, & W. E. Sime. (Eds.), *Principles and Practice of Stress Management* (3rd ed., pp. 57–87). New York: The Guilford Press.

Meland, A. (2016). *Mindfulness in high performance environments*. Dissertation from the Norwegian School of Sport Sciences. ISBN 978-82-502-0533-8.

Meland, A., Fonne, V., Wagstaff, A., & Pensgaard, A. (2015a). Mindfulness-based mental training in a high-performance combat aviation population: a one-year intervention study and two-year follow up. *The International Journal of Aviation Psychology*, 25(1), 48–61. doi: 10.1080/10508414.2015.995572.

Meland, A., Ishimatsu, K., Pensgaard, A., Wagstaff, A., Fonne, V., Garde, A., & Harris, A. (2015b). Impact of mindfulness training on physiological measures of stress and objective measures of attention control in a military helicopter unit. *The International Journal of Aviation Psychology*, 25(3- 4), 191–208, DOI:10.1080/10508414.2015.1162639

Moore, A., & Malinowski, P. (2009). Meditation, mindfulness and cognitive flexibility. *Consciousness and Cognition,* 18, 176–186.

Moran, D. J. (2016). *CBT and Mindfulness*. [Webinar] Tzkseminars: www.tzkseminars.com/Custom/TZKSeminars/Pages/WebinarDetails.aspx?id=6659&Cognitive-Behavior-Therapy-and-Mindfulness:-An-Integrative-Evidence–Based-Approach--3-CEs-

Nestor, J. *Breath: The new science of a lost art*. Riverhead Books (26 May 2020), New York. ISBN-10, 0735213615

Nideffer, R. M. (1992). Psyched to win. Champaign, IL: Leisure Press.

Noble, D. J., & Hochman, S. (2019). Hypothesis: Pulmonary afferent activity patterns during slow, deep breathing contribute to the neural induction of physiological relaxation. *Frontiers in Physiology*, 13(10), 1176. doi: 10.3389/fphys.2019.01176. eCollection 2019

Novaes, M. M., Palhano-Fontes, F., Onias, H., Andrade, K. C, Lobão-Soares, B., Arruda-Sanchez, T., Kozasa, E. H., Santaella, D. F, & de Araujo, D. B. (2020). Effects of Yoga Respiratory Practice (Bhastrika pranayama) on anxiety, affect, and brain functional connectivity and activity: a randomized controlled trial. *Frontiers in Psychiatry*, May 21;11, 467. doi: 10.3389/fpsyt.2020.00467. PMID: 32528330; PMCID: PMC7253694

Oded, Y. (2011). Biofeedback-based mental training in the military—the "Mental Gym™" *Project. Biofeedback*, 39(3), 112–118. https://doi.org/10.5298/1081-5937-39.3.03

Orlick, T. (1990). In pursuit of excellence: Leisure Press. A division of Human Kinetics. Champaign, 11.

Osman, A., Lamis, D. A, Bagge, C. L., Freedenthal, S., & Barnes, S. M. (2016). The mindful attention awareness scale: Further examination of dimensionality, reliability, and concurrent validity estimates. *Journal of Personality Assessment*, 98(2), 189–199. doi:10.1080/00223891.2015.1095761

Pagnini, F., Phillips, D., Bercovitz, K., & Langer, E. (2019). Mindfulness and relaxation training for long duration spaceflight: Evidence from analog environments and military settings. *Acta Astronautica,* 165, 1–8. https:/doi.org/10.1016/j.actaastro.2019.07.036

Pal, G. K., Velkumary, S., & Madanmohan (2004). Effect of short-term practice of breathing exercises on autonomic functions in normal human volunteers. *Indian Journal of Medical Research,* 120, 115–121.

Park, T., Reilly-Spong, M., & Gross. C. (2013). Mindfulness: A systematic review of instruments to measure an emergent patient reported outcome (PRO). *Quality of Life Research*, 22(10), 2639–2659. doi:10.1007/s11136-013-0395-8

Pascoe, M. C., Thompson, D. R., Jenkins, Z. M, & Ski, C. F. (2017). Mindfulness mediates the physiological markers of stress: Systematic review and meta-analysis. *Journal of Psychiatric Research*, 95, 156–178. doi:10.1016/j.jpsychires.2017.08.004

Pattyn, N. (2009). On the persistence of dualism in our so-called unified neurosciences: The case of the autonomic nervous system. *Psychologica Belgica*, 49(2-3), 101–110. DOI: http://doi.org/10.5334/pb-49-2- 3-101

Pattyn, N., Mairesse, O., Cortoos, A., Morais, J., Soetens, E., Roelands, B., van den Nest, A., & Kolinsky, R. (2014). Cardiac reactivity and preserved performance under stress: Two sides of the same coin? *International Journal of Psychophysiology*, Jul;93(1), 30–7. doi: 10.1016/j.ijpsycho.2013.03.008. Epub 2013 Mar 23. PMID: 23528304

Pattyn, N., Migeotte, P.F., Neyt, X., den Nest Av, Cluydts, R. (2010). Comparing real-life and laboratory-induced stress reactivity on cardio-respiratory parameters: differentiation of a tonic and a phasic component. *Physiol Behav*. Sep 1;101(2):218-23. doi: 10.1016/j.physbeh.2010.04.037. Epub 2010 May 6. PMID: 20451535.

Pattyn, N., Van Cutsem, J., Dessy, E., & Mairesse, O. (2018). Bridging exercise science, cognitive psychology, and medical practice: Is "cognitive fatigue" a remake of "the emperor's new clothes"? *Frontiers in Psychology,* 9, Article 1246. https://doi.org/10.3389/fpsyg.2018.01246.

Pelka, M. (2017). *Psychological relaxation techniques in sports: The acute effects of relaxation techniques between physical tasks*. [Doctoral dissertation, Ruhr-Universität Bochum: Fakultät für Sportwissenschaft].

Pineschi, G., & Di Pietro, A. (2013). Anxiety management through psychophysiological techniques: Relaxation and psyching-up in sport. *Journal of Sport Psychology in Action*, 4(3), 181–190. doi:10.1080/21520704.2013.820247

Pozuelos, J. P., Mead, B. R., Rueda, M. R., & Malinowski, P. (2019). Short-term mindful breath awareness training improves inhibitory control and response monitoring. *Progress in Brain Research,* 244, 137–163.

Pradhan, B. (2013). Effect of kapalabhati on performance of six-letter cancellation and digit letter substitution task in adults. *International Journal of Yoga*. Jul;6(2), 128–30. doi: 10.4103/0973-6131.113415. PMID: 23930032; PMCID: PMC3734639

Randall, J., Oswald, F., & Beier, M. (2014). Mind-Wandering, cognition, and performance: A theory- driven meta-analysis of attention regulation. *Psychological Bulletin*, 140(6), 1411–1431.

Rees, B. (2011). Overview of outcome data of potential meditation training for soldier resilience. *Military Medicine*, 176(11), 1232–1242. doi:10.7205/MILMED-D-11-00067

Reiss, N., Warnecke, I., Tolgou, T., Krampen, D., Luka-Krausgrill, U., & Rohrmann, S. (2017). Effects of cognitive behavioral therapy with relaxation vs. imagery rescripting on test anxiety: A randomized controlled trial. *Journal of Affective Disorders,* 208, 483–489. http://dx.doi.org/10.1016/j.jad.2016.10.039

Roeser, R. (2013). Mindfulness and human development: A commentary on the special issue. *Research in Human Development*, 10(3), 273–283. https://doi.org/10.1080/15427609.2013.818490

Rogers, J. M., Ferrari, M., Mosely, K., Lang, C. P, & Brennan, L. (2017). Mindfulness-based interventions for adults who are overweight or obese: A meta-analysis of physical and psychological health outcomes. *Obesity Reviews*, Jan;18(1), 51–67. doi: 10.1111/obr.12461. Epub 2016 Nov 11. PMID: 27862826

Rooks, J., Morrison, A., Goolsarran, M., Rogers, S., & Jha, A. (2017). "We are talking about practice": The influence of mindfulness vs relaxation training on athletes' attention and well-being over high- demand intervals. *Journal of Cognitive Enhancement*, 1(2), 141–153.

Rooks, J. D., Morrison, A. B., Goolsarran, M. Rogers, S. L., & Amishi, P. J. (2007). "We are talking about practice": the influence of mindfulness vs. relaxation training on athletes' attention and well-being over high-demand intervals. *Journal of Cognitive Enhancement*, 1, 141–153. https://doi.org/10.1007/s41 465- 017-0016-5

Röthlin, P., & Birrer, D. (2019). Mental training in group settings: Intervention protocols of a mindfulness and acceptance-based and a psychological skills training program, *Journal of Sport Psychology in Action*, doi: 10.1080/21520704.2018.1557771

Röthlin, P., Birrer, D., Horvath, S., & Grosse Holtforth, M. (2016). Psychological skills training and a mindfulness-based intervention to enhance functional athletic performance: design of a randomized controlled trial using ambulatory assessment. *BMC Psychology*, 4(1), 39–39. https://doi.org/10.1186/s40 359-016-0147-y.

Saoji, A. A, et al. (2017). Effects of yogic breath regulation: A narrative review of scientific evidence. *Journal of Ayurveda and Integrated Medicine*. http://dx.doi.org/10.1016/j.jaim.2017.07.008.

Saoji, A. A., Raghavendra, B. R., & Manjunath, N. K. (2019). Effects of yogic breathing: A narrative review of scientific evidence. *Journal of Ayurveda and Integrated Medicine,* 10(1), 50–58. doi: 10.1016/ j.jaim.2017.07.008. Epub 2018 Feb 1.

Sappington, R., & Longshore, K. (2015). Reviewing the efficacy of mindfulness-based interventions for enhanced athletic performance. *Journal of Clinical Sport Psychology*, 9(3), 232–262.

Schilling, D. J., & Poppen, R. (1983). Behavioral relaxation training and assessment. *Journal of Behavior Therapy and Experimental Psychiatry*, 14(2), 99–107. Doi:10.1016/0005-7916(83)90027-7

Scott, G., Goddard, Christopher J. Stevens, Patricia C. Jackman & Christian Swann (2021). A systematic review of flow interventions in sport and exercise, *International Review of Sport and Exercise Psychology*. DOI: 10.1080/1750984X.2021.1923055

Shannahoff-Khalsa, D. S., Boyle, M. R., & Buebel, M. E. (1991). The effects of unilateral forced nostril breathing on cognition. *International Journal of Neuroscience,* 57, 239–249.

Shapiro, S. L., Carlson, L. E., Astin, J. A., & Freedman, B. (2006). Mechanisms of Mindfulness. *Journal of Clinical Psychology*. 63(3), 373–386.

Sierra-Palmeiro, E., Fernández-Villarino, M., & Freire-Maceiras, R. (2023). Efectos de un programa de yoga en el rendimiento en gimnasia rítmica: un estudio de casos / Effects of a yoga program on perfomance in rhythmic gymnastics: a case study. *Rev. Int. Med. Cienc. Act. Fis. Deporte,* Mar.;23(89), 363–376.

Sime, W. E (Eds.), *Principles and practice of stress management* (3rd ed., pp. 151–174). New York: The Guilford Press.

Small, Dillon. (2015). *Review of the literature regarding mindfulness training as a psychological prophylaxis for military stress*. Dissertation. Biola University.

Smith, J. C. (2005). *Relaxation, meditation, & mindfulness. A mental health practitioner's guide to new and traditional approaches*. New York: Springer Publishing Company.

Smith, J. C., Wedell, A. B., Kolotylo, C. J., Lewis, J. E., Byers, K. Y., & Segin, C. M. (2000). ABC relaxation theory and the factor structure of relaxation states, recalled relaxation activities, dispositions, and motivations. *Psychological Reports,* 86, 1201–1208. doi:10.2466/pr0.2000.86.3c.1201

Soni, S., Joshi, L. N., & Datta, A. (2015). Effect of controlled deep breathing on psychomotor and higher mental functions in normal individuals. *Indian Journal of Physiology and Pharmacology*, 59(1), 41–47.

Sorbero, M., Ahluwalia, S., Reynolds, K., Lovejoy, S., Farris, C., Sloan, J., Miles. J., Vaughan, C., Kandrack, R., Apaydin, E., Colaiaco, B., & Herman, P. (2015). Meditation for depression: A systematic review of mindfulness-based cognitive therapy for major depressive disorder. *RAND Corporation*. Retrieved January 16, 2020, from www.jstor.org/stable/10.7249/j.ctt19w7254

Sovik, R. (2000). The science of breathing — the yogic view. *Progress in Brain Research,* 122, 491–505.

Stanley, E. (2014). Mindfulness-based mind fitness training. In *Amanda Ie*, Christelle Ngnoumen & Ellen Langer (Eds.), *The Wiley Blackwell handbook of mindfulness, first edition*. John Wiley & Sons, Ltd. https:// doi.org/ 10.1002/9781118294895.ch50.

Stanley, E., & Schȧldach, J. (2011). Mindfulness-based Mind Fitness Training (MMFT). *Mind Fitness Training Institute*. Alexandria, VA: Mind Fitness Training Institute.

Stanley, E., Schaldach, J., Kiyonaga, A., & Jha, A. (2011). Mindfulness-based mind fitness training: A case study of a high-stress predeployment military Cohort. *Cognitive and Behavioral Practice,* 18, 566–576.

Stanley, E. A., & Jha, A. P. (2009). Mind fitness and mental armor: Enhancing performance and building warrior resilience. *Joint Force Quarterly,* 55, 144–151.

Stetz, M. C., Kaloi-Chen, J. Y., Turner, D. D., Bouchard, S., Riva, G., & Wiederhold, B. K. (2011). The effectiveness of technology-enhanced relaxation techniques for military medical warriors. *Military Medicine*, 176(9), 1065–1070. doi:10.7205/MILMED-D-10-00393

Strauss, C., Cavanagh, K., Oliver, A., & Pettman, D. (2014). mindfulness-based interventions for people diagnosed with a current episode of an anxiety or depressive disorder: A meta-analysis of randomized controlled trials. *PLoS ONE*, 9(4), e96110. doi:10.1371/journal.pone.0096110

Streeter, C. C., Jensen, J. E., Perlmutter, R. M., Cabral, H. J, Tian, H., Terhune, D. B., Ciraulo, D. A., & Renshaw, P. F. (2007). Yoga Asana sessions increase brain GABA levels: A pilot study. *Journal of Alternative and Complementary Medicine*, May;13(4):419–26. doi: 10.1089/acm.2007.6338. PMID: 17532734.

Streeter, C. C, Whitfield, T. H., Owen, L., Rein, T., Karri, S. K, Yakhkind, A., Perlmutter, R., Prescot, A., Renshaw, P. F., & Ciraulo, D. A, Jensen, J. E. (2010). Effects of yoga versus walking on mood, anxiety, and brain GABA levels: a randomized controlled MRS study. *Journal of Alternative and Complementary Medicine*, Nov;16(11), 1145–52. doi: 10.1089/acm.2010.0007. Epub 2010 Aug 19. PMID: 20722471; PMCID: PMC3111147

Sun, S., Hu, C., Pan, J., Liu, C., & Huang, M. (2019) Trait mindfulness is associated with the self- similarity of heart rate variability. *Frontiers in Psychology*, 10. Article 314. doi: 10.3389/fpsyg.2019.00314

Swift, A. C., Campbell, I. T., & McKown, T. M. (1988). Oronasal obstruction, lung volumes, and arterial oxygenation. *Lancet,* 331(8577), 73–75.

Tang, Y., Holzel, B., & Posner, M. (2015). The Neuroscience of Mindfulness Meditation. *Nature Reviews Neuroscience,* 16(4), 213–225.

Tang, Y., Ma, Y., Wang, J., Fan, Y., Feng, S., Lu, Q., Yu, Q., Sui, D., Rothbart, M., Fan, M., & Posner, M. (2007). Short-term meditation training improves attention and self-regulation. *Proceedings of the National Academy of Sciences of the United States*, 104(43), 17152–5.

Tatum, T., Lundervold, D. A., & Ament, P. (2006). Abbreviated upright behavioral relaxation training for test anxiety among college students: initial results. *International Journal of Behavioral Consultation and Therapy*, 2(4). doi:10.1037/h0101001

Telles, S., Bhardwaj, A. K, Kumar, S., Kumar, N., & Balkrishna, A. (2012). Performance in a substitution task and state anxiety following yoga in army recruits. *Psychol Rep,* 110, 963–976.

Telles, S., Kala, N., Gupta, R. K., Verma, S., Vishwakarma, B., Agnihotri, S., Gandharva, K., & Balkrishna, A. (2019). Effect of yoga on vigilance, self rated sleep and state anxiety in Border Security Force personnel in India. *Work*, 63(2), 243–251. doi: 10.3233/WOR-192925. PMID: 31156205

Telles, S., Raghurai, P., Maharana, S., & Nagendra, H. R. (2007). Immediate effect of three yoga breathing techniques on performance on a letter-cancellation task. *Perceptual and Motor Skills,* 104, 1289–1296.

Telles, S., Singh, N., & Puthige, R. (2013). Changes in P300 following alternate nostril yoga breathing and breath awareness. *Biopsychosocial Medicine*, May 31;7(1):11. doi: 10.1186/1751-0759-7-11. PMID: 23721252; PMCID: PMC3679963.

Thayer, J. F., Ahs, F., Fredrikson, M., Sollers, J. J 3rd, & Wager, T. D. (2012). A meta-analysis of heart rate variability and neuroimaging studies: Implications for heart rate variability as a marker of stress and health. *Neuroscience Biobehavioral Reviews*, Feb;36(2), 747–56. doi: 10.1016/j.neubiorev.2011.11.009. Epub 2011 Dec 8. PMID: 22178086

Tilborg, A., Bijlsma, T., & Muis, S. (2019). Mindfulness in the Dutch military — Train your brain (PDF). Retrieved from: www.researchgate.net/publication/ 334503315_Mindfulness_in_the_Dutch_Military_-_Train_Your_Brain

Tyagi, A., Cohen, M., Reece, J., Telles, S., & Jones, L. (2016). Heart rate variability, flow, mood and mental stress during yoga practices in yoga practitioners, non-yoga practitioners and people with metabolic syndrome. *Applied Psychophysiology Biofeedback*, Dec;41(4), 381–393. doi: 10.1007/s10484-016-9340-2. PMID: 27457341

Udhan, V. D, Wankhede, S. G, & Phatale, S. R. (2018). Effect of yoga on cardio-respiratory health markers: Physical fitness index and maximum oxygen consumption (VO2 max). *Journal of Clinical and Diagnostic Research*, 12, 21–3.

Ungerleider, S. (2005). Mental training for peak performance. Emmaus, PA: Rodale.

Van Diest, I., Verstappen, K., Aubert, A.E., Widjaja, D., Vansteenwegen, D., Vlemincx, E. (2014). Inhalation/Exhalation ratio modulates the effect of slow breathing on heart rate variability and relaxation. *Appl Psychophysiol Biofeedback*, Dec;39(3-4):171–80. doi: 10.1007/s10484-014-9253-x. PMID: 25156003.

Vøllestad, J., Birkeland Nielsen, M., & Høstmark Nielsen, G. (2012). Mindfulness and acceptance- based interventions for anxiety disorders: A systematic review and meta-analysis. *British Journal of Clinical Psychology*, 51, 239–260.

World Health Oranization. (2018). www.who.int/southeastasia/news/detail/20-06-2018-yoga-is-a-valuable-tool-to-increase-physical-activity-and-decrease-noncommunicable-disease

World Health Organization. (2020). www.who.int/southeastasia/news/speeches/detail/international-day-of-yoga-2020

Yadav, G., & Muth, P. K. (2016). Deep breathing practice facilitates retention of newly learned motor skills. *Sci Rep*, 6, 37069. doi: 10.1038/srep37069

Zaccaro, A., Piarulli, A., Laurino, M., Garbella, E., Menicucci, D., Neri, B., & Gemignani, A. (2018). How breath-control can change your life: A systematic review on psycho-physiological correlates of slow breathing. *Frontiers in Human Neuroscience*, Sep 7;12, 353. doi: 10.3389/fnhum.2018.00353. PMID: 30245619; PMCID: PMC6137615

Zanesco, A., Denkova, E., Rogers, S., MacNulty, W., & Jha, A. (2019). Mindfulness training as cognitive training in high-demand cohorts: An initial study in elite military service members. *Progress in Brain Research*, 244, 323–354.

Zautra, A. J., Fasman, R., Davis, M. C., & Craig, A. D. (2010). The effects of slow breathing on affective responses to pain stimuli: an experimental study. *Pain*, 149, 12–18.

Zeidan, F., Johnson, S. K., Diamond, B. J., David, Z., & Goolkasian, P. (2010). Mindfulness meditation improves cognition: Evidence of brief mental training. *Consciousness and Cognition*, 19(2), 597–605. https://doi.org/10.1016/j.concog.2010.03.014

Zou, L., Yeung, A., Quan, X., Boyden, S. D., & Wang, H. (2018). A systematic review and meta-analysis of mindfulness-based (Baduanjin) exercise for alleviating musculoskeletal pain and improving sleep quality in people with chronic diseases. *International journal of environmental research and public health*, 15(2), 206.

Zwaag, J., Naaktgeboren, R., van Herwaarden, A. E., Pickkers, P., & Kox, M. (2022). The effects of cold exposure training and a breathing exercise on the inflammatory response in humans: A pilot study. *Psychosomatic Medicine*, May 1;84(4), 457–467. doi: 10.1097/PSY.0000000000001065. Epub 2022 Feb 23. PMID: 35213875; PMCID: PMC9071023

6 Pharmacological Strategies to Improve Mental Performance

Jeroen Van Cutsem and Nathalie Pattyn

Pharmacology to enhance mental performance, what's in a name?

Considering the current booming use of cognitive enhancers in the general population (Brühl & Sahakian, 2016; Emanuel et al., 2013; Kortekaas-Rijlaarsdam et al., 2019), triggered by their uncontrolled availability through online purchase, defining clear policies and guidelines regarding their use in professional contexts is both necessary and urgent. Whereas these regulations remain a national prerogative, depending on culture and legislation (as described in more detail in Chapter 18), the present chapter aims to provide the scientific evidence base to make informed decisions regarding the benefits of the use of "smart pills" as a mental performance enhancement tool.

Substances that are believed to enhance mental performance are often referred to as "smart pills" or "nootropics", from the Greek "nous" meaning mind and "trepein" meaning turning/bending (Napoletano et al., 2020), and can be defined as drugs that increase the cognitive ability of anyone taking it, independently from whether the user is cognitively impaired (e.g., jet lag, sleep deprived), suffers from a neuropsychiatric disorder (e.g., Alzheimer's disease), or is a healthy person (Smith & Farah, 2011). The present chapter will focus on the latter, the use of pills to enhance mental performance in healthy persons without any medical indication.

Smith and Farah (2011) put forward the Romanian neuroscientist Corneliu Giurgea as the founding father of the concept that smart pills should be developed to increase the intelligence of the general population. Already in the 1960s, Corneliu Giurgea stated that "Man is not going to wait passively for millions of years before evolution offers him a better brain" (Gazzaniga, 2005). A statement that is also shared by Greely et al. (2008), who called for a presumption that mentally competent adults should be able to engage in cognitive enhancement using drugs. However, the present chapter will not go in detail on the ethics of the usage of nootropics; see Chapter 18 for a discussion on this matter.

In this chapter we want to provide the scientific base to make informed decisions regarding the use of "smart pills" as a mental performance enhancement tool. To do so, we will make use of a similar classification as the one provided by Fond et al. (2015). They classified nootropics according to their primary type of action and eventually subdivided nootropics into catecholaminergic drugs, cholinergic drugs, anticholinergic drugs, glutamatergic drugs, histaminergic drugs, melatonininergic drugs, glucocorticoids, and non-steroidal anti-inflammatory drugs (Fond et al., 2015). Fond et al. (2015) did not provide a specific definition of which substances they interpreted to be a drug. However, based on the drugs they reviewed it is obvious that they only included pharmacological smart pill, thereby excluding other biochemical strategies that can enhance mental performance (e.g., nutritional smart pills, e.g., caffeine). This chapter does not serve to elaborate on the exact

DOI: 10.4324/9781003378969-8

definition of a drug, but it should be clear that "drug" is a concept that is interpreted in numerous different ways. Labelling a smart pill as a drug and subdividing it into the pharmacological or nutritional section is often a question of culture and legislation and, therefore, is often arbitrary and disputable. Independently from the definition of the concept "drug", the present chapter, will also include biochemical strategies that are typically referred to as nutritional supplements (e.g., caffeine). In addition, we want to emphasize that, although we want to cast a wide net and discuss as much biochemical strategies as possible, we will not discuss those cognitive enhancing substances on which only anecdotal evidence on their effectiveness to increase cognitive performance in a healthy population has been published. Therefore, we will address the following classifications in the remainder of this chapter: catecholaminergic-based enhancing substances, cholinergic-based enhancing substances, and psychedelic enhancing substances. The last class "psychedelic enhancing substances" we specifically want to add due to growing number of professionals using small doses of psychedelics (e.g., magic mushrooms, or peyote) to boost their productivity and creativity at work (Prochazkova et al., 2018) and because this classification was not addressed in the review of Fond et al. (2015).

In the following sections, we will, based on the above-outlined classification, introduce each nootropic-classification. Moreover, we will also discuss one nootropic in more detail, modafinil. The detailed discussion of modafinil will be structured via five of the seven interdependent dimensions that were put forward by Dresler et al. (2019): (1) mode of action, (2) cognitive domain, (3) personal factors, (4) temporal factors, (5) side effects, (6) availability, and (7) acceptance. In the first dimension "mode of action", background on the mechanism that is thought to underlie the impact of modafinil will be provided. In terms of the second dimension "cognitive domain", it is obvious that the human mind consists of a broad variety of cognitive functions, that no single nootropic enhances every cognitive domain, and that some cognitive domain effects have only been reported in a well-controlled laboratory setting and not in more ecologically valid settings. Therefore, this dimension will provide insights on the cognitive domain(s) that have been found to be particularly impacted by the intake of modafinil. For the third dimension, which we reframe as the "personal and task characteristics" dimension, a focus on the role that individual and task characteristics might play in the impact of modafinil will be adopted. For example, in terms of the use of modafinil as a nootropic, IQ has already been shown to play a role (Randall et al., 2005). The temporal factors dimension will be reframed to the "supplementation protocol specifics" dimension and will take a closer look at the time needed for application and the duration of the effects. In addition, a possible dose-response relation will be discussed. For the dimension "side effects" we will most logically focus on the severity and the form of the known side effects. The detailed discussion of modafinil is included to serve as a case study and provide an example of how the decision-making process to implement or not implement a specific nootropic could be structured.

Concerning the last two dimensions that were put forward by Dresler et al. (2019), the availability and acceptance dimension, we will touch upon those in a more general way in the discussion at the end of this chapter. The availability dimension concerns the legal status and cost of a nootropic, while the acceptance dimension concerns the social acceptance of a nootropic. Moreover, for more detailed information on this last dimension the reader is referred to Chapter 18.

Nootropics

Catecholaminergic-based enhancing substances

A catecholamine is a monoamine neurotransmitter and derives from the amino acid tyrosine. Tyrosine is created from phenylalanine by hydroxylation by the enzyme phenylalanine hydroxylase, and is also ingested directly from dietary protein. Catecholamine-secreting cells use several reactions to convert tyrosine serially to L-DOPA and then to dopamine. Depending on the cell type, dopamine may be further converted to noradrenaline or even further converted to adrenaline (Joh & Hwang, 1987). Catecholamines are often released into the bloodstream in response to stress or fright and prepare the body for "fight-or-flight" and are known to play a crucial role in cognition (Ott & Nieder, 2019).

Catecholaminergic drugs can be defined as substances that may influence catecholaminergic neurotransmitters in the brain, such as dopamine and noradrenaline. However, this positive influence of catecholaminergic drugs on brain neurotransmitter levels should not be interpreted as a linear relation (i.e., the higher the brain neurotransmitter levels the better). As very low and very high levels are often associated with poor performance or even pathologies (Cools & D'Esposito, 2011), neurotransmitter levels are very unlikely to relate to mental performance in a linear fashion (Colzato et al., 2021). In contrast, the fact that poor performance and/or pathologies are associated with very low or very high levels of specific neurotransmitter levels suggests that an inverted-U shaped dose-response effect of catecholamine levels is in place. An inverted-U shaped relation between catecholamine levels and mental performance implies that, for catecholaminergic drugs to be as effective as possible, the state catecholamine level of an individual should be considered. Because, if an individual is at the theoretical optimum of the inverted-U shaped relation, then catecholaminergic drugs will cause the individual to move away from this sweet spot and impair performance.

Substances that are shown to influence the catecholaminergic system include methylphenidate (e.g., Ritalin) and amphetamine-based medications (e.g., Adderall), modafinil, caffeine, and tyrosine (Fond et al., 2015). As a case study for the decision-making process on whether to use a specific nootropic or not, we will provide a detailed discussion of modafinil via the dimensions that were introduced in the introduction of this chapter.

Modafinil

Modafinil or 2-[(diphenylmethyl) sulfinyl] acetamide, commercially known as Provigil® is an eugeroic (i.e., wakefulness-promoting) drug that was approved by the US Food and Drug Administration (FDA) and the European Medicines Agency for the treatment of narcolepsy, excessive sleepiness during daytime due to obstructive sleep apnea, and the shift work sleep disorder (Minzenberg & Carter, 2008). Eugeroic drugs mimic the effects of d-amphetamines by producing high-quality wakefulness, while said to lack the typical unwanted side effects associated with amphetamines (Lagarde et al., 1995). Modafinil, therefore, has quickly found its way to other populations than those with excessive sleepiness due to medical reasons, namely those populations in which sleep deprivation is frequently present (e.g., military personnel, nurses, and medical doctors, being on-call jobs) (Ooi et al., 2019) or in which cognitive performance is highly competitive (e.g., students, academics, or corporate executives) (Teodorini et al., 2020).

MODE OF ACTION

Modafinil is known to have multiple effects on different brain areas and neurotransmitter systems in the brain (Becker et al., 2022; Mereu et al., 2013; Minzenberg & Carter, 2008). Like amphetamines and methylphenidate, it inhibits dopamine reuptake, underlying its positive effects on human performance. Moreover, besides the dopaminergic effects of modafinil, several non-dopaminergic effects of modafinil have been described (e.g., increase of electrical neuronal coupling) that could further explain its efficacy as a wake-promoting and cognitive enhancing substance (Mereu et al., 2013).

COGNITIVE DOMAIN

Regarding attention and vigilance, little evidence is to be found for a positive impact of modafinil (Van Puyvelde et al., 2022). Only in the study of Marchant et al. (2009) was an improvement of rapid attention switching reported, and this only in the most difficult switching tasks. Other studies did not evidence this improvement (Müller et al., 2013; Müller et al., 2004).

It has been suggested that modafinil would specifically be efficient in inhibitory task processes. For example, indications for a beneficial impact on inhibition were reported in Schmidt et al. (2017). Relative to placebo, 600 mg modafinil improved inhibitory performance in a go/no-go task. In addition, Fernández et al. (2015) reported fewer mistakes on the Stroop test after 200 mg intake, and Rattray et al. (2019) reported better reaction times with 400 mg when taking into account time on task. However, in contrast, Mohamed & Lewis (2014) reported significantly longer mean response latencies in participants after intake of 200 mg modafinil for both the response initiation and response inhibition compared to placebo. Notably, modafinil did not enhance accuracy scores and the participants in both the modafinil and placebo groups made a similar number of errors. Based on these results, Mohamed & Lewis (2014) put forward that the effectiveness of modafinil as a putative cognitive enhancer is limited. Besides Mohamed & Lewis (2014), neither did Ikeda et al. (2017), Lees et al. (2017), or Repantis et al. (2021) report any modafinil-associated positive impact on response inhibition or other executive functions.

In terms of the impact of modafinil on creativity and divergent thinking, Müller et al. (2013) conducted a study in which they compared 200 mg intake with placebo, which showed inconsistent findings that did not reach significance regarding the measurements of creativity. In addition, another study by Mohamed (2016) showed ability-dependent results of 200 mg modafinil on convergent thinking and showed a negative impact of modafinil on divergent thinking. They concluded that modafinil cannot be considered a general cognitive enhancer.

PERSONAL AND TASK CHARACTERISTICS

Marchant et al. (2009) reported that 200 mg modafinil promoted the rapid switching of attention only in those conditions that were most demanding. In less demanding conditions, there was no observed benefit. Müller et al. (2013) showed improved performance following the intake of 200 mg modafinil in young healthy volunteers compared to placebo in executive functioning tasks. There were enhancements on spatial working memory, planning, and decision tests, however, only at the most difficult levels. They also reported an improvement in a visual pattern recognition memory task, but only in the delayed testing which is more challenging than the immediate testing. A mediating effect of task difficulty was also reported by Winder-Rhodes et al. (2010). They evaluated the effect of 300 mg of modafinil on several aspects of executive functioning: pattern recognition memory, visual information processing, inhibition of prepotent responses, and spatial planning and working memory. An improvement was only shown on the accuracy factor of the spatial planning and working memory test, and this only at the most difficult level. A study by Esposito et al. (2013) on the impact of 100 mg modafinil on executive functioning showed that 100 mg sufficed to improve the performance on the Raven's Advanced Progressive Matrices II set three hours after administration, in comparison to a baseline, whereas no improvement was observed in the placebo group. The effect was significant for the medium difficulty level. However, close inspection of the raw data shows that the baseline levels were very low, which may indicate that the medium level was the limit of the participants' IQ or ability that was reached. Thus, possibly, the highest level that still allowed for an improvement for the participants was the medium category. Müller et al. (2004) found a positive impact of modafinil in the delayed and possibly more difficult conditions of the testing. Subtle differences in the effect of 200 mg modafinil were identified when considering three difficulty categories of monotonous working memory tasks, for example, a significantly reduced error rate in the long delay condition of the visuo-spatial task and in the manipulation conditions, but not in the maintenance condition of the numeric task. Furthermore, reaction times and attentional control tasks showed no differences.

Besides task difficulty, individual ability may thus play a role as well in the mechanisms of the impact of modafinil. Randall et al. (2005) performed a meta-analysis of their former studies dividing the population into a low and high IQ group. The results showed that the observed improvements in the colour naming of dots and in clock drawing tests only appeared in the lower IQ group. Moreover, the high IQ group showed a small benefit only from the 200 mg condition and not from the 100 mg. Hence, low IQ profiles benefited already from 100 mg, higher IQ profiles only from 200 mg onwards, but this benefit was rather small. Similar results were reported by Finke et al. (2010). They showed that 400 mg modafinil enhanced perceptual processing speed and visual short-term memory storage capacity in low-performing participants. Another study by Mohamed (2016) showed that high scoring persons on the remote Associates Task for convergent thinking did not benefit from 200 mg modafinil, whereas low scoring persons did.

To conclude, only studies that included task-related and individual ability-related aspects as potential moderators pointed to important differentiations. That is, in general, low ability persons benefit more from modafinil than high ability persons and a higher degree of task difficulty or challenge appears to be related with a more consistent positive impact of modafinil. This is an important take home message when considering application in an elite population, which is supposed to already have superior cognitive ability.

SUPPLEMENTATION PROTOCOL SPECIFICS

Most studies used a single 200-mg dose design. Baranski et al. (2004) observed an improvement of detection in a repeated numbers vigilance task and a serial reaction time task in comparison with placebo. These authors chose to provide 4 mg/kg (which is an equivalent of 300 mg on average), since they wanted to study overconfidence, which was clearly present in sleep-deprived subjects that had received 300 mg modafinil.

Turner et al. (2003) found a dose-response effect in the stop-signal paradigm only. Their most important conclusion was that modafinil is a reducer of impulsive response tendencies and that, if the effect were dose-dependent, this would only be the case for response inhibition effects. In 2004, Randall et al. (2004) compared the effect of 100 mg, 200 mg, and placebo in 45 healthy middle aged volunteers. The 200-mg group performed faster on some executive functioning tests, such as the simple colour naming of dots, and the clock drawing test, when compared to placebo. However, in this 200-mg group, significantly more errors were made than in the 100-mg and placebo group, suggesting a different speed-accuracy trade-off. Similarly, in a second study of the same team (Randall et al., 2005) the 200-mg group performed better on the simple colour naming of dots test and the Rapid Visual Information Processing test of sustained attention than the placebo group. The 100-mg group on the other hand improved on digit span forward in comparison with both placebo and 200-mg. Both modafinil groups improved in pattern recognition, however it was accompanied by a slowing of response latency in the 200-mg group. There were no significant effects of modafinil compared with placebo in other tests of long-term memory, executive function, visuospatial and constructional ability, or category fluency. Randall et al. (2005) concluded, again, there were no clear dose-dependent effects.

To conclude, no study showed a clear dose-response effect for modafinil. Moreover, in cases of improved alertness (probably through an underlying increased arousal), accuracy was not guaranteed. However, it may be that task-related aspects play a role within these apparently unclear and sometimes contradictory results, which is an aspect we will explore in the following section.

In terms of multiple dosing studies, only one repeated intake study can be found that examined the impact of repeated daily 400 mg modafinil versus placebo on mood during three subsequent days (Taneja et al., 2005). The authors found a positive impact on some positive mood scales but also on anxiety. Hence, no conclusion can be made with regard to cognitive enhancement in comparison with single-dose studies.

SIDE EFFECTS

In a recent review by Van Puyvelde et al. (2022), a specific focus was put on the possible short- and long-term side effects that could be linked with modafinil intake. It was concluded that, regarding short-term effects, on a somatic level, higher doses induce sympathetic arousal, and on a mental level the risk for overconfidence should be systematically examined in future studies (Van Puyvelde et al., 2022). In terms of long-term effects, no research appears to be available. However, there are indications that modafinil does work on the same neurobiological mechanisms as other addictive stimulants. Hence, the risk for abuse should be investigated, not only on a neurobiological level but also on the level of the subjective user. Both abuse and escalation may lead to higher intakes, likely to induce additional short-term side effects (Van Puyvelde et al., 2022).

CONCLUSION

It is likely that modafinil as a smart pill is effective only in a small scope of persons, most likely those with lower ability to begin with, in a limited domain of task specificities, and it may enhance certain domain-specific aspects but degrade domain-general abilities at the same time, an issue that is further discussed in Chapter 18. One thus might wonder if the limited benefit would be worth the risk. The effect of overconfidence should be examined in a much more rigorous manner. In a sleep-deprived population, overconfidence was reported by Baranski et al. (2004) and Baranski and Pigeau (1997). Although not significant, a tendency towards overconfidence was again found in a non-sleep-deprived population (Baranski et al., 2004). Furthermore, an issue receiving very little attention in the scientific literature, yet of paramount importance for populations like athletes or military personnel, is the effect of modafinil on exercise tolerance, especially in varying environmental temperatures. The briefly described sympathetic effects in a very small number of publications do not bode well in this regard. As suggested by the study of Rattray et al. (2019), the gain in executive function is coupled to a lower perceived effort for physical exercise, however, the increased heart rate and affected sleep quality show there is a trade-off to consider before basing decision on the positive effects.

Other catecholaminergic-based enhancing substances

As a detailed discussion like the one of modafinil would turn this chapter into a book, we will only provide an overview of the other catecholaminergic-based enhancing substances and the other nootropic classifications. For each nootropic, we refer to the most recent research that has been published on the topic.

Kapur (2020) recently conducted a review on the research that is available on the application of methylphenidate to enhance performance in healthy individuals. Methylphenidate is a central nervous system stimulant that acts on both dopaminergic and noradrenergic systems, potentiating their actions through active reuptake transporter inhibition, and facilitating release from reserpine sensitive vesicular stores (Scahill et al., 2004). Kapur (2020) concluded that methylphenidate appears to have dose- and task-dependent effects on a range of cognitive domains such as verbal memory, executive functioning, and attention. In addition, a personal characteristic was also put forward by this author which seems to affect the effectiveness of methylphenidate supplementation, namely pre-intervention cognitive capacity. The role of this personal characteristic has been highlighted by research of Cools et al. (2008), which demonstrated that working memory capacity, as measured with the listening span test, is associated with dopamine synthesis capacity in the striatum. All research considered, Kapur (2020) suggested that individually tailored doses of methylphenidate can confer benefit to some domains of cognition, such as executive function and attention. Neither visual learning nor creative thinking were improved by methylphenidate (Kapur, 2020).

Regarding amphetamines, a recent review was performed by Kassim (2023). Amphetamines are a class of pharmaceuticals that include Adderall, dextroamphetamine, and lisdexamphetamine, which are mainly used for the treatment of attention deficit with or without hyperactivity disorder. When administered acutely, its primary mechanism of action is to enhance the extracellular concentrations of dopamine by blockade of dopamine reuptake. However, besides dopamine, amphetamine intake impacts multiple other systems as well: the serotonergic system, the glutamatergic system, and the cholinergic system (see Hutson et al., 2014, for an overview). Nevertheless, amphetamines are included in the catecholaminergic subdivision due to it being its primary mechanism of action. According to the review of Kassim (2023), acute amphetamine administration was found to enhance information processing speed, attention, executive functioning, inhibitory control, and learning and memory in several studies. However, these results were notably difficult to replicate, which indicates that the cognitive effects of amphetamines are inconsistent. This review also focused on personal characteristics that might play a role in the effectiveness of amphetamines and found that some were correlated (e.g., novelty seeking, impulsivity, reward sensitivity, physical fearlessness, or schizotypy), but that most studies did not report anything on a possible impact of personal characteristics, making it difficult to put forward a hard conclusion on this matter.

Unlike modafinil, methylphenidate, and amphetamines, caffeine is the first nutritional smart "pill" of this list and the first one to not be prescription based. Caffeine intake comes mainly from coffee, tea, energy or sports drinks, and various chocolate products. In addition, it is also commercialized and produced in pills (Sharif et al., 2021). The potential effects of caffeine, at the cellular level, can be explained by three mechanisms of action: the antagonism of adenosine receptors, especially in the central nervous system; the mobilization of intracellular calcium storage; and the inhibition of phosphodiesterases (Cappelletti et al., 2015). Via the first mechanism (i.e., blocking adenosine receptors), caffeine intake results in an increased release of dopamine, noradrenaline, and glutamate and is thought to positively impact cognition (see Cappelletti et al., 2015, for more information). The cognition-enhancing properties of caffeine have been debated (Einöther & Giesbrecht, 2013; Rogers et al., 2013), and to discuss its mental-enhancing properties it is important to emphasize the importance of habitual caffeine consumption as a personal characteristic that impacts the effectiveness of caffeine (Rogers et al., 2013). Overall, caffeine clearly does enhance motor performance (faster) in caffeine consumers. However, it does not appear to improve mental performance (Rogers et al., 2013). In terms of faster reaction times after caffeine intake, follow-up research on the possible role of caffeine to enhance mental performance has been performed (Carswell et al., 2020). This follow-up research focused on the hypothesis that a positive effect of caffeine on mental performance might be genotype-related. For example, Carswell et al. (2020) explained that the P450 enzyme is responsible for 95% of the body's caffeine metabolism (i.e., converting caffeine to its major metabolite paraxanthine) and, subsequently, hypothesized that a polymorphism in the gene which encodes for the CYP1A2 isoform may also be responsible for some interindividual differences. Their results confirmed this hypothesis, as they found that caffeine enhanced CYP1A2 "fast" metabolizers' cognitive performance more than "slow" metabolizers (Carswell et al., 2020).

Tyrosine is another non-prescription nutritional supplement that could potentially enhance mental performance. Tyrosine is an amino acid and the precursor to the catecholamine neurotransmitters dopamine and noradrenaline. Therefore, increasing tyrosine uptake may positively influence catecholamine-related psychological functioning. In 2015 Hase et al. conducted a review on the application of this specific nootropic and put forward that acute tyrosine loading is able to combat the decrements in working memory, slowed information processing, and worsening of mood that might be induced by physically or mentally demanding situations. Moreover, even in the absence of extreme conditions, tyrosine may improve convergent thinking (Hase et al., 2015). However, low sample sizes limit the conclusions of the respective acute loading studies and, therefore, also limit the conclusions of the review. In terms of chronic tyrosine supplementation, one study was included in this review which chronically supplemented tyrosine for two seasons to research station residents in Antarctica, and found that mood improved in the tyrosine group and worsened in the placebo group over the course of the winter (Palinkas et al., 2007). However, considering the profound psychophysiological adaptations triggered by this kind of extreme environment (which are further discussed in Chapter 14), this particular example can hardly be generalized.

Other catecholaminergic-based smart pills are tolcapone, levodopa, pramipexole, guanfacine, and clonidine. However, the research on these substances (some of which are medications with a range of well-known side-effects) regarding their mental performance-enhancing properties is limited. Therefore, these will not be further discussed in the present chapter.

Cholinergic-based enhancing substances

Choline is a primary component of the neurotransmitter acetylcholine, and functions with inositol as a basic constituent of lecithin. Acetylcholine is the primary neurotransmitter in the parasympathetic division of the autonomic nervous system (which is described in Chapter 2). In the brain, three major cholinergic subsystems are described: cholinergic neurons originating from the basal forebrain nuclei innervating mainly the cortex and the hippocampus; cholinergic neurons originating from the brainstem providing innervation to the thalamus and midbrain's dopaminergic areas; and cholinergic neurons originating from cholinergic interneurons in the striatum, providing local innervation (Fond et al., 2015; Woolf, 1991). Thus, cholinergic-based enhancing substances are those substances that mimic the action of endogenously released acetylcholine. In their review, Fond et al. (2015) list acetylcholinesterase inhibitors and acetylcholine precursors and cofactors as the main subdivisions of the cholinergic-based enhancing substances.

Acetylcholinesterase inhibitors (e.g., donepezil, rivastigmine), reversibly bind to the enzyme acetylcholinesterase and thereby inhibit the breakdown of acetylcholine, increasing the availability of acetylcholine at the cholinergic receptors, and subsequently enhancing cholinergic transmission. These drugs are licensed for the symptomatic treatment of dementia in Alzheimer's disease, where treatment demonstrated positive effects in terms of cognitive function, behaviour, and individuals' daily functioning (Birks, 2006). Different studies have investigated the potential neuro-enhancing effects of these drugs (especially donepezil) in healthy individuals. Despite some promising results and reported beneficial effects of donepezil on the retention of training of complex aviation tasks (Yesavage et al., 2002), on the verbal memory for words processed through semantic understanding (FitzGerald et al., 2008), on the episodic memory (Grön et al., 2005), and on the memory and attention deficits after sleep deprivation (Chuah & Chee, 2008; Chuah et al., 2009), transient negative effects on episodic memory were also reported (Beglinger et al., 2004; Beglinger et al., 2005). Overall, Repantis et al. (2010), who reviewed the available literature on this topic in 2010, concluded that, since large longitudinal studies were not available, the use of acetylcholinesterase inhibitors could not be supported nor rejected. Balsters et al. (2011) evaluated drug responses after acute and chronic donepezil administration and reported that donepezil can impair cognitive function in healthy older individuals. Klaassens et al. (2017) measured the effect of another acetylcholinesterase inhibitor (i.e., galantamine), which affected networks and regions that are more involved in learning, memory, and visual perception and processing, but they did not find any change in cognitive performance due to galantamine intake. Lastly, Baakman et al. (2016) performed the first human study with Gln-1062 (i.e., "Memogain"). Gln-1062 is a pharmacologically inactive prodrug of galantamine that preferentially enters the brain, where it is broken down into active galantamine. As such, Baakman et al. (2016) expected Gln-1062 to have fewer peripheral side effects than other cholinesterase inhibitors, with improved effectiveness. Eventually, they demonstrated that Gln-1062 had a dose-dependent positive effect on verbal memory and attention, mainly in the first hours after drug administration. These results warrant further exploration of this compound. However, the current research is still far too limited to support or reject neuroenhancement with acetylcholinesterase inhibitors.

The category acetylcholine precursors and cofactors comprise choline supplements as alpha-glycerophosphocholine, choline bitartrate, lecitine, and citicoline. Choline, identified as an essential nutrient by the FDA, is a precursor of the neurotransmitter acetylcholine. Choline can be found in a broad variety of foods (e.g., fish, dairy products), and is also available in various types of choline supplementation (Kansakar et al., 2023). Despite promising research on these molecules and their cognitive effects, recent reviews (Kansakar et al., 2023; Secades & Gareri, 2022) contain only a few studies where these supplements are really investigated as smart drugs in healthy individuals, with no conclusive results.

Psychedelic enhancing substances

Psychedelics induce distinct states of consciousness that are defined by modified sensory experiences, perceptions, cognitive processes, and self-awareness (Johnson et al., 2019; Nichols, 2016). The classic psychedelics include D-lysergic acid diethylamide (LSD), a synthetic compound first isolated from ergot by Hofmann of the Sandoz Company in 1938; mescaline, the active chemical in a variety of psychoactive cacti, most notably peyote (*Lophophora williamsii*); psilocybin, a psychoactive alkaloid found in a number of mushroom species, most notably psilocybe; and N,N-dimethyltryptamine (DMT), the primary hallucinogenic chemical in the Amazonian brew ayahuasca, also known as yage (Healy, 2021). Psychedelics are agonists or partial agonists for the brain serotonin 5-hydroxytryptamine 2A receptors, and as such, are able to trigger non-ordinary mental states (known as psychedelic experiences or "trips") and an apparent expansion of consciousness. Due to its current illicit status and absence of regulation, accurately determining the dosage of a substance is challenging.

Whereas none of these molecules are new, a fairly recent trend of "microdosing" has emerged. Microdosing refers to the practice of consuming a small fraction of the typical dose of a psychedelic compound. This subperceptual dose is significantly lower than what would be used to induce a "trip" or hallucinatory experience. The absence of a universally acknowledged definition for microdosing of any psychedelic substance poses challenges in conducting systematic research. One definition refers to a quantity that is roughly between 1/5 and 1/20 of a recreational dose (Grinspoon, 2022). Based on empirical evidence, a medium-strength dose of psilocybin is normally 2 to 3 grams of dried mushrooms, whereas a microdose typically would consist of approximately 0.3 grams. An impediment lies in the fact that the potency of mushrooms, for example, can significantly fluctuate, as they obviously lack regulation.

The viability of microdosing psychedelics as a strategy to enhance cognition in healthy individuals was reviewed by Bornemann (2020). Overall, this review evidences a variety of benefits including improvements in mood, focus, and creativity, with some people experiencing no discernible effects or expressing concerns about selective negative consequences like increased anxiety. However, many of the samples drawn in the cited studies were convenience samples and therefore likely biased and unrepresentative of the general population (Bornemann, 2020). Furthermore, considering the mediating effects of mood in these results, the suggestibility and therefore sensitivity to placebo effects warrants extra caution in this interpretation. Healy (2021) conducted a review on the effects of microdosing on memory, and concluded that classic psychedelics dose-dependently impair memory task performance, but may however enhance autobiographical memory. Bonnieux et al. (2023) reviewed both macro- and microdosing effects of psilocybin. One of their main conclusions is the lack of research of sufficient methodological quality. Regarding acute effects of microdosing, their reviewed results rather point towards impairment than improvement. Most recently, proper randomized double-blind placebo-controlled trials have started showing up in published results. These do not bode well for the use of microdosing for mental performance improvement. Cavanna et al. (2022) investigated the acute effects of 0.5 g of dried mushrooms (hence targeting psilocybin) on subjective experience, behaviour, creativity (divergent and convergent thinking), perception, cognition, and brain activity. The results showed noticeable subjective effects and altered EEG rhythms (a decreased power in the theta band), and even a mild cognitive impairment. Mallaroni et al. (2023) conducted a study on the most prevalently used novel serotonergic hallucinogen to date, 2,5-dimethoxy-4-bromophenethylamine (2C-B), a hallucinogenic phenethylamine derived from mescaline. Considering the potential impact of subjective experience, they did not use a placebo control, but rather the more "classical" psilocybin. They compared 2C-B (20 mg) to psilocybin (15 mg) and placebo, in a within-subjects, double-blind, placebo-controlled study of 22 healthy psychedelic-experienced participants. Results demonstrated equivalent psychomotor slowing and spatial memory impairments under either compound compared with placebo.

Although there has been a recent increase in the number of publications, research on this area is still extremely limited. As a result, the findings should be regarded as preliminary. It is important to acknowledge the potential for publication bias to result in the underreporting of negative findings, especially in relation to microdoses. Further investigation is required to examine the enduring effects of psilocybin on cognitive function and creative thinking, as well as on a comprehensive and standardized cognitive evaluation. As per the currently available research, acute effects of psychedelics microdosing seem to result in a mild cognitive impairment.

Conclusion and recommendations

Mental performance is multifaceted and complex. Subsequently, in the search to optimize mental performance, this complexity provides multiple opportunities to impact upon. The application of biochemical strategies to impact specific neurotransmitter levels in the brain is one of those opportunities. Multiple reviews (d'Angelo et al., 2017; Daubner et al., 2021; Fond et al., 2015; Jangwan et al., 2022; Schifano et al., 2022) have been published on the topic and all emphasize the possible benefits of biochemical neuroenhancement. However, they stress as well that "the non-medical use of any potent psychotropic raises serious ethical and legal issues, with nootropics having the potential to become a major public health concern" (Schifano et al., 2022) and "the number of randomized controlled trials is limited, and most of the studies found negative results. Future studies should assess both effectiveness and tolerance of repeated doses administration, and individual variability in dose response (including baseline characteristics and potential genetic polymorphisms)" (Fond et al., 2015).

Therefore, to date, it appears that the possible benefit of biochemical neuroenhancement still does not outweigh the possible risk. The example of modafinil demonstrates that, in terms of research, little to nothing is known about the real risk for abuse and overconfidence in both regular and occasional intake. Moreover, the largest part of the studies in healthy individuals did not investigate possible side effects of modafinil intake (for example, regarding exercise tolerance) and no information is available on long-term effects or possible abstinence effects. These are of course important considerations in the decision-making process of implementing modafinil in high-performance environments, and calls for further action and more research. These limitations are often encountered in the research on other nootropics as well, and form a major concern in advocating the implementation of any nootropic. To address this concern, Colzato et al. (2021) argue in their position paper that a much stronger emphasis on mechanistic theorizing is necessary in guiding future research on both the upsides and the downsides of cognitive enhancement. By doing so, two basic principles should be kept in mind; the neuro-competition principle and the nonlinearity principle. The first principle relates to the simple notion that the brain and its subsystems are both logically and empirically limited in capacity, and improving the efficiency of one particular function or process must imply some kind of loss associated with another function or process or representation. The second principle links back to the inverted-U shaped relation between brain neurotransmitter levels and mental performance that was introduced in the section on catecholaminergic-based enhancing substances. Furthermore, another reasoning error shows up in research questions related to the pharmacological enhancement of performance. It is assuming that a molecule's influence on a particular cognitive modality is linear, with improvements in pathology being extrapolated to healthy individuals.

Despite the majority of the scientific literature agreeing on the fact that pharmacological neuroenhancement in healthy individuals should not yet be implemented, the availability and accessibility of a lot of nootropics has led to a booming use of cognitive enhancers in the general population (Brühl & Sahakian, 2016; Emanuel et al., 2013; Kortekaas-Rijlaarsdam et al., 2019). Detailed national information on diversion and misuse of pharmaceutical stimulants from different regions in the world is limited. As is often the case, legislation and regulation are delayed compared to actual use, as is illustrated by the example of NPSfinder®, a navigating software which was designed to automatically scan the open web for new psychoactive substances (NPS) (Schifano et al., 2021). In their review, Daubner et al. (2021) were able to neatly list a few examples that demonstrate some major evidence for pharmaceutical stimulant misuse and diversion. In the meantime, a few recommendations can be put forward to regulate and control the use of nootropics.

Recommendations

As stated before, accepting or rejecting the use of smart pills for mental enhancement is a matter of national culture and legislation. However, should an individual or a specific organization consider the use of a nootropic, we advocate for applying the following recommendations:

- Treat as a controlled prescription drug regarding custody, transport, and transfer. The same chain of responsibility should be followed as with any other controlled substance.
- Inform and educate the audience regarding potential benefits and risks.
- Considering the underinvestigated individual variability in response, schedule personal tolerance tests documenting all performance-related effects (physical and mental) as well as the occurrence of side effects. This is labour-intensive, yet it familiarizes individuals with the perception of positive and negative effects and builds a trust relationship, where the discussion regarding the use of a nootropic becomes a neutral issue, where the decision is based on the effects, rather than a patronizing attitude regarding drugs.
- If implemented at all, monitor the potential for abuse.

References

Baakman, A. C., 't Hart, E., Kay, D. G., Stevens, J., Klaassen, E. S., Maelicke, A., & Groeneveld, G. J. (2016). First in human study with a prodrug of galantamine: Improved benefit-risk ratio? *Alzheimers Dement (N Y)*, *2*(1), 13–22. https://doi.org/10.1016/j.trci.2015.12.003

Balsters, J. H., O'Connell, R. G., Martin, M. P., Galli, A., Cassidy, S. M., Kilcullen, S. M., . . . Robertson, I. H. (2011). Donepezil impairs memory in healthy older subjects: behavioural, EEG and simultaneous EEG/fMRI biomarkers. *PLoS One*, *6*(9), e24126. https://doi.org/10.1371/journal.pone.0024126

Baranski, J. V., Pigeau, R., Dinich, P., & Jacobs, I. (2004). Effects of modafinil on cognitive and metacognitive performance. *Hum Psychopharmacol. 19*(5), 323–332. https://doi.org/10.1002/hup.596

Baranski, J. V., & Pigeau, R. A. (1997). Self-monitoring cognitive performance during sleep deprivation: effects of modafinil, d-amphetamine and placebo. *J Sleep Res. 6*(2), 84–91. https://doi.org/10.1111/j.1365-2869.1997.00032.x

Becker, M., Repantis, D., Dresler, M., & Kühn, S. (2022). Cognitive enhancement: Effects of methylphenidate, modafinil, and caffeine on latent memory and resting state functional connectivity in healthy adults. *Hum Brain Mapp. 43*(14), 4225–4238. https://doi.org/10.1002/hbm.25949

Beglinger, L. J., Gaydos, B. L., Kareken, D. A., Tangphao-Daniels, O., Siemers, E. R., & Mohs, R. C. (2004). Neuropsychological test performance in healthy volunteers before and after donepezil administration. *J Psychopharmacol. 18*(1), 102–108. https://doi.org/10.1177/0269881104040248

Beglinger, L. J., Tangphao-Daniels, O., Kareken, D. A., Zhang, L., Mohs, R., & Siemers, E. R. (2005). Neuropsychological test performance in healthy elderly volunteers before and after donepezil administration: A randomized, controlled study. *J Clin Psychopharmacol. 25*(2), 159–165. https://doi.org/10.1097/01.jcp.0000155822.51962.b4

Birks, J. (2006). Cholinesterase inhibitors for Alzheimer's disease. *Cochrane Database Syst Rev. 2006*(1), CD005593. https://doi.org/10.1002/14651858.CD005593

Bonnieux, J. N., VanderZwaag, B., Premji, Z., Garcia-Romeu, A., Garcia-Barrera, M.A. (2023). Psilocybin's effects on cognition and creativity: A scoping review. *J Psychopharmacol*. Jul;37(7), 635–648. doi: 10.1177/02698811231179801. Epub 2023 Jul 3. PMID: 37395359; PMCID: PMC10350723

Bornemann, J. (2020). The viability of microdosing Psychedelics as a strategy to enhance cognition and well-being – An early review. *J Psychoactive Drugs*, *52*(4), 300–308. https://doi.org/10.1080/02791072.2020.1761573

Brühl, A. B., & Sahakian, B. J. (2016). Drugs, games, and devices for enhancing cognition: implications for work and society. *Ann N Y Acad Sci. 1369*(1), 195–217. https://doi.org/10.1111/nyas.13040

Cappelletti, S., Piacentino, D., Sani, G., & Aromatario, M. (2015). Caffeine: Cognitive and physical performance enhancer or psychoactive drug? *Curr Neuropharmacol. 13*(1), 71–88. https://doi.org/10.2174/1570159X13666141210215655

Carswell, A. T., Howland, K., Martinez-Gonzalez, B., Baron, P., & Davison, G. (2020). The effect of caffeine on cognitive performance is influenced by CYP1A2 but not ADORA2A genotype, yet neither genotype affects exercise performance in healthy adults. *Eur J Appl Physiol. 120*(7), 1495–1508. https://doi.org/10.1007/s00421-020-04384-8

Cavanna, F., Muller, S., de la Fuente, L. A., Zamberlan, F., Palmucci, M., Janeckova, L., Kuchar, M., Pallavicini, C., & Tagliazucchi, E. (2022). Microdosing with psilocybin mushrooms: A double-blind placebo-controlled study. *Transl Psychiatry*. Aug 2;12(1), 307. doi: 10.1038/s41398-022-02039-0. PMID: 35918311; PMCID: PMC9346139

Chuah, L. Y., & Chee, M. W. (2008). Cholinergic augmentation modulates visual task performance in sleep-deprived young adults. *J Neurosci*, *28*(44), 11369–11377. https://doi.org/10.1523/JNEUROSCI.4045-08.2008

Chuah, L. Y., Chong, D. L., Chen, A. K., Rekshan, W. R., Tan, J. C., Zheng, H., & Chee, M. W. (2009). Donepezil improves episodic memory in young individuals vulnerable to the effects of sleep deprivation. *Sleep*, *32*(8), 999–1010. https://doi.org/10.1093/sleep/32.8.999

Colzato, L. S., Hommel, B., & Beste, C. (2021). The downsides of cognitive enhancement. *Neuroscientist*, *27*(4), 322–330. https://doi.org/10.1177/1073858420945971

Cools, R., & D'Esposito, M. (2011). Inverted-U-shaped dopamine actions on human working memory and cognitive control. *Biol Psychiatry. 69*(12), e113–125. https://doi.org/10.1016/j.biopsych.2011.03.028

Cools, R., Gibbs, S. E., Miyakawa, A., Jagust, W., & D'Esposito, M. (2008). Working memory capacity predicts dopamine synthesis capacity in the human striatum. *J Neurosci*, *28*(5), 1208–1212. https://doi.org/10.1523/JNEUROSCI.4475-07.2008

d'Angelo, L. C., Savulich, G., & Sahakian, B. J. (2017). Lifestyle use of drugs by healthy people for enhancing cognition, creativity, motivation and pleasure. *Br J Pharmacol. 174*(19), 3257–3267. https://doi.org/10.1111/bph.13813

Daubner, J., Arshaad, M. I., Henseler, C., Hescheler, J., Ehninger, D., Broich, K., . . . Weiergräber, M. (2021). Pharmacological neuroenhancement: Current aspects of categorization, epidemiology, pharmacology, drug development, ethics, and future perspectives. *Neural Plast*, *2021*, 8823383. https://doi.org/10.1155/2021/8823383

Dresler, M., Sandberg, A., Bublitz, C., Ohla, K., Trenado, C., Mroczko-Wąsowicz, A., . . . Repantis, D. (2019). Hacking the Brain: Dimensions of Cognitive Enhancement. *ACS Chem Neurosci. 10*(3), 1137–1148. https://doi.org/10.1021/acschemneuro.8b00571

Einöther, S. J., & Giesbrecht, T. (2013). Caffeine as an attention enhancer: Reviewing existing assumptions. *Psychopharmacology (Berl). 225*(2), 251–274. https://doi.org/10.1007/s00213-012-2917-4

Emanuel, R. M., Frellsen, S. L., Kashima, K. J., Sanguino, S. M., Sierles, F. S., & Lazarus, C. J. (2013). Cognitive enhancement drug use among future physicians: findings from a multi-institutional census of medical students. *J Gen Intern Med. 28*(8), 1028–1034. https://doi.org/10.1007/s11606-012-2249-4

Esposito, R., Cilli, F., Pieramico, V., Ferretti, A., Macchia, A., Tommasi, M., . . . Sensi, S. L. (2013). Acute effects of modafinil on brain resting state networks in young healthy subjects. *PLoS One*, *8*(7), e69224. https://doi.org/10.1371/journal.pone.0069224

Fernández, A., Mascayano, F., Lips, W., Painel, A., Norambuena, J., & Madrid, E. (2015). Effects of modafinil on attention performance, short-term memory and executive function in university students: a randomized trial. *Medwave*, *15*(5), e6166. https://doi.org/10.5867/medwave.2015.05.6166

Finke, K., Dodds, C. M., Bublak, P., Regenthal, R., Baumann, F., Manly, T., & Müller, U. (2010). Effects of modafinil and methylphenidate on visual attention capacity: A TVA-based study. *Psychopharmacology (Berl). 210*(3), 317–329. https://doi.org/10.1007/s00213-010-1823-x

FitzGerald, D. B., Crucian, G. P., Mielke, J. B., Shenal, B. V., Burks, D., Womack, K. B., . . . Heilman, K. M. (2008). Effects of donepezil on verbal memory after semantic processing in healthy older adults. *Cogn Behav Neurol. 21*(2), 57–64. https://doi.org/10.1097/WNN.0b013e3181799df1

Fond, G., Micoulaud-Franchi, J. A., Brunel, L., Macgregor, A., Miot, S., Lopez, R., . . . Repantis, D. (2015). Innovative mechanisms of action for pharmaceutical cognitive enhancement: A systematic review. *Psychiatry Res. 229*(1-2), 12–20. https://doi.org/10.1016/j.psychres.2015.07.006

Gazzaniga, M. S. (2005). *The Ethical Brain: The Science of Our Moral Dilemmas*. Dana Press.

Greely, H., Sahakian, B., Harris, J., Kessler, R. C., Gazzaniga, M., Campbell, P., & Farah, M. J. (2008). Towards responsible use of cognitive-enhancing drugs by the healthy. *Nature*, *456*(7223), 702–705. https://doi.org/10.1038/456702a

Grinspoon, P. (2022). The popularity of microdosing of psychedelics: What does the science say? Harvard Health Publishing. www.health.harvard.edu/blog/the-popularity-of-microdosing-of-psychedelics-what-does-the-science-say-202209192819 Retrieved February 21 2024.

Grön, G., Kirstein, M., Thielscher, A., Riepe, M. W., & Spitzer, M. (2005). Cholinergic enhancement of episodic memory in healthy young adults. *Psychopharmacology (Berl). 182*(1), 170–179. https://doi.org/10.1007/s00213-005-0043-2

Hase, A., Jung, S. E., & aan het Rot, M. (2015). Behavioral and cognitive effects of tyrosine intake in healthy human adults. *Pharmacol Biochem Behav. 133*, 1–6. https://doi.org/10.1016/j.pbb.2015.03.008

Healy, C. J. (2021). The acute effects of classic psychedelics on memory in humans. *Psychopharmacology (Berl)*. Mar;238(3), 639–653. doi: 10.1007/s00213-020-05756-w. Epub 2021 Jan 9. PMID: 33420592

Hutson, P. H., Tarazi, F. I., Madhoo, M., Slawecki, C., & Patkar, A. A. (2014). Preclinical pharmacology of amphetamine: Implications for the treatment of neuropsychiatric disorders. *Pharmacol Ther*, *143*(3), 253–264. https://doi.org/10.1016/j.pharmthera.2014.03.005

Ikeda, Y., Funayama, T., Tateno, A., Fukayama, H., Okubo, Y., & Suzuki, H. (2017). Modafinil enhances alerting-related brain activity in attention networks. *Psychopharmacology (Berl). 234*(14), 2077–2089. https://doi.org/10.1007/s00213-017-4614-9

Jangwan, N. S., Ashraf, G. M., Ram, V., Singh, V., Alghamdi, B. S., Abuzenadah, A. M., & Singh, M. F. (2022). Brain augmentation and neuroscience technologies: current applications, challenges, ethics and future prospects. *Front Syst Neurosci. 16*, 1000495. https://doi.org/10.3389/fnsys.2022.1000495

Joh, T. H., & Hwang, O. (1987). Dopamine beta-hydroxylase: Biochemistry and molecular biology. *Ann N Y Acad Sci. 493*, 342–350. https://doi.org/10.1111/j.1749-6632.1987.tb27217.x

Johnson, M. W., Hendricks, P. S., Barrett, F.S., et al. (2019) Classic psychedelics: An integrative review of epidemiology, therapeutics, mystical experience, and brain network function. *Pharmacol Ther*. 197, 83–102.

Kansakar, U., Trimarco, V., Mone, P., Varzideh, F., Lombardi, A., & Santulli, G. (2023). Choline supplements: An update. *Front Endocrinol (Lausanne). 14*, 1148166. https://doi.org/10.3389/fendo.2023.1148166

Kapur, A. (2020). Is Methylphenidate beneficial and safe in pharmacological cognitive enhancement? *CNS Drugs*, *34*(10), 1045–1062. https://doi.org/10.1007/s40263-020-00758-w

Kassim, F. M. (2023). Systematic reviews of the acute effects of amphetamine on working memory and other cognitive performances in healthy individuals, with a focus on the potential influence of personality traits. *Hum Psychopharmacol. 38*(1), e2856. https://doi.org/10.1002/hup.2856

Klaassens, B. L., Rombouts, S. A., Winkler, A. M., van Gorsel, H. C., van der Grond, J., & van Gerven, J. M. (2017). Time related effects on functional brain connectivity after serotonergic and cholinergic neuromodulation. *Hum Brain Mapp. 38*(1), 308–325. https://doi.org/10.1002/hbm.23362

Kortekaas-Rijlaarsdam, A. F., Luman, M., Sonuga-Barke, E., & Oosterlaan, J. (2019). Does methylphenidate improve academic performance? A systematic review and meta-analysis. *Eur Child Adolesc Psychiatry. 28*(2), 155–164. https://doi.org/10.1007/s00787-018-1106-3

Lagarde, D., Batejat, D., Van Beers, P., Sarafian, D., & Pradella, S. (1995). Interest of modafinil, a new psychostimulant, during a sixty-hour sleep deprivation experiment. *Fundam Clin Pharmacol. 9*(3), 271–279. https://doi.org/10.1111/j.1472-8206.1995.tb00295.x

Lees, J., Michalopoulou, P. G., Lewis, S. W., Preston, S., Bamford, C., Collier, T., . . . Drake, R. J. (2017). Modafinil and cognitive enhancement in schizophrenia and healthy volunteers: The effects of test battery in a randomised controlled trial. *Psychol Med. 47*(13), 2358–2368. https://doi.org/10.1017/S0033291717000885

Mallaroni, P., Mason, N. L., Reckweg, J. T., Paci, R., Ritscher, S., Toennes, S. W., Theunissen, E. L., Kuypers, K. P. C., & Ramaekers, J. G. (2023). Assessment of the Acute Effects of 2C-B vs. Psilocybin on Subjective Experience, Mood, and Cognition. *Clin Pharmacol Ther*. Aug;114(2), 423–433. doi: 10.1002/cpt.2958. Epub 2023 Jun 11. PMID: 37253161

Marchant, N. L., Kamel, F., Echlin, K., Grice, J., Lewis, M., & Rusted, J. M. (2009). Modafinil improves rapid shifts of attention. *Psychopharmacology (Berl). 202*(1-3), 487–495. https://doi.org/10.1007/s00213-008-1395-1

Mereu, M., Bonci, A., Newman, A. H., & Tanda, G. (2013). The neurobiology of modafinil as an enhancer of cognitive performance and a potential treatment for substance use disorders. *Psychopharmacology (Berl). 229*(3), 415–434. https://doi.org/10.1007/s00213-013-3232-4

Minzenberg, M. J., & Carter, C. S. (2008). Modafinil: A review of neurochemical actions and effects on cognition. *Neuropsychopharmacology*, *33*(7), 1477–1502. https://doi.org/10.1038/sj.npp.1301534

Mohamed, A. (2016). The effects of modafinil on convergent and divergent thinking of creativity: A randomized controlled trial. *Journal of Creative Behavior*, *50*(4), 252–267.

Mohamed, A. D., & Lewis, C. R. (2014). Modafinil increases the latency of response in the hayling sentence completion test in healthy volunteers: A randomised controlled trial. *PLoS One*, *9*(11), e110639. https://doi.org/10.1371/journal.pone.0110639

Müller, U., Rowe, J. B., Rittman, T., Lewis, C., Robbins, T. W., & Sahakian, B. J. (2013). Effects of modafinil on non-verbal cognition, task enjoyment and creative thinking in healthy volunteers. *Neuropharmacology*, *64*(5), 490–495. https://doi.org/10.1016/j.neuropharm.2012.07.009

Müller, U., Steffenhagen, N., Regenthal, R., & Bublak, P. (2004). Effects of modafinil on working memory processes in humans. *Psychopharmacology (Berl). 177*(1-2), 161–169. https://doi.org/10.1007/s00213-004-1926-3

Napoletano, F., Schifano, F., Corkery, J. M., Guirguis, A., Arillotta, D., Zangani, C., & Vento, A. (2020). The Psychonauts' world of cognitive enhancers. *Front Psychiatry. 11*, 546796. https://doi.org/10.3389/fpsyt.2020.546796

Nichols, D. E. (2016). Psychedelics. *Pharmacol Rev. 68*(2), 264–355. https://doi.org/10.1124/pr.115.011478

Ooi, T., Wong, S. H., & See, B. (2019). Modafinil as a Stimulant for Military Aviators. *Aerosp Med Hum Perform. 90*(5), 480–483. https://doi.org/10.3357/AMHP.5298.2019

Ott, T., & Nieder, A. (2019). Dopamine and Cognitive Control in Prefrontal Cortex. *Trends Cogn Sci. 23*(3), 213–234. https://doi.org/10.1016/j.tics.2018.12.006

Palinkas, L. A., Reedy, K. R., Smith, M., Anghel, M., Steel, G. D., Reeves, D., . . . Reed, H. L. (2007). Psychoneuroendocrine effects of combined thyroxine and triiodothyronine versus tyrosine during prolonged Antarctic residence. *Int J Circumpolar Health. 66*(5), 401–417.

Prochazkova, L., Lippelt, D. P., Colzato, L. S., Kuchar, M., Sjoerds, Z., & Hommel, B. (2018). Exploring the effect of microdosing psychedelics on creativity in an open-label natural setting. *Psychopharmacology (Berl). 235*(12), 3401–3413. https://doi.org/10.1007/s00213-018-5049-7

Randall, D., Shneerson, J., & File, S. (2005). Cognitive effects of modafinil in student volunteers may depend on IQ. *Pharmacology Biochemistry and Behavior*. 82(1), 133–139.

Randall, D. C., Fleck, N. L., Shneerson, J. M., & File, S. E. (2004). The cognitive-enhancing properties of modafinil are limited in non-sleep-deprived middle-aged volunteers. *Pharmacol Biochem Behav. 77*(3), 547–555. https://doi.org/10.1016/j.pbb.2003.12.016

Randall, D. C., Viswanath, A., Bharania, P., Elsabagh, S. M., Hartley, D. E., Shneerson, J. M., & File, S. E. (2005). Does modafinil enhance cognitive performance in young volunteers who are not sleep-deprived? *J Clin Psychopharmacol. 25*(2), 175–179. https://doi.org/10.1097/01.jcp.0000155816.21467.25

Rattray, B., Martin, K., Hewitt, A., Cooper, G., & McDonald, W. (2019). Effect of acute modafinil ingestion on cognitive and physical performance following mental exertion. *Hum Psychopharmacol. 34*(4), e2700. https://doi.org/10.1002/hup.2700

Repantis, D., Bovy, L., Ohla, K., Kühn, S., & Dresler, M. (2021). Cognitive enhancement effects of stimulants: A randomized controlled trial testing methylphenidate, modafinil, and caffeine. *Psychopharmacology (Berl). 238*(2), 441–451. https://doi.org/10.1007/s00213-020-05691-w

Repantis, D., Laisney, O., & Heuser, I. (2010). Acetylcholinesterase inhibitors and memantine for neuroenhancement in healthy individuals: A systematic review. *Pharmacol Res. 61*(6), 473–481. https://doi.org/10.1016/j.phrs.2010.02.009

Rogers, P. J., Heatherley, S. V., Mullings, E. L., & Smith, J. E. (2013). Faster but not smarter: Effects of caffeine and caffeine withdrawal on alertness and performance. *Psychopharmacology (Berl). 226*(2), 229–240. https://doi.org/10.1007/s00213-012-2889-4

Scahill, L., Carroll, D., & Burke, K. (2004). Methylphenidate: Mechanism of action and clinical update. *J Child Adolesc Psychiatr Nurs. 17*(2), 85–86. https://doi.org/10.1111/j.1744-6171.2004.00085.x

Schifano, F., Catalani, V., Sharif, S., Napoletano, F., Corkery, J. M., Arillotta, D., . . . Guirguis, A. (2022). Benefits and Harms of 'Smart Drugs' (Nootropics) in healthy individuals. *Drugs*, *82*(6), 633–647. https://doi.org/10.1007/s40265-022-01701-7

Schifano, F., Chiappini, S., Corkery, J. M., Scherbaum, N., & Guirguis, A. (2021). The e-psychonaut drugs' psychopharmacology. *Curr Opin Pharmacol.* Apr;57, 165–174. doi: 10.1016/j.coph.2021.02.008. Epub 2021 Mar 25. PMID: 33774473

Schmidt, A., Müller, F., Dolder, P. C., Schmid, Y., Zanchi, D., Liechti, M. E., & Borgwardt, S. (2017). Comparative effects of methylphenidate, modafinil, and MDMA on response inhibition neural networks in healthy subjects. *Int J Neuropsychopharmacol. 20*(9), 712–720. https://doi.org/10.1093/ijnp/pyx037

Secades, J. J., & Gareri, P. (2022). Citicoline: Pharmacological and clinical review, 2022 update. *Rev Neurol. 75*(s05), S1-S89. https://doi.org/10.33588/rn.75s05.2022311

Sharif, S., Guirguis, A., Fergus, S., & Schifano, F. (2021). The use and impact of cognitive enhancers among university students: A systematic review. *Brain Sci. 11*(3). https://doi.org/10.3390/brainsci11030355

Smith, M. E., & Farah, M. J. (2011). Are prescription stimulants "smart pills"? The epidemiology and cognitive neuroscience of prescription stimulant use by normal healthy individuals. *Psychol Bull. 137*(5), 717–741. https://doi.org/10.1037/a0023825

Taneja, I., Diedrich, A., Black, B. K., Byrne, D. W., Paranjape, S. Y., & Robertson, D. (2005). Modafinil elicits sympathomedullary activation. *Hypertension*, *45*(4), 612–618. https://doi.org/10.1161/01.HYP.0000158267.66763.63

Teodorini, R. D., Rycroft, N., & Smith-Spark, J. H. (2020). The off-prescription use of modafinil: An online survey of perceived risks and benefits. *PLoS One*, *15*(2), e0227818. https://doi.org/10.1371/journal.pone.0227818

Turner, D. C., Robbins, T. W., Clark, L., Aron, A. R., Dowson, J., & Sahakian, B. J. (2003). Cognitive enhancing effects of modafinil in healthy volunteers. *Psychopharmacology (Berl). 165*(3), 260–269. https://doi.org/10.1007/s00213-002-1250-8

Van Puyvelde, M., Van Cutsem, J., Lacroix, E., & Pattyn, N. (2022). A State-of-the-Art Review on the Use of Modafinil as A Performance-enhancing Drug in the Context of Military Operationality. *Mil Med. 187*(1-2), 52–64. https://doi.org/10.1093/milmed/usab398

Winder-Rhodes, S. E., Chamberlain, S. R., Idris, M. I., Robbins, T. W., Sahakian, B. J., & Müller, U. (2010). Effects of modafinil and prazosin on cognitive and physiological functions in healthy volunteers. *J Psychopharmacol. 24*(11), 1649–1657. https://doi.org/10.1177/0269881109105899

Woolf, N. J. (1991). Cholinergic systems in mammalian brain and spinal cord. *Prog Neurobiol. 37*(6), 475–524. https://doi.org/10.1016/0301-0082(91)90006-m

Yesavage, J. A., Mumenthaler, M. S., Taylor, J. L., Friedman, L., O'Hara, R., Sheikh, J., . . . Whitehouse, P. J. (2002). Donepezil and flight simulator performance: Effects on retention of complex skills. *Neurology, 59*(1), 123–125. https://doi.org/10.1212/wnl.59.1.123

7 Neurostimulation Tools and Approaches

Kristin J. Heaton, Caitlin Ridgewell, Jessica Couse, and William Neumeier

Introduction

The past two decades have seen a marked increase in commercially available products for enhancing mental performance. These approaches are largely device-driven and capitalize on advanced technologies enabling both direct and indirect stimulation of the brain and cranial nerves to influence a range of neural processes, including attention, learning, memory, arousal, and mood. However, as new devices enter the commercial market at a rapid pace, the supporting research needed to document the efficacy and longer-term health impacts of using such technologies often lags.

Elite performers – collegiate and professional athletes, military Special Operation Forces (SOF) personnel, corporate top performers, and first responders – are early adopters and keen consumers of products that can help them achieve and sustain peak mental and physical performance, and more rapidly restore mental fitness after training, deployment, or injuries. It is not surprising then that these individuals are often targeted by product developers and sales representatives, even in cases where empirical investigations related to product efficacy, safety, or health impacts are lacking. Moreover, many commercially available technologies for brain and peripheral nerve stimulation receive minimal oversight by health and safety boards, since these products are marketed non-medical devices.

Certainly, there is a need – and market – for safe, non-addictive methods to build and maintain peak levels of mental performance or to facilitate recovery in elite performers. However, caution must be used when evaluating new and emerging technologies, including neurostimulation devices. The intent of this chapter is to provide an overview of the currently available neurostimulation tools and technologies, as well as considerations for selection and utilization of these approaches based on the current state of science.

Neurostimulation approaches

Neurostimulation represents a broad range of techniques designed to modulate the activity of the central and peripheral nervous system. These approaches can be more or less invasive, ranging from insertion of microelectrodes directly into brain tissue to passing low-level energy current through the skin to stimulate peripheral nerves. Neurostimulation has been used for decades in the treatment of neurological disorders and for pain management. However, based on positive outcomes demonstrated in clinical applications, interest continues to grow in applications aimed at optimizing mental performance in non-clinical settings. This interest has been accompanied by a proliferation of commercially available products claiming to improve cognitive function in healthy adults. In this section, we explore several neurostimulation approaches that have been identified

DOI: 10.4324/9781003378969-9

as having potential or demonstrated benefits for performance improvement. This review is not intended to be exhaustive, but rather aims to provide a broad overview of the technology space and current evidence supporting the efficacy of these approaches.

Transcranial direct current stimulation

The concept of applying electrical currents through the skull and into brain tissue is not new. In fact, electrical stimulation of the brain has been used since the 18th century to treat depression and other psychiatric illnesses (Brunoni, et al., 2012). Today, transcranial direct current stimulation (tDCS), a non-invasive approach that has shown effectiveness in modulating brain activity in both clinical and healthy populations, is commonly used. In this approach, electrical current is passed from electrodes on the scalp through the skin and skull to the underlying cortical tissue, allowing for manipulation of cortical excitability across targeted brain regions (Thair, Holloway, Newport, & Smith, 2017). Typically, the electrical stimulation is mild, with intensities at or below 4 mA (Bikson, et al., 2016; Davis & Smith, 2019). The applied electrical current results in a polarization of neuronal resting membrane potential and therefore, spontaneous excitation or inhibition of entire networks of neurons (Brunoni, et al., 2012; Sparing & Mottaghy, 2008). Whether and to what extent the stimulation excites or inhibits neurons depends upon the selected stimulation parameters. These may include the size of the electrode (Ho, et al., 2016), electrical current flow (anode versus cathode) and current intensity (mA), frequency (how often) and duration of the applied stimulation, and whether the stimulation is applied during (online) or before (offline) a task is performed (Davis & Smith, 2019). Research has shown that online and offline stimulation can elicit different behavioural responses (Feltman, Hayes, & Bernhardt, 2019; Choe, Coffman, Bergstedt, Zeigler, & Phillips, 2016; Barbieri, Negrini, Nitsche, & Rivolta, 2016). In tDCS administration, both anode and cathode electrodes may be used. Anodal current is considered to be "positive" and excites cortical neurons by depolarizing them and generating an action potential; cathodal current is considered to be "negative" and inhibits cortical activity by hyperpolarizing neurons (Thair, Holloway, Newport, & Smith, 2017). This is supported by functional magnetic resonance imaging (fMRI) studies showing increased blood oxygen level-dependent (BOLD) activity in anodally-stimulated regions of interest (Gilam, et al., 2018; Hauser, et al., 2016). The utility of anodal compared to cathodal stimulation depends on the tissue being stimulated and the desired behavioural response. For example, anodal stimulation may be used to increase the likelihood of a behaviour while cathodal stimulation may be used to decrease the likelihood of certain behaviours (Thair, Holloway, Newport, & Smith, 2017). Stimulation may be applied in a single or multiple sessions, with some research suggesting that application over multiple sessions may increase the persistence of effects over time (Shin, Foerster, & Nitsche, 2015). To date, and across tens of thousands of recorded sessions, no serious adverse events have been reported as a result of tDCS administration (Bikson, et al., 2016), although mild transient symptoms, including dizziness, fatigue, and itching, tingling, burning, skin irritation, and scalp pain at the site of stimulation, have been reported (Been, Ngo, Miller, & Fitzgerald, 2007; Feltman, Hayes, & Bernhardt, 2019; Nikolin, Huggins, Martin, Alonzo, & Loo, 2018).

Transcranial direct current stimulation exerts its effects on the brain via generation of action potentials and alterations in synaptic strength via N-methyl-D-aspartate (NMDA) receptors (Brunoni, et al., 2012), changes in the activity of neurotransmitters such as gamma aminobutyric acid (GABA) (Antonenko, et al., 2017; Brunoni, et al., 2012) and dopamine (Fonteneau, et al., 2018), and modulation of intracortical and corticospinal neuron excitability (Brunoni, et al., 2012). Concurrent tDCS-fMRI studies have demonstrated that tDCS increases the efficiency of brain network activity by decreasing functional connectivity between relevant brain structures, which decreases processing effort (Antonenko, et al., 2017; Fiori, Kunz, Kuhnke, Marangolo, &

Hartwigsen, 2018; Wang, et al., 2018). Increases in myoinositol, glutamate, glutamine, and N-acetyl-aspartate that are associated with changes in network connectivity after tDCS (Hunter, et al., 2015) have also been observed using magnetic resonance spectroscopy (MRS) (Clark, Coffman, Trumbo, & Gasparovic, 2011; Rango, et al., 2008). Electroencephalography (EEG) studies have shown alterations in neural oscillation frequency and power change after tDCS stimulation (Accornero, et al., 2014; Jacobson, Ezra, Berger, & Lavidor, 2012). Despite evidence that tDCS induces changes in neural function and activity, at least one systematic review has found no effect of tDCS on outcomes using fMRI, EEG, and other neurophysiological measures (Horvath, Forte, & Carter, 2015a).

A number of studies have explored the effects of tDCS on cognition in healthy individuals, particularly in the areas of learning, attention, memory, and executive functions. In one review, single sessions of anodal tDCS over the dorsolateral prefrontal cortex (dlPFC) were found to improve response times on a variety of cognitive tasks (Dedoncker, Brunoni, Baeken, & Vanderhasselt, 2016). It is important to note that factors such as current intensity (Dedoncker, Brunoni, Baeken, & Vanderhasselt, 2016), repetition (single session versus multiple sessions) (Horvath, Forte, & Carter, 2015b), and both timing (online or offline) and duration of stimulation (Westwood & Romani, 2017) may influence the overall effect of tDCS on cognitive performance. For example, improvements in cognitive function can persist up to three months after training, especially when stimulation is repeated (Shin, Foerster, & Nitsche, 2015). However, results from these studies should be viewed with caution since the studies highlighted may have had insufficient statistical power (Medina & Cason, 2017).

Among the cognitive domains most consistently targeted by both online and offline tDCS are learning, particularly in terms of motor skills, and executive functions (Buch, et al., 2017; Shin, Foerster, & Nitsche, 2015). With respect to learning, procedural and language learning may be enhanced using online, anodal tDCS over the left temporo-parietal junction (Meinzer, et al., 2014) or cerebellum (Ferrucci, et al., 2013) and the left inferior frontal gyrus (De Vries, et al., 2010). Online anodal tDCS over the dlPFC has demonstrated improvements in the acquisition of flight skills during flight simulation (Choe, Coffman, Bergstedt, Zeigler, & Phillips, 2016), as well as information processing and multitasking skills (Nelson, et al., 2016) and cognitive control (Gbadeyan, McMahon, Steinhauser, & Meinzer, 2016). Anodal stimulation over the right and left temporal lobes may also improve navigation efficiency among those who have poor directional sense (Brunyé, et al., 2014). Similarly, attention generally appears to be improved by anodal tDCS, with reviews indicating that cathodal stimulation impairs attention when applied to the dlPFC and parietal cortex, but anodal stimulation applied to the right frontal cortex improves selective attention (Shin, Foerster, & Nitsche, 2015). Offline, anodal tDCS over the right dlPFC has been associated with improved alertness but not orienting or attention (Coffman, Trumbo, & Clark, 2012), while offline, anodal tDCS over the left dlPFC demonstrated improved executive functions, attention, working memory, mood, reaction times, and fatigue after 30 to 36 hours of continued wakefulness (Cheng, et al., 2021; McIntire, McKinley, Nelson, & Goodyear, 2017). Interestingly, these improvements in vigilance appear to be more significant than those achieved through the use of a stimulant such as caffeine (McIntire, McKinley, Nelson, & Goodyear, 2017). Memory, too, may benefit from tDCS, as studies show that offline, anodal stimulation applied to the right dlPFC can improve name recall by up to 50% (Matzen, Trumbo, Leach, & Leshikar, 2015) and stimulation applied to the right occipital cortex enhances memory for faces and objects (Barbieri, Negrini, Nitsche, & Rivolta, 2016). However, the effects of tDCS on episodic memory are less consistent and performance may either be unaffected (Galli, Vadillo, Sirota, Feurra, & Medvedeva, 2019) or impaired (Brunyé, Smith, Horner, & Thomas, 2018) by stimulation. Studies of perception indicate that stimulation over the right inferior frontal gyrus enhances threat detection (Falcone, Coffman, Clark, & Parasuraman, 2012) and stimulation over the right dlPFC enhances visual search accuracy (McKinley, et al., 2013). Additionally, stimulation over the right posterior parietal cortex also improves spatial reorientation (Roy, Sparing, Fink, & Hesse, 2015). Working memory is also affected by tDCS, particularly when applied over the dlPFC. Spatial location-monitoring and verbal identity-monitoring are enhanced after offline, anodal stimulation over the right dlPFC (Trumbo, et al., 2016), while stimulation over the left dlPFC improves working memory accuracy (Hussey, et al., 2020; Shin, Foerster, & Nitsche, 2015).

Another potential target for tDCS is mood state. Studies to date have shown that offline, anodal tDCS over the primary motor cortex is associated with improved vigour (Valenzuela, et al., 2019), while tDCS applied to the frontocerebellar region is associated with improved general mood (Newstead, et al., 2018). Reviews and meta-analyses of the literature have supported these findings, demonstrating decreased depression symptoms in those with depressive disorders, particularly after multiple sessions (Brunoni, et al., 2016; Meron, Hedger, Garner, & Baldwin, 2015). Additionally, in healthy individuals with high trait anxiety, tDCS stimulation over the dlPFC reduces amygdala threat reactivity and increases activity in attentional control regions (Ironside, et al., 2019). Reviews of the literature also indicate that anodal tDCS over the dlPFC and/or ventrolateral prefrontal cortex is associated with reductions in risk-taking behaviour and anger or aggression (Sellaro, Nitsche, & Colzato, 2016; Shin, Foerster, & Nitsche, 2015). And, stimulation over the right frontopolar cortex is associated with improvements in facial emotion identification (Shin, Foerster, & Nitsche, 2015).

Together, these findings suggest that tDCS may have utility for improving mental performance across broad domains of function that are relevant for successful execution of tasks relevant to elite performers. However, few studies have been conducted that focus on elite performers in any field or in relevant contexts.

Transcutaneous electrical nerve stimulation

Transcutaneous electrical nerve stimulation (TENS) involves the application of mild electrical pulses to peripheral nerves through the skin via electrodes placed on the head, neck, and/or face. In contrast to the top-down effects of other cranial stimulation techniques that alter primary cortical activity, such as tDCS, it is hypothesized that TENS modulates brain activity through bottom-up mechanisms via stimulation of cranial nerves, which then connect to the cortex to influence brain activity and support brain plasticity (Rizzo, et al., 2014; Shiozawa, et al., 2014). Currently, stimulation of the vagus (tVNS) and trigeminal (tTNS) nerves have received the most attention in the peer-reviewed literature. The vagus and trigeminal nerves both have extensive connections throughout the brain, via the locus coeruleus (LC) and dorsal raphe nucleus (DR), and stimulation applied to either nerve is believed to affect the locus coeruleus-norepinephrine (LC-NE) system. The LC, DR, and the LC-NE system are largely responsible for the brain's production of the neurotransmitters norepinephrine and serotonin. Norepinephrine and serotonin have widespread impacts on other brain regions, such as the pre-frontal cortex, thalamus, amygdala, and hippocampus. These areas of the brain are associated with attention, arousal, decision-making, vigilance, and memory. Therefore, influencing the trigeminal or vagus nerves with stimulation can impact many areas of the brain related to cognition and mood. While the mechanisms of action for tVNS and tTNS are still being investigated, a growing body of literature demonstrates that both tVNS and tTNS result in therapeutic benefits without adverse effects. Moreover, applications for mental performance optimization are actively being explored (Mercante, et al., 2017).

Primary targets for stimulating the vagus nerve are the auricular branch, referred to as transcutaneous auricular vagus nerve stimulation (taVNS), or the cervical branch, referred to as transcutaneous cervical vagus nerve stimulation (tcVNS or ctVNS). The auricular branch of the vagus nerve (ABVN) can be accessed through the skin of the ear, although the location of taVNS electrode placement on the ear is still a topic of debate (Badran, et al., 2018; Burger & Verkuil, 2018). Stimulation is applied using a clip or electrode placed on the stimulation site for the duration of stimulation, which varies but commonly ranges from 10 to 30 minutes; it is generally limited to the left ABVN, since the right ABVN stimulates the sinus-atrial node of the heart, which may result in bradycardia (Chen, et al., 2015). Stimulation may also be applied to the cervical branch of the vagus nerve by holding a stimulation device to the side of the neck, just lateral to the trachea and medial to the sternocleidomastoid. Stimulation in this manner is generally applied for approximately two minutes, often multiple times per session (Lerman, et al., 2016), and may also be applied bilaterally (Bostrom, et al., 2019; Lerman, et al., 2016; Tarn, Legg, Mitchell, Simon, & Ng, 2019).

Auricular vagal nerve stimulation applies rectangular, alternating electrical pulses at varying levels of intensity and frequencies. Most studies apply currents ranging from 0.3 to 10 mA in intensity (often set to just below the individual's pain threshold) at 25 Hz, with pulse durations between 200 and 1000 μS for 10 to 30 minutes at a time (Badran, et al., 2019). In contrast, cervical vagal nerve stimulation applies five alternating, 5000 Hz sine wave pulses at 25 Hz over two minutes (Simon & Blake, 2017). When applied, these electrical pulses induce depolarization of the neurons along the vagus nerve, thus exciting and activating the nerve. Because the vagus nerve has both afferent (toward brain) and efferent (toward the internal organs) fibres, stimulation results in activation of both pathways. The vagus nerve is also considered to be a parasympathetic nerve as its activation results in reduction of physiological reactivity after stress, to include a reduction in inflammation and circulation of catecholamines, but also increasing digestion and other "resting" bodily functions. Thus, when stimulated by tVNS, the parasympathetic vagus nerve is induced to override sympathetic nerve activity and reduce physiological arousal. It does so by activating the nucleus of the tractus solitarius (NTS), which projects forward to the LC and DR, which release the neurotransmitters norepinephrine and serotonin (Breit, Kupferberg, Rogler, & Hasler, 2018). Upon their release, these neurotransmitters are carried to various cortical tissues, including the hippocampus, hypothalamus, amygdala, and prefrontal cortex (Breit, Kupferberg, Rogler, & Hasler, 2018). Activation of the hypothalamus triggers the hypothalamic–pituitary–adrenal axis release of cortisol, which reduces systemic inflammation while norepinephrine release is shut off to allow the body to return to a state of rest (Breit, Kupferberg, Rogler, & Hasler, 2018). These pro-resting state messages are carried down from the brain to the internal organs, reinstating normal activity levels (Breit, Kupferberg, Rogler, & Hasler, 2018). Brain imaging studies have provided support for these pathways, but research continues to pursue further understanding of neurological changes through the employment of additional brain-imaging techniques, such as MRS and positron emission tomography (PET) (Badran, et al., 2018).

Stimulation of the trigeminal nerve typically focuses on the ophthalmic (V1) branch of the nerve, but may also involve the maxillary (V2) or mandibular (V3) branch endings. Some studies apply anodal stimulation to the ophthalmic branch and cathodal stimulation to the mandibular branch in order to restrict stimulation to the sensory, rather than motor, functions of the trigeminal nerve (Wilson-Pauwels, Akesson, & Steward, 1988). Stimulation is applied using electrodes attached to the right side of the face above the eyes and/or along the jawline for approximately 20 minutes. Although there is considerable cross-study variability, protocols typically recommend rectangular, biphasic pulses, with pulse widths of 250 μs, frequencies of 60–350 Hz, and maximum intensities of 3.5–16 mA for up to 30 minutes (Riederer, Penning, & Schoenen, 2015). As with tVNS, stimulation induces depolarization and excitation of neurons along the trigeminal nerve, thereby activating the trigeminal nerve pathway. This results in activation of several key brainstem nuclei, including the trigeminal sensory nuclear complex (composed of the spinal trigeminal nucleus and motor nucleus of the trigeminal nerve) and the NTS (Bradnam & Barry, 2013; Contreras, Beckstead, & Norgren, 1982). These nuclei project forward to secondary, activating nuclei such as the LC, DR, the pedunculopontine nucleus (PPN), and the nucleus accumbens, thus releasing the neurotransmitters norepinephrine and serotonin and projecting to cortical regions such as the thalamus, amygdala, hippocampus, and hypothalamus (Bari, Chokshi, & Schmidt, 2020; Bradnam & Barry, 2013; Cheyuo, et al., 2011; Contreras, Beckstead, & Norgren, 1982; Feinstein, Kalinin, & Braun, 2016; Ferrucci, Giorgi, Bartalucci, Busceti, & Fornai, 2013; Hagena, Hansen, & Manahan-Vaughan, 2016; Herman, Cruz, Sahibzada, Verbalis, & Gillis, 2009; Lin & Vartanian, 2018; Martinez-Gonzalez, Bolam, & Mena-Segovia, 2011). Moreover, stimulation feeds backward to the spinal cord via the spinal trigeminal tract, which is associated with pain and temperature sense (Marcus, Jacobson, & Sabin, 2014; Walker, 1990). As with stimulation of the vagus nerve, brain imaging studies provide support for these pathways, but understanding of stimulation's effects via additional imaging methodology is still ongoing.

Areas of the brain activated by TENS are also implicated in a variety of medical conditions with neurological foundations. Stimulation of the vagus nerve via implanted devices, which is approved by the US Federal Drug Administration (FDA), has demonstrated clinically beneficial effects for epilepsy, insomnia, anxiety, and depression (Bonaz, Sinniger, & Pellissier, 2016). However, implantation of a device presents risks and side effects. More recently, non-invasive stimulation methods have exhibited positive effects similar to those observed through implanted devices. For example, tTNS has demonstrated efficacy in the treatment of tinnitus, depression, and pain (Mercante, et al., 2017). Low-frequency trigeminal tTNS has successfully been used in the treatment of seizures (DeGiorgio, 2013), depression (Shiozawa, et al., 2014), attention-deficit/hyperactivity disorder (McGough, et al., 2019), and neuralgia (Yameen, Shahbaz, Hasan, Fauz, & Abdullah, 2011). Studies using higher frequency (7–11 kHz), relatively short-term stimulations (~15 minutes) report decreases in sympathetic activity, improvements in mood, decreased stress responses to a conditioned fear stimulus (Tyler, et al., 2015), and improvements in sleep quality (Boasso, Mortimore, Silva, Aven, & Tyler, 2016). These higher frequency stimulations are also reported to produce less discomfort than traditional forms of transcranial direct current stimulation (Paneri, et al., 2016). Therefore, non-invasive stimulation presents an opportunity to increase applications and ease of use while also creating new possibilities for applications of TENS.

As described earlier, areas of the brain that are activated by tVNS and tTNS, including the LC, NTS, PPN, and the corresponding effect on neurotransmitter activity (which can impact hippocampus, amygdala, and thalamus), are implicated in learning, arousal, and vigilance (Tyler, et al., 2015). Recently, researchers have reported effects of tVNS in healthy populations on arousal and vigilance after sleep deprivation (McIntire, McKinley, Goodyear, McIntire, & Brown, 2021), learning and language acquisition (Miyatsu, 2023; Weber, et al., 2021), decision-making and executive functions (Borges, Knops, Laborde, Klatt, & Raab, 2020; Klaming, Simmons, Spadoni, & Lerman, 2020; Ridgewell, et al., 2021), and memory (Giraudier, Ventura-Bort, & Weymar, 2020; Hansen, 2018; Jacobs, Riphagen, Razat, Wiese, & Sack, 2015; Jongkees, Immink, Finisguerra, & Colzato, 2018; Olsen, 2023). While tTNS has also demonstrated positive outcomes for clinical applications, the application of tTNS in non-clinical settings is not yet clear. The ability of both tTNS and tVNS to activate areas of the brain associated with performance and the recent reports of positive outcomes in healthy subjects requires further study, particularly with respect to performance enhancement on military critical skills.

Transcranial magnetic stimulation

Developed over 30 years ago, transcranial magnetic stimulation (TMS) has been used in a variety of populations in order to modulate cortical excitability (Clark & Parasuraman, 2014; George, 2019; Ziemann, 2017). This method of neuromodulation may be used to effect changes in neurophysiological response (Kim, Hong, Kim, & Yoon, 2019; Terao & Ugawa, 2002), to treat psychiatric conditions by attenuating mood (Möbius, et al., 2017; Schaller, et al., 2011), to suppress negative behaviours (Otani, Shiozawa, Cordeiro, & Uchida, 2015), and also to enhance cognitive performance (Luber & Lisanby, 2014; Osaka, et al., 2007; Wagner, Rihs, Mosimann, Fisch, & Schlaepfer, 2006).

A number of good quality reviews have been published pertaining to the methodology and use of TMS (George, 2019; Hallett, 2007; Terao & Ugawa, 2002; Walsh & Cowey, 2000; Ziemann, 2017). In summary, TMS is applied using a coil of insulated wires placed on the surface of the scalp to create a magnetic field that penetrates the skull. The electrical current created by this magnetic field induces a change in neuronal resting membrane activity that may result in depolarization (and a subsequent action potential), hyperpolarization (and a decrease in the likelihood of an action potential to occur), or both (Walsh & Cowey, 2000). Whether the neuronal membrane is depolarized or hyperpolarized depends, at least in part, on the frequency of the stimulation; low-frequency TMS (1–4 Hz) is associated with an increase in resting membrane potential and therefore with cortical inhibition, while high-frequency TMS (5 Hz and greater) is associated with a decrease in resting membrane potential and subsequent cortical excitation (Guse, et al., 2013). Other factors that may contribute to the neuronal response to different frequencies of TMS include characteristics of the stimulation (such as its waveform and pulse intensity) as well as the neuroanatomical (e.g., skull thickness, previous synaptic activity) and characteristics (age and sex) of the person being stimulated (Nicolo, Ptak, & Guggisberg, 2015; Pelligrini, Zoghi, & Jaberzadeh, 2018; Remue, Baeken, & De Raedt, 2016; Valero-Cabré, Amengual, Stengel, Pascual-Leone, & Coubard, 2017).

The specificity and focality of stimulation are dependent upon the shape of the coil of insulated wires that is used to generate a magnetic field (Hallett, 2007). Coils come in several shapes, including but not limited to round, figure-eight, H-, and conical shapes that each generate differently-shaped magnetic fields and thus different patterns (Hallett, 2007) and power or depth (Levkovitz, et al., 2015) of stimulation that may influence performance and behaviour differently (Pell, 2023). Nevertheless, the magnetic field typically only reaches up to two Tesla in strength and pulses are applied very briefly (for seconds or milliseconds at a time) (Hallett, 2007; Klomjai, Katz, & Lackmy-Vallée, 2015). Pulses may be applied individually (single-pulse TMS), in pairs and in rapid succession (paired-pulse TMS), or repeatedly at a regular interval (repetitive TMS, or rTMS), and may be administered on more than one occasion if used in a therapeutic setting or for cognitive enhancement (Klomjai, Katz, & Lackmy-Vallée, 2015; Terao & Ugawa, 2002). rTMS is considered to be the most effective method of TMS as its effects may last well beyond the time of stimulation (George, 2019; Kim, Hong, Kim, & Yoon, 2019; Klomjai, Katz, & Lackmy-Vallée, 2015). Theta-burst stimulation, which applies very high-frequency stimulation at theta frequency (5 Hz), is a type of rTMS that has been noted to be particularly effective. When applied intermittently, theta-burst stimulation increases cortical excitability but when applied continuously, it decreases excitability (Hallett, 2007; Klomjai, Katz, & Lackmy-Vallée, 2015). TMS may also be applied to multiple, related sites using cortico-cortical paired associative stimulation (Hernandez-Pavon, 2023). At this time, research has not yet defined the specific biological processes underlying these effects but suggests that they are the result of changing brain plasticity through long-term potentiation and long-term depression affecting neurotransmission of glutamate and gamma aminobutyric acid (Nicolo, Ptak, & Guggisberg, 2015). Historically, brain regions deep in the brain, such as the striatum, have been inaccessible by TMS but techniques are under development to increase the likelihood of affecting deep brain structures (Wessel, 2023).

TMS is often used in combination with neuroimaging and other neuromodulatory techniques. Stimulation location is commonly determined using functional neuroimaging techniques, such as fMRI and EEG, which help to localize the brain regions responsible for different behaviours and cognitive processes. These techniques are measured prior to the onset of stimulation in order to guarantee that stimulation is applied to the specific region of interest. They can also be used to visualize the effects of TMS. Additionally, techniques such as tDCS may be used before the onset of stimulation in order to "prime" the target neurons to receive TMS (Herpich, Contò, van Koningsbruggen, & Battelli, 2018; Lang, et al., 2007). TMS is also often applied either concurrently with a task (online), which has an inhibitory effect on performance (O'Reardon, et al., 2007) or in advance of a task (offline), which has performance-enhancing effects (Luber & Lisanby, 2014). rTMS is an offline method, applied before the onset of a task in order to enhance performance while other methods of TMS (single-pulse, for example) are often used as online methods to perturb performance (Hartwigsen, et al., 2015). Together, these techniques ensure that the stimulation is as effective and specific as possible and in fact, TMS has very high temporal resolution and spatial resolution, such that regions of interest consisting of mere millimetres may now be targeted (Kim, Hong, Kim, & Yoon, 2019; Walsh & Cowey, 2000). Furthermore, TMS has been deemed to be safe and well-tolerated in clinical trials, with only minimal and transient side effects noted (O'Reardon, et al., 2007; Schulze, et al., 2016).

The direct effects of TMS for cognitive performance optimization are, as yet, unclear. Research indicates that use of rTMS is beneficial for the improvement of perception, psychomotor function, learning, and executive functions (Luber & Lisanby, 2014; Walsh & Cowey, 2000). In healthy young people, rTMS improves decision-making (Hallett, 2007), inhibition and retrieval of memories (Rose, et al., 2016; van den Ven & Sack, 2013), and empathy (Yang, Khalifa, & Völlm, 2018). Inhibitory TMS and intermittent theta-burst rTMS may each be used to improve attention (Bolden, Griffis, Pati, & Szaflarski, 2017; Esterman, et al., 2017), while rTMS applied to the right primary motor cortex leads to a faster rate of learning on motor tasks and enhanced cerebral blood flow in regions associated with skill learning (Narayana, et al., 2014; Ho K. C., 2022; Kolbaşı, 2023). Stimulation is often applied to various regions of the prefrontal cortex due to their involvement in executive functions and cognitive control; it is therefore unsurprising that many studies have explored the effects of rTMS on the dlPFC, finding that it improves selective and divided attention (Guse, et al., 2013) as well as decision-making (Wang, et al., 2021), response inhibition (Kim, Hong, Kim, & Yoon, 2019; Wang, et al., 2018), fluency (Kim, Hong, Kim, & Yoon, 2019; Wang, et al., 2018), memory (Kim, Hong, Kim, & Yoon, 2019; Wang, et al., 2018), working memory (Kim, Hong, Kim, & Yoon, 2019; Wang, et al., 2018; Feng, 2023), and response times (Moscatelli, 2023) in healthy individuals. Similarly, bilateral intermittent theta-burst stimulation over the ventrolateral prefrontal cortex is associated with a reduction in emotional memory encoding, such that negative memories are no longer encoded to a greater degree than positive memories (Weintraub-Brevda & Chua, 2018). Moreover, research from the schizophrenia and depression literature supports findings that working memory, attention, and processing speed are each enhanced by rTMS over the prefrontal cortex (Iimori, et al., 2019; Martin, McClintock, Forster, & Loo, 2016; Schulze, et al., 2016).

In addition, TMS has shown benefit for improving mood, which can indirectly facilitate cognitive performance. A number of controlled clinical trials have shown that TMS can be an effective acute treatment in otherwise treatment-resistant depression, particularly when applied to the left dlPFC (Downar, et al., 2014; Galletly, Gill, Rigby, Carnell, & Clarke, 2016; Krstić, et al., 2014; O'Reardon, et al., 2007). In one study, applying rTMS to the left dlPFC in a sample of individuals with depression each weekday for four weeks resulted in more accurate perceptions of subtle positive affect and a significant decrease in anhedonia compared to sham stimulation (Light, Bieliauskas, & Taylor, 2019). In another study, participants with treatment-resistant major depressive disorder were administered rTMS over the dorsomedial prefrontal cortex, which resulted in substantial improvement on depression and anhedonia measures as well as greater connectivity in the ventral tegmental area (VTA) reward pathway in a subset of participants (Downar, et al., 2014). TMS has also been used with success for treatment of schizophrenia and autism spectrum disorders and anxiety disorders including Post-Traumatic Stress Disorder (Isserles, et al., 2013; Oznur, et al., 2014) and Generalized Anxiety Disorder (Dilkov, Hawken, Kaludiev, & Milev, 2017). TMS is also an FDA-approved treatment approach for obsessive-compulsive disorder (George, 2019). However, there remains a degree of inconsistency in findings across studies (largely due to methodological differences related to stimulation intensity, duration, location, tasks used, and other factors) with regard to the effect of TMS on mood in healthy individuals, with some studies demonstrating enhanced mood after left dlPFC stimulation (Schaller, et al., 2011), and others showing no effect (Mondino, Thiffault, & Fecteau, 2015; Remue, Baeken, & De Raedt, 2016). The evidence does, however, support a role of TMS in modulating emotion processing (reducing perception of negative stimuli) and attentional processing of emotional stimuli (Mondino, Thiffault, & Fecteau, 2015) in healthy people. Furthermore, rTMS may improve increases in hypothalamic–pituitary–adrenal axis activity after sleep deprivation stress (Li, et al., 2021).

In recent years, it has become clear that the impact of TMS on brain function and performance must be considered in the context of current brain or mood state (Sack, 2023) and characteristics of the brain itself. Sleep deprivation, mood and stress levels, and administration of TMS during a task versus at rest affect the real-time activity of the brain circuitry being targeted by TMS (Sack et al., 2023). This points to a need for closed-loop administration of TMS that is dependent on moment-by-moment fluctuations in regional or network-level brain activity. To date, this has been accomplished using monitoring of brain activity using EEG (Gordon, 2021; Zrenner, 2020). Characteristics of the brain, such as cortical thickness (Razza, 2023), may also affect the effectiveness of TMS in cognitive enhancement. Individual differences may contribute to the amount of stimulation required to induce alterations in brain activity (Tik, 2023). Consideration of individual differences in brain structure and function may, therefore, form the basis for personalization of TMS treatment that improves effectiveness.

Overall, the body of the research indicates that TMS techniques may be beneficial and can have enhancing effects on attention and decision-making. However, the expense and lack of portability of TMS technologies limits the feasibility of their use in non-clinical settings. Further study is needed to determine the utility of TMS for performance enhancement purposes in healthy individuals.

Photobiomodulation

Photobiomodulation (PBM) utilizes near-infrared light (0.75–1.4 μm in wavelength) to mitigate inflammation and promote healing, a technology traditionally used in clinical and veterinary contexts (Mitrofanis, 2020). Traditionally, PBM has been used in clinical and veterinary settings to reduce joint swelling, heal wounds, and stimulate hair growth. Recently, its application has extended to enhancing brain function and overall physical wellness (Hamblin, 2018).

The infrared light of PBM activates the photosensitive enzyme cytochrome c oxidase (COX, also called Complex IV), which is the terminal enzyme in the mitochondrial electron transport chain and mediates the transfer of electrons from inside the mitochondrion via the electron carriers nicotinamide adenine dinucleotide (NADH) and flavin adenine dinucleotide (FADH2) to molecular oxygen (Hamblin, 2018; Hennessy & Hamblin, 2017; Salehpour, et al., 2019). It is proposed that when COX absorbs near-infrared light, photodissociation of nitrous oxide (NO) from COX occurs, which increases the availability of electrons for the reduction of oxygen (Hamblin, 2018). This increased availability of electrons also increases adenosine triphosphate (ATP) production and mitochondrial membrane potential, which in turn leads to increased neuronal activity (Maiello, 2019). Stimulation of COX also can activate transcription factors that may act as an exercise mimetic (Hamblin, 2018) (Salehpour, et al., 2023). This therapy also elevates blood oxygen content and cerebral blood flow (CBF), which are critical for fulfilling the substantial energy requirements essential for sustaining cognitive functions (Pan, Liu, Ma, & Yang, 2023). PBM is applied either via LED near-infrared lights to the entire head, or to smaller areas using a direct laser. PBM is considered a safe therapy that is relatively free of adverse side effects (Hennessy & Hamblin, 2017). The most common side effects of PBM are mild headaches and vivid dreams, however, these are rare (Maiello, 2019).

As with other neurostimulation approaches, PBM has typically been used to treat physical and cognitive impairments following brain injury or other neurodegenerative processes, such as Alzheimer's and Parkinson's disease (Hennessy & Hamblin, 2017). However, recent evidence suggests that PBM may also be beneficial for improving cognition in healthy individuals (Salehpour, et al., 2019). For example, Jahan and colleagues (2019) reported that PBM can modulate attention and improve reaction times in healthy adults (as measured using the psychomotor vigilance task or PVT). Barrett et al. (2013), found similar results on PVT performance after the administration of PBM. Similar beneficial effects have been noted for memory (Dougal, Ennaceur, & Chazot, 2021) and working memory (Qu, et al., 2022). In addition to attention modulation, a study by Blanco et al. (2017) noted that rule-based category learning, but not information integration, was improved in healthy adults following transcranial infrared laser stimulation on the forehead. Rule-based category learning is heavily associated with the prefrontal cortex (PFC), whereas information integration is associated with the striatum and the PFC to a lesser degree (Blanco, Saucedo, & Gonzalez-Lima, 2017). It is important to note that in this study, stimulation was applied to the forehead with the intention of targeting the PFC. The results of the study suggest that PBM was beneficial in increasing PFC function, which has significant implications for executive functions.

PBM has also been documented to induce physiological changes within the brain. Based on EEG recordings, PBM significantly changed electrophysiological features in the brain by lowering cortical delta waves, which is associated with increased vigilance (Jahan, Nazari, Mahmoudi, Salehpour, & Salimi, 2019; Salehpour, et al., 2023; Shetty, Shetty, Shettigar, Pagilla, & Maiya, 2023). Zomorrodi and colleagues (2019) reported that PBM reduced delta frequencies while simultaneously raising higher frequencies such as alpha, beta, and theta waves, which are associated with an increase in alertness and attention (Kučikienė, 2018). PBM has also been reported to increase cerebral blood flow in treated brain regions (Carneiro, et al., 2019). Cerebral blood flow is positively associated with an increase in cognitive functioning (Ogoh, 2014). These measurable changes in brain after the administration of PBM support the claim that PBM has the potential to modulate cognition, in particular attention, and expose the underlying etiology of PBM.

Beyond cognitive and physiological benefits, PBM has also shown promise as a method to regulate mood. In patients with generalized anxiety disorder (GAD) PBM was reported to reduce anxiety symptoms when used over 8 weeks (Maiello, 2019). PBM has also been shown to reduce symptoms of depression in patients diagnosed with major depression (Askalsky & Iosifescu, 2019). While most of the research exploring the effects of PBM on mood has been conducted in a clinically depressed population, there is evidence that PBM may improve mood in healthy individuals (Disner, Beevers, & Gonzalez-Lima, 2016). Specifically, research has demonstrated increased positive affect scores on the Positive and Negative Affect Scale (PANAS) (Barrett & Gonzalez-Lima, 2013). In healthy individuals, application of PBM may also increase functional connectivity between the dlPFC and amygdala, suggesting greater emotional control, and decreases in negative mood (Alkozei, et al., 2021).

Overall, PBM represents a safe and innovative approach with minimal side effects for enhancing athletic performance, cognitive function, and emotional well-being. Its application in healthy populations to enhance performance is a burgeoning field, and further research in this area could solidify PBM's role as a key component of modern performance and recovery programs.

Relevance for high performers

Neurostimulation approaches gained early attention for their clinical applications, particularly as means to reduce symptom severity or to improve function in individuals with brain injuries or other neurological or psychiatric conditions. Overall, the majority of studies reviewed for this chapter were clinically-focused; very few studies have examined neurostimulation effects on cognition in healthy adults and even fewer studies have explored the use of such technologies in elite performers. However, existing studies in the clinical and performance domains provide an empirical basis for recommendations regarding the potential utility of these approaches for use by high-performance athletes, military, and first responders.

Neurostimulation approaches are quite attractive for performance enhancement applications since they are relatively non-invasive, easy to use, and boast a range of benefits from better sleep to mood enhancement to performance optimization. In fact, commercially available neurostimulation devices, such as Halo (www.haloneuro.com/) for example, a system that resembles a set of headphones that delivers tDCS to the motor cortex, have been used by professional and collegiate athletes and a number of military groups, including special forces operators. It is also worth noting that although the literature regarding use of neurostimulation approaches to optimize or enhance mental function in healthy adults is limited, there does appear to be some evidence to suggest that these methods can improve certain areas of cognition, particularly in the domains of attention and executive functions, that are relevant to achieving and sustaining peak performance. However, findings across studies are frequently inconsistent. Given the wide range of potential stimulation parameters, including stimulation intensities and durations, peripheral nerve or cranial targets, and timing of stimulation relative to task performance, such inconsistencies are likely the result of methodological differences across individual research protocols, making comparisons across studies difficult. Moreover, since use of neurostimulation approaches to optimize or enhance mental performance is a comparatively new area of study, the specific mechanisms of action and long-term or secondary effects of stimulation are not clear. More importantly, in research protocols the delivery of neurostimulation is often customized for each participant, based on baseline recordings. Commercial applications ignore this need, which is an important corner being cut in the proper use of these techniques.

At this time, the current state of science regarding neurostimulation applications for mental performance enhancement is still developing and use of such technologies by the elite performance community should be viewed with caution. It is important that utilization of commercially available neurostimulation products be guided by both an understanding of the scientific evidence supporting claims of benefit, as well as the potential risks and lack of research examining long-term impacts of brain stimulation.

References

Accornero, N., Capozza, M., Pieroni, L., Pro, S., Davi, L., & Mecarelli, O. (2014). EEG mean frequency changes in healthy subjects during prefrontal transcranial direct current stimulation. *Journal of Neurophysiology, 112*(6), 1367–1375.

Alkozei, A., Dailey, N. S., Bajaj, S., Vanuk, J. R., Raikes, A. C., & Killgore, W. D. (2021). Exposure to blue wavelength light is associated with increases in bidirectional amygdala-DLPRC connectivity at rest. *Frontiers in Neurology, 12*, 625443. doi: 10.3389/fneur.2021.625443

Antonenko, D., Schubert, F., Bohm, F., Ittermann, B., Aydin, S., Hayek, D., . . . Flöel, A. (2017). tDCS-induced modulation of GABA levels and resting-state functional connectivity in older adults. *Journal of Neuroscience, 37*(15), 4065–4073.

Askalsky, P., & Iosifescu, D. V. (2019). Transcranial photobiomodulation for the management of depression: Current perspectives. *Neuropsychiatric Disease and Treatment, 15*, 3255–3272.

Badran, B. W., Brown, J. C., Dowdle, L. T., Mithoefer, O. J., LaBate, N. T., Coatsworth, J., . . . George, M. S. (2018). Tragus or cymba conchae? Investigating the anatomical foundation of transcutaneous auricular vagus nerve stimulation (taVNS). *Brain Stimulation, 11*(4), 947–948.

Badran, B. W., Yu, A. B., Adair, D., Mappin, G., DeVries, W. H., Jenkins, D. D., . . . Bikson, M. (2019). Laboratory administration of transcutaneous auricular vagus nerve stimulation (taVNS). *Journal of Visual Experiments, 143*, e58984.

Barbieri, M., Negrini, M., Nitsche, M. A., & Rivolta, D. (2016). Anodal-tDCS over the human right occipital cortex enhances the perception and memory of both faces and objects. *Neuropsychologica, 81*, 238–244.

Bari, B. A., Chokshi, V., & Schmidt, K. (2020). Locus coeruleus-norepinephrine: Basic functions and insights into Parkinson's disease. *Neural Regeneration Research, 15*(6), 1006–1013.

Barrett, D., & Gonzalez-Lima, F. (2013). Transcranial infrared laser stimulation produces beneficial cognitive and emotional effects in humans. *Neuroscience, 230*, 13–23.

Been, G., Ngo, T. T., Miller, S. M., & Fitzgerald, P. D. (2007). The use of tDCS and CVS as methods of non-invasive brain stimulation. *Brain Research, 56*(2), 346–361.

Bikson, M., Grossman, P., Thomas, C., Zannou, A., Jiang, J., Mourdoukoutas, A., . . . Woods, A. (2016). Safety of transcranial direct current stimulation: Evidence-based update 2016. *Brain Stimulation, 9*(5), 641–661.

Blanco, N., Saucedo, C., & Gonzalez-Lima, F. (2017). Transcranial infrared laser stimulation improves rule-based, but not information-integration, category learning in humans. *Neurobiology of Learning and Memory, 139*, 69–75.

Boasso, A. M., Mortimore, H. M., Silva, R. S., Aven, L., & Tyler, W. J. (2016). Transdermal electrical neuromodulation of the trimgeinal sensory nuclear complex improves sleep quality and mood. *BioRxiv*, 043901.

Bolden, L. B., Griffis, J. C., Pati, S., & Szaflarski, J. P. (2017). Cortical excitability and neuropsychological functioning in healthy adults. *Neuropsychologia, 102*, 190–196.

Bonaz, B., Sinniger, V., & Pellissier, S. (2016). Anti-inflammatory properties of the vagus nerve: Potential therapeutic implications of vagus nerve stimulation. *The Journal of Physiology, 594*(20), 5781–5790.

Borges, U., Knops, L., Laborde, S., Klatt, S., & Raab, M. (2020). Transcutaneous vagus nerve stimulation may enhance only specific aspects of the core executive functions: A randomized crossover trial. *Frontiers in Neuroscience, 14*, 523. doi:10.3389/fnins.2020.00523

Bostrom, A., Scheele, D., Stoffel-Wagner, B., Honig, F., Chaudhry, S. R., Muhammad, S., . . . Kinfe, T. M. (2019). Saliva molecular inflammatory profiling in female migraine patients responsive to adjunctive cervical non-invasive vagus nerve stimulation: The MOXY study. *Journal of Translational Medicine, 17*(1), 53. doi:https://doi.org/10.1186/s12967-019-1801-y

Bradnam, L., & Barry, C. (2013). The role of the trigeminal sensory nuclear complex in the pathophysiology of craniocervical dystonia. *Journal of Neuroscience, 33*(47), 18358–18367.

Breit, S., Kupferberg, A., Rogler, G., & Hasler, G. (2018). Vagus nerve as modulator of the brain-gut axis in psychiatric and inflammatory disorders. *Frontiers in Psychiatry, 9*(44). doi:10.3389/fpsyt.2018.00044

Brinker, M. C. (2013). Rumination, mood and cognitive performance. *Psychology, 4*(3A), 224–231.

Brunoni, A. R., Moffa, A. H., Fregni, F., Palm, U., Padberg, F., Blumberger, D. M., . . . Loo, C. K. (2016). Transcranial direct current stimulation for acute major depressive episodes: Meta-analysis of individual patient data. *British Journal of Psychiatry, 208*(6), 522–531.

Brunoni, A. R., Nitsche, M. A., Bolognini, N., Bikson, M., Wagner, T., Merabet, L., . . . Fregni, F. (2012). Clinical research with transcranial direct current stimulation (tDCS): Challenges and future directions. *Brain Stimulation, 5*(3), 175–195.

Brunyé, T. T., Holmes, A., Cantelon, J., Eddy, M. D., Gardony, A. L., Mahoney, C. R., & Taylor, H. A. (2014). Direct current brain stimulation enhances navigation efficiency in individuals with low spatial sense of direction. *Neuroreport, 25*(15), 1175–1179.

Brunyé, T. T., Smith, A. M., Horner, C. B., & Thomas, A. K. (2018). Verbal long-term memory is enhanced by retrieval practice but impaired by prefrontal direct current stimulation. *Brain and Cognition, 128*, 80–88.

Buch, E. R., Santarnecchi, E., Antal, A., Born, J., Celnik, P. A., Classesn, J., . . . Cohen, L. G. (2017). Effects of tDCS on motor learning and memory formation: A consensus and critical position paper. *Clinical Neurophysiology, 128*(4), 589–603.

Burger, A. M., & Verkuil, B. (2018). Transcutaneous nerve stimulation via the tragus: Are we really stimulating the vagus nerve? *Brain Stimulation, 11*(4), 945–946.

Carneiro, A., Poiani, G., Zaninnoto, A., Lazo, O., Oliveira, M., Paiva, W., & Zângaro, R. (2019). Transcranial photobiomodulation therapy in the cognitive rehabilitation of patients with cranioencephalic trauma. *Photobiomodulation, Photomedicine, and Laser Surgery, 37*(10), 657–666.

Chen, M., Yu, L., Ouyang, F., Liu, Q., Wang, Z., Wang, S., . . . Zhou, S. (2015). The right side or left side of noninvasive transcutaneous vagus nerve stimulation: Based on conventional wisdom or scientific evidence? *International Journal of Cardiology, 187*, 44–45.

Cheng, J.-X., Zhao, X., Qiu, J., Jiang, Y., Ren, J., Sun, S., . . . & Su, C. (2021). Effects of transcranial direct current stimulation on performance and recovery sleep during acute sleep deprivation: A pilot study. *Sleep Medicine, 79*, 124–133.

Cheyuo, C., Jacob, A., Wu, R., Zhou, M., Coppa, G. F., & Wang, P. (2011). The parasympathetic nervous system in the quest for stroke therapeutics. *Journal of Cerebral Blood Flow Metabolism, 31*(5), 1187–1195.

Choe, J., Coffman, B. A., Bergstedt, D. T., Zeigler, M. D., & Phillips, M. E. (2016). Transcranial direct current stimulation modulates neuronal activity and learning in pilot training. *Frontiers in Human Neuroscience, 10*, 34. doi:10.3389/fnhum.2016.00034

Clark, V. P., Coffman, B. A., Trumbo, M. C., & Gasparovic, C. (2011). Transcranial direct current stimulation (tDCS) produces localized and specific alterations in neurochemistry: A 1H magnetic resonance spectroscopy study. *Neuroscience Letters, 500*(1), 67–71.

Clark, V. P., & Parasuraman, R. (2014). Neuroenhancement: Enhancing brain and mind in health and in disease. *Neuroimage, 14*(85, Pt 3), 889–894.

Coffman, B. A., Trumbo, M. C., & Clark, V. P. (2012). Enhancement of object detection with transcranial direct current stimulation is associated with increased attention. *BMC Neuroscience, 13*, 108. doi:https://doi.org/10.1186/1471-2202-13-108

Contreras, R. J., Beckstead, R. M., & Norgren, R. (1982). The central projections of the trigeminal, facial, glossopharyngeal and vagus nerves: An autoradiographic study in the rat. *Journal of the Autonomic Nervous System, 6*(3), 303–322.

Davis, S. E., & Smith, G. A. (2019). Transcranial direct current stimulation use in warfighting: Benefits, risks, and future prospects. *Frontiers in Human Neuroscience, 13*, 114. doi:10.3389/fnhum.2019.00114

De Vries, M. H., Barth, A. C., Maiworm, S., Knecht, S., Zwitserlood, P., & Flöel, A. (2010). Electrical stimulation of broca's area enhances implicit learning of an artificial grammar. *Journal of Cognitive Neuroscience, 22*(11), 2427–2436.

Dedoncker, J., Brunoni, A. R., Baeken, C., & Vanderhasselt, M.-A. (2016). A systematic review and meta-analysis of the effects of transcranial direct current stimulation (tDCS) over the dorsolateral prefrontal cortex in healthy and neuropsychiatric samples: Influence of stimulation parameters. *Brain Stimulation, 9*(4), 501–517.

DeGiorgio, C. S.-L. (2013). Randomized controlled trial of trigeminal nerve stimulation for drug-resistant epilepsy. *Neurology, 80*(9), 786–791. doi:10.1212/WNL.0b013e318285c11a

Dilkov, D., Hawken, E. R., Kaludiev, E., & Milev, R. (2017). Repetitive transcranial magnetic stimulation of the right dorsal lateral prefrontal cortex in the treatment of Generalized Anxiety Disorder: A randomized, double-blind sham controlled clinical trial. *Progression Neuropsychopharmacology and Biological Psychiatry, 78*, 61–65.

Disner, S., Beevers, C., & Gonzalez-Lima, F. (2016). Transcranial laser stimulation as neuroenhancement for attention bias modification in adults with elevated depression symptoms. *Brain Stimulation, 9*(5), 780–787.

Dougal, G., Ennaceur, A., & Chazot, P. L. (2021). Effect of transcranial near-infrared light 1068 nm upon memory performance in aging healthy individuals: A pilot study. *Photobiomodulation, Photomedicine, and Laser Surgery, 39*(10), 654–660.

Downar, J., Geraci, J., Salomons, T. V., Dunlop, K., Wheeler, S., McAndrews, M. P., . . . Giacobbe, P. (2014). Anhedonia and reward-circuit connnectivity distinguish nonresponders from responders to dorsomedial prefrontal repetitive transcranial magnetic stimulation in major depression. *Biological Psychiatry, 76*(3), 176–185.

Esterman, M., Thai, M., Okabe, H., DeGutis, J., Saad, E., Laganiere, S. E., & Halko, M. A. (2017). Network-targeted cerebellar transcranial magnetic stimulation improves attentional control. *Neuroimage, 156*, 190–198.

Falcone, B., Coffman, B. A., Clark, V. P., & Parasuraman, R. (2012). Transcranial direct current stimulation augments perceptual sensitivity and 24-hour retention in a complex threat detection task. *PLoS One, 7*(4), e34993. doi:https://doi.org/10.1371/journal.pone.0034993

Feinstein, D. L., Kalinin, S., & Braun, D. (2016). Causes, consequences, and cures for neuroinflammation mediated via the locus coeruleus: Noradrenergic signaling system. *Journal of Neurochemistry, 139*(Supplement 2), 154–178.

Feltman, K. A., Hayes, A. M., & Bernhardt, K. A. (2019). Viability of tDCS in military environments for performance enhancement: A systematic review. *Military Medicine, 185*(1-2), e53–e60.

Feng, Y. Z. (2023). Does intermittent theta burst stimulation improve working memory capacity? A randomized controlled cross-over experiment. *Behavioural Brain Research, 436*, 114086. doi:10.1016/j.bbr.2022.114086

Ferrucci, M., Giorgi, F. S., Bartalucci, A., Busceti, C. L., & Fornai, F. (2013). The effects of locus coeruleus and norepinephrine in methamphetamine toxicity. *Current Neuropharmacology, 11*(1), 80–94.

Ferrucci, R., Brunoni, A., Parazzini, M., Vergari, M., Rossi, E., Fumagalli, M., . . . Priori, A. (2013). Modulating human procedural learning by cerebellar transcranial direct current stimulation. *Cerebellum, 12*(4), 485–92.

Ferstl, M., Teckentrup, V., Lin, W. M., Kräutlein, F., Kühnel, A., Klaus, J., . . . Kroemer, N. B. (2021). Non-invasive vagus nerve stimulation boosts mood recovery after effort exertion. *Psychological Medicine*, 1–11.

Fiori, V., Kunz, L., Kuhnke, P., Marangolo, P., & Hartwigsen, G. (2018). Transcranial direct current stimulation (tDCS) facilitates verb learning by altering effective connectivity in the healthy brain. *Neuroimage, 181*, 550–559.

Fonteneau, C., Redoute, J., Haesebaert, F., Le Bars, D., Costes, N., Suaud-Chagny, M.-F., & Brunelin, J. (2018). Frontal transcranial direct current stimulation induces dopamine release in the ventral striatum in human. *Cerebral Cortex, 28*(7), 2636–2646.

Galletly, C., Gill, S., Rigby, A., Carnell, B. L., & Clarke, P. (2016). Assessing the effects of repetitive transcranial magnetic stimulation on cognition in Major Depressive Disorder using computerized cognitive testing. *Journal of ECT, 32*(3), 169–173.

Galli, G., Vadillo, M. A., Sirota, M., Feurra, M., & Medvedeva, A. (2019). A systematic review and meta-analysis of the effects of transcranial direct current stimulation (tDCS) on episodic memory. *Brain Stimulation, 12*(2), 231–241.

Gbadeyan, O., McMahon, K., Steinhauser, M., & Meinzer, M. (2016). Stimulation of dorsolateral prefrontal cortex enhances adaptive cognitive control: A high-definition transcranial direct current stimulation study. *The Journal of Neuroscience, 36*(50), 12530–12536.

George, M. S. (2019). Whither TMS: A one-trick pony or the beginning of a neuroscientific revolution? *American Journal of Psychiatry, 176*(11), 904–910.

Gilam, G., Abend, R., Gurevitch, G., Erdman, A., Baker, H., Ben-Zion, Z., & Hendler, T. (2018). Attenuating anger and aggression with neuromodulation of the vmPFC: A simultaneous tDCS-fMRI study. *Cortex, 109*, 156–170.

Giraudier, M., Ventura-Bort, C., & Weymar, M. (2020). Transcutaneous vagus nerve stimulation (tVNS) improves high-confidence recognition memory but not emotional word processing. *Frontiers in Psychology, 11*, 1276. doi:10.3389/fpsyg.2020.01276

Gordon, P. C. (2021). Prefrontal theta-phase synchronized brain stimulation with real-time EEG-Triggered TMS. *Frontiers in Human Neuroscience, 15*, 691821. doi:10.3389/fnhum.2021.691821

Guse, B., Falkai, P., Gruber, O., Whalley, H., Gibson, L., Hasan, A., . . . Wobrock, T. (2013). The effect of long-term high frequency repetitive transcranial magnetic stimulation on working memory in schizophrenia and healthy controls–A randomized placebo-controlled, double-blind fMRI study. *Behavioural Brain Research, 237*, 300–307.

Hagena, H., Hansen, N., & Manahan-Vaughan, D. (2016). Beta-adrenergic control of hippocampal function: Subserving the choreography of synaptic information storage and memory. *Cerebral Cortex, 26*(4), 1349–1364.

Hallett, M. (2007). Transcranial magnetic stimulation: A primer. *Neuron, 55*(2), 187–199.

Hamblin, M. (2018). Mechanisms and mitochondrial redox signaling in photobiomodulation. *Photochemistry and Photobiology, 94*(2), 199–212.

Hancock, P. (1997). Hours of boredom, moments of terror—or months of monotony, milliseconds of mayhem. *9th International Symposium on Aviation Psychology.* Columbus, Ohio.

Hansen, N. (2018). Memory reinforcement and attenuation by activating the human locus coeruleus via transcutaneous vagus nerve stimulation. *Frontiers in Neuroscience, 12*, 955. doi:10.3389/fnins.2018.00955

Hartwigsen, G., Bergmann, T. O., Herz, D. M., Angstmann, S., Karabanov, A., Raffin, E., . . . Siebner, H. R. (2015). Modeling the effects of noninvasive transcranial brain stimulation at the biophysical, network, and cognitive level. In V. Walsh, & S. Bestmann (Eds.), *Progress in Brain Research: Computational Neurostimulation* (Vol. 222, pp. 261–287). Amsterdam, the Netherlands: Elsevier.

Hauser, T. U., Rütsche, B., Wurmitzer, K., Brem, S., Ruff, C. C., & Grabner, R. H. (2016). Neurocognitive effects of transcranial direct current stimulation in arithmetic learning and performance: A simultaneous tDCS-fMRI study. *Brain Stimulation, 9*(6), 850–858.

Hennessy, M., & Hamblin, M. R. (2017). Photobiomodulation and the brain: a new paradigm. *Journal of Optics, 19*(1), 013003.

Herman, M. A., Cruz, M. T., Sahibzada, N., Verbalis, J., & Gillis, R. A. (2009). GABA signaling in the nucleus tractus solitarius sets the level of activity in dorsal motor nucleus of the vagus cholinergic neurons in the vagovagal circuit. *American Journal of Physiology: Gastrointestinal and Liver Physiology, 296*(1), G101-G111.

Hernandez-Pavon, J. C. (2023). Can we manipulate brain connectivity? A systematic review of cortico-cortical paired associative stimulation effects. *Clinical Neurophysiology, 154*, 169–193. doi:10.1016/j.clinph.2023.06.016

Herpich, F., Contò, F., van Koningsbruggen, M., & Battelli, L. (2018). Modulating the excitability of the visual cortex using a stimulation priming paradigm. *Neuropsychologia, 119*, 165–171.

Ho, K.-A., Taylor, J. L., Chew, T., Gálvez, V., Alonzo, A., Bai, S., . . . Loo, C. K. (2016). The effect of transcranial direct current stimulation (tDCS) electrode size and current intensity on motor cortical excitability: Evidence from single and repeated sessions. *Brain Stimulation, 9*(1), 1–7.

Ho, K. C. (2022). Intracortical facilitation and inhibition in human primary motor cortex during motor skill acquisition. *Experimental Brain Research, 240*(12), 3289–3304. doi:10.1007/s00221-022-06496-3

Horvath, J. C., Forte, J. D., & Carter, O. (2015a). Evidence that transcranial direct current stimulation (tDCS) generates little-to-no reliable neurophysiologic effect beyond MEP amplitude modulation in healthy human subjects: A systematic review. *Neuropsychologia, 66*, 213–236.

Horvath, J. C., Forte, J. D., & Carter, O. (2015b). Quantitative review finds no evidence of cognitive effects in healthy populations from single-session transcranial direct current stimulation (tDCS). *Brain Stimulation, 8*(3), 535–550.

Hunter, M. A., Coffman, B. A., Gasparovic, C., Calhoun, V. D., Trumbo, M. C., & Clark, V. P. (2015). Baseline effects of transcranial direct current stimulation on glutamatergic neurotransmission and large-scale network connectivity. *Brain Research, 1594*, 92–107.

Hussey, E. K., Fontes, E. B., Ward, N., Westfall, D. R., Kao, S.-C., Kramer, A. F., & Hillman, C. H. (2020). Combined and isolated effects of acute exercise and brain stimulation on executive function in healthy young adults. *Journal of Clinical Medicine, 9*(5), 1410.

Iimori, T., Nakajima, S., Miyazaki, T., Tarumi, R., Ogyu, K., Wada, M., . . . Noda, Y. (2019). Effectiveness of the prefrontal repetitive transcranial magnetic stimulation on cognitive profiles in depression, schizophrenia, and Alzheimer's Disease: A systematic review. *Progress in Neuropsychopharmacology and Biological Psychiatry, 88*, 31–40.

Ironside, M., Browning, M., Ansari, T. L., Harvey, C. J., Sekyi-Djan, M. N., Bishop, S. J., . . . O'Shea, J. (2019). Effect of prefrontal cortex stimulation on regulation of amygdala response to threat in individuals with trait anxiety: A randomized clinical trial. *JAMA Psychiatry, 76*(1), 71–78.

Isserles, M., Shalev, A. Y., Roth, Y., Peri, T., Kutz, I., Zlotnick, E., & Zangen, A. (2013). Effectiveness of deep transcranial magnetic stimulation combined with a brief exposure procedure in Post-Traumatic Stress Disorder–A pilot study. *Brain Stimulation, 6*(3), 377–383.

Jacobs, H. I., Riphagen, J. M., Razat, C. M., Wiese, S., & Sack, A. T. (2015). Transcutaneous vagus nerve stimulation boosts associative memory in older individuals. *Neurobiology of Aging, 36*(5), 1860–1867.

Jacobson, L., Ezra, A., Berger, U., & Lavidor, M. (2012). Modulating oscillatory brain activity correlates of behavioral inhibition using transcranial direct current stimulation. *Clinical Neurophysiology, 123*(5), 979–984.

Jahan, A., Nazari, M., Mahmoudi, J., Salehpour, F., & Salimi, M. (2019). Transcranial near-infrared photobiomodulation could modulate brain electrophysiological features and attentional performance in healthy young adults. *Lasers in Medical Science, 34*(6), 1193–1200.

Jongkees, B. J., Immink, M. A., Finisguerra, A., & Colzato, L. S. (2018). Transcutaneous vagus nerve stimulation (tVNS) enhances response selection during sequential action. *Frontiers in Psychology, 9*, 1159. doi:10.3389/fpsyg.2018.01159

Kim, T. D., Hong, G., Kim, J., & Yoon, S. (2019). Cognitive enhancement in neurological and psychiatric disorders using transcranial magnetic stimulation (TMS): A review of modalities, potential mechanisms and fucture implications. *Experimental Neurobiology, 28*(1), 1–16.

Klaming, R., Simmons, A. N., Spadoni, A. D., & Lerman, I. (2020). Effects of noninvasive cervical vagal nerve stimulation on cognitive performance but not brain activation in healthy adults. *Neuromodulation*. doi:https://doi.org/10.1111/ner.13313

Klomjai, W., Katz, R., & Lackmy-Vallée, A. (2015). Basic principles of transcranial magentic stimulation (TMS) and repetitive TMS (rTMS). *Annals of Physical and Rehabilitation Medicine, 58*(4), 208–213.

Kolbaşı, E. N. (2023). Enhancement of motor skill acquisition by intermittent theta burst stimulation: a pilot study. *Acta Neurologica Belgica, 123*(3), 971–977. doi:10.1007/s13760-022-02155-0

Krstić, J., Buzadžić, I., Milanović, S. D., Ilić, N. V., Pajić, S., & Ilić, T. V. (2014). Low-frequency repetitive transcranial magnetic stimulation in the right prefrontal cortex combined with partial sleep deprivation in treatment-resistant depression: A randomized sham-controlled trial. *Journal of ECT, 30*(4), 325–331.

Kučikienė, R. P. (2018). The impact of music on the bioelectrical oscillations of the brain. *Acta Medica Lituanica*, 25(2), 101–106. doi: 10.6001/actamedica.v25i2.3763. PMID: 30210244; PMCID: PMC6130927.

Lang, N., Siebner, H. R., Chadaide, Z., Boros, K., Nitsche, M. A., Rothwell, J. C., . . . Antal, A. (2007). Bidirectional modulation of primary visual cortex excitability: A combined tDCS and rTMS study. *Investigative Opthalmology & Visual Science, 48*(12), 5782–5787.

Laqua, R., Leutzow, B., Wendt, M., & Usichenko, T. (2014). Transcutaneous vagal nerve stimulation may elecit anti- and pro-nociceptive effects under experimentally-induced pain: A crossover placebo-controlled investigation. *Autonomic Neuroscience, 185*, 120–122.

Lerman, I., Hauger, R., Sorkin, L., Proudfoot, J., Davis, B., Huang, A. x., & Baker, D. G. (2016). Noninvasive transcutaneous vagus nerve stimulation decreases whole blood culture-derived cytokines and chemokines: A randomized, blinded, healthy control pilot trial. *Neuromodulation, 19*(3), 283–290.

Levkovitz, Y., Isserles, M., Padberg, F., Lisanby, S. H., Bystritsky, A., Xia, G., . . . Zangen, A. (2015). Efficacy and safety of deep transcranial magnetic stimulation for major depression: A prospective multicenter randomized controlled trial. *World Psychiatry*, 14(1), 64–73.

Li, S., Zhou, H., Yu, Y., Lyu, H., Mou, T., Shi, G., . . . Xu, Y. (2021). Effect of repetitive transcranial magnetic stimulation on the cognitive impairment induced by sleep deprivation: A randomized trial. *Sleep Medicine, 77*, 270–278.

Light, S. N., Bieliauskas, L. A., & Taylor, S. F. (2019). Measuring change in anhedonia using the "Happy Faces" task pre- to post-repetitive transcranial magnetic stimulation (rTMS) treatment to left dorsolateral prefrontal cortex in Major Depressive Disorder (MDD): Relation to empathic happiness. *Translational Psychiatry, 9*(1), 217.

Lin, H., & Vartanian, O. (2018). A neuroeconomic framework for creative cognition. *Perspectives on Psychological Science, 13*(6), 655–677.

Luber, B., & Lisanby, S. H. (2014). Enhancement of human cognitive performance using transcranial magnetic stimulation (TMS). *Neuroimage, 15*(85, Pt. 3), 961–970.

Maiello, O. M. (2019). Transcranial Photobiomodulation with Near-Infrared Light for Generalized Anxiety: A Pilot Study. *Photobiomodulation, Photomedicine, and Laser Surgery*, 644–650.

Marcus, E. M., Jacobson, S., & Sabin, T. D. (2014). The Cranial Nerves. In *Integrated Neuroscience and Neurology: A Clinical Case History Problem Solving Approach* (2nd ed., pp. 221–251). New York, NY: Oxford University Press.

Martin, D. M., McClintock, S. M., Forster, J., & Loo, C. K. (2016). Does therapeutic repetitive transcranial magnetic stimulation cause cognitive enhancing effects in patients with neuropsychiatric conditions? A systematic review and meta-analysis of randomised controlled trials. *Neuropsychology Review, 26*(3), 295–309.

Martinez-Gonzalez, C., Bolam, J. P., & Mena-Segovia, J. (2011). Topographical organization of the pedunculopontine nucleus. *Frontiers in Neuroanatomy, 5*(22), 1–22.

Matzen, L. E., Trumbo, M. C., Leach, R. C., & Leshikar, E. D. (2015). Effects of non-invasive brain stimulation on associative memory. *Brain Research, 1624*, 286–296.

McGough, J. J., Sturm, A., Cowen, J., Tung, K., Salgari, G. C., Leuchter, A. F., . . . Loo, S. K. (2019). Double-blind, sham-controlled, pilot study of trigeminal nerve stimulation for Attention-Deficit/Hyperactivity Disorder. *Journal of the American Academy of Child and Adolescent Psychiatry, 58*(4), 403–411.e3.

McIntire, L. K., McKinley, R. A., Goodyear, C., McIntire, J. P., & Brown, R. D. (2021). Cervical transcutaneous vagal nerve stimulation (ctVNS) improves human cognitive performance uner sleep deprivation stress. *Communications Biology, 4*(1), 634.

McIntire, L. K., McKinley, R. A., Nelson, J. M., & Goodyear, C. (2017). Transcranial direct current stimulation versus caffeine as a fatigue countermeasure. *Brain Stimulation, 10*(6), 1070–1078. doi:https://doi.org/10.1038/s42003-021-02145-7

McKinley, R. A., McIntire, L., Bridges, N., Goodyear, C., Bangera, N. B., & Weisend, M. P. (2013). Acceleration of image analyst training With transcranial direct current stimulation. *Behavioral Neuroscience, 127*(6), 936–946.

Medina, J., & Cason, S. (2017). No evidential value in sample of transcranial direct current stimulation (tDCS) studies of cognition and working memory in healthy populations. *Cortex, 94*, 131–141.

Meinzer, M., Jähnigen, S., Copland, D. A., Darkow, R., Grittner, U., Avirame, K., . . . Flöel, A. (2014). Transcranial direct current stimulation over multiple days improves learning and maintenance of a novel vocabulary. *Cortex, 50*, 137–147.

Mercante, B., Enrico, P., Floris, G., Quartu, M., Boi, M., Serra, M. P., . . . Deriu, F. (2017). Trigeminal nerve stimulation induces Fos immunoreactivity in selected brain regions, increases hippocampal cell proliferation and reduces seizure severity in rats. *Neuroscience, 361*, 69–80.

Meron, D., Hedger, N., Garner, M., & Baldwin, D. S. (2015). Transcranial direct current stimulation (tDCS) in the treatment of depression: Systematic review and meta-analysis of efficacy and tolerability. *Neuroscience and Biobehavioral Reviews, 57*, 46–62.

Mitrofanis, J. &. (2020). How and why does photobiomodulation change brain activity? *Neural regeneration research, 15*(12), 2243–2244. doi:10.4103/1673-5374.284989

Miyatsu, T. O. (2023). Transcutaneous cervical vagus nerve stimulation enhances second-language vocabulary acquisition while simultaneously mitigating fatigue and promoting focus. *Neurology, 100*(17 Supplement 2), 1449. doi:10.1212/WNL.0000000000201931

Möbius, M., Lacomblé, L., Meyer, T., Schutter, D. J., Gielkens, T., . . . van Eijndhoven, P. (2017). Repetitive transcranial magnetic stimulation modulates the impact of a negative mood induction. *Social Cognition and Affective Neuroscience, 12*(4), 526–533.

Mondino, M., Thiffault, F., & Fecteau, S. (2015). Does non-invasive brain stimulation applied over the dorsolateral prefrontal cortex non-specifically influence mood and emotional processing in healthy individuals? *Frontiers in Cellular Neuroscience, 9*, 399.

Moscatelli, F. M. (2023). Acute non invasive brain stimulation improves performances in volleyball players. . *Physiology and Behavior, 271*, 114356. doi:10.1016/j.physbeh.2023.114356

Narayana, S., Zhang, W., Rogers, W., Strickland, C., Franklin, C., Lancaster, J. L., & Fox, P. T. (2014). Concurrent TMS to the primary motor cortex augments slow motor learning. *Neuroimage, 14*(85, Pt 3), 971–984.

National Research Council. (2009). *Opportunities in Neuroscience for Future Army Applications.* Washington, DC: The National Academies Press. https://doi.org/10.17226/12500

Nelson, J., McKinley, R. A., Philllips, C., McIntire, L., Goodyear, C., Kreiner, A., & Monforton, L. (2016). The effects of transcranial direct current stimulation (tDCS) on multitasking throughput capacity. *Frontiers in Human Neuroscience, 10*, 589. doi:10.3389/fncel.2015.00399

Nestler, E., Hyman, S. E., Holtzman, D. M., & Malenka, R. C. (2015). Widely Projecting Systems: Monoamines, Acetylcholine, and Orexin. In R. C. Malenka (Ed.), *Molecular Neuropharmacology: A Foundation for Clinical Neuroscience* (3rd ed., pp. 149–183). New York, NY: McGraw-Hill Companies, Inc.

Newstead, S., Young, H., Benton, D., Jiga-Boy, G., Andrade Sienze, M. L., Clement, R. M., & Boy, F. (2018). Acute and repetitive fronto-cerebellar tDCS stimulation improves mood in non-depressed participants. *Experimental Brain Research, 236*(1), 83–97.

Nicolo, P., Ptak, R., & Guggisberg, A. G. (2015). Variability of behavioural responses to transcranial magnetic stimulation: Origins and predictors. *Neuropsychologia, 74*, 137–144.

Nikolin, S., Huggins, C., Martin, D., Alonzo, A., & Loo, C. K. (2018). Safety of repeated sessions of transcranial direct current stimulation: A systematic review. *Brain Stimulation, 11*, 278–288.

Ogoh, H. T. (2014). The effect of changes in cerebral blood flow on cognitive function during excersize. *Pysiological Reports*. doi:https://doi.org/10.14814/phy2.12163

Olsen, L. K.-S. (2023). Vagus nerve stimulation: Mechanisms and factors involved in memory enhancement. *Frontiers in Human Neuroscience, 17*, 1152064. doi:10.3389/fnhum.2023.1152064

O'Reardon, J. P., Solvason, H. B., Janicak, P. G., Sampson, S., Isenberg, K. E., Nahas, Z., . . . Sackheim, H. (2007). Efficacy and safety of transcranial magnetic stimulation in the acute treatment of major depression: A multisite randomized controlled trial. *Biological Psychiatry, 62*(11), 1208–1216.

Osaka, N., Otsuka, Y., Hirose, N., Ikeda, T., Mima, T., Fukuyama, H., & Osaka, M. (2007). Transcranial magnetic stimulation (TMS) applied to the left dorsolateral prefrontal cortex disrupts verbal working memory performance in humans. *Neuroscience Letters, 418*(3), 232–235.

Otani, V. H., Shiozawa, P., Cordeiro, Q., & Uchida, R. R. (2015). A systematic review and meta-analysis of the use of repetitive transcranial magnetic stimulation for auditory hallucinations treatment in refractory schizophrenic patients. *International Journal of Psychiatry and Clinical Practice, 19*(4), 228–232.

Oznur, T., Akarsu, S., Celik, C., Bolu, A., Ozdemir, B., Akcay, B. D., . . . Ozmenler, K. N. (2014). Is transcranial magnetic stimulation effective in treatment-resistant combat related Posttraumatic Stress Disorder? *Neurosciences (Riyadh), 19*(1), 29–32.

Pan, W., Liu, P., Ma, D., & Yang, J. (2023). Advances in photobiomodulation for cognitive improvement by near-infrared derived multiple strategies. *Journal of Translational Medicine, 21*, 135. doi:10.1186/s12967-023-03988-w

Paneri, B., Adair, D., Thomas, C., Khadka, N., Patel, V., Tyler, W. J., . . . Bikson, M. (2016). Tolerability of repeated application of transcranial electrical stimulation with limited outputs to healthy subjects. *Brain Stimulation, 9*(5), 740–754.

Pell, G. S.-Y. (2023). Behavioral and functional brain activity alterations induced by TMS Coils with different spatial distributions. *eNeuro*. doi:10.1523/ENEURO.0287-22

Pelligrini, M., Zoghi, M., & Jaberzadeh, S. (2018). Biological and anatomical factors influencing interindividual variability to noninvasive brain stimulation of the primary motor cortex: A systematic review and meta-analysis. *Reviews in Neuroscience, 29*(2), 199–222.

Qu, X., L. L., Zhou, X., Dong, Q., Liu, H., Liu, H., . . . Niu, H. (2022). Repeated transcranial photobiomodulation improves working memory of healthy older adults: Behavioral outcomes of poststimulation including a three-week follow-up. *Neurophotonics, 9*(3), 035005. doi:10.1117/1.NPh.9.3.035005

Rango, M., Cogiamanian, F., Marceglia, S., Barberis, B., Arighi, A., Biondetti, P., & Priori, A. (2008). Myoinositol content in the human brain is modified by transcranial direct current stimulation in a matter of minutes: A 1H-MRS study. *Magnetic Resonance in Medicine, 60*(4), 782–789.

Razza, L. B. (2023). Cortical thickness is related to working memory performance after non-invasive brain stimulation. *Brazilian Journal of Medical and Biological Research, 56*, e12945. doi:10.1590/1414-431X2023e12945

Remue, J., Baeken, C., & De Raedt, R. (2016). Does a single neurostimulation session really affect mood in healthy individuals? A systematic review. *Neuropsychologia, 85*, 184–198.

Ridgewell, C., Heaton, K. J., Hildebrandt, A., Couse, J., Leeder, T., & Neumeier, W. H. (2021). The effects of transcutaneous auricular vagal nerve stimulation on cognition in healthy individuals: A meta-analysis. *Neuropsychology, 35*(4), 352–365.

Riederer, F., Penning, S., & Schoenen, J. (2015). Transcutaneous supraorbital nerve stimulation (t-SNS) with the Cefaly((R)) device for migraine prevention: A review of the available data. *Pain and Therapy, 4*, 135–147. doi:10.1007/s40122-015-0039-5

Rizzo, V., Terranova, C., Crupi, D., Sant'angelo, A., Girlanda, P., & Quartarone, A. (2014). Increased transcranial direct current stimulation after effects during concurrent peripheral electrical nerve stimulation. *Brain Stimulation, 7*(1), 113–121.

Rose, N. S., LaRocque, J. J., Riggall, A. C., Gosseries, O., Starrett, M. J., Meyering, E. E., & Postle, B. R. (2016). Reactivation of latent working memories with transcranial magnetic stimulation. *Science, 254*(6416), 1136–1139.

Roy, L. B., Sparing, R., Fink, G. R., & Hesse, M. D. (2015). Modulation of attention functions by anodal tDCS on right PPC. *Neuropsychologia, 74*, 96–107.

Sack, A. T. (2023). Target engagement and brain state dependence of transcranial magnetic stimulation: implications for clinical practice. *Biological Psychiatry,* S0006-3223(23), 01571–8. doi:10.1016/j.biopsych.2023.09.011

Salehpour, F., Majdi, A., Pazhuhi, M., Ghasemi, F., Khademi, M., Pashazadeh, F., . . . Cassano, P. (2019). Transcranial photobiomodulation improves cognitive performance in young healthy adults: A systematic review and meta-analysis. *Photobiomodulation, Photomedicine, and Laser Surgery, 37*(10), 635–643.

Salehpour, F., Sadigh-Eteghad, S., Mahmoudi, J., Kamari, F., Cassano, P., & Hamblin, M. (2023). Photobiomodulation for Brain Function in Healthy Young and Aging Adults. In *Photobiomodulation for the Brain. Synthesis Lectures on Biomedical Engineering.* Cham: Springer. doi:10.1007/978-3-031-36231-6_15

Schaller, G., Lenz, B., Friedrich, K., Dygon, D., Richter-Schmidinger, T., Jacobi, A., . . . Kornhuber, J. (2011). Repetitive transcranial magnetic stimulation influences mood in healthy male volunteers. *Journal of Psychiatric Research, 45*(9), 1178–1183.

Schulze, L., Wheeler, S., McAndrews, M. P., Solomon, C. J., Giacobbe, P., & Downar, J. (2016). Cognitive safety of dorsomedial prefrontal repetitive transcranial magnetic stimulation in major depression. *European Neuropsychopharmacology, 26*(7), 1213–1226.

Sellaro, R., Nitsche, M. A., & Colzato, L. S. (2016). The stimulated social brain: Effects of transcranial direct current stimulation on social cognition. *Annals of the New York Academy of Sciences, 1369*(1), 218–239.

Shetty, S. J., Shetty, S., Shettigar, D., Pagilla, V., & Maiya, G. A. (2023). Effect of transcranial photobiomodulation on electrophysiological activity of brain in healthy individuals: A scoping review. *Journal of Clinical Neuroscience, 117*, 156–167. doi:10.1016/j.jocn.2023.09.029

Shin, Y.-I., Foerster, A., & Nitsche, M. A. (2015). Transcranial direct current stimulation (tDCS) – Application in neuropsychology. *Neuropsychologia, 69*, 154–175.

Shiozawa, P., Silva, M. E., Carvalho, T. C., Cordeiro, Q., Brunoni, A. R., & Fregni, F. (2014). Transcutaneous vagus and trigeminal nerve stimulation for neuropsychiatric disorders: A systematic review. *Arquivos de Neuro-Psiquiatria, 72*(7), 542–547.

Simon, B., & Blake, J. (2017). Mechanism of action of non-invasive cervical vagus nerve stimulation for the treatment of primary headaches. *American Journal of Managed Care, 23*(17 Supplement), S312-S316.

Sparing, R., & Mottaghy, F. M. (2008). Noninvasive brain stimulation with transcranial magnetic or direct current stimulation (TMS/tDCS)–from insights into human memory to therapy of its dysfunction. *Methods, 44*(4), 329–337.

Tarn, J., Legg, S., Mitchell, S., Simon, B., & Ng, W. F. (2019). The effects of noninvasive vagus nerve stimulation on fatigue and immune responses in patients wi th Primary Sjogren's Syndrome. *Neuromodulation, 22*(5), 580–585.

Terao, Y., & Ugawa, Y. (2002). Basic mechanisms of TMS. *Journal of Clinical Neurophysiology, 19*(4), 322–343.

Thair, H., Holloway, A. L., Newport, R., & Smith, A. D. (2017). Transcranial direct current stimulation (tDCS): A beginner's guide for design and implementation. *Frontiers in Neurscience, 11*, 641. doi:10.3389/fnins.2017.00641

Tik, M. V. (2023). Concurrent TMS/fMRI reveals individual DLPFC dose-response pattern. *NeuroImage, 282*, 120394. doi:10.1016/j.neuroimage.2023.120394

Trumbo, M. C., Matzen, L. E., Coffman, B. A., Hunter, M. A., Jones, A. P., Robinson, C. S., & Clark, V. P. (2016). Enhanced working memory performance via transcranial direct current stimulation: The possibility of near and far transfer. *Neuropsychologia, 93*(Pt. A), 85–96.

Tu, Y., Fang, J., Cao, J., Wang, Z., Park, J., Jorgenson, K., . . . Kong, J. (2018). A distinct biomarker of continuous transcutaneous vagus nerve stimulation treatment in major depressive disorder. *Brain Stimulation, 11*(3), 501–508.

Tyler, W. J., Boasso, A. M., Mortimore, H. M., Silva, R. S., Charlesworth, J. D., Marlin, M. A., . . . Pal, S. K. (2015). Transdermal neuromodulation of noradrenergic activity suppresses psychophysiological and biochemical stress responses in humans. *Scientific Reports, 5*, 13865.

Usichenko, T., Laqua, R., Leutzow, B., & Lotze, M. (2017). Preliminary findings of cerebral responses on transcutaneous vagal nerve stimulation on experimental heat pain. *Brain Imaging and Behavior, 11*(1), 30–37.

Valenzuela, P. L., Amo, C., Sánchez-Martínez, G., Torrontegi, E., Vázquez-Carrión, J., Montalvo, Z., . . . de la Villa, P. (2019). Enhancement of mood but not performance in elite athletes with transcranial direct-current stimulation. *International Journal of Sports Physiology and Performance, 14*(3), 310–316.

Valero-Cabré, A., Amengual, J. L., Stengel, C., Pascual-Leone, A., & Coubard, O. A. (2017). Transcranial magnetic stimulationin basic and clinical neuroscience: A comprehensive review of fundamental principles and novel insights. *Neuroscience and Biobehavioral Reviews, 83*, 381–404.

van den Ven, V., & Sack, A. T. (2013). Transcranial magnetic stimulation of visual cortex in memory: Cortical state, interference and reactivation of visual content in memory. *Behavioural Brain Research, 236*(1), 67–77.

Wagner, M., Rihs, T. A., Mosimann, U. P., Fisch, H. U., & Schlaepfer, T. E. (2006). Repetitive transcranial magnetic stimulation of the dorsolateral prefrontal cortex affects divided attention immediately after cessation of stimulation. *Journal of Psychiatric Research, 40*(4), 315–321.

Walker, H. K. (1990). Cranial Nerve V: The Trigeminal Nerve. In H. K. Walker, W. D. Hall, & J. W. Hurst (Eds.), *Clinical Methods: The History, Physical, and Laboratory Examinations* (3rd ed.). Boston, MA: Butterworth Publishers.

Walsh, V., & Cowey, A. (2000). Transcranial magnetic stimulation and cognitive neuroscience. *Nature Reviews Neuroscience, 1*(1), 73–79.

Wang, L., Wu, X., Ji, G.-J., Xiao, G., Xu, F., Yan, Y., . . . Wang, K. (2021). Better modulation for risk decision-making after optimized magnetic stimulation. *Journal of Neuroscience Research, 99*(3), 858–871.

Wang, W. C., Wing, E. A., Murphy, D. L., Luber, B. M., Lisanby, S. H., Cabeza, R., & Davis, S. W. (2018). Excitatory TMS modulates memory representations. *Cognitive Neuroscience, 9*(3-4), 151–166.

Wang, X., Wong, W.-W., Fang, Y., Chu, W. C.-W., Wong, K.-S., & Tong, R. K.-Y. (2018). Dynamic influence of ongoing brain stimulation on resting state fMRI connectivity: A concurrent tDCS-fMRI study. *Conference Proceedings of the IEEE Engineering in Medicine and Biology Society*, 1037–1040.

Weber, I., Niehaus, H., Kraus, K., Molitor, L., Peper, M., Schmidt, L., . . . Oehrn, C. R. (2021). Trust your gut: Vagal nerve stimulation improves reinforcement learning. *Brain Communications, 3*(2), fcab039.

Weintraub-Brevda, R. R., & Chua, E. F. (2018). The role of the ventrolateral prefrontal cortex in emotional enhancement of memory: A TMS study. *Cognitive Neuroscience, 9*(3-4), 116–126.

Wessel, M. J.-E. (2023). Noninvasive theta-burst stimulation of the human striatum enhances striatal activity and motor skill learning. *Nature Neuroscience, 26*(11), 2005–2016. doi:10.1038/s41593-023-01457-7

Westwood, S. J., & Romani, C. (2017). Transcranial direct current stimulation (tDCS) modulation of picture naming and word reading: A meta-analysis of single session tDCS applied to healthy participants. *Neuropsychologia, 104*, 234–249.

Wilson-Pauwels, L., Akesson, E. J., & Steward, P. A. (1988). *Cranial Nerves: Anatomy and Clinical Comments.* Toronto, ON: B. C. Decker, Inc.

Yameen, F., Shahbaz, N. N., Hasan, Y., Fauz, R., & Abdullah, M. (2011). Efficacy of transcutaneous electrical nerve stimulation and its different modes in patients with trigeminal neuralgia. *Journal of Pakistan Medical Association, 61*(5), 437–439.

Yang, C. C., Khalifa, N., & Völlm, B. (2018). The effects of repetitive transcranial magnetic stimulation on empathy: A systematic review and meta-analysis. *Psychological Medicine, 48*(5), 737–750.

Ziemann, U. (2017). Thirty years of transcranial magnetic stimulation: Where do we stand? *Experimental Brain Research, 235*(4), 973–984.

Zomorrodi, R., Loheswaran, G., Pushparaj, A., & Lim, L. (2019). Pulsed near infrared transcranial and intranasal photobiomodulation significantly modulates neural oscillations: A pilot exploratory study. *Scientific Reports, 9*(1), 6309.

Zrenner, B. Z.-D. (2020). Brain oscillation-synchronized stimulation of the left dorsolateral prefrontal cortex in depression using real-time EEG-triggered TMS. *Brain stimulation, 13*(1), 197–205. doi:10.1016/j.brs.2019.10.007

8 Computer-assisted Cognitive Training Tools

Kristin J. Heaton, Audrey Hildebrandt, Nicole Ekon, and Erin L. Beatty

Introduction

For elite performers, such as collegiate and professional athletes, military special operations personnel, astronauts, or first responders, the goal of training is to improve performance of real-world tasks – from competition to operations. In the mental performance domain, a range of tools have been developed and marketed that claim to provide positive benefits for cognition across broad domains of function. Computer-based cognitive training tools have, over the past 20 years, proliferated as a global multibillion dollar industry (Cognitive Assessment and Training Market, 2023), which is touted by education, athletic, and military end users for its promise to facilitate cognitive skill development specifically and to enhance real-world performance generally. Such programs have a long history of implementation in academic settings to support and reinforce critical learning objectives, such as computational skills or language (Veloso, Vicente, & Filipe, 2020) (Luis-Ruiz, et al., 2020). Computer-based cognitive training tools also have been employed with reported positive results to aid recovery of cognitive function following brain injury (Fernandez Lopez & Antoli, 2020), or to facilitate maintenance of skills in older adults and individuals diagnosed with cognitive decline due to medical or psychiatric conditions (Zhang, et al., 2019).

Given the popularity of computer-based cognitive training tools for those applications noted above, it is not surprising that applications aimed at improving performance in healthy, high-functioning adults have proliferated. Consumers such as elite college, professional, and tactical athletes are especially keen consumers of novel and innovative training solutions and are frequently targets of aggressive corporate marketing for products promising to deliver them their desired performance advantage. However, scientific evidence supporting the effectiveness of computer-based cognitive training tools is generally limited or not accessible for external scientific verification or validation due to its proprietary nature. Moreover, it is not uncommon that evidence published in the open literature is generated by corporate researchers and others with a vested stake in the commercial product. Moreover, questions remain regarding the incongruence between claims made by corporate marketing and evidence supporting product effectiveness. Specifically, while evidence seems to support the trainability of task-specific performance for some tasks, the applicability or transfer of such performance improvement to more general performance within and across targeted cognitive domains remains questionable (Gobet & Sala, 2023). That is to say, using computer-based cognitive training tools may improve one's score on the test itself, but may not improve performance in any other context.

In this chapter, we highlight a range of currently available computer-assisted cognitive training tools. This review is not intended to be exhaustive, rather it serves to highlight key approaches and

DOI: 10.4324/9781003378969-10

explore strengths and limitations of computer-based cognitive skills training applications more broadly.

Computer-assisted brain training programs

Computer-assisted cognitive training tools are typically gamified versions of standard cognitive tasks targeting basic cognitive functions including attention, memory, and visuomotor control (Li & Chen, 2016), which have been shown to respond positively to training. These tools are widely accessible and generally easy to use, in most cases requiring little training or instruction. The training tasks can range from simple games (e.g., word puzzles) to highly immersive programs (e.g., video games or virtual reality applications). Formats such as driving simulations and first-person shooter games are particularly popular as training aids since they are dynamic and engaging, factors which can support user motivation (Lumsden, Edwards, Lawrence, Coyle, & Munafo, 2016). In the sections that follow, we explore a sampling of popular training programs to highlight both the strengths and limitations of computer-assisted cognitive training approaches broadly.

CogniFit

CogniFit (CogniFit LTD, 2008) is a program designed to support maintenance of cognitive function in adults. The program targets 22 specific cognitive processes, including memory, reasoning, cognitive flexibility, attention, language, neuromotor coordination, and sensory awareness. Each training area evaluates cognitive function using a combination of psychological batteries, questionnaires, and interactive games integrating visual, auditory, and language stimuli. Training modules consist of games that vary in challenge level, goal, and presentation. Training programs can be adapted to user identified areas of concern, life stage (55 years and older), and clinical diagnosis.

CogniFit was identified as one of the two highest-rated tools out of 17 similarly advertised cognitive training programs validated by well-designed, randomized studies published in peer-reviewed journals (Shah, Weinborn, Verdile, Sohrabi, & Martins, 2017). The majority of studies examining the effectiveness of CogniFit for cognitive performance enhancement have involved older adults and individuals with neurological dysfunction. At this time, no studies have examined the use of CogniFit training to improve performance of elite performers. In healthy older adults (55 years of age and older), regular program participation (at least 45 minutes per week) has been shown to improve visuospatial working memory (Shatil, Mikulecka, Bellotti, & Bures, 2014), attention (Peretz, et al., 2011), processing speed (Gigler, Blomeke, Shatil, Weintraub, & Reber, 2013), and coordination (Shatil, Metzer, Horvitz, & Miller, 2010; Shatil, 2013). CogniFit training has also been shown to improve working memory and processing speed in older adults with memory dysfunction (Gigler, Blomeke, Shatil, Weintraub, & Reber, 2013), and enhanced attention, executive function, and processing speed – all of which positively impact gait stability – in a sedentary geriatric population (Verghese, Mahoney, Ambrose, Wang, & Holtzer, 2010). In adult dyslexic readers, error detection improved significantly after training, which researchers suggest is due to improved working memory capacity (Horowitz-Kraus & Breznitz, 2009). However, evidence to date offers weak support for the transfer of improvements on CogniFit tasks to everyday cognitive performance, and research examining the persistence of training improvements over time has yet to be published. In comparison to cognitive performance improvements from playing a roleplaying video game (World of Warcraft), no significant differences were identified in CogniFit-only users (Emihovich, Roque, & Mason, 2020). Moreover, Harris et al. (2018) notes that a large number of these validation studies have been conducted by CogniFit-affiliated researchers, raising concerns of potential bias.

BrainHQ

BrainHQ (Posit Science Corporation, 2002) is another program designed primarily for healthy and cognitively impaired older adults. Similar to CogniFit, BrainHQ was ranked among the top two currently available brain training programs validated by well-designed randomized trials (Shah, Weinborn, Verdile, Sohrabi, & Martins, 2017). The program delivers 29 different adaptive tasks to train skills such as visual search, sustained attention, and categorization, which were designed to target performance across broad domains of function, including attention, processing speed, memory, social cognition, spatial attention, and general intelligence. To date, no studies have explored the use of BrainHQ in elite performers.

A number of studies reported an association between BrainHQ use and improvement in attention (Van Vleet, Hoang-duc, DeGutis, & Robertson, 2010; Smith, et al., 2009; Zelinski, et al., 2011; O'Brien, et al., 2013), auditory and visuospatial attention (Leung, et al., 2015), working memory (Leung, et al., 2015), forward recognition memory span task and global auditory memory scores (Smith, et al., 2009; Zelinski, et al., 2011; Mahncke, et al., 2006), processing speed (Zelinski, et al., 2011; Meltzer, et al., 2023), and executive function (specifically attention switching) (Bamidis, et al., 2015).

Across studies, tasks aimed at improving speed of processing, specifically visually searching for, and identifying objects, showed increased performance, while other training strategies demonstrated minimal positive impact (Ball, et al., 2002). In a longitudinal study of older adults ($n = 2832$), participants were randomly assigned to one of four groups: memory training, reasoning training, processing speed training, or no training. After 10 sessions of training across five to six weeks, participants demonstrated improved performance within the specific domain targeted by training, but not in other, non-trained cognitive domains (Ball, et al., 2002). Training for improved processing speed showed the greatest retention of skill across the domain-specific groups over time. Specifically, participants who received training to improve processing speed exhibited fewer difficulties performing instrumental activities of daily living (Cohen's $d = 0.26$) five years after the initial training sessions (Willis, et al., 2006). After 10 years, participants who received processing speed training continued to perform better on processing speed tasks relative to those who received training to improve memory or reasoning skills; however, differences in instrumental activities of daily living across groups were no longer observed (Rebok & Ball, 2014). Processing speed training was also shown to protect against driving cessation: specifically, three years post training, 9% of participants who received processing speed training ceased driving compared to 14% of controls (Edwards, Delahunt, & Mahncke, 2009). Processing speed training was also associated with a reduction in the number of at fault vehicular accidents, with a rate ratio of 0.55 (Ball, Edwards, Ross, & McGwin, 2010).

Brain Workshop

Brain Workshop (Jaeggi, Buschkuehl, Jonides, & Perrig, 2008; Hoskinson, 2008) is an open-source application released in 2008 that was designed to improve working memory and fluid intelligence using a dual n-back task. The original dual n-back task – the groundwork for this program – involves listening to a continuous audio sequence of letters while watching a continuous sequence of illuminated square positions on a grid, and then responding when a letter or square position matches earlier letters or square positions n-items back in the sequence (Jaeggi, et al., 2010). The program includes 14 different game modes in addition to the default baseline mode and manual mode in which users can set their own gaming parameters. Brain Workshop also includes an interference setting in which a given stimulus feature matches the target on either N-1 or N+1 trials ago, but not on N trials ago, a quarter of the time.

Brain Workshop has an adaptive level-changing model which increases or decreases the n-back level based on performance. A score of 80% or more results in an increase in task difficulty, while a score less than 50% accuracy results in a decrease in difficulty. Scores between 80% and 50% maintain the current n-back level. Users are provided with feedback on performance, including average score plots for each session completed in a day and the average of the last 20 sessions completed by the user. Users can export their saved session histories to track performance over time, but sessions completed in manual mode are not included in progress graphs.

The effectiveness of Brain Workshop use for improving working memory and fluid intelligence has been evaluated in a number of studies in both clinical (PTSD, schizophrenia) and non-clinical (healthy children, healthy young adult, healthy elderly) populations. Some studies found no effect of training on working memory, processing speed, or fluid intelligence (Lawlor-Savage & Goghari, 2016; Redick, et al., 2013). However, others have demonstrated improvements in working memory (Jaeggi, Buschkuehl, Jonides, & Shah, 2011), episodic memory (Rudebeck, Bor, Ormond, O'Reilly, & Lee, 2012), fluid intelligence (Qiu, Wei, Zhao, & Lin, 2009; Rudebeck, Bor, Ormond, O'Reilly, & Lee, 2012), and attention (Lilienthal, Tamez, Shelton, Myerson, & Hale, 2013). One such study found that use of Brain Workshop correlated positively with performance on a task of fluid intelligence (matrix reasoning), but less so with a task of working memory (WMS) (Jaeggi, et al., 2010), providing modest evidence of contrast validity. Performance differences based on age (Salminen, Frensch, Strobach, & Schubert, 2016) and individual characteristics (Jaeggi, Buschkuehl, Jonides, & Shah, 2011) have also been reported.

Near transfer effects of training were measured using either single or dual n-back tasks with different stimuli than those presented in Brain Workshop, and improvements were observed in two controlled investigations (Studer, et al., 2009; Buschkuehl, 2014). In one of these studies, the greatest improvements in performance were observed in participants who trained on a 3-back Brain Workshop module (Buschkuehl, 2014), while the other found no significant transfer from one n-back stimuli to another (Schneiders, et al., 2012). Training-related transfer effects were also evaluated with a digit span task (Jaeggi, Buschkuehl, Jonides, & Perrig, 2008), which found that transfer effects are dependent on the extent of improvement achieved on the n-back working memory task (Jaeggi, Buschkuehl, Jonides, & Shah, 2011). These cognitive transfer effects were replicated using the same cognitive transfer tasks and expanded upon by including transfer into the affective domain using the Emotional Stroop task (Schweizer, Hampshire, & Dalgleish, 2011).

Modest evidence of far transfer of improvements from use of the Brain Workshop program to other cognitive tasks has been demonstrated. Two studies used the forward digit span as an additional measure of far transfer (Schweizer, Hampshire, & Dalgleish, 2011; Jaeggi, Buschkuehl, Jonides, & Perrig, 2008), and another measured affective transfer using the emotional Stroop task (Schweizer, Hampshire, & Dalgleish, 2011). Far transfer effects were observed in both the Bochumer Matrizen-Test and Raven's Advanced Progressive Matrices tasks after training, showing transfer of improvements gained from training on a single n-back task to multiple fluid intelligence tasks (Studer, et al., 2009). Persistence of training effects was also noted in one study in which higher levels of performance on fluid intelligence tasks persisted after a three-month break from any training (Jaeggi, Buschkuehl, Jonides, & Shah, 2011).

Lumosity

Lumosity (Lumos Labs, Inc, 2020), a product of Lumos Labs, includes games purported to train and improve cognitive function in several different domains: memory, attention, processing speed, flexibility, and problem solving. Lumosity, launched in 2007, was presented as an entertaining way to improve cognitive function, the benefits of which are said to transfer to daily tasks "from problem-solving to driving" (Scanlon, Drescher, & Sarkar, 2007). The program boasts 60+ visually engaging games based on an adaptive learning platform that accommodates the learner's desired level of challenge and cognitive domains targeted (Hardy & Scanlon, 2009). As with other cognitive training tools, Lumosity games are rooted in established psychological tests and principles. For example, memory games utilize similar principles as the n-back test, while visual attention games alter difficulty with changes in stimulus duration, eccentricity, and number of distractors (Hardy & Scanlon, 2009).

The effectiveness of Lumosity for improving cognitive function in healthy adults has been explored in a number of studies, the majority of which are focused on older adult and elderly cohorts. Few studies have examined the use of Lumosity to improve performance in elite performers. Overall, evidence supporting the effectiveness of Lumosity to improve performance in healthy adults is inconsistent. Some studies have reported that use of Lumosity across shorter training periods, generally three to ten weeks of training lasting 15 minutes to 1 hour per day (five to seven days per week), is associated with improved performance on tasks involving attention switching (Al-Thaqib, et al., 2018), processing speed, short-term memory, working memory, problem solving, and reasoning (Hardy, et al., 2015), executive functions (Mayas, Partmentier, Andres, & Ballesteros, 2014), and statistical inference and phonetics learning (Kpolovie P. J., 2002; Kpolovie P. J., 2012). Other studies report conflicting results for measures of attention (Ballesteros, et al., 2014; Ballesteros, et al., 2017; Mayas, Partmentier, Andres, & Ballesteros, 2014; Shah, Weinborn, Verdile, Sohrabi, & Martins, 2017), and working and visuospatial memory (Ballesteros, et al., 2014; Toril, Reales, Mayas, & Ballesteros, 2016). Interestingly, Kable and colleagues (2017) reported that participants who completed Lumosity training had similar brain activity (functional magnetic resonance spectroscopy) and risk sensitivity during decision-making as participants who played a non-adaptive video game. Long-term use of Lumosity has been shown to modulate the rate at which participants are able to recognize, process, and react to task-related changes (Stevyers, Hawkins, Karayanidis, & Brown, 2019) and enhance selective attention, attention-switching, and working memory performance (Hardy & Scanlon, 2009; Stevyers & Benjamin, 2019). Use of Lumosity also has been associated with post-training enhancements in general well-being (Ballesteros, et al., 2014), motivation and engagement (Ballesteros, et al., 2017), and alertness (Mayas, Partmentier, Andres, & Ballesteros, 2014). As noted, a few studies have explored use of Lumosity in an elite performer population. One study explored the transfer effects of Lumosity training in a relatively small sample of young professional rugy players with a mixed history of concussion. Players completed five weekly sessions, each lasting 10–15 minutes, across a four-week period. While improvement was observed in visuospatial excutive function, other tasks, including nonverbal strategy initiaton, showed poorer performance after training (Barker & Oledzka, 2021).

Across these studies, the greatest levels of improvement were observed for older adults (Stevyers, Hawkins, Karayanidis, & Brown, 2019) and participants who utilized higher levels of challenge during Lumosity training (Scanlon, Drescher, & Sarkar, 2007). However, studies often consist of small samples and many lacked measures of daily activity transfer effects or persistence of effects over time. In general, evidence suggests that Lumosity users perform better over time on the tasks they trained on (Hardy, et al., 2015; Ruiz-Marquez, et al., 2019; Scanlon, Drescher, & Sarkar, 2007; Stevyers, Hawkins, Karayanidis, & Brown, 2019). For studies that examined longitudinal data, some reported improvements in memory enduring at least three months after training (Toril, Reales, Mayas, & Ballesteros, 2016; Ballesteros, Kraft, Santana, & Tziraki, 2015), while others note that improvements did not persist after training without a "booster" session (Shah, Weinborn, Verdile, Sohrabi, & Martins, 2017).

NeuroTracker

NeuroTracker™ (CogniSens Athletics Inc.) uses multiple object tracking (MOT) in a 3D interface to adaptively train individuals to improve their speed for multiple object tracking while maintaining their response accuracy. There has been limited research conducted on the transfer from NeuroTracker training to real-world performance improvements (Fleddermann, Heppe, & Zentgraf, 2019; Romeas, Guldner, & Faubert, 2016; Moen, Hrozanova, & Pensgard, 2018; Mangine, et al., 2014), although multiple object tracking has been used as an assessment procedure within athletic populations (Faubert, 2013; Mangine, et al., 2014; Park, Klotzbier, & Schott, 2021). Research by Faubert (2013) demonstrated that athletes of different calibres (professional, elite amateur, and recreational) exhibited performance differences in MOT. While each group improved across the course of 15 training sessions, professional athletes had a substantially superior learning curve as they performed better initially and improved more rapidly. Elite amateur athletes started at the same performance average as the recreational athletes; however, they improved more dramatically across sessions. Similarly, Mangine et al. (2014) compared MOT performance to on-court performance of professional basketball players and found that NeuroTracker performance correlated with measures of athletic performance including number of steals and turnovers. Implementing NeuroTracker training in a military special operations population, Vartanian, Coady, and Blacker (2016) found that those trained (supervised) with NeuroTracker demonstrated improvements in working memory, while both active and passive control groups did not. In a follow-on study, Vartanian and colleagues (2021) found that general military personnel utilizing NeuroTracker in an unsupervised setting demonstrated improved simple working memory performance (near transfer) but not more complex multitasking performance (far transfer).

Further, NeuroTracker has been shown to produce both near- and far-transfer effects in athlete populations. NeuroTracker-trained elite volleyball players showed near-transfer post-training improvements in processing speed and sustained attention, but no effect on the volleyball-related decision-making task (Fleddermann, Heppe, & Zentgraf, 2019). University soccer players who underwent NeuroTracker training exhibited a 15% increase in their on-field performance compared with active and passive control groups (Romeas, Guldner, & Faubert, 2016), which implies far-transfer effects since NeuroTracker does not exercise soccer skills. Moen et al. (2018) reported that elite athletes across a number of athletic concentrations saw no improvement in executive function following NeuroTracker training, However, these results should be interpreted with caution given the small group sizes (Romeas, Guldner, & Faubert, 2016) and potential ceiling effects (Fleddermann, Heppe, & Zentgraf, 2019).

Caution is required when considering this device for use with clinical populations as it is not an approved medical device and its safety and efficacy for treatment has not been confirmed. Studies examining the use of NeuroTracker in mild traumatic brain injury cohorts show no clear effect on performance compared with healthy controls (Corbin-Berrigan, Kowalski, Faubert, Cristie, & Gagnon, 2018; Chermann, Romeas, Marty, & Faubert, 2018). As would be expected without treatment, mTBI groups showed lower performance gains using NeuroTracker compared with controls over the training sessions, though this difference was not statistically significant (Chermann, Romeas, Marty, & Faubert, 2018).

To date, the efficacy of NeuroTracker's use for improving operational or sport specific skills (far transfer) is limited and show mixed results at best (Horváth, et al., 2023). These studies have certainly been limited by the challenges inherent in recruiting specialized populations, which leads to statistically underpowered study designs. They also face the challenge of having reliable and sufficiently difficult tasks to represent performance-specific skills that can be administered under controlled research conditions. As an additional consideration, the company's founder is an author on the majority of research that has been conducted involving this tool.

Brain game applications

A quick search of the Apple App and Google Play Stores produces numerous applications for smartphone or tablet devices that are currently marketed as brain games designed to improve mental agility. In most cases, these applications operate on a subscription model with some offering a free starter point combined with more advanced features at the pay level. Many of these applications, which include word games and puzzles, visuospatial reasoning and logic exercises, offer progress tracking and "brain scores", some allow multi-player options, and others display elaborate graphs and plots to visualize performance. Such features are designed to engage users but are not necessarily indicative of scientific rigor. In addition, many applications claim connections with universities and state that their program is based on science. In some cases, the underlying "games" upon which these applications are built may have indeed been developed and validated for clinical or other research purposes. However, it is important to note that there is no standard applied to these applications that requires them to be effective in order to be listed in the mobile app store. Although such applications may be marketed under "educational" or "health and wellness" labels, there is no guarantee that use of the applications will be educational or improve healthy function. Such programs would be more appropriately classified as entertainment. While such applications dominate the commercial market, other more rigorously designed and studied applications are beginning to emerge. Among these are a new smartphone Cognitive Gym application that incorporates a number of cognitive training drills targeting attention, situation awareness, task switching, decision making, cognitive flexibility, among others, that are implemented through a periodized training plan (Aidman, et al., 2022).

Summary

This chapter highlighted a range of commercially available computer-based brain training programs that are commonly referenced in the empirical literature circa 2000–2023. These products boast improved cognitive performance and mental agility with training. However, questions remain regarding the extent to which such claims align with the existing scientific evidence. While data suggest that brain training can lead to improved performance on standard measures of cognitive function, these improvements have been largely limited to the specific tasks that are trained (e.g., near-transfer effects), particularly in the domains of attention, memory, processing speed, working memory, maths, and fluid intelligence (Anguera, Boccanfuso, & Rintoul, 2013; Toril, Reales, & Ballesteros, 2014; Chiu, et al., 2017; Gates N., et al., 2019a; Gates N., et al., 2019b). However, Blacker and colleagues (2019) posit that the near-transfer effects found in basic science trials are likely to offer benefits to tactical athletes, especially when training involves an occupationally relevant task. For example, training with response-inhibition tasks prior to completing a simulated marksmanship trial reduced the occurrence of friendly fire incidents (Biggs, Cain, & Mitroff, 2015). Moreover, while the effects of training may not be readily observable on standard performance measures, mechanisms such as neuroplasticity and functional connectivity have been shown to change with cognitive training (ten Brinke, Davis, Barha, & Liu-Ambrose, 2017; Kühn, Gallinat, & Mascherek, 2019).

In contrast to the observed near transfer effects, objective measurements of performance on untrained tasks have yielded little to no evidence of substantive far-transfer effects (Melby-Lervåg & Hulme, 2013; Hampshire, Sandrone, & Hellyer, 2019; Walton, et al., 2015; Rossignoli-Palomeque, Perez-Hernandez, & González-Marqués, 2018; Tetlow & Edwards, 2017). In fact, the most notable support for far-transfer effects comes from participants' self-reported improvements in social function (Jak, Seelye, & Jurick, 2013; Tetlow & Edwards, 2017). Further, both training program effectiveness and skill transfer specificity has been shown to vary across cognitive performance domains (Jaeggi, Karbach, & Strobach, 2017; Hampshire, Sandrone, & Hellyer, 2019; Kueider, Parisi, Gross, & Rebok, 2012; Lampit, Hallock, & Valenzuela, 2014; Nguyen, Murphy, & Andrews, 2022). Overall, current evidence has failed to support the conclusion that computer-based brain training – regardless of the tool used – can produce generalized improvements in performance on real-world tasks requiring memory, attention, problem solving, or other cognitive abilities that are targeted by training.

Despite limited evidence supporting the effectiveness of brain training tools, research suggests that computer-based training approaches are more effective at reinforcing skill development than more traditional didactic or paper and pencil approaches. In a systematic review conducted by Kueider et al. (2012) focused on brain training in an older adult population, the authors reported that computerized cognitive training appears to be comparable to or better than more traditional, paper-and-pencil cognitive training approaches. This may be due to the adaptive learning nature of many training programs and the gaming format used by most programs, which has been shown to encourage greater task engagement and user motivation (Lumsden, Edwards, Lawrence, Coyle, & Munafo, 2016). Although gamification can enhance motivation, reduce dropout rates, and promote adherence, consideration should be given to each game-task's concurrent and predictive validity (McPherson & Burns, 2008), as well as the type and magnitude of performance differences exhibited after gamified versus non-game training (Lumsden, Edwards, Lawrence, Coyle, & Munafo, 2016; van de Weijer, Kuijf, de Vries, Bloem, & Duits, 2019). Further research is also needed to determine the effect of training duration and intensity on short- and long-term cognitive performance benefits (Rossignoli-Palomeque, Perez-Hernandez, & González-Marqués, 2018; Klimova, 2016; Boot & Kramer, 2014; Gates, Rutjes, & Di Nisio, 2020).

The future of computer-based brain training programs rests fundamentally on continued consumer demand for such products as well as the ability to broaden the existing consumer base. Before this can be accomplished, key gaps and methodological concerns need to be addressed. We begin with the relative absence of studies exploring the use of computer-based brain training programs by elite performers. Over the past two decades, computer-based brain tranining programs have expanded from primarily remediation and rehabilitation applications to a larger community of users, specifically older adults and elderly, seeking solutions to optimize and sustain cognitive performance. The lack of research exploring applications for these programs within the professional sport or other elite performance communities is perhaps more reflective of the current evidence base supporting the effectiveness of these tools, rather than interest in performance enhancement tools per se. As previously noted, on the job performance, whether on the playing field or battlefield, is of considerable importance to elite performers and they are often highly motivated consumers of new and novel solutions with potential to provide a performance advantage. However, given that current evidence supports only modest improvements in cognitive function from computer-based brain training, largely based on studies with healthy older adults, and limited evidence for transfer of effects from computer-based brain training to real-world task performance, it is not surprising that currently available computer-based cognitive training tools may not be seen as viable candidates to achieve meaningful performance enhancement for high-performing individuals.

Other methodological concerns highlighted from the existing literature include generally small study sample sizes (Gobet & Sala, 2023), potential placebo effects of suggestive advertising (Foroughi, Monfort, Paczynski, McKnight, & Greenwood, 2016), lack of active or appropriate control groups (Walton, et al., 2015), the effect of gamification on training efficacy (Lumsden, Edwards, Lawrence, Coyle, & Munafo, 2016; van de Weijer, Kuijf, de Vries, Bloem, & Duits, 2019; McPherson & Burns, 2008), and currently unknown performance moderators (Boot & Kramer, 2014). For those studies relying on convenience samples of brain training program users from the larger community, research findings are further limited to individuals with access to brain training tools. Those who discontinue use of brain training programs early on have a different learning trajectory than those who persist with the programs (Stevyers & Benjamin, 2019). Older adults with poor performance are more likely to drop out than other users (Stevyers & Benjamin, 2019), and even when poor-performing users continue training certain deficits can persist, resulting in different learning trajectories (Guerra-Carrillo, Katovich, & Bunge, 2017; Stevyers, Hawkins, Karayanidis, & Brown, 2019). Potential improvement is further influenced by users' initial (baseline) cognitive performance level and motivation (Scanlon, Drescher, & Sarkar, 2007), as well as many factors that can influence cognitive function regardless of age or proficiency levels, such as history of concussion or brain injury.

To conclude, although evidence is limited regarding the efficacy of computer-based brain training programs for improving global cognitive performance in healthy adult populations, targeted applications may provide some benefit for select tasks. That said, caution should be exercised when recommending the use of computer-based training programs for improving cognitive function broadly, as evidence for this outcome is lacking. Moreover, given the lack of research examining the effectiveness of programs such as those detailed above with high-functioning, healthy adults, we can only recommend that use of such programs be offered as add-ons to existing Human Performance Programs aimed at enhancement of baseline functioning. Further research is needed to better characterize whether such approaches are in fact efficacious for use in elite performers.

References

Aidman, E., Fogarty, G. J., Crampton, J., Bond, J., Taylor, P., Heathcote, A., & Zaichowsky, L. (2022). An app-enhanced cognitive fitness training program for athletes: The rationale and validation protocol. *Frontiers in Psychology, 13*. doi:10.3389/fpsyg.2022.957551

Allaire, J. C., Backman, L., Balota, D. A., Bavelier, D., Bjork, R. A., Bower, G. H., & et al. (2017). *A consensus on the brain training industry from the scientific community.* Retrieved from http://longevity.stanford.edu/a-consensus-on-the-brain-training-industry-from-the-scientific-community-2/

Al-Thaqib, A., Al-Sultan, F., Al-Zahrani, A., Al-Kahtani, F., Al-Regaiey, K., Iqbal, M., & Bashir, S. (2018, April 20). Brain training games enhance cognitive function in healthy subjects. *Medical Science Monitor Basic Research, 24*, 63–69. doi:10.12659/MSMBR.909022

Anguera, J. A., Boccanfuso, J., & Rintoul, J. L. (2013). Video game training enhances cognitive control in older adults. *Nature, 501*, 97–101. doi:10.1038/nature12486

Ball, K., Berch, D. B., Helmers, K. F., Jobe, J. B., Leveck, M. D., Marsiske, M., . . . Willis, S. L. (2002). Effects of cognitive training interventions with older adults: A randomized controlled trail. *Jama, 18*, 2271–2281. doi:10.1001/jama.288.18.2271

Ball, K., Edwards, J. D., Ross, L. A., & McGwin, G. (2010). Cognitive training decreases motor vehicle collision involvement among older drivers. *Journal of American Geriatric Society, 58*, 2107–2113. doi:10.1111/j.1532-5415.2010.03138.x

Ballesteros, S., Kraft, E., Santana, S., & Tziraki, C. (2015). Maintaining older brain functionality: A targeted review. *Neuroscience & Biobehavioral Reviews, 55*, 453–477. doi:doi.org/10.1016/j.neubiorev.2015.06.008

Ballesteros, S., Mayas, J., Prieto, A., Ruiz-Marquez, E., Toril, P., & Reales, J. M. (2017). Effects of video game training on measures of selective attention and working memory in older adults: Results from a randomized controlled trial. *Frontiers in Aging Neuroscience, 9*, 354. doi:doi.org/10.3389/fnagi.2017.00354

Ballesteros, S., Prieto, A., Mayas, J., Toril, P., Pita, C., Ponce de Leon, L., . . . Waterworth, J. (2014). Brain training with non-action video games enhances aspects of cognition in older adults: a randomized controlled trial. *Frontiers in Aging Neuroscience, 6*, Article 277. doi:10.3389/fnagi.2014.00277

Bamidis, P. D., Fissler, P., Papageorgiou, S. G., Zilidou, V., Konstantinidis, E. I., Billis, A. S., . . . Kolassa, I.-T. (2015). Gains in cognition through combined cognitive and physical training: The role of training dosage and severity of neurocognitive disorder. *Frontiers in Aging Neuroscience, 7*, Article 152. doi:10.3389/fnagi.2015.00152

Barker, L., & Oledzka, A. (2021). Visuospatial executive functions are improved by brief brain training in young rugby players – evidence of far transfer effects: A pilot study. *OBM Neurobiology, 5*(2). doi:10.21926/obm.neurobiol.2102093

Biggs, A. T., Cain, M. S., & Mitroff, S. R. (2015). Cognitive training can reduce civilian casualties in a simulated shooting environment. *Psychological Science, 26*, 1164–1176. doi:10.1177/0956797615579274

Blacker, K. J., Hamilton, J., & Roush, G. (2019). Cognitive training for military application: A review of the literature and practical guide. *Journal of Cognitive Enhancement, 3*, 30–51. doi:s41465-018-0076-1

Boot, W. R., & Kramer, A. F. (2014). The brain-games conundrum: Does cognitive training really sharpen the mind? *Cerebrum, 15*, 15.

Buschkuehl, M. H.-G. (2014). Neural effects of short-term training on working memory. *Cognitive, Affective, & Behavioral Neuroscience, 14*, 147–160. doi:10.3758/s13415-013-0244-9

Chermann, J. F., Romeas, T., Marty, F., & Faubert, J. (2018). Perceptual-cognitive three-dimensional multiple-object tracking task can help the monitoring of sport-related concussion. *BMJ Open Sport & Exercise Medicine, 4*, e000384. doi:10.1136/bmjsem-2018-000384

Chiu, H.-L., Chu, H., Tsai, J.-C., Liu, D., Chen, Y., & Yang, H.-L. (2017). The effect of cognitivebased training for the healthy older people: A metaanalysis of randomized controlled trials. *PLoS ONE, 12*(5), e0176742. doi:10.1371/journal.pone.0176742

Clark, C., Lawlor-Savage, L., & Goghari, V. M. (2017). Working memory training in healthy young adults: Support for the null from a randomized comparison to active and passive control groups. *PLoS One, 12*, e0177707. doi:10.1371/journal.pone.0177707

CogniFit LTD. (2008). *CogniFit Personal Coach (CPC) training program and database.*

Cognitive Assessment and Training Market. (2023, Nov 19). Retrieved from MarketsAndMarkets: www.marketsandmarkets.com/Market-Reports/cognitive-assessment-market-1039.html

Corbin-Berrigan, L. A., Kowalski, K., Faubert, J., Cristie, B., & Gagnon, I. (2018). Three-dimensional multiple object tracking in the pediatric population: The NeuroTracker and its promising role in the management of mild traumatic brain injury. *Neuroreport, 29*, 559–563. doi:10.1097/WNR.0000000000000988

Edwards, J. D., Delahunt, P. B., & Mahncke, H. W. (2009). Cognitive speed of processing training delays driving cessation. *Journal of Gerontology, 64*, 1262–1267. doi:10.1093/gerona/glp131

Emihovich, B., Roque, N., & Mason, J. (2020). Can Video Gameplay Improve Undergraduates' Problem-Solving Skills? *International Journal of Game-Based Learning, 10*(2), 21–38.

Faubert, J. (2013). Professional athletes have extraordinary skills for rapidly learning complex and neutral dynamic visual scenes. *Scientific Reports, 3*, 1154. doi:doi.org/10.1038/srep01154

Federal Trade Commission v. Lumos Labs, Inc., and Kunal Sarkar, and Michael Scanlon, 3:16-cv-00001-sk (U.S. District Court for the Northern District of California, San Francisco Division January 8, 2016).

Fernandez Lopez, R., & Antoli, A. (2020). Computer-based cognitive interventions in acquired brain injury: A systematic review and meta-analysis of randomized controlled trials. *PloS One, 15*(7), e0235510. doi:10.1371/journal.pone.0235510

Fischer, M. V., Stone, J., Hawkes, T. D., Eveland, E., & Strang, A. J. (2015). Integrative physical and cognitive training development to better meet airmen mission requirements. *Procedia Manufacturing, 3*, 1580–1586. doi:10.1016/j.promfg.2015.07.445

Fleddermann, M. T., Heppe, H., & Zentgraf, K. (2019). Off-court generic perceptual-cognitive training in elite volleyball athletes: Task-specific effects and levels of transfer. *Frontiers in psychology, 10*, Article 1599. doi:doi.org/10.3389/fpsyg.2019.01599

Foroughi, C. K., Monfort, S. S., Paczynski, M., McKnight, P. E., & Greenwood, P. M. (2016). Placebo effects in cognitive training. *Proceedings of the National Academy of Sciences, 113*, 7470–7474. doi:10.1073/pnas.1601243113

Gates, N. J., Rutjes, A. W., & Di Nisio, M. (2020). Computerised cognitive training for 12 or more weeks for maintaining cognitive function in cognitively healthy people in late life. *Cochrane Database of Systematic Reviews, 2*. doi:10.1002/14651858.CD012277.pub3

Gates, N., Rutjes, A., Di Nisio, M., Karim, S., Chong, L., March, E., . . . Vernooij, R. (2019a). Computerised cognitive training for maintaining cognitive function in cognitively healthy people in midlife. *Cochrane Database of Systematic Reviews, 3*. doi:10.1002/14651858.CD012278.pub2

Gates, N., Rutjes, A., Di Nisio, M., Karim, S., Chong, L., March, E., . . . Vernooij, R. (2019b). Computerised cognitive training for maintaining cognitive function in cognitively healthy people in late life. *Cochrane Database of Systematic Reviews, 8*. doi:10.1002/14651858.CD012277.pub2

Gigler, K. L., Blomeke, K., Shatil, E., Weintraub, S., & Reber, P. J. (2013). Preliminary evidence for the feasibility of at-home online cognitive training with older adults. *Gerontechnology: International Journal on the Fundamental Aspects of Technology to Serve the Ageing Society, 12*, 26–35. doi:10.4017/gt.2013.12.1.007.00

Gobet, F., & Sala, G. (2023). Cognitive training: A field in search of a phenomenon. *Perspectives on Psychological Science, 18*(1), 125–141. doi:10.1177/17456916221091

Guerra-Carrillo, B., Katovich, K., & Bunge, S. A. (2017). Does higher education hone cognitive functioning and learning efficacy? Findings from a large and diverse sample. *PloS one, 12*, e0182276. doi:10.1371/journal.pone.0182276

Hampshire, A., Sandrone, S., & Hellyer, P. J. (2019). A large-scale, cross-sectional investigation into the efficacy of brain training. . *Frontiers in Human Neuroscience* |, *13*, Article 221. doi:10.3389/fnhum.2019.00221

Hardy, J. L., Nelson, R. A., Thomason, M. E., Strenberg, D. A., Katovich, K., Farzin, F., & Scanlon, M. (2015). Enhancing cognitive abilities with comprehensive training: A large, online, randomized, active-controlled trial. *PLoS One, 10*, e0134467. doi:10.1371/journal.pone.0134467

Hardy, J., & Scanlon, M. (2009). *The Science Behind Lumosity.* San Francisco: Lumos Labs.

Harris, D. J., Wilson, M. R., & Vine, S. J. (2018). A systematic review of commercial cognitive training devices: implications for use in sport. *Frontiers in Psychology, 9*, Article 709. doi:10.3389/fpsyg.2018.00709

Horowitz-Kraus, T., & Breznitz, Z. (2009). Can the error detection mechanism benefit from training the working memory? A comparison between dyslexics and controls—an ERP study. *PLoS One, 4*, e7141. doi:10.1371/journal.pone.0007141

Horváth, D., Négyesi, J., Rácz, M., Győri, T., Matics, Z., Puskin, A., . . . Rácz, L. (2023). Feasibility of a novel neurofeedback system: A parallel randomized single-blinded pilot study. *Scientific Reports, 13*(1), 17353.

Hoskinson, P. (2008). *Brain Workshop – a Dual N-Back game*. Retrieved from http://brainworkshop.sourceforge.net/

Jaeggi, S. M., Buschkuehl, M., Jonides, J., & Perrig, W. J. (2008). Improving fluid intelligence with training on working memory. *Proceedings of the National Academy of Sciences, 105*, 6829–6833. doi:10.1073pnas.0801268105%20pna/

Jaeggi, S. M., Buschkuehl, M., Jonides, J., & Shah, P. (2011). Short- and long-term benefits of cognitive training. *Proceedings of the National Academy of Sciences, 108*, 10081–10086. doi:10.1073/pnas.1103228108

Jaeggi, S. M., Karbach, J., & Strobach, T. (2017). Editorial special topic: Enhancing brain and cognition through cognitive training. *Journal of Cognitive Enhancement, 1*, 353–357. doi:10.1007/s41465-017-0057-9

Jaeggi, S. M., Studer-Luethi, B., Buschkuehl, M., Su, Y. F., Jonides, J., & Perrig, W. J. (2010). The relationship between n-back performance and matrix reasoning—implications for training and transfer. *Intelligence, 38*, 625-635. doi:10.1016/j.intell.2010.09.001

Jak, A. J., Seelye, A. M., & Jurick, S. M. (2013). Crosswords to computers: A critical review of popular approaches to cognitive enhancement. *Neuropsychology Review, 23*, 13–26. doi:10.1007/s11065-013-9226-5

Kable, J. W., Caulfield, M. K., Falcone, M., McConnell, M., Bernardo, L., Parthasarathi, T., . . . Lerman, C. (2017). No effect of commercial cognitive training on brain activity, choice behavior, or cognitive performance. *Journal of Neuroscience, 37*, 7390–7402. doi:10.1523/JNEUROSCI.2832-16.2017

Kelly, A., Feltman, K., Nwala, E., Bernhardt, K., Hayes, A., Basso, J., & Mathews, C. (2016). *A systematic review of cognitive enhancement interventions for use in military operations.* Technical Report USAARL 2019-11, Fort Rucker, AL. Retrieved from https://apps.dtic.mil/sti/citations/AD1083490

Klimova, B. (2016). Computer-based cognitive training in aging. *Frontiers in Aging Neuroscience, 8*, Article 313. doi:10.3389/fnagi.2016.00313

Kpolovie, P. J. (2002). *Test, measurement and evaluation in education.* Port Harcourt: Emhai Books.

Kpolovie, P. J. (2012). Lumosity training and brain-boosting food effects on learning. *Education Research Journal, 2*, 186-198.

Kueider, A. M., Parisi, J. M., Gross, A. L., & Rebok, G. W. (2012). Computerized cognitive training with older adults: A systematic review. *PLoS ONE, 7*, e40588. doi:10.1371/journal.pone.0040588

Kühn, S., Gallinat, J., & Mascherek, A. (2019). Effects of computer gaming on cognition, brain structure, and function: A critical reflection on existing literature. *Dialogues in Clinical Neuroscience, 21*, 319–330. doi:10.31887/DCNS.2019.21.3/skuehn

Lampit, A., Hallock, H., & Valenzuela, M. (2014). Computerized cognitive training in cognitively healthy older adults: A systematic review and meta-analysis of effect modifiers. *PLoS Med, 11*, e1001756. doi:10.1371/journal.pmed.1001756

Lawlor-Savage, L., & Goghari, V. M. (2016). Dual n-back working memory training in healthy adults: A randomized comparison to processing speed training. *PloS One, 11*, e0151817. doi:10.1371/journal.pone.0151817

Lenehan, M. E., Summer, M. J., Saunders, N. L., Summer, J. J., & Vickers, J. C. (2015). Does the Cambridge Automated Neuropsychological Test Battery (CANTAB) distinguish between cognitive domains in healthy older adults? *Assessment, 23*, 163–172. doi:10.1177/1073191115581474

Leung, N. T., Tam, H. M., Chu, L. W., Kwok, T. C., Chan, F., Lam, L. C., . . . Lee, T. M. (2015). Neural plastic effects of cognitive training on aging brain. *Neural Plasticity*, 535618. doi:doi.org/10.1155/2015/535618

Li, B. Y., Tang, H. D., Qiao, Y., & Chen, S. D. (2015). Mental training for cognitive improvement in elderly people: What have we learned from clinical and neurophysiologic studies? *Current Alzheimer Research, 12*, 543–552. doi:10.2174/1567205012061507161l2918

Li, R., & Chen, J. (2016). Playing action video games improves visuomotor control. *Psychological Science, 27*(8), 1092-1108.

Lilienthal, L., Tamez, E., Shelton, J. T., Myerson, J., & Hale, S. (2013). Dual n-back training increases the capacity of the focus of attention. *Psychonomic Bulletin & Review, 20*, 135-141. doi:10.3758/s13423-012-0335-6

Luis-Ruiz, S., Caldú, X., Sánchez-Castañeda, C., Pueyo, R., Garolera, M., & Jurado, M. Á. (2020). Is cognitive training an effective tool for improving cognitive function and real-life behaviour in healthy children and adolescents? A systematic review. *Neuroscience & Biobehavioral Reviews, 116*, 268-282. doi:10.1016/j.neubiorev.2020.06.019

Lumos Labs, Inc. (2020). *Lumosity Home*. Retrieved from Lumosity: www.lumosity.com/en/

Lumsden, J., Edwards, E. A., Lawrence, N. S., Coyle, D., & Munafo, M. R. (2016). Gamification of cognitive assessment and cognitive training: A systematic review of applications and efficacy. *JMIR Serious Games, 4*, e11. doi:10.2196/games.5888

Mahncke, H. W., Connor, B. B., Appleman, J., Ahsanuddin, O. N., Hardy, J. L., Wood, R. A., . . . Merzenich, M. M. (2006). Memory enhancement in healthy older adults using a brain plasticity-based training program: A randomized, controlled study. *Proceedings of the National Academy of Sciences of the United States of America, 103*, 12523–12528. doi:10.1073/pnas.0605194103

Mangine, G. T., Hoffman, J. R., Wells, A. J., GonZalez, A. M., Rogowski, J. P., Townsend, J. R., & Fragala, M. S. (2014). Visual tracking speed is related to basketball-specific measures of performance in NBA players. *The Journal of Strength & Conditioning Research, 28*, 2406–2414. doi:10.1519/JSC.0000000000000550

Mayas, J., Partmentier, F. B., Andres, P., & Ballesteros, S. (2014). Plasticity of attentional functions in older adults after non-action video game training: A randomized controlled trial. *PLoS One, 9*, e92269. doi:10.1371/journal.pone.0092269

McPherson, J., & Burns, N. R. (2008). Assessing the validity of computer-game-like tests of processing speed and working memory. *Behavior Research Methods, 40*, 969–981. doi:10.3758/BRM.40.4.969

Melby-Lervåg, M., & Hulme, C. (2013). Is working memory training effective? A meta-analytic review. *Developmental Psychology, 49*, 270-291. doi:10.1037/a0028228

Meltzer, A. J., Rose, M. K., Le, A. Y., Spencer, K. A., Goldstein, L., Gubanova, A., . . . Bialystok, E. (2023). Improvement in executive function for older adults through smartphone apps: a randomized clinical trial comparing language learning and brain training. *Neuropsychology, Development, and Cognition,* 30(2), 150–171.

Moen, F., Hrozanova, M., & Pensgard, A. M. (2018). The effects of perceptual-cognitive training on subjective performance in elite athletes. *The Sport Journal, 60*. Retrieved from http://thesportjournal.org/article/theeffects-of-perceptual-cognitive-training-onsubjective-performance-in-elite-athletes/

Moen, F., Hrozanova, M., & Stiles, T. (2018). The effects of perceptual-cognitive training with Neurotracker on executive brain functions among elite athletes. *Cogent Psychology, 5*, 1544105. doi:10.1080/23311908.2018.1544105

Nguyen, L., Murphy, K., & Andrews, G. (2022). A game a day keeps cognitive decline away? A systematic review and meta-analysis of commercially-available brain training programs in healthy and cognitively impaired older adults. *Neuropsychology review, 32*(3), 601-630.

O'Brien, J. L., Edwards, J. D., Maxfield, N. D., Peronto, C. L., Williams, V. A., & Lister, J. J. (2013). Cognitive training and selective attention in the aging brain: An electrophysiological study. *Clinical Neurophysiology, 124*, 2198-2208. doi:10.1016/j.clinph.2013.05.012

Park, S.-Y., Klotzbier, T. J., & Schott, N. (2021). The Effects of the combination of high-intensity interval training with 3D-multiple object tracking task on perceptual-cognitive performance: A randomized controlled intervention trial. *International Journal of Environmental Research and Public Health, 18*(9), 4862.

Peretz, C., Korczyn, A. D., Shatil, E., Aharonson, V., Birnboim, S., & Giladi, N. (2011). Computer-based, personalized cognitive training versus classical computer games: A randomized double-blind prospective trial of cognitive stimulation. *Neuroepidemiology, 36*, 91-99. doi:10.1159/000323950

Posit Science Corporation. (2002, July). *BrainHQ interactive brain training program.*

Qiu, F., Wei, Q., Zhao, L., & Lin, L. (2009, December 26-28). Study on improving fluid intelligence through cognitive training system based on Gabor stimulus. *First International Conference on Information Science and Engineering* (pp. 3459–3462). Nanjing: Institute of Electrical and Electronics Engineers. Retrieved from https://ieeexplore.ieee.org/abstract/document/5454984

Rebok, G. W., & Ball, K. (2014). Ten-year effects of the ACTIVE cognitive training trial on cognition and everyday functioning in older adults. *Journal of the American Geriatrics Society, 62*, 16. doi:10.1111/jgs.12607

Redick, T. S., Shipstead, Z., Harrison, T. L., Hicks, K. L., Fried, D. E., Hambrick, D. Z., . . . Engle, R. W. (2013). No evidence of intelligence improvement after working memory training: A randomized, placebo-controlled study. *Journal of Experimental Psychology: General, 142*, 359-379. doi:10.1037/a0029082

Romeas, T., Guldner, A., & Faubert, J. (2016). 3D-Multiple object tracking training task improves passing decision-making accuracy in soccer players. *Psychology of Sport and Exercise, 22*, 1-9. doi:10.1016/j.psychsport.2015.06.002

Rossignoli-Palomeque, T., Perez-Hernandez, E., & González-Marqués, J. (2018). Brain training in children and adolescents: Is it scientifically valid? *Frontiers in Psychology, 9*, Article 565. doi:10.3389/fpsyg.2018.00565

Rudebeck, S. R., Bor, D., Ormond, A., O'Reilly, J. X., & Lee, A. C. (2012). A potential spatial working memory training task to improve both episodic memory and fluid intelligence. *Plos One, 7*, e50431. doi:10.1371/journal.pone.0050431

Ruiz-Marquez, E., Prieto, A., Mayas, J., Toril, P., Reales, J. M., & Ballesteros, S. (2019). Effects of nonaction videogames on attention and memory in young adults. *Games for Health Journal, 8*, 414–422. doi:10.1089/g4h.2019.0004

Salminen, T., Frensch, P., Strobach, T., & Schubert, T. (2016). Age-specific differences of dual n-back training. *Aging, Neuropsychology, and Cognition, 23*, 18-39. doi:10.1080/13825585.2015.1031723

Scanlon, M., Drescher, D., & Sarkar, K. (2007). *Improvement of visual attention and working memory through a web-based cognitive training program.* San Francisco: Lumos Labs. Retrieved from https://citeseerx.ist.psu.edu/viewdoc/download?doi=10.1.1.528.8712&rep=rep1&type=pdf

Schneiders, J. A., Opitz B, B., Tang, H., Deng, Y., Xie, C., Li, H., & Mecklinger, A. (2012). The impact of auditory working memory training on the fronto-parietal working memory network. *Frontiers in Human Neuroscience, 6*, Article 173. doi:10.3389/fnhum.2012.00173

Schweizer, S., Hampshire, A., & Dalgleish, T. (2011). Extending brain-training to the affective domain: Increasing cognitive and affective executive control through emotional working memory training. *PloS One, 6*, e24372. doi:10.1371/journal.pone.0024372

Shah, T. M., Weinborn, M., Verdile, G., Sohrabi, H. R., & Martins, R. N. (2017). Enhancing cognitive functioning in healthly older adults: A systematic review of the clinical significance of commercially available computerized cognitive training in preventing cognitive decline. *Neuropsychology Review, 27*, 62-80. doi:10.1007/s11065-016-9338-9

Shatil, E. (2013). Does combined cognitive training and physical activity training enhance cognitive abilities more than either alone? A four-condition randomized controlled trial among healthy older adults. *Frontiers in Aging Neuroscience, 5*, Article 8. doi:10.3389/fnagi.2013.00008

Shatil, E., Metzer, A., Horvitz, O., & Miller, A. (2010). Home-based personalized cognitive training in MS patients: A study of adherence and cognitive performance. *NeuroRehabilitation, 26*, 143-153. doi:10.3233/NRE-2010-0546

Shatil, E., Mikulecka, J., Bellotti, F., & Bures, V. (2014). Novel television-based cognitive training improves working memory and executive function. *PLoS One, 9*, e101472. doi:10.1371/journal.pone.0101472

Simons, D. J., Boot, W. R., Charness, N., Gathercole, S. E., Chabris, C. F., Hambrick, D. Z., & Stine-Morrow, E. A. (2016). Do "brain-training" programs work? *Psychological Science in the Public Interest, 17*, 103-186. doi:10.1177%2F1529100616661983

Smith, G. E., Housen, P., Yaffe, R. R., Ruff, R., Kennison, R. F., Mahncke, H. W., & Zelinski, E. M. (2009). A cognitive training program based on principles of brain plasticity: Results from the improvement in memory with plasticity-based adaptive cognitive training (IMPACT) study. *Journal of the American Geriatrics Society, 57*, 594-603. doi:10.1111/j.1532-5415.2008.02167.x

Stevyers, M., & Benjamin, A. S. (2019). The joint contribution of participation and performance to learning functions: Exploring the effects of age in large-scale data sets. *Behavioral Research Methods, 51*, 1531–1543. doi:10.3758/s13428-018-1128-2

Stevyers, M., Hawkins, G. E., Karayanidis, F., & Brown, S. D. (2019). A large-scale analysis of task switching practice effects across the lifespan. *Proceedings of the National Academy of Sciences, 116*, 17735–17740. doi:10.1073/pnas.1906788116

Studer, B. E., Jaeggi, S. M., Buschkuehl, M., Su, Y. F., Jonides, J., & Perrig, W. J. (2009, November 19-22). Improving fluid intelligence–Single N-back is as effective as Dual N-back. *50th Annual Meeting of the Psychonomic Society*. Boston. Retrieved from www.gwern.net/docs/dual-n-back/2009-jaeggi.pdf

ten Brinke, L. F., Davis, J. C., Barha, C. K., & Liu-Ambrose, T. (2017). Effects of computerized cognitive training on neuroimaging outcomes in older adults: A systematic review. *BMC Geriatrics, 17*, 139. doi:10.1186/s12877-017-0529-x

Tetlow, A. M., & Edwards, J. D. (2017). Systematic literature review and meta-analysis of commercially available computerized cognitive training among older adults. *Journal of Cognitive Enhancement, 1*, 559–575. doi:10.1007/s41465-017-0051-2

Toril, P., Reales, J. M., & Ballesteros, S. (2014). Video game training enhances cognition of older adults: A meta-analytic study. *Psychology Aging, 29*, 706-716. doi:10.1037/a0037507

Toril, P., Reales, J. M., Mayas, J., & Ballesteros, S. (2016). Video game training enhances visuospatial working memory and episodic memory in older adults. *Frontiers in Human Neuroscience, 10*, Article 206. doi:10.3389/fnhum.2016.00206

van de Weijer, S. C., Kuijf, M. L., de Vries, N. M., Bloem, B. R., & Duits, A. A. (2019). Do-it-yourself gamified cognitive training: Viewpoint. *JMIR Serious Games, 7*, e12130. doi:10.2196/12130

Van Vleet, T. M., Hoang-duc, A. K., DeGutis, J., & Robertson, L. C. (2010). Modulation of non-spatial attention and the global/local processing bias. *Neuropsychologia, 49*, 352–359. doi:10.1016/j.neuropsychologia.2010.11.021

Vartanian, O., Coady, L., & Blackler, K. (2016). 3D multiple object tracking boosts working memory span: Implications for cognitive training in military populations. *Military Psychology, 28*, 353–360. doi:doi.org/10.1037/mil0000125

Vartanian, O., Stokes-Hendriks, T., King, K., Rice, E., & Forbes, S. (2021). 3D multiple object tracking or adaptive dual n-back training boosts simple verbal working memory span but not multitasking performance in military participants. *5*, 280-295. doi:10.1007/s41465-020-00201-4

Veloso, A., Vicente, S. G., & Filipe, M. G. (2020). Effectiveness of cognitive training for school-aged children and adolescents with attention deficit/hyperactivity disorder: A systematic review. *Frontiers in Psychology, 10*, 2983. doi:10.3389/fpsyg.2019.02983

Verghese, J., Mahoney, J., Ambrose, A. F., Wang, C., & Holtzer, R. (2010). Effect of cognitive remediation on gait in sedentary seniors. *The Journals of Gerontology, 65*, 1338-1343. doi:doi.org/10.1093/gerona/glq127

Walton, C. C., Kavanagh, A., Downey, L. A., Lomas, J., Camfield, D. A., & Stough, C. (2015). Online cognitive training in healthy older adults: A preliminary study on the effects of single versus multi-domain training. *Translational Neuroscience, 6*, 13–19. doi:10.1515/tnsci-2015-0003

Willis, S. L., Tennstedt, S. L., Marsiske, M., Ball, K., Elias, J., Mann Koepke, K., . . . Wright, E. (2006). Long-term effects of cognitive training on everyday functional outcomes in older adults. *JAMA, 296*, 2805-2814. doi:10.1001/jama.296.23.2805

Zelinski, E. M., Spina, L. M., Yaffe, K., Smith, G. E., Ruff, R., Mahncke, H. W., & Kennison, R. F. (2011). Improvement in memory with plasticity-based adaptive cognitive training: Results of the 3-month follow-up. *Journal of the American Geriatric Society, 59*, 258-265. doi:10.1111/j.1532-5415.2010.03277.x

Zhang, H., Huntley, J., Bhome, R., Holmes, B., Cahill, J., Gould, R. L., . . . Howard, R. (2019). Effect of computerised cognitive training on cognitive outcomes in mild cognitive impairment: a systematic review and meta-analysis. *British Medical Journal Open Access, 9*(8), e027062. doi:10.1136/bmjopen-2018-027062

9 Biofeedback

Martine Van Puyvelde and Nathalie Pattyn

Parts of this chapter were published as *Dessy, E., Van Puyvelde, M., Mairesse, O., Neyt, X. & Pattyn, N. (2018). Cognitive Performance Enhancement: Do Biofeedback and Neurofeedback Work? J Cogn Enhanc 2, 12–42.* doi.org/10.1007/s41465-017-0039-y

Aims and scope of this chapter

Working with biofeedback (BFB) is essentially working with operant conditioning paradigms (described as learning mechanisms in Chapter 10). It thus involves a multiplicity of processes (from attention over learning and memorizing to motivation and reward), and due to this multitude of simultaneous ongoing processes, an involuntary training error may quickly occur.

In Chapter 2 it was stated that mental performance is a window to the brain, being a manner to localize in the brain the processes underlying mental performance. Biofeedback goes one step further. It attempts to train the activity in the localized brain and/or processes in order to optimize mental performance. Biofeedback is the common term for the learning process involved in the acquirement of psychophysiological self-regulation. The main goal of BFB training, regardless of the training modality, is to achieve voluntary control over involuntary physiological processes situated within the central nervous system (CNS) and peripheral nervous system (PNS), involving the somatic nervous system (SNS) and the autonomic nervous system (ANS) (Demos, 2005; Prinzel III et al., 2002; Prinzel III et al., 2001).

Hence, with the topic of BFB training, we enter a research domain with many levels, complexities, and choices that need to be made. There is the level of the training and its design (e.g., type of training, number of sessions, trainer or no trainer, and what type of support, type of biofeedback), the level of ecological validity (real-life field training or laboratory), the level of the feedback device (e.g., type of feedback signal, type of device), the level of the subjects (e.g., motivation, psychological and physiological traits and states, interaction with the device and/or trainer), the level of the targeted improvement (e.g., increased mental performance is a broad concept), and the level of the outcome, to name a few.

Therefore, in the present chapter we will aim to disentangle some of these complexities in the attempt to find an answer to the question: "How to optimize mental performance through the use of biofeedback?". The chapter provides an overview of the description of the relevant techniques, for which the former "Scientific Foundation" chapter (Chapter 2) offers the necessary theoretical physiological constructs. The technical bulk of the chapter is an exhaustive review of the available scientific evidence regarding the use of BFB as an enhancement tool for mental performance. In this overview, we have only included studies on mental performance in a healthy and non-clinical

DOI: 10.4324/9781003378969-11

adult population and we excluded case studies. We also excluded articles of which only an abstract was available in English. Although of interest as well, we did not include studies using functional magnetic resonance imaging (fMRI) biofeedback (see below). The last section of this chapter focuses on the meaning of biofeedback, the caveats, and potential implementations of the technique in a real-life performant context.

Background

Definition and scope

As mentioned above, the main goal of BFB training, regardless of the training modality, is to achieve voluntary control over involuntary physiological processes situated within the central nervous system (CNS) and peripheral nervous system (PNS), involving the somatic nervous system (SNS) and the autonomic nervous system (ANS) (Demos, 2005; Prinzel III et al., 2002; Prinzel et al., 2001). This voluntary control is acquired by means of an operant conditioning procedure during which the trainee receives moment-by-moment feedback information about their own physiological events of interest, associated with the targeted affective and/or cognitive states. This feedback information is commonly displayed in the form of auditory tones or visual representations. By relying on the provided feedback information, the trainee can learn to adjust to the required levels of physiological activation, to gradually gain direct control over his or her own physiological processes and, thus, to optimize his or her psychophysiological functioning (Egner et al., 2004; ; Sutarto et al., 2010; Sutarto et al., 2012; Sutarto et al., 2013).

The most widely applied form of BFB is heart-rate-guided physical training, which has become extremely popular with the widespread use of personal wearables. There are several types of BFB available, such as the electromyographic biofeedback to provide information about muscle activity (e.g., Sharpley & Rogers, 1984), the temperature biofeedback that returns information about the skin's temperature related to blood circulation and the sympathetic nervous system (e.g., Kewman & Roberts, 1980), or the electrodermal biofeedback providing information on skin conductance (e.g., Peek, 2003), to give some examples. Within a non-clinical context, two forms of BFB have been investigated extensively regarding cognitive performance improvement: heart rate variability (HRV) BFB training and the BFB training involving signals from the central nervous system, more commonly called neurofeedback. Neurofeedback was first applied through electroencephalography (EEG) signals, however, this past decade, a growing body of research has applied functional magnetic resonance imaging (fMRI) biofeedback. Regarding both the available evidence and the applicability in ambulatory settings, the current chapter will only discuss HRV BFB and EEG neurofeedback (NFB).

Heart rate variability biofeedback (HRV BFB)

The goal of HRV BFB training is to achieve control over specific cardiorespiratory processes. To summarize in a simplistic way: controlling heart rate through the control of respiration. To understand the real meaning of this type of training, it is important to define heart rate variability. HRV refers to the natural variability that is present in the rhythm of the heart under the influence of the autonomic nervous system (ANS) (Malik et al., 1996) and is defined as the continuous beat-to-beat changes in the inter-beat interval or RR-interval (RRI) (i.e., the time between two successive R-peaks) (Berntson et al., 1997). These autonomic guided beat-to-beat changes of the heart rate offer a window on the interplay between the sympathetic and parasympathetic nervous system (Acharya et al., 2006). This is the founding rationale of the use and investigation of HRV as a source of information concerning a person's ability to adapt to external environmental challenges (Berntson et al., 1997; Malik et al., 1996; Acharya et al., 2006).

To fully understand this relationship between cardiorespiratory regulation on the one hand, and adaptation to our environment on the other hand, it is worthwhile to consider the integrated neuro-visceral or mind-body perspective (Friedman, 2007; Thayer & Lane, 2000, 2009). From the neuro-visceral point of view, the short-term beat-to-beat changes in the heart rate are generated by an interaction between the heart and the CNS. This interaction is mediated by the signalization flow through efferent and afferent pathways of the sympathetic and parasympathetic (vagal) branches of the ANS, which makes HRV a measure of neurocardiac functioning that reflects heart–brain interactions and ANS dynamics (e.g., Friedman, 2007; Thayer & Lane, 2000, 2009). HRV thus not only reflects physiological and psychological flexibility with regard to social, cognitive, and other mental environmental challenges, it has also been associated with creativity (e.g., Gruzelier et al., 2014). In contrast, a reduced level of HRV appears to be related with physical as well as psychological discomfort or disease (e.g., Lehrer et al., 2003; Prinsloo et al., 2013a; Thayer et al., 2010b).

Regarding human performance, and thus the core of this handbook, Caldwell et al. (1994) suggested that cardiovascular information can be useful in the optimization of performance and general well-being, as well as the prevention of accidents or mistakes during difficult task performances. Furthermore, Thayer et al. (2010a) demonstrated a positive relationship between higher levels of resting HRV and executive functioning. In addition, Pattyn et al. (2008) suggested that physiological data can be an interesting predictive measure of real-life performance. Several recent reviews emphasize the link between a higher HRV and better performance and stress management in tactical personnel (Stephenson et al., 2021); better motor function in athletes (Pagaduan et al., 2020); and monitoring stress in first responders (Corrigan et al., 2021). Therefore, increasing the HRV of an individual seems to be a promising way to improve mental performance.

The quantification of HRV is a complex topic because of the variety of methods, something that is lost to most recent publications (where quantification methods are not even described anymore). The two main categories are time-domain methods or frequency-domain methods. Time-domain methods are also called "statistical" because they describe the evolution of the duration of beat-to-beat intervals over time. Frequency-domain methods unravel the signal of the time series of beat-to-beat intervals into different frequency components, which compose the power spectrum of HRV. Two of these components are predominantly discussed in psychophysiology, being the high- (0.15–0.40 Hz) and the low- (0.01–0.15 Hz) frequency component. The high-frequency (HF) component represents primarily parasympathetic influences, whereas the low-frequency (LF) (below 0.15 Hz) component reflects a mixture of sympathetic and parasympathetic autonomic influences. With regard to cognitive performance and related biofeedback training, the HF component is of particular interest since this range primarily reflects the respiration-mediated HRV (Malik et al., 1996; Thayer et al., 2012), namely respiratory sinus arrhythmia (RSA). So, RSA is one component of HRV and expresses the heart rate variability at the respiratory frequency or the coupling between heart rate and respiration. That is, during inspiration, heart rate accelerates, whereas, during expiration, heart rate decelerates. The degree of RSA thus gives an indication of the vagal control of the heart, that is, the more vagal tone, the more pronounced the relationship between HRV and the respiratory cycle, and the higher RSA amplitude becomes (Berntson et al., 1997).

This RSA is what is actually meant by the various applications and biofeedback trainings targeting "cardiac coherence". Cardiac coherence (and its increase through slow-paced breathing) is actually a reflection of the HF component of HRV, or RSA. This is one of the many challenges for an objective appraisal of the field by non-specialists: the fact that the myriad of commercial applications has spread a variety of terminology which is sometimes very remote from the actual physiological description.

Resonant frequency training

A more specific form of HRV biofeedback training is resonant frequency training (RFT). RFT aims to produce maximal increases in RSA amplitude (Lehrer et al., 2000) by teaching the individual to master slow breathing at six breaths per minute (i.e., 0.1 Hz) and to reach a so-called 'resonant frequency' (Lehrer, 2007). The frequency of 0.1 Hz is situated within the low frequency range below 0.15 Hz and is therefore a reflection of activity of both the sympathetic and parasympathetic branches (Berntson et al., 1997). The aim of this specific form of HRV BFB training is to teach the trainees to maximize the respiratory efficiency which helps to improve cardiovascular and autonomic stability (Vaschillo et al., 2006). To do so, trainees must focus on the use of combined diaphragmatically breathing with prolonged exhalation (i.e., inhalation through the nose and exhalation extensively through pursed lips) (Lehrer, 2007).

What's in a name?

In the reviewed literature, HRV, RSA, and RFT were sometimes used to refer to similar psychophysiological processes. However, there are some differences. First, there is a difference between HRV and RSA. As previously described, HRV is the natural beat-to-beat variation in either heart rate or the duration of the R–R interval under influence of the autonomic nervous system (e.g., Berntson et al., 1997; Billman, 2011; Malik et al., 1996). This influence of neural and hormonal inputs on the HRV generates specific observable rhythms that provide a quantitative measure of the autonomic nervous system regulatory action (Magagnin et al., 2010). RSA, however, is only one specific component of this HRV that occurs in relationship to the respiration cycle, being the result of the cardiac regulation by the parasympathetic branch (Berntson et al., 1997). RFT is a specific form of HRV biofeedback training in which the individual is taught to breathe at a frequency of 0.1 Hz (i.e., six breaths per minute).

Neurofeedback

Just like HRV BFB, neurofeedback (NFB) can be best understood in the context of learning and performance. An individual can learn to adjust his EEG activity based on a reward delivered by visual and/or auditory feedback, to mirror a desired pattern of cortical activity, which is related to specific behavioural or cognitive performance components. These changes in the EEG pattern, in turn, are supposed to evoke change in the targeted performance (Vernon, 2005).

In the brain, the transmission of information is based on electrophysiological processes (described in more detail in Chapter 2), and therefore cognitive processes may be described in terms of brain oscillations that are present in specific cortical areas. These brain oscillations, and the considered related cognitive processes, are reflected by different frequency bands (e.g., Klimesch et al., 1998). Although bandwidth definitions can vary (Kaiser, 2007), the following frequency bands can be distinguished: (1) delta (0.5–4 Hz), (2) theta (4–8 Hz), (3) alpha (8–13 Hz), (4) beta (14–40 Hz) and, (5) gamma (>40 Hz) (Klimesch, 1999; Noachtar et al., 1999). The power measured in these frequency bands may be expressed in terms of relative power, absolute power, or a frequency band ratio. The absolute power of a frequency is the actual voltage in the recorded EEG while the relative power is the percentage of power of a specific frequency band compared with the total power in the recorded EEG (e.g., "relative alpha" is the percentage of alpha of the combined sum of delta, theta, alpha, and beta). A frequency ratio (such as theta/beta; alpha/theta; etc.) is the percentage of power in one frequency divided by the percentage of another frequency.

During NFB, one is taught to exert control over specific EEG parameters, and an inference is being made about the influence on associated cognitive functions. In a typical NFB setup, the EEG activity is recorded from a referential (monopolar) montage. During a NFB session, a real-time frequency domain analysis of the EEG is displayed to provide information about the amplitude within each of the different frequency bands. When producing the desired changes in the pre-defined brainwave patterns, the trainee will receive auditory and/or visual reward signals. Over the course of several training sessions, the trainee can gradually develop mental strategies by trial and error to modify the brain activity and to learn to self-regulate their EEG activity.

A specific issue when reviewing the EEG NFB literature is the lack of consistency and consensus regarding terminology and training protocols, something that was acknowledged by an attempt at standardization (Ros et al., 2019). We thus noticed a strong variation in terminology as well as in the range selection regarding the different EEG frequency bands that are supposed to be enhanced or suppressed by training. An overview of some of these differences is summarized here:

- Delta frequency activity varied from 0–4 Hz (Vernon et al., 2003) to 1–4 Hz (Ros et al., 2009).
- Theta frequency activity varied from 3–7 Hz (Beatty, Greenberg, Deibler, & O'Hanlon, 1974), 4–7 Hz (Egner & Gruzelier, 2001; Egner & Gruzelier, 2004; Fritson, Wadkins, Gerdes, & Hof, 2008; Hanslmayr, Sauseng, Doppelmayr, Schabus, & Klimesch, 2005; Kober et al., 2015b; Ros et al., 2009 [group A]; David Vernon et al., 2003; Wang & Hsieh, 2013), 4.5–7.5 Hz (Doppelmayr & Weber, 2011), 4–8Hz (Reiner, Rozengurt, & Barnea, 2014) to 5–8 Hz (Ros et al., 2009 [group B]).
- Alpha band frequency varied from 8–11 Hz (Ros et al., 2009) to 8–12 Hz (Egner & Gruzelier, 2001; Vernon et al., 2003). Moreover, authors distinguished within the alpha band frequency lower and upper alpha activity. The lower alpha frequency was used in Rasey et al. (1996) with a frequency range of 6–10 Hz (Rasey et al., 1996), whereas the upper alpha activity varied from 8–12.5 Hz (Zoefel, Huster, & Herrmann, 2011), 8–12Hz (Hsueh, Chen, Chen, & Shaw, 2016), 8.5–12.5 Hz (Bauer, 1976), 10–12 Hz (Hanslmayr et al., 2005) or even a measure based on the individual alpha frequency (IAF) + 2 Hz (Bazanova et al., 2013; Minguez, 2014; Zoefel et al., 2011).
- Beta band frequency activity varied from 12–15 Hz, 15–18Hz (Rozengurt, Barnea, Uchida, & Levy, 2016) and 18–22Hz (Reiner et al., 2014), 16–22 Hz (Rasey et al., 1996) to 12–20 Hz (Keizer, Verment, & Hommel, 2010a; Keizer, Verschoor, Verment, & Hommel, 2010b). As in the alpha band frequency, within the beta band frequency (13–40 Hz), a distinction needs to be made between lower (which was mostly called SMR, except in two studies of Egner and Gruzelier, 2001, 2004, and one study of Rozengurt et al., 2016, where it was called beta1) and higher beta frequency. The SMR frequency band corresponded with the 12–15Hz range except in the study of Guez et al. (2015) in which SMR ranged from 13–15Hz (Guez et al., 2015), the beta1 frequency band in Egner and Gruzelier studies (2001, 2004) and also in the study of Rozengurt et al. (2016) ranged from 15–18Hz. The high beta frequency bands varied from 22–30 Hz (Egner & Gruzelier, 2001; Egner & Gruzelier, 2003; Ros et al., 2009), 18–22 Hz (Rozengurt et al., 2016; Vernon et al., 2003;), to 21–35Hz (Kober et al., 2015b (Fritson et al., 2008).
- Gamma band frequency activity range of 36–44 Hz was used by Keizer et al. in 2010 and 2010a (Keizer, Verment, et al., 2010a; Keizer, Verschoor, et al., 2010b).

This twofold lack of clarity is a major caveat when attempting to review the available evidence and is definitely not pleading in favour of the field. For the sake of readability in the current chapter, we have chosen a consistent terminology in which we will always first refer to the frequency band (e.g., theta, beta, etc.), then the direction of training (i.e., augment or reduction) to designate the NFB training modality.

Evidence base for mental performance enhancement

Attention, perceptual cognitive, and executive skills are the distinctive cognitive features to excel in elite sport performance (Hodges et al., 2021; Willimas, 2000), military operational performance (Blacker et al., 2019), and musical performance (Anaya et al., 2016; Clayton et al., 2016; Zuk et al., 2014). Therefore, in the attempt to optimize mental performance, researchers have been searching for strong associations between specific brain and/or body activity and the performance output within these cognitive dimensions.

We review the evidence base for mental performance enhancement using HRV BFB and NFB in sport, military operationality, and artistic performance. However, as explained in Chapter 2, mental performance is more than cognition only. An optimal mental performance is highly dependent on one's physiological and psychological state. How the subject perceives the situation (as a threat or a challenge), as well as the balance between the level of this cognitive anxiety and the physiological arousal can be a huge moderator in the outcome of final performance. According to the catastrophe model of Fazey and Hardey (1988), there is a strong negative correlation between cognitive anxiety and performance that may intervene with the aimed inversed U-curve on key moments during a performance. Indeed, several studies (e.g., Mogg et al., 2015; Pacheco-Unguetti et al., 2010) have shown that high (trait) anxiety levels are associated with decreased attention efficiency and impaired reactions of the executive control network. As stated in Chapter 2, "small increases in either physiological arousal or cognitive anxiety can easily push the performer over the cusp and result in detrimental effects on performance."

Hence, in this chapter, we attempt to include both the cognitive and emotional component of the performance. Some studies focused on only one component, whereas others included both. Within the cognitive component, some studies highlighted only one dimension, whereas other studies examined a combination of different cognitive outcomes. It will also become clear that certain cognitive or emotional outputs are studied more than others. Hence, in the text part, it is impossible to present a rigorous taxonomy in function of the known subdivisions. However, in Table 9.1, we will present an overview, listing which cognitive and emotional dimensions were examined in which study and whether the outcome was beneficial or not.

HRV biofeedback (HRV BFB) training

As previously described, it is important to keep in mind that there exists a wide variety of terminology to refer to similar BFB training modalities. Although all the studies applying this type of BFB training essentially had the purpose of augmenting the HRV amplitude, there seems to exist some confusion on the application of terminology regarding HRV, RSA, and RFT. In the following results section, we use the term "HRV biofeedback (HRV BFB) training" as an umbrella-term to refer to any form of cardiorespiratory BFB training.

The studies using HRV BFB training were all based, albeit with some variations, on a conventional training protocol of Lehrer et al. (2000) (i.e., the resonant frequency training or RFT training, see introduction) in which participants practice a slow breathing technique (already described in Chapter 5, in the section regarding breathing).

HRV BFB to enhance attention, memory, and executive functioning

In 2010, Sutarto et al. (2010) showed in two studies the beneficial effect of slow breathing training on memory and executive functional skills, using a Stroop Colour-Word Test (cognitive flexibility), a memory test (verbal memory), and an arithmetic test (decision-making). In the first study, applied in a group of university students acting as simulated industrial operators, a significant

Table 9.1 Overview of the reviewed studies categorized by the cognitive and affective dimensions

	HRV	*Theta*	*Alpha*	*Beta or Gamma*	*SMR only*	*SMR in combi*	*Theta/beta ratio, Theta/alpha ratio and other combi*
PERCEPTION			Nan et al. 2013	Salari et al. 2013, 2014 (Gamma)	Egner & Gruzelier 2004		
ATTENTION	Paul & Garg 2012 (E: shooters)	Beatty et al. 1974	Ros et al. 2014	Egner & Gruzelier, 2004 (Beta)	Egner & Gruzelier 2004	Egner and Gruzelier 2001	Studer et al. 2014
	Sutarto et al. 2010	Wang & Hsieh 2013	Pamplona et al. 2020	Jurewicz et al. 2018 (Beta)	Doppelmayer & Weber 2011	Fritson et al. 2008	
	Sutarto et al. 2012	Toolis et al. 2013 (E: shooting)		Salari et al. 2013, 2014 (Gamma)	Cheng et al. 2015a	Gonçalves et al. 2018	
	Rusciano et al. (2017) (E: soccer)				Cheng et al. 2015b	Kavianapoor et al. 2023 (E: dart)	
	Prinsloo et al. 2011				Cheng et al. 2017	Ros et al. 2009 (E: surgeons)	
	Rose et al. 2021				Vernon et al. 2003 Kober et al. 2015		
EXECUTIVE Core	Prinsloo et al. 2011	Enriquez-Geppert et al. 2014	Berger et al. 2018		Vernon et al. 2003	Egner and Gruzelier 2001	Rasey et al. 1996
	Rusciano et al. (2017) (E: soccer)	Wang & Hsieh 2013	Pei et al. 2018		Egner & Gruzelier 2004		Xiong et al. 2014
	Gruzelier et al. 2014 (E: dance)	Enriquez-Geppert et al. 2014	Shen et al. 2022				
	Sutarto et al. 2010	Eschmann et al. 2022	Barbazzeni et al. 2023				
	Sutarto et al. 2012		Bazanova et al. 2013 Escalano et al. 2012 Gordon et al. 2020 Nawaz et al. 2022				
EXECUTIVE Meta	Paul & Garg 2012 (E: shooters)	Zoefel et al. 2011	Bazanova et al. 2013	Agnoli et al. 2018	Doppelmayer & Weber 2011	Kavianapoor et al. 2023 (E: dart)	Egner & Gruzelier, 2003 (E: music)
	Rusciano et al. (2017) (E: soccer)		Hanslmayer et al. 2005			Ros et al. 2009 (E: surgeons)	Raymond et al. 2005a (E: music)
			Agnoli et al. 2018				

(*Continued*)

Table 9.1 (Continued)

	HRV	*Theta*	*Alpha*	*Beta or Gamma*	*SMR only*	*SMR in combi*	*Theta/beta ratio, Theta/alpha ratio and other combi*
MEMORY	Sutarto et al. 2010	Reiner et al. 2014	Nan et al. 2012		Kober et al. 2015b (RT en LT)		Farnia et al. 2017
	Sutarto et al. 2012	Rozengurt et al. 2016	Hsueh et al. 2016		Guez et al. 2014		Rozengurt et al. 2023
		Reiner et al. 2018	Guez et al. 2014		Hoedlmoser et al. 2008		Tseng et al. 2021
		Vernon et al. 2009	Escalano et al. 2012				Gruzelier et al. 2014 (E: dance)
			Naas et al. 2019				Leach et al. 2008 (E: singers)
			Pei et al. 2018				
			Nawaz et al. 2022				
ANXIETY	Gruzelier et al. 2014 (E: dance)		Hardt and Kamiya (1978)			Ros et al. 2009 (E: surgeons)	
	Makarci et al. 2023		Bazanova et al. 2013				
	Paul & Garg 2012 (E: shooters)		Plotkin and Rice (1981)				
	Prinsloo et al. 2011						
	Wells et al. 2012						
	Prinsloo et al. 2013c						
AROUSAL	Prinsloo et al. 2011		Holmes et al. (1980)				
	Rose et al. 2021						
	Prinsloo et al. 2013c						
MOOD	Makarci et al. 2023	Vasquez et al. 2015	Potolicchio et al. (1979)				
	Paul & Garg 2012 (E: shooters)						
	Prinsloo et al. 2013c						
	Rose et al. 2021						

improvement was observed in verbal memory and decision-making after the BFB training but not in the cognitive flexibility. No control group was used in this study. In the second study, applied in real operators with the use of a control group, the verbal memory and arithmetic tests were replaced by the Sternberg test and D2 attention test. A significantly improved cognitive performance was shown in the HRV BFB group on the response time in the Sternberg test and the concentration performance in the D2 attention test compared to the control group but not in the Stroop test (Sutarto et al., 2010). In their 2012 and 2013 articles, Sutarto et al. (2012; 2013) adapted the RFT training method of Lehrer (2000) and trained participants to breathe at their own "resonant frequency". The individual resonant frequency was determined during the first training session for each participant by measuring HR oscillation amplitudes while the individual breathed at various frequencies (4.5, 5.0, 6.0, and 6.5 breaths/min). They found again a significant improvement in attention and memory tests but not in executive functioning. Furthermore, they observed a significant decrease in the depression, anxiety, and stress scale (DASS). Sutarto et al. (2012; 2013) analyzed the respiratory activity and HRV (Sutarto et al., 2013). These analyses showed that the HRV BFB group consistently used the trained breathing skills during the stress condition even though they were not instructed to do so and that there was an increased activity in the low-frequency band width (i.e., the frequency band that includes the targeted 0.1 respiratory frequency). Hence, these studies found support for a beneficial effect of a series of five to six weekly sessions HRV BFB on attention, memory, and decision-making but not on cognitive flexibility (Stroop test). Moreover, HRV BFB appeared to impact the DASS.

Around the same time, Prinsloo et al. (2011) studied the effect of a 10-minute single HRV BFB session in a population of senior managers. They tested cognitive performance and affect scores during induced stress through a modified Stroop task. The modification concerned updating of the working memory and mental shifting (i.e., the participants needed to count white squares that were randomly shown throughout the Stroop task and give the final sum at the end of the task). The participants were randomized into an HRV BFB intervention group (BIO) and a comparative intervention group (COM). The results showed that, although both groups significantly improved their reaction times, this improvement was more pronounced in the BIO group than in the COM group. However, there was a differentiating result between both groups observed in the working memory. In the COM group, the participants missed as many squares after the intervention as before, whereas in the BIO group, the participants missed any of the squares after the intervention (Prinsloo et al., 2011). Moreover, the participants of the BIO group reported to feel more relaxed, less anxious, and less sleepy than the COM subjects after the intervention.

More recently, Rusciano et al. (2017) showed an improvement in visual search and Stroop test performances in professional soccer players. They executed 15 guided sessions, twice a week and asked the participants to practice a slow breathing exercise daily for five minutes. In comparison to a control group, the HRV BFB group showed significantly better perceptual cognitive, attentional, and executive performance. The cognitive results were supported by the physiological measures, showing a better physiological stress resilience (post-stress recovery of skin conductance, HR, and respiration rate to baseline levels in HRV BFB but not in the control group). Although this recovery was present in SCL, HR, and respiration frequency, it was not reflected in the LF-HRV frequency. Since HF was not measured, it is not clear whether a recovery was reflected in that measure.

HRV BFB as a step towards stress, anxiety, and mood regulation

In 2013, Prinsloo et al. (2013a, 2013b, 2013c) investigated the effect of a HRV BFB single training session on brain activation to understand the potential mechanisms underlying the observed results. In these studies, they used the Stroop test as a stress inducer and considered the HRV BFB training as a form of meditation based on controlled breathing (Prinsloo et al., 2013a, 2013b, 2013c). EEG theta, alpha, beta power, and theta/beta ratio as well as heart rate (HR) and respiratory rate (RR) (to analyze HRV) were measured during the Stroop and rest periods before and after the intervention (HRV BFB training/control) (Prinsloo et al., 2013a). During the intervention, the BIO group showed higher relative theta power, lower relative beta power, and higher theta/beta than the COM group (Prinsloo et al., 2013a). Regarding HRV, there was a great increase in LF during the intervention period in the BIO group in comparison to the COM group (Prinsloo et al., 2013a). Moreover, the COM group responded similarly in the Stroop after intervention than they did before the intervention, namely, an increase in HR and RR, a tendency to decrease in RMSSD and HF power, and no change in LF power. The BIO group showed a different response in the Stroop after the intervention than the one before, namely that while RF increased and LF power decreased, HR, RMSSD, and HF power showed no change. Unfortunately, the Stroop performance was not reported. The study reported a few "group by time" interaction effects for the total scores on energized positive feelings (but not on any of the subscale), mindfulness (but not on any subscale), and one subscale of relaxation, namely feeling rested/refreshed. There were no effects found in STAI/STAT anxiety scales, transcendence, and the total score and other subscale of relaxation (Prinsloo et al., 2013c). Hence, although the immediate impact of one HRV BFB was clearly visible on both physiological and EEG outputs, the subjective reports were not overwhelmingly convincing so far.

When diving further into literature, the results remain indeed rather mixed across studies. In a study by Rose et al. (2021), who also used a single session of HRV BFB, no effect on mood, reaction movement time (measured by Fitlight), or mental workload were observed either. They did, however, observe a decrease in subjectively perceived arousal. In a recent study by Makaraci et al. (2023), six female volley players followed 21 HRV BFB sessions. When comparing pre- and post-intervention measures, the authors found a significant decrease in the DASS and anxiety. However, on a physiological level, there was only a change in midday cortisol levels and no significant changes were observed in the cortisol awakening response, neither in HRV nor HR. Unfortunately, no control group was used. Moreover, the physiological parameters were measured pre-post intervention, whereas the majority of studies measured the impact also during the intervention. In a study by Wells et al. (2012) in a population of musicians, one single HRV BFB session reduced anxiety before performance, but only in highly anxious musicians. The session increased HF and LF/HF ratio in 5 minutes of performance anticipation after the intervention in the highly anxious musicians; hence pointing to potential ceiling effects of HRV BFB impact. Gruzelier et al. (2014) did observe that ten sessions of HRV BFB reduced anxiety in dance performers (see also below).

The impact of HRV BFB in a (semi) ecological setting

Although, the final goal of training for elite performance should be a transition to a real-life effect, we only found three studies that tested the impact of HRV BFB in an ecological setting. In a sport setting, Paul and Garg. (2012), examined the impact of ten daily sessions of HRV BFB on the concentration ability, reaction and movement time, shooting performance, respiration rate, and frequency domain measures of HRV, as well as anxiety, coping, and self-efficacy in basketball players (Paul & Garg 2012). The design consisted of a HRV BFB group, a placebo (watching motivating basketball videos), and control (no treatment) group. They found a significant improvement in all performance parameters at session 10 and after one-month follow-up with regard to session 1 in the HRV BFB group compared to the two other control groups. On a physiological level, the HRV BFB sessions also showed a significant increase in LF and HF and decrease in respiration rate that was not present in the control groups.

In an artistic setting, HRV training and alpha/theta reduction (see further) was trained in a study by Gruzelier et al. (2014) in a ten-sessions protocol. The authors found no impact on the dance performance as judged by a jury of experts. However, the HRV BFB group showed reduced anxiety (measured by scales that focused on autonomic functions, especially cardiovascular activity) and this reduction correlated with improved technique and artistry in performance.

HRV BFB: what can we (not) conclude?

There is no straightforward support for a beneficial impact of HRV BFB on attention processes and executive functions such as working memory. We support the conclusion of Lehrer et al. in 2020 who stated – based on a meta-analysis – that HRV BFB might be a useful training method in addition to other methods. HRV BFB is certainly not sufficient as a stand-alone training method. In Lehrer's (2020) meta-analysis, the Hedges' g effect size for the beneficial impact of HRV BFB on cognitive and executive functioning was small ($g = -0.30$, $p < .02$). Moreover, when going into more detail in those studies that published their physiological raw data, certain data could be interpreted in multiple manners. For instance, in the study of Prinsloo et al. (2013a), one could question whether certain group means might be influenced by outliers that were not removed and/or interindividual differences that were not considered. It is well-known that physiological relationships between respiration and HR/RSA are typically larger within individuals than between individuals. Hence, within-subjects transformations are often used to avoid these types of errors (Grossman et al., 1991). When not applying these techniques, the results may be skewed and even inexplicable from a physiological point of view (e.g., a respiration frequency that increases from 0.14 to 0.33 whereas the heart rate remains identical, without vagal compensation). In psychophysiological research, one should always consider both the group means and the individual differences that may reflect alternative ongoing processes (Dessy et al., 2018). Moreover, both the HRV BFB method (Lehrer et al., 2020) as well as the physiological outcomes (Berntson et al., 2007) are multiply determined and thus reflective of a variety of processes. This multiplicity should always be considered when interpreting data with the purpose of real operational performance training.

Surprisingly, although perceptual cognition is a core feature of several sport, military, and artistic skills performance (Hodges et al., 2021; Willimas, 2000), military operational performance (Blacker et al., 2019), and musical performance (Anaya et al., 2016; Clayton et al., 2016; Zuk et al., 2014), there were only two studies that included a perceptual cognition test (Prinsloo et al., 2011; Rusciano et al., 2017).

Finally, since controlled breathing – which is the base of HRV BFB – is a technique that can be incorporated easily into real-life field applications, research should more often examine the eventual benefits in the real-life world of performers.

Neurofeedback (NFB) training

Theta NFB training

Research into the potential benefits of theta NFB training started with the work of Beatty et al. in 1974. Beatty et al. (1974) observed that a decline in subjects' arousal may be associated with an increase in posterior theta activity (3–7 Hz). Based on this notion, Beatty et al. (1974) made a comparison between the effects of augmented versus reduced theta NFB training. They assigned 19 undergraduate students to either a theta reduction group trained to reduce theta power activity, or a theta augment group trained to increase theta power activity. After the training, participants completed a 12-min radar detection task in two successive sessions, that is, one EEG-regulated monitoring (as learned during the training sessions) and one EEG-unregulated monitoring. The theta NFB training resulted in a selective alteration of the theta activity. Moreover, the performance level was inversely related to the level of theta activity in the occipital area. In the regulated-EEG condition, the theta reduction group performed significantly better than the theta augment group.

During the EEG-unregulated monitoring condition, there was no significant difference between both groups (Beatty et al., 1974).

Theta BFB training to enhance attention, memory, and executive functioning

The above-described study by Beatty et al. (1974) was important to open doors towards potential enhancement training of perceptual cognitive, attention, and executive functioning by theta NFB. However, in later studies, in place of decreasing posterior theta activity, researchers trained the augmentation of frontal-midline theta activity. Wang and Hsieh (2013) studied the impact of frontal-midline theta NFB training on perceptual cognition and attention using the attention network test that examines the alerting component, the orienting component, and the executive component of attention in a young and aging population. They compared 12 sessions of theta NFB augmentation training and sham-neurofeedback (SHAM) training. An increase of theta activity was associated with a significant improvement in the executive component (i.e., decreased conflict score) in both the aged and young group. However, the orienting component only improved in the aging group and no effect was found in alerting scores (Wang & Hsieh, 2013). Toolis et al. (2023) examined the impact of six sessions of frontal-midline theta augmentation training on attention as well. They added a shooting performance test in an ecological context, outdoors on an international-standard biathlon shooting range. They found a small effect on attention that did not transfer to the real-world shooting test. Enriquez-Geppert et al. (2014) tested the impact of frontal-midline theta augmentation on four executive functions, that is, memory updating, set shifting, conflict monitoring, and motor inhibition by testing with the three-back, letter/number task-switching, Stroop, and stop-signal tasks while measuring the EEG. The results showed higher accuracy scores in the three-back task and reduced mixing and shifting costs in letter/number task-switching for the NFB group versus a control group, indicative of a facilitation of the executive functions memory updating and mental shifting. However, no benefits were found in conflict monitoring and motor inhibition.

With regard to memory and memory consolidation, a study by Reiner et al. (2014) examined whether frontal theta augment NFB training might enhance the spatial memory consolidation during sleep. Theta oscillations play a central role in the connectivity between the hippocampus and striatum during consolidation processes; hence the choice for theta augment NFB training to enhance memory consolidation. Memory consolidation was evaluated at five time-points: immediately after a theta NFB training session (T1), at day 1 after one night of sleep (T2), at day 2 and 3 (T3, T4), and at day 5 (T5). The participants were randomly assigned to either a theta augment training group or one out of two control groups (i.e., a beta augment training group or no NFB training group). There was a significant improvement in performance in relation to the baseline in the theta group, but not in the beta and control groups, immediately after the NFB training. After one night of sleep, the performance improved significantly in all the groups, but the improvement in the theta augment training group was significantly higher than in the control groups. On day 7, the improvement of the performance in relation to the baseline was significantly better in the theta than in the control groups. The authors thus suggested a relationship between memory consolidation and theta NFB training (Reiner et al., 2014). Rozengurt et al. (2016) conducted a similar experiment and successfully replicated the results of the previous study. In 2018, Reiner et al. (2018) introduced a more difficult finger tapping memory task. The theta augmentation group showed a significantly larger improvement in speed without losing accuracy immediately after the NFB session in comparison to the control groups. The speed performance did not significantly improve after one, two, or seven nights of sleep but remained stable. Improvement in a finger tapping task was also found in Eschmann et al. (2022) in theta augment responders versus non-responders. However, they could not find any beneficial effect on the cognitive visual n-back working memory task. Finally, in Vernon et al. (2003), a theta augmentation group did not succeed in exhibiting any changes in their EEG and did not show any improvement in a semantic memory test (Vernon et al., 2003).

To conclude, theta NFB training has been used in two manners, a decrease in posterior theta activity to enhance attention processes and an augmentation of frontal-midline theta activity to enhance (working) memory (Eschmann et al., 2022; Wang & Hsieh, 2013) and consolidation processes (Reiner et al., 2014, 2018; Rozengurt et al., 2016). In the section "mixed training", theta augmentation will be further discussed in combination with alpha or beta decrease.

Upper-alpha neurofeedback (NFB) training to enhance attention, memory, and executive functioning

Upper-alpha NFB training has been used in several studies to test its benefit on memory with a starting shot by Bauer (1976), who examined the effect of upper-alpha (8.5–12.5 Hz) augment training on short-term memory performance. The results showed that, despite a significant increase in the percentage of alpha activity, the participants exhibited no change in their level of recall. Bauer (1976) concluded that changes in alpha activity had no apparent functional significance for the learning process itself. Escolano et al. (2012) could not show a positive impact of upper-alpha NFB either. They used a single upper-alpha NFB augment training session compared to a control sham group. After the intervention, both groups had an increased cognitive performance in a large cognitive assessment, with no significant difference between both groups. Further, Pei et al. (2018) tested the impact of alpha (8–12 Hz) augment with five sessions of training compared to a sham control group on memory tested by the word pair task. They did not observe a significant difference between both groups either. In 2019, Naas et al. did not observe a positive impact of a four-session upper-alpha NFB augment training on short-term memory tested by a digit span test either. Recently, Nawaz et al. (2022) did not observe any significant impact of alpha augment (8–13 Hz) on a Stroop task, a mini-mental state exam (MMSE), and the perceived stress scale (PSS), neither after 10 sessions, nor 20 sessions.

However, some other studies did find a beneficial impact on memory tasks. In two studies of Nan et al. (2012, 2013) a significantly positive impact of individual alpha augment training was shown on short-term memory performance (Nan et al., 2012) and a peripheral visual performance task (Nan et al., 2013) compared to a control group. Moreover, in both studies the NFB group showed a significantly increased alpha amplitude and in Nan et al. (2012), the improvement of short-term memory was positively correlated with the increase of the relative amplitude in the individual upper alpha band during training (Nan et al., 2012). Hsueh et al. (2016) also investigated the effect of alpha augment training on memory. Their results indicated that the responders to an alpha augment training significantly improved performance on a word pair memory test in comparison to a control group. Finally, Guez et al. (2015) demonstrated that an upper-alpha NFB training significantly improved the recollection in an associative memory task. Further, Ros et al. (2014) showed that a single session of alpha reduction NFB training can be used to facilitate the acquisition of a procedural motor task. In this study, the subjects performed a serial reaction-time task on two different days, with seven days in-between, in a counterbalanced design, one time with and one time without receiving a 30-min upper-alpha NFB training session. Their results indicated that the alpha reduction group showed a decrease of reaction time across blocks and had an improved rate of learning.

The impact of upper-alpha training has also been tested on visuo-spatial working memory. Hanslmayr et al. (2005) tested the effect of the upper-alpha augment training on a mental rotation test and found a positive correlation between the training success and improvement in performance. However, only the participants that showed a post-training augment in the upper-alpha frequency band compared to the baseline EEG (i.e., responders) performed better on a mental rotation task (Hanslmayr et al., 2005). Zoefel et al. (2011) also showed a positive impact of upper-alpha NFB training on a mental rotation test in students assessed (A3DW, Gittler,

2007). The students were randomly assigned to a NFB group or control group. The cognitive performance improvement was significantly larger for the NFB group than for the control group (Zoefel et al., 2011). Bazanova et al. (2013) also investigated the effect of EEG upper-alpha NFB training on a mental rotation task. The results showed that the impact of upper- alpha NFB training was only present when subjects with an inherent low baseline alpha frequency. In subjects with a high baseline resting alpha frequency, no effects were observed (Bazanova et al., 2013). These responders showed a better performance on the mental rotation task as well as increased cognitive creativity.

Regarding verbal working memory, three studies found a positive and two studies a negative outcome. Pei et al. (2018) found a significant improvement in working memory tested by a backward digit span task after an alpha (8–12 Hz) augment five-session training compared to a sham control group. However, Gordon et al. (2020), who tested the impact of ten sessions of upper-alpha NFB training on different working memory tasks did not find a significant impact of alpha uptraining compared to control groups either. Bazanova et al. (2013) did not find an effect on working memory either. However, Berger et al. (2018) found that larger NFB alpha learning rates were associated with larger decreases in the Gratton effect (i.e., the impact on the Stroop effect of the congruence/incongruence of a stimulus in a preceding trial) and Shen et al. (2022) found a positive impact of alpha augment training on working memory compared to a control group. However, a recent rigorous study by Barbazzeni et al. (2023) reported that there was no impact of alpha NFB training on a working memory task. They demonstrated, however, a relationship between changes in parietal beta oscillations related to cognitive training present during encoding and improvements in accuracy in the working memory tasks. They concluded that cognitive training, but not NFB improves working memory in healthy volunteers.

Finally, Pamplona et al. (2020) examined the impact of alpha NFB training (twice five subsequent sessions) on sustained attention after training. The observed improvement was temporally limited and did not significantly differ from the control group.

Beta neurofeedback (NFB) training to enhance attention, memory, and executive functioning

Beta NFB training is used both in augment and downtraining. A study by Agnoli et al. (2018) showed that beta augment training was linked to divergent thinking. The authors compared a group after a single 2-h session of alpha augment training with one of beta augment training. The alpha NFB did not evoke significant changes in originality of a divergent thinking test, whereas the beta augment training significantly increased originality and fluency in divergent thinking. These results were particularly evident in participants starting with a low creative achievement level.

One of the trained NFB groups in Egner and Gruzelier (2004) learned to enhance low beta activity. The authors reported faster reaction times and increased target P300 amplitudes during a sustained attention test compared to a control group (Egner & Gruzelier, 2004). However, in Jurewicz et al. (2018), no impact on two visual sustained attention tests was found, neither after a beta augment nor beta downtraining. Moreover, the beta augment training appeared to contaminate the alpha activity, challenging the idea of frequency-specific EEG-NFB protocols.

Gamma neurofeedback (NFB) training to enhance attention, memory, and executive functioning

A study by Salari et al. (2013, 2014) showed that increasing gamma band activity (30–40 Hz) promoted a visual processing advantage in a visual perception task in the NFB group and not in a sham control group. There was no impact on a spatial attention task, suggesting that gamma is specifically related to perceptual processing.

Mixed neurofeedback (NFB) training to enhance attention, memory, and executive functioning

There are a variety of studies that tested mixed frequency training designs with several combinations. A frequency that received regular attention in several studies is SMR, sometimes tested as a sole NFB training frequency and sometimes tested in combination with other frequencies.

SMR ONLY

Vernon et al. (2003) investigated the effect of theta augment training and SMR augment training on working memory performance and on attentional processing. A control group did not participate in any neurofeedback session training, but did perform the working memory/attention tests. The participants learned to selectively enhance their SMR activity in the SMR group. The group that was trained to selectively enhance theta activity failed to exhibit any changes in their EEG. Furthermore, only the group training to enhance SMR showed a significant improvement in semantic working memory and focused attentional processing (Vernon et al., 2003). Egner and Gruzelier (2004) showed that SMR training was associated with increased perceptual sensitivity, reduced omission errors and reaction time variability on a sustained attention task compared to a control group (Egner & Gruzelier, 2004). In a study by Doppelmayr and Weber (2011), the impact of 30 sessions of SMR augment NFB training and the theta/beta ratio (TBR) reduction NFB training on attention, reaction times, higher cognitive processes, and creativity were examined. There was also a sham control group. Only the SMR group could successfully induce EEG changes and they significantly improved reaction time tasks and performance on a spatial rotation task after training. There was, however, no impact on creativity. Cheng et al. examined SMR activity in different sport populations. They demonstrated that SMR activity is related to attentional focus in golf players (Cheng et al., 2015a), dart players (Cheng et al., 2015b), and shooters (Cheng et al., 2017). The impact of SMR NFB training on cognitive processing abilities was also shown by Kober et al. (2015b) in a double-blind design with ten training sessions. Participants were randomly assigned to either an SMR NFB group or a sham-feedback group. The SMR group showed increased SMR power over the training as well as in the adjacent beta band (21–35 Hz) course. The SMR group showed significantly better scores in short-term and long-term memory tasks (for verbal material but not for visuo-spatial material) as well as on auditory focused attention performance tasks (Go/No-Go task). In another double-blind sham-controlled design by Guez et al. (2014), a SMR NFB training improved item memory on an item recognition task.

SMR NFB training has also been tested in relation with sleep and declarative memory performance (Hoedlmoser et al., 2008) in a controlled study with ten NFB training sessions in ten consecutive days. The results showed an increase in SMR relative amplitude in the experimental group from the first session towards the last session as well as during sleep. The experimental group also showed a significant decrease of sleep onset and significantly increased retrieval scores on a word-pair association task. The control group data revealed no difference between pre- and post- testing (Hoedlmoser et al., 2008).

SMR IN COMBINATION WITH OTHER FREQUENCIES

Egner and Gruzelier (2001) trained a group of healthy individuals to enhance SMR and low beta, while simultaneously inhibiting theta and high beta. A comparison between pre- and post-training performance on an attention task indicated a significant reduction in commission error rate and a marginal improvement in participants' ability to discriminate potential targets. Furthermore, partial correlations showed a highly positive correlation between enhancing SMR and commission error reduction when controlling for low beta learning; and a negative correlation between enhancing low beta and commission error reduction when controlling for SMR learning; pointing to a counterproductive effect of the latter (Egner & Gruzelier, 2001). Besides, an attention auditory oddball task to elicit P300 event-related potential (ERP) showed a positive relationship between the P300 amplitude and the enhancement of both SMR and low beta (Egner & Gruzelier, 2001). Indeed, authors reported that the mean event-related P300b amplitudes to target stimuli across frontal, central, and parietal scalp regions increased significantly after SMR and low beta trainings. However, Fritson et al. (2008) did not find beneficial effects in attention of a similar SMR NFB training and theta/high beta inhibition. They found a significant post-training change in the experimental group regarding response control, but no significant changes in attention for either the control or treatment group. Gonçalves et al. (2018) compared the impact of a single session theta uptraining/SMR downtraining versus theta downtraining/SMR uptraining (hence, no beta training occurred) on attention processes. They found no impact in either of the groups. Moreover, they only succeeded to uptrain and not to downtrain brain frequency activity. On the contrary, two (partly) ecological studies showed a beneficial effect of SMR augmentation in combination with theta suppression (Ros et al., 2009) (as well as alpha augmentation, Kavianipoor et al., 2023). Ros et al. (2009) assessed the impact of two distinct EEG neurofeedback protocols, i.e., one SMR augment with theta suppression group and another alpha augment and theta suppression group. They reported that the SMR augment with theta suppression group experienced a significant improvement in surgical technique and time on task (Ros et al., 2009). Kavianipoor et al. (2023) used a mixed NFB design (increasing SMR, decreasing theta, and increasing alpha) with 14 sessions in dart players, with a NFB group and control group that only completed the dart-throwing exercise. The authors reported a significant difference in the post-tests of the executive control network (Attentional Networks Test) and dart-throwing skills. They interpreted the latter as being the result of improved attentional performance.

THETA/BETA RATIO, THETA/ALPHA RATIO, AND OTHER COMBINATIONS

Rasey et al. (1996) reported that training to enhance beta and decrease theta and alpha activity in four college students led to a significant improvement in two responders but not in the two other non-responders with regard to several cognitive performance tests of the WAIS. An almost similar design was studied by Farnia et al. (2017), examining the impact of ten 30-minute NFB sessions on working memory (Wechsler Memory Scale) in three groups. Group A received a beta uptraining and theta downtraining, group B low alpha/high alpha ratio, and group C a sham condition. Working memory significantly improved in both the NFB groups compared to the control group.

According to Studer et al. (2014), a theta/beta ratio NFB training did not lead to significant improvements in attentional processes compared to the control group. However, Tseng et al. (2021) observed that a theta/low-beta power ratio NFB training impacted long-term memory processes. In their study, the NFB group showed better episodic and semantic long-term memory than the control group along with significant differences in brain activity during the recall tests. These results were supported by a recent study by Rozengurt et al. (2023). They tested long-term memory three times, i.e., retrieval once immediately after watching a movie (as baseline), 24 hours thereafter; and once again one week later. They reported a significantly better recall in the theta/beta augment NFB group compared to the other control groups. Moreover, the performance output correlated with theta/beta augmentation.

Xiong et al. (2014) tested the hypothesis whether upregulating the theta-to-alpha ratio could improve working memory. The results confirmed their hypothesis, showing that an increase in working memory performance was significantly higher in the NFB than in the control groups.

Combined NFB training designs have shown their benefits in artistic populations or artistic activities. Alpha/theta NFB training significantly enhanced the performances of professional ballroom dancers as judged by a jury compared to a control group (Raymond et al., 2005) and high-level students of the Royal College of Music (Egner & Gruzelier, 2003). In the latter, a theta (5–8 Hz) over alpha (8–11 Hz) NFB augment training showed a significantly greater performance enhancement than in a beta 1 NFB training group, a SMR NFB group, and an Alexander Technique training group. However, a study by Gruzelier et al. (2014) could not – although a clear effect of the NFB training was detected in the EEG activity – evidence a significant improvement on dance performance as judged by four dance experts. There was, however, a significant increase in cognitive creativity measured with the test of unusual uses, but not on insight problems. A study of Leach et al. (2008) showed on the other hand the impact of alpha/theta training in comparison with SMR augment training on the artistic output of novice singers, replicated by Kleber et al. (2008) in conservatory singing students.

NFB/HRV COMBINATION

Dessy et al. (2020) applied a randomized mixed design experiment, with a training period of six weeks and HRV BFB as a control condition to a mixed HRV/NFB training. The HRV/NFB group was instructed to increase sensorimotor (SMR) power (12–15 Hz) and inhibit both theta power (4–8 Hz) and high beta power (21–30 Hz) at central electrode. The authors investigated the evolution of the different EEG frequency bands of the two experimental groups across and within sessions. All the participants exhibited EEG changes across and within sessions. However, within the HRV/NFB training group, untrained EEG frequencies had been significantly modified, unlike some of the trained frequencies. Moreover – similarly to the results of Jurewicz et al. (2018) and Pei et al. (2018) – EEG activity was modified in both the HRV group and the HRV/NFB groups. Hence, the EEG changes were not only circumscribed to the trained frequency bands or to the training modality. The potential benefits obtained after the NFB training could not be attributed to training-specific modifications. This reinforces the importance of the non-specific components of the NFB training to explain the potential benefits. These results show unequivocally that the physiological changes in the EEG obtained through biofeedback are not with certainty defined by the training modalities. As emphasized by the authors, a placebo or Hawthorne effect (i.e., the potential impact of the consequent awareness of being studied; McCambridge et al., 2014) through the coaching process was more likely to subtend the observed changes.

NFB as a step towards stress, anxiety, and mood regulation

There are not a lot of studies that have discussed an impact of NFB on stress, anxiety, or mood regulation within the context of performance and out of a clinical population. Potolicchio et al. (1979) found no changes in mood, as measured by the Profile of Mood States questionnaire (POMS) in alpha NFB responders and Plotkin and Rice (1981) found no difference in improvement as an effect of alpha NFB training in high anxious persons between a treatment versus control group. Holmes et al. (1980) reported alpha NFB training to be ineffective in decreasing levels of arousal during a stressful situation. However, Hardt and Kamiya (1978) observed a reduction in state anxiety due to alpha NFB augment training but only for high trait anxiety participants. More recently, Vasquez et al. (2015) associated the impact of decreased theta with a decrease in negative mood measured by the POMS questionnaire. Further Bazanova et al. (2013) reported an impact on situational anxiety in the NFB alpha augment responders. Accordingly, in Ros et al. (2009) lowered anxiety scores were reported after a SMR NFB augment training in microsurgery performance.

The impact of NFB in a (semi) ecological setting

The studies that were conducted (partly) in an ecological setting were – similarly as for HRV BFB – sparse and their details are discussed above. Most of the ecologically tested studies were in an artistic setting (i.e., Egner & Gruzelier, 2003; Gruzelier et al., 2014; Leach et al., 2008; Raymond et al., 2005) or sport setting (i.e., Cheng et al., 2015a in golf players, 2015b in dart players, 2017 in shooters; Kavianipoor et al., 2023 in dart players). There was also one study in surgeon skills (Ros et al., 2009).

NFB: what can we (not) conclude?

When considering the studies that examined NFB in function of mental performance enhancement, there are some tendencies per targeted frequency. According to Enriquez-Geppert (2014), theta oscillations in an EEG may be considered as the neural "working language" of executive functioning. Frontal-midline theta NFB augment training has indeed shown some benefits in the executive functioning such as task switching and memory updating (Enriquez-Geppert, 2014; Eschmann et al., 2022; Wang & Hsieh, 2013) but the same studies found also negative effects in working memory (Eschmann et al., 2022) and conflict monitoring (Enriquez-Geppert et al., 2014). Cloudt (2020) suggested that the potential influence of frontal midline theta on executive functioning might work through an effect on attention. Indeed, theta NFB impacted attention in Wang and Hsieh (2013) and Toolis et al. (2022). Finally, theta has been shown to play a role in memory consolidation by sleep (Renier et al., 2014; Rozengurt et al., 2016). Alpha NFB is not very convincing with eight studies that showed a negative impact (Barbazzeni et al., 2023; Bauer, 1976; Bazanova et al., 2013; Escalano et al., 2012; Gordon et al., 2020; Naas et al., 2019; Nawaz et al., 2022; Pamplona et al., 2020), two studies that showed mixed results (Hanslmeyer et al., 2005; Pei et al., 2018), and seven studies that showed a beneficial impact (Berger et al., 2018; Guez et al., 2014; Hsueh et al., 2016; Nan et al., 2012, 2013; Ros et al., 2014; Zoefel et al., 2011). Beta NFB is not convincing and we found only one gamma NFB study. Mixed trainings are more common and certainly SMR NFB training has often been examined. In SMR-only and SMR-combined studies, the results often reported a beneficial effect on (perceptual) attention (Cheng et al., 2015a, 2015b, 2017; Egner & Gruzelier, 2004; Doppelmayer & Weber, 2011; Gruzelier et al., 2001; Hoedlmosser et al., 2008; Kober et al., 2015b; Ros et al., 2009) and sometimes on executive functioning (Cheng et al., 2017; Kavianipoor et al., 2023; Kober et al., 2015b; Ros et al., 2009; Vernon et al., 2009). Four studies did not find clear support for SMR NFB training (Dessy et al., 2020; Fritson et al., 2008; Gonçalves et al., 2018).

These results confirm the conclusions of most of the recent meta-analyses. Chiasson et al. (2023) reviewed the impact of NFB in laboratory tasks. Their results showed that there is no real evidence that NFB does have an impactful effect on performance in laboratory tasks. With regard to mental performance, when diving into the details of the results per outcome domain, they found that the proportion reported as significant was 27% on cognitive tasks (on a total of 52 p-values), 38% on perception/attention tasks (on a total of 29 p-values) which is low. A meta-analysis by Brito et al. (2022) on the impact of NFB on cognitive performance and reaction time in athletes (seven randomized controlled trials, $n = 173$) reported a significant improvement in both the intervention and control groups (however, with a larger effect size for the NFB group).

A first important issue to consider, which is seldom addressed, is whether a beneficial impact obtained after a NFB training can be with certainty attributed to the specific trained frequency (Dessy et al., 2020; Enriquez-Geppert et al., 2017; Jurewicz et al., 2018; Pei et al., 2018). Studies that measured and reported brain activity independent from the aims of the NFB protocol observed marginal and even significant activity increases in non-targeted frequencies (Dessy et al., 2020; Enriquez-Geppert et al., 2014, 2017; Jurewicz et al., 2018; Kober et al., 2015b; Pei et al., 2018). It is highly questionable whether the targeted cognitive components in NFB training can be pinpointed to a narrow brain frequency. As stated by Enriquez-Geppert et al. (2017), there exist substantial interindividual differences in brain morphology that obviously may obscure the preciseness aimed at in frequency-specific NFB protocols. Other training errors are possible as well.

An accidental positive reinforcement error was mentioned by Dessy et al. (2020). In their section "Significant Session Events and Participants' Comments", the authors described how one participant experienced increasing their SMR activity by moving their forehead muscles in place of stimulating the frequency band width, and how the experimenter had to reframe the participant to stop training forehead muscles in place of brain activity. This shows how subjects – sometimes without knowing – can wrongly be reinforced for/trained in a non-desired behaviour. It also shows that devices are not able to detect these types of errors, and sometimes even respond to a wrong stimulus. Therefore, an attentive trainer is almost indispensable during training (which however may raise other problems, as we discuss in a following section).

Another training difficulty may arise in professions that are multifaceted. As it has already been raised by Mirifar et al. (2017) and recently again by Horvath et al. (2023), training a certain frequency band is very specific and has a narrow usefulness that depends on the task in question. This may suggest that "the wrong type of activity may not only be ineffective but may also be harmful" (p. 11). Training a specific frequency may be beneficial for one specific competence of the job but may be counterproductive or even dangerous for another part of the job. This further emphasizes the huge gap between laboratory studies and their real-life applications, and the acute shortage of ecological studies. There is a lack of ecological validation to test whether a lab-trained brain activity can indeed approach the required competences in the field, and there is no bulletproof evidence that a NFB or HRV BFB training has a superior value to other training forms to enhance mental performance. Moreover, the results of the small number of studies that were done in elite performance groups were rarely performed within an ecological context. For the purpose of conducting research in an ecological context, real-time NFB would be a very "nice to have" tool. However, an ecological environment is an environment full of uncontrollable aspects (e.g., movement, multi-sensory inputs) that will not only influence the measures but also cause strong artefacts in the physiological signals. For instance, Faller et al. (2019), who used a real-time NFB device in a semi-ecological VR flight environment, recognized that it was impossible to have a continuous reliable clear EEG signal because forehead, face, or neck muscle contractions made the dataset useless. Movement artefacts in EEG are already challenging in laboratory conditions (e.g., Dessy et al., 2020) and semi-ecological conditions (Faller et al., 2019), let alone in real-life military, sport, music, or dance environments where movement is at the base of the performance.

Notably, several studies found responders and non-responders, which means that studying interindividual differences should be high on the research agenda – focusing on the non-responders rather than the responders – to understand why certain persons do not respond. This means that – as it is the case in physiological research – interindividual differences should not be considered as noise but studied as a meaningful signal (e.g., Van Puyvelde et al., 2018,. In some of the studies that mentioned information about responders versus non-responders, it appears that the responders are those subjects that have either their reasons to benefit more from the manipulation or that are highly motivated. For instance, in Bazanova et al. (2013), the responders in an alpha NFB training were the subjects with a low baseline alpha frequency whereas no effects were observed in subjects with a higher baseline frequency. Baseline levels may indeed hinder the training. For instance, in Reichert et al. (2015), participants with lower levels of SMR power were less able to learn increasing SMR power. Similarly, in Naas et al. (2019), participants with high initial alpha levels benefitted more from alpha NFT training. Furthermore, Agnoli et al. (2018), observed an impact of beta NFB augment training on divergent thinking principally in those participants starting with a low creative achievement level. Accordingly, elder persons and persons in need of cognitive rehabilitation benefited more form NFB training than younger healthy adults (e.g., Kober et al., 2015b; Wang & Hsieh, 2013) and a reduction in state anxiety due to alpha NFB augment training was observed only for high trait anxiety participants (Hardt & Kamiya, 1978). These findings might be comparable with one of the conclusions in a recent review on the use of modafinil as a smart drug (van Puyvelde et al., 2022), stating that enhancing effects were beneficial only in persons with an initial lower performance level. Knowing that the costs of a full NFB training sold on the internet can easily rise to 10,000 USD, it would be desirable to know whether you have an eligible profile. Motivation and/or experience in focusing can have an impact on NFB training outcomes as well. For instance, in Witte et al. (2015) the impact of one single NFB session in triathletes was higher than in a matched healthy non-athletic control group. With regard to experience, previous involvement in mindfulness activities appears to facilitate NFB learning (Kober et al., 2015a; Kikkert 2015).

Finally, it would be worthwhile to examine interaction effects between HRV BFB and NFB trainings. Prinsloo et al. (2013) found an impact of HRV BFB training on theta (i.e., increase), beta (i.e., decrease), and the theta/beta ratio (i.e., increase). Bazanova et al. (2013), however, found no unilateral impact of ten sessions of alpha NFB training brain activity training on HRV. They reported that alpha augment training increased HRV only in the subjects with a low baseline alpha frequency. On the other hand, recently, Domingos et al. (2021) found that 12 sessions with a frequency of three sessions per week (but not two session per week) of alpha NFB training increased HRV. Hence, a clear outcome on the direction of influence has not yet been established, and considering the integrative character of physiology, it is overly simplistic to expect a hierarchical relationship between both. However, since HRV BFB is much less expensive, the direction from HRV to NFB could be a path worth investigating (Dessy et al., 2018). Moreover, according to Lehrer et al. (2020) HRV BFB had the largest impact on anxiety, depression, anger, and athletic/artistic performance, suggesting that anxiety and arousal regulation might be an important moderator. When considering the catastrophe model of Fazey and Hardy (1988) and the theory of challenge and threat states in athletes by Jones et al. (2009) in which cognitive and/or physiological arousal is described to intervene with performance (for a more detailed description, see Chapter 2), HRB BFB training may be an ideal complementary training component for performers struggling with cognitive anxiety that negatively influences their peak performances.

HRV BFB and NFB in a military population

Research on BFB in a military population to enhance mental performance is absent. We only found some articles that used fMRI BFB or articles not available in English. Further, publications regarding the use of biofeedback in military populations are related to PTSD treatment or symptom management, which is outside of the scope of the present report.

When targeting specific performance improvement in healthy populations, most of the recent publications retrieved oversell and underdeliver. For example, Oded's (2011) reports on ten years of training application with the "Mental Gym" project in the Israeli army, concluding that the training program is successful, yet no hard evidence is presented with regard to performance. The same holds true for Kizakevich et al. (2018), presenting a mobile application called "PHIT" for duty, or Aidman (2020), presenting the "Cognitive Fitness Framework" developed in collaboration with the Australian Defence Force. Another set of articles present reviews justifying the use of biofeedback and real-time monitoring to support performance management, such as Thomas and Russo's (2007) paper on neurocognitive monitoring in the aviation environment; Blacker et al.'s (2019) review on cognitive training for military applications; or Brunyé et al.'s (2020) review on US Army research contributing to cognitive enhancement in military contexts.

One of the most important sayings in special operations is "Humans are more important than hardware", yet all health and performance practitioners embedded in SOF units will recognize the appetite for hardware solutions of the client units. Biofeedback is an extremely popular method in the military population, and especially so in elite units, be it special forces or fighter pilots, who are more comfortable dealing with a hardware interface when it comes to "fuzzy" concepts like mental performance. This is acknowledged as well by Oded (2011), based on the above mentioned

"Mental Gym" project, which was a pioneer in the field. The use of biofeedback might thus be an adequate "door opener" when training self-regulation. As showed in an experimental investigation of neurofeedback, the adhesion of participants to an intervention is paramount to its effect (Dessy et al., 2020). However, that very same study concluded that the presence of significant effects in both the experimental and the control group showed EEG neurofeedback training to be an expensive placebo.

Conclusion

A summarized in Table 9.1, the two more beneficial BFB forms may be HRV BFB and SMR NFB. Knowing the existing interactions between HRV BFB and NFB, it is worthwhile to consider the physiological aspect of self-regulation as an interesting stepping stone for the implementation of a broader performance management approach. We advocate the use of simple, autonomic nervous system-based biofeedback, such as heart rate variability training, which offers a potentially interesting trade-off between the invested cost, training time, and effect regarding awareness of self-regulation. However, this intervention should be framed by a professional, in order to keep the expectations management realistic and thus credible.

Another aspect that is relevant for both HRV and NFB is the number of sessions needed, and whether these sessions need to be guided or not. In two meta-analyses (Goessl et al., 2017; Lehrer et al., 2020), no significant effect of number of treatment sessions was found. Nevertheless, NFB trainings are learning processes and it is unthinkable that a certain amount of sessions with a high training quality are not determining the training outcome to obtain prolonged effects (Gruzelier et al., 2006; Hammond et al., 2011; Mirifar et al., 2017). The study by Ghaziri et al. (2013) is often cited to show that NFB training induces brain plasticity causing microstructural changes in the brain's white and gray matter. However, it is seldom mentioned that these changes were observed only after 40 intervention sessions (Ghaziri et al., 2013). Besides the number of sessions, it has also been suggested that a more condensed training protocol would lead to better outcomes (Domingos et al., 2021). Surprisingly – as remarked by Enriquez-Geppert (2017) – no study appears to have examined the impact of the established varying intermittent reinforcement schedules. It is nevertheless part of the very basic theory around conditioning mechanisms (which are described in Chapter 10).

Furthermore, the impact of the presence or absence of a personal trainer should not be underestimated. Already in 1995, Kelley pointed out that the personal attention from the trainer may interact with the understanding of the applied breathing techniques and the motivation to practice them (Kelley, 1995). Similarly, Plotkin and Rice found an impact on anxiety of an alpha NFB training both in their intervention and control group. Indeed, in Dessy et al. (2020) a Hawthorne effect was suggested as one of the possible underlying mechanisms to explain the observed EEG changes unrelated to the applied training modalities. Accordingly, in Grosselin et al. (2021), although a significant increase of the individual alpha-band activity was reported in the NFB group only and not in the control group, self-reported effects in terms of increased relaxation and decreased anxiety were observed in both groups.

Considering the literature and its recent evolution, we are confronted with two issues here. The first one is similar to one of the critiques regarding CRM (Crew Resource Management) in the aviation industry. Everybody applies CRM, it is mandatory, yet there are no hard performance data (neither individual nor organizational) showing a clear effect on performance. However, that might be more of a methodological issue on how we measure performance, than a real caveat regarding CRM. The second one is the fact that the spread of personal wearables has made simple biofeedback applications available to everyone, however, there is no quality check whatsoever on the signals, nor the feedback, nor the training. One pragmatic approach could be to use this as a "tangible" approach to breath training (described in Chapter 5), which has demonstrated benefits.

However, if we want the therapeutic relationship to our performers to remain open and honest, and if we claim to use evidence-based techniques, it becomes quite convoluted to justify buying not only hardware, but also monthly subscriptions to subtend what might be either breath training or a sophisticated placebo effect.

Bibliography

Acharya, U., Joseph, K., Kannathal, N., Lim, M., & Suri, J. (2006). Heart rate variability: A review. *Medical & Biological Engineering & Computing*, 44(12), 1031–1051. https://doi.org/10.1007/s11517-006-0119-0

Agnoli, S., Zanon, M., Mastria, S., Avenanti, A., & Corazza, G. E. (2018). Enhancing creative cognition with a rapid right-parietal neurofeedback procedure. Neuropsychologia, 118, 99–106.

Aidman, E. (2020). Cognitive fitness framework: Towards assessing, training and augmenting individual-difference factors underpinning high-performance cognition. *Frontiers in Human Neuroscience*, 13, Article 466. https://doi.org/10.3389/fnhum.2019.00466

Anaya, E. M., Pisoni, D. B., & Kronenberger, W. G. (2016). Long-term musical experience and auditory and visual perceptual abilities under adverse conditions. *The Journal of the Acoustical Society of America*, 140(3), 2074–2081.

Bauer, R. H. (1976). Short-term memory: EEG alpha correlates and the effect of increased alpha. *Behavioral Biology*, 17(4), 425–433.

Barbazzeni, B., Speck, O., & Düzel, E. (2023). Cognitive training, but not EEG-neurofeedback, improves working memory in healthy volunteers. *Brain Communications*, 5(2), fcad101.

Bazanova, O. M., Balioz, N. V., Muravleva, K. B., & Skoraya, M. V. (2013). Effect of voluntary EEG a power increase training on heart rate variability. *Human Physiology*, 39(1), 86–97.

Beatty, J., Greenberg, A., Diebler, W. P., & O'Hanlon, J. F. (1974). Operant control of occipital theta rhythm affects performance in a radar monitoring task. *Science*, 183(4127), 871–873.

Berger, A. M., & Davelaar, E. J. (2018). Frontal alpha oscillations and attentional control: a virtual reality neurofeedback study. *Neuroscience*, 378, 189–197.

Berntson, G., Bigger, J., Eckberg, D., Grossman, P., Kaufmann, P., Malik, M., et al. (1997). Heart rate variability: Origins, methods, and interpretive cavats. *Psychophysiology,* 34, 623–648. https://doi.org/10.1111/j.1469-8986.1997.tb02140.x

Berntson, G. G., Cacioppo, J. T., & Grossman, P. (2007). Whither vagal tone. *Biological psychology*, *74*(2), 295–300. https://doi.org/10.1016/j.biopsycho.2006.08.006

Billman, G. E. (2011). Heart rate variability—a historical perspective. *Frontiers in Physiology,* 2, 86. https://doi.org/10.3389/fphys.2011.00086.

Blacker, K. J., Hamilton, J., Roush, G., Pettijohn, K. A., & Biggs, A. T. (2019). Cognitive training for military application: A review of the literature and practical guide. *Journal of Cognitive Enhancement,* 3, 30–51.

Brito, M. A. D., Fernandes, J. R., Esteves, N. S. A., Müller, V. T., Alexandria, D. B., Pérez, D. I. V., ... & Miarka, B. (2022). The effect of neurofeedback on the reaction time and cognitive performance of athletes: A systematic review and meta-analysis. *Frontiers in Human Neuroscience,* 16, 868450.

Brunyé, T.T., Brou, R., Doty, T.J. et al. A Review of US army research contributing to cognitive enhancement in military contexts. *Journal of Cognitive Enhancement*, 4, 453–468 (2020). https://doi.org/10.1007/s41465-020- 00167-3

Caldwell, J. A., Wilson, G. F., Cetinguc, M., Gaillard, A. W., & Gunder, A. (1994). *Psychophysiological assessment methods*. Neuilly-sur-Seine: Advisory Group for Aerospace Research and Development.

Cheng, M. Y., Huang, C. J., Chang, Y. K., Koester, D., Schack, T., & Hung, T. M. (2015a). Sensorimotor rhythm neurofeedback enhances golf putting performance. *Journal of Sport and Exercise Psychology*, 37(6), 626–636.

Cheng, M. Y., Hung, C. L., Huang, C. J., Chang, Y. K., Lo, L. C., Shen, C., & Hung, T. M. (2015b). Expert-novice differences in SMR activity during dart throwing. *Biological Psychology,* 110, 212–218.

Cheng, M. Y., Wang, K. P., Hung, C. L., Tu, Y. L., Huang, C. J., Koester, D., ... & Hung, T. M. (2017). Higher power of sensorimotor rhythm is associated with better performance in skilled air-pistol shooters. *Psychology of Sport and Exercise,* 32, 47–53.

Chiasson, P., Boylan, M. R., Elhamiasl, M., Pruitt, J. M., Ranjan, S., Riels, K., ... & Keil, A. (2023). Effects of Neurofeedback training on performance in laboratory tasks: A systematic review. *International Journal of Psychophysiology 189*, 42–56.

Clayton, K. K., Swaminathan, J., Yazdanbakhsh, A., Zuk, J., Patel, A. D., & Kidd Jr, G. (2016). Executive function, visual attention and the cocktail party problem in musicians and non-musicians. *PloS ONE*, 11(7), e0157638.

Cloudt, E. F., Schoenmakers, I. S., Van Schie, H. T., & Westerink, I. J. (2020). *Using bi-directional neurofeedback training to explore the causality between frontal midline theta and working memory performance*. Master thesis Eindhoven University of Technology.

Corrigan, S. L., Roberts, S., Warmington, S., Drain, J., & Main, L.C. (2021). Monitoring stress and allostatic load in first responders and tactical operators using heart rate variability: A systematic review. *BMC Public Health*, Sep 18;21(1), 1701. doi: 10.1186/s12889-021-11595-x. PMID: 34537038; PMCID: PMC8449887

Demos, J. (2005). *Getting started with neurofeedback*. New York: WW Norton & Company.

Dessy, E., Mairesse, O., van Puyvelde, M., Cortoos, A., Neyt, X., & Pattyn, N. (2020). Train Your Brain? Can we really selectively train specific EEG frequencies with neurofeedback training. *Frontiers in Human Neuroscience*, Mar 10;14:22. doi: 10.3389/fnhum.2020.00022. PMID: 32210777; PMCID: PMC7077336

Dessy, E., Van Puyvelde, M., Mairesse, O., Neyt, X., & Pattyn, N. (2018). Cognitive performance enhancement: Do biofeedback and neurofeedback work? *Journal of Cognitive Enhancement*, 2(2018), 12–42. https://doi.org/10.1007/s41465-017-0039-y.

Domingos, C., Peralta, M., Prazeres, P., Nan, W., Rosa, A., & Pereira, J. G. (2021). Session frequency matters in neurofeedback training of athletes. *Applied Psychophysiology and Biofeedback*, 46, 195–204.

Doppelmayr, M., & Weber, E. (2011). Effects of SMR and theta/beta neurofeedback on reaction times, spatial abilities, and creativity. *Journal of Neurotherapy*, 15(2), 115–129.

Egner, T., & Gruzelier, J. (2001). Learned self-regulation of EEG frequency components affects attention and event-related brain potentials in humans. *Neuroreport*, 12(18), 4155–4159.

Egner, T., & Gruzelier, J. (2003). Ecological validity of neurofeedback : modulation of slow wave EEG enhances musical performance, *Neuroreport*, 14(9), 1221–1224.

Egner, T., & Gruzelier, J. (2004). EEG biofeedback of low beta band components: Frequency-specific effects on variables of attention, 131–139. https://doi.org/10.1016/S1388-2457(03)00353-5

Enriquez-Geppert, S., Huster, R. J., Ros, T., & Wood, G. (2017). Neurofeedback. In: *Theory-driven approaches to cognitive enhancement*. Springer, Cham. https://doi.org/10.1007/978-3-319-57505-6_11

Enriquez-Geppert, S., Huster, R. J., Scharfenort, R., Mokom, Z. N., Zimmermann, J., & Herrmann, C. S. (2014). *Modulation of frontal-midline theta by neurofeedback. Biological Psychology*, 95, 59–69.

Eschmann, K. C., Riedel, L., & Mecklinger, A. (2022). Theta neurofeedback training supports motor performance and flow experience. *Journal of Cognitive Enhancement*, 1–17.

Escolano, C., Navarro-Gil, M., Garcia-Campayo, J., & Minguez, J. (2014). The effects of a single session of upper alpha neurofeedback for cognitive enhancement: a sham-controlled study. *Applied Psychophysiology and Biofeedback*, 39(3–4), 227–236.

Escolano, C., Olivan, B., Lopez-del-Hoyo, Y., Garcia-Campayo, J., & Minguez, J. (2012). Double-blind single-session neurofeedback training in upper-alpha for cognitive enhancement of healthy subjects. Annual International Conference of the IEEE Engineering in Medicine and Biology Society. IEEE Engineering in Medicine and Biology Society. Annual International Conference, 2012, 4643–4647.

Evans, J. R., & Abarbanel, A. (1999). *Introduction to quantitative EEG and neurofeedback*. Orlando: Academic Press.

Faller, J., Cummings, J., Saproo, S., & Sajda, P. (2019). Regulation of arousal via online neurofeedback improves human performance in a demanding sensory-motor task. *Proceedings of the National Academy of Sciences*, 116(13), 6482–6490.

Fazey, J., L. Hardy. (1988). The Inverted U-hypothesis: A Catastrophe for Sport Psychology British Association of Sports Sciences, Monograph No. 1, The National Coaching Foundation.

Friedman, B. H. (2007). An autonomic flexibility–neurovisceral integration model of anxiety and cardiac vagal tone. *Biological Psychology*, 74(2), 185–199.

Fritson, K. K., Wadkins, T. A., Gerdes, P., & Hof, D. (2008). The impact of neurotherapy on college students' cognitive abilities and emotions. *Journal of Neurotherapy*, 11(4), 1–9.

Ghaziri, J., Tucholka, A., Larue, V., Blanchette-Sylvestre, M., Reyburn, G., Gilbert, G., ... & Beauregard, M. (2013). Neurofeedback training induces changes in white and gray matter. *Clinical EEG and Neuroscience*, 44(4), 265–272.

Goessl, V. C., Curtiss, J. E., & Hofmann, S. G. (2017). The effect of heart rate variability biofeedback training on stress and anxiety: a meta-analysis. *Psychological Medicine*, 47(15), 2578–2586.

Gonçalves, Ó. F., Carvalho, S., Mendes, A. J., Lema, A., Leite, J., & Boggio, P. S. (2018). Neuromodulating attention and mind-wandering processes with multi-session real-time electroencephalogram. *Porto Biomedical Journal*, 3(2).

Gordon, S., Todder, D., Deutsch, I., Garbi, D., Alkobi, O., Shriki, O., ... & Meiran, N. (2020). Effects of neurofeedback and working memory-combined training on executive functions in healthy young adults. *Psychological Research*, 84, 1586–1609.

Grossman, P., Karemaker, J., & Wieling, W. (1991). Prediction of tonic parasympathetic cardiac control using respiratory sinus arrhythmia: the need for respiratory control. *Psychophysiology*, 28(2), 201–216.

Grosselin, F., Breton, A., Yahia-Cherif, L., Wang, X., Spinelli, G., Hugueville, L., ... & George, N. (2021). Alpha activity neuromodulation induced by individual alpha-based neurofeedback learning in ecological context: A double-blind randomized study. *Scientific Reports*, 11(1), 18489.

Gruzelier, J., Egner, T., & Vernon, D. (2006). Validating the efficacy of neurofeedback for optimising performance. *Progress in brain research*, 159, 421–431.

Gruzelier, J. H., Thompson, T., Redding, E., Brandt, R., & Steffert, T. (2014). Application of alpha/theta neurofeedback and heart rate variability training to young contemporary dancers: State anxiety and creativity. *International Journal of Psychophysiology*, 93(1), 105–111.

Guez, J., Rogel, A., Getter, N., Keha, E., Cohen, T., Amor, T., et al. (2015). Influence of electroencephalography neurofeedback training on episodic memory: A randomized, sham-controlled, double- blind study. *Memory*, 23(5), 683–694.

Hammond, D. C., Bodenhamer-Davis, G., Gluck, G., Stokes, D., Harper, S. H., Trudeau, D., ... & Kirk, L. (2011). Standards of practice for neurofeedback and neurotherapy: A position paper of the International Society for Neurofeedback & Research. *Journal of Neurotherapy*, 15(1), 54–64.

Hanslmayr, S., Sauseng, P., Doppelmayr, M., Schabus, M., & Klimesch, W. (2005). Increasing individual upper alpha power by neurofeedback improves cognitive performance in human subjects. *Applied Psychophysiology and Biofeedback*, 30(1), 1–10.

Hardt, J. V., & Kamiya, J. (1978). Anxiety change through electroencephalographic alpha feedback seen only in high anxiety subjects. *Science*, 201(4350), 79–81.

Hodges, N. J., Wyder-Hodge, P. A., Hetherington, S., Baker, J., Besler, Z., & Spering, M. (2021). Topical review: Perceptual-cognitive skills, methods, and skill-based comparisons in interceptive sports. *Optometry and Vision Science*, 98(7), 681–695.

Hoedlmoser, K., Pecherstorfer, T., Gruber, G., Anderer, P., Doppelmayr, M., Klimesch, W., & Schabus, M. (2008). Instrumental conditioning of human sensorimotor rhythm(12-15 Hz) and its impact on sleep as well as declarative learning. *Sleep*, 31(10), 1401–1408.

Horváth, D., Négyesi, J., Rácz, M., Győri, T., Matics, Z., Puskin, A., ... & Rácz, L. (2023). Feasibility of a novel neurofeedback system: a parallel randomized single-blinded pilot study. *Scientific Reports*, 13(1), 17353.

Hsueh, J. J., Chen, T. S., Chen, J. J., & Shaw, F. Z. (2016). Neurofeedback training of EEG alpha rhythm enhances episodic and working memory. *Human Brain Mapping*, 37(7), 2662–2675.

Jones, M., Meijen, C., McCarthy, P. J., & Sheffield, D. (2009). A theory of challenge and threat states in athletes. *International Review of Sport and Exercise Psychology*, 2(2), 161–180.

Jurewicz, K., Paluch, K., Kublik, E., Rogala, J., Mikicin, M., & Wróbel, A. (2018). EEG-neurofeedback training of beta band (12–22 Hz) affects alpha and beta frequencies–A controlled study of a healthy population. *Neuropsychologia*, 108, 13–24.

Kaiser, D. (2007). What is quantitative EEG? *Journal of Neurotherapy*, 10(4), 37–52.

Kavianipoor, H., Farsi, A., & Bahrami, A. (2023). The effect of neurofeedback training on executive control network of attention and dart-throwing performance in individuals with trait anxiety. *Applied Psychophysiology and Biofeedback*, 48(3), 379–391.

Keizer, A. W., Verment, R. S., & Hommel, B. (2010a). Enhancing cognitive control through neurofeedback: A role of gamma-band activity in managing episodic retrieval. *NeuroImage*, 49(4), 3404–3413.

Keizer, A. W., Verschoor, M., Verment, R. S., & Hommel, B. (2010b). The effect of gamma enhancing neurofeedback on the control of feature bindings and intelligence measures. *International Journal of Psychophysiology*, 75(1), 25–32.

Kelley, P. L. (1995). Stress management strategies in the workplace: A meta-analysis of stress intervention techniques. The Pennsylvania State University.

Kewman, D., & Roberts, A. (1980). Skin temperature biofeedback and migraine headaches. *Biofeedback and Self-Regulation*, 5(3), 327–345. https://doi.org/10.1007/BF00999808.

Kikkert, A. (2015). *Predictors of neurofeedback efficacy: An exploratory study to the influence of personality and cognitive characteristics on the efficacy of theta and beta neurofeedback training*. Masters, Psychology, Leiden University.

Kizakevich, P. N., Eckhoff, R., Brown, J., Tueller, S. J., Weimer, B., Bell, S., Weeks, A., Hourani, L. L., Spira, J. L., King, L. A. (2018). PHIT for duty, a mobile application for stress reduction, sleep improvement, and alcohol moderation. *Military Medicine*, Mar 1;183(1), 353–363. doi: 10.1093/milmed/usx157. PMID: 29635566

Kleber, B., Gruzelier, J., Bensch, M., & Birbaumer, N. (2008). Effects of EEG-biofeedback on professional singing performances. Revista Espanola Psichologica, 10, 77–61.

Klimesch, W. (1999). EEG alpha and theta oscillations reflect cognitive and memory performance: A review and analysis. *Brain Research Reviews*, 29(2), 169–195.

Klimesch, W., Doppelmayr, M., Russegger, H., Pachinger, T., & Schwaiger, J. (1998). Induced alpha band power changes in the human EEG and attention. *Neuroscience Letters*, 244(2), 73–76.

Kober, S. E., Schweiger, D., Witte, M., Reichert, J. L., Grieshofer, P., Neuper, C., et al. (2015a). Specific effects of EEG based neurofeedback training on memory functions in post-stroke victims. *Journal Neuroengineering and Rehabilitation*, 12(1), 1. doi:10.1186/s12984-015-0105-6

Kober, S. E., Witte, M., Stangl, M., Väljamäe, A., Neuper, C., & Wood, G. (2015b). Shutting down sensorimotor interference unblocks the networks for stimulus processing: An SMR neurofeedback training study. *Clinical Neurophysiology*, 126(1), 82–95. doi:10.1016/j.clinph. 2014.03.031

Leach, J., Holmes, P., Hirst, L., & Gruzelier, J. (2008). Alpha theta versus SMR training for novice singers/advanced instrumentalists. *Revista Espanola Psichologica*, 10, 62.

Lehrer, P. (2007). Biofeedback training to increase heart rate variability. In P. Lehrer, R.Woolfolk &W. Sime (Eds.), *Principles and practice of stress management* (3rd ed., pp. 227–248). New York: The Guilford Press.

Lehrer, P., Kaur, K., Sharma, A., Shah, K., Huseby, R., Bhavsar, J., Sgobba, P., & Zhang, Y. (2020). Heart Rate Variability Biofeedback Improves Emotional and Physical Health and Performance: A Systematic Review and Meta Analysis. *Applied Psychophysiology and Biofeedback*, 45(3), 109–129.

Lehrer, P., Vaschillo, E., Vaschillo, B., Lu, S., Eckberg, D., & Edelberg, R. (2003). Heart rate variability biofeedback increases baroreflex gain and peak expiratory flow. *Psychosomatic Medicine*, 65, 796–805. https://doi.org/10.1097/01.PSY.0000089200.8196

Lehrer, P. M., Vaschillo, E. G., & Vaschillo, B. (2000). Resonant frequency biofeedback training to increase cardiac variability: Rationale and manual for training. *Applied Psychophysiology and Biofeedback*, 25(3), 177–191. https://doi.org/10.1023/A:1009554825745

Magagnin, V., Mauri, M., Cipresso, P., Mainardi, L., Brown, E., Cerutti, S., ... & Barbieri, R. (2010). Heart rate variability and respiratory sinus Arrhythmia assessment of affective states by bivariate autoregressive spectral analysis. *Computing in Cardiology*, 37(5737930), 145–148.

Makaracı, Y., Makaracı, M., Zorba, E., & Lautenbach, F. (2023). A Pilot Study of the Biofeedback Training to Reduce Salivary Cortisol Level and Improve Mental Health in Highly-Trained Female Athletes. *Applied Psychophysiology and Biofeedback*, 48(3), 357–367.

Malik, M., Bigger, J. T., Camm, A. J., Kleiger, R. E., Malliani, A., Moss, A. J., & Schwartz, P. J. (1996). Heart rate variability: Standards of measurement, physiological interpretation, and clinical use. *European Heart Journal*, 17(3), 354–381. https://doi.org/10.1093/oxfordjournals.eurheartj.a014868

McCambridge, J., Witton, J., & Elbourne, D. R. (2014). Systematic review of the Hawthorne effect: New concepts are needed to study research participation effects. *Journal of Clinical Epidemiology*, 67(3), 267–277.

Mirifar, A., Beckmann, J., & Ehrlenspiel, F. (2017). Neurofeedback as supplementary training for optimizing athletes' performance: A systematic review with implications for future research. *Neuroscience & Biobehavioral Reviews*, 75, 419–432.

Mogg, K., Salum, G. A., Bradley, B. P., Gadelha, A., Pan, P., Alvarenga, P., ... & Manfro, G. G. (2015). Attention network functioning in children with anxiety disorders, attention-deficit/hyperactivity disorder and non-clinical anxiety. *Psychological Medicine*, 45(12), 2633–2646.

Mulert, C., & Lemieux, L. (2009). *EEG-fMRI: Physiological basis, technique, and applications*. Berlin: Springer Science & Business Media.

Naas, A., Rodrigues, J., Knirsch, J. P., & Sonderegger, A. (2019). Alpha Neurofeedback Training with a portable Low-Priced and Commercially Available EEG Device Leads to Faster Alpha Enhancement: A Single-blind, Sham-feedback Controlled Study & Methodological Review. *bioRxiv*, 527598.

Nan, W., Rodrigues, J. P., Ma, J., Qu, X., Wan, F., Mak, P. I., ... & Rosa, A. (2012). Individual alpha neurofeedback training effect on short term memory. *International Journal of Psychophysiology*, 86(1), 83–87.

Nan, W., Wan, F., Lou, C. I., Vai, M. I., & Rosa, A. (2013). Peripheral visual performance enhancement by neurofeedback training. *Applied Psychophysiology and Biofeedback*, 38(4), 285–291.

Nawaz, R., Nisar, H., Yap, V. V., & Tsai, C. Y. (2022). The effect of alpha neurofeedback training on cognitive performance in healthy adults. *Mathematics*, 10(7), 1095.

Newell, A., Carmichael, A., Gregor, P., Alm, N., & Waller, A. (2008). Information technology for cognitive support. In J. Jacko & A. Sears (Eds.), *The human-computer interaction handbook: Fundamentals, evolving technologies, and emerging applications* (2nd ed., pp. 811–828). Mahawa: Laurence Erlbaum Associates.

Niv, S. (2013). Clinical efficacy and potential mechanisms of neurofeedback. *Personality and Individual Differences*, 54(6), 676–686.

Noachtar, S., Binnie, C., Ebersole, J., Mauguière, F., Sakamoto, A., & Westmoreland, B. (1999). A glossary of terms most commonly used by clinical electroencephalographers and proposal for the report form for the EEG findings. *The International Federation of Clinical Neurophysiology Electroencephalography and Clinical Neurophysiology*. Supplement, 52, 21–41.

Oded, Y. (2011). Biofeedback-based mental training in the military—The "Mental GymTM" *Project. Biofeedback*, 39(3), 112–118. DOI: 10.5298/1081-5937-39.3.03

Ogawa, S., Lee, T. M., Kay, A. R., & Tank, D. W. (1990a). Brain magnetic resonance imaging with contrast dependent on blood oxygenation. *Proceedings of the National Academy of Sciences*, 87(24), 9868–9872.

Ogawa, S., Lee, T. M., Nayak, A. S., & Glynn, P. (1990b). Oxygenation sensitive contrast in magnetic resonance image of rodent brain at high magnetic fields. *Magnetic Resonance in Medicine*, 14(1), 68–78.

Onton, J., Delorme, A., & Makeig, S. (2005). Frontal midline EEG dynamics during working memory. *NeuroImage*, 27(2), 341–356.

Pacheco-Unguetti, A. P., Acosta, A., Callejas, A., & Lupiáñez, J. (2010). Attention and anxiety: Different attentional functioning under state and trait anxiety. *Psychological Science*, 21(2), 298–304. https://doi.org/10.1177/0956797609359624

Pagaduan, J. C., Chen, Y. S., Fell, J. W., & Wu, S. S. X. (2020). Can heart rate variability biofeedback improve athletic performance? A systematic review. *Journal of Human Kinetics*, Jul 21;73, 103–114. doi: 10.2478/hukin-2020-0004. PMID: 32774542; PMCID: PMC7386140

Pamplona, G. S., Heldner, J., Langner, R., Koush, Y., Michels, L., Ionta, S., ... & Salmon, C. E. (2020). Network-based fMRI-neurofeedback training of sustained attention. *Neuroimage*, 221, 117194.

Pattyn, N., Mairesse, O., Cortoos, A., Morais, J., Soetens, E., Roelands, B., et al. (2013). Cardiac reactivity and preserved performance under stress: Two sides of the same coin? *International Journal of Psychophysiology*, 93(1), 30–37. https://doi.org/10.1016/j.ijpsycho.2013.03.008

Pattyn, N., Neyt, X., Henderickx, D., & Soetens, E. (2008). Psychophysiological investigation of vigilance decrement: Boredom or cognitive fatigue? *Physiology & Behavior*, 93(1), 369–378.

Paul, M., & Garg, K. (2012). The effect of heart rate variability biofeedback on performance psychology of basketball players. *Applied Psychophysiology and Biofeedback*, 37, 131–144.

Peek, C. (2003). A primer of biofeedback instrumentation. In M. Schwartz (Ed.), *Biofeedback a practitioner's guide* (3rd ed., pp. 43–87). New York: Guilford Press.

Pei G, Wu J, Chen D, Guo G, Liu S, Hong M, Yan T. Effects of an Integrated Neurofeedback System with Dry Electrodes: EEG Acquisition and Cognition Assessment. *Sensors*. 2018; 18(10):3396.

Plotkin, W. B., & Rice, K. M. (1981). Biofeedback as a placebo: Anxiety reduction facilitated by training in either suppression or enhancement of alpha brainwaves. *Journal of Consulting and Clinical Psychology*, 49(4), 590–596.

Posse, S., Fitzgerald, D., Gao, K., Habel, U., Rosenberg, D., Moore, G. J., & Schneider, F. (2003). Real-time fMRI of temporolimbic regions detects amygdala activation during single-trial self-induced sadness. *NeuroImage*, 18(3), 760–768.

Potolicchio, S. J., Zukerman, A. S., & Chernigovskaya, 1200 N. V. (1979). Feedback control of human alpha rhythm from the central area. *Biofeedback and Self-Regulation*, 4(3), 211–219.

Prinsloo, G., Rauch, H., Karpul, D., & Derman, W. (2013a). The effect of a single session of short duration heart rate variability biofeedback on EEG: A pilot study. *Applied Psychophysiology and Biofeedback*, 38(1), 45–56. https://doi.org/10.1007/s10484-012

Prinsloo, G. E., Derman, W. E., Lambert, M. I., & Rauch, H. G. (2013b). The effect of a single session of short duration biofeedback-induced deep breathing on measures of heart rate variability during laboratory-induced cognitive stress: a pilot study. *Applied Psychophysiology and Biofeedback*, 38, 81–90.

Prinsloo, G. E., Derman, W. E., Lambert, M. I., & Rauch, H. G. (2013c). The effect of a single episode of short duration heart rate variability biofeedback on measures of anxiety and relaxation states. *International Journal of Stress Management*, 20(4), 391.

Prinsloo, G. E., Rauch, H. G. L., Lambert, M. I., Muench, F., Noakes, T., & Derman, W. (2011). The effect of short duration heart rate variability (HRV) biofeedback on cognitive performance during laboratory induced cognitive stress. *Applied Cognitive Psychology*, 25(5), 792–801.

Prinzel, L., Pope, A., & Freeman, F. (2001). Application of physiological self-regulation and adaptive task allocation techniques for controlling operator hazardous states of awareness. http://ntrs.nasa.gov/archive/nasa/casi.ntrs.nasa.gov. Langley Research Center Hampton: National Aeronautics and Space administration. Retrieved from https://ntrs.nasa.gov/archive/nasa/casi.ntrs.nasa.gov/20010060397

Prinzel, L., Pope, A., & Freeman, F. (2002). Physiological self-regulation and adaptive automation. *International Journal of Aviation Psychology*, 12(2), 179–196.

Rance, M., Ruttorf, M., Nees, F., Schad, L. R., & Flor, H. (2014). Real time fMRI feedback of the anterior cingulate and posterior insular cortex in the processing of pain. *Human Brain Mapping*, 35(12), 5784–5798.

Rasey, H., Lubar, J. F., McIntyre, A., Zoffuto, A., & Abbott, P. L. (1995). EEG biofeedback for the enhancement of attentional processing in normal college students. *Journal of Neurotherapy*, 1(3), 15–21.

Rauchs, G., Desgranges, B., Foret, J., & Eustache, F. (2005). The relationships between memory systems and sleep stages. *Journal of Sleep Research*, 14(2), 123–140.

Raymond, J., Sajid, I., Parkinson, L. A., & Gruzelier, J. H. (2005). Biofeedback and dance performance: A preliminary investigation. *Applied Psychophysiology and Biofeedback*, 30, 65–73.

Reichert, J. L., Kober, S. E., Neuper, C., & Wood, G. (2015). Resting state sensorimotor rhythm (SMR) power predicts the ability to upregulate SMR in an EEG-instrumental conditioning paradigm. *Clinical Neurophysiology*, 126(11), 2068–2077.

Reiner, M., Lev, D. D., & Rosen, A. (2018). Theta Neurofeedback Effects on Motor Memory Consolidation and Performance Accuracy: An Apparent Paradox? *Neuroscience*, 378, 198–210.

Reiner, M., Rozengurt, R., & Barnea, A. (2014). Better than sleep: Theta neurofeedback training accelerates memory consolidation. *Biological Psychology*, 95, 45–53.

Rogala, J., Jurewicz, K., Paluch, K., Kublik, E., Cetnarski, R., & Wrobel, A. (2016). The do's and don'ts of neurofeedback training: A review of the controlled studies using healthy adults. *Frontiers in Human Neuroscience*, 10, 301.

Ros, T., Enriquez-geppert, S., Zotev, V., Young, K., Wood, G., Wan, F., … Thibault, R. T. (2019). Consensus on the reporting and experimental design of clinical and cognitive-behavioural neurofeedback studies (CRED-nf checklist). *PsyArXiv Preprints*, (January). https://doi.org/10.31234/osf.io/nyx84

Ros, T., Moseley, M. J., Bloom, P. A., Benjamin, L., Parkinson, L. A., & Gruzelier, J. H. (2009). Optimizing microsurgical skills with EEG neurofeedback. *BMC Neuroscience*, 10(1), 1.

Ros, T., Munneke, M. A.M., Parkinson, L. A., & Gruzelier, J. H. (2014). Neurofeedback facilitation of implicit motor learning. *Biological Psychology*, 95, 54–58.

Rose, S., Cacho, F., Wiersma, L., Magdaleno, A., Anderson, N., & Statler, T. (2021). Efficacy of a Brief Biofeedback Intervention on Mood, Arousal, Mental Workload, Movement Time, and Biofeedback Device Preference. *Applied Psychophysiology and Biofeedback*, 46(2), 205–214.

Rosenzweig, M. R., & Bennett, E. L. (1996). Psychobiology of plasticity: Effects of training and experience on brain and behavior. *Behavioural Brain Research*, 78(1), 57–65.

Rota, G., Sitaram, R., Veit, R., Erb, M., Weiskopf, N., Dogil, G., & Birbaumer, N. (2009). Self-regulation of regional cortical activity using real-time fMRI: the right inferior frontal gyrus and linguistic processing. *Human Brain Mapping*, 30(5), 1605–1614.

Rozengurt, R., Barnea, A., Uchida, S., & Levy, D. A. (2016). Theta EEG neurofeedback benefits early consolidation of motor sequence learning. *Psychophysiology*, 53(7), 965–973.

Rozengurt, R., Kuznietsov, I., Kachynska, T., Kozachuk, N., Abramchuk, O., Zhuravlov, O., ... & Levy, D. A. (2023). Theta EEG neurofeedback promotes early consolidation of real life-like episodic memory. *Cognitive, Affective, & Behavioral Neuroscience*, 23(6), 1473–1481..

Ruiz, S., Buyukturkoglu, K., Rana, M., Birbaumer, N., & Sitaram, R. (2014). Real-time fMRI brain computer interfaces: Self-regulation of single brain regions to networks. *Biological Psychology,* 95, 4–20.

Rusciano, A., Corradini, G., Stoianov, I., Neuroplus biofeedback improves attention, resilience and injury prevention in elite soccer players. *Psychophysiology*. 2017;54(6):916–926

Salari, N., Buchel, C., & Rose, M. (2013). Functional dissociation of ongoing oscillatory brain states. *PLoS ONE*, 7, e38090.

Salari, N., Büchel, C., & Rose, M. (2014). Neurofeedback training of gamma band oscillations improves perceptual processing. *Experimental Brain Research,* 232, 3353–3361.

Sharpley, C., & Rogers, H. (1984). A meta-analysis of frontalis EMG levels with biofeedback and alternative procedures. *Biofeedback and Self-Regulation,* 9(3), 385–393.

Shen, L., Jiang, Y., Wan, F., Ku, Y., & Nan, W. (2023). Successful alpha neurofeedback training enhances working memory updating and event-related potential activity. *Neurobiology of Learning and Memory*, *205*, 107834.

Stephenson, M. D., Thompson, A. G., Merrigan, J. J., Stone, J.D., & Hagen, J. A. (2021). Applying heart rate variability to monitor health and performance in tactical personnel: A narrative review. *International Journal of Environmental Research Public Health*, Jul 31;18(15), 8143. doi: 10.3390/ijerph18158143. PMID: 34360435; PMCID: PMC8346173.

Studer, P., Kratz, O., Gevensleben, H., Rothenberger, A., Moll, G. H., Hautzinger, M., & Heinrich, H. (2014). Slow cortical potential and theta/beta neurofeedback training in adults: effects on attentional processes and motor system excitability. *Frontiers in Human Neuroscience*, 8, 555.

Sutarto, A., AbdulWahab, M., & Mat Zin, N. (2010). Heart rate variability (HRV) biofeedback: A new training approach for operator's performance enhancement. *Journal of Industrial Engineering and Management*, 3(1), 176–198. https://doi.org/10.3926/jiem. 2010.v

Sutarto, A., Wahab, M., & Zin, N. (2013). Effect of biofeedback training on operator's cognitive performance. *Work (Reading, Mass),* 44, 231–243.

Sutarto, M., AbdulWahab, M., & Mat Zin, N. (2012). Resonant breathing biofeedback training for stress reduction among manufacturing operators. *International Journal of Occupational Safety and Ergonomics*, 18(4), 549–561. https://doi.org/10.1080/10803548.2012.11076959

Task Force of The European Society of Cardiology and The North American Society of Pacing and Electrophysiology. (1996). Heart rate variability. Standards of measurement, physiological interpretation, and clinical use. *European Heart Journal*, 17(3), 354–381.

Thayer, J., Åhs, F., Fredrikson, M., Sollers, J., & Wager, T. (2012). A meta-analysis of heart rate variability and neuroimaging studies: Implications for heart rate variability as a marker of stress and health. *Neuroscience and Behavioural Reviews,* 36, 747–756.

Thayer, J., Hansen, A., & Johnsen, B. (2010a). The non-invasive assessment of autonomic influences on the heart using impedance cardiography and heart rate variability. In A. Steptoe (Ed.), *Handbook of behavioral medicine: methods and applications* (pp. 723–740). New York: Springer.

Thayer, J., & Lane, R. (2000). A model of neurovisceral integration in emotion regulation and dysregulation. *Journal of Affective Disorders*, 61(3), 201–216.

Thayer, J., & Lane, R. (2009). Claude Bernard and the heart–brain connection: Further elaboration of a model of neurovisceral integration. *Neuroscience & Biobehavioral Reviews*, 33(2), 81–88.

Thayer, J., Yamamoto, S., & Brosschot, J. (2010b). The relationship of autonomic imbalance, heart rate variability and cardiovascular disease risk factors. *International Journal of Cardiology*, 141(2), 122–131.

Thomas, M. L., & Russo, M. B. (2007). Neurocognitive monitors: Toward the prevention of cognitive performance decrements and catastrophic failures in the operational environment. *Aviation Space Environmental Medicine*; 78(5), Suppl.), B144–B152.

Toolis, T., Cooke, A., Laaksonen, M. S., & McGawley, K. (2023). Effects of Neurofeedback Training on Frontal Midline Theta Power, Shooting Performance, and Attentional Focus With Experienced Biathletes. *Journal of Clinical Sport Psychology*, 1(aop), 1–23.

Tseng, Y. H., Tamura, K., & Okamoto, T. (2021). Neurofeedback training improves episodic and semantic long-term memory performance. *Scientific Reports*, 11(1), 17274.

Van Puyvelde, M., Neyt, X., McGlone, F., & Pattyn, N. (2018). Voice stress analysis: a new framework for voice and effort in human performance. *Frontiers in Psychology*, 9, 1994.

Van Puyvelde, M., Van Cutsem, J., Lacroix, E., & Pattyn, N. (2022). A State-of-the-Art Review on the Use of Modafinil as A Performance-enhancing Drug in the Context of Military Operationality. *Military Medicine*, 187(1-2), 52–64. https://doi.org/10.1093/milmed/usab398

Vaschillo, G. E., Vaschillo, B., & Lehrer, P. (2006). Characteristics of resonance in heart rate variability stimulated by biofeedback. *Applied Psychophysiology and Biofeedback*, 31, 129–142. https://doi.org/10.1007/s10484-006-9009-3.

Vernon, D. (2005). Can neurofeedback training enhance performance? An evaluation of the evidence with implications for future research. *Applied Psychophysiology and Biofeedback*, 30(4), 347–364. https://doi.org/10.1007/s10484-005-8421-4.

Vernon, D., Egner, T., Cooper, N., Compton, T., Neilands, C., Sheri, A., & Gruzelier, J. (2003). The effect of training distinct neurofeedback protocols on aspects of cognitive performance. *International Journal of Psychophysiology*, 47(1), 75–85.

Walker, M. P. (2009). The role of sleep in cognition and emotion. *Annals of the New York Academy of Sciences*, 1156(1), 168–197.

Wang, J. R., & Hsieh, S. (2013). Neurofeedback training improves attention and working memory performance. *Clinical Neurophysiology*, 124(12), 2406–2420.

Weiskopf, N., Veit, R., Erb, M., Mathiak, K., Grodd, W., Goebel, R., & Birbaumer, N. (2003). Physiological self-regulation of regional brain activity using real-time functional magnetic resonance imaging (fMRI): Methodology and exemplary data. *Neuroimage*, 19(3), 577–586.

Wells, R., Outhred, T., Heathers, J. A., Quintana, D. S., & Kemp, A. H. (2012). Matter over mind: a randomised-controlled trial of single-session biofeedback training on performance anxiety and heart rate variability in musicians. *PloS ONE,* 7(10), e46597.

Williams A. M. (2000). Perceptual skill in soccer: implications for talent identification and development. *Journal of sports sciences*, *18*(9), 737–750. https://doi.org/10.1080/02640410050120113

Witte, M. (2015, November). With body and soul—A comparison of self-regulatory mechanisms required for neurofeedback in triathletes and healthy controls. In OHBM Alpine chapter symposium and 15th Austrian fMRI symposium.

Witte, M., Kober, S. E., Ninaus, M., Neuper, C., & Wood, G. (2013). Control beliefs can predict the ability to up-regulate sensorimotor rhythm during neurofeedback training. *Frontiers in Human Neuroscience,* 7, 478. https://doi.org/10.3389/fnhum.2013.00478

Xiong, S., Cheng, C., Wu, X., Guo, X., Yao, L., & Zhang, J. (2014). Working memory training using EEG neurofeedback in normal young adults. *Bio-medical Materials and Engineering*, 24(6), 3637–3644.

Zoefel, B., Huster, R. J., & Herrmann, C. S. (2011). Neurofeedback training of the upper alpha frequency band in EEG improves cognitive performance. *NeuroImage*, 54(2), 1427–1431.

Zuk, J., Benjamin, C., Kenyon, A., & Gaab, N. (2014). Behavioral and neural correlates of executive functioning in musicians and non-musicians. *PloS ONE*, 9(6), e99868.

Part 3

Implementing Mental Performance Training

10 Learning Environment

Systemic Approach

Silvia DeGirolamo, Claus Rønnow Pedersen, Jesper Corneliussen, Anders Kjærgaard, and Nathalie Pattyn

Introduction

The purpose of this chapter is to discuss the educational approach to mental performance enhancement. We will discuss education theories and principles of learning that could underpin the development and implementation of a human performance program, as well as explore the teaching techniques and contextual issues specific to operational learning environments (i.e., as opposed to schools, or other educational institutions). The purpose of discussing educational theory in relation to evidence-based mental performance training is to help practitioners and end-users understand how people attain, recall, and acquire pertinent knowledge (i.e., mental skills) so that mental performance programs are grounded in the evidence regarding how people learn.

Everyone has to some degree a theory about how they learn best. However, most educators and researchers on the science of learning have noticed a consistent disconnect between the beliefs of how one learns (a person's personal theories) and what the evidence suggests actually aids learning. Personal theories have the tendency to go awry through two mechanisms: first, individuals hold false beliefs about learning; and second, their metacognitions (a person's thoughts about their thoughts) can be inaccurate. This chapter seeks to join relevant education theories with an exploration of examples of teaching methods in mental performance. When developing mental performance training, combining evidence-based theories and processes layered with a nuanced understanding of specific operational environments will set up the learning environment for success.

Relevant educational theories and learning principles

There is no single education theory which practitioners should use. Rather, educational theory could be reconsidered as an umbrella term that covers many theories and assumptions of learning and retaining information that could influence practice. The following theories are not mutually exclusive. The reader is encouraged to pick and mix the elements that work well within their specific environments to make their programs as effective as possible.

Behaviourism

Behaviourism stems from the underlying principle that human behaviour is the result of conditioned responses to stimuli. From this perspective, human behaviour can be conditioned or shaped through varying techniques that modify the environment. This is specifically used in biofeedback for example, as is described in more detail in Chapter 9. According to behaviourist theorists (e.g.,

DOI: 10.4324/9781003378969-13

B.F. Skinner), people behave in specific ways to elicit a reward (reinforcement) or stop behaving to avoid a punishment. Behaviourism does not address how introspective skills (e.g., goal setting, imagery, self-talk) are acquired, retained, and integrated into habit.

Knowledge of behaviourist theory can be used to reinforce positive behaviour. For example, practitioners could reinforce and reward performers who devote time to practicing skills. Similarly, practitioners could punish negative behaviour. For example, undesirable behaviours observed during group-based practice, such as using personal electronic devices, could be punished. Evaluation, which is a key concept in any performance field, can serve as a positive reinforcement, guidance, or punishment/consequence pedagogy, depending on the situation. In its classic form, this concept has more or less disappeared in today's society, but it is still relevant in extreme learning environments, such as elite military units, where inadequate training and learning ultimately costs lives. Punishment or consequences are sometimes disguised in a strange – and sometimes – fun "extra training" to give the performance a positive, humorous, and educational spirit, while at the same time reflecting a deeper seriousness. It is important to recognize that timing of reinforcement and punishment can moderate the effect. Immediate reinforcement or punishment will have a greater influence on behaviour compared with the same reinforcement or punishment at a later time.

Social constructivism

Social constructivist theorists (e.g., Lev Vygotsky) state that social and cultural interactions play a prominent role in the learning process. Social constructivists believe that knowledge is co-constructed because individuals learn from one another, so the learning takes place in the relationship. When developing an evidence-based mental program, the concepts of "scaffolding" and the "zone of proximal development" can inform performers and practitioners about how they can leverage social and cultural interactions in the learning process.

Practitioners can use the "zone of proximal development" by creating a task or tasks that are too difficult for an individual to master alone. However, with the assistance of leaders or skilled peers, the task can be mastered. As an individual learns, the practitioner can extend the zone of proximal development by setting increasingly difficult tasks. The way in which peers or leaders provide assistance is labelled "scaffolding". Leaders, coaches, and practitioners can scaffold a performer's learning experience by recognizing and adapting how much assistance they provide and by considering whether the timing of assistance can facilitate learning. The zone of proximal development is a relevant analytical tool that can help to elucidate the development of new skills, and is viewed as the meeting between current and potential skills (Sanders & Welk 2005). For example in elite sports, this could describe the relationship between athletes and coaches in the selection phases, but also coach/athlete or athlete/athlete in regard to learning new skills while already performing at a higher level.

In the context of learning mental skills, social constructivism could manifest when performers work in pairs or small groups to develop skills. For example, when learning about adaptive self-talk (as described in Chapter 4) performers could interact and share examples of maladaptive self-talk, beneficial mantras, and times in which application of self-talk has been performance-enhancing. Hence, performers can learn different ideas from one another, they can assist one another, and they can co-construct knowledge.

Coaches and practitioners can intentionally pair novice performers with more experienced ones to help the novices work through their zone of proximal development and to promote the experienced practitioners deeper understanding of the concept. The strength of scaffolding when learning mental skills is that the language/experiences that peers use could be more recognizable and meaningful compared with potentially theoretically laden language that a practitioner might be tempted to use.

Apprenticeship

Apprenticeship could be considered a specific case of social constructivism. Anthropological studies have described the organization of work and the relationships that exist between the participating actors, especially between the master and the apprentice (Lave & Wenger, 1991, Nielsen 2008). Centrally in this perspective are the concepts of situated learning, communities of practice, and legitimate peripheral participation relevant (ibid.). The principles within situated learning arose out of the apprenticeship system that has existed for as long as there has been craftwork; it can be described as the fundamental anthropological-pedagogical form in which those who did not have particular skills learned from those who did.

Traditionally, apprenticeship relates to a given practice and implies that a subject/discipline is learned by working in a context where activity is not only directed towards the education of individuals, but also towards a professional production (Lave 1997, Lave & Wenger 1991). The Master, representing the subject's/discipline's tradition and values, has a natural interest in educating/teaching the apprentice as the survival of the specific community relies on the quality of the apprentice's performance level which ultimately ensures the legacy.

The situated learning perspective can be linked to particular performance contexts and the individual's involvement in this social community of practice, where participation initially is described as legitimate and peripheral and where learning takes place in a mutually interactive relationship. In this context, the novice gradually acquires values and knowledge for the purpose of full membership in the community of practice (ibid.). The peripheral participation is legitimate because the apprentice is accepted as part of the community, but peripheral because the apprentice has not yet mastered the art fully (ibid.). For example, in a military framework, this corresponds to the different phases of selection and basic training up to the final integration with peers. However, even here there will also be a difference among the operators. Newcomers arrive to an often already stable social hierarchy/culture where they, at the starting point, are located at the bottom. An operator comments metaphorically about this position and movement: "I think still we [new members] stand in the doorway looking in. It is not closed … You can see what's going on in there, and they say 'hi' when they pass the door … So, earlier it was just opened occasionally and was slammed again" (Kjaergaard & Pedersen, 2008).

Social-cognitive theory

Social-cognitive theorists (e.g., Albert Bandura) suggest that learning occurs through observing others (i.e., role models); however, learning might not occur immediately after the observation. Learning is an internal process that may or may not lead to a changes in behaviour.

In the context of learning mental skills, people set goals for themselves and direct their behaviour to achieve those goals (i.e., practice visualization). There is an implicit assumption that people are motivated to accomplish those goals. Specifically, the observer is motivated to learn the skills else he would not be observing role models that practice visualization. A key difference between social cognitive theory and earlier behaviourist theories lies in the fact that social-cognitive theorists suggest that behaviour eventually becomes self-regulated. Specifically, people ultimately regulate their own learning and behaviour rather than simply responding to reinforcement and feedback. For example, a musician who is learning a given skill might observe a role model, practice the skill on her own, compare her skills with those of the role model and then recognize in herself when skills are proficient or deficient. While reinforcement and punishment occupy a central role in behaviourist theories of learning, social-cognitive theorists state that punishment and reinforcement have an indirect effect on learning. Individuals form expectations about the probable consequences of future responses, based on how current responses are punished or reinforced. The same may also be true when observing punishment and reinforcement of other people.

From a social-cognitive perspective of learning, the individual performer could be motivated to learn when instructors, or peers, model a desired behaviour. In the context of mental performance programming, for example, in a corporate environment, if a trainer recognizes maladaptive opinions toward psychological development from the performer, he/she can use social-cognitive theory and leverage the potential power of salient role models.

High performers' competitive mindset and continuous focus on being "the best" thus gives learning through imitation a new dimension. Even in what looks like individual disciplines, e.g., chess, performers learn mutually from each other, which can be described as a sort of mini apprenticeship, where the less experienced performer on a particular topic can learn tips and tricks from a more experienced performer. Asked about this phenomenon, a special forces operator indicates: "Interviewer: Do you get something out of looking at the other operators when doing something? Operator: Definitely. When mistakes are made or when they're doing something well. If they make a mistake, then I can see what they are doing wrong, and then I think: I got this, which gives me confidence. If they perform well, then I'm inspired and take it with me. That might be if they have some cool procedures or some nice tricks or just the attitude or way they act" (Kjaergaard & Pedersen, 2008).

Spiral curricula

Jerome Bruner's (1960) spiral curriculum describes how practitioners can design learning experiences around central concepts, which are increased in complexity over time. These core concepts are encountered multiple times throughout the learning process. For instance, if a practitioner was to deliver mental skills training across three separate courses (i.e., beginner, intermediate, advanced) the same concepts would be included in each level of the course; however, the complexity in which skills are learned and applied could differ. New learning therefore has a relationship with old learning and is put in context with the old information. As is described in more detail in the section on "Psychoeducation", this is the approach to Human Factors training in aviation.

When adopting a spiral curriculum, the practitioner selects a fundamental concept that drives deeper understanding in the future. For example, when setting goals, it might be important to start with process and outcome goals. As performers acquire relevant knowledge, the practitioner can spiral the curriculum upward allowing the performer to acquire more advanced knowledge. The performer uses core knowledge of process and outcome goals to build deeper knowledge of other aspects of goal setting (e.g., moderators of the goal setting and performance relationship).

The potential benefits of adopting the spiral curriculum include the reinforcement of core concepts each time the learner revisits the subject. Next, the spiral curriculum permits a logical progression from simpler ideas to more nuanced and complex ideas. Finally, proponents of the spiral curriculum encourage learners to apply knowledge gained in early learning to later learning (i.e., beginner to advanced).

Educational taxonomies

Educational taxonomies are typically sets of educational objectives/outcomes. A prominent example of educational taxonomy is Bloom's (1956) taxonomy, that classifies educational objectives into levels of complexity and specificity in cognitive, affective, and sensory domains.

The utility of any educational taxonomy in the context of evidence-based mental performance training is that the taxonomy can provide both the practitioners and the performer with clear objectives, so that both parties understand the purpose of the educational interchange. For example, Bloom's cognitive taxonomy consists of six objectives, namely knowledge, comprehension, application, analysis, synthesis, and evaluation. The taxonomy is usually presented as a hierarchy, where an understanding of the objective proximal to the base is a precondition for applying a more distal objective. For example, knowledge is required before one can demonstrate comprehension.

Bloom's (1956) taxonomy is not the only education taxonomy that practitioners can apply when developing mental programs. For example, practitioners can adopt the SOLO taxonomy (Biggs & Collins, 2014), which stands for the "Structure of the Observed Learning Outcome", to classify learning outcomes in terms of their complexity. The SOLO taxonomy provides levels of learning in relation to what learners understand. The first level of understanding is labelled "unstructured", where learners acquire one or few aspects of the task. For example, when learning imagery, the performer may pick up the need for relaxation prior to imagery practice, or follow a simple procedure. The next level, labelled "multi-structural", involves understanding several aspects of a task. For example, when learning imagery, the learner may be able to combine sets of procedures into one practice. The next phase, labelled "relational" involves integration of understanding. For example, the learner can apply what they have learned into a novel task or justify a given practice to a novice performer. Finally, the "extended abstract phase" permits the learner to generalize learning to as yet untaught applications. For example, a learner may develop the capacity to theorize and hypothesize how his peers could improve imagery skills.

Overall, taxonomies aim to make the incremental and iterative character of knowledge and skill acquisition explicit, in order for this process to be consciously used and applied by teachers and instructors.

Experiential learning

Lave and Wenger (1991) refer to learning as a change in the relationship between the learner and the organization/community practice. This concept describes a subject's participation in an action system where participants share a common understanding of what they do, and what it means for their lives and for the community. The primary focus is the psycho-constructive formation or modelling of a particular person, shaped by participation in a particular social community (ibid.).

Experiential learning involves learning by doing and then reflecting on the process. Experiential learning theorists, including Dewey, Lewin, and Piaget, maintained that learning is most effective and most likely to lead to change when it begins with experience. Experiential education is based on the belief that active learning is more valuable for the learner because they are directly responsible for, and involved in the process. Proponents of this approach believe that learning is a result of direct experience, and includes the premise that people learn best when they have multiple senses actively involved in the learning experience. Individuals learn when placed outside their comfort zones (i.e., the zone of proximal development: see social constructivism) and into a state of dissonance. This also implies that learning is not a pleasant experience at all times, since it requires a level of discomfort. Learning is then assumed to occur through the changes required to bring the individual back into balance and achieve personal equilibrium. Most theories of experiential learning use reflective practice to transfer the experience into declarative knowledge. For example, Schön (1987) presented a theory of reflective practice as a method of learning that emphasized experiences and connecting with one's feelings.

Schön's theory of experiential learning centres on the construction of domain specific knowledge, through the context of professional practice (i.e., learning via personal experiences). Schön suggested that people learn in two different ways. Firstly, people gain knowledge through what he called reflection in action. Reflection in action, also known as thinking on your feet, involves developing new understandings to inform our actions in the situation that is unfolding. When individuals go about the spontaneous, intuitive performance of actions of everyday life, they demonstrate specific knowledge. However, often this knowledge cannot be articulated; individuals cannot say what they know, they do what they know (i.e., knowledge is in action). For example, a violist will be able to coordinate the multiple bodily movements involved in playing to perfection, whilst timing her breathing and integrating the instructions of the conductor. However, it is unlikely that this performer would be able to articulate how they did this, the timing, coordination, and interplay of skills and knowledge required to achieve this result. It might be that people learn mental skills through experience (e.g., learning self-talk through spontaneous experience), which are then refined through guided reflection. The individual restructures their understanding of the situation and invents new strategies of action. New strategies are then tried out as and when similar situations present themselves.

A different but similar form of experiential learning happens when training of a skill emphasizes transfer of appropriate processing. Specifically, the type of cognitive processing utilized during skills practice should match the way the skill is used after training. Here, the training environment should mimic the real-world experience of the learners as closely as possible so that performers "practice how they play".

Transition from novice to expert

Expertise requires time, practice, and possibly even the right combination of genetic factors (Ullen, Hambrick, & Mosing, 2016) to develop. In fact, evidence suggests that most individuals never reach expert status even though they may have achieved a high level of proficiency in a particular functional domain (Ericsson, 2006; Swanson, O'Connor, & Cooney, 1990).

It is increasingly recognized that expertise reflects more than procedural proficiency. Numerous studies have shown that experts, in contrast with novice learners, exhibit greater fluency, automaticity, and insight in their performance. (Kellerman & Krasne, 2018). Higher order perceptual skills are a key factor in the development of expert levels of performance, allowing the performer to more easily recognize challenges and threats in an evolving situation, without devoting undue cognitive resources to the task (Lerner, et al., 2017). Experts also have a robust network of information, developed over time through practice and experience, from which they can draw. The depth and breadth of their knowledge base influences not only what they perceive in the environment (they perceive more than novice learners), but also how they organize, manipulate, and interpret that information. Indeed, brain imaging studies have suggested that performance at an expert level involves far greater efficiency in complex neural processes than is seen in novice performers. In particular, the cerebellum appears to play a key role in automating and coordinating planning and control of complex movements and operations by integrating sensorimotor inputs (Kim, et al., 2014; Callan & Naito, 2014).

Development of expertise occurs over a series of stages – one cannot move from novice to expert directly. Dreyfus and Dreyfus (2005) describe this process as occurring in five stages: novice, advanced beginner, competent, proficient, and expert. The novice memorizes facts and acquires foundational knowledge, "the Basics", that provide the framework within which further learning can occur. Novice learners are, fundamentally, only able and responsible for following the clearly defined processes and the rules set for them. Advanced beginners, through continued experience, begin to learn heuristics (rules of thumb) to aid performance, leading to increasing automaticity. Information critical to task performance requires less effort to retrieve but formation of linkages between knowledge points still requires outside guidance from more experienced individuals. Competence is achieved through continued experience and is demonstrated through even greater levels of autonomy in day-to-day performance, more independence of thinking and planning, and a broadening of perspective to encompass an expanding range of contingencies. Individuals who reach the proficient stage exhibit greater confidence in their day-to-day actions, feel more accountable for their performance outcomes, and begin to lean on intuitions as a guide for planning and taking action. Proficient operators routinely use intuition to guide decision-making, and are better able to see patterns and deviations from these patterns in their environments (what is normal and what is not normal). Proficient operators have a more highly refined sense of relevance, filtering out irrelevant information more quickly and accurately than less experienced individuals. Expertise in this model is characterized by an intuitive, adaptive thinking style that does not require strict adherence to rules or guidelines. Experts respond more quickly and accurately than those with less experience, drawing from a wealth of information gleaned from experience. They are able to better anticipate problems and respond to them appropriately, with greater efficiency.

As suggested above, moving from novice to expert requires practice. Specifically, Ericsson and colleagues (Ericsson, Krampe, & Tesch-Romer, 1993) note that deliberative practice is central to the transition from novice to expert. Deliberative practice involves the presentation of progressively more complex and challenging problem sets that the learner must work through and master before moving to even more challenging tasks. From this perspective, it is not simply the amount of time spent in practice, but also the quality of that practice, for example, its relevance or applicability to the particular skill being fostered, that determines progression from novice to expert (Kuhlmann & Ardichvili, 2015). Moreover, experts have developed an extensive network of information that is well organized, contextualized based on sets of circumstances, and highly integrated. In contrast, less experienced individuals tend to retain lists of isolated facts and procedural steps tied to specific contexts, requiring more time and effort to access and sort through in order to answer a question or reach a decision point. Experience over time and under varied circumstances helps to decontextualize knowledge, linking pieces of information in memory to more generalized circumstances, making it easier to access and apply to novel conditions or problems. Experts also are more proficient in identifying features and patterns in the environment or decision space more easily than novices. They detect nuances more readily than novice learners and are better able to perceive relationships between features that can more accurately define the situation and its constraints (Persky & Robinson, 2017).

Advances in learning theory and sciences have offered new avenues for improving instructional approaches and accelerating learning on many complex tasks, offering some potential for moving performers from novice to proficient or even expert more efficiently and effectively. Specifically, techniques such as perceptual learning (PL), particularly when coupled with adaptive learning technologies, have become increasingly popular (Kellerman & Krasne, 2018), in part because such approaches target skills that support diverse higher order cognitive process and are trainable. Perceptual learning refers to persistent changes in perception that come about as a function of one's experiences or practice (see Gibson, 1963). Adaptive learning, which, like deliberative practice described above, tune training objectives and challenge to a learner's current functional level, gradually increasing the level of difficulty or challenge as the learner becomes more proficient. These approaches are deeply rooted in behavioural and cognitive psychology and have been used by NASA and the US Army to aid simulation training and education more broadly. Procedural learning approaches aimed at enhancing perceptual process have been successfully applied to enhance aviation (Kellerman & Kaiser, 1994), medicine (Kellerman, 2013), and mathematics (Massey, Kellerman, Roth, & Burke, 2013) instruction.

Learning as transformation of self-identity

Learning means that you become another person in relation to the opportunities provided by these relation systems, hence learning involves construction of self-identity (Lave and Wenger, 1991). The new self-concept gradually occurs in relation to acquiring skills, knowledge and values and culminates with an unconditional sense of belonging to the community of practice. The identity change is also an indication that the performer is simultaneously approved by the community for possessing the attitudes and qualities that are appropriate for that particular sub-culture. Usually, in high-performance domains, 'apprenticeship' is, in comparison with other crafts, clearly defined and directly measurable; the requirements therefore are indisputable. If an athlete after x number of months/years of training cannot break through a given level of competition, they will not be allowed to continue with the training as part of a national team. However, there may also be a case where the athlete, in spite of being able to master the craft, does not fit in socially into the existing community, which ultimately often ends in an exclusion/exit from the framework.

In the context of mental performance training, a performer that holds an identity that is tied to the practice of mental skills is more likely to adopt mental skills practice through habit rather than through planning or goal setting. In a similar vein, a person who identifies as a runner is more likely to go for a run compared with someone who is motivated to run as a means to an end (i.e., weight loss). In the later example, the act of running requires greater regulation of potentially detrimental cognitions (i.e., it's raining, I don't like running in the rain) compared with someone whose identity is tied to being a runner. Practitioners can foster a sense of social and self-identity that is coherent with the practice of mental skills.

"In Order to Be [some Identity], one must act like [some Identity] [...]" (Burke & Reitzes 1981: 90). It is an interesting process when this identification and identity change unfold, as training progresses and new learning is required. For most performers, there will often be a strong identification with the training if "one of their own" works as co-facilitator, because that person represents the standards, working methods, etc. they observe in the system. In the sports world, this is exemplified by the number of athletes who become coaches, in the elite military units instructional functions are only available to former members. This is quite typical in an expert culture that a person internal in the system approves of you, or approves what has to be learned. Then it is ensured that the "inheritance" goes as planned, which is (also) what it is all about.

Process of teaching the content

There are several aspects of the process of teaching mental performance training to consider once the theoretical underpinning of a program is determined. There are many options for teaching modalities, which may be used solely or in combination with other approaches to teaching, many of which are presented in this section and all of which should be considered from a background of the specificities of one's learning environment. Be it for athletes, musicians, corporate executives, special operations operators, astronauts, or jet fighter pilots: specific factors to their performance environments should also be considered when developing programming in order to optimize the learning environment. Several examples of such approaches are discussed in Chapter 11 (team performance) and in the various implementation chapters.

Relevant instructional methods

Education and instruction can be provided through the use of a variety of modalities. Intuitively, individual one-to-one tutoring and training seems a more effective instructional modality than large group education. A series of studies reported on by Bloom (1984) supports this – in a series of elementary school experiments, individual tutoring was two standard deviations more effective for final achievement of students than the more typical class of 30 students per teacher. However, one-to-one tutoring comes at a high resourcing cost. Bloom posed the 2 Sigma problem – what group methods for education could achieve the same results as individual tutoring?

Research into mental skills performance training may not necessarily have the answer to Bloom's question yet, though likely the answer is not as simple as a choice between either group or one-to-one tutoring and may instead be a matter of "it depends". Particular training goals may be better targeted by certain types of instructional modalities. Mental performance program developers, trainers, and their broader organizations will be limited by constraints such as resourcing and time. Additionally, the speed with which technology is advancing has added delivery options never previously available. In this section, specific approaches and examples of instructional modalities are discussed. The reader is also directed to the various implementation chapters in different environments for further discussion of issues to consider when developing and implementing a mental performance training program.

Group vs. individual education

The question of whether to utilize either a group or an individual approach to mental performance training is likely one of the first asked when formalizing a training program and each option has their advantages. Group training is scalable, convenient, and makes most efficient use of resources. And, as noted above, in some contexts (e.g., military) the organization tends to emphasize training of collectives in the form of crews, groups, teams, and units (Fletcher and Chatelier, 2000). Yet, as Bloom (1984) noted long ago, individual one-to-one training can be far more effective in achieving learning outcomes. Additionally, there is a growing body of research regarding the impact of individual differences in baseline performance, motivation, expectations, and responsivity to cognitive training (Blacker, et. al., 2019). As Blacker and colleagues note, a particular challenge of collective training within special forces is the potential for homogeneity. The physical and mental requirements for entry to special operations units are extreme and may result in competencies within the group that are more homogeneous then in other environments.

McCrory, Cobley, and Marchant (2013) describe the use of an individual training approach, developing a multi-modal psychological skills training aimed at improving self-regulation behaviour, self-efficacy, and psychological skill use in 40 military trainee pilots going through remediation training. Pilots had eight to ten hours of one-to-one mentorship over the course of 10 days, supported by a psychological skills training workbook, and supplemented with approximately two hours of intervention training sessions, concurrent with their flight remediation training course. Upon completion of the individual training, participants demonstrated increased self-regulation behaviour, increased self-efficacy and psychological skill use, and reduced anxiety and worry, with changes retained at two-month follow-up.

The Special Operations Mental Agility (SOMA) program is a customized evidence-based mental skills training package developed specifically for the Canadian Special Forces Command (CANSOFCOM) that utilizes, amongst many other components, a group classroom-based training. This enables trainers to harness the impact of peer-to-peer interaction through group discussion, peer-to-peer feedback, and shared experience, as well as for co-facilitators (trained CANSOFCOM members) to present content and share personal experiences. Training groups are moderately sized (between 20 and 40 participants) and include individuals from similar roles within the organization/units to foster individual familiarity and comfort, thereby promoting discussion and disclosure. The program is deserving of description beyond the scope of this section and the reader is directed to Mattie, Jaenen, and Collins (2017), for an in-depth description, as well as to Mattie, Guest, Bailey, Collins, and Gucciardi (2020) for a comprehensive review of the program's robust and evidence-based development process.

There are many additional questions to consider in choosing a target audience for a group training program. For instance, are there aspects of the training that might be impacted by issues of hierarchy or social status? Would athletes who compete against each other be equally as comfortable with disclosure and discussion in the group training? Are the mental performance skills readily transferrable across multiple job types (e.g., different musicians) and effectively presented in a group setting, or would training be more effective if provided to a particular subset? Is the target audience a team who regularly work together (see also Chapter 11 regarding team performance training)? What range of group sizes are typical in this environment, and that in which the audience would most readily absorb knowledge? What is the timing of the training that will maximize group participation and knowledge absorption within the training or usual working cycle?

There may not be a single "right" answer to the question of group vs. individual-based training, but instead the answer will lie in the specific goals, resources, and constraints involved in any given performance environment.

Self-directed learning

Self-directed learning, one in which learners are in control of the information they experience by way of their ongoing decisions (Gureckis and Markant, 2012), has been a learning path for as long as humans have been curious to understand the world around them better. This personal endeavour, the tools for which are increasingly at one's fingertips with the digital transformation, places an emphasis on the learner's inherent needs, wants, and desires to learn rather than a formalized structured or pre-determined curriculum. The learner is able to focus their effort on chosen information they do not yet possess, while also gaining exposure to new information. As this is an active process, the learner is able to encode and retain information better over time. Gureckis and Markant (2012) provide a synthesis of the research on self-directed learning from both cognitive and computational perspectives. As an example of relevance in sports, Culver, Kraft, Din, and Cayer (2019) described a Canadian intervention to address the lack of women in sport coaching and leadership, and offered that female coaches in their program more highly valued self-directed education over passive coaching instruction. The coaches had to be actively engaged in the teaching and learning process to maximize their zone of proximal development, resulting in increased confidence and quality of coaching. Applying this example to mental performance training in other settings, it can be readily imagined that typical high-performing personnel (e.g., conscientious, achievement striving) would have the interest, experience, and motivation to effectively utilize a self-directed mental performance package.

Classroom-based education

Classroom-based education, typically associated with a group training method, can be effective in impacting performance. Barwood, Dalzell, Datta, Thelwell, and Tipton (2006) trained psychological skills over the course of four one-hour sessions on separate days with the goal of improving maximum underwater breath hold in cold water submersion – an important skill/ability for those at risk of finding themselves inverted in the water, such as helicopter pilots. Subjects were instructed in goal setting, arousal regulation, mental imagery, and positive self-talk with the goal of helping them tolerate, and therefore suppress, the respiratory response associated with cold water immersion. Results indicated an 80% increase in maximum voluntary breath hold between the pre- and post-test cold water immersions. Increasing maximum breath hold while underwater can improve the chances of survival following accidental immersion, for instance after an over-water helicopter incident. The reader is also reminded of the Special Operations Mental Agility (SOMA) program described above (Mattie, Jaenen, and Collins, 2017) as another example of effective classroom-based education. It is important to note that even, or especially, within a classroom setting, engaging multiple training modalities (i.e., applied practice, reflection, small and large group discussion) will improve the effectiveness of training (see Knowles, Holton, Swanson, and Robinson, 2020, for an in-depth review of best practices in adult education).

Field-based training

A widely utilized strategy to improve cultural understanding, build credibility, facilitate training or treatment objectives, and foster relationships with performers is to embed with them to some degree. This may be as simple as having one's office in their space rather than a standalone clinic area, or as involved as joining them on trainings and travels abroad (competitions, performances, military deployments). This placement will facilitate access to performers and their schedules in order to be invited to and coordinate training. Applying conceptual knowledge from the classroom, such as mental skills training, to realistic training environments is a codified aspect of military training (U.S. Department of Defense, 2001). There are a variety of opportunities to a weave in mental skills training into existing training exercises, though this may take some creativity by the trainer and a great deal of trust and buy-in by the performers. In the sports world, most nations have implemented this approach through overarching "Sports Institutes" or "Olympic training centres", where trainers and all specialists are available, working side by side with athletes to enhance the quality of the support, and ultimately, of athletic results.

Ideally, field-based training provides the occasion for knowledge application in a supervised, structured, and graduated manner, such as in the evidence-based mental skills training protocol for US Army Infantry Soldiers developed by DeWiggins, Hite, and Alston (2010). Following acquisition of concepts, tools, and techniques in the classroom, as well as development of their Personal Performance Plans (PPP), soldiers went into the field and practiced their PPPs in more realistic surroundings, first slowly and with feedback until standards were met. They then trained to "combat speed" focusing on "full integration of mental tools and skills with physical, technical, and tactical elements...Through multiple practice iterations, execution of the PPP becomes instinctual and reactive" (p. 464). With this training protocol, DeWiggins and colleagues demonstrated a deliberate, applicable, evidence-based approach to field-based training.

Digital platforms

The COVID pandemic has been an exceptional driver of digital technology utilized in instructional capacities. Engagement of digital platforms in the realm of mental performance training can offer a scalable solution to the higher cost, geographical spread, and more limitedly available one-to-one or in-person facilitator/instructor model while still remaining customizable and dynamic.

A growing amount of data over the years has allowed for meta-analytic techniques to assess the effectiveness of computer-assisted instruction (CAI). Fletcher (2009) notes that CAI, when compared with standard classroom learning in military, academic, and industry sectors, reduced the time taken to learn by 24–54%. Translating to dollars saved (2009 dollars at the time of that publication), a 30% reduction in time needed to learn would save the US Department of Defense (DOD) 15–25% of the $4–5 billion spent annually for specialized skill training. Currently, military-developed CAI tends to emphasize portability (allowing digital learning objects to operate across various computer systems) and reusability (on-demand instruction and performance aids). Mental performance training and interventions have utilized CAI in various ways.

Distance learning models offer web-based training, video conferencing, and other non in-person training avenues. However, as cautioned by Salas and Canon-Bowers (2001), these are not always developed from scientific principles or data. Distance learning and CAI offer the opportunity for the trainee to flexibly find time in their "white space" to complete training, rather than having to adhere to rigid or structured scheduling requirements. One of the dangers of computer-assisted instruction becomes the overreliance on minimally guided approaches to the detriment, or outright removal of, direct instructional support. Vogel-Walcutt and colleagues (2013) reviewed the relevant literature on instructional strategies and provide a coherent framework for selecting instructional strategies based on specific military training environment characteristics.

Simulators and simulation-based training are becoming ever more widely utilized, particularly in high-consequence activities. Simulation is an instructional technique to represent the visual, auditory, olfactory, and haptic sensations of the real-life context where any particular skill (e.g., piloting) needs to be conducted. While CAI focuses on teaching, simulation focuses on learning through "real-world" interactive experience. The use of simulation-based training can reduce cost while increasing safety and reproducibility of events. Training can range in cost, fidelity, and functionality (Salas & Cannon-Bowers, 2001). An often cited example of simulation-based training is with the complex task of military aircraft operation. Military pilots must engage abilities related to processing stimuli, attention prioritization, plan adherence, motor control movements, navigation, calculation adjustments based on environmental factors, and avoidance of lethal attacks that can come from anywhere. Simulation-based training can connect trainees (simulators) with simulations virtually anywhere around the world to combine individual training with collective (crew, team, unit) training.

Gaining in applicability and usability are mixed reality platforms, specifically Virtual Reality (VR) and Augmented Reality (AR). VR immerses people in experiences with tools such as headsets or gloves, while AR usually starts with a real-life view of something and projects or inserts images onto a screen. VR creates simulations meant to shut out the real world and fully immerse the viewer. AR inserts or lays over content into the real world using a device like a smartphone or glasses. The exponential growth of the use of augmented/virtual reality, often with little to no evidence base, illustrates the "tech-hungry" aspect of high-performance environments.

However, there are a number of examples of mixed reality mental skill training programs leveraging evidence-based techniques and strategies. In a systematic review of the literature covering the years 2001 to 2016, Pallavicini et al. (2016) found 14 experimental studies testing the effectiveness of virtual reality-based Stress Management Training (SMT) programs within military settings. Their three main observations were (1) VR-based SMT can be effective in training improved management of emotional and psychological responses in high stress situations, thereby maintaining operational performance; (2) VR may be a tool to assess individual responses to stressors and correlated task performance, thereby potentially enabling identification during the selection process for selectively manned military assignments; and (3) combining VR with arousal reduction strategies can increase resilience to stress in military members. The reader is directed to their article for a cogent and comprehensive review of those studies including limitations of such.

There are several intriguing lines of effort being advanced by the Cognitive Fitness Framework (CF2) Foundation (www.cf2foundation.com/), a consortium of sports performance experts in collaboration with the Australian Defence Force developing military-focused mental performance research and training. The reader is directed to a comprehensive review of the Cognitive Fitness Framework hypothesis by Dr. Eugene Aidman (2020), a summary of which is beyond the scope of this chapter. However, one of their areas of development is training mental performance skills to military members within the digital environment. Performance Edge VR is a virtual reality-based stress management training tool (Kluge et. al., 2021). The initial prototype utilizes controlled breathing training and integrated respiratory biofeedback though they plan to develop eight mental performance training modules based upon their BattleSMART stress management and resilience training package delivered in a VR environment. Different from many current VR options, Performance Edge VR provides ongoing instruction and feedback, escalating exercises to challenge the user in specific skills development that is then practiced during the stress scenarios.

Another area of potential advancement from CF2 Foundation is adapting "free-roam" VR (FRVR) technology developed by Zero Latency and incorporating bio-markers in the training of military members (Nalivaiko et al., 2018). While VR setups are "tethered" – users remain seated and attached to a device – FRVR allows users to physically move around a space thereby providing a more immersive and engaging training environment with potential higher stress levels. During the pilot study, eight infantry soldiers were split into teams and given the tactical task of clearing several rooms within a simulated house. Participants could see each other's avatars as well as simulated enemy and civilian avatars. Each "run" over the course of five days was made more stressful and complex by changing the number of enemy and civilian avatars within the rooms and/

or by triggering simulated IED explosions. Despite the limited number of study participants, perhaps one of the most compelling aspects of this study was the reproducible and robust cardiac and respiratory responses of the participants within the FRVR environment – an effect not previously as consistent or strong in other VR studies. This may have significant future training applications. Additionally, there was initial evidence of efficacy of FRVR as a stress inoculation intervention given the repetition of FRVR training over the course of the study resulted in a substantial reduction of cardiac and respiratory responses in most participants.

As the use of these digital platforms has grown, so too has the use of "gamification", or motivational features, within these platforms to increase participant engagement, which can lead to greater enjoyment, persistence through difficult tasks, and eventually better training performance. However, there is also the danger of having too many game design features that then become more distraction than facilitator. Mohammed et al. (2017) provide a thorough review of the utility and limitations of implementing various game elements into mental performance training approaches.

Death by PowerPoint

Roediger, Nestojko, and Smith (2019) stated that PowerPoint and similar applications are used inappropriately in training scenarios. Specifically, Roediger et al. (2019) stated that slides decks are distributed to learners so that they can go through the educational material ad nauseam. However, in practice, learners do not learn the material, rather they demonstrate illusions of learning through the capacity to recall information in the short term. The use of "PowerPoint Karaoke" is also unlikely to help learners retain information. The "PowerPoint Karaoke" practitioner uses the slide deck as an autocue and simply reads what he or she sees. If the learner listens to the same karaoke track several times (i.e., through lecture recording software or a personal recording device) they might gain a sense of comprehension (due to familiarity with the content) but it would be unlikely that the learner can retrieve information, hypothesize, and theorize when needed. Unfortunately, the retention of information is transient and often this type of learning is all too quickly lost. Rather than using PowerPoint, charge people up with information. Roediger at al. recommend helping learning "stick" by asking learners to retrieve information on the fly. That is, practitioners can stimulate the learning of material by quizzing learners and putting them in practical situations where the learner needs to use the information they have learned.

Multi-modal teaching approach

A multi-modal approach to teaching can incorporate a variety of methods in a variety of combinations. Care should be taken to develop programs and interventions from an evidence-based approach, informed by effective service delivery models (for further information, depending on the performance field, we refer to the various implementation chapters). The following are some examples of multi-modal approaches.

As will be described in more detail later in this chapter, Staszewski and Davison (2000) provided expert landmine detection instruction, skill-based practice, and feedback in a controlled facility specially designed for their project. Though the training was physically situated in a specially designed facility, multiple learning methods were engaged. In their case example presented earlier in this chapter, Dewiggins et al. (2010) discuss the need to incorporate application of conceptual knowledge to realistic settings. In general, a three phased approach typically includes education under minimally stressful conditions, an intermediate phase wherein relevant stressors are added for more realistic expectations about field conditions, and then exposure to realistic stressors that approximate the actual environment (e.g., live fire). In the Dewiggins et al. Personal Performance Plan (PPP) model, they first educated participants in a classroom setting on core mental training.

Soldiers translated the concepts to actual tools and techniques by practicing them during each phase of a military task, with the aid of a workbook, guided instruction, and feedback. They then went into the field to practice their plans in more realistic surroundings and slow rehearsals, finally working themselves to "combat speed" during a realistic field exercise. As a final example, the holistic Cognitive Fitness Framework described by Aidman (2020) offers a hypothesized sequence for cognitive training that would encompass a diverse array of mental performance training, monitoring, and recovery to improve real-time task performance and career longevity in high-risk/high-demand occupations (clearly relevant to a military population, but also for example for medical first responders). These are but a few examples of the creative, and evidence-based, ways in which a variety of mental skills training methods and skills can be joined together for optimum training.

Training frequency and skill maintenance

An important and well established finding in the literature is the effect of testing (Rowland, 2014). When individuals study for an exam they often focus on reviewing the material by rereading their notes, the textbook, and highlighting important sections. However, testing an individual's knowledge is actually more effective for learning that information than restudying the material – called the "testing effect" in the literature (Endres & Renkl, 2015, Batsell, Perry, Hanley, & Hostetter, 2017, Kromann, Bohnstedt, Jensen, & Ringsted, 2010). Testing requires the retrieval of information from memory. This act of retrieval does two things, the first is to reinforce the memory for that information, which will make it more likely to be retained over time. Second, it is an effective monitoring process for an individual's learning level (Fernandez & Jamet, 2017). This was mentioned briefly in the introduction when an individual's metacognitive assessment of their own learning was described. Individuals can make errors in their metacognitive assessment, falsely thinking that their feeling of familiarity (thinking "I've read this before; therefore, I know this") instead of asking themselves, "Do I understand this enough that I could explain it to someone else?" For example, learning can and does start in a classroom environment covering the appropriate procedures and process but it rapidly moves outside the classroom to the training floor where procedures are practiced and tested both for conceptual understanding but also through physical demonstration of skills. Importantly this physical demonstration is evaluated, and feedback given. Instructors are interested in "perfect practice" so that individuals learn the proper procedure rather than forming incorrect habits that require remedial training. Even students are expected to be able to analyze operational performance to detect errors in their peers when instructors are not around. The evaluative question here is "have I achieved a degree of skill acquisition that I can produce this procedure accurately under both slow and fast response conditions?" For example, law enforcement environments, and particularly for counterterrorism work, demand speed but an even greater demand is for accuracy. In cognitive psychology performance is considered to be a function of the speed and accuracy trade-off (which is described in Chapter 2); however, within a live-fire training environment students are not allowed to have speed until they can demonstrate accuracy. Fully trained expert operators have developed the metacognitive assessment skills to assess their degree of accuracy at a given speed and calibrate accordingly. Fast and dangerous is not permitted for the safety of the team and the objective.

Another consequence of testing seen from another lens is spaced learning (for a review see Cepeda, Pashler, Vul, Wixted, & Rohrer, 2006). For comparison purposes we consider massed (concentrated) learning versus the same volume of information exposure, but spread out over a longer period. In a traditional university course, students would be taught the material, tested on the midterm and then retested on the final exam. Professors would prefer that students read their assigned reading before class (exposure 1), attend class (exposure 2), study by reading (exposure 3), completing practice tests (exposure 4), completing the midterm (exposure 5), and repeating the process for the final exam (study, practice test, and exam exposures 6, 7, and 8). What we see here is the maximal repeated exposure to course material over the course of a semester. Each repeated processing and retrieval of the information from memory makes the material more likely to be retained and increases the integration of the information into the rest of the student's knowledge. Now university professors understand that not all students will study as thoroughly as outlined here, however, by virtue of the multiple exams in this hypothetical course, instructors ensure students have multiple exposures to the material.

Training courses often include multiple assessments prior to a final assessment. Safety procedures are constantly repeated and reinforced both during a course and during regular professional life in the form of safety briefings prior to an exercise (in military environments, aviation, first responders, etc.). These repetitions all fall within this principle of repeated information exposure to reinforce information and skills.

Potential future learning environment

There are a broad range of possibilities for the future of the learning environment, both in general as well as specifically applied to mental performance training. Schatz et al. (2015) offer a bold, innovative, and sweeping vision of the future of the military learning environment, one that is "an integrated continuum of formal and informal training, education, and operational experience." They posit five enabling conditions necessary for this vision to become a reality, which will be briefly summarized here, though the reader is strongly encouraged to review the original text for a full appreciation of this comprehensive redesign of military learning.

1. Cultivate ubiquitous learner-centric, technology-enabled instruction
2. Build upon the foundations of data-driven learning
3. Foster a learning culture at the organizational level
4. Encourage and empower social learning
5. Draw upon learning science deliberate practices and its body-of-knowledge

They define ubiquitous learning as a "learning context that is pervasive, omnipresent, and transparent", integrating formal and informal learning with more formal modes of instruction. Distinctions blur between training and education, between personal development and operational development. "Operational decision support systems become learning and assessment systems (and vice versa), and all of these technologies also become sensors for detecting context, performance, and tracking lessons learned." Much of learning becomes "continuous, timely, and expressly relevant to each learner's tasks, state, and situation." Mental performance is necessarily woven into this space.

Ubiquitous learning would require extensive performance measurements and evaluations – "data-driven learning enables real-time adaptations, whether in an instructional or operational context…and it will enable organizational adaptability at higher levels." The capture of massive amounts of human performance data, use of performance-sensing technologies, expanded measures, competency-based learning, and traceability of data through layers of the organization (individual readiness as well as prediction of team, collective, or institution level readiness) would all push the system towards data-driven learning. Learning organizations "continuously transform themselves to maintain relevance within changing conditions, respond nimbly to the newest threats, and capitalize upon emerging opportunities" – a great fit for high-performance cultures. Schatz et al. point to literature that indicates organizations with stronger learning cultures outperform peers in employee productivity, response to customer needs, and possessing skills to meet future demands. These outcomes are driven by efficiency, responsiveness, and anticipation – each of which are highly valued high performers.

Social learning serves to augment formally created, or top-down, content. “Individuals need spaces and resources that enable them to engage with one another, to share knowledge peer-to-peer (or bottom- to-top), to co-create meaning, probe new ideas, and create shared narratives.” Social learning already occurs at various levels, as we already discussed in a previous paragraph. Effectively incorporating learning science elements regarding how people learn and how to enhance that learning will function to optimize the learning environment.

Schatz and colleagues admit that they put forth “a big idea” in their vision for the future of the military learning environment. However, even if the fruition of this potential integrated learning and operational space is unlikely to happen soon, it is easier to see that elements are on their way to being actualized. Given the ways in which this vision dovetails with high-performance culture and values, mental performance consultants may consider how to incorporate components into their programming.

Psychoeducation: when the content and the process meet

Overview and relevance

Psychoeducation refers to the process of providing information about psychological processes and skills. Originally the term was used primarily in the context of mental health, however the use of the term has evolved to include any intervention where the primary purpose is to educate and empower through knowledge. Psychoeducation can cover a broad range of topics and is often the basis of further interventions.

In the aviation community, or in the military, the need for training operators on the systems they use would never be questioned, however it has been noted that there are relatively less resources devoted to educating operators in the function of their own executive system – their brain. Practical training in weapons and tactics (for example) involve theoretical and practical applications leading up to real-time, full mission profile activities. This same approach can be applied to education in how human works as a system. This education in the function and limits of the human system is often termed “Psychoeducation”. The aviation world was a pioneer in the field, with courses in “Human performance and limitations” being made mandatory for flight crew licensing as early as 1989 (International Civil Aviation Organization). The rationale behind this approach was that human error has been known for decades as a major cause in over 70% of accidents, and it is widely agreed that a better understanding of human capabilities and limitations – both physical and psychological – would help reduce human error and improve flight safety. This training encompassed components of theoretical knowledge, practical applications, and scenarios adapted to operational settings.

Optimal human performance is not a component of knowledge, it requires self-insight, and thus needs to be applied and practiced as a skill set. It is anticipated that a component of psychoeducation will form the basis of most programs aimed to optimize human performance. In high-performance domains, psychoeducation can be viewed as the process of educating performers on the effects of stress and strain on performance, the constraints and limitations of the human system (e.g., error and decision-making, or sleep and fatigue), techniques for either avoiding or mitigating vulnerabilities, and promoting positive outcomes. High performers across domains usually have high levels of autonomy and initiative, and subsequently could be expected to benefit from programs that empower them to adapt various methods and techniques to suit their individual preferences and specific environment.

Psychoeducation as a performance-enhancing tool

The concept of psycho-education has been around since 1911 (Donley, 1911), however the word itself began being used in clinical settings as from 1941 (Tomlinson, 1941) and became widespread during the 1980s (Anderson, Hogarty & Reiss, 1980). Since this time, psychoeducation has evolved into interventions and programs focusing on effective communication of key information, generally within a cognitive-behavioural framework. Themes of empowerment and coping through improving understanding were proposed by Bauml and colleagues, who developed a model incorporating communication of a basic level of information, with additional elements that could build upon this foundation (Bauml et al., 2006 and 2014).

There is evidence that psychoeducation can be effective in improving behaviour in educational settings (e.g., Harris et al., 2003), well-being (e.g., Hayes et al., 2013), rehabilitation after injury (Gordon et al., 1998), as well as outcomes in mental health settings and clinical settings (Colom et al., 2009; Perry et al., 1999). There is also evidence that psychoeducation can improve life skills and well-being in elite athletes (Danish, Petipas & Hale, 1993; Mosewich et al., 2013).

The bulk of research has focused on the effects of psychoeducation in reducing negative outcomes, however there is some limited evidence supporting the use of psychoeducation to enhance positive outcomes, in a range of occupational settings (Steed, 2014), as well as improving educational outcomes (Perry et al., 1999), for example, reducing test anxiety in students (Rajiah & Saravanan, 2014). Other research in non-clinical populations has shown that psychoeducation can improve social and communication skills (Powell, Parker, Weighall, & Harpin, 2021).

Where there is little current research regarding the use of psychoeducation in high-performance domains, on a closer look, many approaches include empowerment through knowledge, which is known to facilitate skill use in high-performing populations (e.g., Dabovich et al. 2019). It can reasonably be concluded that psychoeducation should be a part of any performance program.

There are two broad goals of psychoeducation: information transfer and facilitating self-help. Achieving these goals will be dependent on the material being customized to the specific environment (e.g., correct use of jargon and relevant examples), and delivered through a credible source. This means that psychoeducation should be based on the lived experience of performers in their specific areas, as well as research and academic literature, and be delivered by those viewed as credible and relatable. This is likely to involve both (former) high performers in the same area; and those with scientific experience and academic qualifications.

Content

Common denominators across psychoeducation programs contain the following elements as a basis or starting point. Where practicable, an iterative approach is recommended, where new knowledge builds on known concepts.

- Physiological effects of stress and mechanisms of arousal. By building an awareness of the physiological and psychological effects of the stress response, individuals can learn when it is appropriate to implement different strategies to manage these effects, for example, behavioural (controlled breathing) or cognitive (self-talk).
- Short- and long-term effects of adrenaline and cortisol. Building an appreciation of the specific effects of stress hormones can increase compliance with behaviours to reduce or manage the stress response ("fight-or-flight"). This can also include building awareness of the long-term effects of a prolonged stress state and of strategies to manage these.
- Mental performance impacts of psycho-physiological response to stress. By increasing understanding of how responses to stress or threat can impact perception, information processing, and decision-making, as well as physical performance (e.g., hand steadiness), individuals can understand how to implement management strategies. This can also include the effects of mood on thought processes and perception.
- Performance impacts of fatigue and fatigue management principles. It is likely that all high performers will be required to operate under conditions of fatigue. By building an appreciation

of how fatigue affects the body and mind, performers can learn when and how to implement risk management strategies.

- Effects of values and beliefs on performance. An understanding of motivation and what drives an individual and groups can aid in maintaining long term performance in demanding conditions.
- Goal setting and performance. A solid grounding in various goal-setting techniques is likely to aid personnel in achieving performance outcomes over both short and long terms.
- Performance and limitations of the human system, including attention, memory, and information processing, as well as bias and the effects of expectations. This will aid individuals in determining their own vulnerabilities and strengths.
- Group dynamics, communication, and conflict resolution. As the team is a central element in many high-performance contexts (for a broader description, see Chapter 11), an understanding of team processes and strategies to maximize team performance is likely to enhance many training interventions.

Recognize the role of sleep

Sleep plays an important role in supporting learning, particularly for the required memory consolidation. Sleep is a time where multiple biological processes occur in the brain that support both the consolidation of information and procedures learned the day before, as well as ready the brain for learning on the upcoming day following sleep (Smith, 2001, Hobson & Pace-Scott, 2002, Fattinger et al., 2017). Research has shown that information recall is reduced if the night following its encoding has a disrupted or shortened sleep period (Curcio, Ferrara & De Gennaro, 2006). Sleep quality and quantity have been shown to relate to student learning capability as well as long-term academic success. Sleep availability on the night following learning is particularly important (Gais, Lucas & Born, 2006). Learning is impaired when an individual has been deprived of sleep following learning even when they have an opportunity to sleep on night two – an individual will have missed their opportunity to fully consolidate during sleep the information learned that day. That is to say, an individual cannot fully make up for nor compensate for reduced or no sleep on Monday by sleeping well on Tuesday night. From an organizational perspective, training is an expensive investment both in terms of direct costs and opportunity costs. High-performance organizations frequently reckon with the consequences of overcommitted, overtaxed performers. Therefore, it is important to consider the context of how much rest is available following a single session or during a multi-day training event, when choosing the timing or duration of your training program and or session. This is starting to become widely acknowledged in the athletic environment (e.g., Day et al., 2024), however, rational information is not enough to change high-performance cultures, where sleep and rest have been viewed for decades as laziness and disengagement (see also Chapter 15 for a description of how this affects corporate environments). Maximizing the investment in training should include a plan to ensure that individuals are able to sleep sufficiently to consolidate the information, procedures, and motor movement patterns that were just so intensively presented and practiced.

Teaching or consulting in high-performance environments

High-performance environments are usually small communities with their unique traditions, cultures, language, mannerisms, resources, and challenges. Though each one is different, there are some commonalities that can be considered when attempting mental performance training. Anyone developing programs or interventions in these environments would be wise to learn more about the subculture and its people, in order to set themselves up for future success. The appropriate use of language can foster rapport and relationship, though misusing phrases or idioms can quickly diminish credibility. Engagement of key leaders or role models will facilitate resourcing and access while including stakeholders, particularly the target audience, in program development will both increase the likelihood that a training will meet the needs of the audience while also increasing their buy-in. Customizing training to performers – the environment, the mission sets, the culture, and the people – can enhance program precision and success.

Walk the walk, talk the talk...but do not fake it until you make it!

Mental performance trainers, researchers, program developers, and practitioners may arrive with a set of assumptions related to different settings. Blacker et al. (2019) suggest several important considerations in individual differences for cognitive training within military populations, particularly with special operations personnel. Both magnification (higher initial scoring individuals show the most improvement) and compensation (lower initial scores though show greatest improvement because they have "room to grow") may boost the performance of individual operators or those seeking to be selected for special operations. Motivation may also be a key factor in the success of cognitive performance efforts. When an intervention or program can be directly tied to positively impacting real-life performance, performers pay attention and become much more engaged. And finally, consult freely and often. No matter how much clinical or academic expertise you bring to the table, seek feedback and ask questions in the spirit of inquisitive curiosity and ongoing development. Harvey describes a number of very useful points to facilitate successful engagement within a special forces unit including "Don't bring your ego...Know the organization and culture...Remember that relationships matter...Show up ready...Don't 'kiss the stone'...Be confident, be clear, and be upfront...Be an honest broker...Be present...Yes, you are being judged" (Harvey, 2019, pp. 84–85). R.E. King (1999) echoes similar guidance, underlining the importance of knowing one's audience in part to avoid inadvertently crossing boundaries or misstepping cultural norms as well as ensuring preparation for what might seem the most innocuous of teaching opportunities. For instance, while walking down the hall to grab a cup of coffee, you come across an operator you're working with who introduces you to their teammate who is "having the same issue I did when we I first talked to you." If you're distracted or unprepared, you may not notice that this is an opportunity to spend a few minutes connecting with this teammate, getting a quick sense of who he is, and "selling" what you can offer as a consultant. This is of course also an informal teaching moment and the novice may take the introduction as just an offhanded interaction and continue on their way to coffee.

Customizing training design for the elite

Tkachuk and colleagues (2003) describe a process of behavioural assessment in sport psychology, where this approach, as compared to a traditional assessment with standardized inventories across a group, so as to harness multiple methods of data collection across time to assess, quantify, and address an individual's performance needs. Within a sports setting, initial information gathering includes behavioural interviewing, across-sport behavioural inventories, within-sport behavioural checklists, and performance profiling. From this initial information gathering stage, the individual, potentially in collaboration with their team leader, mentor, or another appropriate individual with task knowledge chooses target behaviours. A task analysis, as described earlier, will be helpful at this stage to determine how to monitor the chosen behaviour(s). Typical monitoring methods include direct observation of single behaviours (e.g., shoot, don't shoot), behavioural checklists to record multiple behaviours, client self-monitoring, videotaping of practice, pre-performance, or performance behaviours (e.g., detailed analysis of throws in baseball), post-performance videotape reconstruction of verbal behaviour, and computer-assisted data collection. This approach to assessment and monitoring can provide clear applicability to training in high-performance environments, yet its labour intensiveness de facto sets it aside for the categories with the most resources.

Cognitive Engineering Based Upon Expert Skill (CEBES; Staszewski, 2013) is a method to derive an expert model of a process. Based upon an information processing analysis, the equipment manipulations, perceptual information, knowledge, and thought processes used by experts during performance are detailed and then used as a blueprint for training content. Essentially, expertise from experts is elicited and reverse engineered to train other experts, thereby bootstrapping the expert's knowledge and skills. This is different from other training models using introspection and intuition of the training designer, as the model relies instead on analysis of actual expert behaviour.

Cooke and Durso (2008) describe Staszewski's and Davison's use of CEBES in 2000 to derive an expert model of mine detection and clearance operations. They applied cognitive engineering methods to analyze the behaviours and thought processes of an expert in the field using video, verbal records (the expert was told to "think aloud"), and outputs from equipment to better understand what the expert knew about demining, strategies used to detect mines, and specific actions relevant to success. They used this model as a blueprint for training content, which was then combined with explicit methods of instruction (instruction and practice via a series of exercises) and feedback for an actual training program. They studied 22 soldiers who had previously received standard military land mine detection training – half assigned to a training group and the other assigned to a control group (no training). Soldiers were trained for 15 hours over the course of five days under controlled simulated conditions in a facility designed for the project. The experimental group significantly outperformed the control group at the end of initial training and they appeared to have sustained improvement when retested three weeks after completion of training.

Blacker et al. (2019) explore the potential application of cognitive training within military populations beyond typical interventions for medical or psychological disorders. For instance, improving cognitive functioning may have positive preventative implications in mitigation of injury (e.g., traumatic brain injury) or disease. Additionally, they offer examples of unique military situations (e.g., room clearance, battlefield medic tasks) wherein mission success, or simply survival, hinges on the performance of multiple cognitive tasks and offer areas in which cognitive performance interventions or programs can have significant real-world impact. Special attention is paid to the role of baseline performance, motivation, and expectations in individual differences when applying cognitive training, particularly within SOF where some of the skills, competencies, and requirements can be more specialized than in the general military population.

Setting up for success

Salas and Cannon-Bowers (2001) present a review of antecedent training conditions, including individual characteristics, training motivation, and pre-training environment factors to consider for optimum benefit of training. In general, cognitive ability, self-efficacy, and goal orientation positively influence learning outcomes and performance. Motivation to learn and attend training has been shown to affect the skill acquisition, retention, and willingness to apply knowledge, skills, and abilities (KSAs) on the job, though it is a multifaceted factor influenced by individual and situational characteristics. Salas and Cannon-Bowers also describe literature suggesting that the manner in which organizations, leaders, program implementers, and instructors frame training (e.g., remedial versus advanced, voluntary versus mandatory) can also influence subsequent training outcomes.

There are ways in which coaches and consultants can facilitate learning and behaviour change. Tabibnia and Radecki (2018) identify three such "brain-friendly" strategies – positive expectation, growth mindset, and self-affirmation. Expectations have long been known to have a significant capacity to shape experience (i.e., placebo effect). Positive expectation, or a belief that an intervention can lead to a positive outcome, may facilitate the positive outcome's actual occurrence. People with a growth mindset, who believe their abilities are malleable, learn better, improve more, and view their mistakes as opportunities to learn – all critical for feedback-based learning. Self-affirmation, reminding oneself of one's own adequacy, can facilitate positive change by shifting the self-relevance and value of the messages away from negative feedback.

Take-aways and summary

This chapter presented several summarized education theories and principles of learning that could underpin the development and implementation of a mental performance program, and continued with an exploration of the techniques and contextual issues specific to high-performance learning environments. As is illustrated by the variety of examples presented, there are a multitude of evidence-based directions one can take in establishing a mental performance program. There are also several key take-aways that will apply to most, if not all, programs:

- Develop cultural competency for the population
- High stakes environments are all about relationships – always obtain and maintain key stakeholder buy-in and try not to alienate your audience
- Use diverse teaching modalities grounded in the literature and appropriate to the setting
- Collaborate on goals and communicate progress
- Strive to have the training environment to mirror performance environment
- Reflect cultural context – ensure content appropriate for audience
- Implement mental performance training into other events
- Program within the operational tempo
- Consult, consult, consult

High performers work relentlessly to establish expertise in their fundamental tasks so that they can strive to go above and beyond. Mental performance training, especially within a learning environment set up for success, has the promise to contribute to the optimization of an performer's performance as well as to their resilience and longevity.

References

Aidman, E. (2020). Cognitive fitness framework: Towards assessing, training and augmenting individual-difference factors underpinning high-performance cognition. *Frontiers in Human Neuroscience*, 13, 466.

Anderson, C. M., Hogarty, G. E., Reiss, D. J. (1980). "Family treatment of adult schizophrenic patients: A psycho-educational approach". *Schizophrenia Bulletin*, 6(3), 490–505. doi:10.1093/schbul/6.3.490. ISSN 0586-7614. PMID 7403810

Barwood, M. J., Dalzell, J., Datta, A. K., Thelwell, R. C., Tipton, M. J. (2006). Breath-hold performance during cold water immersion: Effects of psychological skills training. *Aviation, Space, and Environmental Medicine,* 77(11), 1136–1142.

Batsell, W. R., Jr., Perry, J. L., Hanley, E., & Hostetter, A. B. (2017). Ecological validity of the testing effect: The use of daily quizzes in introductory psychology. *Teaching of Psychology*, 44(1), 18–23.

Bauml, J., Frobose, T., Kraemer, S., Rentrop, M., & Pitschel-Walz, G. (2006/2014). Psychoeducation: A basic psychotherapeutic intervention for patients with schizophrenia and their families. *Schizophrenia Bulletin.* October, 2006; 32(1), S1–S9. doi: 10.1093/schbul/sbl017. PMCID: PMC2683741

Biggs, J. B., & Collins, K. F. (2014). *Evaluating the quality of learning: The SOLO taxonomy (Structure of the Observed Learning Outcome)*. Academic Press.

Blacker, K., Hamilton, J., Roush, G., Pettijohn, K., & Biggs, A. (2019). Cognitive training for military application: A review of the literature and practical guide. *Journal of Cognitive Enhancement*, 3(1), 30–51.

Bloom, B. S. (1984). The 2 sigma problem: The search for methods of group instruction as effective as one-to-one tutoring. *Educational Researcher*, 13, 4–16.

Bloom, B. S., Engelhart, M. D., Furst, E. J., Hill, W. H., Krathwohl, D. R. (1956). *Taxonomy of educational objectives: The classification of educational goals*. Handbook I: Cognitive domain. David McKay Company.

Bruner, J. S. (1960). *The Process of education*. Cambridge, Mass.: Harvard University Press.

Burke, P. J., & Reitzes, D. C. (1981). The link between identity and role performance. *Social Psychology Quarterly*, 44(2), 83–92.

Callan, D. E., & Naito, E. (2014). Neural processes distinguishing elite from expert and novice athletes. *Cognitive and Behavioral Neurology*, 27(4), 183–188.

Cepeda, N. J., Pashler, H., Vul, E., Wixted, J. T., & Rohrer, D. (2006). Distributed practice in verbal recall tasks: A review and quantitative synthesis. *Psychological Bulletin*, 132(3), 354–380.

Colom, F., Vieta, E., Sanchez-Moreno, J., Palomino-Otiniano, R., Reinares, M., Goikolea, J.M., Benabarre, A., & Martinez-Aran. (2009). Group psychoeducation for stabilised Bipolar disorders: 5-year outcome of a randomised clinical trial. *British Journal of Psychiatry*, 194(2009), 260–265. doi: 10.1192/bjp.bp.107.040485

Cooke, N. J. & Durso, F. (2008). *Stories of modern technology failures and cognitive engineering successes*. Boca Raton, FL: CRC Press, Taylor & Francis Group.

Culver, D. M., Kraft, E., Din, C., & Cayer, I. (2019). The Alberta women in sport leadership project: A social learning intervention for gender equity and leadership development. *Women in Sport and Physical Activity Journal*, 27 (2), 110–117.

Curcio, G., Ferrara, M., & De Gennaro, L. (2006). Sleep loss, learning capacity and academic performance. *Sleep Medicine Reviews*, 10(5), 323–337.

Dabovich, P. A., Eliott, J. A., & McFarlane, A.C. (2019). *The meanings soldiers attach to health and their impacts on primary health-care utilization and avoidance in an Australian high-risk combat unit*. Armed Forces and Society.

Danish, S. J., Petitpas, A. J., & Hale, B. D. (1993). Life development intervention for athletes: Life skills through sports. *The Counseling Psychologist*, 21(3), 352–385. https://doi.org/10.1177/0011000093213002

Day, C., Nishino, N., & Tsukahara, Y. (2024). Sleep in the Athlete. *Clinical in Sports Medicine*, Jan;43(1), 93–106. doi: 10.1016/j.csm.2023.06.007. Epub 2023 Jul 18. PMID: 37949516

DeWiggins, S., Hite, B., & Alston, V. (2010). Personal performance plan: Application of mental skills training to real-world military tasks. *Journal of Applied Sport Psychology*, 22, 458–473.

Donley, J. E. (1911). Psycho-therapy and re-education. The Journal of Abnormal Psychology, 6(1), 1–10. https://doi.org/10.1037/h0071950

Dreyfus, H. L., & Dreyfus, S. E. (2005). Expertise in real world contexts. *Organizational Studies*, 26(5), 779–792.

Endres, T., & Renkl, A. (2015). Mechanisms behind the testing effect: An empirical investigation of retrieval practice in meaningful learning. *Frontiers in Psychology*, 6, Article 1054.

Ericsson, K. A. (2006). *The Cambridge handbook of expertise and expert*. New York: Cambridge University Press.

Ericsson, K. A., Krampe, R. T., & Tesch-Romer, C. (1993). The role of deliberate practice in the acquisition of expert performance. *Psychological Review*, 100(3), 363–406.

Fattinger, S., de Beukelaar, T. T., Ruddy, K. L., Volk, C., Heyse, N. C., Herbst, J. A., & Huber, R. (2017). Deep sleep maintains learning efficiency of the human brain. *Nature Communications*, 8(1), 1–14.

Fernandez, J., & Jamet, E. (2017). Extending the testing effect to self-regulated learning. *Metacognition and Learning*, 12(2), 131–156.

Fletcher, J. D. (2009). Education and training technology in the military. *Science,* 323, 72–75.

Fletcher, J. D., & Chatelier, P. (2000). *An overview of military training*. DOI:10.21236/ada408439

Gais, S., Lucas, B., & Born, J. (2006). Sleep after learning aids memory recall. *Learning & Memory*, 13(3), 259–262.

Gibson, E. J. (1963). Perceptual learning. *Annual Review of Psychology*, 14, 29–56. doi:10.1146/annurev.ps.14.020163.000333

Gordon, S., Potter, M., & Ford, I. W. (1998) Toward a psychoeducational curriculum for training sport-injury rehabilitation personnel. *Journal of Applied Sport Psychology*, 10(1), 140–156, DOI: 10.1080/10413209808406382

Gureckis, T. M., & Markant, D. B. (2012). Self-directed learning: A cognitive and computational perspective. *Perspectives on Psychological Science*, 7(5), 464–481. doi:10.1177/1745691612454304

Hayes, L., Harvey, C., & Farhall, J. (2013). Family psychoeducation for the treatment of psychosis. *Australian Psychological Society*. InPsych: April, 2013, 35, 16–17.

Henry, L., Harris, Altekruse, Michael K., & Engels, Dennis W. (2003). Helping freshman student athletes adjust to college life using psychoeducational groups. *The Journal for Specialists in Group Work*, 28(1), 64–81, DOI: 10.1177/019339202250079

Hobson, J. A., & Pace-Schott, E. F. (2002). The cognitive neuroscience of sleep: neuronal systems, consciousness and learning. *Nature Reviews Neuroscience*, 3(9), 679–693.

Kellerman, P. J. (2013). Adaptive and perceptual learning technologies in medical education and training. *Military Medicine*, 178(10), 98–106. doi:10.7205/MILMED-D-13-00218

Kellerman, P. J., & Kaiser, M. K. (1994). Perceptual learning modules in flight training. *Proceedings of the Human Factors and Ergonomics Society Annual Meeting*, 38(18), 1183–1187.

Kellerman, P. J., & Krasne, S. (2018). Accelerating expertise: Perceptual and adaptive learning technology in medical learning. *Medical Teacher*, 40(8), 797–802.

Kim, W., Chang, Y., Kim, J., Seo, J., Ryu, K., Lee, E., Janelle, C. M. (2014). An fMRI study of differences in brain activity among elite, expert, and novice archers at the moment of optimal aiming. *Cognitive and Behavioral Neurology*, 27(4), 173–182.

King, R. E. (1999). *Aerospace Clinical Psychology*. New York, NY: Routledge.

Kjaergaard, A. & Pedersen, C. (2008). *Internal survey of Danish SOF unit Jaegercorps*.

Kluge, M. G., Maltby, S., Walker, N., Bennett, N., Aidman, E., Nalivaiko, E., & Walker, F. (2021). Development of a modular stress management platform (Performance Edge VR) and a pilot efficacy trial of a bio-feedback enhanced training module for controlled breathing. *PLoS ONE*, 16(2), e0245068. https://doi.org/10.1371/journal.pone.0245068

Knowles, M. S., Holton, E. F., Swanson, R. A., & Robinson, P.A. (2020). *The adult learner. The definitive classic in adult education and human resource development* (9th ed.). Oxon: Routledge.

Kromann, C. B., Bohnstedt, C., Jensen, M. L., & Ringsted, C. (2010). The testing effect on skills learning might last 6 months. *Advances in Health Sciences Education: Theory and Practice*, 15(3), 395–401.

Kuhlmann, D. O., & Ardichvili, A. (2015). Becoming an expert: Developing expertise in an applied discipline. *European Journal of Training and Development*, 39(4), 262-276.

Lave, J. (1997). The culture of acquisition and the practice of understanding. In D. Kirshner & J.A. Whitson (Eds.), *Situated cognition: social, semiotic and psychological perspectives* (pp. 17–36). Erlbaum.

Lave, J., & Wenger, E. (1991). *Situated learning: Legitimate peripheral participation*. Cambridge University Press.

Lerner, N., Gill, M., Kellman, P. J., Burke, T., Older, R. M., & Scott-Parker, B. (2017). *Development of a novice driver training module to accelerate driver perceptual expertise*. Washington, DC: AAA Foundation for Traffic Safety.

Massey, C. M., Kellerman, P. J., Roth, Z., & Burke, T. (2013). Perceptual learning and adaptive learning technology: Developing new approaches to mathematics learning in the classroom. In *Developmental cognitive science goes to school* (pp. 249–263). Routledge.

Mattie C. P., Guest K., Bailey S., Collins J., Gucciardi D. F. (2020). Development of a mental skills training intervention for the Canadian special operations forces command: an intervention mapping approach. *Psychology of Sport and Exercise*, 50, 101720. doi: 10.1016/j.psychsport.2020.101720

Mattie, P., Jaenen, S., & Collins, J. (2017). Special operations mental agility training for the Canadian special operations forces command. *Journal of Science and Medicine in Sport*, 20, Supplement 2, S88.

McCrory, P., Cobley, S., & Marchant, P. (2013). The Effect of Psychological Skills Training (PST) on self-regulation behavior, self-efficacy, and psychological skill use in military pilot-trainees. *Military Psychology*, 25(2), 136–147.

Mohammed, S., Flores, L., Deveau, J., Hoffing, R. C., Phung, C, Parlett, C. M., Sheehan, E., Lee, D., Au, J., Buschkuehl, M., Zordan, V., Jaeggi, S. M., & Seitz, A. R. (2017). The benefits and challenges of implementing motivational features to boost cognitive training outcomes. *Journal of Cognitive Enhancement*, 1(4), 491–507.

Mosewich, A. D., Crocker, P. E., Kowalski, K. C., & DeLongis, A. (2013). Applying self-compassion in sport: An intervention with women athletes. *Journal of Sport and Exercise Psychology*, 35(5), 514–524.

Retrieved 24 February, 2020 from https://journals.humankinetics.com/view/journals/jsep/35/5/article-p514.xml

Nalivaiko, E., Walker, F.R., Harrison, D., Swinsburg, A., & Aidman, E. (2018). *Biomarker-enhanced free-roam VR technology for tactical training, presented at International Conference on Science and Innovation for Land Power (ICSLIP),* Adelaide, Australia, September 2018, accessed at www.dst.defence.gov.au/event/international-conference-science-and-innovation-land-power- 2018/abstracts-and-papers on 21 June 2021

Nielsen, K. (2008). Scaffold instruction at the workplace from a situated perspective. *Studies in Continuing Education*, 30, 247–261. doi: 10.1080/01580370802439888

Pallavicini, F., Argenton, L., Toniazzi, N., Aceti, L., & Mantovani, F. (2016). Virtual reality applications for stress management training in the military. *Aerospace Medicine and Human Performance*, 2016, 87(12), 1021–1030.

Perry, A., Tarrier, N., Morris, R., McCarthy, E., & Limb, K. (1999). Randomised controlled trial of efficacy of teaching patients with Bipolar disorder to identify early symptoms of relapse and obtain treatment. *British Medical Journal*, 1999, 318, 149–153.

Persky, A. M., & Robinson, J. D. (2017). Moving from novice to expertise and its implications for instruction. *American Journal of Pharmaceutical Education*, 81(9), 72–80.

Powell, L. A., Parker, J., Weighall, A., & Harpin, V. (2021). Psychoeducation Intervention effectiveness to improve social skills in young people with ADHD: A meta-analysis. *Journal of Attention Disorders*. https://doi.org/10.1177/1087054721997553

Rajiah, K., & Saravanan, C. (2014). The effectiveness of psychoeducation and systematic desensitization to reduce test anxiety among first-year pharmacy students. *American Journal of Pharmaceutical Education Nov 2014*, 78(9), 163. DOI: 10.5688/ajpe789163

Roediger, H. L., Nestojko, J. F., & Smith, N. (2019). Strategies to Improve Learning and Retention During Training. https://doi.org/10.1093/oso/9780190455132.003.0014

Rowland, C. A. (2014). The effect of testing versus restudy on retention: A meta-analytic review of the testing effect. *Psychological Bulletin*, 140(6), 1432–1463.

Salas, E., & Cannon-Bowers, J.A. (2001). The science of training: A decade of progress. *Annual Review of Psychology,* 52, 471–499.

Sanders, D., & Welk, D. S. (2005). Strategies to scaffold student learning: Applying Vygotsky's zone of proximal development. *Nurse Educator*, 30, 203–207.

Schatz, S., Fautua, D., Stodd, J., & Reitz, E. (2015). *The changing face of military learning. Proceedings of the I/ITSEC*. Arlington, VA: NTSA.

Schön, D. A. (1987). *The Reflective Practitioner: How professionals think in action*. Basic Books.

Smith, C. (2001). Sleep states and memory processes in humans: Procedural versus declarative memory systems. *Sleep Medicine Reviews*, 5(6), 491–506.

Staszewski, J., & Davison, A. (2000). *Mine detection training based on expert skill, Proceedings of 4th International symposium on technology and the mine problem*. Charlottesville, VA: Mine Warfare Association.

Staszewski, J. J. (2013). Cognitive engineering based on expert skill. In J. J. Staszewski (Ed.), *Expertise and skill acquisition: The impact of William G. Chase* (pp. 29–57). Psychology Press.

Steed, R. (2014). A client-centered model of instructional design for psychoeducation interventions in occupational therapy. *Occupational Therapy in Mental Health*, 30(2), 126–143. DOI: 10.1080/0164212X.2014.878536

Swanson, H. L., O'Connor, J. E., & Cooney, J. B. (1990). An information processing analysis of expert and novice teachers' problem solving. *American Educational Research Journal*, 27(3), 533–556.

Tabibnia, G., & Radecki, D. (2018). Resilience training that can change the brain. *Consulting Psychology Journal: Practice and Research*, 70(1), 59–88.

Tkachuk, G., Leslie-Toogood, A., & Martin, G. L. (2003). Behavioral assessment in sport psychology. *The Sport Psychologist*, 17, 104–117.

Tomlinson, B.E. (1941). *The psychoeducational clinician*. New York, NY US: MacMillan Co.

U.S. Department of Defense. (2001). *Instructional systems development/systems approach to training and education. (DoD Publication No. MIL-HDBK-29612-2A)*. Washington, DC: U.S. Department of Defense.

Ullen, F., Hambrick, D. Z., & Mosing, M. A. (2016). Rethinking expertise:. *Psychological Bulletin*, 142(2), 427–446.

Vogel-Wolcutt, J. J., Fiorella, L., & Malone, N. (2013). Instructional strategies framework for military training systems. *Computers in Human Behavior*, 29, 1490–1498.

11 Team Performance

Mental Performance N+1

Deanna Beech, Heikki Mansikka, Don Harris, Kai Virtanen, and Nathalie Pattyn

"No man one is an island."

– John Donne

John Donne's poignant statement from his 1624 work, Meditation, has been frequently cited to underscore the idea that no individual can thrive in isolation. Achieving a fulfilling life and realizing our potential necessitates the aid and guidance of others. Through interactions with friends and mentors, we not only absorb knowledge but also refine it, propelling ourselves toward excellence. In essence, our personal achievements are a testament to the cumulative support and involvement of everyone who has aided us on our journey.

Those that share in supporting us toward our goals, that share this goal with us, can be described as "being on our team". A team is not just a group of associated people. A team is "a distinguishable set of two or more people who interact, dynamically, interdependently, and adaptively toward a common and valued goal/objective/mission" (Salas, Dickinson, Converse, & Tannenbaum, 1992, p. 4). From this generally accepted definition it is clear that even individuals who are performing what appears to be a very individual effort, such as a writer or a pole vaulter, are impacted by the team around them that support their effort toward the shared objective. The impact on the individual is intensified as the interdependence of the individuals increases as is the case with a football team or a specialized military unit.

When a team is performing well, individual members are motivated and engaged. They are receptive to trying new skills and open to learning from others. This not only benefits individual performance, but it also provides social and emotional support to buffer the individual against the intense stress that is present at elite performance levels (Eisenberger et al., 2007; Eisenberger & Cole, 2012). The opposite is also true. When a team is performing poorly, it can have a significant negative impact on the individual. Team members can become unmotivated to work together or even engage in open frustration or hostility, leading to a decrease in mental and physical performance and an increase in stress levels. Studies have even shown that individuals in difficult, negative, or high-conflict team conditions may experience burnout and other mental health issues (Burke et al., 2017; DeChurch, et al., 2010; Gully et al., 2002, Salas et al., 2012; Salanova et al., 2013). As such, it is important to prioritize team performance to maintain and improve individual mental performance. The following chapter focuses on the contributions of team dynamics to performance, team performance theory, and team skills, along with how to assess and intervene to improve team performance.

DOI: 10.4324/9781003378969-14

Compounding stress

Team-based stress and individual performance

Much research has focused on understanding the interplay between the physiological reactions, cognitions, and behaviours that contribute to elite performance. Physiologically, a compelling body of research points to the fact that our actions and reactions are a "set of collaborative processes that strategically deploy resources to preserve functionality in an unpredictable and dynamically changing environment" (Kiely et al., 2018, p. 13). This constant adaptation to the world around us has been described as allostasis. What appears to be homeostasis, also referred to as allostasis, is really the neurobiological imperative to "sensitively pre-empt and respond to emerging challenges by orchestrating multi-level system-wide coordinated compensations" (Kiely et al., 2018, p. 13).

When too much adaptation is required of the individual's system an "allostatic load" is created (McEwen, 2000). For a more detailed description of the physiological and psychological mechanisms subtending this, we refer to Chapter 2 and its section about stress. If this allostatic load is chronic (continually being required to adapt) the chronic over-stimulation of the autonomic nervous system can, over time, result in negative outcomes such as difficulties with sleep, concentration, and poor working memory (Giuliano et al., 2017). Without awareness this trajectory can even lead to physiological illnesses such as hypertension, cardiovascular disease, reduced testosterone, and the development of type II diabetes (Fisher et al., 2009). The psychological costs are also well documented and can include difficulties with insomnia, substance abuse, low self-esteem, reduced energy and motivation, emotional reactivity and anger, hypervigilance, depression, anxiety, sexual dysfunction, cognitive impairments, and combat stress reactions (Frueh et al., 2020). It is clear, failure to effectively incorporate recovery in our performance routines can degrade our ability to reach ideal performance states, and it reduces well-being and longevity in the team (we refer to Chapters 2, 3, and 5 for a more detailed discussion).

Theories of team performance

Our understanding of the various individual and team-based skills that are present in a high-performing team has evolved in an explosion of research on this topic over the last century (Mathieu et al., 2017). However, the starting point is often credited to a foundational series of studies conducted by Harvard University researchers at the Hawthorne Works electrical plant between 1924 and 1933. Originally intended to probe the link between work conditions and employee productivity, these experiments revealed unexpected outcomes. It was found that regardless of whether work conditions were enhanced or degraded, productivity surged. Elton Mayo, who spearheaded the research, discerned that the uptick in productivity wasn't tied to the specific environmental modifications (Gale, 2004). Instead, increased performance stemmed from the workers' awareness that they were under observation which led them to desire to meet or exceed the researchers' expectations. This phenomenon, now coined the "Hawthorne effect", underscores a seminal principle in team performance research: as the act of observation or scrutiny impacts team performance, by aligning these observations with performance metrics and goal achievement, team performance is generally enhanced (Marks et al., 2001; Mathieu et al., 2019; Stewart et al., 2023).

Since these early studies the evolution of team performance research has been described as branching into three distinct trajectories with "very limited cross-pollination" (Mathieu et al., 2017, p. 453; McGrath, 1997; Arrow, McGrath & Berdahl, 2000; Steiner, 1974). In their retrospective analysis for the Journal of Applied Psychology's centennial, Mathieu et al. (2017) delineated these trajectories as the Individualistic Orientation, Group Orientation, and Task Contingency Approach. As makes sense, the research focus of the Individual Orientation branch was on the individual's attitudes and behaviours of the team and its members. From this approach "groups were considered as social influences on individual-level processes" (p. 454). The Group Orientation trajectory focuses on small-group interaction dynamics, often employing complex Interaction Process Analysis (IPA) to yield intricate visualizations of group dynamics after a comprehensive data examination. The third, and perhaps most influential trajectory – the Task Contingency Approach, emphasizes the consistent properties that are found across groups with a primary focus on the factors that enhance task outcomes. It was this perspective that led Hackman and Morris to introduce the Inputs–Process–Outputs (IPO) model in 1975, ushering in a wave of research designed to consider the interplay of team-based skills. They conceptualized inputs as encompassing member characteristics (such as their knowledge, skills, abilities, and values), along with group-level determinants like size and structure, and external influences like stress and task attributes. These inputs, they argued, underwent transformation through group interactions, culminating in performance outputs. This framework was pivotal in shaping subsequent team performance research and mirror our understanding of what has been identified as spontaneously "emerging states" that develop as teams operate. Emergent states reflect a synthesis of team members' emotions, interactions, and behaviours – reflecting elements like trust and team cohesion. As Marks and his team described in 2001, emergent states can be understood as the "cognitive, motivational, and affective states of teams [that are…] dynamic in nature and vary as a function of team context, inputs, processes, and outcomes" (p. 357).

The IPO model was advanced to reflect the increased evidence that the team's processes and emergent states are continuous variables that mediate the inputs brought to the team as the team goes to create the required output. This modification was dubbed the Input–Moderators–Output–Input (IMOI) model by Ilgen et al. (2005), and it was further developed by Mathieu et al. (2008) by drawing attention to the team's Affect, Behaviours, and Cognitions (ABCs) which are seen as central to productive outputs (see Figure 11.1, Grossman et al., 2019, p. 247).

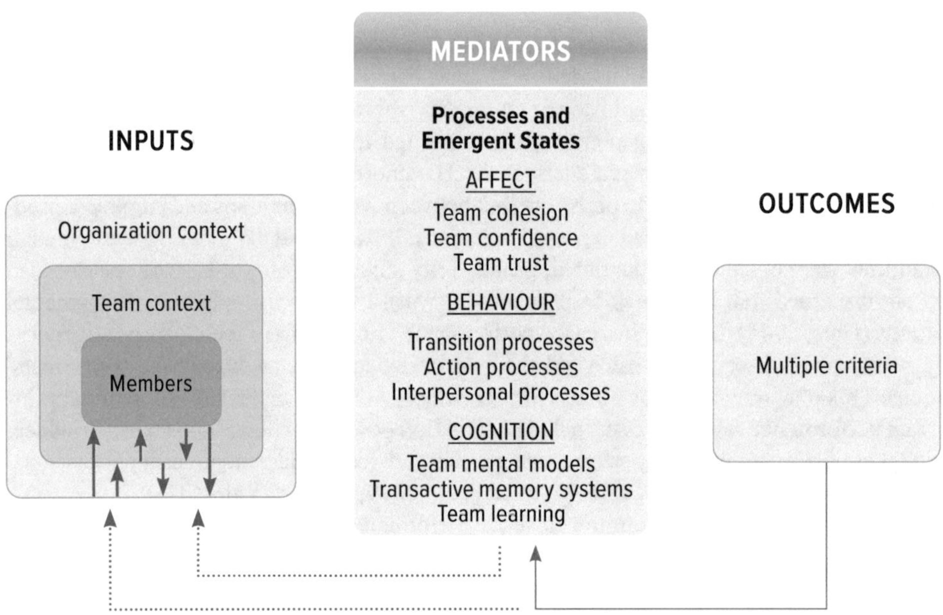

Figure 11.1 Input–Mediator–Output–Input model, originally adapted by Grossman et al., (2019) from the work of Ilgen et al., (2005) and Mathieu et al., (2008) to emphasize the role of affect, behaviour, and cognition in team processing.

Building on foundational research from the IPO/IMOI models, Salas and colleagues proposed their ground-breaking research that began to identify the interactive nature of team processes in the "Big 5 in Teamwork" (2005a). They proposed that team performance takes place through a series of ever present and interactive emergent states (2005a). The model emerged from a thematic analysis of the variables that demonstrated the greatest benefits to team effectiveness. They called the model the "Big 5" to draw attention to the five key Teamwork Components (leadership, mutual performance monitoring, team orientation, back-up behaviours, and adaptability). In addition to these emergent states, their model also identified three Coordinating Mechanisms (shared mental models, communication, and mutual trust). According to the "Big 5" model, each of these factors is important for effective team performance, and each can be developed and improved through training and other interventions. Since 2005 this framework has been instrumental in shaping strategies for enhancing team cohesion, flexibility, and overall performance across diverse settings and continues to influence the conceptualizations of team performance.

Ten years later Salas and his colleagues (2015b) took another look at the literature and expanded their framework. They suggested that there was now sufficient meta-analytic data to support the presence of nine key elements of teamwork – dubbed the "9 C's" (see Figure 11.2, Salas, E., 2015b, p. 602). This framework provides a richer understanding of the various nuances of team performance by integrating the literature into six core Processes and Emergent States

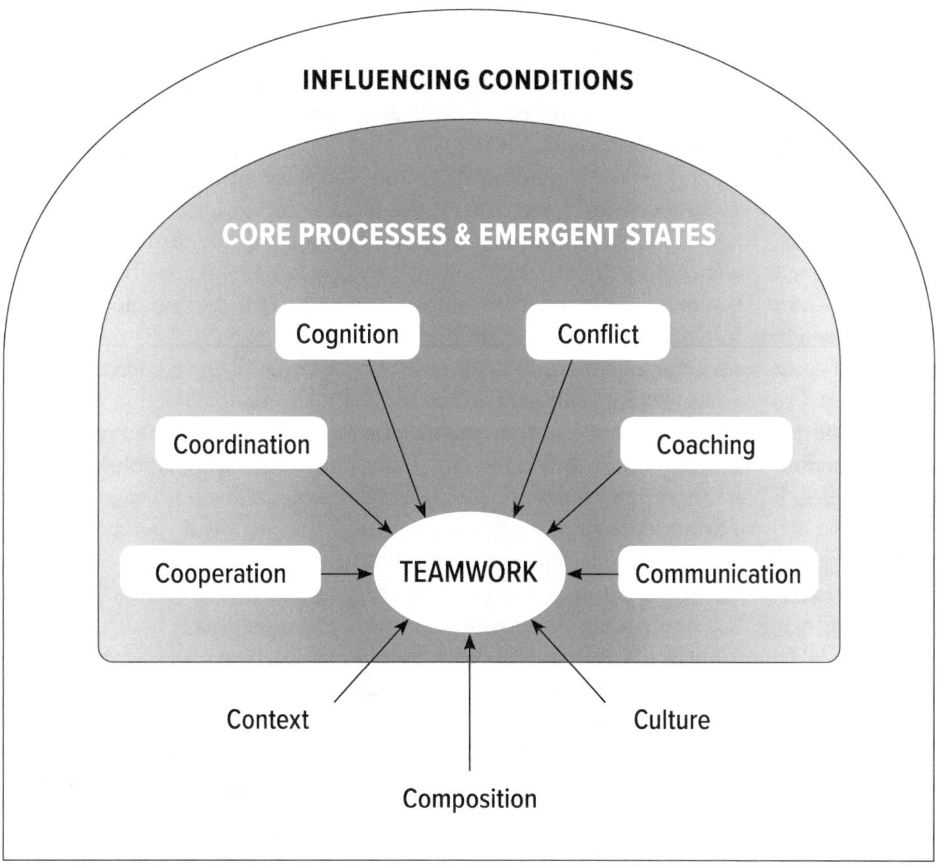

Figure 11.2 Heuristic of the critical considerations of teamwork to illustrate the 9 C's of teamwork as described by Salas, E. (2015).

(cognition, coordination, cooperation, communication, coaching, and conflict) along with three key Influencing Conditions (team context, composition, and culture) (Salas, E., 2015b, p. 602). Each of the processes and emergent states comprise related variables providing an integration of a vast amount of research in this field. For example, the emergent state of Cognition includes the concepts of shared team knowledge, as well as shared understandings (mental models) of the team's roles, norms, and goals. Coordination connotes more than the "behavioral mechanisms necessary to perform a task and transform team resources into outcomes" (Salas, E., 2015b, p. 606); it also involves planning and communication as well as anticipating upcoming needs and adjusting to the circumstances. Cooperation is described as a "motivational driver" of teamwork as it engages the "attitudes, beliefs, and feelings of the team that drive behavioral action" (Salas, E., 2015b, p. 604). Communication involves all the interactive behaviours and thought processes that go into receiving information to form and re-form the team's attitudes, behaviours, and cognitions. Coaching involves the enactment of leadership behaviours to "establish goals and set direction" in a way that empowers the team to reach their goal (Salas, E., 2015b, p. 603). The inclusion of Conflict in these emergent states addresses the inevitable differences of opinion and breakdowns in communication that lead to strife between teammates. Defined as "perceived incompatibilities in the interests, beliefs, or views held by one or more of team member" (Jehn, 1995, p. 257). Conflict, no matter what type, has been found to have a "strong negative correlation with team performance as well as team member satisfaction" (Salas, E., 2015b, p. 605). However, the current understanding of the effect of conflict on team performance is more complicated as relationship conflict consistently has a strong negative correlation to performance outcomes, while task-based conflict has a curvilinear relationship to performance when relationship conflict is low. The implication is that when a team can resolve relationship difficulties, they are able to effectively disagree about ideas related to tasks in ways that improve the eventual solution to the problem by incorporating different perspectives (Caesens et al., 2019).

The three key influencing elements reflect the "factors that have an impact on the core teamwork processes and emergent states"; specifically the team composition, context, and culture (Salas, E., 2015b, p. 610). Team composition is considered critical to the team's success as it is necessary that the team is composed of members with the knowledge, skills, and abilities (KSAs) to achieve the goal. The context in which the team functions serves to "shape the very nature in which team members interact with one another" (Salas, E., 2015b, p. 611). This includes aspects such as whether the team engages with each other in person or virtually, the resources available to the team, as well as the organizational climate within which the team must function. Culture refers to the assumptions held by the people in the organization about how to relate to each other and the environment in which they work. It is a "driving force for [team] member values, norms, and behavior" (Salas, E., 2015b, p. 613). Salas and his colleagues propose this framework to concisely organize a vast body of information pertaining to team performance in a way that makes the information manageable for those trying to enhance team performance.

Recently, team performance research has been working to effectively reflect the interactive nature of team variables, through the development of more dynamic conceptualizations such as the Complex Adaptive Systems (CAS; Ramos-Villagrasa et al., 2018) and small complex systems (Mathieu et al., 2019). These conceptualizations suggest that teams are always in an evolving and adapting state, capturing the creative multilevel expression present in the team's dynamics. For example, the model proposed by Mathieu and his colleagues (2019) organizes team interactions into three primary categories and three overlapping regions. The primary categories include the team's *structural features* (task scope and complexity, interdependence, and knowledge management systems), the *compositional features* (member attributes, diversity, and fault-lines/subgroups), and the *mediating mechanisms* of member interactions (team processes, information sharing/communication, emergent states and conflict). The overlapping regions suggest primary interactions

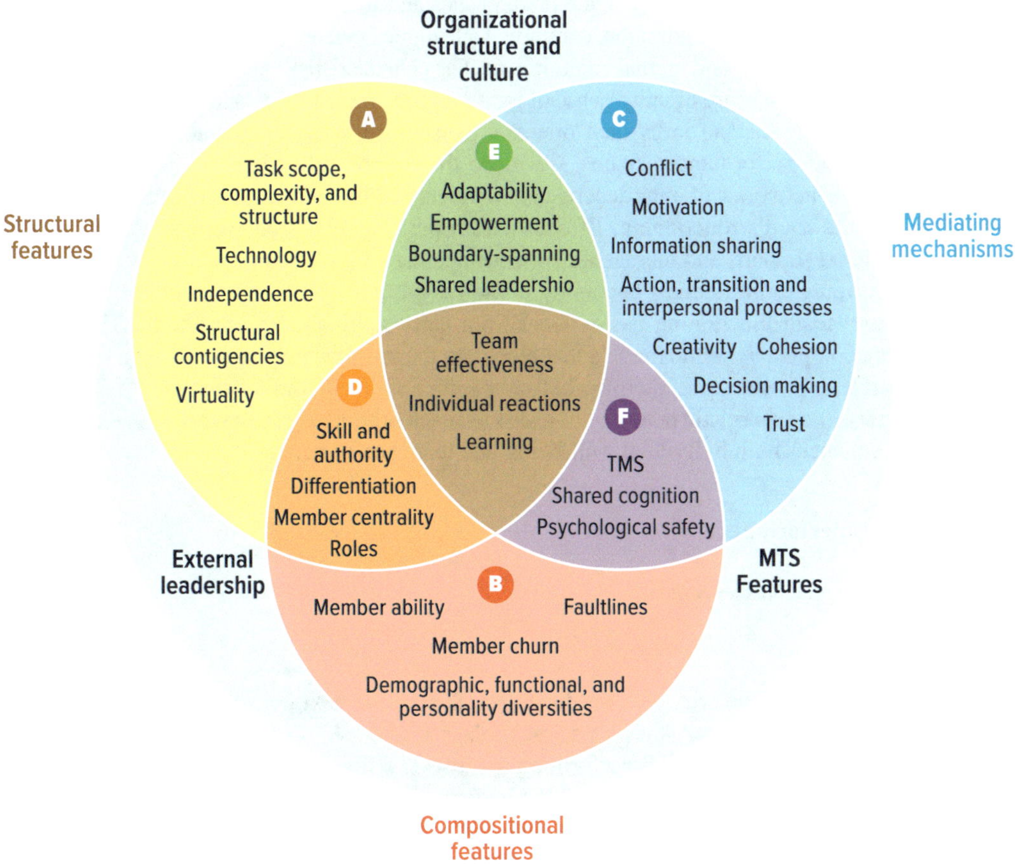

Figure 11.3 Co-evolving team compositional and structural features, mediating mechanisms, external influences, and outcomes. Adapted from Mathieu et al. (2017). Abbreviations: MTS, multiteam systems; TMS, transactive memory system.

between the categories. They proposed that the interplay of these dynamics results in the teams' effectiveness and learning and can even account for individual team member reactions (see Figure 11.3, Mathieu et al., 2017, p. 19).

Further, it has been proposed that when the dynamics are optimal, and a team is in a high-performance moment they experience a state of "flow" that is like that of an individual's flow experience (van den Hout, Davis & Weggeman, 2018). As is true of the subjective experience of the individual who achieves the flow state (Csikszentmihalyi, 1990, 2014; Jackson & Csikszentmihalyi, 1999), to reach this state as part of a team is intrinsically rewarding and enhances the team members' commitment to and satisfaction with the group which perpetuates the teams' continued engagement in high performance. Sawyer pioneered the application of this concept to groups and teams by describing "a collective state that occurs when a group is performing at the peak of its abilities" (Sawyer, 2003, p. 167). Early studies focused on the antecedents to achieving flow in a team (Aubé et al., 2014) and found consistent support for the correlation between flow and high performance of a team (Landhaüßer and Keller, 2012).

Expanding on this, van den Hout and his colleagues conducted a review of this literature and proposed a conceptualization of team flow (2018). They proposed that "team flow be defined as a shared experience of flow derived from an optimized team dynamic during the execution of interdependent personal tasks" (p. 400). They identify seven prerequisites and four characteristics of team flow. The prerequisites include a collective ambition, common goal, aligned personal goals, high skill integration, open communication, safety, and mutual commitment. The characteristics experienced when the group is in a flow state include a sense of unity, sense of joint progress, mutual trust, and holistic focus.

Thus, the principle that no individual operates in isolation is foundational to understanding team dynamics and performance. Teams are more than mere collections of individuals; they represent intricate networks of interdependent members, whose performance can be enhanced or hindered by the team's functioning. Effective team performance promotes individual growth, provides emotional support, and increases resilience against stress. In contrast, poorly performing teams can contribute to individuals becoming unmotivated, poor performing, and burnt out. Our understanding of team functioning has evolved from early seminal research like the Hawthorne studies to more complex dynamic models that elucidate the multifaceted nature of team dynamics. Current research emphasizes the interplay between team structure, composition, and interactions, aiming to harness the synergistic potential of teams to reach optimal performance, where collective participation enhances both individual well-being and team performance.

Assessing team performance

How to know if the team has a problem?

Informal team assessment

As we delve deeper into the crux of team dynamics, the crucial next question becomes – *How to know if the team has a problem?* Answer: actively observe and ask.

When a team has developed high-performing teamwork skills, you can "see" it. The team acts like a cohesive unit with seamless collaboration and communication, team members work fluidly together, proactively supporting each other, and share a deep understanding of their collective goals and norms. They exhibit a strong team identity, seek to work with each other, and show that they enjoy their interactions. Team members willingly offer needed information and feel safe to explore even unpopular viewpoints or differences in opinions trusting that they will continue to be accepted by the team as it seeks to find harmonious solutions and maintain positive interpersonal relationships. Their motivation is aligned with team objectives, and they engage in collective problem-solving, valuing each member's contribution. Shared accountability for outcomes, a clear understanding of individual roles, and supportive leadership are evident, promoting an environment of collective effort. Decision-making is inclusive, ensuring all voices are heard, and the team regularly engages in joint celebrations of successes and reflections for further performance development, reinforcing their unity and commitment to shared success.

Conversely, in low-performing teams, these elements manifest differently. Collaboration is disjointed, communication sporadic and unclear, and there is an evident lack of mutual support and trust. Conflicts go unresolved or may be handled in a way that further damages relationships. The group identity is weak, with members focusing more on individual goals than on the team's objectives. Leadership is often perceived as unsupportive or inconsistent, and decision-making processes are often exclusive, leaving team members feeling undervalued or unheard. Social interactions appear perfunctory or individualized, further eroding the sense of team unity. This stark contrast in behaviours and attitudes helps to highlights the importance of observation in identifying a team's performance level (see Addendum A for a worksheet to organize team observations).

Hopefully, with observations in hand, we can fill in the "what" things are working great, and "why" other things are not by directly asking. With the right questions, in the right setting, the problems are usually volunteered with little prompting. Conducting one-on-one conversations in a secure and private manner to foster honest communication about the team's challenges we can shed light on the difficulties beneath the surface of everyday interactions. A straightforward inquiry like, "How are things on your team?" or "How's the team doing?" can elicit the needed insights. Guaranteeing anonymity for the individual team members by ensuring that all data will be presented in an aggregate format will facilitate a sense of safety in the discussion that may lead to richer disclosure of the team's inner workings.

Another useful structured format for starting these conversations is provided in publicly available work that resulted from an extensive research project conducted by Google. Titled "Project Aristotle" and led by Abeer Dubey, Google set out to determine the attributes of their high-performing teams. This initiative was rooted in the hypothesis that understanding the dynamics behind successful teams could not only enhance collaboration within Google but also provide a blueprint for other organizations striving for excellence. The research was expansive. It spanned several years beginning in 2012 and involved data collection from more than a hundred teams across the company. Their results, published by Charles Duhigg in an article of The New York Times Magazine (2016) and on their website, suggested that the key to effective teams isn't so much who is on the team, but how the members interact, structure their work, and view their contributions. Specifically, the research identified five core dynamics of successful teams: (1) Psychological safety, where team members feel safe to take risks and be vulnerable with each other; (2) Dependability, with peers reliably completing quality work; (3) Structure and clarity, characterized by clear roles, plans, and goals; (4) Meaning, the sense that work has personal significance to each member; and (5) Impact, the belief that one's work makes a difference. Their findings emphasized the importance engaging with teams in support of creating a trusting environment where open communication, dependability, and meaningful work align to produce a significant impact which fundamentally shifts the focus from individual to collective team performance (Duhigg, 2016).

When accessible, supplementary data pertaining to individual team members – encompassing personality assessments, 360-degree feedback, and aptitude evaluations – can enhance a practitioner's comprehension of potential contributions by these members to the challenges currently faced by the team. This information can guide practitioners towards targeted discussions and interventions that may prove advantageous in addressing these issues. For an example of this approach see the case study below titled *Transitioning from Individual to Team Training*.

Formal team assessments

Formal team assessments can be a vital component for any organization striving to ensure their teams are operating at peak efficiency. By methodically evaluating a team's dynamics, performance, and overall effectiveness, practitioners can identify not only areas in need of enhancement but also enhance their strengths. This holistic approach involves selecting appropriate assessment tools, designing the assessment process, collecting and analyzing data, and then sharing the results with stakeholders to get buy-in for a plan of action. Ultimately, such assessments serve as a compass for continuous improvement, aligning resources and goals, identifying difficulties and needed resources, and paving the way for superior team performance and collaboration.

A simple Google search will immediately provide numerous organizations that offer team assessment questionnaires. It is important to vet these sites as most of these questionnaires are not validated instruments. However, several well-researched instruments are available and can be administered for a fee due to their proprietary nature. The benefit of this approach is that the practitioner does not need to be an expert at team performance or assessment and can still obtain actionable information that would support tailored training. Many of these organizations also offer training programs for more in-depth use of the results. One of the most comprehensive of these measures is the Optimizing Team Performance Profile – OTP Profile (Beech, 2023). This instrument is based on an extensive review of the evidence-based team skills that are present in high-performing Special Forces units and assesses the team's Leadership Engagement (Organizational Identification, Leadership Trust, Coaching, and Empowerment), their Mission Focus (Shared Purpose, Shared Vison, Goal Direction, and Roles & Expectations), the team's Action Processes (Monitoring, Joint Action, Communication, and Reasoning), and their Relational Elements (Team Cohesion, Emotional Intelligence, Trust & Safety, and Conflict Repair). The Denison Organizational Culture Model – Denison Model, was developed based on a line of research examining high-performing organizations (Denison & Ko, 2006). This instrument breaks team performance into Adaptability (creating change, customer focus, organizational learning), Mission (strategic direction & intent, goals & objectives, and vision), Consistency (core values, agreement, coordination & integration), and Involvement (empowerment, team orientation, and capacity development). The Team Diagnostic Survey (Wageman et al., 2005) focuses on six team conditions that are broken into three Task Processes (Effort, Strategy, and Knowledge & Skills) and three Criteria of Effectiveness (Quality of Group Process, Member Satisfaction, and Task Performance). The instrument provides an assessment of a team's structure, support, and leadership, along with various indicators of the members' work processes and their emotional responses to the team and its work that is grounded in team research and theory. Other measures of team performance that are focused on specific industries can also be found, such as those for educational institutions like DORA by Algozzine et al. (2012) and medical settings like STAT by Reid et al. (2012).

For those adept at managing survey data, Mathieu et al. (2020) have provided team practitioners with a valid open-source instrument that allows the team practitioner to gather general data on team-based skills. They conducted an extensive review of the literature and identified three critical areas of team processes: transition processes, action processes, and interpersonal processes. Transition processes "occur prior to or between performance episodes and have a dual focus whereby members reflect on and interpret previous accomplishments as well as prepare for the future" (p. 3). This includes questions focused on mission analysis, goal specification, and strategy formulation and planning. The action processes "describe the behaviors that members engage in while working toward goal accomplishment" (p. 4). Included in this section are the team variables of monitoring progress towards goals, systems monitoring, and team monitoring and backup behaviours. The final section, Interpersonal processes includes the team's ability to manage conflict, motivate and build confidence, and affect management. The scale was shown to be valid as a 10-item survey, a 30-item survey, or a comprehensive 50-item survey. Choosing the level of survey would depend on the time requirements and the level of detail needed. The full survey is available in their article (Mathieu et al., 2020). For an example of how to use this method for team assessment and intervention please see the case study below titled *Trouble with Boundary Spanning*.

Team assessment with task analysis

For those with more advanced skill in organizational psychology or human resource management, incorporating an evidence-based understanding of the steps involved in the taskwork that is necessary to meet team objectives (task analysis) can greatly benefit the team assessment by allowing interventions to be more targeted to specific outcomes. Task analysis entails dissecting the team's work into individual tasks, documenting each step, and identifying the requisite KSAs to accomplish them. This detailed breakdown greatly benefits the development of the training program and formal team performance measures can be added to provide a clear picture of the team's current functioning and a baseline from which to judge the effectiveness of the interventions. Those interested in a deeper dive into the methods and benefits of task analysis can refer to "A Guide to Task Analysis" by Kirwan and Ainsworth (1992). The interplay between task analysis and team assessments is exemplified in the case study below titled *Developing High Performing Flight Crews*.

Together, these informal and formal team assessment methods form a tiered approach to identifying the strengths and developmental needs of teams moving toward higher levels of performance. This allows practitioners the flexibility to consider the level appropriate level of interventions given the team's needs, the resources available, and the practitioner's level of experience.

Team training interventions

Extensive research, including meta-analyses by McEwan et al. (2017), Delisa et al. (2010), Lacerenza et al. (2018), and Hughes et al. (2016), indicates that team training interventions yield significant, positive effects on both teamwork and outcome performance. Developing a consultation with a team or organization involves a systematic approach. First, it would be essential to ensure that all stakeholders have "bought in" to the process, and then a thorough team needs assessment is conducted to identify the specific skills and capabilities that need to be improved. This is followed by engaging in detailed discussions with both the team leaders and members to ensure alignment between the training objectives and the stakeholders' expectations, as suggested by Lacerenza et al. (2018).

The next step is to design the training program utilizing a blend of delivery methods, including informational presentations, demonstrations, and practice exercises. Providing a combination of training methodologies is recommended as the most effective approach (Salas et al., 2012). In the program development it is also recommended that the material include a focus on the theoretical framework of team performance to support the transfer of insights to application, as discussed by Hughes et al. (2016) and Lacerenza et al. (2018). For a detailed guide to team training program development see the *Team Training Essentials: A research-based guide* (Salas, E., 2015a). Additionally, while there is an overwhelming number of team training programs available on the internet, they are not all equal. Below is a review of several modalities that have reached the level of well-codified programs with consistent, robust findings for improved team performance: Leadership training, Team coordination and adaptation training, Team building, Crew resource management, and Team debriefing.

Leadership training

Leadership training stands as a cornerstone intervention across organizations, deeply woven into the fabric of operational success. Its pivotal role is not just a matter of consensus, it's also supported by a substantial body of empirical research. Multiple meta-analyses have identified robust findings that support the positive relationship between good leadership and good team performance (Dunst et al., 2018; Fischer & Sitkin, 2023), while bad leadership correlates with poor performance (Burns, 2017; Fischer & Sitkin, 2023; Schyns & Schilling, 2013). Literally hundreds of articles and books have been published on this topic, but if you're looking for a practical guidance on how to develop and implement leadership training programs consider *Leadership Training Design, Delivery, and Implementation: A Meta-Analysis* (Lacerenza et al., 2017) and *Unlocking Human Potential through Leadership Training & Development Initiatives* (Day et al., 2021).

Team coordination and adaptation training

Team coordination and adaptation training aims to enhance team dynamics by teaching members how to streamline their collaborative efforts. The primary focus is on optimizing coordination strategies and minimizing the need for communication while improving efficiency and effectiveness (Salas et al., 2005b). It is suggested that the focus of this training be on the learning cycles embedded within specific team activities to foster such skills. However, a notable problem with this approach is the tendency to provide instructional feedback at an individual level rather than addressing the team as a whole. This individual-centric feedback overlooks the interdependent nature of team processes and fails to reinforce collective behaviours and shared understandings that are critical for team adaptation and synchrony. It's essential for such training to incorporate collective feedback mechanisms that reflect the team's performance as a unit, ensuring that the training outcomes align with the goals of enhanced team coordination and adaptability (Beech et al., 2023).

Team building

Training in team building focuses on cultivating "improvement within a team, providing individuals closely involved with the task with the strategies and information needed to solve their own problems" (Lacerenza et al., 2018, p.13). Team building centres on four basic approaches to team process: goal setting, interpersonal-relationship management, role clarification, and problem-solving.

Interventions focused on goal setting build a context and help to identify components that move the team toward the goal. It is also important that the goal be just challenging enough to focus the team's energy and attention (Vashdi et al., 2013). Maintaining an ongoing dialog about the team's objectives fosters the development of a shared mental model of the objective which, as described above, is one of the most robust variables in team efficacy. It has been proposed that this is accomplished through four specific mechanisms: direct attention and effort toward the goals, energizing the group to meet the goals, fostering effective persistence to keep moving toward the goals, and effecting actions through discovering, sharing, and using knowledge related to goal achievement (Lacerenza et al., 2018).

Interpersonal-relationship management is the process of directly and openly discussing affective interaction to develop a solid trust in the members of the team. As described above, trust enables the team to overcome uncertainty and accept vulnerability which facilitates coordination and communication. Trust does not mean the absence of conflict, rather it enables team members to overcome their uncertainty in expressing their views and accept the vulnerability of not always knowing or being right (DeJong et al., 2016). With solid trust the team can engage in healthy conflict as they problem-solve to reach the objective (Seitchik, 2019).

Role clarification is also thought to develop the teams' shared mental model and coordination by identifying who does what to get to the goal (Salas et al., 2015a). Also, rather than creating rigidity, role clarification allows for a better understanding of individual contributions which fosters the ability for other team members to provide backup behaviours and monitor workload distribution.

Problem-solving emphasizes the involved planning and action of the team members in identifying way to achieve their goals (Klein et al., 2009). This brainstorming provides the team members the opportunity to step back and identify specific processes, outcome levels, and resources needed for their work, which improves motivation and commitment to goal obtainment (Salas et al., 2005a).

Klein and colleagues (2009) conducted a comprehensive review and meta-analysis on team building and found that all of the four components significantly contributed to team process improvements, with goal-setting activities and role clarification showing the greatest benefits. Given the specific focus on processes related to task completion this type of team training can be particularly beneficial for ad hoc teams and newly formed teams.

Crew resource management (CRM) training

CRM was born out of the findings and recommendations from the National Transportation Safety Board's investigation into the preventable crash of United Airlines flight 173 in 1978 (NTSB, 1978). They concluded that the crash was caused by poor communication and situational awareness.

Extrapolating from this report others have also identified the contributions of rigid leadership style in which the captain failed to accept input from junior officers (Jedick, 2014). In response, training in CRM was developed and United Airlines, the airline responsible for the crash, was the first to adopt it. Shortly thereafter all other major airlines began training in CRM and it became mandated by the Federal Aviation Administration, National Aeronautics Space Administration, and Military Aviation. The concept then spread to other industries such as health care (TeamSTEPPS see O'Dea et al., 2014; Epps et al., 2015) and emergency response services (Griffith et al., 2015).

While early meta-analyses into the effectiveness of this approach found questionable results (O'Conner et al., 2008), the training has matured. More recent meta-analyses find that with CRM "positive and significant medium-sized effects were found for teamwork interventions on both teamwork and team performance" (McEwan et al., 2017, p. 1), with a large effect on knowledge and behaviours (O'Dea et al., 2014). Specifically, CRM has been described as:

> A flexible, systematic method for optimizing human performance in general, and increasing safety in particular, by (1) recognizing the inherent human factors that cause errors and the reluctance to report them, (2) recognizing that in complex, high risk endeavours, teams rather than individuals are the most effective fundamental operating units and (3) cultivating and instilling customized, sustainable and team-based tools and practices that effectively use all available resources to reduce the adverse impacts of those human factors (Marshall, 2009, p.22).

The content of the training will vary depending on the team context and specific needs of the intended team, but it usually includes the core variables of teamwork, leadership, situational awareness, decision-making, communication, and personal limitations (Salas et al., 2006). For those interested in establishing a CRM training program the chapter on *The Design, Delivery and Evaluation of Crew Resource Management Training* by Shuffler, Salas, and Xavier (2010) in the book *Crew Resource Management* provides an excellent guide; and Schuermann and Marquardt's 2016 work adds additional support with lessons learned and successful factors for CRM training as identified by expert CRM trainers.

Team debriefs

Team debriefing emerges as a critical mechanism in the learning and development landscape, particularly for collective settings where experience is a shared. Eddy et al. (2013) have positioned debriefing not merely as a reflective practice but as a powerful catalyst for expediting a team's learning curve. This is not hyperbole; Tannenbaum and Cerasoli (2013) quantify this advantage, citing a performance uptick of 20–25% when debriefing is employed effectively. The essence of debriefing lies in its ability to foster a robust shared mental model within the team, clarify roles and responsibilities, reinforce effective strategies, and pinpoint areas needing improvement – all through the prism of active learning (Lacerenza et al., 2018).

The debriefing process entails a collaborative analysis of events or performance periods to dissect outcomes, identify both strengths and weaknesses, and develop actionable strategies for future endeavours. This methodology, with its roots in military applications dating back to the 1970s, has been refined through extensive research, including insights from Morrison and Meliza (1999), to establish evidence-based best practices. A conducive environment characterized by trust, safety, and a tolerance for conflict is pivotal for candid dialogue and constructive feedback, as suggested by Arafeh et al. (2010). Further emphasis on teamwork, alongside task work, ensures a holistic approach to improvement (Reyes et al., 2018).

The structure and leadership of the debriefing session are equally important. While there is value in team-led debriefs, especially when the leader is well-versed in debriefing (Eddy et al., 2013), facilitator-led sessions often yield greater benefits (Fanning & Gaba, 2007). Structured, balanced

1. Set the stage (30 to 60 seconds)

- Explain why you are conducting a debrief and what the team will be discussing.
- "This is a quick opportunity to learn from our experience.
  Let's look at how we handled this [situation, project, event, meeting, shift]: what we did well or could improve."
- "Let's consider how we worked as a team, in addition to any technical issues"
- If there are any boundaries or "non-negotiables," let the team know what's off limits.Identify our main tasks?

Basic assumption: "We're all competent and well intentioned people who want to do our best. This is about getting better at what we do."
Identify the key challenges that we expect to face?

2. Ask the team for their observations (5-20 seconds)

- What **happened**?
- What did we do **well**? What **challenges** did we face?
- What should we do differently or focus on +?
- What could **help us** be more effective? Anything we need?

3. Add your observations/recommendations and confirm understanding (5-10 minutes)

- Reinforce their observations, or if you noticed something different, share your view of what happened or needs to happen in the future.
- Be sure any feedback you provide is clear, actionable, and focuses on the work, not personal traits.

4. Summarize any agreed-upon actions or focus for the future (5 minutes)

- Be clear about who will do what, when...and how this will help the team.
- Specify when and how you will follow up to assess progress (e.g., next debrief?).

Tip 1: Ask the team for their perceptions first. Then if possible, acknowledge one thing that you could have done differently or that you will focus on in the future. This will make it easier for team members to voice their own observations or concerns.

Tip 2: Tip: If the team doesn't discuss teamwork, ask "how well did we work together as a team?" Perhaps ask one or two specific questions such as:

HOW WELL DID WE...	HOW CLEAR WERE OUR...
• Communicate/share info • Monitor/provide backup • Coordinate with "outsiders" • Speak up/challenge one another • Ask for/offer help • Handle conflict • Share/allocate resources • Prepare/plan	• Roles/assignments • Goals/priorities

Figure 11.4 Quick Team Debrief Outline. Originally published by Reyes, Tannenbaum, and Salas (2018, p.50). Adapted from www.gOEbase.com. Permission granted.

discussions that methodically address both the highs and lows of performance, as advocated by Lacerenza et al. (2018) and Reyes et al. (2018), culminate in a more productive debrief. Documentation of the outcomes serves as a vital reference point for continuous improvement.

Considering the substantial benefits for the relatively minimal investment of time, averaging around 18 minutes (Tannenbaum & Cerasoli, 2013), the case for integrating team debriefing into routine practice is compelling. For organizations looking to implement or refine debriefing procedures, Reyes, Tannenbaum, and Salas (2018, p. 50) offer an invaluable resource in their guide, *Team Development: The Power of Debriefing* (see Figure 11.4). This guide lays out a pragmatic framework for debriefing, encompassing preparatory considerations, a detailed debriefing protocol, and strategies for post-debriefing follow-up, making it an essential tool for any team committed to continuous growth and performance excellence.

A strong body of evidence supports the conclusion that interventions designed for training teams are fundamental in enhancing both teamwork and overall performance. Such interventions begin with a needs assessment, followed by aligning training objectives with stakeholder expectations, and employing varied training methods for effective learning. Leadership training is central to team goal setting and outcome measurement, and team coordination and adaptation training emphasizes collaborative efficiency, shifting towards collective feedback to enhance team synchrony. CRM has been successfully extended to various industries, improving teamwork and performance through core teamwork principles. Team building activities are tailored to improve problem solving, goal setting, role clarification, and interpersonal relationships, and have been shown to be particularly effective for new teams. Lastly, team debriefing acts as a critical learning tool, significantly enhancing performance through structured, reflective practices that are documented for continuous improvement.

Case study: transitioning from individual to team training

A pilot project with a special operations forces team

This case study focuses on the implementation of a pilot project conducted with the Belgian Special Forces Group. The fundamental purpose of the program was to connect various divides: bridging the divide between physical and mental training; closing the gap between the curative/preventive medical approach and an approach focused on enhancing performance; and linking individual training with team training. The following summary will focus on the third objective, transitioning the operator's focus from individual effort to excellent teams, toward an identity as a team striving for excellence. For a full review of the development and implementation of this comprehensive Human Performance Program in a tier 1 Special Forces Unit see Pattyn et al. (2022).

Special Operations Forces (SOF) operators and elite athletes both demonstrate a wholehearted dedication to their respective professions. Historically, the process of selecting and training operators has been focused on cultivating their skills and abilities with the goal of achieving individual excellence. Therefore, transitioning from a solely individual-focused approach to performance management, while maintaining high personal standards, necessitated a change in mindset. Our human performance program aimed to take this additional stride.

To steer the program development process our team adopted the Intervention Mapping (IM) approach, as the benefits of this approach had been highlighted by Mattie et al. (2020) in their development of a human performance program for Canadian Special Forces. This method, delineated by Bartholomew Eldridge et al. (2016), involves six steps: needs assessment, setting objectives, designing the program using evidence-based methods, pilot testing, planning for sustainable implementation, and program evaluation. To this we added two additional aspects that we felt were essential – the incorporation of a multidisciplinary team approach that brings together all subject-matter experts in the human performance domain and a focus on co-creation with end-users, ensuring ethical and practical alignment.

This process was then broken into two stages, methods and results, and each of these was subdivided into two steps. The methods stage was broken into a needs assessment step and a program objective step. The first step of the results stage identified the program design contributions of each discipline including the specific assessment tools, training methods, and outcomes measures that would be utilized in the program, and the final step was implementation of the pilot project (see Table 11.1, Pattyn et al., 2022, p. 5).

Table 11.1 Overview of the four steps of the Intervention Mapping methodology

Methods	
STEP 1 Needs assessment	• Establish a multidisciplinary expert and stakeholders team to design the program. • Determine the current need based on real-life participant observation and analysis.
STEP 2 Determine program objectives	• Setting-up the program within a holistic approach regarding health and performance. • Define an individualized tailor-made approach to customize the whole support. • Address physical activity, nutrition and sleep needs to facilitate healthy lifestyle choice and performance improvement. • Support injury prevention and healthy coping mechanisms.
Results	
STEP 3 Program design according to each area of expertise	• Physiotherapy ◦ Identify body regions discomfort and potential musculoskeletal injuries through a first screening questionnaire. ◦ Provide an overall whole body functional movements assessment. ◦ Offer a detailed assessment for specific injuries involving lower back, cervical or lower/upper limb dysfunctions. • Physical training ◦ Define a detailed individualized physical performance assessment. ◦ Provide a specific, validated and practical test battery ◦ Create an evaluation tool to be used by the PTI, the operator and the physiotherapists. ◦ Provide individualized physical training programs. ◦ Adapt specific nutrition and hydration knowledge to the particular constraints of the population. • Performance psychology ◦ Determine the specific psychometry assessment need. ◦ Specify the most adequate validated trait and state assessment tools. ◦ Provide a customized individual feedback. ◦ Dispense a team workshop to provide feedback and determine possible interventions
STEP 4 Implementation in a pilot project	• Conceive a modular training program about the impact of human factors on the individual and team functioning. • Integrate an evolution from individual functioning to team functioninig; and from participant operator receiving expert advice to autonomous actor of their own performance management. • Distribute the program throughout the year, according to the modular built-up principles discussed earlier: ◦ Four weeks at the unit (January – April – June – December) ◦ Two deployment periods (3 weeks/3 months) with embedded experts.

Adapted from the original (Patton et al., 2022).

Step 1: Needs assessment

To ensure a comprehensive focus on all aspects involved in human performance, professionals from across the fields of clinical medicine, physiotherapy, physical training, nutrition, and performance psychology were brought together to create the program design team. We capitalized on our psychologist's specialization working therapeutically with networks of individuals, resulting in our approach being rooted in psychotherapeutic systems thinking.

To initiate our project, we arranged multiple coordination sessions where all collaborators prioritized their involvement despite other commitments. The first critical step involved each specialist gaining an in-depth understanding of others' fields, recognizing the distinct contributions of each discipline to the program. Specialists demonstrated how their expertise enhanced human performance, detailing their assessment techniques, feedback processes, and intervention strategies. This exchange aimed to achieve two primary objectives: firstly, to develop a comprehensive grasp of the program as a whole, identifying synergies and effective strategies for guiding operators in each domain; and secondly, to showcase the concrete impact of each expert's involvement, underscoring the collaborative essence of the program. We acknowledged that while expanding the scope of expertise beyond their individual interventions might initially appear demanding for our specialists, it is essential to recognize that performance is a holistic concept. Addressing all the "pillars of health" is fundamental to optimizing client performance effectively.

Step 2: Determine program objectives

As the primary approach for the program development process, we adopted a non-hierarchical co-creation approach, actively involving both specialists and the client. This process included unit representatives, team leaders, and key stakeholders in collaborative discussions to foster program relevance, acceptance, and long-term sustainability (Gergen, 2008; Jorgensen, 1989; McTaggart, 1991; McIntyre, 2007; Spradley, 2016). An important aspect of this stage was the deliberate shift of focus from individual clients to the team as the primary beneficiary in aligning with the program's ultimate objectives.

The involvement of clients and stakeholders is crucial in this context. Their buy-in is essential for several reasons. First, it ensures that the program is responsive to the actual needs and expectations of both the individuals and the team as a whole. When clients and stakeholders are involved in the program's design, they are more likely to feel a sense of ownership and commitment to its success. This sense of ownership is vital for the program's acceptance and longevity. Additionally, stakeholders provide valuable insights into the broader organizational context and goals, ensuring that the program aligns with strategic objectives. Their support is also crucial in providing necessary resources, facilitating implementation, and championing the program within the organization. Gaining buy-in and participation from clients and stakeholders as a component of developing the human performance program increases the likelihood of successful implementation, sustained engagement, and the achievement of desired outcomes (Mattie et al., 2020; Pattyn et al., 2022).

Step 3: Program design

Psychological assessments were to first serve as the basis for developing greater individual awareness and then would provide insights into interpersonal styles as they are shared with the team. This process was broken into a three-tiered approach. In the first-tier individual assessments were conducted and the results were mapped using psychometric measures. The second tier focused on providing personalized feedback to each individual. Finally, the third tier involved integrating the assessment results at the team level, which included a psychoeducational approach aimed at fostering self-regulation within the team.

In the study of human performance, the definition or specification of what one should assess is the most essential challenge, whether for individual or crew performance, as Hollnagel (1998) described more than two decades ago. Measurements must be possible, trustworthy, relevant, and valid. Few practical measurements meet all of these conditions, so this continues to be a challenge for those looking to assess team performance. Additionally, the quality of the expert who provides comments and uses the information is often disregarded when analyzing assessment outcomes. A trained systemic psychotherapist and a performance psychologist individually interviewed each participant, followed by a joint feedback session with both professionals. This interdisciplinary collaboration, though uncommon in psychology, was deemed essential based on our previously established criteria.

After consideration of various psychological instruments, including those previously completed by the operators, the psychometric tools chosen for effective team feedback and interventions included the NEO-PI-R, EQi, and the MBTI. The Revised NEO Personality Inventory (NEO-PI-R), was central to this methodology, offering an in-depth analysis of five major personality traits and facets underpinning these traits (Young & Schinka, 2001). To measure emotional intelligence we used the Bar-On Emotional Quotient Inventory (EQi), a tool assessing emotional intelligence across a range of competencies including intrapersonal, interpersonal, stress management, adaptability, and general mood (Bar-On, 1997, 2004). Alongside these, the Myers's-Briggs Type Inventory (MBTI; Boyle, 1995) was incorporated, despite wide skepticism of the its usefulness among psychologists, typified in the theoretical criticism of the MBTI outlined by Stein and Swan (2019). The researchers selected the MBTI primarily because it was familiar to the operators from a previous international training, and in part to leverage its popularity to promote self-awareness and bridge communication gaps between different assessment dimensions.

Considering the team's small and egalitarian structure, a unique "third person" assessment technique was implemented. This involved team members completing the MBTI for each other, aiming to explore the differences between self-perception and how others perceive them. This strategy proved crucial in examining social desirability and authenticity, key elements in maintaining effective team dynamics and coping mechanisms.

The concept of social desirability in assessments, often viewed as a bias, was addressed through the dual categories of self-deception and impression management, as defined by Paulhus (1984). While impression management involves a conscious effort to project a positive image, self-deception is characterized by respondents believing their positive self-reports. Understanding the importance of these aspects in various contexts, including military settings, the researcher included the Balanced Inventory of Desirable Responding (BIDR; Paulhus, 1984, 1991) in the evaluation process. This measure aimed to raise participant awareness of their behavioural tendencies.

Step 4: Implementation blueprint

The implementation of the pilot program was designed to be structured in a modular manner, consisting of six distinct training times over the course of a year. The initial training was scheduled for the only time in the year when the entire team operates together in a standard work environment, commonly known as the "administration and logistics" weeks. We selected this time to start the program, ensuring the availability of all team members for the training. There were also two distinct training programs during deployments that were spread over the one-year period. The first deployment training involved a three-week mountain training session, during which the physical training instructor served as the embedded expert. The second period encompassed a three-month operational deployment, during which the medical doctor assumed the role of the embedded expert for a duration of one month. During these trainings the focus began to shift in emphasis from the individual to the collective entity, specifically the team. Table 11.2 presents a comprehensive summary of the team members' timetable and organization, excluding any consideration of the preliminary work and collaboration among the specialists (Pattyn et al., 2022, p.19). Over the course of the year, the process transitioned from a model in which experts provided guidance to a collaborative approach involving the team, which was informed by emerging insights and accumulated experience.

Table 11.2 Blueprint

Administration and logistics weeks			
BLOCK 1	1 week (Jan)	Education (team classroom sessions)	1. introduction to the program and goalsetting (1 h) 2. exercise physiology and training principles (4 hrs) 3. information processing and learning processes (4 hrs)
		Individual assessment	1. initial medical interview 2. psychometry tools 3. individual intake interview with the clinical psychologist 4. VO2 max testing at the sports physiology laboratory 5. individual physiotherapy screening: questionnaire and consultations
		Team Intervention	first team training session with PTI to illustrate training principles (half day)
BLOCK 2	1 week (Apr)	Education (team classroom sessions)	1. nutrition basics (4 hrs) 2. communication and team cognition (2 hrs) 3. sleep and fatigue management for optimal performance (2 hrs)
		Individual assessments	1. full physical assessment with PTI 2. repeat sleep aspects of psychometry
		Individual Intervention/ Feedback	individual consultation with physiotherapist and PTI to discuss customized training program based on the assessments of block 1.
		Workshop/Practical exercise	1. nutrition: analysis of the different types of field rations used by the unit 2. exercise on determination of metabolic needs in function of different types of settings and activities (based on real exercises/deployments) 3. sleep and fatigue: scheduling examples based on observational data from the mission of the previous year
		Feedback	individual interview with the psychologists regarding the psychometry results from block 1.
		Team intervention	1. introducing the concept of team performance management and the team assessments 2. group workshops around personality types, behavioural preferences, and team dynamics
BLOCK 3	1 week (Jun)	Individual intervention	1. individual follow-up with physiotherapist and PTI on customized training program 2. individual pre-deployment interview with clinical psychologist
		Team intervention/ workshop	1. how to implement the Human Performance Program on deployment. 2. team cognition, performance and human error: how to reframe error analyses (with real-cases examples). 3. team training session with PTI

(*Continued*)

Table 11.2 (Continued)

Administration and logistics weeks			
BLOCK 4	1 week (Dec)	Individual assessment	repeat of the full physical assessment to evaluate impact of deployment
		Individual intervention	follow-up with physiotherapist and PTI on customized training program follow-up consultation with ad hoc experts based on individual needs
		Team intervention/ workshop:	1. debriefing on human performance aspects on deployment: physical activity, nutrition, sleep and fatigue 2. education refresher regarding nutrition and sleep (2 x 2 hrs) based on feedback during deployment
Deployment periods			
Mountain training period	3 weeks (Feb)	• Mixed education/intervention with PTI: • Injury prevention and recovery applied to a technical and tactical setting. • Physical activity as a means (technical), an end (tactical), and a recovery resource (mountaineering activity during the free week-end). • Emphasis on the importance of managing physiological resource spending and acceptable pain thresholds depending on the context. • Illustration of nutrition choices depending on the type of activity.	
Operational deployment	3 months (Aug-Nov)	• Interventions: • Managing nutrition in a resource-constrained environment, based on the previous lectures and workshops; • Adapting sustained operations schedule to the team set-up in terms of chronotype and sleep need; • Individual physical training schedules depending on available time and space. • Availability of the experts (PTI, MD, Physiotherapists, Psychologists) for reach back guidance and support.	

To facilitate the paradigm shift our team workshops drew an initial comparison between Chris Hadfield's memoir detailing his experiences as an astronaut (Hadfield, 2015) and the professional trajectory of an operator. In his narrative, Hadfield provides a lucid account of the transformation in his cognitive framework, wherein he transitions from a competitive and individualistic fighter pilot to a member of a space crew. This shift in perspective leads him to see that his survival prospects in the space environment are contingent upon the collective efficacy of the crew, rather than solely relying on his own capabilities. Hadfield employs the terms "how to be a zero" to depict this transformation in mindset: his transition from striving to be the standout individual in any given system, to endeavouring to function as a highly adaptable and efficient component within a significantly intricate apparatus.

The program built on the insights gained in the individual psychological feedback sessions by facilitating discussion of the information collectively with team members sharing with each other their strengths and weaknesses. In this process the teams were able to begin developing mental maps of how to support each other and utilize each other's strengths. The conclusion of the program involved an interactive classroom activity in which we critically analyzed authentic instances of performance evaluations and human errors from past courses and deployments, drawing upon our first-hand participant observations from embedded experts. This encompassed evaluations of performance in physical or tactical difficulties within training programs, as well as insights derived from post-deployment after-action reports. This phase facilitated the demonstration that individuals who may have appeared to be "high performers" were, in fact, reliant on the system (team, unit) in which they operated to achieve genuine high performance. Further, the team's active engagement in arriving at this understanding demonstrated their ability to apply the concepts covered in the activities beyond our human performance program to real-world scenarios, an essential step for demonstrating the success and effectiveness of the workshop.

Results achieved

The primary positive outcome for the team entailed the enhanced quality of the team dynamics, insights, and self-awareness, thereby instilling a sense of fortitude through the identification of distinct strengths and flaws, as well as the strategic means to rectify them. The successful application of the selected knowledge and behavioural skills was demonstrated through the effective transfer of information across individual interventions, team workshops, and classroom sessions to real-life settings. Nevertheless, the participants also expressed a significant degree of dissatisfaction over the perceived "culture clash" within the unit, which presented challenges in effectively implementing their acquired knowledge. This underscores the necessity for the successful implementation of such a program to encompass all levels of end users and management in decision-making and program development. Given the scale of an organization such as Defence, certain decision-making procedures cannot be effectively decentralized and efforts such as this must be viewed as an iterative process. This type of program could perhaps be facilitated within the context of a sports team setting, with a higher autonomy, or in a more decentralized organization.

Case study: trouble with boundary spanning

The Officer in Charge (OIC) of an Intelligence Department at a military unit sought help to address problems with burnout that were plaguing his team. Military intelligence is a specialized branch of the armed forces focused on the collection, analysis, and dissemination of information that is vital for military decision-making. They play a critical role in all military operations. Personnel in military intelligence are tasked with gathering data through various means, analyzing this information, and then providing the analysis to the command as part of their planning processes. Their work requires that they collaborate with other teams, the command group, and external agencies to provide a comprehensive understanding of potential threats and security issues related to the mission.

To get an understanding of what was going on in this intelligence team we began with the administration of the 30-item Team Process Survey (Mathieu et al., 2019) and included four open-ended questions. Specifically, which elements of your team's performance are key to your current success? What areas of teamwork does your team need to improve to optimize performance? What type of resources does your team need to perform better? And, is there another question/issue that should be asked about how this team works together? The survey is on a five-point Likert scale and results under 3 were considered a weakness while above 4 were considered a strength. The results are indicated below (see Table 11.3 below). The outcomes from the open-ended questions were analyzed to determine the team dynamics they represented. The findings aligned with the survey results and offered insights directly from the team members, expressed in their own words.

As is evident, the team was having significant difficulty identifying their priorities. Material from the open-ended questions suggested that they specifically had a hard time prioritizing which actions were most important, as they felt that it was their responsibility to respond to all requests that came to the department. They did not feel empowered to say no to any unit member who requested their support. This resulted in an unmanageable workload that led to all the team members putting in extreme hours. They provided good backup behaviour to each other in their effort to cover everything and showed good ability to manage their relationships with each other, but the stress was clearly evident.

Table 11.3 Intel "Team Process Survey" results

	Transition Processes: 3.16	
	Mission Analysis:	3.36
1	Identify our main tasks?	3.36
2	Identify the key challenges that we expect to face?	3.45
3	Determine the resources that we need to be successful?	3.55
	Goal specification:	2.79
6	Set goal for the team?	2.55
7	Ensure that everyone on our team clearly understand our goals?	2.82
8	Link our goal with the strategic direction of the organization?	3.0
	Strategy Formulation and Planning:	3.24
9	Develop an overall strategy to guide our team activities?	2.73
10	Prepare contingency ('if then') plans to deal with uncertain situations?	3.73
11	Know when to stick with a given working plan, and when to adopt a different one?	3.27
	Action Processes: 3.16	
	Monitoring Progress Toward Goals:	3.22
12	Regularly monitor how well we are meeting our team goals?	2.36
13	Use clearly defined metrics to assess our progress?	2.18
14	Seek timely feedback form stakeholders (e.g. customers, top, management, other organizational units) about how well we are meeting our goals?	2.91
	Systems Monitoring:	3.36
15	Monitor and manage our resources (e.g. equipment, manpower, etc. …)?	3.18
16	Monitor important aspects of our work environment (e.g. inventories, equipment and process operations, information flows)?	3.27
17	Monitor events and conditions outside the team that influence our operations?	3.64
	Team Monitoring and Backup:	3.82
18	Develop standards for acceptable team member performance?	4.00
19	Balance the workload among our team members?	3.18
20	Assist each other when help is needed?	4.27
	Coordination:	3.48
21	Communicate well with each other?	3.36
22	Smoothly integrate our work efforts?	3.64
23	Coordinate our activities with one another?	3.45
	Interpersonal Processes: 3.62	
	Conflict Management:	3.97
24	Deal with personal conflicts in fair and equitable ways?	3.82
25	Show respect for one another?	4.45
26	Maintain group harmony?	3.64
	Motivating and Confidence Building:	3.67
29	Take pride in our accomplishments?	3.18
30	Develop confidence in our team's ability to perform well?	3.91
31	Encourage each other to perform our very best?	3.91
	Affect Management:	3.21
32	Share a sense of togetherness and cohesion?	3.73
33	Manage stress?	2.73
34	Keep a good emotional balance in the team?	3.18

A one-day workshop was developed to address these concerns. In the workshop the team was broken into work groups to discuss how to communicate with other teams and clients when their requests are not aligned with the command's priorities and would draw away resources from primary tasks. Each work group gave a report of their discussion, and then the team came to a shared understanding of how they will collectively communicate with the command group, other teams, and unit members. They agreed to a common phrasing that they would use to set a clear boundary that would help others recognize when what they were asking for was not focused on the units strategic priorities. As a result, the team was able to feel empowered to address their situation which improved morale and reduced their perceived stress level.

In this case summary the Team Process Survey and four open-ended questions were used to gather data on the difficulties faced by a military Intelligence Department facing intense stress. The results were used to develop a one-day workshop in which the team developed their own way of addressing their situation which empowered the team, boosting morale and reducing stress levels.

Case study: developing high-performing flight crews

Traditionally, the performance of a team is associated with taskwork and the products of taskwork in the sense of how well the team achieves the objectives of its tasks. However, when trying to comprehensively understand team performance, it is appropriate to look at more than simply the outcome of the team's task. Focusing only on output performance will provide a narrow view about the performance of team members and the team as a whole. This approach potentially misses the complexity of the task environment, behaviour of the team members during the task, as well as team processes and emergent states leading to the output.

In air combat, teams operate in a constantly changing, probabilistic environment and decisions are often made with incomplete information. As a result, a team might achieve the desired result in almost any decision-making activity even with incorrect decisions. On the other hand, an undesirable outcome can be reached after making all the right decisions. In both cases, the team members could have good or poor perceptions of each other's actions and knowledge about the environment when conducting the task; their cognitive resources could be completely depleted, or their mental workload may be low. Considerations of this type, some of which are also related to teamwork (i.e., how the team does a task) must be taken into account in order to draw a holistic view of team performance. This following case study discusses how to obtain a comprehensive estimate for team performance by using task performance, normative performance, team situation awareness, and mental workload as supplementary measures for the team's output performance. These metrics are illustrated with examples, and their measurement practices are introduced. This section also considers effects of explicit coordination on teamwork, i.e., the communication of team members, as well as implicit coordination based on their shared knowledge, or team situation awareness. Affective concepts, such as cooperation and psychological safety, as well as some concepts related to teamwork, such as backup behaviour and mutual performance monitoring, are not addressed. The measures discussed in this section are summarized in Figure 11.5.

Output performance (OP)

The most traditional way of assessing team performance is to measure a team's output performance (OP) after its action period. A sales department's OP can be evaluated by reviewing the sales at the end of the quarter, or the output performance of a football team can be assessed by simply looking at the scoreboard at the end of the second half. OP is the most used measure in air combat when evaluating the performance of a flight. A flight is the standard team used in air combat. It comprises

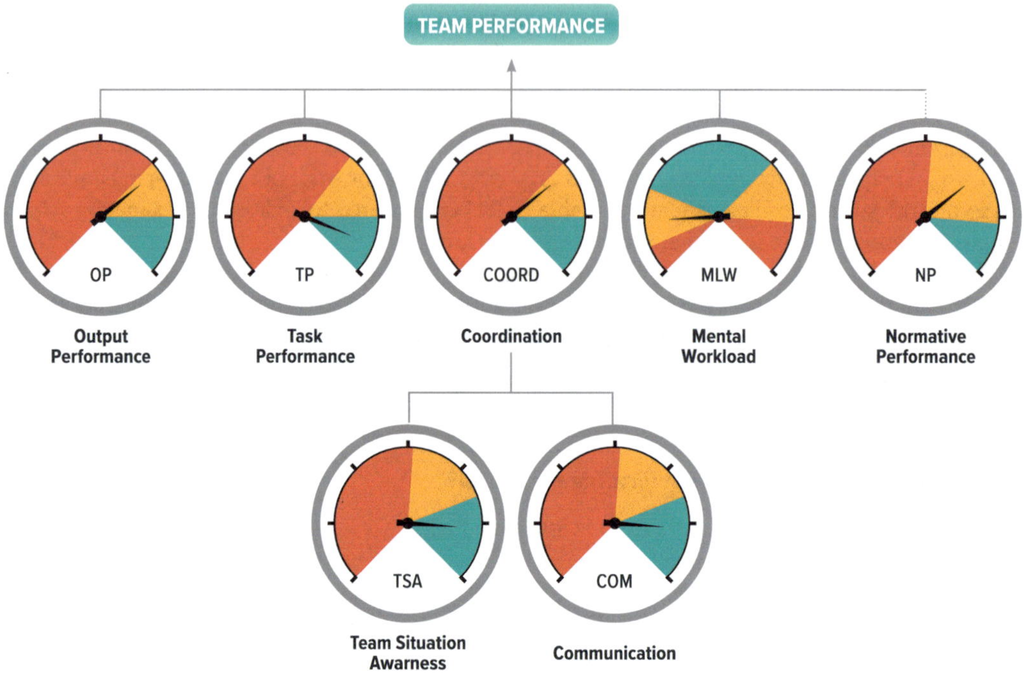

Figure 11.5 Air Combat Team Performance. Summary of measures used to evaluate team performance. The measures include output performance (OP), task performance (TP), coordination (COORD), team situation awareness (TSA), communication (COM), mental workload (MWL) and normative performance (NP).

four aircraft arranged in two sections with two aircraft (lead and wing) in each. The most typical OP measure used is the ratio between the number of enemy aircraft shot down to the number of friendly aircraft lost. While it is the measure of performance most directly related to the objectives of the mission, it only provides a relatively narrow insight concerning the team's performance and it potentially misses the complexity of air combat. It does not reflect the flight's taskwork using tactical operating procedures, the team's competency and the applicability of the aircraft systems utilized (Mansikka et al., 2021a). One way to gain a better understanding about a team's performance is to evaluate its task performance.

Task performance (TP)

Task performance (TP) can be best explained with an example. Imagine that the national football team of England plays two practice games against France. The manager of England decides to play the first game using one set of tactics and the second game using another, whereas France uses the same tactics in both games. From all other aspects, both teams are assumed to perform similarly in both games. The final score in both games is 0-0. Does this mean that both the English national team tactics were equally good in both matches? Not necessarily, because the final score itself does not say much about what happened during the game. It could be that in the first game England was constantly just inches away from scoring a goal, whereas France may have dominated the second game but were just unlucky. To gain an insight about team performance and the dynamics of the game, we need other indicators in addition to the OP.

One way to do this is to measure the team's TP. When TP is measured, the team's task must be divided into recognizable and measurable phases or stages. Using the same football example again, TP could be described as a hierarchical construct where during the first phase the English team must gain possession of the ball. In the next phase, the team must move the ball into France's defensive zone. Then, in the third phase, the English team must pass the ball and position the players such that the French defensive line is broken and an attempt on goal is made. Finally, if the English team successfully completes the fourth phase and a goal is scored, this is reflected in both teams' OP.

Any TP measurement should start by identifying the hierarchical phases or stages impacting the OP of the team. There is no global way to describe the progress of teams' taskwork. In air combat, the flight's taskwork can be described as the management of two parallel processes called the live-chain and kill-chain (Joint Chief of Staff 2013). On one hand, the flight tries to shoot down the enemy fighters, but on the other hand it tries to deny the enemy from killing members of the friendly flight. Both friendly and enemy pilots can engage a number of opposing aircraft at the same time. Every friendly pilot has a kill-chain against each enemy aircraft. The management of a kill-chain can be assigned to a single pilot, or the management of a single kill-chain can be a joint effort between several flight members. However, at the same time, each pilot has only one live-chain.

TP describes how close or how far the team is from achieving its overall goal, such as destroying the enemy aircraft while staying alive. In air combat, the kill-chain can be divided into phases such as find, target, engage, and assess. During the find phase, the flight attempts to find the enemy aircraft with its radar. Once found, the enemy aircraft is targeted. This means that the follow-on management of the kill-chain is assigned to a flight member or a group of flight members. The responsible flight member (or members) manoeuvres into a position where they can launch weapons against the targeted enemy aircraft. As the launch parameters are satisfied, a weapon is launched and the engage phase begins. The engage phase continues until the weapon hits or misses the enemy aircraft. At this point, the flight's kill-chain progresses to the assess phase. During the assess phase, the flight evaluates whether a satisfactory effect on the enemy has been achieved or does its kill-chain need further management? It is important to note that TP is a hierarchical construct, where the preceding phase must be satisfied for the following phase to be reached. As such, the phases associated with TP can move dynamically back and forth. For example, in air combat, the friendly team can lose track of the enemy aircraft in the middle of the target phase. If this happens, the kill-chain against that enemy aircraft reverts to the find phase.

In air combat, the live-chain is essentially about denying the opposing team's kill-chain from progressing. Due to the equilibrium of the chains, the live-chain has phases which mirror the phases of the kill-chain. The phases of the live-chain can be described as deny-find, deny-target, deny-engage, and deny-assess. Each time the phase of the kill-chain changes, it also changes the opposing side's live-chain. From the perspective of TP, any force-on-force setup, such as air combat, is a zero-sum game: both teams have similar kill- and live-chains, where a gain in a one team's kill-chain results in an equal loss in the other team's live-chain and vice versa.

As noted earlier, teams with different pilots, aircraft systems, or tactics might achieve equivalent OP but this does not mean their TPs are similar. If TPs are dissimilar but OPs are similar, the flight who has kept its members' live-chains more intact will have maintained a greater survival margin. In the same vein, a flight whose kill-chains have progressed further will have been closer to achieving the desired effect on the enemy. In summary, it is more informative to evaluate TP based on the progression of the kill- and live-chains than just OP alone (Mansikka et al., 2021a).

When the phases in the TP measurement involve cognitive characteristics, such as situation awareness, it is essential to differentiate the machine phases from the human-machine phases. For example, an aircraft's sensor may have detected an enemy aircraft, but the pilot may have allocated his/her attention elsewhere and thus be completely unaware of the changed machine phase. If the phase changes can be unambiguously observed from the system with which the team members interact, the measurement of the machine TP can be evaluated in real time by simply logging the system status or events associated with the chain changes. However, the measurement of the human-machine TP can be laborious and time-consuming. In air combat, the task situation can be highly dynamic and chaotic as the multiple kill-chains and the live-chains of individual pilots move constantly back and forth. Real-time evaluation of the phases of the kill- and live-chains can seriously disrupt the execution of the primary task. It is therefore essential that the human-machine TP is evaluated after the task. To do this the flight members must be able to recall what happened during the task execution and to verbalize how they understood the kill- and live-chains to have evolved. To avoid the TP measurement from turning into a memory recall task, it is recommended to replicate or reconstruct the progression of the tasks and thereby assist the flight members in recalling how the tasks evolved from the perspective of TP. With relatively little practice, trained pilots can usually provide highly accurate assessment of their TP phases.

Compared to OP, TP provides a far more diagnostic measure of team performance. With TP, it is possible to differentiate the competencies of teams, the procedures they follow, and the effectiveness of the tools and systems they use, even when these differences cannot be identified from OP. In addition, TP can reveal if the team performance was closer to being good or closer to being bad as evaluated by the team's OP.

Normative performance (NP)

Normative performance (NP) describes the level of adherence to the team's tactics, techniques, and procedures (TTPs), i.e., how accurately they are followed during a team's task execution (Mansikka et al., 2021d). While NP is not a measure of team performance per se, it plays a critical role when the utility of TTPs, the competence of teams, or the applicability of a team's tools and systems are evaluated and compared. NP also considers the impact that non-adherence of TTPs has on task accomplishment, i.e., OP.

While the concept of NP was originally developed for the assessment of air combat TTPs, the principles of NP can be extended beyond air combat. For example, let us consider the previous football example again. As discussed, the head coach of England tried two different tactics. But let us also assume that the head coach was stuck in traffic on the M25 motorway around London and could not see the game. Could s/he still draw conclusions about the effectiveness of those two tactics based on OP and TP alone? Probably not. This is because without the knowledge of the team's NP, the head coach would not know whether the team had followed the tactics they were supposed to follow. As this example highlights, the concept of NP can be used in many different domains. However, for the sake of clarity, the rest of the section deals only with the adherence of air combat TTPs.

For NP measurement to be possible, the directed TTP must be documented in sufficient detail, and it must be possible to identify possible TTP adherence violations during or after its execution. The NP measurement starts by identifying the core tasks a flight must undertake to be successful in air combat. Depending on the depth and breadth of the analysis, a large number of tasks may be identified.

Almost every task in air combat is somehow regulated and could thus be included in the assessment of NP. However, as it would be impractical to assess the team's adherence to every possible task it in which it engages, the number of tasks evaluated with NP measures must be reduced to a manageable level (Mansikka et al., 2021b). Subject matter experts (SMEs) can assist in identifying the most relevant tasks. SMEs can also help in reducing the number of nominated tasks by combining and grouping them into meaningful units and removing possible duplicates. This process may require several iterations. The selection of the most relevant tasks can be conducted by rating the tasks based on their impact on the flight's OP. A decision-tree format based on the Cooper-Harper scale (Cooper & Harper 1969) can be useful when doing this – especially when each rating in the decision tree is associated with a verbal description. Figure 11.6 (adapted from Mansikka et al., 2021b) illustrates a Cooper-Harper type tool for rating the tasks based on their importance for the flight's air combat mission. In this figure, the importance of the tasks ranges from 1 (low importance) to 5 (high importance). Based on the resulting ratings, the tasks can be shortlisted such that the NP measurement captures a desired number of tasks with known importance to the flight's OP.

NP is measured by comparing the flight's task execution with that described for each sub-task. If the automatic measurement of NP is not possible (as is often the case) the NP measurement can best be conducted post-task. Post-task NP measurement requires that the flight's task execution can be recorded or otherwise tracked and reviewed. It can also be done by using observer ratings or the flight members can conduct the NP measurement by themselves. Usually SME observers

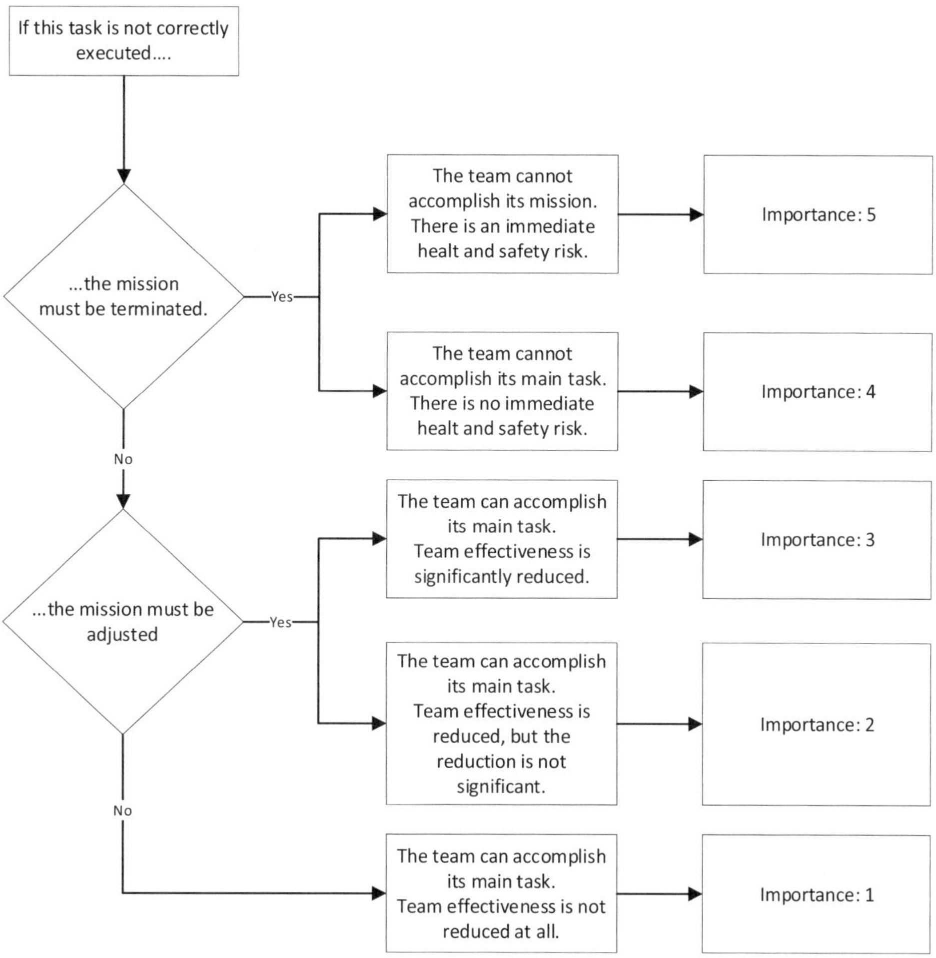

Figure 11.6 Cooper-Harper type tool for rating the tasks based on their importance for the flight's air combat mission (adapted from Mansikka, H., Virtanen, K., Mäkinen, L. and Harris, D. (2021b). Normative Performance Measurement in Simulated Air Combat. Aerospace Medicine and Human Performance, 92(11), 908-912).

are preferred, as the measurer must be capable of evaluating how the degree of adherence or non-adherence affects the flight's overall task accomplishment.

To enable scoring of NP, questions tapping the execution correctness of each sub-task must be generated. For example, an adherence question evaluating an aircrew's engine start-up procedure could read as: "Did the crew follow the established standard operating procedure for engine start-up?" As the team's NP is reviewed, each time a nominated sub-task is performed, an associated adherence question is introduced and the NP regarding that sub-task is scored (Mansikka et al., 2021b). The NP score is based on the level of process or procedure adherence and the impact that a possible nonadherence has on the overall task accomplishment. While there is no global scale for NP, a scale ranging from 0 (low NP) to 3 (high NP) has proven to be practical (Mansikka et al., 2021b). Within the scale, each score is associated to a verbal description as follows:

- 0 = Did not adhere to an established process or procedure. The non-adherence had a negative impact on the overall task accomplishment. The negative impact was significant;
- 1 = Did not adhere to an established process or procedure. The non-adherence had a negative impact on the overall task accomplishment. The impact was not significant;
- 2 = Did not adhere to the process or procedure. The non-adherence had no impact on the overall task accomplishment;
- 3 = Did adhere to the process or procedure.

Once all the shortlisted sub-tasks have been assigned a NP score, an overall NP score for each flight member can be formed by averaging the individual scores. The level of an acceptable NP must be determined on a case-by-case basis.

To summarize, whenever a new work process, procedure or tool is introduced, one should always make sure that the new workflow is being followed and executed accordingly before drawing any conclusions concerning whether it is effective or not. Unless satisfactory NP is verified, all other team performance measures may have little or no meaning as it could be that the team never did what it was supposed to do.

Mental workload (MWL)

Mental workload (MWL) characterizes the demands imposed by the tasks on limited mental resources when the desired performance is to be maintained (Vicente et al., 1987; Parasuraman et al., 2008). From the perspective of performance, too low or too high workload is not desirable and the optimal level of cognitive resource expenditure lies somewhere between the two extremes.

The available cognitive resources define the portion of such resources to achieve a desired level of performance. The variations of task demand cause variations in the amount of resources required to satisfy that demand. From the perspective of an individual, the task demand can be managed by, for example, either lowering or increasing the personal desired level of performance, i.e., varying the amount of effort invested on the task, and/or by changing the strategy used for executing the task. However, in air combat and many other safety critical tasks, the satisfactory level of performance cannot be lowered and if the task demand increases, the predefined level of performance must be maintained by investing more resources and greater voluntary effort. Unfortunately, once the pilot's cognitive resources have been depleted, performance will begin to deteriorate regardless of the amount of effort invested. In many dynamic tasks, working memory is often the most performance-limiting cognitive resource.

An unbalanced MWL has a negative impact on both individual and team performance. A team has several ways to manage its members' MWL. First, a team may try to organize and allocate its tasks such that the team members are not exposed to an undesirable level of task demands. Second, a team may attempt to lower the MWL experienced by team members by changing the teams' operating strategy. Third, assuming that overload is a problem, the team could release team members with too low cognitive capacity and replace them with individuals with higher capacity. For a team to be aware whether MWL is an issue, the MWL of team members must be measured.

MWL cannot be measured directly. Most empirical measures can be categorized either as behavioural (or performance based), subjective, or physiological. Behavioural measures can be broadly divided into primary and secondary task measures (Paas et al., 2003). When secondary task measures are used, an operator is given both a primary task and a secondary task. The operator is expected to maintain his/her performance on the primary task and to use any excess cognitive capacity on the secondary task (Casner & Gore, 2010). Variations in the secondary task performance are assumed to reflect the amount of spare capacity – and hence the MWL caused by the primary task (Verwey & Veltman, 1996; Ogden et al., 1979; Brown, 1978). The secondary task measures are, by their nature, disruptive and cannot be safely utilized in high-risk environments when the MWL is high (O'Donnell et al., 1986; Casali & Wierwille, 1984). The primary task measures are based on the assumption that the pilot's primary performance is related to MWL. The sensitivity of the primary task measures decreases as MWL moves towards the high or low extremes. All secondary task-based measures are unique to the scenario and the secondary task used. There is no MWL metric that can be generalized from such measures.

Physiological measures of MWL are based on the physiological changes caused by arousal, effort, and general activation level. As different tasks cause different physiological responses, not all physiological measures are sensitive to MWL in all tasks. A wide range of measures tapping physiological changes in either the central nervous system or the peripheral nervous system have been developed. These include measures such as electroencephalographic (EEG) activity (Berka et al., 2007), event-related brain potentials (ERPs) (Kramer et al., 1987), electrooculographic (EOG) standing potentials (Ryu & Myung, 2005), functional near-infrared spectroscopy (fNIRS) (Hamann & Carstengerdes, 2022), heart rate (HR) (Reimer & Mehler, 2011), heart rate variability (HRV) (Mehler et al., 2011), electrodermal activity (EDA) (Setz et al., 2010), and electromyography (EMG) (Roman-Liu et al., 2013).

HR and HRV are probably the most widely used physiological measures of MWL. HR measures the heart's beat-to-beat sinus rhythm or interval, whereas HRV measures the differences between these intervals (Sampson & McGrath, 2015; Houghton & Gray, 2014; Ivanov et al., 1999). While physiological measures allow objective, continuous, and real-time monitoring of the pilot's state, which does not intrude on performance, their sensitivity may become limited when used during a flight. For example, pupillary diameter may be affected not only by variations in the information processing demands, but also by variations in the eye's fixation distance or ambient lightning. In a similar fashion, cardiological responses can be affected by blood pressure variations, body temperature, and arterial pressure. In fighter aviation, factors like extreme cockpit temperatures, exposure to direct sunlight and high G-loads can generate physiological responses which can, if not properly controlled, be falsely interpreted as MWL responses. In addition, the instrumentation used for physiological MWL measuring is often bulky, disruptive, and requires expensive aircraft integration and flight approval. Physiological responses are also unique to the individual and once again, there is no generalizable metric of MWL. All MWL measures are relative to the various task conditions. While HR and HRV have been successfully used to measure MWL in a simulator environment (Mansikka et al., 2019a; 2016a; 2016b), recent developments in smart rings and other wearable technologies may open new possibilities for physiological MWL measurement during a flight as well (see Kinnunen et al., 2020; Kinnunen & Koskimäki, 2018; Stone et al., 2021).

Subjective measures of MWL, on the other hand, are easy to employ in simulated and real fighter missions, and they generally enjoy high face validity with wide operator acceptance. However, subjective measures have been criticized for their inherent tendency to generate time-related errors as the data collection is typically conducted after the activity. In addition, subjective measures typically rely on a MWL rating scale of some sort. This mechanism is a source of bias as the subjects must memorize their past sensations and arrange them to a rating scale (Annett, 2002). In addition, the number of different task features and the phasing of high and low task demand events can affect subjectively sensed MWL (Wierwille et al., 1985). Subjective, post-task measures have been criticized as it is often unclear if the rating reflects average workload for the task, peak workload during the task, or is a measure of the user's experience of MWL during the latter stages of the task. Furthermore, the potentially negative outcomes of unbalanced workload may limit the willingness to report MWL honestly (Mansikka et al., 2019a).

NASA-TLX (Task Load Index) is the most widely used subjective MWL measurement method. It is a multidimensional method, where MWL is assessed across six dimensions. Despite its popularity, it has some serious challenges. For example, the original NASA-TLX weighting technique based on pairwise comparisons of MWL dimensions' importance does not allow directly expressing two or more dimensions as equally important. Also, if pairwise comparisons are conducted consistently, there exists only one possible importance order for the dimensions. Finally, with consistently conducted pairwise comparisons, a weight of 0.33 is artificially forced on the most important dimension and the least important dimension is given a zero weight. Thus, in practice, the contribution of one of the dimensions is not considered at all. These challenges can be overcome by determining weights of load dimensions with the Swing weighting method (see Virtanen et al., 2021 for details of how to apply Swing weighting with NASA-TLX).

In summary, both subjective and physiological MWL measures may be effective and sensitive in certain situations but highly ineffective or unreliable in others. While Mansikka et al. (2019a) have demonstrated HR/HRV and subjective measures to be equally sensitive when assessing flight members MWL in an air combat environment, the final selection of the type of MWL measure(s) should be assessed on a case-by-case basis.

In flight, no obtrusive measures or ones that require divided attention on the part of the pilot should be used. These may be acceptable in a simulator, but care needs to be taken that they do not impinge on the flight task being evaluated. In general, most physiological measures associated with the collection of ECG, respiration rate, or blood pressure can be used at any time. However, there can often be problems associated with locating and securing the equipment safely in the aircraft itself, especially in smaller types. In general, EEG, EOG, and electrodermal responses are impractical to collect in flight. To help improve reliability of MWL measures, particularly intra-rater reliability, consideration should be given to performing a series of workload ratings on a number of reference tasks (of varying levels of workload) to help "calibrate" the pilots, prior to making the workload assessments on the tasks of interest. This also helps to avoid "errors of severity" or "errors of leniency" when making assessments.

(Team) situation awareness (T)SA, communication (COMM) and coordination

Various definitions of situation awareness (SA) have been proposed. All relate to the acquisition of task specific information for integration into a dynamic mental model to support a pilot's dynamic decision-making processes. SA is not "achieved"; it is constantly being revised and updated during a flight in light of new task-relevant information. Endsley's (1988; 1995) three-level model of SA is perhaps the most frequently cited theory. In this SA is defined as "...the perception of the elements in the environment within a volume of time and space [SA level 1], the comprehension of their meaning [SA level 2], and the projection of their status in the near future [SA level 3]" (Endsley, 1995; p. 36). At level 1, SA is based on the perception of the basic building blocks of data obtained from the environment, cockpit systems, and tactical communications, etc. At the second level, obtained data are integrated to form a holistic understanding of the situation, aiming to achieve the comprehension of all significant elements within it: data start to become information (Ackoff, 1989). Level 3 SA addresses the pilot's understanding of the tactical situation and how it will evolve in the near future. Ensley's model is essentially hierarchical in nature, with each level building upon the preceding lower level; poor SA at a lower-level results in low SA at subsequently higher levels (e.g., Endsley and Garland, 2000). SA forms the basis of pilot decision-making.

In a flight, each pilot will have their own SA, however, the flight also has a collective team SA (TSA). TSA is more complex than individual SA. There are many definitions of TSA. Endsley (1995) defined TSA as "the degree to which every team member possesses the SA required for his or her responsibilities" (p. 39). Salas et al. (1995) suggested that "TSA is at least in part the shared understanding of a situation among team members at one point in time" (p. 131). Wellens (1993) defined it as "the sharing of a common perspective between two or more individuals regarding current environmental events, their meaning and projected future status" (p.6). Salmon et al. (2008) suggested that TSA comprised the SA of individual members; their shared SA (the elements of a common mental model combined with an appreciation of individual responsibilities), and the emergent, "common picture" which was the combined SA of the whole team.

A flight uses its TSA to understand and predict the progress of an air combat engagement, and hence to select appropriate TTPs to enable the execution of kill- or live-chains (Rouse & Morris, 1986; Mansikka et al., 2023b). TSA builds upon the theory of transactive memory (Wegner, 1985) and shared cognition (Rogers, 1997). A transactive memory system (TMS) has two basic components: the knowledge resident in each team member, and a set of transactive processes concerning what members collectively understand about the knowledge held by others. The knowledge possessed by team members can be highly variable and redundant. Rogers (1997) further illustrated the generic properties of cognition in teams, describing how members interact, allowing them to pool their cognitive resources and share knowledge through both implicit and formal communication, building upon their prior knowledge of each other.

The measurement of TSA in a fast-moving, dynamic context such as air combat poses several difficulties. Techniques which require pausing activities to make SA measurements (e.g., Cooke et al., 1997; Bolstad & Endsley, 2003; Sulistyawati et al., 2009) are not always possible, especially during a live exercise. Salmon et al. (2009) criticized the validity of this approach, suggesting it was unclear if it was SA or recall memory being assessed. Sulistyawati et al. (2009) also used combat performance measures to assess TSA effectiveness, but this can be a misleading as there is often a dissociation between SA and OP, TP or both (see Mansikka et al., 2019b).

Self- or peer-appraisal assessment techniques (e.g., Weigl et al., 2020) do not intrude on TP, but have been criticized as they may reflect pilot confidence or knowledge rather than TSA (Lichacz, 2006; Prince et al., 2007). Fowlkes et al. (1994), Salas et al. (1995), Bolstad and Endsley (2003), and Gorman et al. (2006) all argue that TSA is an emergent state, rather than a product of teamwork. As a result, the best method to assess TSA is by examining teamwork behaviours. Rosenman et al. (2018) developed a measurement approach based upon post-task probes of SA. The score was based upon the response accuracy to these questions, and the TSA metric was derived from averaging the pairwise agreement for each dyad in the team.

To address some of these measurement issues Mansikka et al. (2021c; 2023a) developed a TSA measurement technique based upon Endsley's freeze-probe SAGAT (Situation Awareness Global Assessment Technique; Endsley, 1988) combined with a shortened form of the critical decision-making (CDM) interview approach (Crandall et al., 2006). During a post-sortie debrief, an instructor pilot (IP) would reconstruct the mission using cockpit video, simulator flight trajectories, sensor tracks, weapon simulations, etc. At significant decision points the post-sortie replay would be paused, and a set of questions based upon relevant attributes relating to different levels of SA would be asked. With the help of deepening probes, the pilots were assisted to compare their expectations with the manner in which the simulated combat situation evolved.

In contrast to other measures of TSA, Mansikka et al. (2021c; 2023a) derived two related metrics: TSA accuracy (TSA ACC) and TSA similarity (TSA SIM). TSA ACC is a measure of how closely the flight's collective knowledge is aligned with the ground truth and TSA similarity (TSA SIM) is a measure of the similarity of team members' SA (Mansikka et al., 2021c).

To assess TSA ACC, each pilot's SA accuracy for a relevant attribute at a decision point was established. To do that, the accuracy of the pilot's cognitive model of the situation was compared to the simulation ground truth. The SA accuracies were scored, and scores were aggregated to provide an overall SA accuracy score for a single pilot (see Mansikka et al. 2021c; 2023a for further details). Separate scores were calculated for each SA level. By summing the individual pilots' SA accuracy scores at each SA level, level 1-3 TSA ACC indexes for the flight were obtained. TSA SIM was determined by making pairwise comparisons of level 1-3 SA accuracy at each decision point between all members of the flight (Mansikka et al., 2023a). A higher score was associated with a higher similarity.

For most purposes, the evaluation of TSA ACC is adequate but taken alone it does not portray a complete picture of the shared situational knowledge possessed by the flight. If TSA ACC is high, the flight's TSA is closely aligned with the ground truth, and in such a situation, the SA of each flight member must also be very similar. If TSA ACC is low, however, flight members can have similar or dissimilar SA.

It was found that a flight's TP showed a curvilinear relationship with TSA ACC (Mansikka et al., 2021c; 2023a). As TSA accuracy increased, there were diminishing returns in TP. Gains in TP decreased disproportionately with increases in TSA. Furthermore, the strongest predictors of OP or TP (or both) were level 1 TSA measures. Low TSA SIM was found to have a negative impact on combat performance both offensively and defensively (Mansikka et al., 2023a). These findings were consistent with Endsley's hierarchical model of SA.

The main challenge in achieving high TSA is the coordination of the flight members (Mansikka et al., 2023b; 2023c). If both aspects of TSA are high (ACC and SIM) the pilots can anticipate the actions of other flight members without communication. Explicit coordination depends upon active communication, whereas implicit coordination relies on the flight coordinating its members' actions without such verbal efforts. Implicit coordination is based on members' shared knowledge about each other, the task, and the task environment. In so doing this enables flight members to anticipate each other's actions without need for overt communication (Entin & Serfaty, 1999; Rico et al., 2008; Stout et al., 2017). Team members require common knowledge about the task situation during the action phase while they are updating their knowledge by ongoing situation assessment. Implicit coordination enables a flight to rapidly synchronize its activities.

Team training has been found to facilitate the formation of TMSs as well as TSA. For stable groups, such as a flight, the effect of team training also extends beyond the task for which they are initially trained (Lewis et al., 2005). On the other hand, communication facilitates the encoding, storage, retrieval, and update of information drawn from individual memory system components. Peltokorpi and Hood (2019) observed that the frequency of communication decreases over time as teams increase in familiarity. Mansikka et al. (2023a) examined the relationship between within-flight communications, TSA and OP. During simulated engagements TSA ACC nonlinearly increased with a concomitant decrease in the number of SA-related communication acts. In a similar vein, when TSA started to deteriorate, additional communication as a means to recover TSA was observed not to be effective; increased communication was associated with poorer TSA. There was less communication in successful engagements as measured by OP compared to unsuccessful engagements. In highly time-pressured, high-workload, and extremely dynamic situations such as air combat, attempts at explicit coordination may be counterproductive. In such cases, implicit coordination based upon the common knowledge developed during team training is the better option.

Dissociation of SA, MWL, and OP

Both Vidulich and Wickens (1986) and Yeh and Wickens (1988) noted that MWL can become dissociated from performance, particularly if the task is resource limited. The relationship between SA and performance (OP and TP) can also be complex and unclear (Sulistyawati et al., 2009; Mansikka et al., 2019b). A pilot's awareness of the task demands, which is predicated upon their SA, will partially determine their MWL. Mansikka et al. (2019b) observed that when pilots had low awareness of the tactical situation, they also exhibited a combination of low workload and poor OP and/or TP: they were not aware of the need to invest more cognitive effort to enhance their SA. Furthermore, in a highly dynamic and uncertain environment such as air combat, both success and failure can occasionally be a product of chance (Mansikka et al., 2021a).

In summary

Focusing only on the outcome of a team's task, i.e., the product of taskwork, may give a biased estimate for the performance of a team and provide little explanation for the observed level of performance. A much richer picture of team performance can be obtained by also considering taskwork processes and teamwork, including the coordination mechanisms of team members. Such a holistic performance evaluation can be carried out with the five-dimensional measurement approach discussed. It offers a way to explain why a specific performance level has, or has not, been achieved in an understandable, transparent, and traceable manner. This kind of insight can be utilized in many ways, for example, when identifying means to improve the performance of a team. It should be noted that dependences between the performance metrics discussed, as well as the utility of any metric depends on the context in which the team performance is evaluated. All of them might not be used in all cases but it is important to acknowledge the availability of these complementary measurement techniques when assessing performance of teams undertaking complex tasks.

Conclusion

Team performance, as we have seen, is more than mere aggregates of individual performance. Teams are complex networks where each member's performance, well-being, and development are inextricably linked to the collective functioning of the group. The synergy that emerges from effective team dynamics transcends individual capabilities, leading to enhanced performance, resilience, and fulfilment.

From the foundational work at the Hawthorne Works to the innovative approaches in special operations forces and flight crews, the evolution of team performance research and application demonstrates a continuous quest to understand and optimize the interplay of individual skills, team processes, and environmental factors. The progression of our understanding of linear IPO models to a more dynamic conceptualization of teams as complex adaptive systems reveals a deepening appreciation of the nuanced interrelations that define team performance.

Real-world applications further illustrate a practical process for developing team training programs. These case studies highlight the critical role of team assessments, both informal and formal, in diagnosing and enhancing team performance. They show how tailored interventions, based on a deep understanding of team dynamics and individual contributions, can significantly improve both team effectiveness and member satisfaction.

In summary, this chapter illuminates the complexities and rewards of effective team performance. It underscores the importance of understanding and nurturing the intricate dynamics within teams to harness their full potential. The profound truth that no one is an island finds its embodiment in the realm of teams, where the collective interplay of skills, knowledge, and emotions shapes not only the outcomes of team endeavours but also the personal growth and resilience of each member. As we continue to explore and apply these insights, we contribute to a world where teams not only achieve their goals but also foster environments of collaboration, innovation, and mutual support.

References

Aubé, C., Brunelle, E., & Rousseau, V. (2014). Flow experience and team performance: The role of team goal commitment and information exchange. *Motivation and Emotion*, 38(1), 120–130.

Ackoff, R. (1989). From data to wisdom. *Journal of Applied Systems Analysis*, 16(1), 3–9.

Annett, J. (2002). Subjective rating scales: Science or art? *Ergonomics*, 45(14), 966–987.

Arafeh, J. M., Hansen, S. S., & Nichols, A. (2010). Debriefing in simulated-based learning: facilitating a reflective discussion. *The Journal of Perinatal & Neonatal Nursing*, 24(4), 302–309.

Arrow, H., McGrath, J. E., & Berdahl, J. L. (2000). *Small groups as complex systems: Formation, coordination, development, and adaptation*. Sage Publications.

Bar-On, R. (1997). *The Emotional Intelligence Inventory (EQ-i): technical manual*. Toronto, Canada: Multi-Health Systems.

Bar-On, R. (2004). *The Bar-On Emotional Quotient Inventory (EQ-i): Rationale, description and summary of psychometric properties*. In G. Geher (Ed.), Measuring emotional intelligence: Common ground and controversy (pp. 115–145). Nova Science Publishers.

Boyle, G. J. (1995). Myers-Briggs type indicator (MBTI): Some psychometric limitations. *Australian Psychologist, 30*(1), 71–74.

Beech, D. (2023). The development and validation of the Optimizing Team Performance Profile — OTP Profile. Retrieved on 19 Nov 2023 from www.otpprofile.com/profile-validation-and-research

Beech, D., Gist, R., & Corneliussen, J. (2023). Optimizing Team Performance. In R. Hauffa., & N. Pattyn (Eds.), *Optimizing Human Performance in NATO SOF Personnel Through Evidence-Based Mental Performance Programming*. NATO HFM-308 Working Group.

Berka, C., Levendowski, D., Lumicao, M., Yau, A., Davis, G., Zivikovic, V., Olmstead, R., Tremoulet, P., & Craven, P. (2007). EEG correlates of task engagement and mental workload in vigilance and memory tasks. *Aviation, Space and Environmental Medicine*, 78(5), Supplement 1, 231–244.

Bolstad, C., & Endsley, M. (2003). Measuring shared and team situation awareness in the army's future objective force. *Proceedings of the Human Factors and Ergonomics Society Annual Meeting*, 47(3), 369–373.

Brown, I. (1978). Dual task methods of assessing workload. *Ergonomics*, 21(3), 221–224.

Burke, M. J., Salvador, R., Smith-Crowe, K., Chan-Serafin, S., Smith, A., Kataria, N., & ... Halvorsen-Ganepola, M. D. K. (2017). The dread, fatigue, and prediction of team performance: An integrative model. *Journal of Occupational Health Psychology,* 22(3), 363–372. doi:10.1037/ocp0000053

Burns Jr, W. A. (2017). A descriptive literature review of harmful leadership styles: Definitions, commonalities, measurements, negative impacts, and ways to improve these harmful leadership styles. *Creighton Journal of Interdisciplinary Leadership*, 3(1), 33–52.

Caesens, G., Stinglhamber, F., Demoulin, S., De Wilde, M., & Mierop, A. (2019). Perceived organizational support and workplace conflict: The mediating role of failure-related trust. *Frontiers in Psychology*, 9, 2704.

Casali, J., & Wierwille, W. (1984). On the measurement of pilot perceptual workload: A comparison of assessment techniques in a simulated flight task emphasizing communications load. *Human Factors*, 25(6), 623–641.

Casner, S., & Gore, B. (2010). *Measuring and evaluating workload: A primer. NASA technical memorandum 2010-216395*. San Jose, CA: NASA Ames Research Center.

Csikszentmihalyi, M. (1990). *Flow: The psychology of optimal experience*. New York, NY: Harper & Row.

Csikszentmihalyi, M. (2014). *Flow and the foundations of positive psychology*. Springer.

Cooke, N., Stout, R., & Salas, E. (1997). Broadening the measurement of situation awareness through cognitive engineering methods. *Proceedings of the Human Factors and Ergonomics Society Annual Meeting*, 41(1), 215–219.

Cooper, C., & Harper, R. (1969). *The use of pilot rating in the evaluation of aircraft handling qualities*. (NASA TN-D-5153). Moffett Field, CA: NASA Ames Research Center.

Costa, P. T., Jr., & McCrae, R. R. (2008). The Revised NEO personality inventory (NEO-PI-R). In G. J. Boyle, G. Matthews, & D. H. Saklofske (Eds.), *The SAGE handbook of personality theory and assessment*, Vol. 2. Personality measurement and testing (pp. 179–198). Sage Publications, Inc. https://doi.org/10.4135/9781849200479.n9

Crandall, B., Kein, G., & Hoffman, R. (2006). *Working minds: A practitioner's guide to cognitive task analysis*, MIT Press, Cambridge, CA.

Day, D., Bastardoz, N., Bisbey, T., Reyes, D., & Salas, E. (2021). Unlocking human potential through leadership training & development initiatives. *Behavioral Science & Policy*, 7(1), 41–54.

DeChurch, L. A., & Mesmer-Magnus, J. R. (2010). The cognitive underpinnings of effective teamwork: A meta-analysis. *Journal of Applied Psychology*, 95(1), 32–53. https://doi.org/10.1037/a0017328

de Jong, B., Dirks, K. & Gillespie, N. (2016). Trust and team performance: A meta-analysis of main effects, moderators and covariates. *Journal of Applied Psychology*, 101(8). DOI: 10.1037/apl0000110

Delise, L. A., Allen Gorman, C., Brooks, A. M., Rentsch, J. R., & Steele-Johnson, D. (2010). The effects of team training on team outcomes: A meta-analysis. *Performance Improvement Quarterly*, 22(4), 53–80. https://doi.org/10.1002/piq.20068

Denison, D. R., Janovics, J., Young, J., & Cho, H. J. (2006). Diagnosing organizational cultures: Validating a model and method. *Documento de trabajo. Denison Consulting Group*, *1*(1), 1–39.

Donne, J. (1624). Devotions upon emergent occasions: No. 17. Meditation. In J. M. Dent & Co. (Eds.), *Collected poems of John Donne* (pp. 404). (Originally published in 1624).

Donne, J. (2001). *The complete poetry and selected prose of John Donne*. Modern library.

Duhigg, C. (2016). What google learned from its quest to build the perfect team. *The New York Times*. Retrieved on 8 November 2023 from www.nytimes.com/2016/02/28/magazine/what-google-learned-from-its-quest-to-build-the-perfect-team.html

Dunst, C. J., Bruther, M. B., Hamby, D. W., Howse, R., & Wilkie, H. (2018). Meta-analysis of the relationships between different leadership practices and organizational, teaming, leader, and employee outcomes. *Journal of International Education and Leadership*, 8(2), n2.

Eddy, E. R., Tannenbaum, S. I., & Mathieu, J. E. (2013). Helping teams to help themselves: Comparing two team-led debriefing methods. *Personnel Psychology*, 66(4), 975–1008. https://doi.org/10.1111/peps.12041

Eldredge, L. K. B., Markham, C. M., Ruiter, R. A., Fernández, M. E., Kok, G., & Parcel, G. S. (2016). *Planning health promotion programs: An intervention mapping approach*. John Wiley & Sons.

Eisenberger, N. I., & Cole, S. W. (2012). Social neuroscience and health: Neurophysiological mechanisms linking social ties with physical health. *Nature Neuroscience*, 15(5), 669–674. https://doi.org/10.1038/nn.3086

Eisenberger, N. I., Taylor, S. E., Gable, S. L., Hilmert, C. J., & Lieberman, M. D. (2007). Neural pathways link social support to attenuated neuroendocrine stress responses. *Journal of Personality and Social Psychology*, 93(1), 7–19. https://doi.org/10.1037/0022-3514.93.1.7

Endsley, M. (1988). Design and evaluation for situation awareness enhancement. In *Proceedings of the Human Factors Society annual meeting*, 32(2), 97–101.

Endsley, M. (1995). Toward a theory of situation awareness in dynamic systems. *Human Factors*, 37(1), 32–64.

Endsley, M., & Garland, D. (2000). *Situation awareness: Analysis and measurement*. Mahwah, NJ: Lawrence Erlbaum Associates.

Entin, E., & Serfaty, D. (1999). Adaptive team coordination. *Human Factors*, 41(2), 312–325.

Epps, H. R., & Levin, P. E. (2015). The TeamSTEPPS approach to safety and quality. *Journal of Pediatric Orthopaedics*, 35, S30–S33.

Fanning, R. M., & Gaba, D. M. (2007). The role of debriefing in simulation-based learning. *Simulation in Healthcare: Journal of the Society for Simulation in Healthcare*, 2(2), 115–125. https://doi.org/10.1097/SIH.0b013e3180315539

Fischer, T., & Sitkin, S. B. (2023). Leadership styles: A comprehensive assessment and way forward. *Academy of Management Annals*, 17(1), 331–372.

Fisher, J., Young, C., & Fadel, P. J. (2009). Central sympathetic overactivity: Maladies and mechanisms. *Autonomic Neuroscience*, 148(1), 5–15. https://doi.org/10.1016/j.autneu.2009.02.003

Fowlkes, J., Lane, N., Salas, E., Franz, T., & Oser, R. (1994). Improving the measurement of team performance: The TARGETs methodology. *Military Psychology*, 6(1), 47–61.

Frueh, B.C., Madan, A., Fowler, J. C., Stomberg, S., Bradshaw, M., Kelly, K., Weinstein, B., Luttrell, M., Danner, S. G., & Beidel, D. C. (2020). "Operator syndrome": A unique constellation of medical and behavioral health-care needs of military special operation forces. *International Journal of Psychiatry in Medicine*, 55(4), 281–295. https://doi.org/10.1177/0091217420906659

Gale, E. A. (2004). The Hawthorne studies—a fable for our times?. *Qjm*, 97(7), 439–449.

Gergen, K. J., & Gergen, M. M. (2008). Social construction and research as action. *The Sage handbook of action research: Participative inquiry and practice*, 159–171. Ed Bradbury, Thousand Oaks, Sage.

Giuliano, R., Gatzke-Kopp, L. M., Roos, L. E., & Skowron, E. A. (2017). Resting sympathetic arousal moderates the association between parasympathetic reactivity and working memory performance in adults reporting high levels of life stress. *Psychophysiology*, 54(8), 1195–1208. https://doi.org/10.1111/psyp.12872.

Gorman, J., Cooke, N., & Winner, J. (2006). Measuring team situation awareness in decentralized command and control environments. *Ergonomics*, 49(12–13), 1312–1325.

Griffith, J., Roberts, D., & Wakeham, R. (2015). A Meta-Analysis of crew resource management/incident command systems implementation studies in the fire and emergency services. *Journal of Aviation/Aerospace Education & Research*, 25(1), 1–25. https://doi.org/10.15394/jaaer.2015.1647

Grossman, R., Friedman, S., & Suman, K. (2019). Teamwork Processes and Emergent States. In E. Salas, R. Rico, & J. Passmore (Eds.). *The Wiley Blackwell handbook of the psychology of team working and collaborative processes* (pp. 245–269). Wiley Blackwell Publishing.

Gully, S. M., Incalcaterra, K. A., Joshi, A., & Beaubien, J. M. (2002). A meta-analysis of team-efficacy, potency, and performance: Interdependence and level of analysis as moderators of observed relationships. *Journal of Applied Psychology*, 87(5), 819–832. https://doi.org/10.1037/0021-9010.87.5.819.

Hadfield C. (2015). *An astronaut's guide to life on Earth*. MacMillan.

Hamann, A., & Carstengerdes, N. (2022). Investigating mental workload-induced changes in cortical oxygenation and frontal theta activity during simulated flights. *Scientific Reports*, 12(1), 6449.

Hollnagel, E. (1998). Cognitive reliability and error analysis methodology. London: Elsevier.

Houghton, A., & Gray, D. (2014). *Making sense of the ECG: A hands-on guide*. CRC Press, Boca Raton, FL.

Hughes, A. M., Gregory, M.E., Joseph, D.L., Sonesh, S.C., Marlow, S.L. (2016). Saving lives: a meta-analysis of team training in healthcare. *Journal of Applied Psychology*, 101, 1266–304

Ilgen, D., Hollenbeck, J., Johnson, M., & Jundt, D. (2005). Teams in organizations: From input-process-output models to IMOI models. *Annual Review of Psychology*, 56, 517–543.

Ivanov, P., Amaral, L., Goldenberger, A., Havlin, S., Rosenblum, M., Struzik, Z., & Stanley, H. (1999). Multifractality in human heartbeat dynamics. *Nature*, 399(6735), 461–465.

Jackson, S. A., & Csikszentmihalyi, M. (1999). *Flow in sports*. Human Kinetics.

Jedick, R. (2014). United Airlines 173 — The need for CRM. *Go flight Medicine*. https://goflightmedicine.com/united-airlines-173/

Jehn, K. A. (1995). A multimethod examination of the benefits and detriments of intragroup conflict. *Administrative Science Quarterly*, 40(2), 256–282.

Joint Chief of Staff. (2013). *Joint Publication 3-60: Joint Targeting*. Washington, DC: US Joint Chief of Staff.

Jorgensen, D.L. (1989). *Participant Observation. A Methodology for Human Studies*. Sage Publications.

Kiely, J. (2018). Periodization theory: Confronting an inconvenient truth. *Sports Medicine (Auckland)*, 48(4), 753–764. https://doi.org/10.1007/s40279-017-0823-y

Kinnunen, H., & Koskimäki, H. (2018). The HRV of the ring-comparison of nocturnal HR and HRV between a commercially available wearable ring and ECG. *Sleep*, 41(1), 120.

Kinnunen, H., Rantanen, A., Kenttä, T., & Koskimäki, H. (2020). Feasible assessment of recovery and cardiovascular health: Accuracy of nocturnal HR and HRV assessed via ring PPG in comparison to medical grade ECG. *Physiological Measurement*, 41(4), 1–9.

Kirwan, B., & Ainsworth, L. K. (Eds.). (1992). *A guide to task analysis: the task analysis working group*. CRC press.

Klein, G. (2009). *Streetlights and shadows: Searching for the keys to adaptive decision making*. Cambridge, MA: MIT Press.

Kramer, A, Sirevaag, E., & Braune, R. 1987. A psychological assessment of operator workload during simulated flight missions. *Human Factors*, 29(2), 145–160.

Lacerenza, C. N., Marlow, S. L., Tannenbaum, S. I., & Salas, E. (2018). Team development interventions: Evidence-based approaches for improving teamwork. *American Psychologist*, 73(4), 517–531. https://doi.org/10.1037/amp0000295

Lacerenza, C. N., Reyes, D. L., Marlow, S. L., Joseph, D. L., & Salas, E. (2017). Leadership training design, delivery, and implementation: A meta-analysis. *Journal of Applied Psychology*, 102(12), 1686–1718. https://doi.org/10.1037/apl0000241

Landhaüßer, A., & Keller, J. (2012). Flow and its affective, cognitive, and performance-related consequences. In S. Engeser (Ed.), *Advances in flow research* (pp. 65–85). Springer Science.

Lewis, K., Lange, D., & Gills, L. (2005). Transactive memory systems, learning, and learning transfer. *Organization Science*, 16(6), 581–598.

Lichacz, F. (2006). An examination of situation awareness and confidence within a distributed information sharing environment. *Proceedings of the Human Factors and Ergonomics Society Annual Meeting*, 50(3), 344–348.

Mansikka, H., Simola, P., Virtanen, K., Harris, D., & Oksama, L. (2016a). Fighter pilots' heart rate, heart rate variation and performance during instrument approaches. *Ergonomics*, 59(10), 1344–1352.

Mansikka, H., Virtanen, K., & Harris, D. (2019a). Comparison of NASA-TLX scale, modified Cooper–Harper scale and mean inter-beat interval as measures of pilot mental workload during simulated flight tasks. *Ergonomics*, 62(2), 246–254.

Mansikka, H., Virtanen, K., & Harris, D. (2019b). Dissociation between mental workload, performance, and task awareness in pilots of high performance aircraft. *IEEE Transactions on Human-Machine Systems*, 49(1), 1–9.

Mansikka, H., Virtanen, K., & Harris, D. (2023a). Accuracy and similarity of team situation awareness in simulated air combat. *Aerospace Medicine and Human Performance*, 94(6), 429–436.

Mansikka, H., Virtanen, K., & Harris, D. (2023c). What we got here, is a failure to coordinate: Implicit and explicit coordination in air combat. *Journal of Cognitive Engineering and Decision Making*, 17(3), 279–293.

Mansikka, H, Virtanen, K., Harris, D., & Jalava M. (2021a). Measurement of team performance in air combat — have we been underperforming? *Theoretical Issues in Ergonomics Science*, 22(3), 338–359.

Mansikka, H., Virtanen, K., Harris, D., & Järvinen, J. (2023b). Team performance in air combat: A teamwork perspective. *International Journal of Aerospace Psychology*, 33(4), 232–246.

Mansikka, H., Virtanen, K., Harris, D., & Salomäki, J. (2021d). Live–virtual–constructive simulation for testing and evaluation of air combat tactics, techniques, and procedures, Part 1: Assessment framework. *Journal of Defense Modeling and Simulation*, 18(4), 285–293.

Mansikka, H., Virtanen, K., Harris, D., & Simola, P. (2016b). Fighter pilots' heart rate, heart rate variation and performance during an instrument flight rules proficiency test. *Applied Ergonomics,* 56, 213–219.

Mansikka, H., Virtanen, K., Mäkinen, L., & Harris, D. (2021b). Normative performance measurement in simulated air combat. *Aerospace Medicine and Human Performance*, 92(11), 908–912.

Mansikka, H., Virtanen, K., Uggeldahl, V., & Harris, D. (2021c). Team situation awareness accuracy measurement technique for simulated air combat- Curvilinear relationship between awareness and performance. *Applied Ergonomics,* 96, 103473.

Marks, M. A., Mathieu, J. E., & Zaccaro, S. J. (2001). A temporally based framework and taxonomy of team processes. *Academy of Management Review*, 26(3), 356–376.

Marshall, D. (2009). *Crew resource management: from patient safety to high reliability*. Safer Healthcare Partners, LLC.

Mathieu, J., Gallagher, P., Domingo, M. & Klock, E. (2019). Embracing Complexity: Reviewing the Past Decade of Team Effectiveness Research. *Annual Review of Organizational Psychology and Organizational Behavior.* 6, 17–46.

Mathieu, J., Hollenbeck, J., van Knippenberg, D. & Ilgen, D. (2017). A century of work teams in the journal of applied psychology. *Journal of Applied Psychology*, 102 (3), 452–467.

Mathieu, J. E., Luciano, M. M., D'Innocenzo, L., Klock, E. A., & LePine, J. A. (2020). The development and construct validity of a team processes survey measure. *Organizational Research Methods*, *23*(3), 399–431.

Mathieu, J., Maynard, M. T., Rapp, T., & Gilson, L. (2008). Team effectiveness 1997–2007: A review of recent advancements and a glimpse into the future. *Journal of Management*, 34, 410–476. http://dx.doi.org/10.1177/0149206308316061.

Mattie, C. P., Guest, K., Bailey, S., Collins, J., & Gucciardi, D. F. (2020). Development of a mental skills training intervention for the Canadian Special Operations Forces Command: An intervention mapping approach. *Psychology of Sport and Exercise*, 50, 101720.

McEwan, D., Ruissen, G., Eys, M., Zumbo, B. & Beauchamp, M. (2017). The effectiveness of teamwork training on teamwork behaviors and team performance: a systematic review and meta-analysis of controlled interventions. *PLoS ONE*. 12(1), e0169604. doi:10.1371/journal. pone.0169604

McEwen, B.S. (2000). Allostasis and allostatic load: Implications for neuropsychopharmacology. *Neuropsychopharmacology*, 22, 108–24.

McGrath, J. E. (1997). Small group research, that once and future field: An interpretation of the past with an eye to the future. *Group Dynamics: Theory, Research, and Practice*, 1, 7–27. http://dx.doi.org/10.1037/1089-2699.1.1.7

McIntyre, A. (2007). *Participatory action research*. Sage.

McTaggart, R. (1991). Principles for participatory action research. *Adult Education Quarterly*, 41(3), 168–187.

Mehler, B., Reimer, B., & Wang, Y. (2011). A comparison of heart rate and heart rate variability indices in distinguishing single task driving and driving under secondary cognitive workload. Proceedings of the Sixth International Driving Symposium on Human Factors in Driver Assessment, *Training and Vehicle Design*, 590–597.

Morrison, J. E., & Meliza, L. L. (1999). Foundations of the after-action review process (Special Report 42). Alexandria, VA: U.S. Army Research Institute for the Behavioral and Social Sciences. https://apps.dtic.mil/dtic/tr/fulltext/u2/a368651.pdf

National Transportation Safety Board (1978) *Aircraft accident report: United Airlines*, Inc. NTSB-AAR-79-7. Retrieved from www.ntsb.gov/investigations/ AccidentReports/Reports/AAR7907.pdf

O'Connor, P., Campbell, J., Newon, J., Melton, J., Salas, E., & Wilson, K. A. (2008). Crew resource management training effectiveness: Ameta-analysis and some critical needs. *The International Journal of Aviation Psychology*, 18(4), 353–368.

O'Dea, A., O'Connor, P., & Keogh, I. (2014). A meta-analysis of the effectiveness of crew resource management training in acute care domains. *Postgraduate Medical Journal*, 90(1070), 699–708. https://doi.org/10.1136/postgradmedj-2014-132800

O'Donnel, R., Eggemeier, F., & Thomas, F. (1986). Workload assessment methodology. In Boff, K., Kaufman, L., and Thomas, J. (Eds.), *Handbook of Perception and Human Performance* Vol 2: 42, 1–49. Wiley Interscience, New York, NY.

Ogden, G., Levine, J., & Eisner, J. (1979). Measurement of workload by secondary tasks. *Human Factors*, 21(5), 529–548.

Paas, F., Tuovinen, J., Tabbers, H., & van Gerven, P. (2003). Cognitive load measurement as a means to advance cognitive load theory. *Educational Psychologist*, 38(1), 63–71.

Parasuraman, R., Sheridan, T. B., & Wickens, C. D. (2008). Situation awareness, mental workload, and trust in automation: Viable, empirically supported cognitive engineering constructs. *Journal of Cognitive Engineering and Decision Making*, *2*(2), 140–160.

Pattyn, N., Van Cutsem, J., Lacroix, E., Van Puyvelde, M., Cortoos, A., Roelands, B., Tibax, V., Dessy, E., Huret, M., Rietjens, G., Sannen, M., Vliegen, R., Ceccaldi, J., Peffer, J., Neyens, E., Duvigneaud, N., & Van Tiggelen, D. (2022). Lessons from special forces operators for elite team sports training: How to make the whole greater than the sum of the parts. *Frontiers in Sports and Act Living*, 4, 780767. doi: 10.3389/fspor.2022.780767

Paulhus, D. L. (1984). Two-component models of socially desirable responding. *Journal of Personality and Social Psychology*, 46(3), 598–609. https://doi.org/10.1037/0022-3514.46.3.598

Paulhus, D. L. (1991). Measurement and control of response bias. In J. P. Robinson, P. R. Shaver, & L. S. Wrightsman (Eds.), *Measures of personality and social psychological attitudes* (pp. 17–59). Academic Press. https://doi.org/10.1016/B978-0-12-590241-0.50006-X.

Peltokorpi, V., & Hood, A. (2019). Communication in theory and research on transactive memory systems: A literature review. *Topics in Cognitive Science* 11(2019), 644–667.

Prince, C., Ellis, E., Brannick, M., & Salas, E. (2007). Measurement of team situation awareness in low experience level aviators. *International Journal of Aviation Psychology*, 17(1), 41–57.

Ramos-Villagrasa, P., Marques-Quinteiro, P., Navarro, J., & Rico, R. (2018). Teams as complex adaptive systems: Reviewing 17 years of research. *Small Group Research*, 49(2), 135–176. https://doi.org/10.1177/1046496417713849

Reid, J., Stone, K., Brown, J., Caglar, D., Kobayashi, A., Lewis-Newby, M., ... & Quan, L. (2012). The simulation team assessment tool (STAT): Development, reliability and validation. *Resuscitation*, 83(7), 879–886

Reimer, B., & Mehler, B. (2011). The impact of cognitive workload on physiological arousal in young adult drivers: A field study and simulation validation. *Ergonomics*, 54(10), 932–942.

Reyes, D. L., Tannenbaum, S. I., & Salas, E. (2018). Team development: The power of debriefing. *People & Strategy*, 41(2), 46–52.

Rico, R., Sánchez-Manzanares, M., Gil, F., & Gibson, C. (2008). Team implicit coordination processes: A team knowledge–based approach. *Academy of Management Review*, 33(1), 163–184.

Rogers, Y. (1997). A brief introduction to distributed cognition. Retrieved from http://yvonnerogers.com/wp-content/uploads/2014/07/dcog-brief-intro.pdf

Roman-Liu, D., Grabarek, I., Bartuzi, P., & Choromanski, W. (2013). The influence of mental load on muscle tension. *Ergonomics*, 56(7), 1125–1133.

Rosenman, E., Dixon, A., Webb, J., Brolliar, S., Golden, S., Jones, K., Sachita, S., Grand, J., Kozlowski, S., Chao, G., & Fernandez, R. (2018). A simulation-based approach to measuring team situational awareness in emergency medicine: a multicenter, observational study. *Academic Emergency Medicine*, 25(2), 196–204.

Rouse, W., & Morris, N. (1986). On looking into the black box: Prospects and limits in the search for mental models. *Psychological Bulletin*, 100(3), 349–363.

Ryu, K., & Myung, R. (2005). Evaluation of mental workload with combined measure based on physiological indices during a dual task of tracking and mental arithmetic. *International Journal of Industrial Ergonomics*, 35(1), 991–1009.

Salanova, M., Llorens, S., Cifre, E., & Martínez, I. M. (2013). We need a hero! Toward a validation of the healthy and resilient organization (HERO) model. *Group & Organization Management*, 38(5), 569–598.

Salas, E. (2015b). *Team training essentials: A research-based guide*. Routledge.

Salas, E., Bowers, C. A., & Cannon-Bowers, J. A. (1995). Military team research: 10 years of progress. *Military Psychology*, 7(2), 55–75.

Salas, E., Dickinson, T. L., Converse, S. A., & Tannenbaum, S. I. (1992). *Toward an understanding of team performance and training*. CRC Press.

Salas, E., Priest, H., & DeRouin, R. (2005a) Team building. In N. Stanton (Ed.), *Handbook of human factors and ergonomics methods.* (pp. 465–470). CRC Press.

Salas, E., Shuffler, M. L., Thayer, A. L., Bedwell, W. L., & Lazzara, E. H. (2015a). Understanding and improving teamwork in organizations: A scientifically based practical guide. *Human Resource Management*, 54(4), 599–622.

Salas, E., Sims, D., & Burke, C. (2005b). Is there a "Big Five" in Teamwork?. *Small Group Research*, 36(5), 555–599.

Salas, E., Tannenbaum, S. I., Kraiger, K., & Smith-Jentsch, K. A. (2012). The science of training and development in organizations: What matters in practice. *Psychological Science in the Public Interest*, 13(2), 74–101. https://doi.org/10.1177/1529100612436661

Salas, E., Wilson, K. A., Burke, C. S., Wightman, D. C., & Howse, W. R. (2006). Crew resource management training research, practice, and lessons learned. *Reviews of Human Factors and Ergonomics*, 2(1), 35–73.

Salmon, P., Stanton, N., Walker, G., Baber, C., Jenkins, D., McMaster, R., & Young, M. (2008). What really is going on? Review of situation awareness models for individuals and teams. *Theoretical Issues in Ergonomics Science*, 9(4), 297–323.

Salmon, P., Stanton, N., Walker, G., Jenkins, D., Ladva, D., Rafferty, L., & Young, M. (2009). Measuring situation awareness in complex systems: Comparison of measures study. *International Journal of Industrial Ergonomics*, 39(3), 490–500.

Sampson, M., & McGrath, A. (2015). Understanding the ECG Part 2: ECG basics. *British Journal of Cardiac Nursing*, 10(12), 588–594.

Sawyer, R. K. (2003). *Group creativity music, theater, collaboration*. Erlbaum Associates.

Schuermann, V., & Marquardt, N. (2016). Adaptation of crew resource management training in high-risk industries. *International Journal of Safety and Security Engineering*, 6(2), 341–350.

Schyns, B., & Schilling, J. (2013). How bad are the effects of bad leaders? A meta-analysis of destructive leadership and its outcomes. *The Leadership Quarterly*, 24(1), 138–158.

Seitchik, M. (2019). The Goldilocks approach to team conflict: How leaders can maximize innovation and revenue growth. *The Psychologist-Manager Journal*, 22(1), 37–45. https://doi.org/10.1037/mgr0000082

Setz, C., Armrich, B., Schumm, J., La Marca, R., Troster, G., & Ehlert, U. (2010). Discriminating stress from cognitive load using a wearable EDA device. *Information Technology in Biomedicine*, 14(2), 410–417.

Shuffler, M. L., Salas, E., & Xavier, L. F. (2010). The design, delivery and evaluation of crew resource management training. In Kanki, B., Helmreich, R.,; Anca, J. (Eds) *Crew resource management* (pp. 205–232). Academic Press.

Spradley, J. P. (2016). *Participant obs*ervation. Waveland Press.

Stein, R, Swan, A. B. (2019). Evaluating the validity of Myers-Briggs Type Indicator theory: A teaching tool and window into intuitive psychology. *Social and Personality Psychology Compass*, 13, e12434. https://doi.org/10.1111/spc3.12434.

Steiner, I. D. (1974). Whatever happened to the group in social psychology? *Journal of Experimental Social Psychology*, 10, 94–108. http://dx.doi.org/10.1016/0022-1031(74)90058-4

Stewart, V.R., Snyder, D.G., Kou, C.Y. (2023). We hold ourselves accountable: A relational view of team accountability. *Journal of Business Ethics*, 183(3), 691–712. doi: 10.1007/s10551-021-04969-z. Epub 2021 Nov 18. PMID: 34812211; PMCID: PMC8600914

Stone, J., Ulman, H., Tran, K., Thompson, A., Halter, M., Ramadan, J., & Hagen, J. (2021). Assessing the accuracy of popular commercial technologies that measure resting heart rate and heart rate variability. *Frontiers in Sports and Active Living*, 37.

Stout, R., Cannon-Bowers, J., & Salas, E. (2017). The role of shared mental models in developing team situational awareness: Implications for training. In *Situational Awareness* (pp. 287–318). London, UK: Routledge.

Sulistyawati, K., Wickens, C., & Chui, Y. (2009). Exploring the concept of team situation awareness in a simulated air combat environment. *Journal of Cognitive Engineering and Decision Making*, 3(4), 309–330.

Tannenbaum, S. I., & Cerasoli, C. P. (2013). Do team and individual debriefs enhance performance? A meta-analysis. *Human Factors*, 55(1), 231–245. https://doi.org/10.1177/0018720812448394

van den Hout, J., Davis, O. & Weggeman, M. (2018). The conceptualization of team flow. *The Journal of Psychology*, 152(6), 388–423, DOI: 10.1080/00223980.2018.1449729

Vashdi, D. R. (2013). Teams in public administration: A field study of team feedback and effectiveness in the Israeli public healthcare system. *International Public Management Journal*, 16(2), 275–306.

Verwey, W, & Veltman, H. (1996). Detecting short periods of elevated workload: A comparison of nine workload assessment techniques. *Journal of Experimental Psychology*, 2(3), 270–285.

Vicente, K., Thornton, D., & Moray, N. (1987). Spectral analysis of sinus arrythmia: A measure of mental effort. *Human Factors*, 29(2), 171–182.

Vidulich, M., & Wickens, C. (1986). Causes and dissociation between subjective workload measures and performance. *Applied Ergonomics*, 17(4), 291–296.

Virtanen, K., Mansikka, H., Kontio, H., & Harris, D. (2022). Weight watchers: NASA-TLX weights revisited. *Theoretical Issues in Ergonomics Science*, 23(6), 725–748.

Wageman, R., Hackman, J. R., & Lehman, E. (2005). Team diagnostic survey: Development of an instrument. *The Journal of Applied Behavioral Science*, 41(4), 373–398.

Weigl, M., Catchpole, K., Wehler, M., & Schneider, A. (2020). Workflow disruptions and provider situation awareness in acute care: An observational study with emergency department physicians and nurses. *Applied Ergonomics*, 88, 103155.

Wegner, D. M., Giuliano, T., & Hertel, P. T. (1985). Cognitive interdependence in close relationships. In W. J. Ickes (Ed.), Compatible and incompatible relationships (pp. 253–276). New York: Springer-Verlag.

Wellens, A., 1993. Group situation awareness and distributed decision making: from military to civilian applications. In: Castellan Jr., N.J. (Ed.), Individual and Group Decision Making: Current Issues. Lawrence Erlbaum Associates Inc, Hillsdale, NJ, pp. 267–291. https://doi.org/10.4324/9780203772744.

Wierwille, W. W., Rahimi, M., & Casali, J. G. (1985). Evaluation of 16 measures of mental workload using a simulated flight task emphasizing mediational activity. *Human factors*, *27*(5), 489–502.

Yeh, Y. Y., & Wickens, C. D. (1988). Dissociation of performance and subjective measures of workload. *Human factors*, 30(1), 111–120.

Young, M. S., & Schinka, J. A. (2001). Research validity scales for the NEO-PI-R: Additional evidence for reliability and validity. *Journal of personality Assessment*, 76(3), 412–420.

12 Mental Performance and Mental Health

Robin Hauffa

Introduction

When Robert Enke, professional soccer goalkeeper and member of the German national team, committed suicide in 2009, the discussion on mental health in elite athletes was brought into the spotlight. Media and many experts saw him as the number one for the upcoming World Cup in South Africa. Despite battling depression for a long time, his performance on the field was outstanding. How could an athlete suffering from severe depression perform so well? Apparently, the connection between elite-level performance and mental health is far more complex than popular opinion would have us believe.

While the use of psychological expertise to improve performance has a long history in elite sports (e.g., Triplett, 1898; and see Chapter 16 for more details), sports psychiatry is a relatively young field. The International Society for Sports Psychiatry was founded in 1994, whereas the European Federation of Sport Psychology has been around since 1969. Having a sport psychologist or mental performance consultant within the coaching team is now considered a standard at elite level sports. The primary focus of such efforts is to enable athletes to perform to the best of their ability. It is a common belief that high-level performance requires above the average motivation, resiliency, and dedication. Early models therefore postulated a linear approach, having health, well-being, and high performance on one side and illness, injury, and impaired performance on the other (Lardon & Fitzgerald, 2013). While these models have a lot of face validity, they lack the backing of scientific evidence. At the same time, military organizations all over the world have massively increased their efforts in preventing and treating adverse mental health outcomes related to military service. This was mainly driven by US experiences in Vietnam and skyrocketing prevalence numbers for post-traumatic stress disorder (PTSD), depression, and other conditions following deployments in Iraq and Afghanistan. Given the high exposure to potentially traumatic events, most nations focused on improving their service members' ability to cope with such experiences, but also to increase readiness und performance. Many nations adopted a linear model ranging from well-being to injured. Naturally there is a considerable overlap between programs that aim to optimize performance and those that are intended to prevent adverse mental health outcomes. Many common psychological techniques have been validated for their use in psychotherapeutic, resiliency enhancing as well as performance enhancing settings (e.g., arousal management techniques, visualization, goal setting, self-talk, mindfulness related interventions – all of which are covered in the specific technical chapters of the present handbook). Assuming the connection between performance and mental health as a linear continuum, it is not far-fetched to assume that the use of such techniques will likely be helpful to move an individual towards the high-performance pole of the continuum, independent of the current position of this individual.

DOI: 10.4324/9781003378969-15

Over the last years, criticism of this foundational linear model has been growing. Leading organizations have published consensus statements on mental health care for athletes, highlighting that peak performance does not equal the absence of mental disorders (Moesch et al., 2018; Van Slingerland et al., 2019). On the contrary, mental health symptoms and disorders are considered common among elite athletes (Reardon et al., 2019). Chang et al. (2020) argue that elite athletes are exposed to additional risk factors, with some of these also being instrumental in their success. Organizational and environmental factors are also relevant and can have a positive or negative effect on an athletes' mental health in a an elite setting (Henriksen et al., 2020).

Can overachieving be healthy?

Individual and social factors, as well as performance related factors, are even associated with a specific vulnerability (Frank et al., 2013). Baum proposed three possible relationships between the athlete and an existing mental health issue: "(i) athletes may obtain high levels of success in spite of a coexistent primary psychiatric disorder; (ii) athletes may have chosen the athletic arena as a means of coping with a disorder; or (iii) athletes may have psychiatric illness precipitated or worsened by sport itself" (Baum, 2000; Baum, 2003; Reardon & Factor, 2010). This is also transferrable to other high-performance areas. Especially the bullets (ii) and (iii) require a closer investigation with regard to the role of performance-enhancing techniques in setting off, sustaining, or worsening adverse mental health outcomes in elite populations.

To elaborate on the topic, we are taking an "Acceptance and Commitment Therapy"-based transdiagnostic approach to mental illness, focusing on psychological inflexibility[1] as a relevant factor in the genesis of mental disorders (Hayes et al., 2006; Levin et al., 2014; Tavakoli et al., 2019). Psychological inflexibility is defined as the "rigid dominance of psychological reactions over chosen values and contingencies in guiding action" (Bond et al., 2011), whereas psychological flexibility is "the process of contacting the present moment fully as a conscious human being and persisting or changing behaviour in the service of chosen values" (Hayes et al., 2006). Experiential avoidance is recognized as a relevant part of psychological inflexibility (Hayes et al., 2006) and the subsequent development of psychopathology (Hayes et al., 1996). It is defined as "the phenomenon that occurs when a person is unwilling to remain in contact with particular private experiences (e.g., bodily sensations, emotions, thoughts, memories, behavioral predispositions) and takes steps to alter the form or frequency of these events and the contexts that occasion them" (Hayes et al., 1996).

The association between psychological inflexibility and mental illness has been well documented (e.g., Venta et al., 2012). Mental performance programs and the interventions utilized will ideally lead to an increase in psychological flexibility and thus reduced vulnerability to develop a mental disorder. So how do interventions aimed at improving performance affect psychological flexibility and what are possible pitfalls practitioners should be aware of when applying these interventions?

Can mental performance training serve mental health?

One of the main components of mental performance programs is often a combination of psychoeducation on stress and the implementation of stress/arousal management techniques (as demonstrated by the technical part of the present handbook, and the various implementation chapters). For the purpose of this chapter, we include mindfulness and meditation-based interventions, specific relaxation techniques (like progressive muscle relaxation, autogenic training, or behavioural relaxation training), breathing techniques, and yoga into this category. Looking at

1 There is currently no universally accepted definition of the concept of psychological flexibility (Malo et al., 2022).

the connection between stress and performance (which is described in Chapter 2), there is sufficient evidence to consider restorative techniques as part of the performance-enhancing arsenal. There is plenty of evidence for the benefit of stress management techniques to reduce stress in healthy populations (Gaab et al., 2003; Gaab et al., 2006; Murphy, 1996; Richardson & Rothstein, 2008) (Brinkborg et al., 2011; Jamieson et al., 2012; Wersebe et al., 2018). These interventions have also been shown to be helpful in patient populations (Shah et al., 2014). Many interventions aim to increase knowledge on physiological and psychological processes underlying the perception of stress, which is described in more detail in Chapter 10 (Learning environment: psychoeducation). Even if only through providing reappraisal instructions, participants showed physiological and cognitive benefits (Jamieson et al., 2012) and reduced negative affect (Beltzer et al., 2014). Most protocols also include specific interventions based on Cognitive Behavioural Therapy (CBT; Meichenbaum, 1985) and/or mindfulness (Kabat-Zinn & Hanh, 2009), that have shown to reduce measures of stress (Goldin & Gross, 2010; Saranapala et al., 2022). Both approaches aim to reduce the negative influence of dysfunctional cognitive patterns on one's psychological reaction to different stressors. While there is (to the author's knowledge) no scientific evidence that specifically links a reduction in stress response to psychological flexibility, we hypothesize that a reduction in maladaptive stress responses can lead to less rigid psychological reaction patterns, and thus to increased psychological flexibility, as was hypothesized by Friedman as well (2007) with his autonomic flexibility-neurovisceral integration model of anxiety and cardiac vagal tone. If, on the other hand, stress management is mainly utilized to improve experiential avoidance, the result is often a decrease in psychological flexibility, as avoidance always reduces the possible courses of action. Subsequently, such an approach will likely increase the risk for developing an adverse mental health outcome. This is especially relevant in individuals who engage in a certain sport or other activity to cope with an underlying disorder (reference bullet (ii)) or where the desired behaviour can precipitate or worsen a mental health condition (reference bullet (iii)). For example, many people utilize mindfulness apps as an attempt for a quick fix to a problem they are experiencing (Clarke & Draper, 2020; Laurie & Blandford, 2016). However, if stress management techniques are used to reduce negative affects and stress experiences, chances are that experiential avoidance is the relevant factor for their short-term success. Research results have confirmed this, showing that brief mindfulness exercises can have negative effects in the moral domain, like easing a bad conscience (Schindler et al., 2019), as well as reduce empathy, especially in people with narcissistic or autistic traits (Ridderinkhof et al., 2017). The subjective effect of yoga and meditation on well-being has been shown to be caused by increasing self-enhancement bias (Gebauer et al., 2018). While these effects can be very helpful in high-performance settings, e.g., prior to or during an important event like a sports competition, a military mission, or a business presentation, it can also cause negative long-term consequences for mental health. Especially when the experienced stress that needs to be managed derives from internal or external problems that need to be attended to. This is often the case in persons where performance or success has an important role in coping with an underlying disorder or dysfunctional thought patterns (e.g., "I am only respected when I am successful", "I am useless if I can't even do my job"). Interventions to help keeping up or improving the performance level in such cases often do not properly address deeply rooted internal problems, but tend to avoid them. This easily leads to unintentional reinforcement of dysfunctional patterns and reducing psychological flexibility for the short-term benefit of stabilizing a potentially pathogenic system. The subsequently following long-term consequence is then likely the enhancement of the underlying problem.

Many soldiers, for instance, describe a significant reduction in perceived stress levels while on deployment or mission, as compared to routine duty (Ungerer et al., 2015). This reduction in perceived stress is partially explained by a lower exposure to the burdens of "daily business" during deployment. In special forces, it is part of the culture to prioritize the mission and the team before one's own needs (Blaber, 2010). Therefore, many clients request counselling to better deal with distracting daily stressors so they can focus on their job and get ready for the next mission. This can have detrimental effects on the client's overall situation, e.g., when the root of the distraction are family conflicts or financial issues that are avoided instead of attended to.

When looking at high performers across all areas that are discussed in the present handbook, there is one fundamental difference between military and other elite populations like sports, business, or art that needs to be addressed when looking at potential harmful effects of stress management techniques. In addition to generally non-dangerous sources of stress (e.g., performance anxiety, social pressure, intrinsic stressors), these populations are consciously exposed to potentially traumatic and life-threatening situations as regular part of their job. While managing trauma-related symptoms to allow patients to reach a level of functioning or partake in trauma therapy is well established and beneficial, the management of symptoms to stay deployable increases the likelihood of developing a significant mental health problem. Prior exposure to trauma and prior psychological problems are significant risk factors for developing combat-related PTSD (Xue et al., 2015). A recent meta-analysis also evidenced that stress control interventions had no significant impact on PTSD rates or PTSD symptom scores (Maglione et al., 2021). The already significant risk for adverse mental health outcomes in this population can therefore be increased even further by uncritical application of stress management techniques.

The displayed mechanisms regarding stress management procedures can also be translated to other interventions utilized in mental performance programming. In addition, the use of many techniques is not limited to the management of stress and arousal, but also can be utilized to help in specific situations or with specific tasks (e.g., the use of imagery to practice certain motions or movements). Goal setting is an extremely useful technique (as described in more detail in Chapter 4) that is well established in clinical practice as well as in mental performance programs. Adverse mental health effects can result from performance goals that are either not in line with other personal goals or personal values, or have negative second-order effects.

In summary, the positive effects of psychoeducation and stress management techniques on well-being and performance are plausible and not harmful per se. In certain constellations, they can also lead to a decrease in psychological flexibility and subsequently to an increased vulnerability for mental illness, despite a positive impact on performance. While this may seem trivial, clinical practice has proven that humans are often not aware of all their personal goals, motivators, and values, making it difficult to identify possible conflicts ahead of time. To complicate the matter, social desirability, and institutional pressure to perform are often relevant yet concealed factors in one's motivational constructs. Given that neither prevention strategies nor interventions specifically designed for depression in the workplace have been shown to be effective based on clinical standards (Dietrich et al., 2012; Furlan et al., 2012), the effect of non-specific interventions on the prevention of adverse mental health outcomes seems questionable. We conclude that mental performance training can have positive and negative impacts on mental health, but is not likely to improve or prevent mental illness. A sophisticated mental performance program is therefore no replacement for effective screening and treatment protocols for mental disorders. A current trend is to move the performance management responsibility away from the medical field. However, precisely because this screening needs to be present throughout the program, we need clinicians able to detect when performance management should give way to treatment.

Organizational environments

Institutional features can yield another risk factor for adverse effects of mental performance interventions at the workplace. While there is some evidence, that implementation of stress management training at the workplace is associated with improved stress reactivity (Limm et al., 2011), psychological health and job satisfaction (Kröll et al., 2017), as well as in promoting a healthy and positive work environment (Tetrick & Winslow, 2015), most studies neither address elite populations nor are they looking for long-term effects (e.g., over the life cycle of an entrepreneur, an elite athlete, or a special forces operator). There is also a missing differentiation of results that primarily benefit the organization versus results that are beneficial to the individual. This potential conflict of interest is elaborated upon in Chapter 18. While the official goals of human performance programs often include the reduction of adverse health outcomes even after retirement, the authors' experience shows that leaders often focus on the short-term effects of keeping people in the job, even if this implies a higher mental health cost to the individual after the short-term goal has been secured. This problem has been acknowledged by the French Armed Forces, who created a free, 24/7 reachable phone number for military personnel, veterans, but also families; "Ecoute Défense" has existed since 2012 (www.defense.gouv.fr/sga/au-service-agents/soutien-aux-blesses/guide-du-blesse/je-suis-membre-famille-dun-militaire-blesse-malade-0).

Paired with the high motivation to excel in elite populations, negative long-term consequences are easily neglected. When interventions mainly target the results of organizational stressors or their management, without properly targeting the root cause, negative effects are not unlikely. A prime example are measures to reduce the impact of sleep deprivation in the military. While the available knowledge on the need for sufficient sleep is widely available and has been partly generated by military research, organizational measures have not yielded in military members getting enough sleep (Mysliwiec et al., 2013; van den Berg et al., 2023) and measures to improve sleep quality, reduce other causes of sleep impairment (e.g., mental illness, sleep apnea) or combat performance effects of sleep deprivation are a major focus (Good et al., 2020). Another example is a recently published scientific recommendation to mitigate the effects of a shortage of teachers in the German school system. While acknowledging objective stress factors associated with the job (one of them being personnel shortages) one of the recommendation was the implementation of additional health promotion measures such as mindfulness training and communication training to reduce perceived stress to fight attrition (Köller, 2023). Without denying the positive impacts such mitigating interventions, they also yield a significant potential to contribute to long-term negative outcomes in some individuals. This issue of mental performance promotion to alleviate toxic work conditions is also discussed in Chapter 15, regarding the mental performance training in corporate environments.

Mental health implications of organizational "image preservation"

One of the most common stressors in some elite populations like athletes or astronauts is the constant pressure of being in the public eye. While praise and recognition are mostly tied to actual achievements, e.g., winning a competition, closing a big business deal, or successfully completing a mission, failures or mistakes often have a huge impact, even when they are not related to the actual performance. While "being in the spotlight" and feeling a pressure to perform is well recognized in the sports community as a potential stressor (Frank et al., 2013), this is only one aspect of the issue. Even minor or just alleged misconduct can lead to negative (social) media coverage with severe consequences for the individual and subsequently for the organization as well. Especially when public opinion, political support, funding, or shareholder trust is at risk, organizations can be tempted to avoid negative publicity regardless of the consequences for the individual. Regardless of the legal or ethical evaluation of specific actions, these circumstances must be taken into account when looking at performance or mental health issues. One common area of conflict is often seen in military populations. Molendijk (2019) described the impact of avoiding political risk during a mission in Afghanistan, even if it was associated with a higher risk for overall casualties, on the burden of moral injuries in Dutch soldiers. She argues that the experience of institutional betrayal needs to be included into respective theories. Moral injury is defined as "perpetrating, failing to prevent, bearing witness to, or learning about acts that transgress deeply held moral beliefs and expectations" (Litz et al., 2009). While the term is often used in close connection with trauma-related mental illness, we strongly believe that the concept should be utilized in a broader sense. In the context of this book, it might become especially relevant, when measures taken for image preservation create a conflict between institutional actions and personal values. This can easily happen when admitting a mistake is anticipated to harm the organization or the public relations section is creating a heroic narrative that doesn't fit the personal experience of involved individuals. An extreme, but well-known example is the institutional denial or covering up of clear evidence of physical, emotional, and sexual violence in elite sports organizations over the past decades. Regardless of moral implications, it is essential to understand that these abusive behaviours are very likely to happen in high-performance environments. Especially when a certain level of secrecy is mandatory (e.g., in special operations or possible industrial espionage), the risk for perceived organizational betrayal and moral injury with subsequent detrimental effects on performance as well as mental health is considerable. While we strongly believe that covering up (criminal) misconduct (e.g., sexual harassment) in the name of image preservation must be condemned, we also acknowledge, that there is often a grey area. The creation of "safe spaces" for affected individuals to articulate their issues and concerns is necessary to mitigate negative effects and reduce attrition.

Conclusion and practical recommendations

Good mental health is not a prerequisite for elite-level performance. It is possible to suffer from severe mental illness without significant effects on achievement potential. In some individuals, factors associated with elite performance are also linked to preexisting mental health conditions, or a respective vulnerability. At the same time, measures intended to improve performance and well-being can have a negative effect on long-term or even short-term mental health outcomes. Furthermore, there are substantial barriers to seeking help with mental health problems in elite athletes (Gulliver et al., 2012) as well as in the military (Sharp et al., 2015). In order to mitigate potential harmful side effects while using mental performance training or interventions, we recommend the following measures to be considered when admitting individuals into a mental performance program:

1. Multidisciplinary teams should include mental health expertise (Pattyn et al., 2022), i.e., a clinical psychologist or a psychiatrist, to reduce barriers to diagnostic procedures and care for individuals, but also for early identification of personnel at risk. In order to keep the clinical perspective, this mental health expert should not have the role of performance psychologist/mental performance training provider and should solely act as an advocate for the client (or the client's health and safety), independent of institutional requirements.
2. Implementation of regular, mandatory mental health screenings for all personnel enrolled in a mental performance program. The easiest and most common way is questionnaires asking for the frequency and/or severity of specific symptoms relevant to mental health (e.g., the Patient Health Questionnaire PHQ (Spitzer et al., 1999) or Symptom Check List 90-Revised SCL-90R (Derogatis, 1975)). While psychometric measures have several limitations, one of the most relevant being their inability to detect dissimulation, we feel that they are superior to mandatory interviews in elite populations. Questionnaires offer the opportunity to signal the need for support without actively seeking for an appointment and thus might reduce barriers to initial counselling. Mandatory interviews, on the other hand, often become a nuisance to individuals and undermine the relationship of trust in the mental health professional. In particular, personnel with high internal stigma often report fears of being "taken off the team" when speaking openly about negative emotions and personal struggles during such an interview.

3. Create opportunities for "off the record" counselling, where individuals can get a professional opinion on their mental health status and recommendations on how to proceed. Circumstances on when and how the "off the record"-status needs to be breached must be openly communicated up front. We recommend that such a breach is only undertaken in cases of an immediate endangerment of self or others, which is in most nations the condition for involuntary admission to a psychiatric hospital. While such an approach is often seen with great skepticism by leadership and parts of the medical community, it is rather common in mental health care. Many patients present with severe mental health issues but refuse treatment despite strong recommendations to do so. In our opinion, the reduction of barriers to care supersedes the institutional risk of not taking action. While suicides are generally rare, most patients actually have contact with the medical system shortly prior to suicide (Luoma et al., 2002; Pirkis & Burgess, 1998). Subsequently, a low-level "off the record" approach probably prevents more suicides and other catastrophic outcomes than risks adverse reporting policies with increased barriers to care.
4. Implementation of a multidisciplinary case review board to allow for development of individually tailored approaches for personnel at risk (e.g., drop in performance, serious injury, maladaptive behaviour, exposure to critical incidents) or with relevant mental health symptoms. This is for example adopted by military elite units, or space agencies, as described in Chapters 13 and 14.
5. Embedding mental health professionals as part of the integrated performance and health care team with a regular presence at workplace and training place to allow building of a trustful relationship, which is also discussed in Chapter 16 on Olympic athletes.
6. Provide mental health literacy trainings tailored for athletes/operators/clients, coaches, leadership, and members of the human performance and health care teams. Even for health care providers, psychiatry is often seen as a distant and exotic part of the medical spectrum, whereas mental health is a continuum rather than a binary categorization.

References

Baum, A. (2000). Psychopharmacology in athletes. *Sport psychiatry*. New York: WW Norton & Company, 249–259.

Baum, A. L. (2003). Sport psychiatry: How to keep athletes in the game of life, on or off the field. *Current Psychiatry*, *2*(1), 51–56.

Beltzer, M. L., Nock, M. K., Peters, B. J., & Jamieson, J. P. (2014). Rethinking butterflies: The affective, physiological, and performance effects of reappraising arousal during social evaluation. *Emotion*, *14*(4), 761–768. https://doi.org/10.1037/a003632610.1037/a0036326.supp (Supplemental)

Blaber, P. (2010). *The Mission, The Men, and Me: Lessons from a Former Delta Force Commander*. Penguin Publishing Group.

Bond, F. W., Hayes, S. C., Baer, R. A., Carpenter, K. M., Guenole, N., Orcutt, H. K., & . . . Zettle, R. D. (2011). Preliminary psychometric properties of the acceptance and action Questionnaire–II: A revised measure of psychological inflexibility and experiential avoidance. *Behavior Therapy*, *42*(4), 676–688. https://doi.org/10.1016/j.beth.2011.03.007

Brinkborg, H., Michanek, J., Hesser, H., & Berglund, G. (2011). Acceptance and commitment therapy for the treatment of stress among social workers: A randomized controlled trial. *Behaviour Research and Therapy*, *49*(6), 389–398. https://doi.org/https://doi.org/10.1016/j.brat.2011.03.009

Chang, C., Putukian, M., Aerni, G., Diamond, A., Hong, G., Ingram, Y., & . . . Wolanin, A. (2020). Mental health issues and psychological factors in athletes: detection, management, effect on performance and prevention: American Medical Society for Sports Medicine Position Statement—Executive Summary. *British Journal of Sports Medicine*, *54*(4), 216–220. https://doi.org/10.1136/bjsports-2019-101583

Clarke, J., & Draper, S. (2020). Intermittent mindfulness practice can be beneficial, and daily practice can be harmful. An in depth, mixed methods study of the "Calm" app's (mostly positive) effects. *Internet Interventions*, *19*, 100293. https://doi.org/https://doi.org/10.1016/j.invent.2019.100293

Derogatis, L. R. (1975). *SCL-90-R: Symptom Checklist-90-R: Administration, scoring, and procedures manual*. NCS Pearson.

Dietrich, S., Deckert, S., Ceynowa, M., Hegerl, U., & Stengler, K. (2012). Depression in the workplace: a systematic review of evidence-based prevention strategies. *International Archives of Occupational and Environmental Health*, *85*(1), 1–11. https://doi.org/https://doi.org/10.1007/s00420-011-0634-7

Frank, R., Nixdorf, I., & Beckmann, J. (2013). Depression in elite athletes: Prevalence and psychological factors. *Deutsche Zeitschrift für Sportmedizin*, *64*(11), 320–326. https://doi.org/10.5960/dzsm.2013.088

Friedman, B. H. (2007). An autonomic flexibility-neurovisceral integration model of anxiety and cardiac vagal tone. *Biological Psychology*, Feb;74(2), 185–99. doi: 10.1016/j.biopsycho.2005.08.009. Epub 2006 Oct 27. PMID: 17069959

Furlan, A. D., Gnam, W. H., Carnide, N., Irvin, E., Amick, B. C., Derango, K., & . . . Bültmann, U. (2012). Systematic review of intervention practices for depression in the workplace. *Journal of Occupational Rehabilitation*, *22*(3), 312–321. https://doi.org/10.1007/s10926-011-9340-2

Gaab, J., Blättler, N., Menzi, T., Pabst, B., Stoyer, S., & Ehlert, U. (2003). Randomized controlled evaluation of the effects of cognitive–behavioral stress management on cortisol responses to acute stress in healthy subjects. *Psychoneuroendocrinology*, *28*(6), 767–779. https://doi.org/https://doi.org/10.1016/S0306-4530(02)00069-0

Gaab, J., Sonderegger, L., Scherrer, S., & Ehlert, U. (2006). Psychoneuroendocrine effects of cognitive-behavioral stress management in a naturalistic setting—a randomized controlled trial. *Psychoneuroendocrinology*, *31*(4), 428–438. https://doi.org/https://doi.org/10.1016/j.psyneuen.2005.10.005

Gebauer, J. E., Nehrlich, A. D., Stahlberg, D., Sedikides, C., Hackenschmidt, A., Schick, D., & . . . Mander, J. (2018). Mind-Body practices and the self: Yoga and meditation do not quiet the ego but instead boost self-enhancement. *Psychological Science*, *29*(8), 1299–1308. https://doi.org/10.1177/0956797618764621

Goldin, P. R., & Gross, J. J. (2010). Effects of mindfulness-based stress reduction (MBSR) on emotion regulation in social anxiety disorder. *Emotion*, *10*(1), 83–91. https://doi.org/10.1037/a0018441

Good, C. H., Brager, A. J., Capaldi, V. F., & Mysliwiec, V. (2020). Sleep in the United States military. *Neuropsychopharmacology*, *45*(1), 176–191. https://doi.org/10.1038/s41386-019-0431-7

Gulliver, A., Griffiths, K. M., & Christensen, H. (2012). Barriers and facilitators to mental health help-seeking for young elite athletes: A qualitative study. *BMC Psychiatry*, *12*(1), 157. https://doi.org/10.1186/1471-244x-12-157

Hayes, S. C., Luoma, J. B., Bond, F. W., Masuda, A., & Lillis, J. (2006). Acceptance and commitment therapy: Model, processes and outcomes. *Behaviour Research and Therapy*, *44*(1), 1–25. https://doi.org/10.1016/j.brat.2005.06.006

Hayes, S. C., Wilson, K. G., Gifford, E. V., Follette, V. M., & Strosahl, K. (1996). Experiential avoidance and behavioral disorders: A functional dimensional approach to diagnosis and treatment. *Journal of Consulting and Clinical Psychology*, *64*(6), 1152–1168. https://doi.org/10.1037/0022-006X.64.6.1152 (Development of Theoretically Coherent Alternatives to the DSM-IV)

Henriksen, K., Schinke, R., Moesch, K., McCann, S., Parham, William D., Larsen, C. H., & Terry, P. (2020). Consensus statement on improving the mental health of high performance athletes. *International Journal of Sport and Exercise Psychology*, *18*(5), 553–560. https://doi.org/10.1080/1612197X.2019.1570473

Jamieson, J. P., Nock, M. K., & Mendes, W. B. (2012). Mind over matter: Reappraising arousal improves cardiovascular and cognitive responses to stress. *Journal of Experimental Psychology: General*, *141*(3), 417–422. https://doi.org/10.1037/a0025719

Jason, B., Luoma, M. A., Catherine, E., Martin, M. A., & Jane L. Pearson, Ph.D. (2002). Contact with mental health and primary care providers before suicide: A review of the evidence. *American Journal of Psychiatry*, *159*(6), 909–916. https://doi.org/10.1176/appi.ajp.159.6.909

Kabat-Zinn, J., & Hanh, T. N. (2009). *Full catastrophe living: Using the wisdom of your body and mind to face stress, pain, and illness*. Delta.

Kröll, C., Doebler, P., & Nüesch, S. (2017). Meta-analytic evidence of the effectiveness of stress management at work. *European Journal of Work and Organizational Psychology*, *26*(5), 677–693. https://doi.org/10.1080/1359432X.2017.1347157

Köller, O. (2023). *Empfehlungen zum Umgang mit dem akuten Lehrkräftemangel* www.kmk.org/fileadmin/Dateien/pdf/KMK/SWK/2023/SWK-2023-Stellungnahme_Lehrkraeftemangel.pdf

Lardon, M. T., & Fitzgerald, M. W. (2013). Performance Enhancement and the Sports Psychiatrist. In *Clinical Sports Psychiatry* (pp. 132–146). https://doi.org/https://doi.org/10.1002/9781118404904.ch13

Laurie, J., & Blandford, A. (2016). Making time for mindfulness. *International Journal of Medical Informatics*, *96*, 38–50. https://doi.org/https://doi.org/10.1016/j.ijmedinf.2016.02.010

Levin, M. E., MacLane, C., Daflos, S., Seeley, J. R., Hayes, S. C., Biglan, A., & Pistorello, J. (2014). Examining psychological inflexibility as a transdiagnostic process across psychological disorders. *Journal of Contextual Behavioral Science*, *3*(3), 155–163. https://doi.org/https://doi.org/10.1016/j.jcbs.2014.06.003

Limm, H., Gundel, H., Heinmuller, M., Marten-Mittag, B., Nater, U. M., Siegrist, J., & Angerer, P. (2011). Stress management interventions in the workplace improve stress reactivity: A randomised controlled trial. *Occupational and Environmental Medicine*, *68*(2), 126–133. https://doi.org/10.1136/oem.2009.054148

Litz, B. T., Stein, N., Delaney, E., Lebowitz, L., Nash, W. P., Silva, C., & Maguen, S. (2009). Moral injury and moral repair in war veterans: A preliminary model and intervention strategy. *Clinical Psychology Review*, *29*(8), 695–706. https://doi.org/https://doi.org/10.1016/j.cpr.2009.07.003

Maglione, M. A., Chen, C., Bialas, A., Motala, A., Chang, J., Akinniranye, O., & Hempel, S. (2021). Combat and operational stress control interventions and PTSD: A systematic review and meta-analysis. *Military Medicine*, *187*(7-8), e846–e855. https://doi.org/10.1093/milmed/usab310

Malo, R., Acier, D., & Bulteau, S. (2022). Psychological flexibility: Toward a better understanding of a key concept. *Trends in Psychology*. https://doi.org/10.1007/s43076-022-00188-1

Meichenbaum, D. (1985). Stress inoculation training. New York, Pergamon Press.

Moesch, K., Kenttä, G., Kleinert, J., Quignon-Fleuret, C., Cecil, S., & Bertollo, M. (2018). FEPSAC position statement: Mental health disorders in elite athletes and models of service provision. *Psychology of Sport and Exercise, 38*, 61–71. https://doi.org/https://doi.org/10.1016/j.psychsport.2018.05.013

Molendijk, T. (2019). The role of political practices in moral injury: A study of Afghanistan Veterans. *Political Psychology*, *40*(2), 261–275. https://doi.org/10.1111/pops.12503

Murphy, L. R. (1996). Stress management in work settings: A critical review of the health effects. *American Journal of Health Promotion*, *11*(2), 112–135. https://doi.org/10.4278/0890-1171-11.2.112

Mysliwiec, V., Mcgraw, L., Pierce, R., Smith, P., Trapp, B., & Roth, B. J. (2013). Sleep disorders and associated medical comorbidities in active duty military personnel. *Sleep*, *36*(2), 167–174. https://doi.org/10.5665/sleep.2364

Pattyn, N., Van Cutsem, J., Lacroix, E., Van Puyvelde, M., Cortoos, A., Roelands, B., & . . . Van Tiggelen, D. (2022). Lessons from special forces operators for elite team sports training: How to make the whole greater than the sum of the parts. *Frontiers in Sports and Active Living*, 4. https://doi.org/10.3389/fspor.2022.780767

Pirkis, J., & Burgess, P. (1998). Suicide and recency of health care contacts: A systematic review. *The British Journal of Psychiatry*, *173*(6), 462–474.

Reardon, C. L., & Factor, R. M. (2010). Sport Psychiatry. *Sports Medicine*, *40*(11), 961–980. https://doi.org/10.2165/11536580-000000000-00000

Reardon, C. L., Hainline, B., Aron, C. M., Baron, D., Baum, A. L., Bindra, A., & . . . Engebretsen, L. (2019). Mental health in elite athletes: International Olympic Committee consensus statement (2019). *British Journal of Sports Medicine*, *53*(11), 667–699. https://doi.org/10.1136/bjsports-2019-100715

Richardson, K. M., & Rothstein, H. R. (2008). Effects of occupational stress management intervention programs: A meta-analysis. *Journal of Occupational Health Psychology*, *13*(1), 69–93. https://doi.org/10.1037/1076-8998.13.1.69

Ridderinkhof, A., De Bruin, E. I., Brummelman, E., & Bögels, S. M. (2017). Does mindfulness meditation increase empathy? An experiment. *Self and Identity*, *16*(3), 251–269. https://doi.org/10.1080/15298868.2016.1269667

Saranapala, D. M. M. K., Baranoff, J., Rushworth, R. L., Westley, I., Collins, K., Burke, A. L. J., & . . . Torpy, D. J. (2022). The effect of cognitive behavioral stress management on perceived stress, biological stress markers and weight loss/regain, from a diet-induced weight loss program: A randomized controlled trial. *Comprehensive Psychoneuroendocrinology*, *10*, 100124. https://doi.org/https://doi.org/10.1016/j.cpnec.2022.100124

Schindler, S., Pfattheicher, S., & Reinhard, M.-A. (2019). Potential negative consequences of mindfulness in the moral domain. *European Journal of Social Psychology*, *49*(5), 1055–1069. https://doi.org/https://doi.org/10.1002/ejsp.2570

Shah, L., Klainin-Yobas, P., Torres, S., & Kannusamy, P. (2014). Efficacy of psychoeducation and relaxation interventions on stress-related variables in people with mental disorders: A literature review. *Archives of Psychiatric Nursing*, *28*, 94–101. https://doi.org/10.1016/j.apnu.2013.11.004

Sharp, M.-L., Fear, N. T., Rona, R. J., Wessely, S., Greenberg, N., Jones, N., & Goodwin, L. (2015). Stigma as a barrier to seeking health care among military personnel with mental health problems. *Epidemiologic Reviews*, *37*(1), 144–162. https://doi.org/10.1093/epirev/mxu012

Spitzer, R. L., Kroenke, K., Williams, J. B. W., & Group, a. t. P. H. Q. P. C. S. (1999). Validation and utility of a self-report version of PRIME-MD. The PHQ primary care study. *JAMA*, *282*(18), 1737–1744. https://doi.org/10.1001/jama.282.18.1737

Tavakoli, N., Broyles, A., Reid, E. K., Sandoval, J. R., & Correa-Fernández, V. (2019). Psychological inflexibility as it relates to stress, worry, generalized anxiety, and somatization in an ethnically diverse sample of college students. *Journal of Contextual Behavioral Science*, *11*, 1–5. https://doi.org/https://doi.org/10.1016/j.jcbs.2018.11.001

Tetrick, L. E., & Winslow, C. J. (2015). Workplace stress management interventions and health promotion. *Annual Review of Organizational Psychology and Organizational Behavior*, *2*(1), 583–603. https://doi.org/10.1146/annurev-orgpsych-032414-111341

Triplett, N. (1898). The dynamogenic factors in pacemaking and competition. *The American Journal of Psychology*, *9*(4), 507–533. https://doi.org/10.2307/1412188

Ungerer, J., Kowalski, J. T., Kreim, G., Hauffa, R., Kropp, S., & Zimmermann, P. L. (2015). Chronischer Stress bei Spezialkräften der Bundeswehr: Chronischer Stress bei Spezialkräften der Bundeswehr. *9*(3), 236–243. https://elibrary.klett-cotta.de/article/99.120130/tg-9-3-236

van den Berg, N. H., Michaud, X., Pattyn, N., & Simonelli, G. (2023). How sleep research in extreme environments can inform the military: Advocating for a transactional model of sleep adaptation. *Current Psychiatry Reports*, *25*(2), 73–91. https://doi.org/10.1007/s11920-022-01407-3

Van Slingerland, K. J., Durand-Bush, N., Bradley, L., Goldfield, G., Archambault, R., Smith, D., & . . . Kenttä, G. (2019). Canadian Centre for Mental Health and Sport (CCMHS) position statement: Principles of mental health in competitive and high-performance sport. *Clinical Journal of Sport Medicine*, *29*(3), 173–180. https://doi.org/10.1097/jsm.0000000000000665

Venta, A., Sharp, C., & Hart, J. (2012). The relation between anxiety disorder and experiential avoidance in inpatient adolescents. *Psychological Assessment*, *24*(1), 240.

Wersebe, H., Lieb, R., Meyer, A. H., Hofer, P., & Gloster, A. T. (2018). The link between stress, well-being, and psychological flexibility during an acceptance and commitment therapy self-help intervention. *International Journal of Clinical and Health Psychology*, *18*(1), 60–68. https://doi.org/https://doi.org/10.1016/j.ijchp.2017.09.002

Xue, C., Ge, Y., Tang, B., Liu, Y., Kang, P., Wang, M., & Zhang, L. (2015). A Meta-analysis of risk factors for combat-related PTSD among military personnel and veterans. *PLOS ONE*, *10*(3), e0120270. https://doi.org/10.1371/journal.pone.0120270

13 Implementing Mental Performance Programs in Elite Military Units

Paige Mattie, Anders Kjærgaard, and Nathalie Pattyn

Introduction

This chapter will discuss opportunities, challenges, and considerations for program development and service delivery in the context of mental performance training within elite military units and organizations. A high-level overview of theoretical and applied frameworks to guide program development and implementation is offered, and the applied experiences of subject matter experts who have worked in or supported applied mental performance programs within military establishments are summarized.

Special Operations Forces (SOF) operatives are confronted with the challenge of sustaining peak performance consistently, despite the escalating demand for their services. This heightened demand underscores the critical need to prioritize the optimization of their job performance, which in many cases has a mental component.

The prevailing SOF landscape features counterterrorism and counterinsurgency operations bolstered by advanced technology, underscoring the heightened complexity faced by both special operations and conventional military units. Consequently, this evolving complexity in the SOF milieu places the operators in a precarious position, requiring them to acquire increasingly intricate skills without compromising their performance during high-stakes operations.

The formulation and execution of mental performance initiatives can be seen as an important initiative to help maintain the high performance level of the operator. However, such capabilities necessitate a methodical approach encompassing a comprehensive planning. This planning phase should encompass input from diverse sources, including peer-reviewed literature, subject matter experts, command authorities, end-users, and other relevant stakeholders. Such meticulous deliberation and collaboration are imperative to ensure the integration of these programs into a holistic strategy aimed at optimizing occupational performance, extending the operational life span of operators, and mitigating enduring health consequences. Key elements underpinning this process include:

Program Objectives: Clearly defining the goals and objectives of the mental performance program.

Intervention Selection: Identifying the specific interventions, tools, or techniques to be employed, along with the intended outcomes of these strategies.

Expert Involvement: Determining the appropriate experts and professionals who are proficient in delivering the program effectively.

DOI: 10.4324/9781003378969-16

Program Evaluation: Establishing robust methods for evaluating the efficacy and impact of the mental performance program, ensuring continuous refinement and improvement.

Various program implementation options have been employed by military institutions to date which may constitute a valuable starting place to identify implementation approaches and strategies to ensure effective and sustainable program uptake. In planning for the implementation of mental performance training and services with military constituents, consideration should be given to *what* the training will entail based on intended program outcomes, *who* will deliver the training, and *how* it will be implemented in consideration of military-specific opportunities and constraints.

Theoretical frameworks for implementation

Selection of a guiding framework

Simply getting off the starting block, or knowing where and how to begin, can be a significant barrier to any group of experts or lone practitioner initiating military mental training programs of any size or scale. Oftentimes, experts trained in the field of sport psychology or other related fields are employed as consultants in their work with athletes, sport organizations, or corporations. For the consultant embarking on an organization-level effort or government-funded initiative in support of military members, the expectations imparted on them with respect to articulating and documenting their intentions, consulting stakeholders, and obtaining requisite support and approval may be unfamiliar and even unsettling, particularly for those accustomed to a more independent style of practice.

What follows is a description of several available frameworks from a variety of fields, which may prove a valuable starting place to provide inspiration or guidance to a practitioner or group in the development of mental performance programs for military organizations.

Applied sport psychology

The field of applied sport psychology provides a useful foundation upon which to conceptualize mental performance training with the aim of facilitating performance excellence in the military operational context. However, the culture of elite military units is different from conventional military organizations, and certainly has distinguishing features from sport (Goodwin, 2008). Therefore, planning for mental performance training in this domain demands consideration of the unique culture of military institutions. In particular, the consistently high operational tempo maintained by elite military personnel provides limited access to unit members on a consistent or reliable basis, inhibiting implementation of a typical sport psychology intervention. Planning for mental performance programs in military organizations must carefully consider barriers and enablers to implementation that extend beyond the sport performance literature. Specifically, in a real-world military context, program implementers must be sensitive to such opportunities and challenges as existing training and operational schedules and the availability of personnel.

The standard process for implementing mental skills training within athletic populations typically includes three distinct phases: *Education,* whereby participants learn the influence of psychological skills on performance; *Acquisition*, during which performers develop various psychological skills; and the application or *Practice* phase, where psychological skills are applied and practiced in the performer's specific context (Weinberg & Gould, 2007). In general, mental skills training is considered most effective when administered across the long term, and initiated in the off-season, when real or perceived performance pressure is relatively low (Weinberg & Gould, 2007). Training is conducted with individuals and/or groups, and can include individual assessment and training as well as the integration of mental training within other areas of development (e.g., physical or technical training).

Partington and Orlick's (1987) early guidance for sports psychology consultants in setting the stage for success rings as true today for consultants in military settings as it did for those in 1987 elite sports:

> First, have the coach or contact person set a positive expectation about you and your service before you become involved. Second, be sure your first contact with the athlete or team is at an appropriate time (e.g., when athletes are relaxed, rested, and attentive, as opposed to being forced to face tired athletes between their other training or competitive demands). Third, provide individual sessions that focus on the needs of individual athletes. And fourth, attend some training sessions and competitions to gain both credibility and understanding of the demands these athletes face. (p. 315)

Indeed, initial relationship building with leadership, command teams, and military personnel is integral to establishing key stakeholder buy-in and setting appropriate expectations in a military context. Individualization of services will be expected, as cookie-cutter approaches are oftentimes not well received amongst high-performing military constituents. In the early stages, a mental performance practitioner or specialist will want to be visible, available, and demonstrate interest in learning the unit or organizational culture, in order to begin fitting into the culture of the unit and establishing professional credibility.

Cropley, Hanton, Miles, and Niven (2010) employed focus group and consensus validation procedures to explore the process of effective practice for applied sports psychologists, and put forth the following definition:

> *Effective practice in applied sport psychology concerns meeting the needs of the client(s). Effective practice is therefore a process where (a) a working alliance is developed between client(s) and practitioner, (b) clients goals are clear and agreed by all stakeholders, (c) appropriate evidence-based interventions are undertaken to achieve goals, and (d) goals are achieved or reformulated. Honest evaluation and reflection on the process then occurs to inform future practice, which requires the consultant to pro-actively seek sincere feedback. (p. 527)*

A strength of this definition is the provision of specific guidance for the consultant establishing a mental performance initiative, namely the importance of relationship building, goal clarification, evidence-based intervention, self-reflection, and feedback seeking.

In a detailed sport psychology service delivery heuristic-revised (SPSD-R), Poczwardowski and Sherman (2011) identify 18 elements of effective sports psychology service delivery, expanded from an original 11 factor model (Poczwardowski, Sherman, & Henschen, 1998). In this revised model, the authors integrated the empirical and practice-based literature from sport psychology and counselling psychology with an analysis of interviews with experienced consultants. The revised SPSD heuristic (SPSD-R) consists of three fundamental factors; the foundation of service, the process and service (which is further delineated into entry and conceptualization, implementation, and conclusion and termination), and working interpersonal alliance. Each item of the 11 factor model resides amongst the three fundamental factors.

The SPSD-R is both broad in scope, ranging from the formative training of a consultant to the conclusion of actual service provision, as well as detailed in focused element areas. The reader is referred to the SPSD authors' original works (Poczwardowski, Sherman, & Henschen, 1998; Poczwardowski & Sherman, 2011) for further details of the literature from which it was drawn, the heuristic itself, and additional special considerations.

Table 13.1 The revised SPSD heuristic (SPSD-R)

The foundation of service	• Professional Philosophy • Professional Ethics • Education and Training • Professional Experience
The process and service	Entry and conceptualization • Making Contact • Assessment • Conceptualizing Athletes' Concerns and Potential Interventions Implementation • The Range Type & Organization of Service • Program Implementation • Managing the Self as an Intervention Instrument Conclusion and termination • Program and Consultant Evaluation • Conclusions and Implications • Leaving the Setting
Working interpersonal alliance	• Consultant-Client Relationship • The Consultant Variables • The Client Variables • Immersion • The Goodness of Fit

Mental health training

Castro and Adler (2011) contend that effective mental training should be synonymous with mental health training and resilience training, emphasizing the interconnectedness of these concepts. Both mental health and resilience training are pertinent to performance enhancement, stress management, and overall well-being, as further detailed in Chapter 12 on mental performance and mental health, and in Chapter 16 illustrating the concept in Olympic athletes. Numerous initiatives have been introduced in various military SOF settings with a shared overarching objective to empower SOF personnel with cognitive and behavioural strategies, enabling them to effectively navigate the challenges inherent in military service.

Castro and Adler (2011) have outlined fundamental principles of mental health training and implementation, within which 10 general principles on mental health training and 15 principles of implementation are listed. This guidance may serve as a useful checklist in the development phase of mental performance initiatives, in particular where mental health education or mental health literacy is included as a program objective.

Program planning and implementation

The program planning and implementation literature offers an additional perspective for implementing mental performance programming within military organizations. Intervention Mapping (IM; Bartholomew Eldridge et al., 2016) is an approach commonly applied within the health promotion literature as a framework to guide program development and implementation and has been applied across a variety of health promotion domains. By using IM as a methodological framework, the likelihood of later successful implementation and the achievement of desired outcomes can be enhanced (Bartholomew Eldridge et al., 2016; Fernandez, Ruiter, Markham & Kok, 2019). Notably, this approach has been employed to guide the development of

Table 13.2 Fundamental principles of mental health training and implementation (adapted from Castro & Adler (2011, p. 327)

Principles of mental health training	*Principles of implementation*
• Strength based	• Integration into the organizational culture
• Relevant purpose and content	• Appropriate in timing
• Based on experience	• Quality control
• Explanatory	• Train-the-trainer program
• Team-based approach	• Exportable and scalable
• Action-based strategies	• Training guidelines
• Developmental approach	• Refresher training
• Comprehensive and integrated training	• Mobile training teams
• User acceptability	• Sustainability
• Evidence-based and validated	• Program improvement
	• Policy

mental performance programming in several SOF communities (Mattie, Guest, Bailey, Collins & Gucciardi, 2020; Pattyn et al., 2022).

The IM framework is an iterative process involving six phases, each comprising several tasks/steps: (1) needs assessment, (2) identification of program outcomes and objectives, (3) program design, (4) program production, (5) program implementation, and (6) development of an evaluation framework. It can be used as a stand-alone framework or be used to supplement phase one of the MRC guidance, described later, by providing practical guidance and pinpointing essential components for developers to make informed decisions regarding intervention development (Bartholomew Eldridge et al., 2016; Fernandez et al., 2019).

Strengths of this approach include the provision of a structured framework by which to include evidence-based and theoretically informed principles of performance and behaviour change, the inclusion of a needs assessment phase to identify program outcomes and the inclusion of key stakeholders throughout the development and implementation process. A noteworthy advantage of this approach within the SOF context is the ongoing consultation with the end-user (i.e., SOF members/operators) throughout the iterative program development process, which ensure relatability and program uptake (Mattie et al., 2020). A notable drawback of the IM approach is that the process has been considered time-consuming by some program developers (e.g., Mattie et al., 2020; McEachan, Lawton, Jackson, Conner, & Lunt, 2008).

User-centred design literature

Another lens through which to plan implementation of mental performance programming is within the user-centred design literature. Broadly speaking, user-centred design is a design process that involves end-user influence in how the design takes shape. The principle outcome of this approach is usability (i.e., "the extent to which a product can be used by specified users to achieve specified goals with effectiveness, efficiency, and satisfaction in a specified context of use", put forth by the International Standards Association (1998) and cited in Lyon & Koerner, 2016, p. 183). The application of this approach is apparent within the elite military culture, given these groups typically comprise individuals who are mission focused, goal oriented, and without much need for frills. The philosophy and methodology of user-centred design are becoming more widely applied outside of traditional product development. Lyon and Koerner (2016) outline the design concepts that can be applied to psychosocial interventions (specifically with evidence-based therapies). The concepts include (a) clear identification of end users and their needs, (b) prototyping/rapid iteration, (c) simplifying existing intervention parameters/procedures, and (d) exploiting natural constraints.

Table 13.3 The Intervention Mapping (IM) approach (adapted from Bartholomew et al., 2016)

EVALUATION	Step 1: Logic Model of the Problem	• Establish and work with a planning group • Conduct a needs assessment to create a logic model of the problem • Describe the context for the intervention, including the population, setting, and community • State program goals
	Step 2: Program Outcomes and Objectives – Logic Model of Change	• State expected outcomes for behaviour and environment • Specify performance objectives for behavioural and environmental outcomes • Select determinants for behavioural and environmental outcomes • Construct matrices of change objectives • Create a logic model of change
	Step 3: Program Design	• Generate program themes, components, scope, and sequence • Choose theory- and evidence-based change methods • Select or design practical applications to deliver change methods
	Step 4: Program Production	• Refine program structure and organization • Prepare plans for program materials • Draft messages, materials, and protocols • Pretest, refine, and produce materials
	Step 5: Program Implementation Plan	• Identify potential program users (adopters, implementers, and maintainers) • State outcomes and performance objectives for program use • Construct matrices of change objectives for program use • Design implementation interventions
	Step 6: Evaluation	• Write effect and process evaluation questions • Develop indicators and measures for assessment • Specify the evaluation design • Complete the evaluation plan

National Collaborating Centre for Methods and Tools

The National Collaborating Centre for Methods and Tools out of Canada offers a comprehensive package of methods and tools to plan, implement, and evaluate public health programs, which may also be applicable to applied mental performance programs in elite military settings. The Getting to Outcomes (GTO) approach, designed to help programs improve accountability and program quality comprises ten accountability questions or steps that cover planning, evaluation, and improvement/sustainment data.

Planning for implementation should encompass the identification of internal groups or sections responsible for various critical aspects, such as (1) managing the program or capability itself, (2) overseeing service delivery, and (3) assessing the effectiveness of training or capability, including ensuring program fidelity and maintaining quality control. The order and sequence in which these questions are addressed can be flexible and adapted to the specific context. This process can be likened to an iterative feedback loop, wherein lessons learned and insights gained can inform and improve earlier stages of planning. Furthermore, it is strongly recommended that practitioners consider and incorporate the cultural characteristics, norms, and values of the target population. By doing so, this approach can be effectively applied to military populations, facilitating the development of programs that are tailored to meet the unique needs and demands of this specific setting and population.

Table 13.4 The Getting to Outcomes (GTO) approach

1	Needs and Resources: What are the underlying needs and conditions in the community?
2	Goals: What goals, target populations and objectives (i.e., desired outcomes) will address the needs and change the underlying conditions?
3	Best Practice: Which evidence-based models and best practice programs can you use to reach your goals?
4	Fit: What actions do you need to take so that the selected program "fits" the community context?
5	Capacities: What organizational capacities are needed to implement the program?
6	Plan: What is the plan for this program?
7	Process: How will you assess the quality of program implementation?
8	Outcomes: How well did the program work?
9	Continuous Quality Improvement: How will you incorporate continuous quality improvement strategies?
10	Sustainability: How will effective programs be sustained?

Development of complex interventions

A final perspective to consider as an overarching framework is the methodological guidance provided by the UK Medical Research Council (MRC) for developing complex interventions (Skivington et al, 2021). This framework has gained international recognition and has seen widespread use in health and social care services, public health practice, and other social and economic policy domains that influence mental health outcomes. The MRC guidance includes four phases centred around six core elements which should be considered in each phase shown in Table 13.5.

Each of the above listed approaches offer a unique framework for conceptualizing, defining, or structuring effective practice or consultation which, when used to inform development prior to implementation, can provide the consultant or program developer with an opportunity to consider factors influencing program success and to identify constraints to implementation in advance, thereby optimizing the opportunity for successful program uptake.

While each is unique in perspective and methodology, several key themes emerge. Specifically:

- the importance of stakeholder involvement
- the requirement to consider context and cultural characteristics
- employing an iterative process/ feedback loops to program development
- assessing for feasibility and acceptability of the interventions; and
- planning for program evaluation.

These themes collectively underscore the need for a structured and adaptable approach when implementing mental performance programs in military organizations. Successful implementation involves understanding the unique military culture, employing evidence-based practice, engaging stakeholders, setting clear goals, and continuously improving the program based on feedback, program evaluation metrics, and end-user consultation.

Mental performance initiatives are typically subsumed within larger organizational human performance optimization (HPO) efforts in high-performance military settings. As Deuster, Lunasco and Messina (2019) comment, "HPO is a continuous process – it is not a program – and it involves and requires continuous learning as new information and technologies unfold" (p. 103). As such, planning for implementation can be considered a continuous process requiring regular monitoring and adjustment.

Table 13.5 The MRC framework for complex interventions (adapted from Skivington et al., 2021)

	FEASIBILITY Assessing feasibility and acceptability of intervention and evaluation design in order to make decisions about progression to next stage of evaluation	
DEVELOP INTERVENTION Either developing a new intervention, or adapting an existing intervention for a new context, based on research evidence and theory of the problem **OR** **IDENTIFY INTERVENTION** Choosing an intervention that already exists (or is planned), either via policy or practice, and exploring its options for evaluation (evaluability assessment)	**CORE ELEMENTS** Consider context Develop, refine, and (re)test programme theory Engage stakeholders Identify key uncertainties Refine intervention Economic considerations	**EVALUATION** Assessing an intervention using the most appropriate method to address research questions
	IMPLEMENTATION Deliberate efforts to increase impact and uptake of successfully tested health innovations	

Applied considerations

The following section provides recommendations for program implementation from the applied perspectives of an international group of subject matter experts (SMEs), each of whom have been involved in mental performance programs in military populations, from the perspective of design and implementation, oversight, or uptake.

Identification of program scope, goals, and objectives

Critical questions to consider include, for example, where did this initiative originate (e.g., who is driving it, where did the request come from?), is the initiative primarily focused on prevention or enhancing performance to prepare operators for upcoming mission, or perhaps both, and specifically which outcomes or effects is the effort aiming to achieve (e.g., enhanced performance, operational readiness, resilience, care seeking)? The identification of clear program objectives holds significance for both the unit and the consultant or coach, as it establishes a common anchoring point and shared framework in measuring outcomes.

Explicit identification of the target population from the outset is critical to ensure a program is developed that meets the needs of the target end-user (i.e., operator constituents, all serving military members of a military unit, family members of serving military, potential or incumbent members of elite units, etc.).

The intended scope or reach of a mental performance program will influence the nature of training administration. A common approach to implementing wide-spread mental training initiatives geared toward entire organizations is the Train the Trainer Model, as is used in the US Army Comprehensive Solder Fitness (CSF; Reivich, Seligman & McBride, 2011) and the Master Resilience Trainer (MRT) delivery models, as well as the Canadian Road to Mental Readiness Program (R2MR) program. Some of these programs offered mirrored programs to family members of active duty personnel, thereby encouraging a similar skillset to be applied to a family unit.

Other initiatives have specifically addressed candidates embarking on physically and psychologically challenging selection and assessment processes. For instance, within the US Navy SEAL selection process, candidates are provided with a variety of psychological skills and cognitive strategies which are integrated within the selection pipeline (Robson & Manacapilli, 2014).

Including the end-user in program development and implementation

Subject matter experts in the human performance field are great assets within a military organization, offering a wealth of experience pertaining to performance optimization. We offer that, in order to successfully create a human performance program within elite units, the involvement and expertise of the actual end-user, the SOF operator, is equally important as the guidance of the human performance expert.

The end-user offers the necessary knowledge and experience to identify and prioritize current gaps from a cultural and operational point of view, and can advise on relevant issues in training and operations, which might differ substantially from the assumptions of subject matter experts and/or leadership. Thus, involving operators in all phases of planning, implementation, execution, and evaluation of the program is critical to ensure program acceptance.

Specifically, experienced operators involved with the mental performance program can help fine-tune teaching materials for an appropriate level of scientific detail, relatable language, and context-specific examples. Importantly, they offer the necessary organizational knowledge to identify formal and informal leaders who can assist in ensuring program hype and interest. Their role as force multipliers is a highly valuable, essential function within any human performance effort, as without their involvement, even the best designed, evidence-based program may struggle with user acceptance and therefore program uptake.

In summary, early and ongoing involvement with the end-user, conducted either formally or informally, is essential for creating an effective and culturally relevant intervention. Including SOF operators in the development process allows program developers to gain an understanding of the specific needs, preferences, and challenges of the target audience, which is essential for tailoring the program to their unique requirements. Further, it ensures relevance and relatability to the military members who will receiving the training, allowing for the creation of meaningful content that directly resonates with their operational experience. Finally, when operators have a sense of ownership in the program, there may be a higher likelihood of buy-in from the target audience.

Identification and inclusion of relevant stakeholders

As previously mentioned within the description of available guiding frameworks, planning for implementation must include identification of which internal group(s) or section(s) will assume responsibility for such aspects as the program/capability itself, service delivery, evaluating effectiveness of the training/capability, and ensuring program fidelity and quality control. It is critical to clearly identify, and formally document, which stakeholder(s) are driving the initiative. Within military installations, the ongoing turnover of military members, leaders, and often human performance staff is inevitable. Therefore, documenting the evolution of a program, including key decision-making processes and outcomes, will anchor the initiative in a systematic way, to help prevent lost or duplicated effort. A top-down (i.e., leader-directed) approach can ensure that the intent of senior leadership is reflective in the initiative, and that the mental performance capability aligns with the broader organizational priorities related to performance and wellness. Alternatively, or potentially concurrently, programs that are bottom-up informed will enable the end-user (i.e., military constituents) to influence all phases of development.

In military settings, especially within the fast-paced environment of SOF, concise and to-the-point communication is the standard. External subject matter experts often have difficulties with specific military communication styles and staffing procedures. To obtain stakeholder support for a program, a sufficient communication strategy which includes correct formatting and language, as well as appropriate timing, is essential. When strategizing implementation, it's important to collaborate with colleagues within the organization to gain insights into the preferred communication methods and channels typically used, such as email, brief updates during meetings, or formal briefings to decision-makers. Furthermore, it's essential to understand the communication expectations of key stakeholders, both in terms of frequency and style. You may find that after investing significant time in creating a detailed and compelling PowerPoint presentation, the unit commander prefers a concise three-minute pitch. Generally, stakeholders may only have time for the "Bottom Line Up Front" (BLUF). Informal opportunities may also present to explain your vision and project to key enablers. These unexpected opportunities provide the prepared practitioner with informal channels to relay progress, gather valuable feedback, address issues like resource allocation, and obtain valuable information regarding command priorities.

Pilot testing training programs

Pilot testing a training package prior to widespread implementation allows for program developers to trial the content for feasibility and acceptance, make any required adaptations to training content, identify logistical considerations with program delivery, and to obtain feedback from the SOF community on the relevance of content. When conducting pilot testing, it is helpful to have a monitoring and information capturing system in place such that feedback from users and facilitators, as well as program activities and outcomes can be tracked. The pilot testing phase helps uncover any flaws, errors, or issues in the program's design, content, or delivery and to refine and improve program content, materials, and delivery methods. Finally, pilot testing allows organizations to test the processes and procedures related to program delivery, such as registration, scheduling, communication, and data collection. Oftentimes, data collected during the pilot phase can serve as a baseline for evaluating the program's effectiveness. This information can be used to assess changes in knowledge, behaviour, or outcomes after full-scale implementation. A practical example is offered by Pattyn et al. (2022) in their description of a pilot-test of an interdisciplinary human performance program in the Belgian tier 1 SOF unit.

Service delivery approaches

One of the essential elements in planning to implement a mental performance capability within any organization is identifying the expert(s) who will deliver mental performance training or service and the role they hold within an organization. Consideration should be given to the specific intent of the training (i.e., performance enhancement, promote resilience, or mental health literacy), the available resources, and the specific needs of the organization. This section discusses various options/approaches with respect to service delivery and the opportunity and drawback associated with each.

Mental performance specialists

Embedded or contracted mental performance specialists are the core of any mental performance program. Their role is to develop, implement, and evaluate all mental performance efforts within the unit, and to remain on top of advancements or trends within the field of practice. The professional background of these practitioners is usually sports science or psychology. While medical professions are highly regulated in many parts of the globe, the standards for mental performance providers differ widely. As a general rule, the authors suggest that a mental performance team should be led by individuals with at least a master's degree in sports science or psychology and specific training including practical application of mental performance techniques under supervision. When applicable within the nation, accreditation by an official body that regulates training, education, and professional conduct should be mandatory. Professional oversight by such a provider is especially important when training elements are delivered by individuals without the respective professional background.

DEDICATED, EMBEDDED EXPERTS

The employment of full-time, embedded practitioners with expertise and relevant qualification and certification in sport/performance psychology is viewed as the "gold standard" in mental performance training. This is consistent with models of mental performance training in elite sport, where it has become commonplace for professional and elite amateur athletes, teams, and sport organizations to employ mental performance practitioners on a full-time, dedicated basis. Typically, these mental performance specialists are integrated within the context of multidisciplinary health or human performance teams, enabling holistic service provision across multiple disciplines.

The embedded service provision model offers opportunities to both the organization (i.e., SOF members, SOF enterprises) and the service provider. When regular access to a mental performance practitioner is ensured, traditional models of mental training typical of those applied in a sport context (e.g., phased, progressive training) can be employed, and the members gain familiarity with the provider and the field of practice, possibly via the mere exposure effect. Concurrently, embedding a service provider within a SOF unit or organization affords that practitioner the opportunity to acquire context, establish relationships, and appropriately identify client needs. Finally, embedding a provider on a full-time basis ensures the practitioner will have the time available for the many activities required of them. As mental/cognitive performance coaches, a primary focus is mental performance training and supporting it, such as crafting individual training plans and creating educational content. Oftentimes, they are sole representatives of their job description within the unit or military installation. In addition to activities of the trade, they may also find themselves engaged in ancillary activities like managing program budgets, drafting work statements for hiring staff, composing operating procedure memorandums, data entry and analysis, briefing command chains on program status, evaluating the scientific basis of new tools, or producing articles and white papers on mental performance topics of interest. These additional responsibilities, along with the time-consuming tasks of building relationships and networking, are crucial. Being visible within SOF units is also of paramount importance. Successful mental performance providers invest a significant portion of their time attending meetings, training sessions, observing work processes, and engaging with colleagues. Cultivating relationships is vital, and it's essential to allocate time in one's daily schedule for this purpose.

Offsetting the noted strengths of this approach are several challenges, such as the resource investment/logistics required to employ a dedicated provider on a sustained basis, and the need for integration of the position into existing organizational structure (e.g., where does the position reside, who has authority for it). Added to this is the importance of having the function, initiatives, and tasks of the position clearly outlined and formally approved. In cases where the integrated consultant suddenly disappears, a void may be left in the organization if there is no curriculum or process to fall back on.

Some considerations in the selection of appropriate embedded service providers include (1) what is the requisite level and type of training/education relative to the identified organizational need; (2) how can person/organizational fit be identified; (3) does this position required certification with appropriate accreditation organization or groups (e.g., AASP, FEPSAC, CSPA); (4) what are conditions of full-time employment; and (5) are resources secured to employ this expert on an ongoing basis. The selection of personnel should be based on academic credentials, professional expertise, and personal fit. The ability to work in a team, see the bigger picture, and prioritize the overarching goal is essential for an embedded specialist.

CONTRACTING EXTERNAL PROVIDERS.

A second approach to service delivery is the short-term (i.e., one-off) or ongoing contracting of industry experts from relevant disciplines to deliver mental performance training. This approach has been employed at the unit (i.e., tactical) level within various SOF organizations. A strength in contracting industry leaders is the perception of "street-credibility' among operators when the provider has a significant background in elite sport performance. Additionally, the option of contracting may be logistically simpler than hiring a full-time embedded provider. It is recommended that when contracting external providers, that embedded personnel with appropriate expertise and who are trusted agents within the organization be tasked with overseeing the hiring, service delivery, and outputs of contracted external providers.

Several challenges of this approach should be noted. With training delivered in a 'one-off' manner, there is no continuity of service or option to follow-up with the provider. Secondly, it is common for contracted providers to deliver a training package with little documented evidence of a needs assessment or program evaluation. Thirdly, external consultants are often expensive, which even in SOF environments is something that must be taken into account. Organizations considering external industry experts are advised to determine the specific education training and experience required to meet their training needs, and to ensure any contracted provider is fully vetted to fulfil those needs. Finally, caution should be used in contracting providers whose marketing prowess may exceed their actual qualification or expertise.

Secondary duties of health and human performance providers

Another approach is for existing assets within SOF units to deliver mental performance training as a secondary responsibility. This could reasonably be conducted by professionals working in other areas of psychological service or human performance teams. Indeed, there is considerable overlap between various branches of psychology and mental performance enhancement. Critically, service providers must deliver services for which they have received explicit training and hold appropriate certification. While this model is more cost-effective than hiring a dedicated service provider, drawbacks to this model include time constraints on the part of the provider (i.e., s/he would not be dedicated to mental performance effort full-time, given competing responsibilities), dual role challenges, and the depth of expertise they can offer this capability.

Not all those spearheading mental performance initiatives have it as their primary duty. Many are operational psychologists who manage mental performance programming as an "additional duty" or are innovators working to develop it within their units. Operational psychology is a specialized field applying psychological principles to the operational activities of national security, defence, and public safety. These experts cover a range of areas, from command consultation to personnel assessment and selection, training, performance optimization, clinical care approaches, data analysis, program management, leadership or team training, and other "duties as assigned".

They often participate in training exercises and deployments with their units, collaborate with operational psychologists from other units, and are on call 24/7 for consultations on urgent personnel or mission matters.

Mental performance training, though recognized as valuable, may sometimes take a back seat to other pressing operational priorities, depending on resource availability within a unit. Given the diverse responsibilities operational psychologists have, mental performance training may not always be at the forefront of their priorities. While the SOF units tend to break down some stigma associated with behavioural health care, the clinicians may still find themselves inundated with addressing behavioural health needs.

Clinical psychologists, who primarily focus on patient care, are also involved in mental performance initiatives. They offer clinical care to service members and their families, including therapy sessions, group sessions, collaboration with multidisciplinary teams, medical reporting, communication with community providers, and referrals. They may participate in various activities such as family readiness group meetings, or wellness workshops to promote soldier or family well-being. Clinical behavioural health providers can be essential assets to a SOF unit, but they may find it challenging to allocate time for prevention and enhancement efforts amid the pressing need for clinical care. To address these performance enhancement and prevention objectives, operational psychology experts are often dedicated to such pursuits and can more readily allocate time.

In the military, individuals often juggle multiple responsibilities alongside their primary roles and personnel are adept at optimizing their limited resources to accomplish their mission, even if it means assisting with tasks that would not typically fall within their job description in other contexts. Additionally, within these organizations, it's common for individuals to wear multiple hats, leading to dual role conflicts. Providers often find themselves grappling with the question of whether they are in a clinical, consultative, or teaching role. Determining when to transition from one role to another is a critical decision with potential ethical implications for both the provider and the client. For instance, when a mental performance coach becomes aware of an operator's combat-related nightmares and drinking issues, determining the extent of intervention and disclosure to other providers can be complex.

Providers bear the responsibility of understanding their ethical boundaries and obligations, seeking consultation from trusted experts, and engaging with industry-specific ethics organizations to navigate these complex situations, prioritizing the principle of "First, do no harm".

MEDICAL PROVIDERS

Medical professionals in performance optimization primarily focus on prevention, rehabilitation, and medical considerations related to performance enhancement. In most cases, medical providers operate independently from the unit's human performance program, fulfilling essential performance-related functions alongside their primary duties. Medical teams typically comprise primary care providers, nurses, and physical therapists. There is a growing trend in SOF units to include mental health professionals (e.g., clinical psychologists, psychiatrists, clinical social workers) to offer diagnostic and therapeutic support to operators. The diagnosis and treatment of medical conditions, particularly the assessment of medical readiness, should be distinct from the human performance functions, and clear separation between clinical aspects and performance enhancement efforts should be assured.

However, the coordination of service provision across the spectrum of health and human performance should be prioritized, such that referral of members to the correct provider occurs seamlessly, for example, between strength and conditioning, physiotherapy, and medical care, and between mental performance specialists, operational psychologists, and clinical behavioural health providers. Such a structure lends itself to an integrated and holistic human performance service, whereby all services within a human performance program are easy to access, and a seamless referral pathway is in place for all providers within human performance and healthcare. This "No Wrong Door Approach" ensures an operator need only ask for help one time, and the risk of an individual falling through the proverbial cracks is minimized. Additionally, health and human performance practitioners can work to understand the scope of each domain or area of practice, ensure the use of similar and consistent terminology with their clients/patients, and where appropriate, reinforce messaging from other domains in their own practice.

PHYSICAL TRAINING INSTRUCTORS

Physical performance teams focus on physical aspects, such as strength training, conditioning, injury prevention, and rehabilitation. The education and titles of physical performance providers may vary between organizations, but accreditation and certification systems are typically well-established. Military regulations often govern physical training closely, with oversight usually provided by professionals holding graduate-level training in sports science or exercise physiology. In units where unsupervised physical training takes place, it's advantageous to train operators within the teams to supervise and align training with coaching staff recommendations.

Mental performance efforts can be reinforced through practical application during physical training. For example, visualization training can be integrated into physical activities, reinforcing techniques throughout training programs. Collaboration among experts and practitioners from various domains (mental performance, physical training, etc.) during content development ensures inclusivity and informed training. The presence of mental performance specialists during content delivery facilitates participant engagement and Q&A.

This service delivery approach is most effective when theory and training in a specific technique precede physical activity sessions. Written materials can be provided to participants up front, with applied skills and techniques progressively integrated throughout training programs, and applied to the context of physical preparation (e.g., goal-setting specific to physical training outcomes, arousal regulation to "pump oneself up" in a gym session).

Advantages of this approach include emphasizing the integrated nature of human performance, resource efficiency, and presentation flexibility. Additionally, including mental training within the context of physical condition may destigmatize mental preparation and reinforce it as a regular and expected form of training from which anyone can benefit. Potential disadvantages may involve a shift toward the presenter's dominant domain (e.g., strength and conditioning) and a lack of in-depth expertise, which can be mitigated by involving experts from all relevant domains and emphasizing a collaborative and holistic approach during training sessions.

OPERATORS/TRAINING CADRE

An alternative approach for delivering mental training is to involve military personnel in program delivery. Typically employed using a Train the Trainer model, this method capitalizes on the credibility and real-world experience of military members who are familiar with the SOF environment. When a credible operator leads these initiatives, the others are listening. As such, these members can be force multipliers in generating acceptance of what is often a new area of training. While a benefit of this approach is the availability and interest of service personnel, especially where reservists or former operators are available, a common drawback is that mental performance training typically falls outside their primary training and expertise, limiting the depth of knowledge they can provide compared to qualified subject matter experts. Further, "creeping excellence" can take form, where instructors may adapt or expand teaching material based on personal interest, knowledge, or experience.

SOF technical training instructors generally operate independently from the human performance framework. However, technical training is an ideal setting for operators to practice applying mental performance techniques in real-world scenarios. Therefore, it's crucial to include training instructors in the planning process when implementing or revising a mental performance program. Ideally, mental performance skills should be seamlessly integrated into technical training as early as possible along a training or selection pipeline, such as visualization before a house clearing task, breathing techniques before a shooting drill, or distancing techniques during SERE training. Training instructors should be adequately equipped to encourage students to use these techniques in specific situations, to model skill usage, and to assist with their practical application. They can also offer valuable insights to the mental performance team on when and how these techniques could be beneficial for students/operators due to their in-depth understanding of the subject matter. These trained individuals subsequently serve as peer support and act as a bridge, as needed, between service providers and military constituents.

Interdisciplinary human performance teams

The primary objective of human performance programs within military institutions is to enhance battlefield performance, increase resilience to physiological and psychological stress, expedite return to duty following injury, and improve overall health and well-being. These programs span various domains, including technical, physiological, mental, social, ethical/moral, and medical practice, each representing dedicated fields but often exhibiting significant overlap in the context of health and human performance. A multidisciplinary human performance team comprises specialists from diverse backgrounds, such as coaches, mental performance specialists, physical therapists, and physicians.

As mentioned, the technical domain in military organizations typically operates independently of human performance sections or departments. However, regardless of the organizational structure, close cooperation and coordination among various professions and functions within the human performance framework, as well as with the medical and technical domains, are crucial for the success of human performance programs, as is illustrated as well in Chapter 16 regarding Olympic athletes.

Ideally, these domains would work together in symbiosis, actively integrating their expertise to expand upon an organizational body of knowledge. Such an approach, referred to as interdisciplinary, fosters collaboration, intellectual stimulation, and cross-fertilization of ideas. Creating a climate of cooperation and collaboration is essential in environments that may naturally foster competition and conflict. Prioritizing interdisciplinary coordination and cooperation helps manage competing interests, such as organizational concerns like funding, staff positions, or influence. A potential lack of coordination among different providers in health and human performance domains carries several risks, including the duplication of effort, interference, uncoordinated training and information, and the potential to undermine the credibility of all involved parties. Successful coordination demands professionalism, modesty, and, at times, a willingness to compromise from all service providers. It requires a commitment to collaboration within interdisciplinary teams, which involves clearly defining shared spaces and professional boundaries. In human performance domains, there is often significant overlap, resulting in shared spaces that encompass the mental domain in human performance, operational psychology, mental health (as part of the medical domain), and, to some extent, the social and moral/ethical domain. It is of utmost importance to establish well-defined shared spaces, professional boundaries, and a framework for oversight and accountability when developing a mental performance program.

Summary

As evident from the descriptions above, there are numerous human resource challenges involved in developing, implementing, and sustaining mental performance initiatives. A unit, or even an entire military installation, might only have one dedicated mental performance coach or provider, or they may rely on an operational or clinical psychologist taking on these initiatives as a secondary duty. When planning mental performance initiatives or programs, it is essential to carefully assess the sustainability of long-term requirements, hire the right practitioners, and manage organizational resources effectively.

Lessons learned

A unit-specific mental performance capability is a critical component of a holistic, overarching human performance program. Implementing such a program is not without its challenges and recognizing that the process takes time, investment, and support from all levels of an organization is essential to the successful implementation of a program or area of service.

The experiences of authors who have implemented, or are in the process of implementing, a mental performance program provide valuable lessons learned. This section summarizes these lessons learned and recommendations submitted by the authors, as well as members of the technical team represented on the NATO Research Task Group on mental performance training in special operations personnel (RTG-HFM-308). These are included in an effort to pre-empt or minimize challenges faced by other organizations/practitioners and to identify features or approaches that could save other program implementers time and effort. It should, however, be recognized that all units are different and a thorough needs analysis of any unique organization and of the intended end-user will be required.

Secure leadership (i.e., top-down) and end-user (i.e., bottom-up) support/buy-in

Documented, long-term financial support and buy-in from multiple rather than a single Command individual, are essential when developing, implementing, and sustaining a mental performance program. Senior leadership must understand the intent of the program, as well as that of any broader human performance initiative, in order to ensure that sufficient resources are allocated, and that an internal interest in supporting high performance, recovery, and excellence is developed and maintained. For example, without Command support, ensuring that personnel are available to receive training or support, or that schedules are adapted where necessary, may be a continued challenge.

Using focus groups or surveys with end-users and stakeholders identifies needs, perceived barriers, and beliefs and also serves to generate buy in, ownership, and motivation. Operators will have more incentive to commit to a program if they have been involved in its design, and command will be more likely to facilitate a program's success and adequately resource it if their opinions and ideas have been incorporated.

Identifying program champions or "cultural architects", amongst leadership, a training cadre, or actively deploying members, who genuinely believe in and promote the program, is an effective tool to enhance program engagement and success.

Ensure continuous communication

Effective communication is crucial in all aspects of military training and operations. Continuous and clear communication of goals and expectations among all stakeholders, including providers, operators, and leadership, is vital to enhance buy-in and prevent later confusion or dissatisfaction. It's important to document and communicate successes and challenges through regular, concise briefings to command. Inadequate communication within the unit regarding program content and implementation can lead to mixed messages within the unit and potentially affect the perception of the program.

Implement an overall program manager

Having a dedicated Human Performance Program Manager, who has oversight of an entire human performance and/or health program(s) can help achieve the program requirements previously mentioned (e.g., stakeholder engagement, leadership briefings, communication). This oversight can help to mitigate duplication of effort with other sections, and can facilitate coordination and collaboration amongst various providers and areas of practice.

A dedicated program manager can further ensure that a strategic approach to continuous program/capability development is employed, and that findings from research, training opportunities, and conferences are disseminated widely, for the benefit of all practitioners and the program.

Include a comprehensive evaluation framework

Failing to conduct a thorough program evaluation means missing the opportunity to showcase its effectiveness and, most importantly, the return on investment. It is critical that well-structured evaluations be developed early on in the programming process, to provide evidence for program outcomes and to ensure continuous program improvement. Program developers should establish an evaluation framework from the beginning, which should encompass plans for data collection, management, and analysis. Alongside the evaluation of program uptake, user satisfaction, program fidelity, or changes in relevant mental performance and mental health outcomes, it's important to include operationally relevant performance metrics, where feasible.

By ensuring that comprehensive program evaluation measures are in place, ongoing support for the program can be justified and sustained. Regular evaluations can quickly identify underperforming programs, allowing for quick adaptation or withdrawal, thereby turning failed ideas into valuable learning experiences. Ultimately, ongoing evaluation should keep a watchful eye on changing needs of the end-user, and the organizational and operational requirements, enabling the program to evolve as necessary.

Adapt to specific organizational and individual needs

Customizing interventions to align with the unique requirements of an organization, military section, or trade is essential. There is no cookie-cutter or universal solution in mental performance training, and practitioners must ensure that a program or initiative addresses the specific needs of a unit, irrespective of its success in other contexts.

However, it's worth noting that an 80% effective solution can serve as a solid foundation for implementing a valuable idea, allowing room for enhancements and adjustments. To begin, consider examining what already works well and building upon it, a complete overhaul may not be necessary.

Embed providers into the unit

Many organizations have found that an embedded, holistic approach to the delivery of a mental performance program is highly effective, with the mental performance specialist working closely with other human performance, medical, family liaison personnel, etc. within the unit. This can also help with continuity of provision, whereby embedded providers, assuming they are a good organizational fit, may have more longevity than temporary or fixed-term contractors.

Future proof the program

To ensure program sustainability, it's vital to future-proof them against the potential departure of key individuals, such as mental performance providers or senior leadership. Securing a broad base of high-level supporters and establishing formal policies is essential. This approach guarantees that the program remains stable in the face of personnel changes or adjustments to organizational priorities. Both long-term and short-term planning and policy development are crucial. Dependence on goodwill has its limits and should be minimized.

Allow for quick adaptations

The program should be quickly tailored to fit the specific characteristics of the target group, such as their cultural norms and everyday language. It's important to remain responsive to feedback, which might involve adjusting the training duration or modifying content to ensure the target group's engagement. These adaptations should align with the core training objectives and be the product of discussions grounded in scientific and training principles. Conducting focus-group consultations with the end-user, or pilot tests of the training material before full implementation can aid in fine-tuning the program to better meet the needs of the target group.

By incorporating ideas, tools, equipment, and techniques from innovative research, training can establish itself as cutting-edge and suitable for an elite performing group. However, to achieve this successfully, a balance between innovation and evidence is required. This balance is maintained by ensuring there is at least proof of concept data, often drawn from student or civilian populations, and by avoiding the use of SOF personnel as guinea pigs for entirely unproven concepts. Any new approaches should be grounded in sound theoretical principles. Having a scientific or research advisor evaluate potential training innovations can be particularly helpful.

Align with and incorporate into existing training

Mental performance content should directly relate to the specific tasks of the target audience. For instance, when operators are about to face high-risk and unfamiliar activities (e.g., parachuting or deep-water diving), focusing on arousal management is suitable. During phases that require them to diagnose a device or assess a target, content concerning perceptual or attentional limitations, problem-solving, and decision-making processes becomes more relevant.

Whenever feasible, it appears most effective to integrate the content into existing military training rather than presenting it exclusively as standalone training. This approach serves a dual purpose: it provides ongoing education and practical application of mental performance training, while also continually showcasing its tactical value and encouraging the use of mental skills in the specific SOF performance context.

Obtain baseline assessment of relevant health and human performance factors

Baseline assessments play a pivotal role in the realm of health and human performance. These assessments are not just beneficial, but essential to identifying the specific requirements of a human performance program. Moreover, baseline assessments serve as the bedrock for depicting the accurate health and performance status of operators, providing a clear snapshot of where an individual stands in terms of physical, mental, and overall well-being before embarking on any performance improvement initiatives. Without baseline data, it becomes challenging to measure progress, set meaningful goals, and make informed decisions about the most effective interventions, and demonstrate usefulness of an initiative or return on investment.

Ensure appropriate resource investment

In order to achieve both initial success and sustainability, it is imperative that initiatives receive appropriate resourcing. In some instances, the support for establishing mental performance initiatives relies significantly on goodwill from individuals already tasked with a complete workload, and who are associated with the military unit. However, if this investment is not acknowledged by the organization, for example, by formally requesting support from higher-ranking authorities and thus validating the importance of the invested personnel, goodwill tends to diminish over time.

Resources encompass not only financial allocation and personnel, but also time and prioritization. Conversely, program developers and managers bear the responsibility of being accountable to the organization or institution funding the initiative. They should demonstrate a clear return on investment resulting from their efforts, thereby ensuring that the initiative remains well-supported and sustainable.

Ensure HP activities are protected in the training template

Allocating dedicated time to human performance initiatives is essential to prevent them from being overshadowed by already packed schedules. Frequently, a shortage of available time leads to a lack of structured scheduling for human performance activities. Instead, human performance time slots often serve as backup weeks for organizing administrative follow-up tasks, unit meetings, or any other activities that can't find a proper place in the schedule. This situation demands a significant degree of flexibility from both operators and human performance experts. Unfortunately, this approach ultimately hampers the ability to conduct the intended work at the necessary standards.

Develop unit-wide/organization-wide initiatives

In order to realize a substantial and transformative impact, a human performance or mental training initiative should extend its reach beyond the individual and team levels, encompassing the entirety of the unit or organization. This broad approach can result in a valuable cultural shift within the organization, which is essential for the initiative to achieve its full potential and drive holistic improvements in performance and well-being throughout the entire unit.

Constant innovation

SOF operators and organizations are known for their relentless pursuit of excellence, ongoing improvement, and for pushing boundaries. This drive extends beyond military skills to encompass a strong desire for innovative methods to optimize and enhance performance. Human performance providers frequently encounter operators and leadership introducing new ideas for inclusion in the human performance program. Balancing openness to novel approaches with maintaining critical professional judgment is paramount. In this dynamic environment, gaining approval for beneficial, evidence-based interventions can be just as challenging as preventing the adoption of non-evidence-based and potentially harmful practices. For instance, it may require a similar level of effort to advocate for well-founded interventions as it does to discourage practices that lack scientific merit.

Collaboration with existing stakeholders vs. empire building

As mentioned earlier in this section, many services integral to an interdisciplinary, holistic human performance program are already available within the military, and in some cases, within a SOF unit itself. This pre-existing infrastructure significantly influences the process of developing, implementing, and executing a human performance program within the organization.

External stakeholders may at times lack the understanding required to support the unique needs of an SOF unit. They are typically constrained by regulations and leadership directives tailored to the much larger conventional forces. Effecting the necessary changes in support of an elite unit can be a laborious and frustrating endeavour, particularly when the specific concerns of SOF are not prioritized within the supporting organization. Achieving success in this regard hinges on continuous education of external stakeholders, the active involvement of leadership, and fostering transparency to cultivate a collaborative and mutually beneficial arrangement. Regrettably, these efforts don't always yield the desired outcomes within the expected timeframes.

In certain situations, it may seem justifiable to seek alternative, SOF-specific solutions rather than relying on existing stakeholders. While this may provide short-term benefits, it often has counterproductive long-term effects, especially when met with significant resistance. One example involves contracting or hiring external specialists operating within the domain of responsibility of external stakeholders (e.g., nutrition, psychoeducation, mental skills training) but operating independently. This approach grants these personnel a high degree of autonomy but results in the creation of parallel structures, uncoordinated efforts, and the potential for real or perceived lack of professional oversight. This scenario, especially when undertaken without coordination with current stakeholders or against their wishes, can complicate or even preclude future cooperation with those stakeholders.

It's essential to avoid transforming disagreements over professional approaches into politically charged disputes about influence, resources, or jurisdiction. Such conflicts divert attention from the primary goal: providing the best possible environment for operators to perform their duties effectively.

Summary

This chapter has provided an overview of various frameworks available for developing mental performance programs tailored to elite military units. It has also delved into practical considerations crucial for implementing such programs successfully. Additionally, we've gleaned insights and lessons from an international cohort of collaborators who have been involved in similar initiatives.

To ensure the effective implementation of mental performance programs, systematic planning is paramount. The approach should be thoughtfully crafted to align with the organization's priorities and available resources. It is essential to involve the end-users in the program's implementation, while also securing the unwavering support of leadership. A systematic planning phase, taking into account program objectives, subject matter expertise, evidence-based practices, and organizational needs, lays a strong foundation for success. Moreover, it's imperative to design the program to be culturally relevant, specifically tailored to the unique culture of special operations force.

In addition to cultural alignment, mental performance efforts should seamlessly integrate with other human performance and health services. This integration is best achieved within a holistic model of service delivery, allowing for smooth referrals when necessary. Furthermore, continuous innovation and staying abreast of developments in the field are vital. Remaining attuned to the evolving needs of the organization and its operators is equally crucial for the sustained success of mental performance programs.

References

Bartholemew-Eldridge, L. K., Markham, C.M., Ruiter, R.A., Fernadex, M.E., Kok, G. & Parcel, G. S. (2016). *Planning Health Promotion Programs: An Intervention Mapping Approach* (4th Ed.). Hoboken NJ: Wiley.

Castro, C. & Adler, A. (2011). Military MHT. Building resilience. In: Southwick et al.. *Resilience and Mental Health. Challenges across a Lifespan*. Cambridge University Press. ISBN: 9780521898393

Cropley, B., Hanton, S., Miles, A., & Niven, A. (2010). Exploring the relationship between effective and reflective practice in applied sport psychology. *The Sport Psychologist*, 24, 521–541.

Deuster, P.A., Lunasco, T., & Messina, L.A. (2019). Optimizing warfighter lethality through human performance education. *Journal of Special Operations Medicine*, 19(2), 100–104.

Fernandez, M. E., Ruiter, R. A. C. C., Markham, C. M., & Kok, G. (2019). Intervention mapping: Theory-and evidence-based health promotion program planning: Perspective and examples. *Frontiers in Public Health*, 7(AUG). https://doi.org/10.3389/fpubh.2019.00209

Goodwin, G. F. (2008). Psychology in sports and the military: Building understanding and collaboration across disciplines. *Military Psychology*, 20(1), S147–S153.

International Standards Organization. Ergonomic requirements for office work with visual display terminals (VDTs) – Part 11: Guidance on usability. International Organization for Standardization, 9241; 1998.

Lyon, A.R. & Koerner, K. (2016). User-centered design for psychosocial intervention development and implementation. *Clinical Psychology: Science and Practice*, 23(2), 180–200.

Mattie, C. P., Guest, K., Bailey, S., Collins, J. & Gucciardi, D. (2020). Development of a mental skills training intervention for the Canadian Special Operations Forces Command: An intervention mapping approach. *Psychology of Sport & Exercise,* 50(16), 101720. https://doi.org/10.1016/j.psychsport.2020.101720

McEachan, R. R. C., Lawton, R. J., Jackson, C., Conner, M., & Lunt, J. (2008). Evidence, theory and context: Using intervention mapping to develop a workplace physical activity intervention. *BMC Public Health*, 8, 326. https://doi.org/10.1186/1471-2458-8-326.

Partington, J. & Orlick, T. (1987). The Sport Psychology Consultant Evaluation Form. The Sport Psychologist, 1, pp. 309–317.

Pattyn, N., Van Cutsem, J., Lacroix, E., Van Puyvelde, M., Cortoos, A., Roelands, B., Tibax, V., Dessy, E., Huret, M., Rietjens, G., Sannen, M., Vliegen, R., Ceccaldi, J., Peffer, J., Neyens, E., Duvigneaud, N., & Van Tiggelen, D. (2022). Lessons from special forces operators for elite team sports training: How to make the whole greater than the sum of the parts. *Frontiers in Sports and Active Living*, 4, 780767. doi: 10.3389/fspor.2022.780767

Poczwardowski, A. & Sherman, C.P. (2011). Revisions to the sport psychology service delivery (SPSD) heuristic: Explorations with experienced consultants. *The Sport Psychologist*, 25, 511–531.

Poczwardowski, A., Sherman, C.P., & Henschen, K.P. (1998). A sport psychology service delivery heuristic: Building on theory and practice. *The Sport Psychologist*, 12, 191–207.

Reivich, K. J., Seligman, E. P. & McBride, S. (2011). Master resilience training in the U.S. *Army. American Psychologist*, 66, 25–34. Doi: 10.1037/a0021897

Robson, S. & Manacapilli, T. (2014). Enhancing performance under stress: Stress inoculation training for battlefield airmen. *RAND.*

Skivington, K., Matthews, L., Simpson, S A., Craig, P., Baird, J., Blazeby, J. M., et al. (2021). A new framework for developing and evaluating complex interventions: update of Medical Research Council guidance, *BMJ*, 2021, 374, n2061. doi:10.1136/bmj.n206

Weinberg, R. S. & Gould, D. R. (2007). *Foundations of Sport & Exercise Psychology*. Champaign, IL, Human Kinetics, 2007.

14 Mental Performance in Extreme Environments (Space and Antarctica)

Findings and Countermeasures

Nathalie Pattyn, Susan Charlesworth, and Dietrich Manzey

Why is mental performance relevant in extreme environments?

The duration of a round-trip to Mars is currently estimated to last up to 18 months. A few important factors in life sciences limit the possibility to expose humans to such long-duration flights, e.g., the effects of long-duration exposure to cosmic radiation, microgravity, and the "human factor". To mitigate the issues related to this human factor, the operator's resilience and adaptivity to isolated, confined, and extreme (ICE) environments has been the focus of space agencies' sponsored research for several decades, with the aim of safeguarding crew health and operational safety during long-duration missions. More specifically, psychological training and support of crews is provided in order to maintain an optimum mental performance state of humans in space. Mental performance, as understood here, includes all aspects related to efficient human performance during space missions, ranging from the efficiency of basic cognitive and psychomotor functions to overall behavioural health of astronauts, reflected in individual mood, well-being, and interpersonal behaviour.

Indeed, besides microgravity, space operators are known to be affected by the cumulative effect of multiple stressors (Manzey & Lorenz, 1998; Manzey, 2018; Smith, 2023), such as isolation, confinement, increased workload, fatigue, and circadian desynchronization. The following section gives a more detailed description of these specific stressors. To disentangle these multiple stressors of an ICE-environment, research has been organized in several locations on earth utilized as space-analogue environments (e.g., different types of polar expeditions, caves, submarine missions, and space simulation environments in Antarctica and non-Antarctic regions) (e.g., Sandal et al., 2006; Palinkas & Suedfeld, 2008, 2021; Van Ombergen et al., 2021; Golden et al., 2018; Mogilever et al., 2018; Pagnini et al., 2023). In comparison to real spaceflight, these space-analogue ICE-environments share similar characteristics from a psychological point of view. That is, the combination of being isolated from family and friends and being confined with a small group of people on a limited surface, but also being exposed to changes in the somatosensory stimulation due to specific physical characteristics of the natural environment (Casler & Cook, 1999; Sandal et al., 2006; Palinkas & Suedfeld, 2008; Van Puyvelde et al., 2022). Moreover, ICE-environments have the advantage to be less expensive and less technically complex than a space research station (Palinkas & Suedfeld, 2021). However, every ICE environment, be it in space or on earth, as well as each crew and the engaged external organizations, have their specific characteristics which may nevertheless create marked differentiations (Palinkas & Suedfeld, 2021). In this research community, the term "mental performance" is seldom used, and publications will more often refer to "Human Behaviour and Performance", which is a term that will be further illustrated in the case study.

DOI: 10.4324/9781003378969-17

In the current chapter, we focus on both Antarctica and long-duration human spaceflight, where the following three factors are combined in terms of extreme environment: the need for autonomy, as crew cannot always be readily evacuated; the actual operational duty, as crew have duties to perform beyond simulation and scientific research; and the constant risk to life, as crew depend on a life-support technical infrastructure. These features are associated with a number of stressors that can have an impact on physiological and psychological health. Since human behaviour and performance are the acknowledged areas of major risks for operational safety and efficiency (Pagnini et al., 2023), all space agencies have created programs to train current and future astronauts in recognizing these potential stressors and acquiring a new range of cognitive and behavioural skills to cope with them. This is particularly important in successfully preparing for long-duration spaceflight, including future exploration missions to Mars. In addition, specific psychological support programs have been developed and applied during current orbital space missions to help astronauts in maintaining an optimum mental performance state while in space.

Space and Antarctica as extreme environments?

Astronauts work in harsh circumstances and face several stressors. Some stressors affect specifically astronauts' physiological and physical health, but others may also negatively impact their mental performance state. Two types of stressors exist. The first encompasses all spaceflight-specific characteristics that make space a unique environment, which humans are not natively equipped for. Microgravity, the altered dark–light cycle in an orbiting spaceship, and space radiation without Earth's protection are the biggest stressors. Other pressures astronauts face during a space mission are common to all hostile environments on Earth. For instance, these stressors include all aspects of living in an ICE environment, which are also present in submarines, Antarctic outposts, and underwater habitats. Most of these stressors are not unique to spaceflight, yet they can influence astronauts' mental performance. Space-specific stresses normally affect astronauts more during short-term space missions and the early adaption period of long-term missions, although most have significant psychological impacts after some time in space, and some have long-lasting health consequences.

Our brief description of the most common space-specific and space-relevant stressors astronauts face is a shortened version of the description of critical mission factors provided by Manzey (2018). A more detailed description of relevant mission factors impacting astronauts during their living and working in space stations is provided by Messerschmid & Bertrand (1999, in Manzey 2018).

Why does space qualify as an extreme environment?

Microgravity

The continuous gravitational force (9.81 m/s^2 = 1g) has shaped all life on Earth. However, during a spaceflight this gravitational force is significantly reduced. For example, during an orbital spaceflight, the spaceship must travel at about 28,000 km/h to maintain a low-Earth orbit. At this speed, the centrifugal force impacted on the spaceship is so large that the opposite gravitational force pulling the spaceship back to Earth is almost cancelled out, leading to a state of microgravity in the spaceship. As a consequence, the astronauts and all other objects on board become weightless, causing them to float if not fixed. This change in gravitational pull requires profound physiological adaptations, particularly from the vestibular, cardiovascular, and musculoskeletal systems (Clément, 2011). Cognitive, and more specifically, psychomotor functions might be affected as well (Manzey, 2017). During future Moon and Mars explorations, humans will face microgravity during their transfer flights from Earth. On the Lunar surface astronauts will be exposed to gravitational forces of only 0.166g, on Mars the gravitational force will be reduced to about 0.33g. Even if this hypogravity is not as extreme as microgravity, it will require another adaptive process after the transfer flights, and likely also affect the general performance state of astronauts, at least during this adaptive phase.

Photoperiod: the natural rhythmic pattern of daylight and darkness

Due to Earth's rotation, much of its surface has a 24-hr dark–light cycle, and a photoperiod defined as the alternation of one night and one day in a 24-hr period, another natural constant for life. During evolution, humans, like almost all other living organisms on Earth, have adapted to this light regime. This is reflected in rhythmic fluctuations of physiological and hormonal processes, as well as psychological performance functions across the 24-hr day, which are referred to as circadian rhythms. However, an orbiting spacecraft lacks the natural 24-hr cycle of sunlight and darkness. By cycling in about 90 minutes around the Earth, the 24-hr cycle gets compressed to only about 90 minutes. This variation in natural lighting cannot be fully compensated by the artificial light in a spaceship, and thus represents a significant change which may affect astronauts' sleep and performance. For future Moon and Mars missions, natural dark–light cycles may also shift, especially during transfer flights. In addition, even more extreme changes need to be expected on the Lunar surface. Here, depending on what side of the Moon they stay, astronauts will experience either everlasting sunlight or darkness, just like we know it from the polar summer and winter on Earth. However, on the surface on Mars, astronauts will be exposed to an Earth-like natural light regime, as the usual Martian day lasts 24.37 hours.

Cosmic radiation

Without having the Earth's atmosphere as natural protection, space radiation, especially ionizing radiation, can directly impact living cells, making space a hazardous living environment for people. Such radiation comes from galactic cosmic rays, solar particle events, and trapped belt radiation and can cause cataracts and cancer in humans if they are not properly protected. Recent rodent space research reveals that space radiation might also harm the central nervous system, impairing cognitive skills such as learning, memory, attention, and sensorimotor coordination (Nelson, Simonsen, & Huff, 2016). Within a spaceship, the hull of the habitat provides protection which significantly lowers the impact of radiation on astronauts. However, during extravehicular activities an efficient protection is difficult to achieve. On the International Space Station, several measurement systems, including personal dosimeters, are available to monitor the crew's radiation stress and assess its health risks.

Analogue environments: sharing other stressors with space

Isolation and confinement

As with other habitats for humans in extreme environments, spacecraft are sealed facilities with limited living, working, and moving space. For example, on board the ISS, seven crewmembers usually stay within a habitat of 400 m^3 of pressurized and liveable capacity. During visiting missions or hand-over periods, the crew size can even increase up to 11 astronauts. This characteristic of being confined in a sealed environment is not specific for space missions but holds also true for crews working in other extreme environments, like Antarctic outposts, submarines, or saturation diving chambers on offshore platforms. The main physical and psychological effects of such ICE environments include hypokinesis and sensory and social monotony. For humans living in

ICE environments for a long time, these elements can not only impair cognitive functions, but also cause manifest psychosomatic complaints, including insomnia and depressive episodes (Palinkas & Suedfeld, 2008; Suedfeld & Steel, 2000).

Ambient air quality

The ambient air on Earth contains only 0.04% CO_2. However, inside sealed habitats like a space station or submarine, this CO_2 concentration can increase considerably, due to the exhalation of CO_2, depending on the number of people. An additional stress factor is that crew members thus rely on life-support systems for air quality, something that needs to be actively monitored and adapted to ensure the survivability of the crew.

Empirical evidence shows that visuo-motor performance and subjective alertness of humans can decrease if CO_2 levels in the ambient air rise above 1% or 7.6 mmHg partial pressure (Manzey & Lorenz, 1998). This supports the definition of the Spacecraft Maximum Allowable Concentration (SMAC) of 1% CO_2 on the ISS for chronic exposure during long-duration stays there. However, recent reports from ISS missions suggest that crew members' subjective well-being can become already impaired by chronically elevated levels of 0.4–0.5%, or 3-4 mmHg partial pressure. Daily environmental parameter reports during ISS operations suggest that the CO_2 levels can be maintained below 3 mmHG most of the time (author observation). Exceptions with greater levels of 3-4 mmHg are not unusual, though, especially in case of technical failure or an increase of crew size to greater than seven. Depending on their air quality sensitivity, such an increase can be a significant stressor for individual astronauts.

Noise

All spacecraft are noisy, which is the case for some other technical ICE environments as well, such as submarines. Life-support system fans, which run 24/7 to maintain airflow, and other hardware, such as experiment equipment, are major noise generators. Another environment where the effect of noise on health is currently being investigated is intensive care units, where the high levels of ambient noises that some patients can be continuously exposed to (from cumulative mechanical life-support systems like ventilation, monitoring, or the likes of extra-corporeal membrane oxygenation) are now showing decremental effects (e.g., Drouot, 2023).

Chronic exposure to high noise levels can stress humans and harm both health and performance. These effects can be directly aural, like increased hearing thresholds, or indirectly extra-aural, like speech intelligibility interference affecting voice communications, alarm audibility, or performance impairments. Most aural impacts have been observed at 8-hr average (equivalent) noise levels above 75 dB. However, extra-aural effects may be important at far lower levels. On the ISS, the noise levels during work time are in the range of 64–72 dB. During the night on station, this noise level is significantly reduced (54–62 dB) but still higher than the 50 dB threshold, which is usually considered as the maximum that still allows for peaceful sleep (Limardo, Allen & Danielson, 2015). The ambient noise only falls below the crucial limit (approximately 48 dB) within the private crew quarters (the capsule-like tiny "bedrooms" of astronauts, which are described in more detail in the following section). While overall noise levels on ISS still remain below medical concern thresholds, they are considerably higher than noise levels at typical working environments in offices or laboratories on ground, and definitely higher than any citizen of a Western country will experience in their bedroom. The persistent exposure to this relatively high noise around the clock makes the ISS a psychological stressful environment for humans.

Personal hygiene and privacy

Personal space and privacy are limited in capsule habitats. The ISS has a total of six permanent crew quarters (two of them in the Russian module) and one additional inflatable one which give at least some personal space for permanent crews staying six months or longer.

These crew quarters have noise dampening walls and individually controlled lighting and ventilation to promote sleep and seclusion. In addition, the permanent crew quarters provide some extra protection for radiation. Although these crew quarters are small (about 2 m^3), they do provide at least some privacy and possibilities of withdrawal for sleep, private communication, and storage of private items, which crew members generally welcome (Schlesinger et al., 2013). While this might not be sufficient to fully eliminate stress related to lack-of-privacy issues, it can be expected to reduce this stress to some extent.

However, the ISS has only two waste and hygiene compartments for the seven crew members, one in the Russian segment and one in the US(OS) segment. These compartments include fan-driven suction toilets for weightless use. Unlike the former Russian Mir station, the ISS has no crew showers, though. Crew members can only clean with wet towels, even after physical exercise. Although these living conditions appear to be quite uncomfortable for long-term stays under confinement and isolation, and can be perceived as a potential psychological stressor, astronauts' complaints about lack of privacy and restricted facilities for personal hygiene are rare (Stuster, 2010, which probably is more an indicator of astronaut "culture" than of crew quarters' comfort.

Workload

Finally, workload and time-pressure need to be considered as relevant stressors during space missions, like in many other high-stakes environments. Individual astronaut activity assignments by mission control usually include a mixture of housekeeping, (technical) maintenance, scientific experiment execution, and daily physical exercising which is crucial for preventing microgravity-related osteoporosis (loss of bones) and muscle atrophy. This list of activities is often complemented with e-mailing, photo-, and video activities to serve outreach and public relations, which astronauts partially perform in their spare time. Dependent on the tightness of scheduling of the different activities, astronauts need to deal with time-pressure and task-switching. On the ISS, official restrictions and medical requirements have been put in place to prevent the astronauts from being overwhelmed by work. Currently, astronauts on the ISS work five days a week for 6.5 hours each day, with an additional 2.5 hours scheduled daily for physical exercise (including donning and staffing). Weekend work is limited to one hour per weekend, usually on Saturday to avoid Sunday. However, due to operational demands, these working times often become expanded to some degree.

Antarctica as a natural terrestrial analogue for space

For those with knowledge of the Antarctic environment, the enumeration of spaceflight stressors is familiar. Whereas the specificity of these stressors differs, the distinction of stressors which are specific for the environment and others shared by other extreme environments as well, also applies to long-duration Antarctic missions, where crew spend between 12 and 24 months on continuous so-called "overwintering" missions. Although there is no microgravity present in Antarctica, there are obvious similarities with spaceflight related to the harshness of the environment, such as extreme outside temperatures, large variations in photoperiod (the normal alternation of light and darkness during a 24-hr period at moderate latitudes), remoteness and isolation, and reliance on a technical life-support system for survival. Antarctica thus provides an environment similar to space, where particularly the effects of true isolation and confinement on individual and group coping can be studied. It makes a good comparison with space because of the common stressors it shares relating to habitat, mission, and the social situation. Considering these environmental challenges, habitats are therefore limited spaces of "viable" environment, relying on a life-support system to supply energy, and thus heat and light. Stressors related to the mission include variable workload and re-supply and support operations, which are conducted by logistical multi-national agents for both human spaceflight and Antarctic stations. The social situation of Antarctic winter-over crews closely mimics a long-duration exploration flight: being isolated and confined within a small group of people, with reduced or no real-time communication and limited mission abort and rescue capability. Space agencies have therefore included Antarctica in the list of useful analogue environments. For example, the Human Research Program of NASA, which covers topics such as psychosocial and behavioural health, has found long-duration Antarctic expeditions to be useful space analogues. Similarly, the European Space Agency (ESA) supports life science research at Concordia station (a French-Italian continental station) that is environmentally relevant, creating physiological and psychological issues which mimic those encountered during long-duration spaceflights.

The similarity between the challenges of long-duration spaceflight and overwintering warrants that similar approaches may be needed in the psychological preparation for both. There are many examples of exploration, including space exploration, that have failed due to human factors issues being underestimated (Bishop et al., 2016).

It should be noted that, despite the very strong similarities in environment and challenges, there are very few similarities in crew types between human spaceflight environments and Antarctic environments. Indeed, whereas astronaut candidates undergo an extensive selection process, a lengthy and thorough training and are part of a group with a very strong cultural identity culture; Antarctic over-winterers form a much more heterogeneous group, both in terms of background and in terms of group culture. This is a major caveat in the use of Antarctica as an analogue in space-related research on psychological processes, since both the individual characteristics and the team processes are completely different between the two environments.

Mental performance in extreme environments: what's in a name

Cognitive and psychomotor performance

Across the last three decades, various spaceflight studies were performed to investigate the possible impact of the extreme environment in space on the cognitive and psychomotor performance of astronauts. Two lines of research can be distinguished: the first line includes neurocognitive experiments which have addressed specific effects of microgravity on perceptual functions, spatial cognition, and psychomotor functions (e.g., Leone, 1998; Bock, Fowler & Comfort, 2001; see for a review Clement & Ngo-Anh, 2013). The second line included so-called performance-monitoring studies (Manzey, 2000). In these latter studies, different cognitive and/or psychomotor functions are repeatedly probed during a space mission by means of laboratory tasks to investigate any performance changes throughout the entire mission, compared to usual performance on ground. In contrast to neurocognitive studies, performance-monitoring studies do not focus specifically on the impact of microgravity but on the overall impact of the multi-stressor environment in space on the performance of astronauts. Performance functions probed in this research have included a variety of functions ranging from basic cognitive functions (e.g., choice reaction time, visual search, memory, time estimation, mental arithmetic, logical reasoning) and spatial cognition (e.g., spatial orientation, mental spatial imagery) to psychomotor (e.g., tracking) and higher executive functions (e.g., dual-tasking) (see for reviews Casler & Cook, 1999; Manzey, 2017;). Although, the overall number of empirical spaceflight studies is still limited and the validity of results is sometimes difficult to assess due to usually small sample sizes, at least some preliminary conclusions can be drawn. First, the available data from performance-monitoring studies provide converging evidence that at least basic cognitive functions remain largely intact during spaceflight, i.e., does not show significant performance decrements under the impact of the extreme working and living conditions in space (e.g., Benke et al. 1993; Eddy et al. 1998; Kelly et al. 2005; Manzey et al. 1993, 1998; Ratino et al. 1988). As is suggested by neurocognitive research, this also seems to be true for processes involved in spatial imagery and object recognition which did not show obvious alterations in space compared to Earth (e.g., Leone, 1998; de Schonen et al., 1998). Second, in direct contrast to basic cognitive functions, performance decrements were consistently found in spatial perception and orientation (e.g., Oman, 2007) and fine-motor control tasks (e.g., pointing, tracking; Bock, Fowler, & Comfort, 2001; Bock, Weigelt, & Bloomberg, 2010; Manzey, Lorenz, Thiele, & Schiewe, 1993; Manzey, Lorenz, Heuer, & Sangals, 2000). Most alterations of spatial perception and orientation reflected in different sorts of perceptual illusions; Oman, 2007) seem to be directly related to microgravity-induced changes in the vestibular system. Most of these illusions only occur during the primary adaptive phase in space. In contrast, performance decrements observed in fine-motor control during spaceflight are assumed to reflect both the impact of microgravity on sensorimotor processes (Bock & Cheung, 1998) and the impact of other unspecific stressors like sleep loss and high workload (Manzey et al., 2000). Because of the scarcity of data from long-term space missions, it is not yet clear whether these performance decrements only represent transient phenomena which disappear after three to four weeks in space (Manzey et al., 1998), or persist during an entire long-term space mission (Bock, Weigelt & Bloomberg, 2010). Third, there are at least some data from spaceflight studies suggesting that also higher cognitive (executive) functions might suffer from the impact of the multi-stressor environment in space. For example, this is suggested by repeated findings of impaired performance in dual-tasks (Manzey et al., 1993, 1998), or other cognitive interference tasks (e.g., Pattyn, Migeotte, Demaeseleer, Kolinsky, Morais & Zizi, 2005). However, here the current data base is still smaller and more contradictory than for the other performance aspects mentioned above.

Having drawn these conclusions one needs to consider that most of the available data about cognitive and psychomotor performance in space are from short-term spaceflights, only. This holds particularly true for performance-monitoring of basic cognitive functions. Only two performance-monitoring studies from long-term space missions are available, thus far (Manzey et al., 1998; Garrett-Bakelman et al., 2019). Both support the assumed high resilience of basic cognitive functions found in short-term spaceflight also for a 12–14-month-long stay in space. However, both studies were single-case studies, and we certainly need more data before any final conclusions about cognitive performance during such long-term stays in space can be drawn. At least the fact that these studies have been performed with different astronauts on different space stations (Mir and ISS) give some validity to the findings.

Considerably less systematic performance data are available from polar expeditions and overwintering campaigns in Antarctica (for a review see Strangman et al., 2014). Furthermore, these studies suffer from a higher variety of assessment approaches than the spaceflight studies reviewed above. However, at least data from some performance-monitoring studies are available also from overwinterings in Antarctica (e.g., Defayolle, et al., 1985; Le Scanff, Larue & Rosnet, 1997; Palinkas et al., 2007; Reed et al., 2001; Taylor & Duncum, 1987). As in the spaceflight studies reviewed above, these studies investigated possible alterations of a variety of cognitive functions including, e.g., visual perception, attention, memory, spatial imagery, while staying for several months in this harsh multiple-stressor environment. Apart from a single finding of mild memory impairments (Reed et al., 2001), none of these studies reported any obvious performance decrements in either function. This supports the high resilience of these functions in extreme environments which also was found in space. Almost no data are available for performance aspects like fine-motor control or higher executive functions during expeditions to Antarctica, though.

The authors hypothesize that, due to the known bias in publication, negative results are likely to be underreported, as they have knowledge of several protocols investigating cognitive performance during Antarctic overwinterings, which never showed published results. One exception is the study by Le Scanff et al. (1997) which also probed tracking and dual-task performance in a group of overwinterers in Antarctica. No performance impairments were found in these tasks either. This suggests that the findings of motor impairments from spaceflight might indeed rather be related to the differences of gravitational force in this environment, than just the effects of being in a confined and isolated environment.

Mood and social behaviour

The psychosocial impact factor has important ramifications for several components of future spaceflights (Kanas et al., 2001, 2009). The specific psychosocial impact of isolation and confinement is variable over the different types of missions, and although it is sometimes discussed in the margin, it may actually be a variable of greater importance than is often considered (Kanas et al., 2001, 2009; Golden et al., 2018; Pattyn et al., 2018; Somaraju et al., 2022). The combination of isolation and confinement in the specific situation where people work and live together for a longer period may trigger exaggerated reactions to (sometimes minor) job-related or personal daily events or disputes (Jehn, 1995; Jehn & Chatman, 2000; Suedfeld & Weiss, 2000; Palinkas & Suedfeld, 2008; Driskell et al., 2018; Golden et al., 2018; Somaraju et al., 2022). Being separated from family and friends, while not being able to escape from the crew when feeling the urge to, may block the capacity to put things into perspective (Palinkas & Suedfeld, 2008, 2021; Driskell et al., 2018; Golden et al., 2018) and to separate normal professional discussions from personal interpersonal tensions (Jehn & Chatman, 2000). For instance, these types of cumulating dynamics resulted during the "105-day Simulation of the Flight of International Crew and Space Station-1999" (SFINCSS-99) in a physical fight among crewmembers and sexual harassment (Vanhove et al., 2015). Concerning the latter, a recent study on gender experiences in women that were involved in an Antarctic Australian mission reported striking statistics, namely that 36% of the interviewees had observed inappropriate or sexual remarks to colleagues and 63% received these types of remarks themselves. Nevertheless, none of these women specified their experiences in open response questions (Nash et al., 2019). All these types of tensions, which usually remain "under the radar" during missions, may become a dangerous hotbed of further conflicts, but also a source of individual distress. For instance, in a recent study (Somaraju et al., 2022), it was shown how current-day relationship conflicts predicted next-day individual strain and vice versa. Moreover, high workload worsened this negative spiral, whereas low workload decreased the association (Somaraju et al., 2022); hence showing how the different levels of functioning on station may interact with one another. Furthermore, initial efforts to install a positive group cohesion from the start of the mission appear to be crucial. Not only has a crew more motivation and energy in the first half of the mission to build group cohesion, negative relations established early in isolation appear to remain stable over time of a mission (Sandal et al., 1995). This can be confounded by observable dips in crews' morale and cohesion in the second half (Wood et al., 1999; Palinkas and Houseal, 2000; Kanas et al., 2001, 2009; Sandal, 2001; Palinkas & Suedfeld, 2008; Supolkina et al., 2021) and third quarter of a mission (Bechtel & Berning, 1991). Hence, when considering the literature, one can state that the existing variability over ICE-environments may be interpreted as a function of the prominence of each of its three respective factors (isolation, confinement, or environment) in which isolation and confinement may refer rather to the psychosocial characteristics; and extremeness to the physical characteristics of the ICE-environment (Van Puyvelde et al., 2022). Recently, the interaction between the isolation-confinement (IC) factor and the extremeness (E) factor of ICE-environments was highlighted, stating that the impact of both factors may mutually reinforce one another when individual vulnerabilities are challenged (Van Puyvelde &

Mairesse, 2022; van den Berg et al., 2023). In Antarctica, the most stringent example of ICE, sleep complaints still rank as the most important individual adaptation issues (Pattyn et al., 2018). When looking at fundamental research, several studies have shown that sleep curtailment accounts for operational deteriorations which are part of the daily performance of ICE-personnel. For instance, vigilance decrements combined with poor attention and concentration (Van Dongen et al., 2004), visuo-motor disturbances (Van Dongen et al., 2004), decreased reaction time (Choo et al., 2005), poor memorizing and memory consolidation (Nilsson et al., 2005; Stickgold, 2005), and impaired decision-making (Killgore et al., 2006; Venkatraman et al., 2007) may threaten daily routine safety procedures, scientific efficiency, and specific technical operations, as well as job satisfaction, a factor that has been indicated as a crucial motivator in long-term isolation since other social roles in normal daily life are limited or eliminated (Natani et al., 1973). On the other hand, day-to-day worries about internal and external problems such as within-crew conflicts (Somaraju et al., 2022), harassment (Vanhove et al., 2015; Nash et al., 2019), problems in family context, or missing loved ones (Palinkas & Suedfeld, 2008; Kanas et al., 2009; Temp et al., 2020) may amplify the environmental-induced problems (e.g., poor sleep, seasonal depression). Finally, an indispensable factor is consciousness. That is, most individuals are seldom aware, neither of their increasing fatigue and performance impairment (Van Dongen et al., 2004; Mallis & DeRoshia, 2005; Yoo et al., 2007), nor of their isolation impact (Suedfeld & Weiss, 2000), possibly endangering their operational functioning on the station (e.g., Nilsson et al., 2005; Killgore et al., 2006; Orzeł-Gryglewska, 2010; Brown et al., 2013; Boivin & Boudreau, 2014). The risk for developing behavioural and psychiatric problems that may result in human errors exist in space and isolated analogue missions (McPhee & Charles, 2009). For instance, some studies reported one incident per every 2.86 person/years for shuttle missions (Billica, 2000), one incident per every 1.3 person-years in the MIR station (Marshburn, 2000), and 0.44–2.8 incidents per person-year in submarines (Thomas et al., 2000). In Antarctica, 12.5% of the personnel were reported to meet DSM-IV criteria for mental disorders after deployment (Palinkas et al., 2004). Human errors in operational settings, including ICE-environment, can be life-threatening and extremely expensive (Horneck et al., 2003; Manzey, 2004), hence, to safeguard optimal adaptation of operational personnel in simulation missions is of indisputable importance. Therefore, all Space Agencies have created programs – partially based on human factors approaches from the aviation world – to train future astronauts in recognizing these potential stressors and acquiring a new range of behavioural skills to cope with them. However, in space-analogue environments, these types of trainings are rather underdeveloped if not non-existent, as if the space-analogue environment is considered as the arena of training itself. Nevertheless, the crew of these simulation missions are exposed to similar environmental difficulties and hazards. One exception – although not comparable with the exhaustive astronaut preparatory trainings – could be found for some time at Concordia station, where a "Human Behaviour and Performance" (HBP) training was supported for several years by the European Space Agency (ESA) team. The training was based on the "International Space Station Human Behavior & Performance Competency Model" (Bessone et al., 2008a,b) in which individual and interpersonal competencies (e.g., self-management, communication, cross-culturalism, teamwork, leadership, conflict management, decision making, problem solving) are put forward as required capacities to participate in long-duration missions. This program will be described in more details in the upcoming section describing implementation at the European Space Agency.

Real-life performance reports

While most reports of operational failures are merely anecdotal, describing errors in conducting experiments, equipment handling, or losses of experimental data (Manzey, Lorenz, Schiewe, Finell & Thiele, 1995), a couple of publications exist analyzing cosmonauts' errors and behavioural problems. The "lack of official reports of behavioural disorders or significant performance decrements during spaceflights" described by Manzey et al. (1995) contrasts with these reports. Two of these studies were conducted during Skylab missions in the 1970s (hence, originating from US authors), and another one was based on analyses of crew errors during Mir missions (Russian authors).

Regarding the Antarctic environment, as it was under far less scrutiny until recently, there are no scientific publications regarding real-life performance. Van Puyvelde et al. (2022) is the only one addressing how the environment and mission stressors might affect performance, based on 24 qualitative interviews with former ICE-crew members. Unsurprisingly, the impact of the different stressors was deemed huge (for a detailed analysis, we refer to the original publication), and an interesting feature which emerged from the interview was the additional pressure induced by the sense of responsibility derived from being in such an exceptional position.

Garriott and Doerre (1977) analyzed the "crew efficiency" of Skylab astronauts, which they computed by comparing the number of working hours spent on defined tasks divided by the number of hours awake. Over time, crew efficiency improved considerably from an efficiency ratio of about 0.5 during the first week (where decrements were related to the prevalence of space motion sickness, a known adaptation phenomenon to microgravity); to a ratio of up to 0.75 at later mission phases. However, this measure of "crew efficiency" does not reveal any detailed information about the actual performance of the astronauts, as it is a quantitative measure of how time is spent rather than an actual measure of the quality of performance.

Kubis et al. (1977) performed time-and-motion studies for different defined operational tasks in space and compared the results with the data obtained on these same tasks during pre-flight training. Tasks included assembling and using a camera system; or experimental and exercise equipment; or food preparation. These are obviously ecologically valid, however, one could argue that an astronaut selected based on their exceptional cognitive abilities might not be tested in the most relevant way by these seemingly trivial tasks. The authors found a significant slowing of performance only for the first execution in space. These results thus demonstrate a psychomotor adaptation effect to microgravity. In line with the results from cognitive neuroscience and performance-monitoring studies, most of these disturbances thus related to transient impairments of fine-motor skills and showed a rapid recovery. Most of the tasks could be performed as fast as on the ground during the second trial in-flight, which usually was scheduled during the second week of the mission. Again, this hardly qualifies as mental performance in this particular population.

Several reports from the Russian space program analyze crew errors, being defined as a deviation from the standards of performance, including incorrect execution of procedures, forgetting of necessary actions, or conducting unnecessary actions (Kubasov et al., 1985, in Nechayev et al., 1998; Baydin & Stepanov, 1993, in Nechayev et al., 1998). This error analysis showed dependence on phase of orbital flight, task complexity, crew size, and experience with other crew members (Nechayev et al., 1998) as well as on psychophysiological state (being an aggregate numerical evaluation compiling scoring of general behaviour, motor activity, speech, sleep, mood, general condition, manifestation of emotional reactions, sensory disorders, deprivation phenomena, adequacy, demands, and complaints) and general tension (being an aggregate numerical evaluation compiling scoring of shifts in sleep-wake phase, surplus workload, and manifestations of psychosomatic discomfort). The conclusion on reviewing the available information stemming from Russian research in the field is thus that there is a measurable occurrence of real-life errors during spaceflight, and that the rate of occurrence mainly varies in function of adaptation processes, workload and sleep/work schedules (Nechayev et al., 1998).

More recently, Chinese authors (Chen et al., 2018) have adopted an engineering perspective on human error, using human reliability analysis to investigate the space-specific performance shaping factors, and leverage those.

As emphasized by Chen et al. (2018), and similarly to the aviation world, 80% of all accidents, incidents, and mishaps in space relate to the human factor. Astronauts' subjective evaluations of their own performance often report impairment in flight (Bluth, 1984) or challenging cognitive workload (Burgess, 2000). Dijk et al. (2001) reported a better subjective self-evaluation post-flight than pre-flight and in-flight, and significantly poorer in-flight assessment of one's own performance. Subjects also rated themselves less well-coordinated, less relaxed, and marginally less quick-witted in-flight vs. post-flight. Kelly et al. (2005) reported subjective fatigue ratings through the POMS (Profile of Mood Scale) and a VAS (Visual Analogue Scale) to be significantly higher in-flight. Eddy et al. (1998) also reported higher fatigue ratings (through a 7-point scale) in-flight, which co-occur with some of their performance decrements.

Thus, anecdotal reports on operational performance, subjective self-evaluations, and naturalistic analysis of real-life performance have shown decrements during spaceflight. The question for operational psychologists then becomes: how can astronauts be prepared, i.e., trained, and supported to maintain optimum mental performance, both regarding cognitive aspects and psychosocial aspects, of individuals who have already been selected for their superior abilities.

The European Space Agency's approach to mental performance

Currently, there are three aspects of astronauts' basic training that relate to mental performance: the "Human Behaviour and Performance" training, which was defined and standardized through interagency collaboration in 2008; a psychoeducation approach on "Human Factors" training, and a specific briefing on insights and conclusions drawn from research in space psychology. Capitalizing on this, more advanced training is provided via specific field and outdoor trainings which are either provided by ESA or other space agencies involved in the ISS program (e.g., NASA). All of these trainings are provided in an early phase of an astronaut's career, independent of a specific assignment to space missions. During an actual space mission, these trainings then are complemented by a specific mission support provided to the astronauts which also can be considered an important measure to help astronauts keeping an optimum mental performance state in space.

Basic human behaviour and performance training

The current training stems from the requirements laid out in the "Human Behaviour and Performance competency model for long-duration spaceflight" (ISS Mission Operation Directorate ITCB Working Group, 2008), jointly developed by the Canadian Space Agency (CSA), the European Space Agency (ESA), the Japanese Space Agency (JAXA), the US (NASA), and Russia (Roskosmos). The purpose of this model is to define the competencies and behaviours required of astronauts/cosmonauts who participate in ISS expeditions and other international long-duration missions. It was developed in response to the Multilateral Crew Operations Panel (MMOP) request to develop common and standardized training requirements across partner nations for the International Space Station (ISS). In no other high-performance field is there such a degree of standardization and cross-cultural collaboration. The topics of HBP training are the following: Self-Care and Self-Management; Communication; Cross Cultural; Teamwork and Group Living; Leadership; Conflict Management; Situational Awareness; Decision-Making and Problem Solving. The HBP requirements for each category, the delivery of training, and the assessment of the outcome are outlined in Volume II of the Human Behaviour and Performance Competency Model Guide (ISS Mission Operation Directorate ITCB Working Group, 2008). This reference document describes exhaustively each identified competency in the eight categories, which we will not reproduce here. To illustrate the methodology and rationale behind this standardization effort, we will describe one of the competencies of the first category (Self Care and Self-Management). This competency is "Manage stress", which is further detailed in three behavioural markers: "Identifies symptoms and causes of personal stress"; "Takes action to prevent and mitigate stress, negative mood or low morale"; and "Uses calm and flexible approach in dealing with unfamiliar situations". Zooming in on the first of this behavioural markers, "Identifies symptoms and causes of personal stress", it is further detailed in the following behaviours: "Is aware of the adverse influences of stress such as physiological changes and sleep issues on own condition and identifies the causes of stress"; "Pays attention to the changes in physiological and psychological status and emotions, and identifies their causes"; and "Determines sources of current stress". The underpinning knowledge and attitudes are also defined, which, in this example, lists for "Knowledge": "Stress symptomology [physiological and emotional] [Comprehend]"; and "Awareness of personal stress symptoms and triggers [Apply]". Finally, attitudes related to this behavioural marker are defined as: "Recognition that symptoms of stress are not evidence of weakness or inadequacy [Value]"; "Interest in seeking root sources of and contributors to own stress [Value]"; "Acknowledgement that stress impacts performance [Value]". The whole description of the eight categories is conceptualized as a table, allowing for an exhaustive description of competencies, behavioural markers, examples of behaviours, and underpinning knowledge and attitudes.

As illustrated by the list of topics covered by HBP training, the majority of it targets team training (e.g., Noe, Dachner, Saxton & Keeton, 2011). Indeed, in team-based work environments, individual knowledge, skills, and abilities (KSAs) may not be sufficient to allow team members to efficiently and successfully communicate and coordinate with other team members and perform complex tasks that require integration of team members' competencies (Delise et al., 2010). As emphasized by Ellis et al. (2005) for team training, the success of any training program depends on the quality of the skills inventory to identify needed competencies.

HBP Team Training is offered by ESA, NASA, and Roskosmos to astronauts and cosmonauts from all international partner agencies. This occurs during the non-assigned training phase, during basic training in ESA's case. At that time, the training is non-specific, because the astronaut is not yet preparing for a well-defined mission (for requirements see Bessone et al., 2008). HBP reinforcement is provided during subsequent technical training. Reinforcement is provided throughout the astronauts' training by instructors who undergo HBP "Observer" training (ESA), Spaceflight Resource Management (SFRM) observers (NASA), and psychologists (Roskosmos). ESA's Ground Control Crew also undergo a basic HBP course so that they can work effectively as a team with each other, and with astronauts when on the ISS. ISS emergency crew training is provided to all members of two three-person crews. This consists of realistic simulations of ISS emergencies with participation of two subsequent crews along with flight control personnel, performed prior to launch for all ISS crews. ESA uses a computer simulation to observe whether crew's HBP skills are successfully applied during a simulated space-like mission. After each simulation, a debriefing is held and feedback is given as to how to improve the use of such skills and apply more successful strategies in future simulated and real situations. Training consists of various missions to reinforce and improve the HBP competences taught during the seven days of HBP seminars during basic training.

Basic human factors training

The 2022 selection of ESA "career" astronauts also received Human Factors training, in addition to the HBP training. This focused on what Human Factors is: the safety impact in safety-critical industries such as space, aviation, rail, etc.; and methods and tools to assess Human Factors, e.g., cognitive workload, teamwork assessments; reinforcing their learning from the HBP course and giving the astronaut candidates more formal ways of assessing the human element in operations. The second part of the Human Factors course looked more specifically at spaceflight examples, such as interfaces they might find on the ISS, the hardware and equipment aboard, and habitability aspects to living and working in space. The course lasted one week and was given after the HBP training.

The Human Factors course was based on a number of publications, most specifically NASA-STD-3001 and NASA's Human Integration Design Handbook (HIDH). These documents outline in detail the standards and guidelines for integrating humans into the design of human interfaces in spacecraft. Intended users include human factors practitioners, engineers and designers, crews and flight controllers, and training and operations developers.

The topics covered ranged from physiological and mental capabilities of crew to interaction with physical aspects of the space station, hardware, and equipment onboard. For example, training was given on anthropometrics, biomechanics, and strength, how these factors are affected during spaceflight and therefore how crew should prepare for, e.g., loss of strength or change in body posture during different gravity environments. The crew were also prepared for how mental capabilities are affected during spaceflight, such as their visual and auditory perception changing; and also how cognitive workload increases during particular phases of flight.

The crew were introduced to the physical interfaces they would encounter on the ISS (in particular), including the hardware and equipment onboard. For example, the restraints and mobility aids that will enable them to translate through the ISS; the racks and drawers; fasteners and connections; and the crew personal protective equipment. They also explored the different controls and displays they will encounter during spaceflight – visual, auditory, and tactile.

These topics were interlaced with real examples of spaceflight – e.g., case studies, photos of the physical hardware they will encounter; and also research that has been done to test the physiological and mental capabilities in different gravity environments.

Basic space psychology briefing

The third HBP-related element of the basic training of ESA astronaut candidates includes a six-hour introduction to and briefing on the important findings of space psychological research (Kanas & Manzey, 2008). Similar to the Human Factors training, this briefing focuses on specific issues and psychological challenges which might arise during a long-term stay in space. In addition, the briefing also includes a description of important training and means of psychological in-flight HBP support which they might expect to get during their further career and most important their stay in space. The briefing is structured into three parts which are presented in separate 135-minute sessions. The first two parts are dedicated to a review about the impact of spaceflight on different aspects of mental performance, with the first part addressing the impact of spaceflight on cognitive and psychomotor performance, and the second part addressing issues of sleep and circadian rhythm in space, as well as the impact of confinement and isolation in a space habitat mood, well-being, and crew interactions. In both parts, first, a short summary of important knowledge about the specific challenges, followed by hints of how to cope with them and/or what practical consequences during the mission might be related to them. The third part of the briefing then is dedicated to a description and discussion of psychological countermeasures available for the different psychological issues in space. One important element of this part is a description of all the means available during long-term orbital missions to ISS which are of psychological relevance (see the "In-flight mission support" section below). The basic rational behind providing this briefing already as part of the Basic Training of astronaut candidates is so that astronaut candidates from the very beginning shall develop proper expectations about the possible psychological challenges of space missions, as well as the resources available for them to cope with it. Building such proper expectations about challenges and resources is considered as a first step to develop appropriate strategies to cope effectively with the challenges using the available resources. As this element of basic training is provided by the psychologists, who actually are involved in ESA mission support and will also stay in contact with the astronauts during phases without mission assignment, the briefing also paves the way for a trustful and supporting relationship between psychologists and astronauts during their further career and their future space missions.

Field and outdoor training

A more advanced HBP training module, which is offered by ESA to all astronauts and cosmonauts of the space agencies contributing to ISS, includes outdoor training referred to as ESA CAVES (**C**ooperative **A**dventure for **V**aluing and **E**xercising Human Behavior and Performance **S**kills) training (Klein & Bessone, 2008). Based on a field-exercise the training, which includes living and working together in a small team underground in a large system of caves, reinforces important HBP skills under real challenges, analogue to those of a short-term spaceflight, and, at the same time, prepares astronauts for the specific mental performance challenges to be expected during a space mission. Overall, the training lasts for 12 days which are structured as five days preparatory didactic training, six days underground scientific expedition, run according to typical ISS operations, and one day of scientific reporting. A total of six ISS astronauts and cosmonauts from all partners attend each year, accompanied by an instructor. Some are astronaut candidates, others have already flown and are able to provide mentoring. The main characteristic of this training is that it combines technical and scientific activities with advanced HBP challenges, including exercises on multicultural influences, teamwork, situational awareness, and decision-making. Daily team debriefings occur based on the ISS HBP Competency Model (ISS Mission Operation Directorate ITCB Working Group, 2008), provided by the HBP instructor and alternating peers. Continuity within the instructor team from HBP basic to outdoor training is intended throughout training, to reinforce the link between basic classroom training and its applications. Similar training is also offered by other international partners and sometimes also attended by ESA astronauts (e.g., NASA outdoor training in the wilderness of the Rocky Mountains or in the underwater habitat Aquarius).

Other HBP-related field training of ESA astronauts are the land and sea survival trainings which represent a requirement for assigned crews. These trainings have been offered by the Russian Space Agency for all crews using the Soyuz spacecraft for their flight to the ISS. Although the main focus of the training is on the acquisition of (technical) survival skills, also HBP-related debriefs are provided to the crews by a psychologist observing the training and this represents another direct way of reinforcing HBP skills, which is also discussed by Canadian astronaut Chris Hadfield in his memoir (2013). Typically, this training also starts with two days didactic training and introduction, followed by the practical exercises either in a forest or on sea which last two to three days. The trainings are particular as they do not focus just on improving the individual team skills but also directly involve whole crews.

In-flight mission support

Already with the first permanent orbital space stations becoming operational with the space agency of the former Soviet Union, a psychological support program was put into place to support astronauts in maintaining an optimum mental performance state during their month-long stays in space (Kanas, 1991). With the start of ISS operations, this program was adopted by the space agencies of the other international partners (e.g., Sipes & Vander Ark, 2005). Today, astronauts and cosmonauts staying for several months on the ISS are provided with in-flight HBP support based on different resources and interactive support measures, which have been defined as medical requirements of ISS operations (ISS Medical Operations Requirements Document, 2003). This is also considered to serve as a model for future exploration missions to Moon and Mars (Doarn et al., 2021). More specifically, these measures include: (1) countermeasures for possible issues of boredom and monotony, comprising various resources to support leisure activities, like libraries of e-books and videos, music, recreational software, and music instruments (e.g., keyboard); (2) countermeasures for social monotony and isolation, including flexible access to email and internet phone, uplink of news in native language according to individual interests on regular schedule, provision of crew care packages with re-supply flights, crew discretionary events (i.e., private meeting with specific individuals like actors, musicians, or scientists as wished by the crew member), and weekly private family conferences (PFC), i.e., confidential video-conferences with family and friends; and (3) bi-weekly private psychological conferences with a psychologist or other HBP expert on the ground. The latter represents an interactive support measure which ensures a continuous contact between the individual astronaut and a specifically assigned support person on the ground. It enables monitoring of the mental performance state of the astronaut while in space and provision for consultation if needed. This element of in-flight support is usually based on at least three pre-flight meetings during the year before the launch, and three follow-up meetings after the flight.

Conclusions

Although the presented concept of HBP training and support might not fully avoid the emergence of mental performance issues, primarily resulting from some negative individual reactions or interpersonal issues during spaceflight, it seems to be very successful in preventing these issues becoming a serious danger to the success and safety of orbital spaceflights. At least during the almost 20 years of experience with ESA long-term missions to ISS, we are not aware of any big issues related to an impaired mental performance of astronauts. In the following paragraph, we share some of the lessons learned according to our experience.

First, the combination of a didactic HBP training as part of the Basic Training of astronauts with practical experiences in simulations and follow-ups by more advanced field and outdoor trainings, seem to be essential to support a transfer of the didactic HBP training in practical action. Second, the decision to integrate also a briefing on Space Psychology focusing on specific effects of the space environment on cognitive and psychomotor performance, sleep, mood, and crew interactions already in the Basic Training of AsCans (Astronaut Candidates), was motivated by the insight that this might help to support the building of realistic expectations about the specific psychological challenges of staying in space already at an early stage in their career. Third, for the Human Factors training, it was important that the material and examples were as up-to-date and relevant as possible. The area of space exploration is changing so fast – and two big factors in particular: the commercial space companies in the US designing new spacecraft and new ways of doing things; and the future Artemis missions to the Moon. For commercially sensitive reasons, a lot of the designs of new spacecraft and missions are confidential. Whilst most commercial companies are still using the NASA STD-3001 as a guideline, it is still a guideline and things are changing rapidly. For example, during the time it took to create the Human Factors course ready for delivery, the design of spacesuits for the moon changed three times (NASA[3]) and the interface of the Orion control panels were constantly developing and updating. Fourth, with respect to HBP in-flight support and particularly the acceptance and success of PPCs, several success factors could be identified, including the building of a trustful relationship between the astronaut and HBP expert on the ground based on mutual respect and strict confidentiality, a clear definition of the role of the HBP expert and the astronaut as a sort of coach–coachee relationship instead of any therapeutical relationship, an understanding of PPCs as non-clinical events which focus on a general understanding of the mental performance state of the astronaut and what might be needed to optimize this state, and to finally leave the astronauts with full control of what they want to share and how to use this support tool. Related to this latter lesson learned, finally, a fifth and overarching one is to take care to fully uncouple HBP training and support from any sort of selection of astronauts or decisions affecting their career. Only with such uncoupling is it ensured that astronaut candidates and astronauts perceive the training and support as opportunities of development and ways of improvement rather than as assessment and with fear of failure.

Unlike the standardization and collaboration effort undertaken by space agencies, no international initiatives exist so far to pool resources to cope with human behaviour and performance issues in Antarctica. The similarity between the challenges of long-duration spaceflight and overwintering warrants that similar approaches may be needed in the psychological preparation for both. From our experience in the field, we noticed a discrepancy between HBP training for human spaceflight (even for short duration missions), and HBP training for overwintering in Antarctica, as is explained in detail in Van Puyvelde et al. (2022). This is striking because, as is evident from our literature review, and based on our own experience, many problems in ICE-environments are human factors problems, although those which derive from organizational issues may vary widely between nations.

The current chapter has dealt with the mental performance of humans in extreme environments, that is environments humans are not naturally suited for. Examples of such environments considered included Antarctica and the near-Earth orbit. Mental performance was understood in a very broad range, from basic cognitive and psychomotor performance to behavioural health, reflected in mood, well-being, and social behaviour. As becomes evident from the currently available evidence from these environments, basic cognitive functions per se seem to remain very resilient even to drastic environmental changes like an alteration of gravitational forces or dark–light cycles. This is remarkable given the fact that humans have been optimized for life on Earth with gravity and a 24-hour day defined by sunlight and darkness for billions of years. If at all, decrements of cognitive performance in extreme environments seem to reflect indirect effects of impairments of mood, sleep, well-being, or interpersonal relationship induced by the multi-stressor environment of a sealed habitat and, thus, a more general impairment of mental performance state. As a consequence, current training and support programs for humans working and living in these environments primarily focus on improving the individual adaptive skills needed for living in small crews in confinement and isolation, such as self-management skills, teamwork skills, leadership skills, and cross-cultural skills if necessary. This shall improve the general stress resilience of humans in extreme environments, and thus ensure that they can maintain an optimum mental performance state, as understood here, even under the extreme working and living conditions as represented by spaceflight or an overwintering in the Antarctic.

While this seems to be a proper approach for current expeditions in the extreme environments considered, despite the existing shortcomings related to the Antarctic environment, as emphasized by Van Puyvelde et al. (2022), it might not be sufficient for even more extreme endeavours like a stay on the Lunar surface or a flight to Mars. Such future exploration activities will involve new and more extreme challenges than known thus far. This will be particularly true for missions to Mars, which will represent a much more extreme psychological challenge for humans than any other expedition before, related, for example, to the extreme duration of missions of up to three years, a much higher crew autonomy given significantly less options for support from ground, and a much higher internal and external decoupling from Earth which will even not be seen any more (e.g., Manzey, 2004). As a consequence, even more effort need be made for preparing crews for these new challenges and to enable them to maintain an optimum mental performance state even under those conditions. This might also include the development of new training and support technologies, for example, to enable individuals maintaining critical cognitive and psychomotor skills learned on Earth for application on Mars, to support proper autonomous decision-making, and to advise individuals and crews in phases of internal or external crises.

References

Bechtel, R. B., and Berning, A. (1991). "The third-quarter phenomenon: do people experience discomfort after stress has passed?," in *From Antarctica to Outer Space*, ed A. A. Harrison (New York: Springer New York LLC), 261–266.

Benke, T., Koserenko, O., Watson, N.V., Gerstenbrand, F. (1993). Space and cognition: The measurement of behavioral functions during a 6-day space mission. *Aviation, Space and Environmental Medicine*, 64, 376–379.

Bishop, S., Häuplik-Meusburger, S., Guined, J. & Peldszus, R. (2016). Bionomic Design Countermeasures for Enhancing Cognitive and Psychological Functioning and Crew Performance in Isolated and Confined Habitats. 46th International Conference on Environmental Systems 10-14 July 2016, Vienna, Austria. ICES-2016-375

Bock, O., and Cheung, B. S. K. (1998). Control of isometric force in hypergravity. *Aviat. Space Environ. Med.* 69, 27–31.

Bock, O., Fowler, B. & Comfort, D. (2001). Human sensorimotor coordination during spaceflight: an analysis of pointing and tracking responses during the "Neurolab" space shuttle mission. *Aviation, Space and Environmental Medicine*, 72, 877–883.

Bock, O., Weigelt, C., Bloomberg, J.J. (2010). Cognitive demand of human sensorimotor performance during an extended space-mission: a dual-task study. *Aviation, Space, and Environmental Medicine*, 81, 819–824.

Casler, J. G., and Cook, J. R. (1999). Cognitive performance in space and analogous environments. *Int. J. Cogn. Ergon.* 3, 351–372. doi: 10.1207/s15327566ijce0304_5

Choo, W. C., Lee, W. W., Venkatraman, V., Sheu, F. S., and Chee, M. W. L. (2005). Dissociation of cortical regions modulated by both working memory load and sleep deprivation and by sleep deprivation alone. *Neuroimage* 25, 579–587. doi: 10.1016/j.neuroimage.2004.11.029

Clément, G. 2011. Fundamentals of Space Medicine. Springer New York, NY

de Schonen, S., Leone, G. & Lipshits, M. (1998). The face inversion effect in microgravity: is gravity used as a spatial reference for complex object recognition? *Acta Astronautica*, 42, 287–301.

Defayolle, M., Boutelier, C., Bachelard, C., Rivolier, J. & Taylor, A.J . (1985). The stability of psychometric performance during the International Biomedical Expedition to the Antarctic (IBEA). *Journal of Human Stress*, 11, 157–60.

Doarn, C.R., Polk, J.D., Grigoriev, A., Comtois, J-M., Shimada, K., Weerts, G., Dervay, J.P., Taddeo, T.A. & Sargsyan, A. (2021). A framework for multinational medical support for the International Space Station: a model for exploration. *Aerospace Medicine and Human Performance*, 92(2), 129–134.

Driskell, T., Salas, E., and Driskell, J. E. (2018). Teams in extreme environments: alterations in team development and teamwork. *Hum. Resour. Manag. Rev.* 28, 434–449. doi: 10.1016/j.hrmr.2017.01.002

Drouot, X. (2023). Le sommeil en réanimation, enjeu crucial mais méconnu [Sleep in intensive care: a crucial but little-known issue]. *Rev Prat*. Jun;73(6), 669–675. French. PMID: 37458561

Eddy, D. R., Schiflett, S. G., Schlegel, R. E., & Shehab, R. L. (1998). Cognitive performance aboard the life and microgravity spacelab. *Acta Astronautica,* 43, 193–210.

Garriott, O.K. & Doerre, G.L. (1977). Crew efficiency on first exposure to zero gravity. In R.S. Johnston & L.F. Dietlein (Eds.), *Biomedical results from Skylab (NASA-SP377)*, Washington: National Aeronautics and Space Administration.

Garrett-Bakelman, F.E. et al. (2019). The NASA Twins Study: A multidimensional analysis of a year-long human spaceflight. *Science*, 364, eaau8650.

Golden, S. J., Chang, C. H., and Kozlowski, S. W. J. (2018). Teams in isolated, confined, and extreme (ICE) environments: review and integration. *J. Organ. Behav*. 39, 701–715. doi: 10.1002/job.2288

Hadfield, C. (2013). *An astronaut's guide to life on Earth*. Macmillan, NY, USA.

International Space Station Human Behavior & Performance Competency Model - Mission Operations Directorate, ITCB HBP Training Working Group - Loredana Bessone, Emily Coffey, Natsuhiko Inoue, Maureen Gittens, Chiaki Mukai, Sharon O'Connor, Leena Tomi, Victor Ren, Lacey Schmidt, Walter Sipes, Steve Vander Ark, Alexander Vassin NASA/TM–2008–214775 Vol 1 & Vol 2.

ISS Mission Operations Directorate ITCB Training Working Group (2008). *Human behaviour and performance competency model Working Group Document*. Vol. I. Houston: Johnson Space Center. [available from: https://ntrs.nasa.gov/api/citations/20080018552/downloads/20080018552.pdf; 29 November, 2023]

ISS Mission Operations Directorate ITCB Training Working Group (2008b). *Volume II, Human behaviour and performance competency model guide Working Group Document*, Vol. II. (NASA TM 2008-20080018551). Houston: Johnson Space Center. [available from: https://ntrs.nasa.gov/api/citations/20080018551/downloads/20080018551.pdf; 29 November 2023]

Jehn, K. A. (1995). A multimethod examination of the benefits and detriments of intragroup conflict. *Adm. Sci. Q*. 40, 256–282. doi: 10.2307/2393638

Jehn, K. A., and Chatman, J. A. (2000). The influence of proportional and perceptual conflict composition on team performance. *Int. J. Confl. Manag.* 11, 56–73. doi: 10.1108/eb022835

Kanas, N. (1991). Psychosocial support for cosmonauts. *Aviation, Space, and Environmental Medicine*, 62, 353–355.

Kanas, N., Salnitskiy, V., Grund, E. M., Weiss, D. S., Gushin, V., Bostrom, A., et al. (2001). Psychosocial issues in space: results from Shuttle/Mir. *Gravit. Space Biol. Bull.* 14, 35–45.

Kanas, N., Sandal, G., Boyd, J. E., Gushin, V. I., Manzey, D., North, R., et al. (2009). Psychology and culture during long-duration space missions. *Acta Astronaut.* 64, 659–677. doi: 10.1016/j.actaastro.2008.12.005

Kanki, B, Clervoy, J & Sandal, G. (Eds.), *Space safety and human performance* (pp. 185–199). Amsterdam: Elsevier. ISBN 978-0-08-101869-9

Kelly, T. H., Hienz, R. D., Zarcone, T. J., Wurster, R. M., & Brady, J. V. (2005). Crewmember performance before, during, and after spaceflight. *Journal of the Experimental Analysis of Behavior,* 84, 227–241.

Killgore, W. D. S., Balkin, T. J., and Wesensten, N. J. (2006). Impaired decision making following 49 h of sleep deprivation. *J. Sleep Res.* 15, 7–13. doi: 10.1111/j.1365-2869.2006.00487.x

Klein, N.G. & Bessone, L. (2008). Training for space endeavours: Designing behavioural training for individuals and teams in high risk environments. In *Proc. 3rd IAASS conference: Building a safer space together*. www.spacebooks-online.com/product_info.php?cPath=104&products_id=17269&osCsid=sscldrhw

Kubis, J.F., McLaughlin, E.J., Jackson, J.M., Rusnak, R., McBride, G.H. & Saxon, S.V. (1977). Task and work performance on Skylab missions 2, 3, and 4: time and motion study – experiment M151. In R.S. Johnston & L.F. Dietlein (Eds.), *Biomedical results from Skylab (NASA-SP377)*. Washington: National Aeronautics and Space Administration.

Leone, G. (1998). The effect of gravity on human recognition of disoriented objects. *Brain Research Review*, 28, 203–214.

Le Scanff, C., Larue, J. & Rosnet, E. (1997). How to measure human adaptation in extreme environments: The case of Antarctic wintering-over. *Aviation, Space, and Environmental Medicine*, 68, 1144–1149.

Limardo-Rodriguez, J.G., Allen, C.S., & Danielson, R.W. (2015). Status: Crewmember Noise Exposures on the International Space Station. NASA Technical report 20150011048 . Johnsons Space Centre

Manzey, D. (2017). Cognitive and psychomotor performance. In R. Hilbig, A. Gollhofer, O. Bock & D. Manzey (Eds.), *Sensory motor and behavioral research in space*. Heidelberg: Springer.

Manzey, D. (2018). Mission factors. In B. Kanki, J. Clervoy & G. Sandal (Eds.), *Space safety and human performance* (pp. 185–190). Amsterdam: Elsevier. ISBN 978-0-08-101869-9

Manzey, D., & Lorenz, B. (1998). Mental performance during short-term and long-term spaceflight. *Brain Research Reviews,* 28(1-2), 215–221. https://doi.org/10.1016/S0165-0173(98)00041-1

Manzey, D., Lorenz, B., Heuer, H. & Sangals, J. (2000). Impairments of manual tracking performance in space: More converging evidence from a 20-day space mission. *Ergonomics*, 43, 589–60.

Manzey, D., Lorenz, B., Schiewe, A., Finell, G., & Thiele, G. (1993). Behavioral-Aspects of Human Adaptation to Space - Analyses of Cognitive and Psychomotor Performance In-Space During An 8-Day Space Mission. *Clinical Investigator,* 71, 725–731.

Mogilever, N. B., Zuccarelli, L., Burles, F., Iaria, G., Strapazzon, G., Bessone, L., et al. (2018). Expedition cognition: a review and prospective of subterranean neuroscience with spaceflight applications. *Front. Hum. Neurosci.* 12, 1–26. doi: 10.3389/fnhum.2018.00407

NASA (1). The Human Integration Design Handbook (HIDH), NASA/SP-2010-3407/REV1

NASA (2) Space Flight Human-System Standard, Volume 2 of NASA-STD-3001 Revision D Human Factors, Habitability, and Environmental Health. https://standards.nasa.gov/standard/NASA/NASA-STD-3001-VOL-2

NASA (3) "Spacesuit for NASA's Artemis III Moon Surface Mission Debuts" www.nasa.gov/feature/spacesuit-for-nasa-s-artemis-iii-moon-surface-mission-debuts

Natani, K., Shurley, J. T., and Joern, A. T. (1973). "Interpersonal relationships, job satisfaction, and subjective feelings of competence: their influence upon adaptation to Antarctic isolation," in *Polar Human Biology*, eds O. G. Edholm and E. K. E. Gunderson (London: Heinemann), 384–400.

Nelson, G.A., Simonsen, L., and Huff, J.L. (2016). Evidence Report: Risk of Acute and Late Central Nervous System Effects from Radiation Exposure. NASA Technical Report 20160004368. Johnson Space Centre.

Nilsson, J. P., Söderström, M., Karlsson, A. U., Lekander, M., Åkerstedt, T., Lindroth, N. E., et al. (2005). Less effective executive functioning after one night's sleep deprivation. *J. Sleep Res.* 14, 1–6. doi: 10.1111/j.1365-2869.2005.00442.x

Oman, C. (2007). Spatial orientation and navigation in microgravity. In: F. Mast & L. Jaencke (Eds.), *Spatial processing in navigation, imagery and perception* (pp. 369–387). Springer: Berlin.

Pagnini, F., Manzey, D., Rosnet, E., Ferrante, D., White, O. & Smith, N. (2023). Human behavior and performance in deep space exploration: Next challenges and research gaps. *npj Microgravity*, 9(27). https://doi.org/10.1038/s41526-023-00270-7.

Palinkas, L. & Suedfeld, P. (2008). Psychological effects of polar expeditions. *The Lancet*, 371, 153–163.

Palinkas, L.A., Reedy, K.R., Smith, M., Anghel, M., Steel, G.D., Reeves, D., Shurtleff, D., Case, H.S., van Do, N. & Reed, L. (2007). Psychoneuroendocrine effects of combined thyroxine and triiodothyronine versus tyrosine during prolonged Antarctic residence. *International Journal of Circumpolar Health*, 66, 401–17.

Palinkas, L.A., Suedfeld, P. (2021). Psychosocial issues in isolated and confined extreme environments. *Neurosci Biobehav Rev.* Jul;126:413–429. doi: 10.1016/j.neubiorev.2021.03.032. Epub 2021 Apr 6. PMID: 33836214.

Pattyn, N., Migeotte, P.F., Demaeseleer, W., Kolinsky, R., Morais, J. & Zizi, M. (2005). Investigating human cognitive performance during spaceflight. *Journal of Gravitational Physiology*, 12, P39–P40.

Pattyn, N., Van Puyvelde, M., Fernandez-Tellez, H., Roelands, B., and Mairesse, O. (2018). From the midnight sun to the longest night: sleep in Antarctica. *Sleep Med. Rev.* 37, 159–172. doi: 10.1016/j.smrv.2017.03.001

Ratino, D. A., Repperger, D. W., Goodyear, C., Potor, G., & Rodriguez, L. E. (1988). Quantification of Reaction-Time and Time Perception During Space-Shuttle Operations. *Aviation Space and Environmental Medicine,* 59, 220–224.

Reed, H.L., Reedy, K.R., Palinkas, L.A., Van Do, N., Finney, N.S., Case, H.S., Homer, J.L., Wright, J. & Thomas, J. (2001). Impairment in cognitive and exercise performance during prolonged Antarctic residence: Effect of thyroxine supplementation in the polar triiodothyronine syndrome. *Journal of Clinical Endocrinology & Metabolism*, 86, 110–6.

Sandal, G.M., Leon, G.R. & Palinkas, L. Human challenges in polar and space environments. *Rev Environ Sci Biotechnol* **5**, 281–296 (2006). https://doi.org/10.1007/s11157-006-9000-8

Schlesinger, T., Rodriguez, B.R., and Borrego, M. (2013). ISS Crew Quarters On-Orbit Performance and Sustaining Activities. 43rd International Conference on Environmental Systems, Vail, CO, July 14-18. https://doi.org/10.2514/6.2013-3515

Sipes, W.E. & Vander Ark, S.T. (2005). Operational behavioral health and performance resources for international space station crews and families. *Aviation, Space, and Environmental Medicine*, 76(6), B36–41.

Smith, N., Peters, D., Jay, C., Sandal, G.M., Barrett, E.C., Wuebker, R. Off-World Mental Health: Considerations for the Design of Well-being–Supportive Technologies for Deep Space Exploration. JMIR Formative Research 7 (1), e37784.

Somaraju, A. V., Griffin, D. J., Olenick, J., Chang, C. H., and Kozlowski, S. W. J. (2022). The dynamic nature of interpersonal conflict and psychological strain in extreme work settings. *J. Occup. Health Psychol.* 27, 53–73. doi: 10.1037/ocp0000290

Stickgold, R. (2005). Sleep-dependent memory consolidation. *Nature* 437, 1272–1278. doi: 10.1038/nature04286

Strangman, G. E., Sipes, W., and Beven, G. (2014). Human cognitive performance in spaceflight and analogue environments. *Aviat. Sp. Environ. Med.* 85, 1033–1048. doi: 10.3357/ASEM.3961.2014

Stuster, J. (2010). *Behavioral issues associated with long-duration space expeditions: Review and analysis of astronaut journals (Experiment 01-E104 (Journals): Final Report)*. Houston: Nasa.

Stuster, J. (2016). *Behavioral issues associated with long-duration space expeditions: Review and analysis of astronaut journals (Experiment 01-E104 (Journals): Phase 2 Final Report)*. Houston: Nasa.

Suedfeld, P., & Steel, G.D. (2000). The environmental psychology of capsule habitats. *Annu Rev Psychol.* 51, 227–53. doi: 10.1146/annurev.psych.51.1.227. PMID: 10751971.

Suedfeld, P., and Weiss, K. (2000). Antarctica: natural laboratory and space analogue for psychological research. *Environ. Behav.* 32, 7–17. doi: 10.1177/00139160021972405

Taylor, A.J.W. & Duncum, K. (1987). Some cognitive effects of wintering-over in the Antarctic. *New Zealand Journal of Psychology*, 16, 93–4.

van den Berg NH, Michaud X, Pattyn N, Simonelli G. How Sleep Research in Extreme Environments Can Inform the Military: Advocating for a Transactional Model of Sleep Adaptation. Curr Psychiatry Rep. 2023 Feb;25(2):73–91. doi: 10.1007/s11920-022-01407-3. Epub 2023 Feb 15. PMID: 36790725.

Van Dongen, H. P. A., Maislin, G., Mullington, J. M., and Dinges, D. F. (2004). Erratum: THE cumulative cost of additional wakefulness: dose-response effects on neurobehavioral functions and sleep physiology from chronic sleep restriction and total sleep deprivation (Sleep (March 2003) 26, 2. *Sleep* 27, 600. doi: 10.1093/sleep/26.2.117

Van Ombergen A, Rossiter A, Ngo-Anh TJ. 'White Mars' - nearly two decades of biomedical research at the Antarctic Concordia station. Exp Physiol. 2021 Jan;106(1):6–17. doi: 10.1113/EP088352. Epub 2020 Jul 27. PMID: 32662901.

Van Puyvelde, M., and Mairesse, O. (2022). Do C-tactile afferents go to sleep? A potential role for somatosensory stimulation in sleep regulation. *Curr. Opin. Behav. Sci.* 43, 62–68. doi: 10.1016/j.cobeha.2021.08.006

Van Puyvelde, M., Gijbels, D., Van Caelenberg, T., Smith, N., Bessone, L., Buckle-Charlesworth, S. & Pattyn, N. (2022). Living on the edge: How to prepare for it? *Front. Neuroergon.*, 3, 1007774. doi: 10.3389/fnrgo.2022.1007774

Vanhove, A. J., Herian, M. N., Desimone, J. A., Harms, P. D., Luthans, F., and DeSimone, J. A. (2015). Examining psychosocial well-being and performance in isolated, confined, and extreme environments final report. *Natl. Aeronaut. Sp. Adm.* 1–134.

Venkatraman, V., Chuah, Y. M. L., Huettel, S. A., and Chee, M. W. L. (2007). Sleep deprivation elevates expectation of gains and attenuates response to losses following risky decisions. *Sleep* 30, 603–609. doi: 10.1093/sleep/30.5.603

Wood, J., Lugg, D. J., Hysong, S., and Harm, D. L. (1999). Psychological adaptation to extreme environments : effects of team composition on individual adaptation. *Environm* 31, 299–337. doi: 10.1177/00139169921972128

15 Mental Performance Programs in the Corporate World

Aisha Cortoos and Maarten Bocksteins

Introduction

As mentioned before, mental performance is important to any area that depends on tasks performed by humans. It relies on optimal brain functioning and the way mental skills are used. In the corporate world, unlike sports or the military, the most important instrument for performance is the brain, as there is no physical component to performance. However, these "brain-workers" have little to no knowledge about their instrument. Similarly to a military context, where Pattyn (2020) mentioned "You would never consider to deploy an operator with a new weapon system without the appropriate training, would you? Regardless, this is what is done in most Special Operating Forces (SOF) units right now, they are sent to war with a weapon they don´t even realize they are carrying – their brain." The same goes for the corporate world.

The goal of this chapter is to guide the reader through the necessary knowledge about implementing mental performance programs into a corporate environment; the similarities and differences between a corporate context and the military or sport environment; and the areas requiring specific attention when trying to implement mental performance programs in this specific context.

To illustrate the choice of topics we covered in the present chapter, we choose to start with a testimony of a client's perspective on existing mental performance initiatives:

> People working jobs in fast-paced professional environments like consulting, investment banking, C-levels in large corporates, high-demand commercial functions, etc. are typically required to keep multiple balls in the air. While running from one (client) meeting and from one deadline to another, they need to (i) stay focused when switching between tasks/topics, (ii) be "present" and stay "on top of things" at all times while dealing with a never-ending mail trail and with a multitude of ad-hoc demands from Board, ExCo, clients and other stakeholders, (iv) stay energetic while working long hours in order to get everything done, (v) be clear in communication and priority setting towards their teams, and be experts in delegation (vi) show leadership and vision while being attentive for group dynamics and team issues, (vii) be able to adapt and connect with a variety of personalities, (viii) manage politics and corporate culture, and (ix) stay resilient in an ever changing context. On top of that, they are required to balance professional and private lives to also meet the needs of their life partners, their kids, their family and their friends.
>
> It comes without saying that "corporate performance" is not only about being focused and about working efficiently. It's a neat balance between "hard" and "soft" skills, whether it's about excelling in people- & stakeholder management, communication & presentation skills, time- &

DOI: 10.4324/9781003378969-18

stress management, being a leader and influencer, project management skills, technical know-how and expertise, having the ability to develop a broad network, about ambition and the eager to move forward while exceling in quality of delivery, the ability to show "flexibility in mind" and resilience, understand the latest technical and business advancements, master the ability to shift between in-depth analysis and synthesis, ... and all this while maintaining a perfect physical and mental wellbeing. Easy, no?

Those same executives are often coached and advised by (sport)coaches, (former) athletes, explorers... personalities of all kind that tell them how to apply techniques and "tips & tricks", in order to achieve their corporate objectives. However, the context where such executive professionals are working in, seems quite different from those "advisors". Why? Many of those coaches are solely focusing on "what works" for a top sports or a mental coach, while applying their "tips & tricks" in an isolated environment, focused on one outcome and with "perfect" conditions (which does not mean they do not meet adversity...). In isolation, all those techniques will for sure demonstrate their added value, whether it's breathing techniques and mindfulness, physical exercise and the use of healthy meals, being your authentic self to create a safe psychological environment for teams to excel, showing and communicating leadership & vision, structuring and presenting presentations, developing insights on your own personality (MBTi®, Social styles®, etc.) in order to understand your "red flags" and improve the ability to connect with a variety of people along the day, learn about time management, etc. However, the busy agenda of the executive doesn't allow of being able to be attentive to all those aspects. Furthermore, one could argue that "one size" doesn't necessarily fit all purposes: a finance director may have different corporate objectives and will need to show a different skillset (financial & technical expertise, team management) than a commercial director (being connected, commercial acumen, presentation skills).

I guess that you could compare the executive professionals with a sprinter who's running the 100 meter multiple times per day, during 220 working days per year, while being distracted by some cheering audience (board, peers, clients, family & friends, team, etc.) and with the need of being attentive for the position of other sprinters. Therefore, other rules apply, and the advice for professionals should be holistic. How can you stay performant while running multiple sprints every day, all year long, while continuously being distracted? I assume that, except if everyone is a kind of superman, the only thing that can really work is a holistic program adapted to the specific needs of the executive and which takes into account the individual corporate objectives of that person. A program that identifies the most commonly needed skills, and focuses on those that are important. The corporate performance is a combination of health, focus, EQ, IQ, etc.

I guess that the cooling down period between the different sprints are crucial, and that performance coaching is about rearranging an agenda as such that those cooling down periods are build-in, that the professional is not only coached on physics and focus, but also on communication, empathy, leadership, etc. The performance of a top executive requires therefore a multifaceted approach which addresses focus, recuperation, health, wellbeing, communication, team leadership, etc. whereas the advice of many "coaches" only focuses on one aspect. In parallel with a nutritionist that adapts the menu to the type of sports, e.g., powerlifting versus endurance training. A top-down approach, starting from the objectives of the executive professional should be translated into a sub-set of the menu the various "coachings" are offering.

Corporate environments and corporate athletes: similarities with sports and military contexts

The previous chapters have focused mainly on areas such as the military and sports elite performers. In the corporate world, a similar group of people exist, the so-called corporate athletes

(Loehr & Schwartz, 2001). We will use the term "corporate high mental performers" to refer to business leaders, entrepreneurs, C-level corporates or managers who are in the higher hierarchy of a business. It is known that high mental performers typically work very hard for long hours and are confronted with uncertainty, ambiguity, and stress (Morris, 1998; Mueller & Thomas, 2001). Specifically for business leaders or entrepreneurs, the process of transforming an idea or mental construct into a well-functioning enterprise is definitely a process with peaks and valleys regarding stress levels and unforeseen events, which depends heavily on mental performance and skills. Schindehutte, Morris, and Anderson (Schindehutte et al., 2006) show that entrepreneurship can be regarded as an extreme experience where peak performance, peak experiences, and states of flow go hand in hand. Moreover, Crecente, Sarabia, and del Val (Crecente et al., 2021) explain that there exists quite some overlap between characteristics and learned skills of military personnel and those skills necessary to engage in entrepreneurship or the environment of a business leader. In a military or combat environment, abilities such as innovation, risk taking, flexibility, adaptation to new environments, mutual support, and self-efficacy are crucial, which are also valuable or even necessary skills in a high mental performance environment (Avrahami & Lerner, 2003). Indeed, when evaluating how venture capitalists, for example, decide which new venture they will invest in, it appears the characteristics of the entrepreneur are more important, rather than the idea or business concept being proposed (Cardon et al., 2009). The most important characteristic for venture capitalists is the capacity to function effectively under stress (Wright et al., 1997) and the process towards funding and starting a new venture is designed to select people who possess this strength. Again, we see a similar environment and procedure as in military contexts.

The cognitive psychology of mental performance in corporate life

High mental performers often juggle several roles and responsibilities, must be able to make rational and sound decisions under pressure, solve sudden and complex problems, and find new ideas or solutions for clients, as well as maintain a professional relationship with partners, clients, and team members. Selection of these leaders or managers has mainly focused on distinguishing intelligence, attained skills, and judgement capacities. The problem here lies in the fact that all these capabilities highly depend on the functioning of our core and higher-order executive functions (see Chapter 2 for a detailed description).

In neuroscience, mental performance is the result of the efficient use of our three core executive functions: working memory, inhibition, and cognitive flexibility or shifting. Working memory refers to the capacity to keep information in mind and mentally work with it; inhibitory control makes it possible to suppress all irrelevant stimuli or behavioural responses; and cognitive flexibility builds on the two previous executive functions allowing us to change perspective, look at something from a different angle, or admit we were wrong. It is the opposite of cognitive rigidity (Cristofori et al., 2019; Diamond, 2013). These core executive functions in turn allow one to use more high-level executive functions, such as decision-making, goal setting, and metacognition. It is clear that all these skills are necessary in a corporate environment, however, there is a lack of scientific research evaluating the use of these mental skills in a corporate life, especially in business executives or C-level executives, the top mental performers in corporate life. One of the possible reasons why organizational research has overlooked assessment of executive functions within this context is because they are often seen as the same as assessments of general intelligence, or the idea that executive functions are difficult to measure or asses in organizations (Chan et al., 2021).

Regulating one's attention is crucial for any part or aspect of mental performance. However, it is a limited resource that must be regulated and controlled (see Chapter 2 for a detailed description). Executive functions drive the efficient management of attention (Diamond, 2013). Only when the core executive functions efficiently work together, is sustained attention possible.

Executive functions will play a major role for organizational leaders or managers when they need to perform under pressure in a rapidly changing environment with many responsibilities and a high load of stress, combined with the necessity of accurate and effective performance. They play a crucial role in task-oriented, relations-oriented and change-oriented behaviour. With regard to task-oriented behaviour, the most important ones are decision-making, planning and monitoring, and problem solving. With regard to decision-making, executive functions help us to pay attention to the relevant information. Working memory is engaged to keep the necessary information online, and inhibition helps to suppress irrelevant information or solutions. The second step in decision-making is to rationally and deliberately process this information. High performers have to be aware of certain framing heuristics that can impact the decision-making process, or suppress intuition if necessary (Del Missier et al., 2012). Key within this process is efficient attention management. Planning and monitoring, another task-oriented behaviour of leaders or managers, requires meta-cognitive tracking: are we still progressing towards the goal, and if not, can we adjust our strategy or the goal? Working memory keeps all the factors in mind that contribute to goal progress versus goal hindrances (Fernandez-Duque et al., 2000). Especially in a rapidly changing environment, executive functions will help to decide if a change in strategy or goal is necessary. Next to meta-cognitive tracking, self-regulation is key. It allows one to use the information from metacognitive tracking and implement changes, which results in changes in behaviour and goals. Inhibition and mental flexibility are important executive functions within this adaptation process (Masicampo & Baumeister, 2011).

Leaders and managers need to be able to handle tough negotiations, with clients, business partners, or team members. This falls into the category of relations-oriented behaviour. There are five important skills involved in successful negotiating. The first is *perspective taking*: the ability to take the perspective of the other person while making an accurate assumption about their intentions. Inhibition and working memory need to work along in order to keep the different perspective in mind and to suppress the tendency to solely pay attention to their own perspective (Wardlow, 2013). The second skill is *emotion regulation*: this allows us to suppress our own needs, as well as the emotions that might arise if confronted with a situations where our needs need to wait. Emotion regulation also allows us to focus on positive emotions, which will positively impact the process of negotiating. It is clear that this skill depends on our ability to use working memory and inhibition. Without them, it would be impossible to suppress anger and angry reactions during negotiations (Hofmann et al., 2008). *Metacognitive evaluation* is the third skill involved in negotiations. Through metacognitive evaluation we can evaluate ourselves and our performances in a realistic way. Working memory and inhibition allow us to pay attention to our own behaviour and performances. Fourthly, *seeking outcomes* means we actively look and think about possible outcomes that can be beneficial for all involved parties. Inhibition is of particular importance to inhibit wrong impressions about people and their intentions, which would lead to negative emotions and make it much more difficult to find the common ground (Radvansky et al., 2010). Finally, strategic concealment is a skill that can be important when negotiating, because of the necessity to conceal sensitive information. This is a task that is cognitively demanding and needs sharp executive functions (Gombos, 2006).

Finally, high mental performers in corporate life function in rapidly changing, high-pressure environments. A key aspect to survive is innovation, the ability to develop new strategies, solutions, or ideas in response to changing situations. From an organizational point of view, innovation is often related to the characteristics of novel or creative thinking, open to new experiences and unconventional mindsets. However, without strong executive functions, innovation will stay mediocre. Inhibition is crucial in suppressing conventional and "known" ideas or approaches. Mental flexibility is needed to think out of the box and allow a different set of rules in the creative process. Working memory is needed to keep all the information (new and old) in mind and connect the dots towards the process of true innovation. In summary, strong core and higher-level executive functions lead to planned and deliberate decision-making, allow leaders to adjust strategies or goals if necessary, support prioritizing competing demands, find solutions for complex problems, help negotiations, and lead to truly innovative behaviour.

Stress in high-paced corporate environments

Working as a business executive or entrepreneur is an exciting experience which demands a lot of effort, creativity, perseverance, and cognitive flexibility. High mental performers in corporate life are exposed to many potential stressors. It is characterized by high unpredictability, rapid and unforeseen changes, high risk levels and work load, and many responsibilities, especially when you have employees working for you. Given this occupational environment, the first conclusion might be that corporate mental performers experience high levels of stress, and as such are at a higher risk for burn-out or other mental health problems. This was also evidenced in a study by Buttner (Buttner, 1992), where he found higher levels of stress and lower job satisfaction in entrepreneurs compared to employees. However, this finding has not been researched systematically and the result is a lack of empirical evidence that supports this statement. More recent research evaluating both entrepreneurs (Baron et al., 2016) as well as people in high leadership positions (Sherman et al., 2012) shows a different picture: high mental performers in high leadership positions appear to show lower levels of stress. Both psychological levels of stress, such as anxiety, as well as physiological levels of stress, evaluated by cortisol, were lower (Sherman et al., 2012). One important mediating factor according to this last study, is the sense of control. Leaders in a high position experience more autonomy and control, which is known to have a positive and buffering impact on stress levels. Moreover, it is hypothesized that people with exceptional stress coping strategies are best suited for these leadership positions and, as such, are more often selected for these positions. Baron et al. (2016) suggest the "Attraction–Selection–Attrition (ASA) theory" to explain this seemingly contradictory finding of lower stress in high mental performers. This theory was originally designed to explain the finding that organizations tend to become increasingly homogenous over time with respect to the knowledge, skills, abilities, and other characteristics of their employees (Bretz Jr et al., 1989; Ployhart et al., 2006). However, it also been used to look into the reasons why people tend to choose to enter and remain in particular careers and occupations. The attraction–selection–attrition theory suggests that individuals choose careers or occupations to which they are initially attracted because the requirements are well aligned with their personal skills, characteristics, and motives. Following the attraction, selection will be responsible for actually entering the career of occupation, because individuals will decide they are in fact suited. The final step is attrition, which occurs when individuals actually discover that their skills, characteristics, or interests do not align with the requirements of the career or occupation. The result is that they will withdraw from it. According to this theory, the existing population of C-level executives and entrepreneurs have been formed by this process because certain characteristics of the job needs certain individual abilities. One of these characteristics is the capacity to tolerate and manage stress.

An interesting question here is to look into the specific characteristics that help corporate mental performers in experiencing lower levels of stress. One of those characteristics is psychological capital reflecting four underlying components: self-efficacy, optimism, hope, and resilience (Luthans et al., 2005). Psychological capital is related to superior performance, positive work-related attitudes, and reduced turnover in employees (Peterson et al., 2011), and also appears negatively related to experienced stress (Avey et al., 2011). This finding in employees was also confirmed in entrepreneurs by Baron et al. (Baron et al., 2016), who indicated that the higher entrepreneurs are in psychological capital, the lower their reported stress was. It creates a buffer against high levels of stress and, as such, protects mental performance in entrepreneurs. If we take another look at the four underlying components of psychological capital, these are also important aspects of what we call a "growth mindset", a concept predicting motivation and self-regulatory strategies, especially under stressful conditions (Molden & Dweck, 2006).

A final remark that deserves some attention is the fact that within the population of top executives, chronic stress, and especially the consequences it can have on mental performance and general well-being, still remains a taboo (Manzoni & Florent-Treacy, 2012). Talking about stress or coping strategies is often seen as a weakness that can have a negative impact on the continuation of one's career path. However, ignoring stress puts too much strain on the physiological system, resulting in a decrease of mental performance, and eventually even mental health problems such as anxiety, depression, sleep complaints, and burnout. Moreover, the impairment of the executive functions and sustained attention due to burnout can persist for three years or more even after the disappearance of the stressor (Jonsdottir et al., 2017). To conclude, high mental performers in corporate environments appear to be more resilient and are able to manage high levels of stress. However, they also seem reluctant to talk about it, which might lead to an underestimation of stress levels and the need for coping strategies and techniques. More specifically, stress regulation is part of a good strategy to improve and maintain high mental performance, and definitely not a sign of weakness.

Mental health and mental performance

Although mental health is not the topic of this handbook, it is a major topic in corporate environments (see Chapter 12 for a detailed description of the relationship between mental health and mental performance). Many high mental performers, such as business leaders or entrepreneurs, reach out to experts not because of poor performance, but rather because they are performing very well, but at a certain cost: their mental health. They experience symptoms of decreased mental health with preserved performance. Rumination, constant worrying, catastrophizing, sleep complaints, and the inability to relax are some of the most common reasons to seek help.

Entrepreneurs and top mental performers in the corporate world are focused on action, progress, moving on, achieving new goals, and so on. That is one of their assets, which allows them to excel at performing. However, as we know from the functioning of our nervous system, recovery is crucial to be able to perform optimally in the long term. In order to do so, we must actively engage our prefrontal cortex and the executive functions. However, the most prevalent mental health disorders, such as anxiety disorder and depression are known to have a negative impact on cognitive functions and specifically executive functions of the prefrontal cortex (Gotlib & Joormann, 2010; Park & Moghaddam, 2017; Rolls et al., 2020).

The previous chapters have focused specifically on aspects of mental performance, assuming that the basic needs in order to use these skills are already met. However, when it comes to corporate life, we feel we need to revisit them, because from our experience, they are often one of the reasons why mental health issues and problems with sustainable high mental performance arise. Corporate top mental performers need to be reminded of one of the most important prerequisites of mental performance: Recovery.

Pillars of health: prerequisites revisited

It is well-known that nutrition, sleep, and physical activities have an impact on our mental performance (Burkhalter & Hillman, 2011; Philip et al., 2012). In the military as well as the world of top athletes, physical activity is part of their daily functioning, even their job. However, in corporate life, sedentary behaviour is the norm. Corporate athletes work while sitting, almost all the time. This is why it is so important to raise the awareness regarding the importance of physical activity for cognition and mental performance. In the last decades, entrepreneurs and business leaders have become more aware of the need for physical activity. Indeed, the amount of businesses focusing on improving physical activity in the corporate life has grown.

Research shows that engaging in regular physical activity improves cognition, mainly the executive function, and protects against cognitive decline which co-occurs with aging (e.g., Arida & Teixeira-Machado, 2021). Furthermore, sedentary behaviour is also related to an increased risk of cardiovascular disease and a higher cortisol response to an acute stressor (e.g., Chauntry et al., 2022). As such, paying attention to regular movement and decreasing sedentary behaviour can contribute to improved mental performance.

However, since top mental performers tend to focus on performance, the combination of business performance and high expectations of physical performance often results in strain and ignores the concept of recovery. One of the consequences is that top mental performers ignore the need for rest and sleep. One might assume that there is an overactivation of the sympathetic nervous system and an underactivation of the parasympathetic nervous system. Taking time to recover by allowing enough rest and qualitative sleep is an important issue in a corporate environment.

Recovery: the value of sleep and rest

In the process towards top mental performances, neuroplasticity is crucial. The plasticity of the brain refers to the capacity to change its neural organization based on experience, exposure to stimuli, learning processes, and results in changed behaviour or new behavioural responses (Debarnot et al., 2014) (see Chapter 2 for a more in-depth discussion). Due to brain plasticity, a novice can evolve to become an expert. Consolidation of new information and skills is crucial in this process, and sleep appears to play a crucial role (Rasch & Born, 2013; Walker & Stickgold, 2010). Moreover, sleep deprivation is known to negatively impact the prefrontal cortex, which is crucial for our executive functions and mental performance, as well as emotion regulation (Yoo et al., 2007). As such, the need to invest in qualitative sleep is a prerequisite for optimal mental performance. More importantly, the need to understand that sleep is not a waste of time, but rather an investment in recovery and mental performance, needs a shift in mindset. We can offer many tips and tricks, but if we don't change our initial mindset on the value of recovery, brain workers will not change their behaviour.

In the corporate world, sleep has long been regarded as "a waste of time", it is often one of the first things that is sacrificed for work. Short nights are a sign of grit and work engagement. Top mental performers have a tendency to pay attention to sleep, only when they have time for it. Moreover, there still is a tendency to highlight the concept of waking up very early in order to be productive. The so-called 5AM clubs are an example of this myth. However, this does not take into account the role of the biological clock or circadian rhythm in mental performance, neither the fact that our sleep need is genetically determined and cannot be altered by training. Sleep is too often regarded as a luxury, not a priority. So what is the benefit of investing in sleep?

First of all, during wakefulness there is a build-up of harmful metabolites, such as amyloid beta in the brain. During sleep, and mainly deep sleep, cerebrospinal fluid is responsible for flushing out all the metabolites (Fultz et al., 2019). Researchers are even evaluating the possibility that chronic partial sleep deprivation is correlated with the development of neurodegenerative diseases in later life, such as Alzheimer's or dementia (Sabia et al., 2021).

Regarding mental performance, self-control is a crucial skill, as mentioned before. Sleep deprivation results in a decrease of top-down control processes which in turn results in a decrease of attention regulation, as well as memory processes and learning ability (Jackson et al., 2013). Sleep is crucial for the functioning of our prefrontal cortex and our core executive functions. It allows for the consolidation of new information in long-term memory and as such increases learning potential.

Sleep deprivation results in an increased activation of the amygdala when confronted with negative stressful stimuli, resulting in a decreased emotion regulation (Yoo et al., 2007). Concretely, partial sleep deprivation makes it more difficult to suppress unwanted, negative thoughts, which makes it much more difficult to regulate our stress system and control our behaviour. In other words, it impacts our self-control, a necessary skill for any top mental performer.

To summarize, sleep affects every aspect of the mental skills necessary to perform. Neglecting this basic need of the brain will have a negative impact on mental performance. It is no surprise that fatigue and exhaustion come into play at some point, especially when sleep is sacrificed. Exhaustion refers to a lack of energy and the feeling that one's resources are depleted (LePine et al., 2004), impairing the process of mental performance because exhaustion can result in decreased motivation, less desire to complete tasks, and lower achievement striving (Halbesleben & Bowler, 2007). Fatigue can be triggered by a lack of sleep, but also by continuous mental performance and a lack of recovery (Caldwell et al., 2019; Krausman et al., 2002).

The challenge for top mental performers in corporate life is to find efficient strategies that can be implemented in their specific professional environment and schedule to improve recovery, and as such, support top mental performance. They have to become experts in recovery.

Mental performance in the business world: where is the science?

When researching mental performance in the workplace or more specifically, in business executives, the first striking observation is that the result almost always mentions "mental health" instead of "mental performance". There is a striking lack of research specifically on the topic of mental performance in the workplace. Possibly, because mental health and mental performance are often used interchangeably, or because people believe that mental health always leads to optimal mental performance (more on this confusion can be found in Chapter 12). Studies evaluating specific interventions always start with pointing out that mental well-being has become a serious problem in the workplace. The increasing demands for high performance and demanding work conditions result in higher prevalence of anxiety, stress, emotional exhaustion and burnout, which is then related to a decrease in work performance (Bakker et al., 2005; Schaufeli et al., 2009). Currently, the focus lies on improving mental health and well-being, in order to improve work performance. Studies have mainly been done with employees, but not with business executives or the top mental performers within a company.

Furthermore, what is completely lacking is a holistic and multifaceted mental performance program that is tested in a real-life corporate environment. We see some studies evaluating isolated programs regarding mindfulness (Johnson et al., 2020; Kersemaekers et al., 2018; Passmore, 2019), or breathing (Eslami et al., 2023; Tavoian & Craighead, 2023), or emotional intelligence (Cherniss et al., 2010; Gilar-Corbi et al., 2019; Slaski & Cartwright, 2003), but no program that encompasses all skills necessary for optimal mental performance exists in scientific literature.

Mental performance in the corporate environment: what attributes are we talking about?

Cognitive functions

An important question in the realm of high mental performers is: "Why are some people more successful in high mental performer roles than others?" or "What attributes determine who will make a superior leader or manager?" The answer to this question is not a simple one and brings together many different factors such as individual characteristics, environmental and market conditions, as well as interactions between these factors. However, in research the main focus has been on the one thing we can control: the individual characteristics of the mental performer, the nature and origins of exceptional performance.

Many people used to assume that exceptional performance is mainly related to a superior talent or intelligence and/or a growing experience in the field. However, research shows this is not the case. Yes, talent, intelligence, and experience play a role, but appear not to be the defining factor for exceptional performance. With regard to experience, we even see a decline in performance after a while. Research shows that initially experience results in rapid increments of performance, followed by a plateau, and sometimes even a decline (Ericsson, 2006; Ucbasaran et al., 2009). Performance goes beyond typical or average levels only when individuals engage, actively and intently, in a particular form of learning, which is called deliberate practice (Ericsson et al., 2018). On a more concrete level, deliberate practice is characterized by (Colvin, 2010; Ericsson et al., 2018):

1. Sustained attention and focus: deliberate practice demands a high mental effort. The person needs to be fully absorbed in the effort, also referred to as "being mindful".
2. The task needs to be designed to improve performance. This means that weaknesses must be identified and efforts must be made to improve these. As such, it is more than just repeating a known performance.
3. It must continue for long periods of time and it must be repeated, it is a continuous process.
4. Continuous feedback on results is imperative.
5. The performance must be prepared in advance. As such, accurate and concrete goal-setting is an important skill, focused on both the process of performance, as well as the outcome.
6. Metacognition is a key aspect: self-observation and self-reflection are necessary in the process towards excellent performance.
7. Careful reflection on performance after practice: the newly achieved performance must be compared with predefined goals in order to adapt the next performance to optimally adapt and evolve towards a better performance.

Deliberate practice, as such, is an effortful form of learning which relies on the executive functions of the brain. Moreover, deliberate practice results in an enhancement of these basic cognitive processes necessary for entrepreneurial learning and venture performance. Train "the muscle", and it becomes stronger and more skilled.

As discussed, this kind of learning demands a lot of effort, as such, it is difficult to engage in this kind of activity for more than a few hours a day (Ericsson, 2006; Zimmerman, 2006). This is what is called "focus time" in corporate settings. Time to engage in deliberate practice with sustained attention, using working memory optimally to keep new information online and retrieve old information from long-term memory, while at the same time using inhibitory processes to suppress irrelevant stimuli, information, and responses in order to engage fully in creative, innovative, and controlled goal-oriented behaviour. An important note to this, individuals show great variation in their capacity to engage in deliberate practice, which means that only the people who can pursue this type of learning vigorously and persistently for a long time, will achieve top mental performance. This raises the question as to what kind of factors play a role in the individual capacity to engage in deliberate practice?

First of all, *achievement motivation* plays an important role in the development of exceptional levels of mental performance. The will and grit to go beyond the normal and continue to strive for excellence. Secondly, *self-efficacy* – the belief that one can accomplish what one has set out to accomplish (more information on self-efficacy can be found in Chapter 3). The amount of self-efficacy can be related to the appraisal process during stress: do I perceive the stressor as a possible harm or rather as an opportunity to grow, and do I have enough coping skills to achieve the goal? Thirdly, self-regulatory mechanisms that allow to regulate one's own behaviour in order to achieve specific personal goals (Winne, 1997). One of the self-regulatory mechanisms that has received a lot of attention is *self-control*. An important remark with regard to this factor is the fact that self-control is a cognitive resource that can be exhausted. If we use self-control for one specific task, we will show less self-control in other areas or tasks (Wan & Sternthal, 2008).

The benefit of deliberate practice is that it enhances basic cognitive resources necessary for excellent performance. It enhances aspects of perception which allow top mental performers to make finer discriminations of incoming information, and recognize complex patterns. The result is that the top performer can use their attentional recourses more quickly and efficiently (Baron & Henry, 2010). Secondly, it improves working memory, which allow the top performer to store new information efficiently in memory in a more organized way and at deeper levels. Furthermore, they are better at retrieving information that is relevant to the current situation, which allows them to effectively combine this information with new information, resulting in efficient goal-oriented behaviour. Thirdly, deliberate practice enhances metacognition and intuition. Experts and top mental performers excel in self-reflection which increases their understanding of the factors that influence their performance. As a result, they are better at defining current and future tasks consistent with their current knowledge, skills, and abilities (Hacker, 2003). Moreover, it protects them from hubris, which refers to the combination of overconfidence and excessive optimism (Hayward et al., 2006). Metacognition is a skill that is crucial for mental simulations – creating a mental image of the result of future actions. This allows them to be more flexible and adapt the course of action to changing situations (Hogarth, 2001). Finally, deliberate practice enhances intuition, also known as offline processing among cognitive scientists. The result is that expert mental performers who engage regularly in deliberate practice acquire enhanced access to a wealth of information in the long-term memory, as well as enhanced capacities to recognize complex information. This combination is also referred to as mature intuition (Baylor, 2001).

One important aspect of being a corporate mental performer is the fast paced environment they work in, characterized by ambiguity, uncertainty, and high risks, which does not allow them to engage in long periods of deliberate practice. Entrepreneurs and business leaders do not specialize in one specific domain, such as an athlete, musician, or researcher. Similarly to elite military performers, they are generalists, not specialists, which makes it difficult to pinpoint the exact skills that need to be trained by deliberate practice. In light of this, MacNamara and colleagues (Macnamara et al., 2014) performed a large meta-analysis on the correlation between deliberate practice and performance. Surprisingly, within the field of professions, there was no significant relation between deliberate practice and performance. Less than 1% of the variance in performance was explained by deliberate practice. This does not imply that deliberate practice has no value in corporate life. It does show there are definitely issues with the research methodologies, which were also raised by the authors: within corporate life, there is no clear definition on how to measure deliberate practice, there was no control over the level of previous knowledge and gained abilities compared to the specific skills that were measured in the studies (participants were already performing very well and didn't need deliberate practice to become better), the unpredictability of corporate life makes it more difficult to examine the effect of deliberate practice, and finally, methodological differences in measurement methods played a role. It is clear that there is a need to further explore, define, and develop research methodologies to evaluate the role of deliberate practice in corporate environments. However, we can assume that the main executive functions of the prefrontal cortex are necessary skills, even for generalists. The ability to use working memory optimally, to inhibit irrelevant information and show excellent self-control, the use of metacognition to constantly evaluate one's own performance in light of well-defined concrete future goals. As such, it is proposed by Baron and Henry (Baron & Henry, 2010) that these skills can be trained and enhanced in other areas than entrepreneurship, and transferred to the corporate environment. Moreover, vicarious learning, referring to the learning process that occurs through observation of the actions and outcomes of others, is another way for top mental performers in the corporate world to enhance their mental performance. This means that top mental performers in the corporate world can engage in deliberate practice by exposure to a large number of pertinent, realistic, and highly relevant examples. This can be comparable with certain routines and habits in other fields, like intervision in psychotherapy. We also see a similar form of learning within the field of chess masters, where they study the games of excellent players to learn from them and improve their own game.

An example of a company focusing on exactly this, is Rubicon in Belgium. They have built a community of entrepreneurs who come together every month and discuss specific difficulties in entrepreneurial life. Within a psychologically safe environment, small groups of five to six entrepreneurs discuss these topics under the guidance of an experienced facilitator/coach. During these group sessions, the model of "reflecting team" is used, which teaches the entrepreneurs to first ask observational questions and stay curious instead of immediately giving advice. Entrepreneurs are able to discuss cases and difficulties, as well as learn from one another. At the same time they also learn basic coaching skills they can use within their company and with their teams.

The role of affect

As described in Chapter 3 on ideal performance state, top mental performance will address emotion regulation in some way. Mental performance depends on our ability to use cognitive functions and skills and to enhance them in order to constantly evolve and grow in the way we perform. With regard to this, the concept of general mental ability, referring to the general information-processing capacity that results in reasoning, problem solving, and other higher-order thinking skills (Gottfredson, 1997), is strongly related to the cognitive recourses and skills previously described. For a long time, the main focus has been on general mental ability as the main predictor of mental performance and entrepreneurial success. However, in the last decades more attention has been paid to another skill that seems to be important for top mental performances, especially in a corporate or entrepreneurial environment, namely emotional intelligence (EI). Although the definitions used to investigate this concept still remain a topic of debate, it is clear that our affect – our feelings and emotions – impact our cognitive processes and as such, our mental performance. Originally, the concept of emotional intelligence was first introduced by Mayer and Salovey (Salovey & Mayer, 1990) as a concept that can be divided into four specific interrelated abilities (Ability-based model): first, the ability to *perceive emotions* within themselves and others. Second, facilitating thought, referring to the ability *to use emotions*, which is based on the knowledge about the impact of emotions on our thinking processes. This is important to facilitate problem-solving. Thirdly, the *ability to understand emotions*, which helps a person to understand the causes and consequences of emotions and how they develop over time. Fourthly, the *ability to manage emotions*, which is about regulating one's own and others' feelings to better attain specific goals (Salovey et al., 2004). There are, however, also trait-based models of EI, where EI is viewed as emotion-related dispositions, that determine the way people behave in emotional situations (Petrides et al., 2007). Besides these two approaches, there are so-called mixed models of EI, such as Bar-On´s Emotional Social Intelligence (ESI) model (Bar-On, 2006) which suggests that ESI is a multifactorial set of competencies, skills, and facilitators that determine how people express and understand themselves, understand and relate to others, and respond to daily situations. Goleman´s model of emotional competences (Boyatzis et al., 2000) is another mixed model, which includes other non-cognitive features like social skills, motivation, self-esteem, or personality aspects. Finally, integrative models of EI attempt to reconcile and combine different theoretical approaches to EI. Integrative EI models are, for instance, Mikolajczak, Quoidbach, Kotsou, and Nélis´s (Mikolajczak, 2009) tripartite model of EI, Fiori´s (Fiori, 2009) dual process approach to EI, or Joseph and Newman´s (Joseph & Newman, 2010) cascading model of EI. Independent from the theoretical approach or model, most of the EI experts agree that EI refers to measurable individual differences in experiencing and processing emotions and emotion-related information.

As mentioned before, corporate high mental performers work in environments characterized by unpredictability and rapid change, which are situations where affect has an impact on cognition and behaviour. In stressful situations, our emotions and feelings will have a stronger impact on the actions we take or the decisions we make (Phelps, 2006). Moreover, affect has been shown to influence our creativity, persuasion, decision-making and judgements, and the way we form relationships, all tasks and activities very relevant in the corporate world (Forgas & George, 2001). Recent studies have shown that people with higher EI are better at performing in high emotional situations, compared to those with a lower EI (Checa & Fernández-Berrocal, 2019; Megías et al., 2017). In other words, emotional intelligence is key in cognitive control processes, especially in situations characterized by a high emotional load. A recent meta-analysis also showed that EI is positively related to organizational commitment, organizational citizenship behaviour, job satisfaction, and job performance, and negatively related to job stress (Doğru, 2022).

One observation we can make is that top mental performers do not always understand the need to pay attention to their emotions. They see them as irrelevant or even an obstacle for performance. However, as our behaviour is often guided by emotions, especially in stressful situations, this means that by ignoring emotions, people are only using half of the data given by their body to make decisions. Moreover, when stress increases, the functioning of the prefrontal cortex is hampered and the emotional circuit in the brain becomes more dominant. This will then influence memory and cognitions. To understand emotions, to be able to reflect on them, instead of ignoring them, will give more freedom of choice as to the actual decision process and consequently behavioural response.

Being able to be conscious of emotions and reflect on them, does not imply the need to follow them or, as I have often heard, become "emotional". Again, a common misunderstanding about emotions lies in the difference between "being emotionally aware and transparent" and "being emotional". The latter is more related to expressing the emotional response without control or reflection. The first is about the capacity to feel emotions, reflect on them and use language to express them in a non-judgemental way, as well as having the language to explain where the emotion comes from and how it is related to the situation. If people are unaware of their emotions, the downside is that reactions or behaviour will occur that are directed towards short-term control and not long-term control and goals. Short-term control is often focused on immediate gratification or avoiding uncomfortable situations or feelings. With regard to high mental performers, research shows that leadership is a highly emotional process and the skill to manage one's own and other's emotions is crucial. Emotional intelligence plays an important role in three critical leadership outcomes (Walter et al., 2012): First, emotional intelligent has a positive impact on leader emergence. In other words, emotional intelligence is the most important factor in predicting whether or not a person takes the lead within his or her team. Second, emotional intelligence results in the actual exhibition of productive leadership behaviours. In other words, a higher emotional intelligence results in more transformation leadership behaviours. Third, emotional intelligence improves leadership effectiveness.

If we link this to mental skills, reflection and metacognition are crucial skills to be able to deal with emotion and show self-control. One interesting model within psychology that is often used to increase self-awareness, self-consciousness, and self-control, is the Rational Emotive Behavioural Training (REBT) (Ellis, 1995) model, originally developed by Albert Ellis as the Rational Emotive Therapy (RET) (Ellis, 1974). This model assumes that dysfunctional beliefs are the key for dysfunctional behaviour. As such, adjusting negative or disrupting self-talk is one of the key aspects of this model, which in turn impacts the appraisal process when confronted with a stressful event. This model uses the well-known ABC model to describe the internal information processing: "A" referring to an Adverse event or trigger, which is not the actual situation, but an interpretation of an observed situation. This is then followed by "B", the activation of certain rigid beliefs. These beliefs will have Consequences (C), both on an emotional, as well as a behavioural level.

Adverse Event (A) → Beliefs (B) → Emotion (C) → Behaviour (C) This model teaches us to reflect on the internal information process and become aware of more than just the input (A) and the output (behaviour, C). It makes us aware that our behaviour is influenced by our beliefs and consequently the emotions triggered by our beliefs and cognitions. The goal is not to change A in order to then change our behaviour, but rather to become conscious of disruptive negative and rigid cognitions and change those thinking patterns so as to create behaviour that is more aligned with our long-term goals.

Improving focus: the goal of mental performance training

The digital revolution has made it possible to become more efficient, minimizing distance and transmission times and thus improving our performances, but on the other hand it has created an environment that puts our attentional system under great pressure. More specifically, our capacity to stay focused and use our inhibition processes in order to deep dive in a work flow is at risk. It is shown that intensive digital media use results in a reduction of working memory capacity (Moisala et al., 2016), an increase in psychological problems such as anxiety and depression (Turkle , 2011), and has a negative impact on text comprehension while reading on screens (Uncapher et al., 2017). Heavy media multitaskers exhibit a decreased ability to inhibit irrelevant external stimuli or memory representations. As a result, heavy media multitaskers experience problems with their task switching ability. Moreover, heavy media multitaskers experience increased impulsivity, less empathy, more anxiety, and poorer memory function. This means that for top mental performers in the corporate world, where it is a necessity to work in an environment characterized by an overload of (digital) stimulation, the aim is to become an expert in focus management. To balance out the need to engage in this digital world, and use their finite cognitive resources as efficiently as possible. In order to do this, corporate performers have to become aware of the different obstacles for focus, mostly related to all aspects that put the core and higher level executive functions under pressure.

Interventions aimed at recovery and improving mental skills

As we mentioned before, high mental performers and entrepreneurs tend to perceive stressful situations more as challenges, rather than harmful. The appraisal process appears to be more positive, which reduces the aspect of negative stress. However, it is not because a situation is seen as challenging that the pure physiological strain on the nervous system is not present. Therefore a distinction must be made between the concept of stress as a negative state, and the concept of physiological stress referring to the continuing high arousal levels while performing. In light of the latter perspective, the need to recover and restore cognitive resources that drive our mental skills is an important topic. Corporate mental performers experience a high degree of engagement which is fuelled by a high degree of autonomy, meaningfulness, and personal identification with their work (Shir et al., 2019; Van Gelderen & Jansen, 2006; Wiklund et al., 2019). These concepts are typically related to the positive impact on mental performance (Stephan et al., 2020). However, in a high-performing corporate environment, this can also lead to being overly absorbed with their work. The result is a 24/7 activated mental performer, who is no longer capable of recovery, and as such is decreasing the optimal use of their mental skills.

Some of the described interventions to improve mental performance in the previous chapters have a twofold impact: they allow for efficient recovery and sharpen the executive functions necessary to perform optimally. In the following part we will describe some of these interventions that have been tested and evaluated within a corporate environment. However, as described previously, there is still a serious lack of research evaluating these strategies within a specific corporate environment. The programs that have been evaluated were focused on mindfulness, individual coaching, and emotional intelligence.

Yoga

Yoga has gained much interest as an intervention to improve stress management and general well-being. There are, however, no studies available on yoga as an intervention in a corporate context that evaluated the effects on mental performance. However, since stress management is an important aspect of mental performance, we will describe the main findings of the studies on stress regulation and general well-being.

All current studies incorporated the three main components of yoga: postural exercises, breathing control, and meditation (Puerto Valencia et al., 2019). There is a great variability with regard to the frequency and length of the training, going from once a week for a total period of six weeks, up to six sessions a week over a total period of six months. Furthermore, most studies had small sample seizes and an unclear risk of bias. In general yoga appears to have a positive effect on stress but there is a need for more studies with larger sample sizes. Since this book is mainly focused on the top mental performer, we have to point out that there are no studies at the moment that evaluate the use of this technique within this specific corporate population. For more information about yoga as a performance-enhancing tool, we refer to Chapter 5.

Mindfulness

As described in Chapter 5, mindfulness is a promising tool to improve mental performance. Within a corporate environment it has gained interest because of the positive effects on attention, mood, and stress regulation (Tang & Posner, 2014). Mindfulness intervention programs in the workplace result in a reduction of mental health symptoms related to decreased performance, such as anxiety, stress, and burnout (Johnson et al., 2020). It is a strategy that helps regulate stress and as such will have an impact on mental performance. Furthermore, mindfulness training also has an impact on group functioning by having a positive effect on relationship and performance within a team (Yu & Zellmer-Bruhn, 2018). However, there is still a lack of research into the specific improvements of mental performance in a corporate environment. In order to truly become a standard technique within organizations, it is necessary to provide clear scientific evidence of the effects on job performance, more specifically on the cognitive functions such as the executive functions, sustained attention, emotion regulation, and stress management within a specific corporate context (Passmore, 2019). Furthermore, the concrete application and implementation of easy-to-use mindfulness exercises within a corporate working environment need to be evaluated.

Individual or executive coaching

Executive coaching refers to an individualized approach to support leaders improve their capabilities, enhance their effectiveness, and maximize their personal and professional potential in their organization (Richardson, 2010; Williams & Lowman, 2018). The aim of executive coaching is to improve performance by facilitating continuous learning, providing emotional support and feedback. The current research on executive coaching shows a lack of consistency, possibly due to the different research designs and a varying outcomes evaluated. Theeboom (Theeboom et al., 2014) recently highlighted the need for defining relevant outcomes dimensions for executive coaching to tackle this inconsistency. In a recent meta-analysis on executive coaching, Nicolau and colleagues (Nicolau et al., 2023) used an outcome taxonomy based on the work of Bosco (Bosco et al., 2015) that divides executive coaching outcomes in five categories (see Figure 15.1). Executive coaching has a moderate positive effect on all outcome dimensions, with the strongest

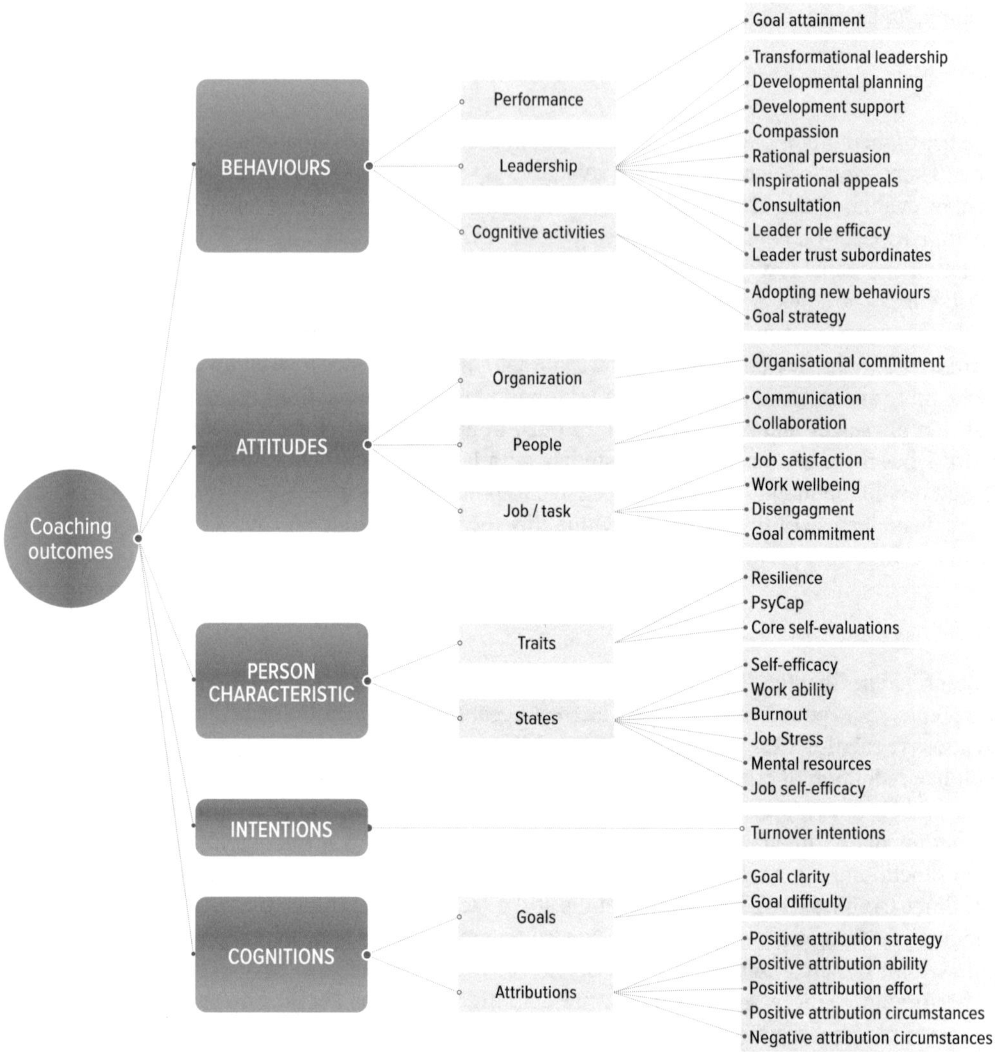

Figure 15.1 Executive coaching outcome classification.

effect for behaviour outcomes, and more specifically the cognitive activities within this category (Nicolau et al., 2023). Cognitive outcomes, such as developing planning and goal strategy, are essential in promoting change on a behavioural level. Executive coaching has positive effects on specific outcomes such as goal attainment, self-efficacy, psychological capital, and resilience. Given the role of all these concepts within mental performance, executive coaching seems a very strong intervention for high mental performers in a corporate context to improve their mental performance.

However, executive coaching should not solely focus on mental performance, but also try to implement aspects of mental health. The solution-focused cognitive-behavioural framework is an approach that implements both approaches (Grant, 2017). It uses the performance/well-being matrix (Figure 15.2). The two orthogonal dimensions in this model are (1) performance (high–low), and (2) well-being (high–low), which results in four quadrants.

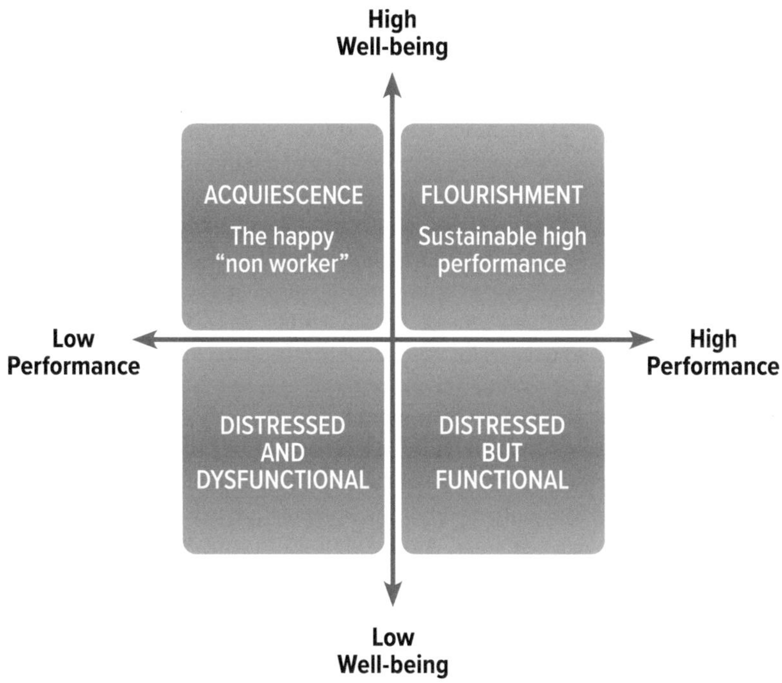

Figure 15.2 Performance/well-being matrix.

The distressed but functional corporate performer is characterized by high performance but low mental well-being. Performance in this quadrant can range from average to high performance, while mental well-being can vary from moderately distressed to very high distress. In order to identify possible mental health problems, a thorough clinical or counselling education is necessary, because the presence of anxiety or depressive symptoms might be difficult in this group (Cavanagh, 2005). The goal of executive coaching in this quadrant is reducing distress levels and enhancing well-being, while maintaining performance levels.

If mental well-being is not tackled or improved, people within this quadrant can shift towards the left, the distressed and dysfunctional performer.

The distressed and dysfunctional mental performer can be found in the left bottom quadrant and is characterized by low work engagement, the presence of severe mental health issues, as well as high levels of physical and mental exhaustion. Given the presence of severe mental health issues, a referral to a licensed psychotherapist is often necessary.

The happy "non-worker" is characterized by a high level of well-being, but lacking a high level of performance. There is a lack of commitment and mental effort and there is a lack of engagement with the goals of the organization. However, this quadrant can also be seen a "break" for the high performer with low mental health. The need for recovery after intense periods of stress and performance is well known, as such allowing people to stay in the Acquiescent zone for a short period of time, can have a beneficial effect on long-term high performance, as well as improvement of mental well-being. The main objective for the coach is to recognize when mental performers need to move into or out of this quadrant. A low performer will need to receive coaching focused on increasing mental performance to move towards the upper right quadrant, while high performers, especially those characterized by a high degree of perfectionism, should move into this quadrant and become more aware of the need of recovery. Coaching focused on rest, sleep and stress management techniques can be helpful.

Finally, individuals in *the **flourishing quadrant***, which equals sustainable high performance, are characterized by a high level of engagement, they find their work meaningful and are able to maintain positive relationships with colleagues. However, sustainable high performance can be related to an increase in quantity of work, but also a focus on improving quality of work. Corporate performers within this quadrant are often in need or searching for challenges, growth, and development. The goal of executive coaching is to first identify possible obstacles for the aspirations and ambitions of the mental performer. Several organizational characteristics are at play, such as the level of bureaucracy, organizational values, work culture, etc. Secondly, it is important to understand that it is impossible to stay in this quadrant all the time. A fluctuation in performance levels should be allowed and accepted. When to move out, and how to move back in are necessary coaching topics for people within this quadrant. Thirdly, and maybe most importantly, organizations should realize that not all employees can be or stay all the time in this quadrant. A sustainable high-performance culture within an organization is characterized by low levels of distress, fatigue, and burnout, for which only a part of the organization needs to reside in this fourth quadrant. Furthermore, realistic goals, coaching, and psychological support for both mental health as well as mental performance, ideally are in place to support individual and organizational growth.

Improving emotional intelligence

As previously discussed, Emotional Intelligence has an impact on mental performance through the ability to recognize and regulate emotions, hence improving self-control, a necessary skill for corporate high mental performers. This has given rise to an increase in EI interventions. However, there still exist quite some differences between the studies depending on the model of EI that is used: ability-based, trait-based, or mixed models. A recent meta-analysis (Hodzic et al., 2018) showed that EI interventions have moderate effects on actual EI, with a higher efficacy of ability-based interventions, compared to trait or mixed interventions. With regard to the content, an EI intervention should incorporate sessions that focus on the different EI abilities, with a combination of group workshops, individual sessions, and role-playing to improve skills. A recent study (Gilar-Corbi et al., 2019) used a program of seven weeks with an individual approach, however, they failed to improve two dimensions of EI, namely interpersonal and adaptability skills. This possibly means that the seven-week training was enough to improve the intrapersonal skills and awareness of their own emotions, but that the interpersonal skills need more training. As such we advise to implement EI training that combines both knowledge and exercises over a longer time period, with frequent follow-ups.

Concluding remarks

The corporate world demands excellent mental performance, but lacks an individualized evidence-based approach to support the high performers. There are definitely interesting initiatives that try to fill the current gap between scientific knowledge and real-life implementation. However, as is concluded in many chapters of the present handbook, research designs are not always consistent, there is a lack of control groups, methodological aspects are not described in detail, or different techniques are used for the same outcome (e.g., different breathing techniques between studies). Moreover, the current studies only focus on implementing one single technique to improve mental performance, but there is no study that evaluates a complete mental performance program. As was described at the beginning of this chapter, in the client's testimony, mental performance in corporate life relies on a complex interaction of different skills, abilities and strategies within very different contexts. As such, a mental performance program should implement all these components and allow the opportunity to be customized, based on the actual needs of mental performers. Moreover, performance improvement is limited, performance cannot be infinitely improved. The question arises whether organizations accept that there is a limit with regard to what a person can do or perform, as well as the fact that not everyone will be able to become a top mental performer. Furthermore, a workplace culture characterized by high psychological safety to ensure the process of improving mental performance with respect for mental health is a necessity (Edmondson, 2018). The delicate balance between mental health and sustainable mental performance is one of the biggest challenges in current corporate life, as in all high-performance environments. A responsibility lies within the organization itself to create a culture which allows for this.

Based on current literature and the needs of corporate life, a mental performance program should focus on:

1. Psycho-education on brain functioning and mental performance (we refer to Chapter 10 for a more detailed description on this kind of intervention).
2. The need for recovery in order to fully use the potential of the brain: workshops on rest and recovery are crucial, as well as individualized concrete applications and strategies, and a management approach that allows for the application of said knowledge and skills.
3. Focus strategies: how can we support the executive functions of the brain in order to completely focus when necessary?
4. Emotional Intelligence interventions: teach people to become more aware of their emotions, how they impact their behaviour and the behaviour of others, learn emotion regulation techniques, and engage in difficult conversations with emotional intelligence.
5. Stress management techniques: education on how high chronic stress decreases mental performance, and which techniques can be used to regulate stress. Here the emphasis should be on efficient activation of the parasympathetic nervous system. High mental performers are very good at accelerating, but often lack training in disconnection and relaxation. They have to become excellent in this area.
6. Mental health and well-being: strategies to improve mental health and the link with sustainable mental performance.
7. Cultural change and implementation of psychological safety.
8. If the program is for business leaders and the top mental performers of an organization, individual coaching will have the most impact, especially since it is often very difficult to organize group workshops or trainings, due to the different agendas. If the program focuses on middle managers and leaders, individual coaching is often too expensive and group interventions can be a better option.

What a mental performance program is NOT: a way to fix toxic management.

References

Arida, R. M., & Teixeira-Machado, L. (2021). The contribution of physical exercise to brain resilience. *Frontiers in Behavioral Neuroscience*, 14, 279.

Avey, J. B., Reichard, R. J., Luthans, F., & Mhatre, K. H. (2011). Meta-analysis of the impact of positive psychological capital on employee attitudes, behaviors, and performance. *Human Resource Development Quarterly*, *22*(2), 127–152.

Avrahami, Y., & Lerner, M. (2003). The effect of combat service and military rank on entrepreneurial careers: The case of Israeli MBA graduates. *Journal of Political & Military Sociology*, *31*(1), 97–118.

Bakker, A. B., Demerouti, E., & Euwema, M. C. (2005). Job resources buffer the impact of job demands on burnout. *Journal of Occupational Health Psychology*, *10*(2), 170.

Bar-On, R. (2006). The Bar-On model of emotional-social intelligence (ESI) 1. *Psicothema*, 18 suppl, 13–25.

Baron, R. A., Franklin, R. J., & Hmieleski, K. M. (2016). Why entrepreneurs often experience low, not high, levels of stress: The joint effects of selection and psychological capital. *Journal of Management*, *42*(3), 742–768. https://doi.org/10.1177/0149206313495411

Baron, R. A., & Henry, R. A. (2010). How entrepreneurs acquire the capacity to excel: Insights from research on expert performance. *Strategic Entrepreneurship Journal*, *4*(1), 49–65.

Baylor, A. L. (2001). A U-shaped model for the development of intuition by level of expertise. *New ideas in psychology*, *19*(3), 237–244.

Bosco, F. A., Aguinis, H., Singh, K., Field, J. G., & Pierce, C. A. (2015). Correlational effect size benchmarks. *Journal of Applied Psychology*, *100*(2), 431.

Boyatzis, R. E., Goleman, D., & Rhee, K. (2000). Clustering competence in emotional intelligence: Insights from the Emotional Competence Inventory (ECI). *Handbook of Emotional Intelligence*, *99*(6), 343–362.

Bretz Jr, R. D., Ash, R. A., & Dreher, G. F. (1989). Do people make the place? An examination of the attraction-selection-attrition hypothesis. *Personnel Psychology*, *42*(3), 561–581.

Burkhalter, T. M., & Hillman, C. H. (2011). A narrative review of physical activity, nutrition, and obesity to cognition and scholastic performance across the human lifespan. *Advances in Nutrition*, *2*(2), 201S–206S.

Buttner, E. H. (1992). Entrepreneurial stress: Is it hazardous to your health? *Journal of Managerial Issues*, *4*, 223–240.

Caldwell, J. A., Caldwell, J. L., Thompson, L. A., & Lieberman, H. R. (2019). Fatigue and its management in the workplace. *Neuroscience & Biobehavioral Reviews*, *96*, 272–289.

Cardon, M. S, Wincent, J, Singh, J., & Drnovsek, M. (2009). The Nature and Experience of Entrepreneurial Passion, *Academy of Management review*, 34, 511–532.

Cavanagh, M. (2005). Mental health issues and challenging clients in executive coaching. *Evidence-Based Coaching*, *1*, 21–36.

Chan, T., Wang, I., & Ybarra, O. (2021). Leading and managing the workplace: The role of executive functions. *Academy of Management Perspectives*, *35*(1), 142–164.

Chauntry, A. J., Bishop, N. C., Hamer, M., Kingsnorth, A. P., Chen, Y.-L., & Paine, N. J. (2022). Sedentary behaviour is associated with heightened cardiovascular, inflammatory and cortisol reactivity to acute psychological stress. *Psychoneuroendocrinology*, *141*, 105756.

Checa, P., & Fernández-Berrocal, P. (2019). Cognitive control and emotional intelligence: Effect of the emotional content of the task. Brief reports. *Frontiers in Psychology*, *10*, 195.

Cherniss, C., Grimm, L. G., & Liautaud, J. P. (2010). Process-designed training: A new approach for helping leaders develop emotional and social competence. *Journal of Management Development*, *29*(5), 413–431.

Colvin, G. (2010). *Talent is Overrated: What Really Separates World-Class Performers from Everybody Else*. Penguin.

Crecente, F., Sarabia, M., & Teresa del Val, M. (2021). The hidden link between entrepreneurship and military education. *Technological Forecasting and Social Change*, *163*. https://doi.org/10.1016/j.techfore.2020.120429

Cristofori, I., Cohen-Zimerman, S., & Grafman, J. (2019). Executive functions. *Handbook of Clinical Neurology*, 163, 197–219.

Debarnot, U., Sperduti, M., Di Rienzo, F., & Guillot, A. (2014). Experts bodies, experts minds: How physical and mental training shape the brain. *Frontiers in Human Neuroscience*, *8*, 280.

Del Missier, F., Mäntylä, T., & De Bruin, W. B. (2012). Decision-making competence, executive functioning, and general cognitive abilities. *Journal of Behavioral Decision Making*, *25*(4), 331–351.

Diamond, A. (2013). Executive functions. *Annual Review of Psychology*, *64*, 135–168.

Doğru, Ç. (2022). A meta-analysis of the relationships between emotional intelligence and employee outcomes. *Frontiers in Psychology*, *13*, 611348.

Edmondson, A. C. (2018). *The fearless organization: Creating psychological safety in the workplace for learning, innovation, and growth*. John Wiley & Sons.

Ellis, A. (1974). *Rational-emotive theory: Albert Ellis.*

Ellis, A. (1995). Changing rational-emotive therapy (RET) to rational emotive behavior therapy (REBT). *Journal of Rational-Emotive & Cognitive-Behavior Therapy* 13, 85–89.

Ericsson, K. A. (2006). The influence of experience and deliberate practice on the development of superior expert performance. *The Cambridge Handbook of Expertise and Expert Performance*, *38*(685-705), 2–2.

Ericsson, K. A., Hoffman, R. R., & Kozbelt, A. (2018). *The Cambridge handbook of expertise and expert performance*. Cambridge University Press.

Eslami, A., Nassif, N. T., & Lal, S. (2023). Neuropsychological performance and cardiac autonomic function in blue-and white-collar workers: A psychometric and heart rate variability evaluation. *International Journal of Environmental Research and Public Health*, *20*(5), 4203.

Fernandez-Duque, D., Baird, J. A., & Posner, M. I. (2000). Executive attention and metacognitive regulation. *Consciousness and Cognition*, *9*(2), 288–307.

Fiori, M. (2009). A new look at emotional intelligence: A dual-process framework. *Personality and Social Psychology Review*, *13*(1), 21–44.

Florent-Treacy, E., & Manzoni, J.-F. (2012). *Stress and the city (B). Antonio Horta Osorio*, CEO Lloyds Banking Group. INSEAD Case Study.

Forgas, J. P., & George, J. M. (2001). Affective influences on judgments and behavior in organizations: An information processing perspective. *Organizational Behavior and Human Decision Processes*, *86*(1), 3–34.

Fultz, N. E., Bonmassar, G., Setsompop, K., Stickgold, R. A., Rosen, B. R., Polimeni, J. R., & Lewis, L. D. (2019). Coupled electrophysiological, hemodynamic, and cerebrospinal fluid oscillations in human sleep. *Science*, *366*(6465), 628–+. https://doi.org/10.1126/science.aax5440

Gilar-Corbi, R., Pozo-Rico, T., Sánchez, B., & Castejón, J.-L. (2019). Can emotional intelligence be improved? A randomized experimental study of a business-oriented EI training program for senior managers. *PloS One*, *14*(10), e0224254.

Gombos, V. A. (2006). The cognition of deception: The role of executive processes in producing lies. *Genetic, Social, and General Psychology Monographs*, *132*(3), 197–214.

Gotlib, I. H., & Joormann, J. (2010). Cognition and depression: Current status and future directions. *Annual Review of Clinical Psychology, 6*, 285–312.

Gottfredson, L. S. (1997). Why g matters: The complexity of everyday life. *Intelligence*, *24*(1), 79–132.

Grant, A. M. (2017). Solution-focused cognitive–behavioral coaching for sustainable high performance and circumventing stress, fatigue, and burnout. *Consulting Psychology Journal: Practice and Research*, *69*(2), 98.

Hacker, W. (2003). Action regulation theory: A practical tool for the design of modern work processes? *European Journal of Work and Organizational Psychology*, *12*(2), 105–130.

Halbesleben, J. R. B., & Bowler, Wm. M. (2007). Emotional exhaustion and job performance: The mediating role of motivation. *Journal of Applied Psychology*, *92*(1), 93–106. https://doi.org/10.1037/0021-9010.92.1.93

Hayward, M. L., Shepherd, D. A., & Griffin, D. (2006). A hubris theory of entrepreneurship. *Management Science*, *52*(2), 160–172.

Hodzic, S., Scharfen, J., Ripoll, P., Holling, H., & Zenasni, F. (2018). How efficient are emotional intelligence trainings: A meta-analysis. *Emotion Review*, *10*(2), 138–148.

Hofmann, W., Gschwendner, T., Friese, M., Wiers, R. W., & Schmitt, M. (2008). Working memory capacity and self-regulatory behavior: Toward an individual differences perspective on behavior determination by automatic versus controlled processes. *Journal of Personality and Social Psychology*, *95*(4), 962.

Hogarth, R. M. (2001). *Educating intuition*. University of Chicago Press.

Jackson, M. L., Gunzelmann, G., Whitney, P., Hinson, J. M., Belenky, G., Rabat, A., & Van Dongen, H. P. (2013). Deconstructing and reconstructing cognitive performance in sleep deprivation. *Sleep Medicine Reviews*, *17*(3), 215–225.

Johnson, K. R., Park, S., & Chaudhuri, S. (2020). Mindfulness training in the workplace: Exploring its scope and outcomes. *European Journal of Training and Development*, *44*(4/5), 341–354.

Jonsdottir, I. H., Nordlund, A., Ellbin, S., Ljung, T., Glise, K., Währborg, P., Sjörs, A., & Wallin, A. (2017). Working memory and attention are still impaired after three years in patients with stress-related exhaustion. *Scandinavian Journal of Psychology*, *58*(6), 504–509.

Joseph, D. L., & Newman, D. A. (2010). Emotional intelligence: An integrative meta-analysis and cascading model. *Journal of Applied Psychology*, *95*(1), 54.

Kersemaekers, W., Rupprecht, S., Wittmann, M., Tamdjidi, C., Falke, P., Donders, R., Speckens, A., & Kohls, N. (2018). A workplace mindfulness intervention may be associated with improved psychological well-being and productivity. A preliminary field study in a company setting. *Frontiers in Psychology*, *9*, 195.

Krausman, A. S., Crowell, H. P., & Wilson, R. M. (2002). *The effects of physical exertion on cognitive performance*. Army Research Laboratory.

LePine, J., LePine, M., & Jackson, C. (2004). Challenge and hindrance stress: Relationships with exhaustion, motivation to learn, and learning performance. *Journal of Applied Psychology*, *89*(5), 883–891. https://doi.org/10.1037/0021-9010.89.5.883

Loehr, J., & Schwartz, T. (2001). The making of a corporate athlete. *Harvard Business Review*, *79*(1), 120–129.

Luthans, F., Avolio, B. J., Walumbwa, F. O., & Li, W. (2005). The psychological capital of Chinese workers: Exploring the relationship with performance. *Management and Organization Review*, *1*(2), 249–271.

Macnamara, B. N., Hambrick, D. Z., & Oswald, F. L. (2014). Deliberate practice and performance in music, games, sports, education, and professions: A meta-analysis. *Psychological Science*, *25*(8), 1608–1618.

Masicampo, E. J., & Baumeister, R. F. (2011). Unfulfilled goals interfere with tasks that require executive functions. *Journal of Experimental Social Psychology*, *47*(2), 300–311.

Megías, A., Gutiérrez-Cobo, M. J., Gómez-Leal, R., Cabello, R., & Fernández-Berrocal, P. (2017). Performance on emotional tasks engaging cognitive control depends on emotional intelligence abilities: An ERP study. *Scientific Reports*, *7*(1), 16446.

Mikolajczak, M. (2009). Going beyond the ability-trait debate: The three-level model of emotional intelligence. *E-Journal of Applied Psychology*, *5*(2), 25–31.

Moisala, M., Salmela, V., Hietajärvi, L., Salo, E., Carlson, S., Salonen, O., Lonka, K., Hakkarainen, K., Salmela-Aro, K., & Alho, K. (2016). Media multitasking is associated with distractibility and increased prefrontal activity in adolescents and young adults. *NeuroImage*, *134*, 113–121.

Molden, D. C., & Dweck, C. S. (2006). Finding" meaning" in psychology: A lay theories approach to self-regulation, social perception, and social development. *American Psychologist*, *61*(3), 192.

Morris, M. H. (1998). *Entrepreneurial Intensity: Sustainable advantages for individuals, organizations and societies*. Quorum Books.

Mueller, S., & Thomas, A. (2001). Culture and entrepreneurial potential: A nine country study of locus of control and innovativeness. *Journal of Business Venturing*, *16*(1), 51–75. https://doi.org/10.1016/S0883-9026(99)00039-7

Nicolau, A., Candel, O. S., Constantin, T., & Kleingeld, A. (2023). The effects of executive coaching on behaviors, attitudes, and personal characteristics: A meta-analysis of randomized control trial studies. *Frontiers in Psychology*, *14*, 1089797.

Park, J., & Moghaddam, B. (2017). Impact of anxiety on prefrontal cortex encoding of cognitive flexibility. *Neuroscience*, *345*, 193–202.

Passmore, J. (2019). Mindfulness in organizations (part 1): A critical literature review. *Industrial and Commercial Training*, *51*(2), 104–113.

Pattyn, N. (2020). *Keynote sessions 'Mental Performance'*. 2nd International SOF Human Performance Symposium, Quebec, Ca.

Peterson, S. J., Luthans, F., Avolio, B. J., Walumbwa, F. O., & Zhang, Z. (2011). Psychological capital and employee performance: A latent growth modeling approach. *Personnel Psychology*, *64*(2), 427–450.

Petrides, K. V., Pita, R., & Kokkinaki, F. (2007). The location of trait emotional intelligence in personality factor space. *British Journal of Psychology*, *98*(2), 273–289.

Phelps, E. A. (2006). Emotion and cognition: Insights from studies of the human amygdala. *Annu. Rev. Psychol.*, *57*, 27–53.

Philip, P., Sagaspe, P., Prague, M., Tassi, P., Capelli, A., Bioulac, B., Commenges, D., & Taillard, J. (2012). Acute versus chronic partial sleep deprivation in middle-aged people: Differential effect on performance and sleepiness. *Sleep*, *35*(7), 997–1002.

Ployhart, R. E., Weekley, J. A., & Baughman, K. (2006). The structure and function of human capital emergence: A multilevel examination of the attraction-selection-attrition model. *Academy of Management Journal*, *49*(4), 661–677.

Puerto Valencia, L. M., Weber, A., Spegel, H., Bögle, R., Selmani, A., Heinze, S., & Herr, C. (2019). Yoga in the workplace and health outcomes: A systematic review. *Occupational Medicine*, *69*(3), 195–203.

Radvansky, G. A., Copeland, D. E., & Von Hippel, W. (2010). Stereotype activation, inhibition, and aging. *Journal of Experimental Social Psychology*, *46*(1), 51–60.

Rasch, B., & Born, J. (2013). About sleep's role in memory. *Physiological Reviews*. 93(2):681–766

Richardson, T. M. (2010). *Solution-focused brief coaching as an executive coaching intervention: A quasi-experimental study*. University of Phoenix.

Rolls, E. T., Cheng, W., Du, J., Wei, D., Qiu, J., Dai, D., Zhou, Q., Xie, P., & Feng, J. (2020). Functional connectivity of the right inferior frontal gyrus and orbitofrontal cortex in depression. *Social Cognitive and Affective Neuroscience*, *15*(1), 75–86. https://doi.org/10.1093/scan/nsaa014

Sabia, S., Fayosse, A., Dumurgier, J., van Hees, V. T., Paquet, C., Sommerlad, A., Kivimäki, M., Dugravot, A., & Singh-Manoux, A. (2021). Association of sleep duration in middle and old age with incidence of dementia. *Nature Communications*, *12*(1), 2289. https://doi.org/10.1038/s41467-021-22354-2

Salovey, P., Caruso, D., & Mayer, J. D. (2004). Emotional intelligence in practice. In: Linley, P.A., Joseph, S., eds. *Positive Psychology in Practice*, (pp. 447–463) John Wiley & Sons.

Salovey, P., & Mayer, J. D. (1990). Emotional intelligence. *Imagination, Cognition and Personality*, *9*(3), 185–211.

Schaufeli, W. B., Bakker, A. B., & Van Rhenen, W. (2009). How changes in job demands and resources predict burnout, work engagement, and sickness absenteeism. *Journal of Organizational Behavior: The International Journal of Industrial, Occupational and Organizational Psychology and Behavior*, *30*(7), 893–917.

Schindehutte, M., Morris, M., & Allen, J. (2006). Beyond achievement: Entrepreneurship as extreme experience. *Small Business Economics*, *27*(4-5), 349–368. https://doi.org/10.1007/s11187-005-0643-6

Sherman, G. D., Lee, J. J., Cuddy, A. J., Renshon, J., Oveis, C., Gross, J. J., & Lerner, J. S. (2012). Leadership is associated with lower levels of stress. *Proceedings of the National Academy of Sciences*, *109*(44), 17903–17907.

Shir, N., Nikolaev, B. N., & Wincent, J. (2019). Entrepreneurship and well-being: The role of psychological autonomy, competence, and relatedness. *Journal of Business Venturing*, *34*(5), 105875.

Slaski, M., & Cartwright, S. (2003). Emotional intelligence training and its implications for stress, health and performance. *Stress and Health*, *19*(4), 233–239.

Stephan, U., Tavares, S. M., Carvalho, H., Ramalho, J. J., Santos, S. C., & Van Veldhoven, M. (2020). Self-employment and eudaimonic well-being: Energized by meaning, enabled by societal legitimacy. *Journal of Business Venturing*, *35*(6), 106047.

Tang, Y.-Y., & Posner, M. I. (2014). Training brain networks and states. *Trends in Cognitive Sciences*, *18*(7), 345–350.

Tavoian, D., & Craighead, D. H. (2023). Deep breathing exercise at work: Potential applications and impact. *Frontiers in Physiology*, *14*, 23.

Theeboom, T., Beersma, B., & van Vianen, A. E. (2014). Does coaching work? A meta-analysis on the effects of coaching on individual level outcomes in an organizational context. *The Journal of Positive Psychology*, *9*(1), 1–18.

Turkle, S. (2011). *Alone together: Why we expect more from technology and less from each other*. Basic Books.

Ucbasaran, D., Westhead, P., & Wright, M. (2009). The extent and nature of opportunity identification by experienced entrepreneurs. *Journal of Business Venturing*, *24*(2), 99–115.

Uncapher, M. R., Lin, L., Rosen, L. D., Kirkorian, H. L., Baron, N. S., Bailey, K., Cantor, J., Strayer, D. L., Parsons, T. D., & Wagner, A. D. (2017). Media multitasking and cognitive, psychological, neural, and learning differences. *Pediatrics*, *140*(2), S62–S66.

Van Gelderen, M., & Jansen, P. (2006). Autonomy as a start-up motive. *Journal of Small Business and Enterprise Development*, *13*(1), 23–32.

Walker, M. P., & Stickgold, R. (2010). Overnight alchemy: Sleep-dependent memory evolution. *Nature Reviews Neuroscience*, *11*(3), 218–218.

Walter, F., Humphrey, R. H., & Cole, M. S. (2012). Unleashing leadership potential: Toward an evidence-based management of emotional intelligence. *Organizational Dynamics*, *41*(3), 212–219.

Wan, E. W., & Sternthal, B. (2008). Regulating the effects of depletion through monitoring. *Personality and Social Psychology Bulletin*, *34*(1), 32–46.

Wardlow, L. (2013). Individual differences in speakers' perspective taking: The roles of executive control and working memory. *Psychonomic Bulletin & Review*, *20*, 766–772.

Wiklund, J., Nikolaev, B., Shir, N., Foo, M.-D., & Bradley, S. (2019). Entrepreneurship and well-being: Past, present, and future. *Journal of Business Venturing*, *34*(4), 579–588.
Williams, J. S., & Lowman, R. L. (2018). The efficacy of executive coaching: An empirical investigation of two approaches using random assignment and a switching-replications design. *Consulting Psychology Journal: Practice and Research*, *70*(3), 227.
Winne, P. H. (1997). Experimenting to bootstrap self-regulated learning. *Journal of Educational Psychology*, *89*(3), 397.
Wright, M., Robbie, K., & Ennew, C. (1997). Venture capitalists and serial entrepreneurs. *Journal of Business Venturing*, *12*(3), 227–249.
Yoo, S.-S., Gujar, N., Hu, P., Jolesz, F. A., & Walker, M. P. (2007). The human emotional brain without sleep—A prefrontal amygdala disconnect. *Current Biology*, *17*(20), R877–R878.
Yu, L., & Zellmer-Bruhn, M. (2018). Introducing team mindfulness and considering its safeguard role against conflict transformation and social undermining. *Academy of Management Journal*, *61*(1), 324–347.
Zimmerman, B. J. (2006). Development and adaptation of expertise: The role of self-regulatory processes and beliefs. *The Cambridge Handbook of Expertise and Expert Performance*, *186*, 705–722.

16 Psychological Support for Olympic Athletes

Paul Wylleman

From its early beginnings at the end of the 19th and the beginning of the 20th century (Seiler & Wylleman, 2009) the scientific discipline of sport psychology has focused on the psychological aspects of sport, physical activity, and physical education. Especially in Europe and North America research and publications treated themes such as personality and character development, the relation between physical strain and mental performance, pathological effects of physical activity, and contributions to training and competition. In competitive sport, and more particularly at the Olympic level, it is interesting to note that Pierre de Coubertin, the founder of the Olympic Games of the modern era, is reported not only to have introduced the term "sport psychology" (*psychologie sportive* in French) in 1900, but also to have organized the first international congress on sport psychology in 1913 in Lausanne, Switzerland (Comité International Olympique, 1913 in Nitsch et al., 2000). It is in fact at the Olympic level that the role of psychology recently became front page news. Not only due to the fact that one of its most prominent athletes, Simone Biles, decided to opt out of a team final due to a mental challenge, but also due to the occurrence of the COVID-pandemic and its impact on the mental health (MH) of athletes, coaches, and staff members. As such the 2020 Tokyo Olympic Games actually became labelled as the "mental games" and as a "game-changer in how we view athletes' mental health" (CNN, 2021). Taking this increased focus on the role of the mental side of performing at the Olympic Games (OGs) in general, and on the provision of psychological support to Olympic athletes in particular, this chapter will provide an overview of some of the recent developments in the application of sport psychology at Olympic level and in view of the OGs. We will not address performance psychology, as this is extensively covered in the other chapters: our focus will be on the relationship between mental performance and mental health, a topic discussed in detail in Chapter 12.

Psychologists' support provision at Olympic level

As the scientific field of sport psychology developed and started to focus on high-level competition sport, three major domains received sport psychologists' attention, namely the talent and career development (e.g., Collins et al., 2019; Stambulova & Wylleman, 2019), the performing (e.g., Cotterill et al., 2010; Kukidome et al., 2021), and the mental health and welfare (e.g., Moesch et al., 2018; Purcell et al., 2021) of athletes. While in research the focus was generally on one of these three domains, from an applied perspective a stronger emphasis on their interrelationship and interactions was found to be crucial in optimizing the provision of psychological services at Olympic level (e.g., Wylleman, 2019; Wylleman et al. 2015). This applied emphasis led to several major developments in support provision which impact the role of psychologists.[1] In the next sections three such developments and their application at Olympic level will be described.

DOI: 10.4324/9781003378969-19

A holistic and life span approach to support provision at Olympic level

A first development consists of the fact that psychology services shifted gradually from focusing on one theme (e.g., performance enhancement) or one specific challenge (e.g., optimizing the pre-competition mental routine) to using a holistic and life span approach in order to take a broader focus on some of the different challenges to be tackled by Olympic athletes at the same time or in close concurrence. This holistic and life span perspective allows for a broader overview of the challenges Olympic athletes may face. Representing this perspective, the Holistic Athletic Career (HAC) model (Wylleman et al., 2020) provides an overview of major career stages (i.e., initiation, development, mastery, discontinuation) as well as of several (normative) career transitions (e.g., junior-to-senior, initial participation at the OGs, end-of-career) athletes will face at different domains of development (i.e. athletic, psychological, psychosocial, academic and vocational, financial, legal). The HAC model also allows to identify the possible impact of non-normative transitions (i.e., which some elite-level athletes may experience) on the different domains of development such as an injury, initiating a dual career as elite student-athlete, or starting a family. Each of these different stages and transitions can in fact be characterized by the specific challenges or barriers they pose to athletes. To enhance their possibilities for a continued development, athletes will require strategies and resources to cope with these possible challenges and barriers in order (Stambulova et al., 2020). As these challenges may occur at each of the different domains of development in concurrence or in close sequence to each other, a continued process of coping may be essential. This process may then impact not only athletes' development in each of the different domains, but also their mental health (MH) as this coping may have a debilitating effect or even end up in a mental crisis. For example, final-year junior athletes may find themselves frustrated, anxious, and stressed due to increased (and perhaps self-imposed) performance expectations to make it to the senior level, while at the same time being faced with their transition from secondary education to university, changing from home to a student home, the accompanying changes in peer group relationships with students and new friends, the financial requirements to study at university, the changing of coaches and training venues, and of course the combination of an academic study and elite sport. These challenges may, possibly in combination with physical challenges (e.g., overload, overtraining), lead to specific MH challenges or even (sub-)clinical psychological problems (Kegelaers et al., 2022; Wylleman et al., 2015).

This holistic life span approach has been used in providing psychology support to athletes and coaches in view of performing at the OGs. Considering the OGs as a non-normative transition for elite athletes, the approach consisted of allowing athletes to prospectively describe their cognitive, affective, and behavioural responses to challenges and opportunities they perceived at four levels of development (i.e., athletic, psychological, psychosocial, academic/vocational) during the three major specific phases related to the Olympic experience, namely prior, during, and after the OGs. These phases and levels of development were delineated in collaboration with the head coach and the staff so as to capture the most important aspects for support provision. This collaboration ensured that all relevant within-transitions that could have a psychological impact on athletes were also included. Within transitions prior to the OGs included, for example, the different international competitions which could lead to Olympic qualification as delineated by the international federation; once this qualification was met, athletes could be pre-selected by their national Olympic Committee (i.e., named in the short-list for participation in the OGs); athletes on this short-list were then presented for accreditation as an athlete to compete at the OGs; and the departure from home to the base camp (i.e., the holding camp grouping all delegation members before travelling to the Olympic Village or the different Olympic competition venues). During the OGs within transitions were, for example, the arrival in the Olympic Village and settling down in the residence allotted to their Olympic team, getting acquainted with the Olympic Village, and using the training and competition venues. The changes perceived by athletes prior to the OGs included, for example, an increased training load and changes in sport technical training at athletic level; and an increased feeling of pride, self-confidence, as well as pressure from the media, combined with an exclusive focus on their sport at the psychological level. During the OGs athletes perceived boredom and pre-competition pressure at the psychological level as well as difficulty relating to other athletes or to their family at the psychosocial level. Finally, post-OGs athletes perceived the opportunity to take a long break away from competitions at athletic level; at the psychological level they perceived increased self-confidence and motivation to continue competing as a result of having achieved personal bests during the OGs; this was coupled with a feeling of being recognized as such by their family, public, and the media at the psychosocial level; and also an return to study or their professional job at academic and vocational level.

While understanding the role of psychology support during each phase separately (e.g., Birrer et al., 2012; Elsborg et al., 2015; Howells & Lucassen, 2018; Mitchell et al., 2021) remains beneficial, the added value of this combined dynamic and a holistic perspective for psychologists is that it provides for a more detailed insight into athletes' perceptions and the accompanying cognitions, affections, and behaviour. This allows psychologists (as well as the coach and staff) to understand, recognize, and provide situation-specific support – a type of support provision which is deemed essential when working at the Olympic level (e.g., Birrer et al., 2012; Elsborg et al., 2015), ensuring greater effectiveness and efficiency psychologists.

A dual continuum approach to mental health at Olympic level

A second development is related to the changing perspective on mental health (MH). More particularly, while MH has generally been represented as being bipolar with high positive MH and active mental illness being at opposite ends of the same continuum, the perspective has shifted towards a dual continua model (i.e., the continuum "high positive to low positive" and the continuum "absence or presence of mental illness"). While the bipolar continuum perspective assumed a person to be either mentally healthy or mentally ill, the dual continua perspective acknowledges that a person can still experience high levels of positive MH and well-being even with a measure of a mental illness present (Keyes, 2014). This model, which follows the WHO conceptualizations of MH (World Health Organization, 2001/2013), is now being used in research on athletes' MH (e.g., Kegelaers et al., 2022; Kuettel & Larsen, 2020; Perry et al., 2021). By enabling a stronger differentiation between athletes regarding their MH status (e.g., high positive MH with mental illness, low positive MH with no mental illness), more proactive MH interventions (e.g., MH literacy) are made feasible. Furthermore, information on MH (e.g., being resilient in performance contexts, supportive interpersonal relationships in career development, life satisfaction as an athlete) can now be distinguished from information on mental illness. In this way, this model contributes also to an integrated approach in the provision of psychology support services at Olympic level, for example, by establishing goals for sport psychologists as well as for counselling or clinical psychologists (Wylleman, 2022).

A first application of this dual continuum approach to MH is that it allows psychologists to provide more explicitly a proactive rather than (only) a reactive support to athletes. While this latter approach focuses on how to reduce mental illness symptoms, the proactive approach entails, for example, providing athletes with competences (i.e., knowledge, skills, attitude) to enhance their MH and to reduce the possibilities for mental illness symptoms. A first example is strengthening athletes' MH literacy and thus increase athletes' knowledge and beliefs about MH and MH problems. For example, the MH Literacy Workshop for elite dual career athletes (Kegelaers et al., 2022) consists of the following five steps: (a) talking about stigma with regard to MH, (b) providing information and asking questions about common myths and realities of MH, (c) discussing how is it to live with MH challenges, (d) a MH quiz, and (e) specific information about getting professional MH expert support. This approach is especially relevant for athletes who have a poor attitude towards understanding and recognizing MH issues, who have little knowledge about preventative strategies regarding MH disorders, and who are also uncertain about where to seek appropriate support (e.g., Breslin et al., 2017; Chow et al., 2021; Vella et al., 2021). Such a MH literacy workshop can, after having received the appropriate training, be led by the coach, staff member, or sport psychologist.

A second application is rooted in the holistic life span perspective. Based upon the challenges in the different career stages, athletes are initiated and trained in a set of psychological competences (i.e., knowledge, skills, attitude, experience) which facilitate their holistic development, enhance their performance, and strengthen their MH (Blijlevens, Elferink et al., 2018; Blijlevens, Wylleman et al., 2018). These competences include, for example, adapting to changes, taking decisions, focusing, persevering, problem-solving, being process-focused, setting and guarding own boundaries, self-confidence, performing under pressure, maintaining an optimal development, and self-reflection. As the type and number of challenges differs not only between each of the career stages but also between sport disciplines, coaches are trained to initiate and make their athletes stronger in specific psychological competences which are presented in a specific sequence and which are built one-upon-the-other. For example, in gymnastics such a sport-specific and multi-year development plan includes goal-orientation, problem-solving, adaptability to changes, taking decisions, performing under pressure as part of gymnasts' talent development. At the elite level, gymnasts' psychological competences of problem-solving, adaptability, taking decisions and performing under pressure are targeted. In beach volleyball communicating, optimal balancing of sport and other activities, and performing under pressure are put forward. This competency-building approach is fully integrated in athletes' multi-year multidimensional (e.g., physical, technical, mental) training process led and supervised by coaches. These coaches receive specialist education and training (via master classes, workshops), will have specific information (e.g., fact sheets, podcasts, videos) and tools (e.g., competency-specific observation tool) made available to them, and will be supported by sport psychologists to tackle issues arising in individual athletes' development and in the use of these competences.

A third application is directly related to the expertise of psychologists required in the provision of support to elite athletes. With the dual continua MH model as basis, it becomes clear that different specialists will be required to provide the appropriate support. When athletes' MH can be considered as "enhanced" (i.e., high positive MH with no mental illness) then sport psychologists can provide support in, for example, maintaining an optimal holistic development, maximizing level of performance, enabling fulfilling relationships, and continuously strengthening their (robust and rebound) resilience (Wylleman, 2023a). When athletes' MH is "challenged" (i.e., low positive MH with no mental illness) then not only the sport psychologist but also the counselling psychologist can provide appropriate expertise, for example, on the quality of interpersonal relationships between coach and athlete, or with regard to eating patterns. However, when athletes' MH is "reduced" (i.e., high positive MH with mental illness) (e.g., adverse alcohol use, anxiety attacks) or even "lacking" (i.e., low positive MH with mental illness) (e.g., eating disorder, post-traumatic stress disorder, autism spectrum disorder), then clinical psychologists, neuropsychologists, and psychiatrists will be required, with sport psychologists remaining available and attending the possible needs in development and/or performance. With 80% of consultations related to enhanced and challenged MH, and 20% of consultations related to mental illness, there is a clear need for psychologists with different specialized expertise (Gouttebarge et al., 2017; Wylleman, 2022).

An inter- and intradisciplinary approach to mental health at Olympic level

The "monodisciplinary" approach to support provision, whereby one type of (sport) scientific support expertise is provided directly to the athlete and/or coach, has been for a long time the standard approach to support provision in elite sport (e.g., the sport nutritionist working one-on-one with the athlete). Slowly this "specialist silo" approach has been developing into a "multidisciplinary" approach with different experts (e.g., medical doctor, sport physiotherapist, sport psychologist) supporting directly the athlete and/or coach (e.g., Van Slingerland et al., 2022). The step currently taken by support teams working with Olympic coaches and athletes is to have an interdisciplinary team (IDT) where different (sport) scientific experts collaborate and confer in order to present the coach or athlete with an integrated support plan. These experts may also positioned in a primary (e.g., medical doctor, physiotherapist, sport psychologist) and secondary circle (e.g., biomechanical expert, performance analyst, media officer) or in a performance coaching (e.g., head coach, sport technical staff) or performance management team (e.g., medical doctor, physiotherapist, psychologist) (Arnold et al., 2019; Meckbach et al., 2022). IDT members thus require, among others, competences to provide and apply their own expertise as well as to recognize the added value of the other IDT members, to ensure interaction and collaboration within the IDT, to communicate openly with each team member, to cope with possible intragroup processes (e.g., tunnel vision), and to accept the management and leadership of the expert – or the coach – leading the IDT (Burns & Collins, 2023; Verhaegen et al., 2020).

Applying the principle of an IDT to psychology support can lead to establishing an *intra*disciplinary team (IaDT) where psychologists with different expertise (e.g., sport psychologist, counselling psychologist, clinical psychologist, neuropsychologist) join their expertise (Wylleman, 2023). Although this type of support team seems relatively easy to constitute, the challenge is that these psychology experts may use not only different theoretical frameworks (e.g., performance enhancement, counselling) but also apply different time frames in their working relationship with athletes (e.g., short-term behavioural changes, long-term clinical therapy).

A second application of the IDT and the IaDT during the Olympic Games is when the Welfare Officer, as clinical sport psychologist, will be part of an IDT with the Chief Medical Officer, other medical doctors, different physiotherapists, a nutritionist, and a physiologist. At the same time, the Welfare Officer will have to coordinate and consult with other sport psychologists on-site or at home. This intradisciplinary collaboration is required in view of ensuring, among others, that all reasonable steps are taken to ensure the athletes' mental and physical well-being, to act as focal point for all matters related to mental health and well-being, and to provide support appropriate to the different types of MH as specified by the dual continua MH model.

Conclusions

The elite sport career requires athletes to be able to cope with a diversity of demands and challenges. As these occur at different levels of development and during different periods of development, it is clear that there is no one-size-fits-all type of support. As mental health is indeed part of an athlete's development and performance, psychologists with specialized expertise will be able to contribute in a structured and continuous way. As presented in this chapter this contribution can be based first upon a holistic and life span approach allowing consideration and focus on those concurrent challenges Olympic athletes may face throughout their athletic career, as well as on a stage-by-stage basis, and by providing for the development and use of psychological competences. Secondly, by using a multi-phase approach as depicted by the dual continua MH model rather than using the classical single continuum in considering Olympians' mental health and well-being. Third, by being integrated in an IDT as well as by taking up the required collaboration with other psychologists within an IaDT, thus broadening the provision of expertise at the Olympic level and ensuring high-quality psychology support provision prior, during, and after the Olympic Games. Finally, while absolutely required for Olympic athletes, this expertise should also be made available for coaches, staff members, and by extension to those of the members of the athletes' entourage (Kegelaers et al., 2021).

Note

1 The term 'psychologist' (single or plural) refers to a professional having acquired (at minimum) a Master degree in Psychology and can include a specialization in, for example, clinical or occupational psychology. The term 'sport psychologist' (single or plural) refers to a psychologist having specialized (e.g. at Master or post-graduate level) in sport psychology. Combinations are possible (e.g., clinical sport psychologist is a clinical psychologist with specialization in sport psychology) and are explicitly stated as such when specifically required. A sport psychologist generally focuses on performance enhancement while the clinical (sport) psychologist will generally focus on (sub-) clinical mental health issues. A sport psychologist without clinical education and training will refer (sub-) clinical mental health issues to a clinical (sport) psychologist. This may of course differ by country or by individual choice.

References

Arnold, R., Collington, S., Manley, H., Rees, S., Soanes, J., & Williams, M. (2019). "The Team Behind the Team": Exploring the organizational stressor experiences of sport science and management staff in elite sport. *Journal of Applied Sport Psychology, 31*, 7–26. https://doi.org/10.1080/10413200.2017.1407836

Birrer, D., Wetzel, J., Schmid, J., & Morgan, G. (2012). Analysis of sport psychology consultancy at three Olympic Games: Facts and figures. *Psychology of Sport and Exercise, 13*, 702–710. https://doi.org/10.1016/j.psychsport.2012.04.008

Blijlevens, S., Elferink-Gemser, M., Wylleman, P., Bool, K., & Visscher, C. (2018). Psychological characteristics and skills of top-level Dutch gymnasts in the initiation, development and mastery stages of the athletic career. *Psychology of Sport & Exercise, 38*, 202–210. https://doi.org/10.1016/j.psychsport.2018.07.001

Blijlevens, S., Wylleman, P., Bool, K., Elferink-Gemser, M., & Visscher, C. (2018). Acquisition and maintenance of excellence: The challenges faced by Dutch top-level gymnasts throughout different stages of athletic development. *Sport in Society, 23,* 577–594. https://doi.org/10.1080/17430437.2018.1524106

Breslin, G., Shannon, S., Haughey, T., Donnelly, P., & Leavey, G. (2017). A systematic review of interventions to increase awareness of mental health and well-being in athletes, coaches and officials. Breslin et al. *Systematic Reviews, 6*, 177.

Burns, A., & Collins, D. (2023). Interdisciplinary practice in performance sport: A scoping review of evidence of collaboration. *European Journal of Sport Science*. https://doi.org/10.1080/17461391.2023.2201812

Chow, G.M., Bird, M.D., Gabana, N.T., Cooper, B.T., & Swanbrow Becker, M.A. (2021). A Program to reduce stigma toward mental illness and promote mental health literacy and help-seeking in national collegiate athletic association division I student-athletes. *Journal of Clinical Sport Psychology, 15*, 185–205.

CNN (2021, August 8). Will Tokyo Olympics be a game-changer in how we view athletes' MH? https://eu.usatoday.com/story/sports/olympics/2021/08/08/tokyo-olympics-game-changer-athletes-and-mental-health/5523250001/

Collins, D., MacNamara, A., & Cruickshank, A. (2019). Research and practice in talent identification and development—some thoughts on the state of play. *Journal of Applied Sport Psychology, 31*, 340–351, https://doi.org/10.1080/10413200.2018.1475430

Comité International Olympique. (1913). *Congrès international de psychologie et physiologie sportives. [International congress of psychology and physiology of sport]*. Lausanne: Imprimerie E. Toso.

Cotterill, S.T., Sanders, R., & Collins, D. (2010). Developing effective pre-performance routines in Golf: Why don't we ask the Golfer? *Journal of Applied Sport Psychology, 22*, 51–64. http://dx.doi.org/10.1080/10413200903403216

Elsborg, P., Diment, G.M., & Elbe, A-M. (2015). Sport psychology consultants' perceptions of their challenges at the London 2012 Olympic games. *The Sport Psychologist, 29*, 183–195. https://doi.org/10.1123/tsp.2013-0105

Gouttebarge, V., Jonkers, R., Moen, M., Verhagen, E., Wylleman, P., & Gino Kerkhoffs (2017). The prevalence and risk indicators of symptoms of common mental disorders among current and former Dutch elite athletes, *Journal of Sports Sciences, 35*, 2148–2156. https://doi.org/10.1080/02640414.2016.1258485

Howells, K., & Lucassen, M. (2018). 'Post-Olympic blues' –The diminution of celebrity in Olympic athletes. *Psychology of Sport & Exercise, 37*, 67–78. https://doi.org/10.1016/j.psychsport.2018.04.008

Kegelaers, J., Wylleman, P., Defruyt, S., Praet, L., Stambulova, N., Torregrossa, M., Kenttä, G., & De Brandt, K. (2022). The MH of student-athletes: A systematic scoping review. *International Review of Sport and Exercise Psychology,* published online 13 Jul 2022. https://doi.org/10.1080/1750984X.2022.2095657

Kegelaers, J., Wylleman, P., van Bree, B., Wessels, F., & Oudejans, R. (2021). Mental health in elite-level coaches: Prevalence rates and associated impact of coach stressors and psychological resilience. *International Sport Coaching Journal*, 8, 338–347. https://doi.org/10.1123/iscj.2020-0066

Keyes, C.L.M. (2014). MH as a complete state: How the salutogenic perspective completes the picture. In C.L.M. Bauer, & O. Hämmig (Eds.), *Bridging occupational, organizational and Public health: A transdisciplinary approach* (pp. 179–192). Springer Science. https://doi.org/10.1007/978-94-007-5640-3

Kuettel, A., & Larsen, C.H. (2020). Risk and protective factors for MH in elite athletes: A scoping review. *International Review of Sport and Exercise Psychology, 13*, 231–265. https://doi.org/10.1080/1750984X.2019.1689574

Kukidome, T., Noguchi, Y., Katagami, E., Kegelaers, J., & Wylleman, P. (2021). Performance behaviour improvement with the focus on cognitive readiness in high performance sport. *Japan Journal of Physical Education, Health and Sport Sciences* (Advance publication). https://doi.org/10.5432/jjpehss.20141

Meckbach, S., Wagstaff, C.R.D., Kenttä, G., & Thelwell, R. (2022). Building the "team behind the team": A 21-month instrumental case study of the Swedish 2018 FIFA World Cup team, *Journal of Applied Sport Psychology, 35*, 521–546. https://doi.org/10.1080/10413200.2022.2046658

Mitchell, L.A., Knight, C.J., Morris, R., & Mellalieu, S.D. (2021). "Maybe I'm just not good enough?": British swimmers' experiences of attempting to qualify for the Olympic Games. *Scand J Med Sci Sports, 00*, 1–16. https://doi.org/10.1111/sms.13953

Moesch, K., Kenttä, G., Kleinert, J., Quignon-Fleureth, C., Cecili, S., & Bertollo, M. (2018). FEPSAC position statement: Mental health disorders in elite athletes and T models of service provision. *Psychology of Sport & Exercise, 38*, 61–71. https://doi.org/10.1016/j.psychsport.2018.05.013

Nitsch, J.R., Gabler, H., & Singer, R. (2000). Sportpsychologie: ein Überblick. [Sport psychology: An overview]. In H. Gabler, J.R. Nitsch, & R. Singer (Eds.), *Einführung in die Sportpsychologie. Teil 1: Grundthemen. [Introduction into sport psychology: Part 1: Fundamental themes]* (pp. 11–42). Schorndorf: Hofmann.

Perry, C., Champ, F.M., Macbeth, J., & Spandler, H. (2021). Mental health and elite female athletes: A scoping review. *Psychology of Sport and Exercise, 56*, 101961. https://doi.org/10.1016/j.psychsport.2021.101961

Purcell, R., Gwyther, K, & Rice, S.M. (2021). A systematic review and meta-synthesis of mental health position statements in sport: Scope, quality and future directions. *Psychology of Sport and Exercise, 55*, 101946. https://doi.org/10.1016/j.psychsport.2021.101946

Seiler, R., & Wylleman, P. (2009). FEPSAC's role and position in the past and in the future of sport psychology in Europe. *Psychology of Sport and Exercise, 10*, 403–409. https://doi.org/10.1016/j.psychsport.2009.02.009

Stambulova, N., Schinke, R.J., Lavallee, D., & Wylleman, P. (2020). The COVID-19 pandemic and Olympic/Paralympic athletes' developmental challenges and possibilities in times of a global crisis-transition. *International Journal of Sport and Exercise Psychology, 20,* 92–101. https://doi.org/10.1080/1612197X.2020.1810865

Stambulova, N. & Wylleman, P. (2019). Psychology of Athletes' dual careers: A state-of-the-art critical review of the European discourse. *Psychology of Sport and Exercise, 42*, 74–88. https://doi.org/10.1016/j.psychsport.2018.11.013

Van Slingerland, K.J., DesClouds, P., Durand-Bush, N., Boudreault, V. & Abraham, A. (2022). How collaborative mental health care for competitive and high-performance athletes is implemented: A novel interdisciplinary case study. *Frontiers in Psychology, 13,* 994430. https://doi.org/10.3389/fpsyg.2022.994430

Vella, S.A, Swann, C., Batterham, M., Boydell, K.M., Eckermann, S., Ferguson, H., Fogarty, A., Hurley, D., Liddle, S.K., Lonsdale, C., Miller, A., Noetel, M., Okely, A.D., Sanders, T., Schweikle, M.J., Telenta, J., & Deane, F.P. (2021). An Intervention for mental health literacy and resilience in organized sports. *Medicine & Science in Sports and Exercise, 53*, 139–149. https://doi.org/10.1249/MSS.0000000000002433

Verhagen, E. Mellette, J., Konin, J., Scott, R., Brito, J., & McCall, A. (2020). Taking the lead towards healthy performance: The requirement of leadership to elevate the health and performance teams in elite sports. *BMJ Open Sport & Exercise Medicine, 6*, e000834. https://doi.org/10.1136/bmjsem-2020-000834

World Health Organization (2001). *Strengthening MH promotion*. Geneva: World Health Organization.

World Health Organization (2013). *Comprehensive MH action plan 2013–2020*. Geneva: World Health Organization.

Wylleman, P. (2019). An organizational perspective on applied sport psychology in elite sport. *Psychology of Sport and Exercise, 42*, 89–99. https://doi.org/doi.org/10.1016/j.psychsport.2019.01.008

Wylleman, P. (2022, October 26). *Mental health in elite sport*. Presentation during the Mental Health Symposium. Lisbon: Portuguese Olympic Committee.

Wylleman, P. (2023, October 18). *Performance and mental health in high-performance cultures*. Presentation during the 4th Sports Psychology Forum 'In between pushing limits towards achieving excellence and the MH of elite athletes in the context of the Olympic Games.'. Bucharest: Romanian Olympic & Sports Committee.

Wylleman, P., De Brandt, K., & De Knop, P. (2020). Career development of elite athletes. In D. Hackfort and R. Schinke (Eds.), *Routledge International encyclopedia of sport and exercise psychology: Volume 2: Applied and practical measures* (pp. 89–106). New York, NY: Routledge.

Wylleman, P., Rosier, N., & De Knop, P. (2015). Transitional challenges and elite athletes' MH. In J. Baker, P. Safai and J. Fraser-Thomas (Eds.), Health and elite sport. Is high performance sport a healthy pursuit? (pp. 99–116). Oxon, UK: Routledge.

17 Program Evaluation

How to Determine the Success of an Intervention

Erin L. Beatty, Silvia DeGirolamo, and Martin I. Jones

Introduction

The evaluation of mental skills programs is an integral part of professional practice and should be built into program design from the beginning and applied throughout the program. When developing and implementing a program, it is essential to consider whether the program outcomes are valuable and desired by the program participants. The reason being is that an intervention program faces an uphill battle for change if the participants themselves do not value the program outcomes. Similarly, it is vital to contemplate whether the program works as intended and whether the program can be improved. Other important questions might be related to the costs of the program and whether the benefits are worth the costs. Furthermore, practitioners might ponder whether participants can achieve the desired results in alternative (cheaper and quicker) ways and whether the program might have unintended (positive and negative) consequences. These questions and considerations might be deliberated by practitioners during the design phase, during the implementation, and once the program ceases. Program evaluation is, therefore, not something that succeeds as an afterthought. Nor is program evaluation something that can only occur at the end of a program. Practitioners should strive for the systematic assessment of their work before, during, and after a program (Anderson, Mahoney, Miles, & Robinson, 2002; CDC, 1999; Coyle, Boruch, & Turner, 1991). This chapter will strive to lay out the practical steps for how to achieve a feasible and meaningful program evaluation plan while also acknowledging that even sizable organizations can fail to follow these best practices in the name of expediency. There can often be pressures to deliver something quickly rather than ensuring it is the best thing to deliver. Unfortunately, this can undermine the value of mental performance interventions generally in the eyes of the client if the program has poor fit with the needs and then fails to have an impact on the participants.

Given that mental performance training for elite performers is fundamentally about indirectly changing performance through improvements in cognition, emotions, and behaviour; practitioners, or their managers, need to be able to show when improvements have been made, under which circumstances, and by how much if we are to claim that our work has been successful. Practitioners, therefore, require feedback systems (i.e., program evaluation) that allow for learning and ongoing improvement to occur. The need to evaluate is vital for the operator (i.e., gauging personal development), for the practitioner (i.e., providing feedback about what to repeat or change), and for policymakers (i.e., funding decisions). Whether the purpose of the evaluation is to gauge program effectiveness or whether it is to build a business case for the future, it is essential that program developers have a clear plan for the evaluation of their work.

Mental performance practitioners in elite performance contexts need to be accountable and responsible for providing a service that is rigorous and ethical. Furthermore, practitioners must also

DOI: 10.4324/9781003378969-20

recognize that their practice could influence perceptions of mental performance as a profession. Poor service could limit future uptake of mental programming. By integrating program evaluation into their work, mental performance practitioners in elite performance contexts can document their effectiveness and provide an audit trail of how they have provided a rigorous and ethical service.

The following chapter describes various aspects of program evaluation to help to increase practitioners' evaluation literacy and competency. In doing so, we hope that practitioners are given guidance to understand why they need to evaluate programs and ideas for what should be pursued for an evaluation to be effective. The first half of the chapter will focus on the evaluation of programs and how to design such an evaluation. The latter half of the chapter will look at evaluating individual service providers. There is a lack of domain-specific mental performance evidence from the literature for either program evaluation or consultant evaluation. This chapter will rely heavily on general evaluation principles as well as sport research as is appropriate.

What is program evaluation?

Program evaluation involves the systematic collection of information that assists stakeholders to understand a program better, improve its effectiveness, and make decisions about future program planning.

Program evaluation is an assessment of a program's procedures and outcomes, carried out to improve the effectiveness (i.e., doing the right things) and efficiency (i.e., doing things right) of a program. For example, in the context of mental programming for elite performers, program evaluation might consider whether the program achieves a predetermined goal in a prescribed time. The outcome of such an assessment would then influence the decision-making on continuation, future program design, and implementation. Despite "calls to arms" in the sport psychology (e.g., Anderson, Mahoney, Miles, & Robinson, 2002; Smith, 1989; Strean, 1998) and public health (e.g., CDC, 1999) literature, it remains unclear whether program evaluation is practiced consistently. Moreover, it is unclear if sport psychology practitioners sufficiently integrate program evaluation into the planning and implementation of most "mental skills" programs.

Phases of an effective program evaluation

Several program evaluation frameworks exist that are both general (Centers for Disease Control and Prevention, 1999) and specific to particular domains of practice (Anderson, Miles, Robinson, & Mahoney, 2004). Program effectiveness and efficiency can only be demonstrated by practitioners if they (or someone independent from the program design/delivery team) collect and analyze data rigorously and transparently so that the effects of the program can be observed. The data typically collected by practitioners focus on program activities (i.e., procedural fidelity) and outcomes (i.e., changes in desired markers of performance). However, the purpose of the evaluation could be diverse and multifaceted (e.g., accountability, improvement, learning, cost). Regardless of the intention of the evaluation, it must be planned and agreed on by relevant groups (e.g., planners, delivers, stakeholders) before the evaluation commences. Experience has shown that when this agreement is not achieved both the success of the evaluation well as the credibility of the evaluation can be put in jeopardy. For example, if your providers are unhappy with the direction of the evaluation they can disincentivize the individual program participants from completing the evaluation (e.g., interview or survey). Or if the organization does not value the outcome measures selected the evaluation conclusions (be it positive or negative) can be disregarded.

Within the sport and exercise psychology literature, where the focus of psychological programming is often on the development of mental skills, there are a scant number of well-formed evaluation frameworks and relatively sparse coverage of program evaluation research. Typically, the focus has been on evaluating consultant effectiveness and social validity (Anderson, Miles, Robinson, & Mahoney, 2004; Sharp & Hodge, 2011), rather than on procedural fidelity and effectiveness of program aims. Consultant effectiveness can be formal (e.g., through carefully designed surveys), informal (e.g., through chats about effectiveness), and reflective (e.g., consultant reflects on his/her performance). One might surmise that the primacy of consultant effectiveness as an evaluation approach in sport psychology is due to the lack of real-world measures of effect in the sports domains. Thus, where practitioners cannot measure program outcomes (i.e., makes the athletes stronger, faster) they might choose to measure their effectiveness as a consultant instead. In some high-performance contexts, such as the military, these real-world markers might be more tangible than in sport and while this does not mean that consultant effectiveness should be abandoned, it probably does mean that consultant effectiveness should be used as an adjunct assessment of program quality, rather than the sole means. More discussion of evaluating consultant effectiveness can be found in the latter half of this chapter.

Given the lack of domain-specific evaluation frameworks we will take a domain general approach in this chapter. A crucial part of the program evaluation process is to consider the purpose of the evaluation. Evaluations typically answer either (or a combination) of two questions. Firstly, "what is the outcome of the program (i.e., satisfaction, real-world impact)?" Secondly, "how did the program achieve the outcomes as mentioned earlier (i.e., what were the procedures and were they implemented as intended)?" The "what" and "how" of program evaluation is also known as the program theory. The program theory essentially explains how and why a program is supposed to work. Evaluators can use the program theory as a yardstick to compare what was intended with what happened. If the evaluation is being planned long after the program has been deployed the evaluation team can be left trying to develop a program theory absent any existing framework.

What program evaluation is not?

There are a few points to cover on what we are not discussing before delving too deeply into the process of program evaluation. Although publishable research matches many of the hallmarks of functional program evaluation (i.e., systematic, rigorous) and uses many of the same methods, research and program evaluation are different because they have a different intent. That is not to say that program evaluations are unpublishable, far from it. Instead, most program evaluators do not set out to publish the findings from their evaluation. People who intend to publish results are often (although not always) motivated by testing theory and producing reproducible outcomes. Consequently, research questions are typically research-driven (i.e., addressing gaps in existing knowledge), and the results of those research questions should contribute to the knowledge base. Evaluators are motivated by determining the effectiveness and efficiency of a specific program, which is inevitably unique in terms of program leaders, timings, and situational constraints. Therefore, program evaluations are often not reproducible, but that is their nature – it is not a limitation. The questions that form a program evaluation are not necessarily research-driven like publishable research. Instead, the questions originate from the key stakeholders and the intended users of the program. Finally, the test of value comes from the capacity to improve the program, not to contribute to the published literature.

Program monitoring is also not the same as program evaluation. Program monitoring is the ongoing (in)formal assessment of a program that is focused on examining and ensuring the efficiency of the program. It can be relatively informal, sometimes reactive (rather than planned), can involve observational methods and occurs continuously throughout the program. This type of monitoring could comprise reflections of leaders, casual observations of participants, or observation of attendance records. Program monitoring is short term, in that it only lasts for the length of the program, and is conducted by those directly involved in the program. Program evaluation is different from program monitoring because the focus of the evaluation is on both effectiveness and efficiency, and data collection is rigorous and pre-planned. The results are both short (i.e., within program) and long term (i.e., future iterations of a program and program development), and ideally, the evaluation data are collected by practitioners who are independent of the program design/delivery team. In theory, external evaluations should be able to examine the procedures and outcomes with a greater degree of objectivity than internal evaluators can.

In the real world, the separation of program monitoring and evaluation is a false dichotomy. Most people adopt aspects of both approaches in unequal measures, depending on the circumstances at hand. For example, when external evaluators are not available, it makes sense to "make do and mend" rather than to abandon evaluation altogether. An internal evaluation, undertaken by those involved in the program design and delivery, can focus on specific issues that might be hidden from external evaluators (i.e., group dynamics and culture) that influence the effectiveness and efficiency of the program. In practice, external evaluators may not be financially accessible for some groups and the program may have to rely on internal people to staff an evaluation. Experience has shown this can create conflict between time spent on the evaluation versus time spent on service delivery. If you are reading this chapter, it may be obvious that there is value in time spent on both delivery and evaluation services, but institutional pressures may value these activities differently. Contracting the evaluation out to an external group can reduce this tension in resourcing and allocation of staff time. However, we would argue that even if you are a sole provider working alone it is worth the time investment to make a plan on how to evaluate your program and collect information to substantiate the impact of your work. You need not conduct a full randomized control trial to collect information on the behaviour change among your clients. Small amounts of data collected systematically can go a long way to showing the value-add of your services to decision-makers considering your contract renewal. With that said let us turn to how to go about doing this work.

How do we evaluate?

At its core mental performance interventions seek to do a very ordinary thing: support behaviour change. Now the unusual part of the equation comes from the people, i.e., highly skilled elite performers and the context, i.e., national teams, surgical suites, counterterrorism missions, and Olympic finals. Due to the lack of elite performance specific evaluation frameworks and the underlying common characteristic of behaviour change for our purposes, here we will present an evaluation process that comes from the public health. One of the benefits of recent world events is that everyone has come into contact with some type of public health intervention in the post COVID-19 period. We have all likely witnessed that interventions with the best of intentions have a variety of outcomes once they were rolled out to the general public. This can perhaps motivate us all to look at our own interventions with a critical lens and ask ourselves: What were the intended and unintended consequences of this program?

The Centers for Disease Control and Prevention (CDC) recommends the following steps within program evaluation:

Step 1: Engage stakeholders.
Step 2: Describe the program.
Step 3: Focus the evaluation design.
Step 4: Gather credible evidence.
Step 5: Justify conclusions.
Step 6: Ensure use and share lessons learned.

Since public health interventions can have such diverse intents this process is not context- or domain-specific, thus it provides an appropriate process that can be customized for program evaluation within an elite performance context. For the purposes of this section we are going to describe the process taking the position that an external examiner or team of examiners has been hired to evaluate your program; however, the process is the same for internal evaluators.

Step 1: Engage stakeholders, aka talk to the people!

Stakeholders are individuals or organizations that have a vested interest in what will be learned through the course of the evaluation and how that information will be used. Not involving stakeholders from the start risks missing important program elements and perspectives in the evaluation. It also risks producing an evaluation that does not meet the needs of decision-makers. There can often be considerable variation in people's understanding of a mental performance program's intended purpose. The greater the level of internal disagreement the more important it is to know about this early in the evaluation process. Generally speaking, stakeholders include: those parties involved in program operations, those served and impacted by the program, and those who will use the information generated by the evaluation; this latter group may or may not include the funding individual. These engagements can take the form of sit downs with leadership teams, focus groups with customers (i.e. elite performers), in-depth conversation with Human Performance team members and other relevant teams like Medical and/or Psychological Services, and informal conversations with various groups about their perceived needs. A key element here is reinforcing buy-in in the evaluation process. Any reputable evaluator will take the time to determine what the stakeholders' value as outcomes from the evaluation process.

Step 2: Describe the program, aka what are the people trying to do?

It is important to generate a detailed understanding of the goals and strategies of the program. It is necessary to determine the development stage of the program; for example, is the program new and not yet completely formalized in its administration or is it a long-standing program that has been running for years? What is the perception of the program's role in creating change? Is it an education program with broad informational goals? Or is it a targeted intervention aimed at improving a specific aspect of performance such as diaphragmatic breathing? Understanding the program development stage as well as the program goals influences the evaluation design. Having a consensus regarding the program description among the stakeholders is very important lest the evaluation start from a false premise in the eyes of stakeholders. Having a fundamental disagreement about these concepts between the stakeholders and the evaluation team can gravely compromise the value of any evaluation activities. Programs can be over hyped where they promise grand effects when in practice they improve related smaller skills. This can be marketing puffery to increase buy-in but it can complicate evaluation designs. For example, say we have a hypothetical Use of Force Training program. This program promises to improve use of force judgement (excellent – military and police personnel need to be highly accurate in their use of force) but the content of the course focuses only on arousal management. While arousal management is a part of the use of force judgement it is most certainly not the only factor. Such a discrepancy between the advertised program claims and the program content highlights the value in this initial process of building consensus among stakeholders and evaluators. Should the program be evaluated based on the marketing claims? Or based on improving the skills taught on the course? We would suggest it depends on the consensus view of the program's purpose and goals.

The program description should include a statement on the problem or the need that the program addresses, including the size of the problem, the population impacted, and the projected manner of desired change. What are the expected effects of the program? How are these effects expected to take place? What is the minimum required impact for the program to be considered impactful? There is a need to consider the impact over time, i.e., what are the immediate expected impacts and those over a longer period of time? Some consideration should also be given to unintended consequences. The standard by which the program will be judged is set during the process of answering these questions. These standards will come back into play when the data is collected and being assessed in Step 5.

As part of the program description you should create detailed lists of the program activities and who is responsible for each activity. It is important to consider how the program may be impacted by external factors. For example, have the necessary critical investments for the program been made? If not it may be very difficult for the program to succeed. These investments can include time, talent, technology, equipment, information, and money. From an organizational perspective if these investments are not yet made this should influence the type of evaluation to be conducted. How mature is the program? Is it in the planning, implementation, or established phase? If you are planning, then the goal is to inform those plans. If the program is implemented, then the evaluation can document the program's actual conditions and inform revisions. If the program is established and has been running, then the evaluation can assess the intended and unintended outcomes of the program. It is important to consider the context of the program. What is the history of mental performance programing at the unit? How do various service providers work together? Has there been turmoil or turnover in the service delivery space? After gathering all of the above information you should be able to construct a logic model for your program, the logic model clearly states the sequence of events that lead to the outcomes of the program. The model gives the clear depiction of the mechanism of change that drives the hypothesized results of the program. The model should depict the required resources (infrastructure, staff, time) required for the successful implementation. This model gives the ability to connect the intermediate activities to the initial and longer-term outcomes of the program. It can also allow for critical reflection during program development about the magnitude of impact expected, considering the anticipated mechanism of change and the level of investment in the program. This logic model is critical in designing the program evaluation. The following figure is an example of a logic model for a school counselling program (Figure 17.1). Similar to a mental performance program evaluation in the military or national sport organization you can see the clear depiction of the program inputs (foundational elements and program resources), the activities of the program (direct member services, indirect services, program management), as well as the program outputs (athlete change, family involvement, coaching staff competence, organizational policies and procedures, program improvements, administrative support), and finally program outcomes (athlete performance, resilience, and retention, training improvements, increased program resources). The arrows indicate the hypothesized relationships between the activities, outputs, and outcomes of the program. The take-away point from this example is how complicated the causal relationships can be within the program activities and outputs and the outcomes that are the ultimate goal to influence.

Step 3: Focus the evaluation design, aka choose the right path forward!

Now that the program has been described and everyone has come to a consensus the next step is to consider is the purpose the evaluation. Formal full-scale evaluations can be tremendously effortful and resource intensive. It is important to ensure that the evaluation is fit for purpose, meaning it will generate the information required by decision-makers. This is a decision point that ultimate directs the outcome of the evaluation. Changing the evaluation purpose later will usually cost significant amounts of funding and time so it is best to be thoughtful and realistic at this stage about both the state of your program and what you can actual accomplish within your evaluation effort with the resources you can realistically devote. Generally, there are four purposes to program evaluation. Perhaps you are early on in the process of designing your mental performance program and you want to use the evaluation as an opportunity for innovation and to learn from previous evaluations. In that case a formative evaluation will help inform your program development implementation and give you ways to improve your program design (Coyle, Boruch, & Turner, 1991).

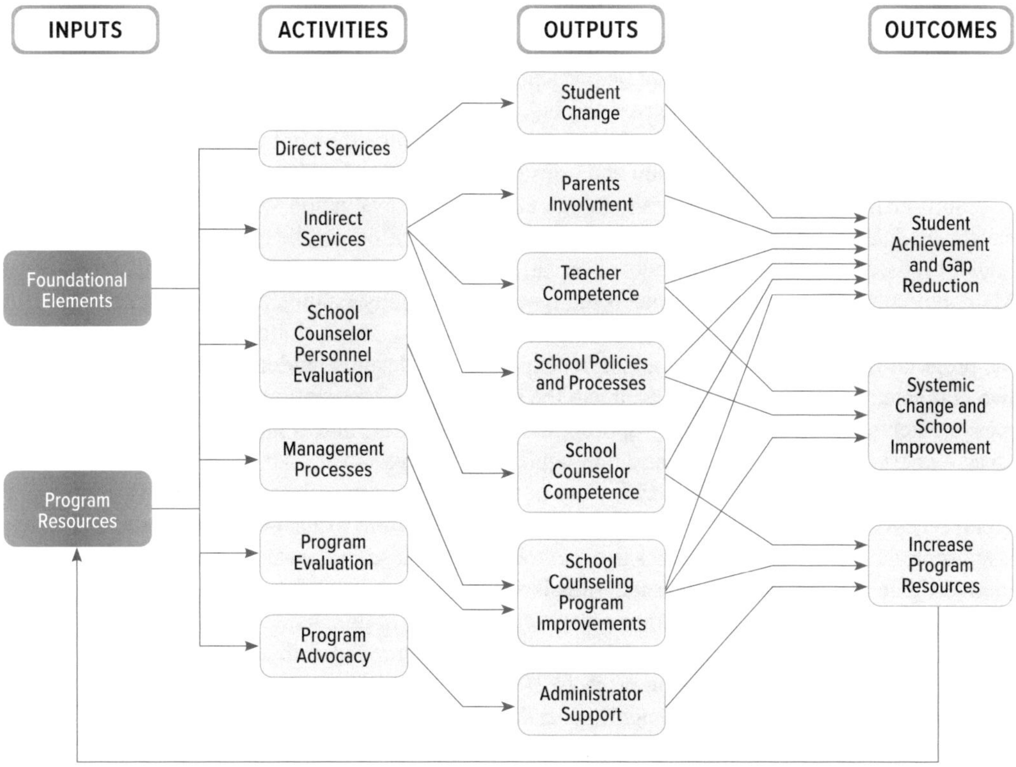

Figure 17.1 Logic model reproduced here with permission from Martin and Carey (2014) this logic model depicts the national model for school counselling program from the American School Counselor Association.

Secondly, a process evaluation can help in assessing a program that has been running for a while and has recently seen some staff change over. You may want to ensure that the program is still being delivered in the manner that it was intended and you are looking for opportunities to improve the program's implementation. In this case a process evaluation is likely what you need. You can answer questions like: what was done? To whom was it done? And how was it done? If you have a standard program being run at multiple sites by different delivery personnel it is reasonable to run a process evaluation periodically to ensure that the program is still being implemented as expected (Coyle, Boruch, & Turner, 1991). A third purpose is to examine program effects. This is appropriate for mature programs with a sufficient run time to allow for potential effects to occur as well as sufficient population trained to display the desired outcomes. Evaluation outcomes may include: assess skills development among program participants, conduct cost benefit calculations, and determine who benefits most from the program. The fourth purpose of conducting an evaluation is to influence those people who would participate in the exercise. An evaluation for this purpose can be conducted at any point in the development process of a training program. Outcomes can include: stimulate communication and awareness among stakeholders, reinforce program messaging, develop evaluation skills among existing staff, and support organizational change. As we said above, but it bears repeating, it is this stage that directs the rest of the evaluation activities so it is important to be clear on who the evaluation is for and what they need to use the information to do. The use case needs to be very specific to ensure that the evaluation asks the right questions to inform the existing motivation for the evaluation. Questions themselves need to be agreed upon at the outset of the program evaluation design; which are feasible and how many can be addressed in a single evaluation. One stakeholder might be interested in the effect of a particular sub-component of the program, while funders might be particularly focused on the efficacy of the program given the cost to provide the program across the organization. Sometimes these disparate interests are compatible and you can do all things for all people. More often than not you cannot accommodate every request into a single evaluation and priorities will need to be identified.

Additionally, in this step the methodological design for evaluation will be selected. That is to say the evaluation team will have to decide how the information will be collected. Common methodologies used in evaluations include: observation, quasi-experimental, and experimental designs. Methodological choices need to match the research questions established during the framing of the evaluation design. They also need to take into consideration the organizational context of the program being evaluated. For example, experimental designs randomly assign individuals to two equivalent groups in order to establish the effect of the intervention on the selected outcome measurements. This method is only appropriate if you have sufficient individuals for two groups. Quasi-experimental designs compare non-equivalent groups (such as intervention group to wait list controls) or interrupted time series data. In some organizations it is not palatable to give one group access to training that another is denied. In these situations a quasi-experimental intervention is appropriate. Observational designs use methods such as case studies and cross-sectional surveys to investigate features of particular individuals who have participated in programing. While these research methods are common within social science, each requires specific expertise on the part of the researcher to be carried out properly. It is not recommended that individuals without any research training take on evaluation projects. If you would like to do some more detailed reading on methodology we recommend Langdridge and Hagger-Johnson's (2013) Introduction to research methods and data analysis in psychology.

Practical Tip!

Agreements, contracts, protocols, or memorandums of understanding should be in place before the evaluation begins, regarding clearances, permissions, roles, and support to ensure that all involved parties understand the requirements to support a successful evaluation administration. As stated earlier, evaluations are time and resource heavy. This cost is magnified if a lack of shared understanding and support from stakeholders at the beginning requires adjustments midway through the process.

Step 4: Gather credible evidence, aka get the right information!

The challenging work of consultation, shared understanding, and agreements about purpose and process established thus far will pay dividends later. Evaluations can produce controversial information; certain aspects of the program may not function as predicted, while stakeholders may have investments in particular outcomes for professional or personal motives. Using multiple sources of information is advisable; it can increase the confidence in the results if multiple indicators support the same conclusions. It can also make the design more robust to the harsh reality of data collection within a dynamic environment (if athlete personnel changes make 25% of your sample unavailable at least you have that data from the earlier time point in the program). Collecting as high-quality data as possible is also recommended as it improves the quality of the evaluation and thus the strength of the conclusions (e.g., use validated reliable scales rather than making your own). It also protects the evaluation results from criticism later. Bringing in outside advisors for the evaluation design and data analysis should be considered when the consequences of the outcome are high (such as cancelling a program due to negative efficacy results or vice versa, continuing a potentially ineffective program). However, if that is unattainable for whatever reason, the evaluator could consult with an external expert on the method selection, the data analysis could be contracted to an internal or external person at arm's length to the program or the analysis plan can be preregistered to ensure it is not modified later to influence the results. The crucial aspect here is to ensure that the person with the most to gain or lose professionally is not in charge of the evaluation without a serious review process or consultation. No matter the direction of the evaluation outcome, be it positive or negative, the perception of a conflict of interest can taint the results. The program logic model used in Step 3 above is very useful in providing direction as to where the data is best collected. Indicators of the impact of a program which are identified as being significant toward the expected mechanism of program impact (i.e., behaviour change model) are a good place to start. While there is such a thing as tracking too many indicators, as the data collection can become burdensome, a reasonable number should be included. Indicators should be specific, observable, and measurable. Example indicators include how often the program can be delivered, what is the participation rate, and changes in participant behaviour. It is important to have a balance of indicators from different phases of the project. Input requirements can include funding and staffing. Process indicators can include the activities of the program such as enrolment numbers. Outcome indicators can include expected changes in the medium and long term. The people who can be sources for the indicator information are going to vary and can include: program participants, program staff, key informants, documents, such as administrative records, needs assessments, and previous evaluation reports; and direct observation of sessions, job performance, and service encounters.

Step 5: Justify conclusions, aka no funny business!

The evaluation conclusions are based on the information gathered which is then connected to the standards set in Step 2 by the evaluation team and the stakeholders. The conclusions must rely on transparent standards, data analysis, interpretation, judgement, and recommendations. Standards could include: participant needs, expectations, norms, program objectives, sustainability, resource efficiency, and institutional goals. The conclusions should be warranted based on the data being interpreted in light of significance and the values and/or standards of the stakeholders. Recommendations include actions that should be considered given the results of the evaluation. Recommendations are greater in scope than that of the evaluation itself as they should consider the larger context of the organization, competing priorities, and affective alternatives. Recommendations should be well supported by evidence lest they undermine the credibility of the evaluation.

Step 6: Ensure use and share lessons learned

Methods to put the knowledge gained through the evaluation into practice are not always immediately obvious to the stakeholders. Deliberate effort must be made to ensure that the findings are shared with all stakeholders. While a final written report is a standard output, it is not always the best method to share the results with all stakeholders. Evaluation results are constrained by the context in which they were collected. Results should not be misused for other purposes or other contexts. Consider as an example a mental skills program that is delivered across the entire Army but the program evaluation is limited to only an Army recruit population. Negative evaluation results would only reflect the program as administered to recruits and should not be used to invalidate all versions of the program with all populations. In another case, say an evaluation demonstrates the effectiveness of a small group in-person intervention. These results should not be used to claim that a digital administration of the same content is effective even for the same population as the program administration context has changed significantly. One of the many challenges in conducting and sharing results of program evaluations in specific elite communities are the inherent differences and unique characteristics of each community. When you have evaluated one program in an elite performance group, you have evaluated just one program in an elite performance group. Some generalizations could potentially be made, though evaluators should be explicit and transparent when presenting conclusions.

Standards for program evaluation

The CDC has a detailed description of 30 specific standards for program evaluation which they organize into four groups (Centers for Disease Control and Prevention, 1999) and these are worthy of a detailed read. To summarize briefly, the CDC recommends the following groupings for standards for evaluations: utility, feasibility, propriety, and accuracy. The utility principle states that the information needs of the evaluation user must be met. The feasibility principle states that evaluation must be practical and deploy non-destructive procedures. The principle of propriety states that the evaluation should be ethical, taking consideration of the welfare of human participants, disclosing information in a balanced manner, and addressing conflicts of interest openly. The principle of accuracy states that the findings ought to be correctly generated by appropriate methodologies and analyzed fairly, without bias and all conclusions properly justified. Taken together these standards can be used to judge if the evaluation will be effective.

Program evaluation requires a mastery of technical research skills (methodological design and data analysis). Equally important is the understanding of the program context within the organization and the management of the people involved in the program (elite performers, leaders, service providers and their managers). You have to ensure the people are invested in the evaluation and are realistic about the potential outcomes in order to ensure that the outcome of the evaluation is taken on board. However, formal mental performance programs may not exist within your organization so from here we will turn our attention to evaluating individual consultants which is a situation you are likely to find yourself in.

Evaluation of individual consultation interventions

Not only can (and should) we evaluate mental performance programs, but we can (and should) evaluate the individuals providing that consultation service. Consultants can utilize a variety of service delivery formats, including a more structured group format, informal or formal individual formats, or some combination thereof. There are a number of advantages to each of these approaches. For instance, Anderson et al. (2004) performed semi-structured interviews with 30 elite United Kingdom athletes from a range of sports to identify how they perceive the effectiveness of sports psychologist consultation, including service delivery format. Some athletes thought the group work was helpful in terms of sharing ideas, developing a better understanding of the team, and getting an introduction to particular techniques. Athletes who typically would not speak with a consultant on their own had the opportunity to listen to information in the group without needing to offer any individual input, thereby receiving education they would not otherwise. Disadvantages were that group work was found to be too brief, or that individuals were uncomfortable sharing in a group setting. Individual consultations were viewed as an opportunity for more in-depth and individualized work, focused on adapting the training to the athlete's needs thereby increasing effectiveness. These consultations were perceived as more private and confidential, allowing for reticent or shy individuals to speak more freely and be more open about their perceived weaknesses or mistakes.

Elite organizations typically offer the opportunity to utilize various service delivery formats, including individual, team, large group, as well as classroom based instruction, or some combination thereof. So, understanding that individual and team performance arises from a multifactorial system and is not a direct correlate of consultant or program effectiveness, the challenge becomes: how do we assess effectiveness of a consultant and/or their intervention? Individual consultation can be such a fluid and dynamic exchange that structuring a standardized research protocol to conduct an evaluation can be challenging. The following discussion will first review the limited research on the assessment of consultation practices and secondly review the assessment of characteristics of effective consultants.

Assessing effective practice

The flexible and dynamic nature of many individual consultation practices does not easily lend itself to standardized evaluation protocols. However, Cropley and colleagues (2010) explored the process of effective practice for applied sports psychologists using focus group and consensus validation procedures with accredited and trainee sport psychologists. Through that process, they developed the following definition of effective practice:

> Effective practice in applied sport psychology concerns meeting the needs of the client(s). Effective practice is therefore a process where: (a) a working alliance is developed between client(s) and practitioner, (b) client goals are clear and agreed by all stakeholders, (c) appropriate evidence-based interventions are undertaken to achieve goals, and (d) goals are achieved or reformulated. Honest evaluation and reflection on the process then occurs to inform future practice, which requires the consultant to pro-actively seek sincere feedback. (p. 527)

This multidimensional process incorporates reflection as a key component in the assessment of one's practice and the reader is directed to the Cropley et al. (2010) article for a detailed exploration of reflective practice in effective applied sport psychology practice. Their findings also indicated a differentiation between competence and effectiveness of applied sport psychologists, noting that competence refers to theoretical knowledge and the ethical implementation of that knowledge, while effectiveness refers to being able to apply and adapt that knowledge "to the specific context in which they find themselves to meet the needs of the client" (p. 528). As such, assessing practice competence is not sufficient in assessing effectiveness. Assessing effectiveness in one's practice is multidimensional, layered, and complex. The above definition of effective practice gives the consultant a place to start.

As the provider/consultant proves themselves to be an asset to the organization (i.e., effective), their role will expand and they will become an increasingly sought-after resource. As such, another approach to evaluating a component of effectiveness is to track consultant utilization over time, as a *de facto* measure of perceived usefulness by the user population. Birrer et al. (2012) examined the utilization of the sport psychology consultant of the Swiss team for the Olympic Games of 2006, 2008, and 2010. Daily meetings, interventions, and personal experiences were tracked at each of the Games. Planned and scheduled interventions were labelled as formal interventions, while unplanned and non-scheduled contacts greater than 15 minutes and related to a psychological issue were labelled informal. Contacts were differentiated by client group (individual athlete, team, coach/head coach, member of the medical team, executive board member, or other), intervention issues (number and category), client name, and client sex (see Birrer et al. for further details). With appropriate data analysis, they were able to more meaningfully examine the consultant practice and inform future practice and recommendations from a data-driven perspective. This approach is easily translatable to working with elite organizations and, in fact, some programs may require this type of data to justify ongoing funding. Data that is gathered for one reason (i.e., program justification) can be incorporated into the multidimensional and layered assessment of effective practice described above. This also illustrates the importance of collecting objective, performance-based data as part of an evaluation program.

Poczwardowski and Sherman (2011) extended their earlier work on a sports psychology service delivery heuristic (Poczwardowski, Sherman, & Henschen, 1998) to include several new key components of applied work. Though part of the original heuristic, they also expanded upon the modalities of program and consultant evaluation. They note that evaluation is an ongoing process and not a one-time event at the end of a relationship or program. Through interviewing ten experienced sports psychology consultants, they learned that a variety of evaluation methods were utilized including, among others, existing psychometric measures, consultants' own evaluation forms, visible behavioural changes in the client, client application of learned techniques, and client successes. Additionally, client requests for additional sessions when new issues arose, as well as getting new referrals from clients, were discussed as indicators of consultation effectiveness. Indeed, this parallels the experience of many providers – clients who have found the consultant to be effective will return when they are faced with other issues and many will be quite open with their peers if the consultant has been helpful in some way. Though there are two sides to this coin – word will also spread if the consultant is found to be unhelpful (also very helpful to those tasked with evaluating service efficacy).

The pursuit of effective individual consultation and the variety of novel settings and scenarios a consultant can find themselves in may lead the consultant into areas of ethical concern, such as multiple roles, informed consent, confidentiality, and maintaining one's practice within one's areas of competence to name a few. The reader is directed to Moore's (2003) review of the ethical concerns that frequently arise in sports psychology consultation and useful approaches to address such, which is informed in part by the military psychology ethics literature. Additionally, Moore provides an "Ethical Self-Awareness Checklist for Sport Psychologists" to serve as an assessment or guide to ethical self-awareness of oneself and one's consultation practice. The reader may also consider reviewing Johnson et al.'s (2006) exploration of the unique, multiple role dilemmas military health care providers may be challenged by in elite performance settings.

As noted by Fortin-Gouchard et al. (2018) and others, the literature identifying the characteristics of effective sports psychology consultants is fairly subjective in nature and is dependent upon stakeholder perceptions. They note that future studies using quasi-experimental designs, validated questionnaires and observable, measurable benefits could further the understanding of effective consultants and programs. Anderson et al. (2004) suggest future research exploring whether client's preferred characteristics and activities of consultants are actually associated with performance improvement or other positive change. Many questions within this space remain unanswered in the existing literature. Given the parallels between consultation with athletic and with SOF populations, advances in the assessment of applied sport psychology consultants and their practices would inform and forward the assessment of consultants and practices in SOF settings.

Assessing characteristics of an effective consultant

As Gardner (2001) noted in his exploration of the team psychologist role in professional sports, "The psychologist needs to become comfortable with informal and sometimes short sessions, in elevators, on side-lines, on airplanes, and in hotel restaurants at breakfast during road trips. Consultations are provided when requested or when necessary and are rarely formally set up as 45-min in-office sessions" (p. 35). This is not dissimilar to the working environment for service providers with elite groups. Cognitive performance coaches and other members of the support team are expected to be available for individual consultation as needed and sometimes in unanticipated scenarios, for instance on a plane while traveling to a training exercise with the team, in the organization's dining facility while making a lunch plate at the salad bar, or even when showering after a workout in the unit gym (true story).

Most of the literature in applied sport psychology regarding effective consultation is focused on the identification and assessment of the characteristics of effective consultants. Despite this being a focus area within the literature, the available work is limited and there are few tools to support examining the characteristics of effective applied sports psychology consultants (see Anderson et al., 2004, for a succinct review). Researcher's exploration into this area began as anecdotal reports from successful consultants in the field, which then evolved into more formal approaches, specifically evaluations of interviews done with coaches and athletes. As is supported in the literature in other service provision areas (e.g., clinical psychology), relationship factors between consultant/provider and client are key contributors to positive change (Norcross & Wampold, 2011). Given this link, evaluating the characteristics of consultants that are perceived as effective by their clients/stakeholders provides useful information when assessing overall effectiveness of individual consultation.

Among numerous other contributions, Partington and Orlick (1987) developed the first assessment tool to measure effectiveness of sports psychology consultants, the Sports Psychology Consultant Evaluation Form (CEF). The CEF rates 10 consultant characteristics, including useful knowledge, positive attitude, and trustworthiness, as well as two effectiveness ratings (for self and for team). The specific items were based on interviews about sports psychology consultant effectiveness with 75 Olympic athletes and 17 national team coaches as part of a large-scale survey of Canadian athletes' mental readiness for the 1984 Olympic Games. Derived from using the CEF in interviews with athletes and coaches, their model of an effective sport psychology consultant was an individual who provided clear, practical, and concrete knowledge, was relatable and trustworthy, fit in with the team, met individual needs, drew on strengths, was flexible, and had a positive-constructive attitude. Partington and Orlick advised that consultants use the CEF to identify strengths and weaknesses for their professional development, as well as to provide a "springboard" for further conversations with coaches and athletes to identify improvement suggestions. There are several limitations to the original tool, however, including validity outside the original sample group of Canadian Olympic athletes and coaches, as well as the overlap of many items thereby tapping into highly similar constructs (Anderson, Miles, Robinson, & Mahoney, 2004).

United States Olympic Committee (USOC) sport psychology staff used Partington and Orlick's CEF as a foundation for the evaluation of their consultation program (Haberl & McCann, 2012). They modified the CEF to include questions on effective team building and practice attendance, as well as questions relating to the Olympic environment for both athletes and coaches. Additionally, they included qualitative, open-ended questions to ask what the consultants should keep doing, stop doing, and start doing (of note, the keep/stop/start model of feedback is a format widely used in the military). They have also adapted the paper and pencil version to a Web-based version so that either format can be utilized while facilitating electronic capture of data when able. Finally, they have explored athlete/team evaluations of their services after workshops and camp presentations during the Olympic cycle, as well as after individual consultations. Peer consultation prior to and during six Olympic Games have been a helpful part of the evaluation process. These assessment tools and approaches have had significant impact on consultant effectiveness – guiding adjustments to their program, shifting approaches used with specific teams, coaches, and athletes, and facilitating the professional development of the consultants themselves.

Fortin-Guichard and colleagues (2018) reviewed the peer-reviewed scientific articles in English that examined, among other topics, sport psychology consultants' (SPC) effectiveness. They found that most of the research on this topic centred on the characteristics SPCs possessed that helped to make an intervention successful. The literature supported that athletes assessed SPCs as effective when the consultant had a positive attitude, good communication skills, a friendly/informal approach, and was trustworthy and flexible. Coaches assessed SPCs as effective when they had knowledge of the sport, were trustworthy, had good listening skills, and were able to integrate the team's culture.

Based on the research reviewed above, it seems likely that a formalized tool, based on sound theory and scientific principles, is a useful adjunct when considering how to assess consultants.

This will also have the benefit of reducing risks of bias from, for example, poorly designed survey evaluations or other extraneous factors. There will be a need for flexibility in applying this formalized approach of course, given the varied nature of services that can be provided and the changing needs of the target population.

Relevance to elite performers and organizations

Program evaluation is an aspect of service delivery within elite organizations that is often overlooked or underperformed. At times, programs and initiatives are implemented as "good ideas" without a great deal of forethought for evaluation. In agile organizations, 80% solutions are commonplace – this speaks to the flexibility, adaptability, and high operational tempo that these organizations must maintain. Most programs and initiatives are developed and intended for that small team or group alone due to the relatively small and individualized nature of many elite teams. There typically is not time or funding to dedicate to program evaluation as that is usually not built into budgets and resourcing allocation. Oftentimes, the practitioner(s) developing and implementing human performance initiatives is also designing the program evaluation component which can lead to somewhat less time and attention being spent on this important aspect. Time and funding can be quite limited for mental performance initiatives in the military or other elite organizations as oftentimes those sections are either staffed "one deep" or are an additional duty for an interested and somewhat trained existing practitioner. Even if all you have is a single provider, developing a logic model for how mental performance services could work within your organization can help shape the prioritization of the activities of that one provider and can call attention to where new resources could be deployed in future. However, as has hopefully been made clear throughout this chapter, program evaluation is an integral component to both large- and small-scale mental performance programs and interventions, as well as for individual consultants, in elite organizations that can demonstrate effectiveness, efficiency, and return on investment to ensure future resourcing.

Summary

Program evaluation is an assessment of a program's procedures and outcomes, carried out to improve the effectiveness (i.e., doing the right things) and efficiency (i.e., doing things right) of a program. Program evaluation is an important step in developing and maintaining a mental performance program. In the program development phase you can use evaluation to ensure that your program is on track to meet the needs identified within the population. If your program is established you can evaluate the consistency of the implementation by different staff members or across different sites. Finally, if your program is completed you can assess the impact of the program on individuals including intended and unintended outcomes. Furthermore, you can and should evaluate the services from individual consultants. Staffing costs can be significant and not all consultants offer equal value to your organization. To what degree does the consultant exhibit the characteristics of an effect consultant? How much are the services utilized? These are questions that can be answered through an evaluation. The distilled key principles for the evaluation of mental skills programs and individual consultants:

- Evaluations should examine both advantages and disadvantages of potential programs.
- Evaluation should be based, wherever possible, on objective, data-driven measures.
- It is important to consider the purpose of the evaluation carefully before embarking on such an effort.
- Evaluation should be ongoing throughout programs, and not just a one-off event.
- The competence of the consultant as well as the efficacy of the program should be evaluated.

- Utilization of services can be an effective measure, however this should be balanced with an outcomes focus.
- Evaluation should take into account the unique characteristics of the context in which the consultation is to be delivered.
- Evaluation should include consideration of the ethical standards.

Having the information generated by an evaluation can be of value when advocating for additional resource investment. Evaluations can take a lot of time for the individual doing the work itself. If possible we recommend using an outside provider with experience conducting program evaluations so that staff can focus on service delivery. Using internal staff capacity can look cheaper than using an outside provider, however, costs nonetheless can exist through reduced availability for service provision and or much slower evaluation progress.

References

Anderson, A., Miles, A., Robinson, P., & Mahoney, C. (2004). Evaluating the athlete's perception of the sport psychologist's effectiveness: What should we be assessing? *Psychology of Sport and Exercise, 5*, 255–277. doi: 10.1016/S1469-0292(03)00005-0

Anderson, A. G., Mahoney, C., Miles, A., & Robinson, P. (2002). Evaluating the effectiveness of applied sport psychology practice: Making the case for a case study approach. *The Sport Psychologist, 16*, 432–453. doi: 10.1123/tsp.16.4.432

Birrer, D., Wetzel, J., Schmid, J., & Morgan, G. (2012). Analysis of sport psychology consultancy at three Olympic Games: Facts and figures. *Psychology of Sport and Exercise, 13*, 702–710. doi: 10.1016/j.psychsport.2012.04.008

Centers for Disease Control and Prevention. (1999). *Framework for program evaluation in public health.* Georgia: U.S. Dept of Health & Human Services. Retrieved from: www.cdc.gov/mmwr/PDF/rr/rr4811.pdf

Coyle, S. L., Boruch, R. F., & Turner, C. F. (1991). Design and Implementation of Evaluation Research. In *National Research Council, In Evaluating AIDS Prevention Programs: Expanded Edition.* USA: National Academies Press. doi: 10.17226/1535

Cropley, B., Hanton, S., Miles, A., & Niven, A. (2010). Exploring the relationship between effective and reflective practice in applied sport psychology. *The Sport Psychologist, 24,* 521–541. doi: 10.1123/tsp.24.4.521

Fortin-Guichard, D., Boudreault, V., Gagnon, S., & Trottier, C. (2018). Experience, effectiveness, and perceptions toward sport psychology consultants: A critical review of peer-reviewed articles. *Journal of Applied Sport Psychology, 30,* 3–22. doi: 10.1080/10413200.2017.1318416

Gardner, F. (2001). Applied sport psychology in professional sports: The team psychologist. *Professional Psychology: Research and Practice, 32*, 34–39. doi: 10.1037/0735-7028.32.1.34

Haberl, P., & McCann, S. (2012). Evaluating USOC sport psychology consultant effectiveness: A philosophical and practical imperative at the Olympic Games. *Journal of Sport Psychology in Action, 3,* 65–76. doi: 10.1080/21520704.2012.683095

Johnson, W. B., Bacho, R., Heim, M., & Ralph, J. (2006). Multiple-role dilemmas for military mental health care providers. *Military Medicine, 171*, 311–315. doi: 10.7205/MILMED.171.4.311

Langdridge, D., & Hagger-Johnson, G. (2013). *Introduction to research methods and data analysis in psychology* (3rd ed.). Pearson Education.

Martin, I., & Carey, J. (2014). Development of a logic model to guide evaluations of the ASCA national model for school counseling programs. *The Professional Counselor, 4*, 455–466. doi: 10.15241/im.4.5.455

Moore, Z. (2003). Ethical dilemmas in sport psychology: Discussion and recommendations for practice. *Professional Psychology: Research and Practice, 34*, 601–610. doi: 10.1037/0735-7028.34.6.601

Norcross, J. C., & Wampold, B. E. (2011). Evidence-based therapy relationships: Research conclusions and clinical practices. *Psychotherapy, 48*, 98–102. doi: 10.1037/a0022161

Partington, J., & Orlick, T. (1987). The sport psychology consultant evaluation form. *The Sport Psychologist, 1,* 309–317. doi: 10.1123/tsp.1.4.309

Poczwardowski, A., & Sherman, C. P. (2011). Revisions to the sport psychology service delivery (SPSD) heuristic: Explorations with experienced consultants. *The Sport Psychologist, 25,* 511–531. doi: 10.1123/tsp.25.4.511

Poczwardowski, A., Sherman, C. P., & Henschen, K. P. (1998). A sport psychology service delivery heuristic: Building on theory and practice. *The Sport Psychologist, 12*, 191–207. doi: 10.1123/tsp.12.2.191

Sharp, L. A. & Hodge, K. (2011). Sport psychology consulting effectiveness: The sport psychology consultant's perspective. *Journal of Applied Sport Psychology, 23*, 360–376. doi: 10.1080/10413200.2011.583619

Smith, R. E. (1989). Applied sport psychology in an age of accountability. *Journal of Applied Sport Psychology, 1,* 166–180. doi: 10.1080/10413208908406413

Strean, W. (1998). Possibilities for qualitative research in sport psychology. *The Sport Psychologist, 12,* 333–34 doi: 10.1123/tsp.12.3.333

18 Ethical Caveats Surrounding Mental Performance Enhancement

Marion Trousselard, Koen Hogenelst, and Nicholas van den Berg

Introduction

Ethics is often considered the science of morality, or the art of good conduct and moral behaviour. This behaviour is determined by the decisions we make, thus ethical considerations are akin to moral decision-making. Indeed, whereas the Greek etymology for "ethics" (*ethos*) means behaviour or custom, "decided" (*prohaireton*) refers to something that is chosen (*-haireton*) before any other (*pro-*). A decision is therefore a preferential choice, and the use of ethics we question this preference. For elite professionals such as military personnel, ethics can, in some way, be considered the ultimate objective, insofar as "positioning itself one degree higher than morals. It is what is required from everyone outside of the sense of obligation" (Briole, 1996).

Ethics falls within the realm of moral philosophy. This branch of philosophy aims to understand three components: (i) what is right and wrong (i.e., fundamental or meta-ethics); (ii) what to do or not to do, (i.e., normative ethics); and (iii) how to apply normative ethics to specific areas, such as the workplace (i.e., applied ethics). The second component – normative ethics – is prescriptive, and therefore judges. This component can be further divided into three major families, all of which have implications for the military. The first is *deontology*. This Kantian-inspired field refers to absolute norms, obligations, and prohibitions. This ethics of conviction provides a code of conduct that requires universal rules of behaviour to be respected (e.g., dignity), whatever the consequences. The second is *consequentialism*, which unlike deontology, judges an action by its foreseeable consequences at the time it is taken. Here, the aim is to achieve the best possible results for the community. Finally, *virtue ethics* is inherited from Aristotelian thought. It focuses on the individual, and his or her perfection as a virtuous moral agent. These three families coexist without a hierarchical structure or order of precedence.

In many military situations, conflicting decisions can arise depending on the ethical framework to which the decisions apply. Applied ethics frameworks help us to answer ethical questions, also known as ethical dilemmas. Ethical dilemmas arise when the theory does not help us to map out a rational way forward, but a decision must be made. They arise when a moral value or principle is at stake in the context of a question or situation that requires a definitive response. For military personnel, both their status and their missions can evoke situations which raise ethical dilemmas and in turn, increase risk of error and misjudgement. Examples of the latter include the use of child soldiers and human shields, invisible enemies, and a mismatch between orders and reality on the ground.

In this chapter, we apply ethical frameworks that help guide moral decisions on the use of scientific and technological advances in the military context. We do not attempt to provide a clear answer to ethical dilemmas, rather we raise several considerations that can be found regarding

DOI: 10.4324/9781003378969-21

mental performance enhancement in humans. The ethical frameworks as described above are woven throughout the present chapter, particularly when reviewing examples of the various tools used to enhance mental performance. Indeed, several of these tools rely on identifying norms and convictions of society or the individual (i.e., deontology), weighing cost–benefit analysis of applied methods (i.e., consequentialism), and through emphasis on the individual as an autonomous moral agent capable of making decisions (i.e., virtue ethics).

Human optimization: enhancement, modification, or adaptation?

A recent report by the Multinational Capability Development Campaigns (MCDC) outlines the use of science and technology to optimize or even exceed the biological potential of individuals, to enhance operational effectiveness among soldiers (Haggenmiller, 2021). The report distinguishes between Human Performance Optimization (HPO) as *reaching* the individual's biological potential, in contrast to Human Performance Enhancement (HPE) as *exceeding* the biological potential. This distinction has implications for ethical considerations when manipulating mental performance.

The operational demands of military personnel can be challenged by expectations that breach societal or personal rules for ethically acceptable behaviour. Importantly, these challenges are not exclusive to the military setting, as the same challenges can be found among athletic, academic, industrial, religious, and other domains. The ethical considerations for an operational demand differ between at least three actors: (i) the command – or manager in the broadest sense – who formulates the demand, mission, purpose or ambition; (ii) the individual(s) involved as an autonomous person, who determines their own level of contribution; and (iii) the practitioner, doctor, coach, or mental trainer, who monitors the autonomous individual's optimization or enhancement process.

The ethical considerations of HPE compared to HPO, and the potential breach of ethics to consider for all actors, are both exemplified through the field of psychopharmacology (see also *Pharmaceuticals*, below). Indeed, with recent developments in this field, use of pharmaceuticals is no longer limited to simply treating issues (i.e., HPO), but has moved towards enhancing human performance (i.e., HPE). This example of HPE involves all three actors: the autonomous individual who receives the treatment does so on the demands of the command, and through execution of the practitioner. This introduces ethical considerations from several perspectives: (i) transcendental, i.e., whether the modification is morally acceptable as considered by the human community; (ii) behavioural, to ensure the various actors behave according to their social mandate (e.g., the laws of the country, the professional code of ethics, etc.); and (iii) emotional, i.e., the recognition of an otherness that establishes the medical act as a loyal partnership. These ethical perspectives can occasionally conflict, for example, the absolute autonomy of the individual might be at odds with an organizational "push" towards enhancement. Nevertheless, the prerequisite for each of these standpoints is the absolute autonomy of the individual, as this is the only way a true "informed consent" can be given.

Importantly, the outcomes of HPE must be considered holistically. If several factors are not considered, any attempt at HPE risks either deterioration of the individual's functioning, or costs outweighing the benefit. For example, improving particular brain functions in support of one effect might result in another imbalance, suggesting the overall systemic functioning will not necessarily be improved. In this way, human performance might be *modifiable*, but pure *enhancement* is hard to obtain if the change is not considerate of the holistic effects. From a Kantian ethics perspective, this suggests that enhancement is not an end in itself, therefore HPE as a means requires holistic ethical considerations. These holistic considerations can be grouped into three categories: increasing a biological capacity at the risk of functional impairment, enhancing human nature (stimulating evolution if we perceive it has plateaued), and improving the way that an individual finds fulfilment in their life. Ideally, an individual's performance is enhanced while maintaining holistic biological potential, without harming human nature. None of this has currently been achieved.

Part of the holistic considerations necessary for successful HPE regards the enactive framework, i.e., humans' dynamic interaction with the environment (Varela et al., 1991). In fact, the decision of whether to engage in HPE often occurs when the environment is no longer suitable. Accordingly, HPE as it relates to the environment requires adaptation. Adaptation can be measured through allostatic load – a psychological homeostatic process which minimizes the effects of environmental stressors (McEwen, 1998). If we consider adaptation in this way, an "enhanced" human with little allostatic load would demonstrate proactive adaptation to the stressors of their environment. However, psychological adaptation involves an interplay between individual perception and collective norms (e.g., the decision to wear a coat to protect from the cold could be impaired if nobody else is wearing one). This leads to geographical adaptation (e.g., migration, or technological advances in habitat or clothing development), to better guarantee homeostasis, in turn preventing allostatic overload. Thus, the ethics surrounding HPE not only requires an enhancement of the factor in question, but to do so while maintaining low allostatic load from the stressors of the constantly-changing environment.

The case of cognitive optimization and enhancement

What is cognition?

Mental performance encompasses a range of cognitive processes. Cognition is extensively described in Chapter 2 of this handbook, and specific methods for increasing the cognitive potential of an individual are described throughout Part 2. Here, we regard cognition as a collective process that encompasses various skills to successfully engage with information and realize cognitive tasks. Such skills include acquiring information (perception), selection (attention), consideration (representation), remembering (memory), and by confronting what is expected of oneself (detection and error) or others (social confrontation). These skills are used to engage in managing our behaviour, resolving problems, and making decisions (executive functions) in the anticipation of – and reaction to – reward and punishment. To realize a simple cognitive task, the performance is assessed by what is expected of oneself or others (i.e., the "error rate"). For complex tasks, measuring the error rate relies on carrying out specific simple tasks which scaffold the overall problem. This involves several cognitive functions to help make sense of the task at hand (e.g., supported and shared attention, distraction, auto-calculation, judgement, executive functions, etc.). In this way, cognitive capabilities are shaped by societal norms, often within a population holding shared socio-demographic characteristics.

While this definition of cognitive performance might apply to an average population, it does not necessarily apply to members of an extreme population, including specialized military personnel. Indeed, although this definition applies to the military context insofar as it avoids deterioration of performance when under stress (i.e., maintaining HPO), it remains unclear whether the classical view of cognitive performacnce is appropriate when the goal is to enhance mental performance (i.e., HPE). One must therefore ask what the objective of mental performance training is: to develop exceptional performances in a situation of psychic calm but extreme fragility in a situation of duress, or to develop a long-term resistance by protecting the standard performances of which he is disposed (i.e., hardening existing traits)? These remarks are valid for certain elites such as military personnel who might face life-threatening situations, but also top athletes or elites in certain high-stakes negotiations. The one who remains calm and capable of discernment is often the one who prevails.

Available arsenal of means to enhance mental performance

The available arsenal of methods to increase an individual's cognitive potential is vast. Whereas several of these methods are described in depth in Part 2 of the present handbook, here we consider

Table 18.1 Non-exhaustive list of the existing arsenal according to its societal acceptance

<table>
<tr><th>Conventional means of cognitive enhancement largely accepted</th><th>Unconventional means tend to evoke moral and social concerns</th></tr>
<tr><td>Education, enriched environments and general health
Prenatal and perinatal enhancement
Mental training & coaching</td><td>External hardware software systems
Nanotechnologies Nanomedicine
Collective intelligence Connective intelligence
Genetic modifications</td></tr>
<tr><td colspan="2" align="center">Drugs</td></tr>
</table>

the ethics of what is and what is not acceptable when considering different types of techniques used to enhance cognition. The increase in human capacities in the context of cognitive enhancement includes tools of societal norms (e.g., education), but primarily mechanisms of the traditional pharmacological approach, as well as those of neurobiological conditioning. Some tools are commonly accepted, others much less so, regardless of the cultural, religious, and ethical reasons (Table 18.1).

Education, enriched environment, and state of health

Education is a strategy that trains an individual to better participate in an independent or societal activity. Children who grow up in an area of enriched development with little biological or psychological stress will optimize their biopsychosocial capabilities and increase their capability to resist duress. This optimization that installs itself in prenatal, perinatal, or post-natal periods has the advantage of being perennial (Roubertoux, 2004). Basic education is a pre-requirement so that armies, sports teams, or corporations can employ personnel with the emotional stability facing duress. It enables the development of a thought process to allow for clear judgement when deciding on acts to undertake. Developing individual citizens to be fully responsible for their actions is therefore the first means of ethically improving cognitive performances under duress. Put differently, education can instil one's moral compass regarding individual and societal norms.

Mental training

Whereas education focuses on general knowledge, mental training is a vast collection of grouping techniques aimed at acquiring specific aptitudes. Mental training can be directed towards controlling emotional states, through controlling the cerebral activation level by mastering the body awareness and/or breathing control. This training for mental control improves performance by mitigating stressors. Contrary to training for specific cognitive tasks, this type of exercise improves overall quality of life to better manage reactions to a breadth of phenomena. In this way, mental training can strengthen awareness and emotional control to optimize ethics-related faculties such as decision-making.

Nutritional supplements

Cognitive performance has benefitted from a nutritional approach coupled with genetics, as ideal supplements can be identified according to the genome of each individual (Helland et al., 2003). In a military context, nutritional supplements can be taken during the time of exposition to stress, which can inhibit deleterious effects while maximizing performance (e.g., caffeine to increase vigilance) to the threat.

The ethical question regards the right moment to use a (nutritional) substance. The ethics of its use does not reside in the substance itself, but in the intentions of the act. For example, if the aim is HPO, alleviation is justified. By contrast, if the intention is HPE, ethical considerations must occur on a case-by-case basis. This requires best judgment from the actors involved at the time of the constraint, to consider the situation itself as well as the cost–benefit of using the substance in the short and long term. Generally, nutritional supplements are low-risk for violating ethical standards.

Pharmaceuticals

The use of mind-altering substances to benefit from their effects has been found even in ancient customs. From a technical point of view, this topic is described in detail in Chapter 6. The field of pharmaceuticals has changed radically with the use of stimulants such as amphetamines and modafinil. Their use for enhancement illustrates certain ethical issues to a larger scale than nutritional supplements. Indeed, these substances were developed by the pharmaceutical industry with therapeutic purposes in mind. Independent of any ethical considerations or efficiency criteria, the use of these substances – particularly in an elite and competitive context – presents ethical considerations.

First, these substances were evaluated in a pathological context, for both their therapeutic efficiency and in a physiological context for their harmlessness for daily usage. By contrast, their use in an acute or threatening environment poses the problem of the pharmacology of a brain under stress; not only does stress modify pharmacokinetic characteristics and thus pharmacodynamics, it modifies the function of the brain independent of the intended customs or actions of the substance. This can produce potential effects that transition from a controlled and harmless dose into risk. It is necessary to know their pharmacological characteristics under stress so that whoever takes them in a state of stress does not risk any unwanted side effects.

The second neurophysiological problem lies in their neurobiological specificity and their selective impact on certain functions. This returns to the idea of considering the holistic effects of HPE, rather than just the targeted effect. For example, the dopaminergic system is strongly involved in the evaluation of risk and reward. Modifying this specific function by these substances directly impacts safety, particularly in the event of decision-making under intense psychological duress. It is therefore essential to know the impact of these substances on the elementary cerebral function in a stressful situation. Furthermore, the same dose of a substance does not necessarily have the same effects from one individual to another. This variability must be accounted for in evaluating individual risk.

Overall, with the emergence of nootropics, we as ethical actors must understand the risk/benefit balance. Keeping an individual stimulated carries obvious benefits in a survival situation, but stimulation can be questionable when this is not the case, especially in sporting or corporate environments. Nonetheless, competitive humans will always aim to gain an advantage over their peers, and we currently see these nootropics being accessed almost freely through the digital economy.

Genetic modifications

Since performance is a direct consequence from the brain's function, it is obvious that any modulation of the genome can have an impact on certain aspects of this performance. Still, there is no direct and linear relationship between the importance of genetic modification and impact on behaviour (de Quervain & Papassotiropoulos, 2006). Among animals, relationships exist between expression modes of the glutamatergic receptors NMDA and memory capability, but human studies on the same genetic targets calculate their role in the modifications on the capabilities at 5% (Craig & Plomin, 2006; de Quervain & Papassotiropoulos, 2006).

Alternatively, alleles of certain genes crucial to behaviour (e.g., glucocorticoides MR receptors, and recapture sites for serotonin) can become modification carriers which affect a small number of nucleotides. This in turn can deeply modify the function of the resulting protein, thus altering human behaviour. This modification can be an advantage, or can be deleterious, but naturally, individuals are typically selected if they are most apt at a particular function; however, the modification to support the function can either be advantageous or deleterious. The biomedical perspective can in no way caution this selection. Instead, it remains that the use of genetic knowledge can only be therapeutic (an individual carrying such a polymorphism and presenting a pathology could need a heavier treatment) or possibly preventative to a recurrence (the presence of this polymorphism increases the chances of risk of recurrence).

Collective intelligence

Improving cognitive capabilities concerns not only the individual, but also their community. Tools and procedures are developed to improve the intellectual collaboration between individuals by focusing on communication systems and representations formed within the group. Currently, connective intelligence is taking advantage of information communication (Surowiecki, 2004; Warwick et al., 2003). It is the objective of the digital giants Google, Apple, Facebook (Meta), and Amazon to advocate such collective advantage of social networks while reassuring the benefits (e.g., social connection) outweigh the costs (e.g., privacy and security).

An individual's competencies can be shared in a group to increase the group's cognitive performance. However, leveraging collective intelligence to heighten the potential of a group can evoke ethical considerations. For example, an excessive specialization reduces the individual to a tool for the group's service (i.e., a means to an end) rather than working synergistically. This tailoring strategy has possible repercussions on mental health and, subsequently, on physical health. Human society assumes that individuals work in intelligence, that is, that they use their knowledge and know-how for a common aim and they react to the consequences of their actions. Everything resides in the balance between specialization and versatility. This balance should be kept in mind when considering individual or group enhancement.

Nanotechnologies and nanomedicine

Nanomedicine equates to "a domain consecrated to health, which uses knowledge acquired in medicine, biology and nanotechnology" (Chouard et al., 2008). It opens up a myriad of possibilities of encapsulating cells, which under electromagnetic stimulation, could free neurotransmitters, in turn increasing cognitive capabilities. The potential health and well-being benefits of nanomedicine is fascinating, yet the risks are often unknown. The stakes are both complex and major, ethically, legally, socially, and politically.

The nanosciences are not necessarily a product of a scientific revolution, but the inevitable result of technological development. The exponential rate at which this technology is developing risks cutting short formal sociological reflection that is indispensable to ethical consideration. This question goes back to the source of ethical thought, which confronts how technological development – as stimulated by medical interests – may help or hinder either society or small group goals when attempting to achieve their aims. The ethical risk of agreeing to these advances is the neglect to consider the cultural and societal norms to which they belong.

Furthermore, the use of technological developments by professional elites stretches the limitations on these ethical considerations. Aside from the limitations in efficiency, the use of such technologies may represent limits to societal acceptance. Though the ethical considerations for professional elites vary by context and necessity of its use (e.g., sports vs. national security or survival), it is again important to consider the cost–benefit on a case-by-case basis.

Enhancement and doping

Having explored our arsenal of tools used to enhance mental performance, the ethical considerations for some of the tools test the differentiation between acceptable enhancement and doping. The etymology of the word "doping" refers to the word "doop" which means broth, mixture, or blend and is said to come from a patois used by Dutch immigrants who, in 1666, built the city of New Amsterdam (present-day New York). This broth possessed exceptional stimulating qualities that made it possible to work tirelessly and without apparent fatigue. The composition of this drink is not known, but it is known that it sometimes caused fatal tachycardia, which forced the bosses of these tireless pioneers to prohibit its use.

The professionalization of sport has led to the emergence of doping, even as the development of the practice of sport has revolved around this quest to surpass oneself "naturally". Doping was considered an aberration that was taken into account by the legislator as early as 1965. The Public Health Code defines doping as "the use, during or with a view to participating in competitions and sporting events, of substances or procedures likely to artificially modify performance which may be detrimental to sporting ethics and to the physical and psychological integrity of the athlete." From this definition, it follows that an athlete who resorts to doping harms not only sport as a whole by failing to respect equal opportunities, but the athlete and their individual health. This law has a repressive side which sanctions the use of stimulants in competitions. Whereas the ban on doping currently concerns only the profession of athletes, the use of doping substances concerns society as a whole, and particularly the working environment in situations of professional overwork.

Whereas doping in athletic competition invokes unfair advantage to human performance (i.e., an HPE rather than HPO), the threshold for what is ethically acceptable is higher in other areas such as the military context, which involves life-threatening situations and the prevention thereof. *Thou shalt not dope* is thus not a universally acknowledged ethical commandment for all pursuits of performance enhancement. The etymology, "per-formare", means to give form, to make real, or to give life to ideas and projects. Performance thus calls on specific abilities – as the linguistic use of the word "performance" attests – which is tantamount to putting "skills" to work. "Skills" therefore also define its scope: there can be no performance without the corresponding competence. Moreover, the prefix *per-* indicates that the necessary shaping or implementation required by performance is part of a process of progress or surpassing. Performance must therefore be seen as an essential property of *homo faber*, and therefore of the sportsman who surpasses himself. Performance calls to mind the idea of man as machine; perhaps the legislator wanted to emphasize the utilitarian nature of doping, which distances man from his *homo faber* qualities.

Perspectives

Interoception: a target of enhancement guaranteeing human integrity?

Recent neuroscience data pose two relevant frameworks for reflections on enhanced man. The first is the enactivism framework – the interplay between the body/environment (Varela et al., 1991). If the individual "gives shape to his environment", "he is at the same time shaped by it". Literally, our environment constitutes us. In fact, each event leaves a trace in the brain and any intense or prolonged constraint transforms the brain morphology durably. Indeed, the brain is, permanently, enacted; the increase can thus only be thought of in an incarnated and situated way. The second framework is that of the probabilistic human brain. The individual does not tolerate uncertainty; he constantly makes inferences from the information that his brain filters and interprets to make predictions about the state of the world. In return, he adjusts these predictions according to the deviation from what he expected from his predictions. A high-level individual is therefore an individual who predicts well, as well as perceives and judges the smallest deviation to improve

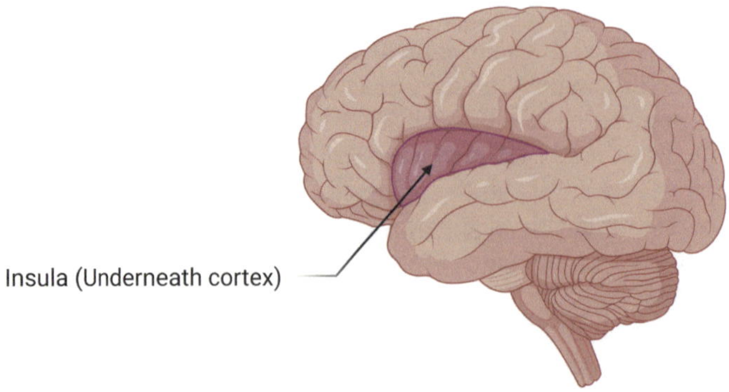

Figure 18.1 Sagittal view of the insula.

subsequent predictions. These inference loops are based on an adjusted perception of the state of interoception – the perception of information coming from the body, or the ability to perceive the physiological state of the body (heartbeat and breathing rhythm, state of satiety, etc.). Awareness of one's physiological state, moment-by-moment, allows for appropriate inferences to be made.

This ability to relate to one's internal feelings has a well identified neurofunctional substrate. Specifically, the insula is nested at the front of the brain between each hemisphere, and is dedicated to the integration of interoceptive information (Figure 18.1). The insula is a probabilistic brain supervisor at the heart of the prediction system. It allows for a moment-by-moment estimate of the balance between the body's available functional resources and needs (metabolic, immunological, etc.). Concurrently, the insula participates in the emergence of emotions and the resulting behaviours in order to restore/maintain the balance between the demands of the environment and the subject evolved (Riva et al., 2019). Given its functions, it is tempting to consider the insula as a principal substrate for weighing ethical considerations in the face of threatening situations.

Care ethic and stakeholder ethic as a safeguard?

Recent years have seen the emergence of reflections on the value of developing an ethic of care within competitive structures. Subscribing to a care ethic implies "being aware that relationships between individuals give rise to a recognition of the responsibilities we have towards one another, and a perception of the need to respond to the needs of others" (Garrau, 2010, p. 43). This ethical framework offers an analytical tool for enriching reflections on what the ethics of augmentation can be to open up new organizational and social practices. However, the values underlying these virtues can also be discussed in the theory of moral philosophy known as the "ethic of care". This ethical framework places "The Other" at the centre of our actions, based on the assumption that individual autonomy is not independent but, on the contrary, completely interdependent on our relationships with others. In other words, this ethic leads us to give priority to satisfying the needs of those for whom we feel responsible. This kind of responsibility towards others is fully reflected in the solidarity between athletes in a competitive team or in corporate governance.

The word "care" has two facets. First, it is a way of expressing concern and worry for others (a disposition) and, secondly, it expresses taking practical action (Tronto, 2013). The two sentences "I care for you" (care as a moral disposition) and "I take care of you" (a concrete action) reflect an engagement in the individual's personal and professional daily life. This interdependence between individuals, alongside its mutual responsibility, has consequences at the institutional level insofar as it posits a social contract in general and, in the competitive context, a contract that binds the fate of individuals to the institution they serve. Care ethics can be understood as a voluntary effort to de-centre oneself in an attempt to understand reality from the perspective of another (Noël, 2018). "It is the person, not his or her actions or traits subsumed under general rules, that constitutes a guide in our motivation to act; hence, the attention we pay to him or her, our reactions to him or her reflect a moral commitment oriented towards the person rather than based on the observance of rules" (Paperman & Laugier, 2005, p. 65).

This voluntary effort to take account of the other's point of view chimes calls for a certain change in perspective. Rather than evaluating the elite's actions with reference to independent growth virtues that are ingrained by training and correspond to social and entrepreneurial ideals (e.g., own it, do better than perfect, be successful, be courageous), the focus is on raising awareness of, and even embodying, interdependence at all levels – from the memberships, to his or her leaders. The aim is to provide neither a predetermined content, nor a theoretical answer, but to lead each elite to consider their responsibilities towards their partners, along with other stakeholders, whether in a context of confrontation or competition (Murat, 2013).

When applied to the complex, tense, and often inextricable situations that elite personnel repeatedly find themselves in, care ethics provides a more comprehensive understanding of the challenges for each stakeholder, and can improve decision-making. A moral dialectic acts as a counterbalance to the means-ends dialectic, in that it challenges each person's commitment both as a moral agent, and as an end in itself. More than any other elite leader, the ethical elite must be fully aware of his or her responsibilities, which are interdependent with those of others: On the one hand, the leader must take care of the partners and colleagues under their command insofar as he or she is accountable for decisions that involve them; on the other hand, they must also take into account interdependencies with other mission stakeholders, be they allies, religious, political or intellectual leaders, or even the media (Noël, 2018). Finally, while the leader is part of the institutional system, he or she must be recognized as a legitimate and autonomous actor; hence, they cannot turn a blind eye to an order, action, or policy that is unjust or contrary to human ethics. Any oversight in this respect must have consequences for the functioning of the system, consisting of each of the actors involved, given that they have a responsibility towards everyone else.

An ethical–legal–societal aspects framework for application in military context

As mentioned previously, enhancing military capability and survivability in threatening situations carries obvious benefits. Moreover, as opposed to other fields including sports, a military organization does not seek a level playing field but a strategic and tactical advantage over its opponents. It is therefore not surprising that in order to maximize human performance, defence forces continue to explore, develop, and apply HPE methods, ranging from pharmaceuticals to (bio)technological enhancement. Yet, even though the military context differs in many ways from civil contexts, ethical, legal, as well as societal concerns need to be addressed. This requires the organization of a careful reflection and deliberation process, with relevant stakeholders at an institutional level. A framework deriving ethical aspects from various streams of thought (deontology, consequentialism, virtue ethics), legal aspects from legislation and conventions (e.g., international law, human rights law), and societal aspects drawing from technology assessment and responsible innovation (Rip & Robinson, 2013; van Est, 2017), may guide such a careful reflection and deliberation process.

Ethical aspects may include:

- Necessity: is this HPE technology or application a military necessity? This is one of the primary concerns to be addressed by the military. Necessity closely follows a (proportionate) benefit to risk analysis, including effectiveness of HPE, potential side effects, and potential negative

health impacts. It also includes the discussion of subsidiarity, i.e., can the effect not be achieved by other means. If the necessity of HPE is not clear, there is no further need to consider the military use of a certain HPE.
- Dignity: how does the HPE affect human dignity of soldiers who use/undergo it?
- Fairness: are benefits (pluses) and costs (minuses) of this technology distributed fairly, e.g., between different units of the military organization, or between individual soldiers?
- Agency and Autonomy: considering the agency of soldiers, do they possess the ability of to make his or her own decisions?
- Responsibility: how does the HPE affect the responsibility of soldiers, e.g., during an operation?

Legal aspects may include:

- Legality: what is the legal basis for using this HPE technology or application? Does it impinge on the right to life? If so, can its use be sufficiently justified?
- Autonomy: how does this HPE technology or application affect an individual's autonomy? Whereas also discussed from an ethical perspective, here the focus is on dignity from human rights perspective as well as rights to privacy and to bodily integrity.
- Accountability: how does this technology affect the accountability of the military organization? Who is ultimately accountable for a decision made to allow a certain HPE to be used?

Societal aspects may include:

- Impact: what are the technology's positive or negative effects on the broader society, e.g., through spill-over effects into the private, family or social lives of solders, outside or after service?
- Democratic control: to what extent and how can democratic institutions, notably the legislature and the executive branch, review and steer the development and deployment of this technology?
- Alignment: to what extent is this technology aligned with values in society, e.g., public values, and to what extent can the technology be modified to better align with these values?
- Support: is there support for this technology in society? Can we organize societal engagement, so that citizens (or CSOs or NGOs) can influence the development and deployment?

The aspects listed above may guide (military) institutions in deliberation and decision-making regarding human enhancement. Note that the process and discussion around certain aspects may vary depending on the level at which decisions are made. Indeed, deliberation and decision-making regarding policy (i.e., does military policy allow for equipping military personnel with enhancement options to be used?) is likely to differ from decision-making regarding the actual application (i.e., the decision on whether or not to apply the enhancement option that is at a commander or military operator's disposal). The former process (i.e., regarding policy formulation) likely requires a group of higher-level accountable representatives, including heads of legal, medical and operational affairs, subject matter experts, and people in communication and personnel roles. Realistic military scenarios may also be useful to guide the discussion. The latter process (i.e., regarding application) is more or less decision-making by the commander and/or military operator that follows the previously formulated policy, with accurate situation assessment, responsibility, and accountability playing an important role at this "lower" level.

It should be expressed that the military context is currently the only context that takes the human enhancement consideration process this far, i.e., to actually consider the use of HPE. As mentioned earlier, it is within the nature of Defence organizations to gain a strategic advantage over (potential) enemies and, in order to do so, have an "arsenal" at their disposal (e.g., akin to nuclear weapons) that hopefully never have to be used.

Conclusion

Effective high-level cognitive functions are crucial for adapting to the operating environment. These functions are sensitive to the frequent high-stress situations in which they are found, in turn deteriorating perception and decision-making. A minimal requirement towards any intervention targeting these functions would be to ensure these other faculties of perception and decision making are maintained. Enhancement techniques must therefore ensure that the acceptable level of mental load is maintained to allow for adjusted functioning.

Stress is inseparable from operational life, but its consequences on high-level cognition can be disastrous. This high-level cognition can be extremely effective in a nominal situation, even if it is highly dependent on individual qualities. It develops and is maintained by its permanent ecological interaction with the environment. The enactive framework suggests that any modifications of the interactions of humans with their environment are likely to be part of the very long-term perspective. This makes it necessary to take into account a risk of the increase of performances altering the natural adaptation mechanisms, among which include recovery mechanisms. This enactive framework leads one to consider the relevance of the ethic care and stakeholder ethics for the cognitive individual and collective enhancement. With military capability and survivability being important drivers of human enhancement considerations, the military setting is a sector par excellence that benefits from a framework for deliberation and decision-making regarding human enhancement. The ethical considerations and frameworks discussed in this chapter may be of great value here.

Altogether, these reflections bring our attention to the new technologies that reduce global cognitive capacity by targeting the increase of a precise function – possibly at the detriment of a systemic and respectful consideration of human beings. Any exogenous increase of cognitive function that is not aligned with homeostatic functioning actually constitutes an aggression. The only acceptable increase is when it is voluntarily chosen by the autonomous individual, and that creates a state of improved awareness of their capacities of stress regulation via an optimization of emotional skills in a stakeholder ethic.

References

Briole, G. (1996). Ethics in Military Medicine (Ethique en médicine militaire). *Médecine & Armées, 24(8),* 649–657.

Chouard, C., Cabanis, E., Chambron, J., Milgrom, E., Adolphe, M., Ardaillou, R., et al. (2008). Nanosciences et médecine. *Bulletin de l'Académie Nationale de Médecine, 192*, 1253–1259. Doi: 10.1016/S0001-4079(19)32726-8

Craig, I., & Plomin, R. (2006). Quantitative trait loci for IQ and other complex traits: single-nucleotide polymorphism genotyping using pooled DNA and microarrays. *Genes, Brain and Behavior, 5*, 32–37. Doi: 10.1111/j.1601-183X.2006.00192.x

de Quervain, D. J. F., & Papassotiropoulos A. (2006). Identification of a genetic cluster influencing memory performance and hippocampal activity in humans. *Proceedings of the National Academy of Sciences, 103(11)*, 4270–4274. Doi: 10.1073/pnas.0510212103

Garrau, M., & Le Goff, A. (2010). *Care, justice and dependence: An introduction to care theories.* (Care, justice et dépendance: introduction aux théories du care). Coll. Philosophies, Paris: Presses Universitaires de France.

Haggenmiller, C. (2021). *Human performance optimization and enhancement.* 2021-03-22_MCDC_HPEO_Project_Report_final-1.pdf (gids-hamburg.de)

Helland, I. B., Smith, L., Saarem, K., Saugstad, O. D., & Drevon, C. A. (2003). Maternal supplementation with very long chain fatty acids during pregnancy and lactation augments children's IQ at 4 years of age. *Pediatrics, 111(1)*, 39–44. Doi: 10.1542/peds.111.1.e39.

McEwen, B. S. (1998). Stress, adaptation, and disease: Allostasis and allostatic load. *Annals of the New York academy of sciences, 840(1)*, 33–44. Doi: 10.1111/j.1749-6632.1998.tb09546.x

Murat, G. (2013). Understanding military ethics through care ethics and stakeholder theory. *Death Studies, 144(2)*, 27. Doi: 10.3917/eslm.144.0027

Noël, J. F. (2018). *The ethic of care: The hidden face of military ethics in the Canadian Armed Forces*. (L'éthique du care: la face cachée de l'éthique militaire au sein des Forces armées canadiennes). Thesis in philosophy. Ottawa, Canada: Saint Paul University.

Paperman, P., & Laugier, S. (2005). *Caring for others: The ethics and politics of care.* (Le souci des autres: éthique et politique du care). Raisons pratiques: épistémologie, sociologie, théorie sociale. Éditions de l'École des hautes études en sciences sociales. Paris; France.

Rip, A., & Robinson, D.K. R. (2013). *Constructive Technology Assessment and the methodology of insertion.* In *Early engagement and new technologies: Opening up the laboratory*, edited by Neelke Doorn, Daan Schuurbiers, Ibo van de Poel and Michael E. Gorman, 37–53. Dordrecht, The Netherlands: Springer Science+Business Media.

Riva, G., Wiederhold, B. K., & Mantovani, F. (2019). Neuroscience of Virtual Reality: From Virtual Exposure to Embodied Medicine. *Cyberpsychology, behavior, and social networking*, *22*(*1*), 82–95. Doi: 10.1089/cyber.2017.29099.gri.

Roubertoux, P. (2004). *Do comportemental genes exist?* (Existe-t-il des gènes du comportement?). Paris: Odile Jacob.

Surowiecki, J. (2004). *The wisdom of crowds: Why the many are smarter than the few and how collective wisdom shapes business, economies, societies, and nations.* Doubleday & Co.

Tronto, J. C. (2013). *Caring democracy: Markets, equality, and justice*. New York: New York University Press.

van Est, R. (2017). Responsible Innovation as a source of inspiration for Technology Assessment, and vice versa: The common challenge of responsibility, representation, issue identification, and orientation. *Journal of Responsible Innovation, 4(2),* 268–277. Doi: 10.1080/23299460.2017.1328652

Varela, F. J., Thompson, E., & Rosch, E. (1991). *The embodied mind.* Cambridge MA: The MIT Press.

Warwick, K., Gasson, M., Hutt, B., Goodhew, I., Kyberd, P., Andrews, B., Teddy, P., & Shad, A. (2003). The application of implant technology for cybernetic systems. *Archives of Neurology, 60(10)*, 1369–1373. Doi: 10.1001/archneur.60.10.1369

19 Conclusion

In many of our practical implementation chapters in various environments, both experts and end-users emphasized the importance of a basic cornerstone, being the confidentiality of the process. The fact that none of the assessment results (clinical, physical, or mental) are part of the performer's official record (be it for military operators, pilots, astronauts, or elite athletes), and the fact that they had the assurance that these data were actually their property were paramount to the success of any mental performance training project. In order to work on one's own functioning, it is an absolute necessity to face one's limitations, failures, and weaknesses. However, in an evaluation context (e.g., regarding professional fitness qualifications, or in a sports team, regarding player trading decision-making), there is no room for such openness, no room for individuals to lay open their vulnerabilities. This determines the mutual trust relationship, the absolute honesty in assessment situations (for both clinical interviews and questionnaires); and the overall feeling that the programme is an alliance between professional experts and operators to provide operators with the best possible support both on an individual and team level, which is the definition of a therapeutic alliance. The fact that many performance management programmes in the high-performance environments are designed or managed without this clinical background and care deontology in mind is a point of attention, as this seems essential in the success of the endeavour.

The past two decades have witnessed a steady growth in programs, tools, and technologies that seek to modify aspects of central nervous system function (either directly or indirectly) with the goal of improving mental and physical performance, productivity, and well-being. These commercial products often have low levels of regulatory oversight, which has created an environment where product developers' claims regarding product efficacy and safety may not have been subjected to the same scientific scrutiny as comparable medical devices or treatment approaches currently on the market. Even so, many products for mental optimization are widely available at price points that make them attractive to a large swath of the consumer market. Many with unsubstantiated claims to deliver a decisive performance advantage to users, so high performers across all professional domains embracing such devices or products is not surprising.

The rapid proliferation of new technologies and tools with purported benefit for optimizing, even enhancing, cognitive performance and brain function, raises a number of challenges for trainers, program managers, leadership, and individual users. Given a seemingly unending array of devices and programs to choose from, decisions regarding which approach to select, and for what purpose, can be anything but straightforward. At present, evidence supporting the efficacy of individual approaches for cognitive improvement or optimization in healthy adult populations is inconsistent, and almost non-existent in elite high performers. Although there may be considerable research exploring certain classes of technologies, such as transcranial direct current stimulation (tDCS) and transcranial magnetic stimulation (TMS), two common neurostimulation approaches,

DOI: 10.4324/9781003378969-22

the effectiveness of individual commercially available devices employing such technology must be independently tested and verified. In some cases, the proprietary nature of device software and hardware components may limit access by researchers not affiliated with the company to conduct independent evaluations of the device. While studies conducted by internal research and development teams may be of high quality, it is not unbiased and the research may not be accessible for review or critique, impeding independent assessment of the device's efficacy.

As demonstrated by the concluding remarks of each of our technical chapters in Part 2, there is typically a lack of methodological consensus across the broader scientific literature pertaining to any given device or approach which often results in inconsistent findings. Moreover, for many products, there is little consensus regarding the most appropriate or optimal methods for implementation with healthy individuals, let alone healthy high-functioning elite performers. Such inconsistencies can make it difficult to determine a product's true efficacy. Conversely, depending on which studies one may have access to or rely on, it is possible to deem a device suitable for use when in fact there is no evidence to support it. Finally, it is important to note that many products currently on the market are not subjected to regulatory oversight by government agencies, such as the US Food and Drug Administration (FDA) or the European Agency for the Evaluation of Medicinal Products. This lack of, or limited oversight means that for many products, monitoring of safety, effectiveness, and long-term health outcomes is left to the company to implement or not. Unfortunately, not every company is able or willing to conduct such monitoring, even though doing so may be beneficial for the company's longer-term viability. Ultimately, it is the job of device developers, manufacturers, and distributers to sell their products. Decisions made by the user community that are based on a marketing pitch, and not on careful scrutiny of the science can lead, at best, to disappointment in performance outcomes, and at worst, to unanticipated side effects or longer-term health consequences. It will be some time before the science behind many of these newly emerging technologies and approaches catches up with the marketing.

One caveat to keep in mind when attempting to evaluate the cost/benefit balance of the implementation of a new technique, is that time is an extremely spare resource in high-performance environments. Whereas national health authorities may not feel it necessary to intervene in the marketing of seemingly harmless devices promoting performance enhancement, the fact that the use of such device (or techniques) in high-performance environments will be at the cost of a potentially beneficial approach is actually harming the performer. This is a major difference between high performers and a more general audience, and the reason why this group of authors decided to bundle forces to gather all the evidence in one single handbook.

At the crux of this question is an understanding that the drive to gain and sustain optimal functional status – a tactical edge – will continue to fuel the demand for new technologies and products with potential to enhance training effectiveness. We sincerely hope to have provided practitioners and program managers with enough background to make informed decisions in the best interest of their performers.

Index

Note: Numbers in *italics* indicate figures.

Made in the USA
Monee, IL
23 March 2026

46621520R00219